Politics and Ideology in Canada
Elite and Public Opinion in the Transformation
of a Welfare State

Politics and Ideology in Canada examines a period of crucial historical change in Canada, beginning in the mid-1970s, when the crisis of the Keynesian welfare state precipitated a transition to a new political order based on the progressive "downsizing" of state involvement in the economy and society. Using class and ideology as key concepts, Michael Ornstein and Michael Stevenson examine this transition in terms of the nature of hegemony and hegemonic crisis and the conditions of political order and instability. These concepts guide the interpretation of three large surveys of representative samples of the Canadian public and two unique elite surveys, conducted between 1975 and 1981. The surveys cover an exceptionally broad spectrum of political issues, including social programs, civil and economic rights, economic policy, foreign ownership, labour relations, and language issues and sovereignty.

A wide-ranging analysis of public and elite attitudes reveals a hegemonic order through the early 1980s, built around public support for the institutions of the Canadian welfare state. But there was also widespread public alienation from politics. Public opinion was quite strongly linked to class but not to party politics. Regional variation in political ideology on a broad range of issues was less pronounced than differences between Quebec and English Canada. Much deeper ideological divisions separated the elites, with a dramatic polarization between corporate and labour respondents. State elites fell between these two, though generally more favourable to capital. The responses of the business elites reveal the ideological roots of the Mulroney years in support for cuts in social programs, free trade, privatization, and deregulation.

MICHAEL ORNSTEIN is associate director of the Institute for Social Research and associate professor of sociology, York University.
MICHAEL STEVENSON is vice-president (Academic Affairs) and provost of York University.

Politics and Ideology in Canada

Elite and Public Opinion in the Transformation of a Welfare State

MICHAEL ORNSTEIN AND
H. MICHAEL STEVENSON

McGill-Queen's University Press
Montreal & Kingston · London · Ithaca

Legal deposit second quarter 1999
Bibliothèque nationale du Québec

Printed in Canada on acid-free paper

This book has been published with the help of a grant from
the Humanities and Social Sciences Federation of Canada,
using funds provided by the Social Sciences and Humanities
Research Council of Canada.

McGill-Queen's University Press acknowledges the financial
support of the Government of Canada through the Book
Publishing Industry Development Program (BPIDP) for its
activities. We also acknowledge the support of the Canada
Council for the Arts for our publishing program.

Canadä

Canadian Cataloguing in Publication Data

Ornstein, Michael D.
    Politics and ideology in Canada: elite and public opinion in
    the transformation of a welfare state
    Includes bibliographical references and index.
    ISBN 0-7735-1829-0
    1. Canada – Politics and government – 1980– 2. Canada –
    Social conditions – 1971– 3. Welfare state – Political aspects
    – Canada. 4. Elite (Social sciences) – Canada – Attitudes.
    I. Stevenson, H. Michael II. Title.
    JA84.C3075 1999   971.064   C99-900495-6

This book was typeset by Typo Litho Composition Inc.
in 10/12 Times Roman.

Contents

Acknowledgments

This book has grown out of a research project entitled "Social Change in Canada," which the authors designed and directed, together with Tom Atkinson and Bernard Blishen. The book would not have been possible, or a great deal of what may be useful in it would be missing, were it not for our association with these two colleagues and their expertise in fields outside of our competence. We appreciate their commitment to major shares of the administrative burden of the project and their good-natured tolerance of our peculiar interests in a project that they conceived in essentially different terms. Jeri Lee and later Darla Rhyne gave us invaluable help as administrative assistants to the project.

We are also indebted for assistance with this research project to members of the staff of the Institute for Social Research at York University, where the project was undertaken. We are grateful in particular to Frieda Marsden, Mirka Ondrack, Anne Oram, and John Tibert, who contributed in major ways to the survey fieldwork, data archiving, and data processing for this project. We hope in return that this work will do something to indicate the enormous value of academic social research centres like the Institute for Social Research, especially in the field of public opinion research. Without them the exclusive control by governments and commercial enterprises of public opinion data will threaten the quality of public debate and public policy based upon readings of public opinion, and the democratic promise of public opinion research will be vitiated by political manipulation and ideologically biased interpretation.

In addition to those who worked on the project, our most helpful colleagues, whom we cannot name, are the thousands of Canadians who so graciously allowed an invasion of their time in order to give us their opinions about Canadian life and politics. We hope that those who do not recognize themselves or their views in this account will find comfort in statistical anonymity, and will otherwise find some insight into what troubles and moves their society. Those who do find some recognizable representation of their interests and positions will, we hope, find comfort in our assumption that these are matters of significance, even when the burden of our analysis is to criticize them.

We are also indebted to numerous friends and colleagues not directly involved in the project, whose advice, criticism, or collaboration has been of great assistance to us, whether or not they know or approve of it, and whether or not we have made adequate use of it. In this regard we acknowledge the assistance of Frank Andrews, Sylvia Bashevkin, David Bell, Robert Brym, Val Burris, Robert Cox, Bill Johnson, Robert McDermid, Ken McRoberts, Leo Panitch, Peter Rossi, Paul Sniderman, the late Donald Smiley, David Shugarman, and Reg Whitaker. Paul Williams served as a research assistant to this project and worked with us on the earlier versions of material. He is responsible for much of the research, analysis and documentation of part of chapter 1. Our references throughout the text indicate our obligations to other colleagues with whom we have had no direct communication on the substance of this book, but whose work has prepared the way for us.

While these obligations to people are primary, our work has depended most, perhaps, upon the institutional support of York University and the Social Sciences and Humanities Research Council of Canada, both of whom gave us very generous financial assistance. We hope that our efforts here will help advertise the value of large-scale, long-duration, collaborative, and interdisciplinary research projects, of which there are too few. In addition to our own work, others have used the data generated by this project in numerous books, theses, articles, and papers. Although we believe the collective results have justified the funding involved, we are very conscious of our debt, especially now that government funding of social research has been so seriously curtailed by comparison with the years in which we were supported. Of course no one of those who assisted us so generously bears responsibility for deficiencies of this work and, especially, for the delay in the publication of a volume that was essentially completed a decade ago.

Politics and Ideology in Canada

Introduction

This book has three interrelated objectives. First, we set out to understand a crucial historical change in Canada: the crisis of the Keynesian welfare state, beginning in the mid-1970s, and the transition thereafter to a new political order based on the progressive dismantling or "downsizing" of state involvement in economy and society. Second, we seek to comprehend this historical transition from the perspective of a theoretical argument about the nature of hegemony and hegemonic crisis, or in other words about the conditions of political order and instability. This theoretical argument emphasizes the importance of class and ideology as keys to the understanding of such questions. Third, we seek to establish the plausibility of this very general theoretical argument by reference to a very particular body of information derived from surveys of a panel sample of the Canadian public and of selected leaders of government, business, trade unions, and other institutions, conducted over the period 1975–81.

The last year, 1981, coincidentally marked the beginning of a major economic recession in Canada, and the setting in motion of political changes that we seek to explain. In terms of causal logic, seeking to explain a phenomenon by reference to prior conditions is perfectly reasonable. Inevitably, however, much of our analysis is influenced by hindsight, and this book is very much a retrospective examination of historically limited survey data. Nevertheless we believe that the data are intrinsically interesting and unique, and that they contribute to a fundamental rethinking of the merits of theoretically informed survey research, as well as to a theoretically and empirically improved perspective on the politics of Canada and similar societies.

Like any work of political analysis, this book reflects a particular intellectual and political milieu. Intellectually it reflects our professional training in sociology and political science in the late 1960s and early 1970s. Like political sociologists everywhere we were struck by the glaring inability of the dominant theory of pluralist democracy, especially in its "end of ideology" variants, to explain events in advanced capitalist societies during this period. That theory was clearly unprepared for the ideological ferment of the "new left" as it developed in all these countries through the 1960s. Nor was it prepared for the threats to economic growth that emerged in the mid-1970s, and the associated rise of the neo-conservative critique of the traditional Keynesian welfare state, a critique as fundamental as that put forward on the left. Coupled with the internal loss of confidence and direction in established political organizations, these pressures from the new left and right produced an instability in party politics and government not seen in advanced capitalist countries since before the Second World War.

As Canadians we had a particular experience of these political and ideological developments. We witnessed, first, the swift rise and fall of Trudeaumania between 1968 and 1972. Then followed the growing difficulties of our economy, with unemployment and inflation rates higher than elsewhere in the developed world during the late 1970s. The political and economic uncertainty was intensified by the U-turns of the Pierre Trudeau government on incomes and social policy after the 1974 election, and by the increasingly visible power and militancy of Quebec nationalism after the election of the Parti Québécois in 1976. Trudeau stumbled to defeat in 1979, only to be resurrected within a year by the still more stumbling performance of his successor. Relatively radical attempts at a new national policy by the new Trudeau government intensified political and ideological conflict and were doomed in the face of the serious recession of 1981–82. Subsequently we witnessed the coming to power of Prime Minister Brian Mulroney, with a dramatic swing towards more neo-conservative emphases on the stimulation of private investment, the privatization of public corporations, welfare state cut-backs, the free-trade integration of Canada in the North American economy, and a resurgence of Quebec nationalism.

By 1975, when we began the design of this study, it took no intellectual acuteness to see that the coming decade would likely be a period in which were condensed some of the most pressing problems, the most exciting political agenda, the most intense political conflict, and the most far-reaching political change in Canadian history. As a result, in collaboration with other colleagues in an interdisciplinary research program, the Social Change in Canada project, we applied for and obtained very generous financial support to monitor social changes over a five-year period. As a means of monitoring complex social change, we proposed to conduct a series of surveys of a large national panel of randomly selected Canadians, to be interviewed and reinterviewed in 1977, 1979, and 1981, as well as surveys of elite decision makers in 1977 and 1981: senior politicians and bureaucrats at the federal, provincial, and municipal levels of government, the chief executive officers of the largest Canadian corporations, medium- and small-business people, senior partners of the major Canadian law firms, publishers and owners of the major mass communication media, leading academics, and leaders of the major trade union and agricultural organizations.

Commonly referred to as the "Quality of Life" surveys, these interviews focused on subjective perceptions of the quality of life in Canada, and on attitudes towards a wide range of public policy issues. We sought to understand what ordinary Canadians thought about the problems of their everyday and public life, and their attitudes towards what governments should do or had done to affect their quality of life. At the same time we sought to understand the response to public opinion of elites with the capacity to influence public policy. Our interest in the perceived quality of life reflected the concern, widely shared in government and academic circles in the mid-1970s, in Canada and internationally, with what appeared to be an emerging crisis of public confidence and discontent in all Western countries, and the associated belief that the key to understanding the problem lay in subjective perceptions of the quality of life (cf. Campbell, Converse, and Rodgers 1976; Andrews and Withey 1976). According to the emerging quality of life paradigm, the ideological and political ferment of the late 1960s and early 1970s was in part attributable to the emergence of new needs, demands, and dissatisfactions geared to changing standards of quality, rather than to the traditional, quantitative concerns with economic growth. It was still recognized, though, that much of the frustration and discontent articulated in mass politics was rooted in the failure of economic growth to keep pace with traditional expectations.

This problematic of the quality of life is certainly one of the concerns addressed in this book. But at the risk of appearing intellectually opportunistic, or ungrateful to our very generous financial supporters, we should say that we never believed that questions about the contemporary politics of countries like Canada could properly be answered by socio-psychological alternatives to the classical traditions of political economy and political sociology. Rather, we approached such questions using key terms from these classical traditions – state, class, and ideology. This approach reflects an understanding of historical events and theoretical developments in the social sciences that we develop throughout the book, but that we outline here by way of introduction.

We start with a view of historical changes in capitalist countries, and of recent change in Canada, that gives primacy to the phenomena of class and ideology. This view derives theoretically from the concept of hegemony, which we understand, following Antonio Gramsci, as a condition of political order in which class rule in capitalist societies is based on a preponderance of consent rather than coercion. That condition is achieved when the divided classes in capitalist societies are united in an ideological understanding about the justifications for the existing, unequal distribution of power and wealth – an understanding maintained by material conditions and political leadership that makes plausible the justice imagined in ideological discourse. Unlike the conceptualizations of social integration and political culture in non-Marxist theory, as independent factors that give social systems their essential political stability, the Gramscian concept of hegemony makes popular consent to the rule of capital dependent upon certain material and political conditions, and subject to the crisis tendencies of capitalist economy (see the discussion and references in chapter 1).

In these terms the reproduction of hegemony is always problematic. Classes and class conflict limit both the orderly growth of material production and the sustained legitimation of the power relations embedded in production relations. Hegemony, though a measure of the stability of the society, is itself always unstable. Economic and political crisis recurs periodically in capitalist society, magnifying the internal contradictions and tensions within the ideological discourse that justifies the consent of subordinate classes to the rule of dominant classes. In such circumstances the restoration of hegemony requires new economic and political arrangements, as well as changes in ideological discourse to motivate and legitimate such change.

This conception of problems of hegemony is associated with a particular concept of the state and politics. The state, in these terms, is *the* site of class conflict, and the arena in which hegemonic relations are produced. In order to produce hegemonic solutions to class conflict, state policies must satisfy the interests of the dominant class while at the same time appearing to be in the universal interest of society as a whole. The creation of hegemony, or attempts at it, therefore involves the relative autonomy of politics and ideology as realms of discourse and institutional activity that cannot be reduced to the interests and determination of singular classes. The progressive autonomization of the state, politics, and ideology can be traced through historical phases of crisis and political adjustment throughout the development of modern capitalist societies, and the political problems addressed in this book – the political problems of Canada in the late 1970s and early 1980s – can be given a very general theoretical formulation as the results of a hegemonic crisis, or of tendencies toward such crisis. The way in which we apply this theoretical perspective to the understanding of Canadian politics can be summarized as follows.

Chapter 1 is taken up with these theoretical questions of ideology and hegemony, and with a summary review of the historical development of Canadian politics in these terms. We outline the broad conceptualization of hegemony in Gramsci's work, emphasizing that this conceptualization avoids a strict isolation of ideological from economic and political matters, and the ways in which it points to the continuous dialectical inversion of the sometimes coherent, but always contradictory, ideological discourse in which political consent is expressed. To give these concepts concreteness we give a sketch of Canadian political history, from Confederation to the present time, that illustrates the changing character of hegemonic regimes and the ideological discourse sustaining them.

We argue that the hegemony established through the national policy, inaugurated in 1867 with the founding of Canada as an independent nation, involved a contradictory mix of ideological commitments to state-initiated economic nationalism as well as to the classic liberal doctrines of the limited, night-watchman state. By the turn of the century these contradictions were magnified by the growing powers of large-scale agricultural and manufacturing capital, represented in the Liberal party's championing of *laissez-faire* doctrines against the nationalist, statist, and aristocratic inheritance of the Conservative party. The ideological and political difficulties of the limited capitalist state were further magnified through the long period of economic and political instability following the First World War. These difficulties were finally resolved through the introduction of a new hegemonic regime: the Keynesian welfare state.

The development of this new hegemonic regime during and after the Second World War was the product of protracted class and ideological struggle, mediated by the unique political institutions of the Canadian federal state. The policy blueprints of the 1940s were not fully implemented until the passage of the 1967 medical services insurance legislation, and, barely properly in place, the Canadian welfare state began to suffer from escalating political conflicts of the kind it was supposed to end. The effervescence of the 1968 Trudeau electoral victory was rapidly extinguished, and the period with which we are concerned in this book involves the Trudeau government's uncertain, inconsistent, and unsuccessful attempts to maintain the welfare state it inherited, and its final desperate attempt to establish a new basis of hegemony with a new national policy defined by more pronounced economic interventionism and constitutional reform. This period is marked, we shall argue in subsequent chapters, by sharp ideological conflict over the traditional defence of the welfare state – conflict evident in class divisions of public opinion, and much more so in the divisions among elites over questions concerning public policy. It is the beginning of a period, like the long period of instability following the First World War, in which a hegemonic regime becomes unravelled in political and ideological conflict, and in which a new hegemonic project begins to be formulated.

Chapter 1 sets out, both in theory and in the historical background to contemporary political problems in Canada, the interrelationship of economic, political, and ideological processes in the establishment and destabilization of hegemonic regimes. The rest of this book is devoted to the least well investigated of these interrelated processes: the ideological. Despite the central importance of the concepts of ideology and ideological class conflict in the definition of hegemony, there are serious problems, in the work of Gramsci and later Marxist theorists influenced by him, in the conceptualization of what is meant by class and ideology, as well as serious weaknesses in empirically identifying class and ideological divisions. Chapters 2 and 3 are devoted, therefore, to an investigation of contending approaches, Marxist and non-Marxist, to the conceptualization and empirical study of class and ideology.

Chapter 2 deals with conceptual problems in the Marxist analysis of ideology. Three general problems are raised: the definition of ideology, the theoretical identification of the relative autonomy of ideology, and the empirical identification of the content and intensity of ideological divisions in modern capitalist society. The problem of definition derives from the metaphoric conception of ideology as "false" consciousness, and the associated conception of the opposition between ideological distortions and scientific or objective truths about society. We argue that such conceptions are neither a valid reading of Karl Marx's original specification of the concept nor an adequate starting point for the analysis of ideological conflicts in contemporary society. The theoretical identification of the relative autonomy of ideology is related to the problem of definition, deriving more particularly from the metaphoric conception of ideology as part of a society's superstructure, reflecting and justifying the relations of exploitation in its economic base. In these deterministic formulations, the content and intensity of ideological divisions between classes, regions, genders, and so on requires little attention, but we discuss a variety of important attempts to reorient the Marxist analysis of politics and ideology away from this deterministic dead end. Unfortunately, the most significant of these theoretical efforts, that of Louis Althusser and his school, failed to open analysis to the empirical complexities of ideological conflicts in concrete societies, and we argue that it is only in the work of neo-Marxists who have attempted concrete, empirical analysis of ideological changes in capitalist societies that we come to a more adequate understanding of the phenomenon.

Here we refer to the work of C.B. Macpherson, Jürgen Habermas, Stuart Hall, and Claus Offe as the best guides to the ideological conflicts in capitalist societies after the mid-1960s. Their work needs to be understood in the context of the problematic, but increasingly rich, empirical identification of changes in public opinion that is available in the work of liberal political sociologists. We therefore review a number of revisions to liberal political sociology that point to the emergence of new value conflicts in capitalist societies, and to the difficulties faced by liberal states in responding coherently to the social forces generated by these "cultural contradictions." Where these

revisions speak clearly to the need to reconsider the role of ideology in political affairs, other strains of liberal revisionism have also pointed to the entrenched bias of liberal politics in the perpetuation of inequalities of wealth
and power, and to the emergence of non-democratic, corporatist arrangements for maintaining this bias. These arguments establish the need to reconsider the exclusion of class from liberal political analysis, and for a
consideration of the special content of ideological discourse justifying class
cooperation.

The most fruitful vocabulary for reconsidering these questions comes,
however, not from liberal but from Marxist-inspired writers like those we refer to above. Their analysis of the historical development of liberalism as the
dominant ideology in capitalist society, and of the particular contradictions
constraining that development after the emergence of the modern welfare
state, is the most coherent approach to the subject. Indeed their theoretical
arguments have been so convincing that they are increasingly appropriated
by non-Marxists. We argue, however, that these highly promising theoretical
developments in the Marxist analysis of ideology have been limited in their
impact, and have allowed for an easy and distorting appropriation by non-
Marxist scholars, because of the weaknesses of empirical research in Marxist
scholarship.

Empirical research in the development of a Marxist understanding of
problems of ideology and hegemony is bedevilled by major epistemological
controversy, particularly by methodological attacks on the value of systematic survey research as a means of dealing with problems of ideology. In
chapter 3 we take up such criticisms of the empirical methodology used in
this book. We argue for a recognition of the primacy of theory in social research, but for the necessity of an independent empirical method, or discipline, in the evaluation of theoretical argument. We argue, further, that the
key issues in the analysis of hegemony – of understanding ideology outside
of the simplifications of the dominant ideology thesis, of understanding class
outside of economistic categories, and of understanding the state outside of
the instrumental identification of government agents with specific class
backgrounds or involvements – can only be resolved by serious empirical investigation based on data systematically collected to deal with such questions. In particular we argue for the usefulness and importance of survey
research as a means of addressing these questions.

The empirical analysis of hegemony and hegemonic crisis must involve an
investigation, first, of the extent to which classes are united by agreement to
basic ideological presuppositions; second, of the extent to which the majority, non-ruling classes are incorporated in, or alienated from, the political
process by the mediating influences of material consumption and satisfaction; and, third, of political leadership and public policy. Bearing in mind the
critical qualification that if class and ideology are important to political life

then they must entail political practice and organization, it is nevertheless clear that an exclusive focus upon the active class organizations in a society is not sufficient for a precise understanding of hegemony. Because hegemony involves a balance of organized conflict and disorganized incorporation within the political system, understanding that balance demands a sense of the overall structure of political consciousness and involvement. Survey measures are ideal for this purpose, despite the difficulties of and controversies over the measurement of class and ideology.

Chapter 3 outlines the conceptual and operational definitions of class and ideological divisions used in this book. Conceptually, our mapping of ideological conflict is based upon the articulation of conflicting interests in the triadic relationships between the state, capital, and labour. These relationships define ideological conflicts over state economic regulation, social welfare policy, and labour relations. In addition to these basic dimensions in which ideological *conflict* is structured, the key dimensions in which ideological *incorporation* is structured have to do with conceptions of civil liberty and what Habermas calls the syndrome of civil and familial privatism. These dimensions of ideological discourse are operationalized by questions dealing with the scope of individual freedoms from the state, as well as the collective liberties defined by new and not so new social movements concerned with language, race, gender, peace, and other issues; by questions about public confidence in government, satisfaction with governmental performance, and the responsiveness of the political regime to individual political participation; and by attitudes defining satisfaction with everyday private life in its numerous domains of family, work, and leisure activity.

Our surveys of elites and the general public tap these various dimensions of ideological discourse in Canada, but the logic underlying this operational specification of the content of ideology, as well as our analysis of the survey data, requires a knowledge of how ideological divisions are rooted in social classes. Chapter 3 ends, therefore, with a discussion of how social classes can be identified from survey data. Although classes cannot be reduced to empirically distinctive locations in the structure of production relations, we argue in this chapter for an operational conception of social classes that *is* restrictive in this sense. After surveying the contributions of Nicos Poulantzas, Guglielmo Carchedi, Eric Olin Wright, and others to the conceptualization and empirical identification of social classes, we adopt a modified typology of class positions suggested by Wright. In addition we argue for the utility of elite surveys, as a supplement to sample surveys of the general population, for understanding the nature of ideology and ideological division within the ruling class. Although elite "theory" proper is explicitly anti-Marxist, we argue that the methodology of elite or "positional" surveys is not, even if the method has so far largely been developed in non-Marxist political sociology.

To summarize, the first three chapters of this book introduce the framework of our analysis. The guiding strategy of our analysis is to recast the general theoretical and historical understanding of problems of hegemony as a set of questions about the structure of ideological divisions between classes and other social groupings. We examine class and ideology as dimensions of conflict internal to the state, conditioning the shape of political affairs. We look behind the surface of political institutions and events, trying to understand how Canadians made sense of the problems and changes confronting them in a period of evident turmoil: how the somewhat distant world of political affairs became the lived experience of ordinary men and women, how public figures directly concerned with those affairs understood the manifold crisis of the times, and how they envisaged solutions to it. The concern underlying these questions is to understand how, in times of evident threats to the orderly management of a capitalist society, political conflict was articulated and regulated: over what issues conflicts of interest were expressed, the extent of such conflict, and the ways in which past political and ideological commitments, and new political and ideological initiatives, mediated such conflict.

Our analysis of these questions, using opinion survey data, is divided into two parts. Part 2 of this book deals with popular ideology, and with the balance of consent and dissent in the mass public. Part 3 deals with the opinions on public policy questions of state, corporate, labour, and other elites. The analysis in these two parts enables us to distinguish analytically (1) the content of a still relatively well-established, if not fully hegemonic, consensus uniting the majority of Canadians in support of some, though not all, welfare state principles; (2) the weakly organized, although still significant, class divisions in support of these principles in the mass public; and (3) the much more sharply defined breakdown in hegemonic consensus among elites influential in politics, or directly involved in the management of the state, who our data show to be sharply divided over questions of the justification and future direction of the welfare state.

Chapter 4 investigates the contours of public ideology in Canada. It begins with a review of arguments for the *in*significance of ideological divisions in Canadian politics – arguments, obviously, that suggest the difficulty (and futility) of the enterprise on which we are embarked. The argument in liberal scholarship assumes the functional autonomy of the state and politics from social and economic affairs, the independent derivation of state interest and policy within the agencies of government, and the dominant role played by the state in shaping the character of economic and political life. Within very narrow limits, public participation in the political process is institutionalized by a party system that brokers power among competing elites, whose constituencies are not directly involved in questions of public policy.

As the core explanation of our political affairs, this pluralist tradition emphasizes the multiplicity of group interests and the competition between multiple elites running functionally separated institutions in society, as well as the competition between governments in the Canadian federal system. In conditions of economic restraint, the demands of the divided interest groups intensify, the capacity of governments to meet these demands is overloaded, governmental agencies struggle to defend their turf and budgets, and political compromises are reached through incremental change. Divisions of class and ideology are displaced by an emphasis on the rational identification of interest with individual or functional group membership, and the rational accommodation of governments to the expression of interests. To the extent that it touches on questions of ideology, the liberal tradition assumes a political culture that justifies a liberal state regulating private markets, with minimal interference in the everyday lives of citizens. Within this broad consensus there is little or no ideological awareness among citizens, although much commentary emphasizes the generally more "left-liberal," even social democratic orientation of the Canadian political culture, particularly as compared to the United States. Tensions about how to carry out the regulation of economy and society are articulated by government elites, largely concerned with their own institutional self-interest in holding and expanding power.

In contrast, Marxist scholarship, and Canadian research in the broad political economy tradition, tends to assume the functional fusion of state and economy, the formulation of public policy in the interest of the capitalist ruling class, and the manipulation of mass support for class rule. That manipulation is assisted by a dominant ideology that camouflages class power. As a corrective to the extreme voluntarism characteristic of liberal scholarship (the state does what it wants), the political economy tradition substitutes an extreme economism (the state does what economic forces impel it to do). As argued in earlier chapters, this is no particular gain. Indeed it has meant that radical scholarship in Canada has barely touched upon questions of ideology.

In order to make some headway against these arguments, in the bulk of chapter 4 we provide an empirical outline of the contours of popular ideology. In contrast to the liberal picture of a left-liberal or social democratic consensus, the analysis in this chapter suggests a predominantly petty bourgeois ideology in Canada, confirmed by an emphasis on individual civil liberties and the satisfactions of private life, with an ambiguous and alienated perspective on the state and political power. On the one hand there is widespread opposition to all forms of political power, in government, big business, and organized labour, and on the other hand a commitment to the state as the proper locus of responsibility for social and economic welfare. Ideological support for the social welfare state is, in these terms, limited to concepts of welfare capitalism rather than embracing a more fundamental, social democratic reform of capitalism on the basis of a settlement between labour and capital. Our data show widespread support for social welfare programs and for measures of state economic regulation oriented towards national objectives rather than the strict market determination of economic activity, but only limited support for principles of labour relations that would imply a genuine sharing of power between capital and labour. Furthermore, despite the magnitude of economic and social change in the period that we examine, this pattern of support for the central principles of the postwar settlement in the areas of labour relations, social welfare policy, and economic regulation is remarkably stable.

The aggregate patterns described in chapter 4 nevertheless conceal substantial variation in the attitudes of Canadians, indicating the limitations of the orthodox liberal or political economy assumptions of ideological consensus in Canada. Before investigating what explains such variation, we examine the hypothesis that these variations are purely random, and that our survey data cannot, therefore, sustain the conclusions we make from them regarding the structure of ideology in Canada. At issue here is an argument that has been a key corollary to the "end of ideology" thesis in liberal political sociology. The argument has it that although survey methods and public opinion data are on their face methodologically well suited to the study of political ideology, there is no ideological coherence in the political consciousness of most people. The mass public in liberal democracies, it is said, is not ideologically constrained. "Constraint," here, is taken to mean the ability to use a coherent set of abstract ideological principles in evaluating political issues. The evidence invoked against such an ability has to do with the lack of correlation between "logically related" opinions on political issues. If true, this argument would represent a formidable obstacle to the assumption in this book that it makes sense to look at ideological divisions in mass politics. We show in chapter 4, however, that the argument is far from convincing, and that our surveys indicate substantial ideological constraint among Canadians.

With these arguments about the non-existence of ideology out of the way, in chapter 5 we investigate the nature of ideological divisions among Canadians. Here we come to grips with the standard arguments about the irrelevance of class and ideological divisions in Canadian political culture. These arguments emphasize the greater importance of non-class factors, particularly language, religion, and region, to the explanation of such divisions as exist. After a critical review of these arguments, on the basis of our empirical analysis of the national surveys we establish: first, that regional differences in Canadian popular ideology are largely accounted for by the marked differences between Quebec and English Canada; second, that regional differences are less pronounced than class differences in key dimensions of popular ideology; and third, that the effects of social class, including the internal differentiation of classes by income and autonomy in the determination of work, are as important as the effects of region in determining patterns of ideological division in Canadian political life.

The survey analysis suggests that the organization of public ideology can be conceived in terms of three levels – moving from the most concrete attitudes towards governments and parties, to more abstract concerns about political efficacy and participation, to the most abstract questions about the proper goals to be pursued in political action – and that these levels are differently affected by class divisions. We show, that is, that there are reasonably strong statistical associations between measures of class and ideological divisions on the fundamental ideological issues of civil liberties, political participation, and the nature of the postwar settlement, although not on questions of satisfaction with government and everyday life.

These results suggest that liberal political sociologists' insistence on the irrelevance of class and ideology in Canada has much to do with a failure to investigate political attitudes outside of a narrow focus upon electoral behaviour. Surveys like ours, which focus upon a wider set of political concerns, do show coherent ideological divisions meaningfully related to class. We also qualify the standard Canadian thesis about the dominance of regionalism by showing that regional divisions are not uniformly more important than class divisions in the political culture, and that there are important senses in which the language of regionalism is an ideological screen against the perception of national divisions in Canada. In Quebec, peculiarly ideological class conflict has been accentuated by the coincidence of class and ethnicity, producing a more deeply entrenched commitment to the welfare state's mediation of class conflict. In this sense the language of regionalism conceals not only the national question, but the way in which regionalism in Canada expresses a complex, underlying pattern of class conflict. Finally, we show that age, religion, occupation, and income have important influences on political ideology net of the influence of class, but that this is no reason to dispense with the argument for the importance of class divisions in understanding the organization of political ideology in Canada.

We do not, however, want to exaggerate the extent of these class divisions. In statistical terms they are only moderately large. Part of the explanation for only moderate effects of class on political attitudes is, of course, related to the prior conclusions of chapter 4: there cannot be both very strong class divisions and a consensus in public attitudes in the direction of a petty bourgeois ideology. Any hegemonic structure to popular ideology reduces the extent to which class divisions will be evident, and the evidence in chapters 4 and 5 is, therefore, consistent. Still more important, we argue, is the mediating influence of party politics in depressing class divisions in Canadian ideology. Chapter 6 explores this argument.

Here we confront two of the principal arguments for the irrelevance of class and ideology in Canadian politics: that the party system in simple plurality electoral systems like Canada's produces only minor product differentiation in the market for votes, and that the traditions of brokerage politics have been particularly strong in Canada for reasons related to its peculiarly marked social, geographical, and economic diversity. Our analysis substantially confirms this view of the electoral and party system as essentially removed from the social forces of class and ideology. There are only very weak relationships between party identification, class, and ideological orientation. We suggest that there may be important class dynamics, and ideological colourations, inherent in shifts over time in popular identification with different political parties. But these effects of class and ideology are also weak, and significant only in relation to the potentially great importance of even small shifts of partisan identification to the outcome of elections.

The lack of ideological polarization in party politics is not the same, however, as the insignificance of ideological polarization in the Canadian political culture. In the context of our evidence of ideological and class cleavages in political attitudes, we agree with many other commentators that the explanation for the lack of polarization among political parties must lie in the use of the party system to avoid articulating the divided interests of classes.

But this strategy is not fully implementable, and there is a continuing expression of the divisions of class and ideology we document in the strikes, protests, lobbying, and other organized political activity that recurs between isolated episodes of electoral activity. These expressions of conflict and struggle must be resolved in public policy. The rest of the answer to the question of how political order is maintained by the containment of class divisions must therefore be sought in an assessment of the balance of these class forces in the state, and of the ways in which these forces produce policy that satisfies the "general" interest. We must look, that is, behind the democratic consensus defined by majority public opinion, and behind the struggles or pressure-group practices articulating different class interests, into the institutional matrix of power relations through which different social interests are given a distorted but legitimate representation in the public policy process. Public opinion and organized political protest set limits on the state, but they are limits that are mediated by the structure of opinion and interest representation in the state.

Mediation, like much of the vocabulary in the contemporary theory of the state, is an overworked word. Not because it does not refer to something vital – the complex transformation of social interests into state activity through processes of conflict regulation and minimization – but because it is rarely given any concrete content in political analysis. In part 3 of this book we attempt to specify the concept by analyzing elite ideology: evaluating the extent of ideological conflict between business and labour leaders; the articulation of these conflicting positions by the leaders of the intermediary institutions of the law, academia, and the mass media; and their representation by politicians and bureaucrats who run the state machinery.

In making this transition from the structure of ideological conflict in the mass public to questions of the state mediation of such conflicts or contradictions, we have to deal with a raft of competing theoretical formulations of the ways in which the capitalist state works. Chapter 7 reviews these formulations, broadly distinguishing liberal from Marxist arguments, and within each camp a number of significantly diverging positions. We attempt to show how these opposing positions entail different hypotheses, explicit or implicit, about the distribution of elite ideology and the nature of the state's mediation of conflicting interests in society. Naturally, part of chapter 7, as well as the subsequent data analysis, involves a defence of elite analysis as an appropriate methodology, not just for liberal theory, which uses the concept "elites," but for Marxist theory, which denies its validity. Our purpose, as in part 1, is to use the kinds of methods and data typical of liberal political sociology, but to demonstrate with them the greater explanatory power of Marxist arguments about the ways in which political order is organized.

Chapter 8 shows that elite ideology, measured in the same dimensions as for the general public in chapter 3, is not more consensual than popular ideology, as much liberal political sociology would have it in order to explain political order in capitalist societies. On the contrary, we show that the ideological class struggle identified in popular ideology is much more clearly demarcated in the systematically opposing positions on the right and left of business and labour elites, and by differences among political and bureaucratic elites. Second, we show that corollaries of the elite consensus model – that elites are more constrained and more liberal (tolerant and democratic) in their outlook than the mass public, thereby explaining the stability of a liberal democratic social order – are invalid, and that the anti-democratic conclusion from this model of the appropriate stratification of political power on the basis of the greater political sophistication and tolerance of elites cannot be sustained.

These findings are inconsistent with key arguments in pluralist theories of the liberal democratic state. They add credence to our general strategy, following Marxist theories of the state, of looking for the representation by elites of relatively coherently organized ideological divisions in the mass public. The balance of such forces among elites in the institutions of civil society and the state is critical to explaining the direction and stability of public affairs.

While our findings in chapter 8 raise serious difficulties for many versions of liberal theory, they do not decisively dismiss sophisticated, neo-pluralist accounts of the capitalist state, which can in all essential respects anticipate the descriptions we provide of inter-elite differences in public policy perspectives. Further, these findings are broadly consistent with an instrumental Marxism that sees a clear division of interest between business and labour leaders and an uneven representation, favouring business, of these interests within the state. In order to add weight to our preference for a Marxist theory of the autonomy of the state – a theory in which the ideological orientation and discourse of state officials and the leaders of significant institutions in civil society make a difference to public policy, which cannot be reduced to the interests of capitalists – in chapter 9 we proceed to examine a number of auxiliary arguments about divisions among elites that differentiate pluralist from Marxist theories of the autonomy of the state. We then proceed in chapter 10 to examine the key assumptions that differentiate, within Marxism, among instrumental and structural theories of the state.

In chapter 9 we show that there is no evidence for either of two standard arguments by pluralists for the autonomy of the state: the functionalist hypothesis of the differences among politicians (more ideologically conflictual) and bureaucrats (more centrist, impartial); or the institutionalist hypothesis of differences among levels of government. Among bureaucrats and politicians there is significant variation in ideological orientations towards public policy issues, reflecting the representation of interests in society at large, but these divisions do not coincide with the functional divisions of government. Ideological variation among state elites is more pronounced than among business or labour elites, but the extreme positions held by business and labour elites are not widely held by government leaders. The pattern of state elite policy preferences tends, therefore, to suggest in rather straightforward statistical terms a tendency for these elites to adopt intermediate or mediating positions on issues.

This is not simply a reflection of a tendency towards compromise, and a mechanical sorting of middle positions. State officials tend to articulate a coherent ideological position that logically integrates approaches to diverse public policy issues. In these terms chapter 9 concludes with an empirically refined demonstration of the ideological distance between state and capital in the late years of the Trudeau regime, based upon an empirically more sophisticated model of elite ideology, which demarcates the complex arguments of neo-conservatives from neo-Keynesians and social democrats. We show how a form of *dirigiste* welfare capitalism became the dominant position in Canadian government at the beginning of the 1980s, uniting the great majority of state officials with a minority of capitalists and labour leaders. The majorities of business and labour adopted sharply conflicting neo-conservative and neo-Keynesian positions. This picture of elite ideology suggests how the Canadian state and its vacillating public policy in this period can be seen as an attempt, however unsuccessful and short-lived, to confront the constraints in popular ideology and the conflicts in elite ideology that developed in the context of mounting economic difficulties in this period.

Although these findings are quite unlike the predictions of instrumental Marxism, they do not directly confront the basic tenets of that kind of Marxist theory. In chapter 10, therefore, we show in opposition to Marxist instrumentalism that state elites are not ideologically tied to capitalists – either to the class as a whole, or to any particular, dominant fraction. The uneven structure of representation of the conflicting interests of business and labour by state officials is not, that is, tied to the variation in class background of the state officials, nor to the extent of communication and interaction between them and clients representing different class interests.

At least modally, it is possible to distinguish the different elite groups, in terms of their class backgrounds, and the patterns that we observe are compatible with the directions of past Canadian research in the tradition of John Porter's famous study, *The Vertical Mosaic* (1965). By the beginning of the 1980s, however, our surveys show dramatically less class bias in recruitment to elite positions in state and economy than Porter and others have observed. Also, perhaps as a result of some opening up of recruitment channels to elite positions (though, of course, there is no previous empirical evidence on this point), the social background of elites proves to have little independent effect on their ideological orientation. We take this as compelling evidence against instrumentalist interpretations of political ideology and confirmation of the wisdom of structurally locating elite ideological orientations in the context of the concrete institutional interests they serve, the balance of political and ideological forces in the wider society, and the political alliances and organization forged among elites. On this last matter, our findings in chapter 9 suggest a much stronger connection of party identification to ideological orientation among elites than among members of the mass public.

Our findings in chapters 9 and 10 are therefore consistent with, although they cannot alone demonstrate, structuralist arguments for the state as a field of class struggle, and for the autonomy of the state as based, at least in part, upon the relative autonomy of ideological discourse among elites, its manifestation in political party activity and in business and labour organizations, and its relatively autonomous translation or application by state officials in public policy decision making. Evidence of the sharp conflict between business and labour, and the absence of any evidence for an instrumental connection of such positions to state officials through recruitment to state office from different classes or more concentrated interaction of state officials in different agencies with members of different classes, leads in this direction.

The essential problem of pluralist theory and of instrumentalist Marxism is that these perspectives contain no logic of change. Pluralist theory does not indicate why there should be any change in the balance of group interests, and instrumentalist Marxism and radical neo-pluralism, which share similar perspectives, offer no clue as to why, as in the Canadian case we discuss, the state should attempt a program strongly opposed by capitalists, or why the latter should have any reason to oppose a state that they control.

To move beyond static reproduction of political power in capitalist society and its "efficient" translation into public policy, we have to move to a more dynamic conception of the relative autonomy and contradictory unity of the state, the limited nature of attempts by the state to construct a hegemonic order through public policy, and the struggles within the state to formulate new hegemonic projects in the midst of crisis.

More broadly, we interpret the ideological divisions in the general public and among the leaders of the major institutions in Canadian society as reflecting problems of hegemony in Canada in the transition from the 1970s to the 1980s – from an order defined in terms of the regulation of national economies by independent welfare states to one redefined in terms of the regulation of interdependent national states by the international economy of flexible specialization. Chapter 11 summarizes this perspective.

Three essential arguments are made here. First, our analysis of the surveys of the general public in part 2 reveals the contradictory and unstable character of the hegemonic order built around the Keynesian welfare state in this period. Public opinion in Canada, though strongly in favour of institutional commitments to social insurance and economic equity, remained heavily petty bourgeois in its support for private, capitalist, as opposed to public, state-directed, arrangements for the organization of economic life, and substantially uncommitted to institutional aspects of the welfare state that protected labour against capital. Further, by the mid-1970s public opinion had become fundamentally estranged from the political institutions, parties, and governments that had sustained the Keynesian welfare state. The public defence for this kind of state was, therefore, inadequate by the 1980s for a truly hegemonic order, that is for the consensual and stable support of a particular form of state and economy.

Second, our analysis shows that by the beginnings of the 1980s the business class in Canada had become radically disengaged from the core commitments of the Keynesian welfare state, developing instead a neo-conservative perspective favouring a quite different form of state and economy. Here again our analysis underlines problems for hegemony in Canada when at this time a coherent and unified assault on the principles of the Keynesian welfare state was mounted by the most powerful class in society.

Finally, we infer from these two conclusions, a third: the attempt at a new hegemonic project visible in the new national policy of the late Trudeau regime (and in our descriptions of the distinctive ideological orientation of Canadian government officials in this period) was doomed to failure in the context of the weaknesses in public support for a renewed welfare state, and the strengths of business opposition to such a project. Our description of this very uneven balance of forces sets the stage for developments that lie beyond the scope of this book: the subsequent coming to power of a new alliance of business and right-wing political forces, with a shift from *dirigisme* to a neo-Conservative emphasis upon free trade and supply-side incentives to business investment. This was not, of course, a purely ideological development, explained by the greater coherence of ideological perspective on one side rather than another in the debate over the future of the Keynesian welfare state. It was as much the product of a profound economic collapse in the recession of 1981–82 and the only faltering recovery thereafter, as it was the product of important new developments in political organization and leadership. It was still, however, an ideological development, which our analysis should help comprehend.

We are aware of the serious pitfalls entailed in an attempt to move from an emphasis on the ideological positions of individuals to an interpretation of large historical issues of political change. Our narrow focus on the empirical analysis of ideology is problematic. No matter how clear it may be that ideology is a crucial ingredient of hegemonic crisis in theory and in historical fact, it is only *an* ingredient, not *the* ingredient, or even the most important ingredient. And even accepting the narrowing of focus to questions of ideology, there are, we are well aware, other problems in bridging from our micro-analytic emphasis on the structure of individuals' political consciousness to the macro-analytic concepts of hegemony and hegemonic crisis. The gap between theory and data analysis may often seem too large. But there are always such gaps in the analysis of social phenomena. Survey data, like all data, never speak for themselves. They must be interpreted in light of a priori theoretical arguments, and an associated understanding of the historical context from which they derive. If we have erred on the side of interesting speculation rather than a narrow preoccupation with data that obscures the forest for the trees, we will have done what we set out to do.

Perhaps it is helpful to make explicit the relationship between the text of this book and the very numerous tables giving the survey results – simple profiles of the responses to the questions, but also more abstract statistical analysis designed to discern abstract patterns in the data. The text is intended to stand on its own. While we refer to the sources of figures in specific tables, we have attempted to write a book about ideology and politics that could be read without direct reference to the statistical material. The tables, however, are our evidence. Not only do they provide more detail and subjects for thought than could ever be covered in a text, they allow the reader to pass judgement on our *interpretation* of the survey results and to develop her or his own views. A basic knowledge of multiple regression is required to fully understand some of the argument in chapters 5, 6, and 10, since regression is used to separate the "effects" of competing factors – for example to compare the impact of social class and region in chapter 5. The more complex material is confined to parts of these chapters and we have done our best to put the results in non-technical terms.

PART ONE

Theory, Context, and Methods

1 The Problem of Hegemony in Theory and History: An Introduction

In this book we seek to discover something about the character of political life in Canada by looking at surveys of the opinions held by Canadians concerning their political affairs during the period 1977–81. As in all research, what we "discover" is critically affected by what we assume is there to be discovered. This is especially true for the interpretation of surveys, because the opinions we discuss are not so much evidence about an objective, external world given to us (as in the Latin *data*) as they are facts that we have constructed about the social world (as in the Latin *facta*). The opinions we discuss are answers to questions we have posed: they reflect our opinions about what one should be opinionated about, and they are stated in our own language, not the language of the persons whose opinions we want to know. Further, our interpretation of these data reflect our opinions of what motivates the opinion of our respondents, not their own explanations of why they think the way they do.

In chapter 3 we go more deeply into the problems of and justification for dealing with these kinds of materials, but want at the very beginning to introduce the reader to the assumptions and opinions that have shaped our surveys of public opinion, and the interpretation we put upon them. These assumptions and opinions arise out of a theoretical argument about the nature of political order and change in capitalist societies, and out of an interpretation of Canadian history framed in terms of that argument.

Put briefly, in this chapter we argue that the period 1975–81 saw the erosion of a hegemonic order that had been established in Canada after the Second World War through the institutionalization of a Keynesian welfare state. The erosion prompted attempts by the Pierre Trudeau government at reform, but these attempts failed. Trudeau's successors, both within his own Liberal party and still more within the soon-victorious Progressive Conservative party, proceeded not to consolidate or entrench but to reduce and replace the Keynesian welfare state. We will argue that the conflicts over the welfare state described in this chapter were reflected in public opinion, and in the attitudes of decision makers in Canadian government, business, labour, and other organizations. As a result our surveys of the balance of forces arrayed on different sides of these conflicts during the period 1977–81 are a useful guide to understanding the redirection of Canadian politics thereafter.

In developing this argument we introduce, first, Antonio Gramsci's conceptualization of the nature of hegemony and hegemonic crises in capitalist societies. Second, we sketch the historical development of Canadian politics as a dialectical progression of attempts to establish hegemonic regimes and crisis tendencies undermining such hegemony, with special emphasis on the construction and erosion of the Keynesian welfare state. We conclude the chapter by emphasizing the importance of ideology in understanding these developments and by outlining the key questions about the structure of ideological conflict raised by our sketch of recent Canadian political history, which we investigated in our surveys of public and élite opinion.

THE QUESTION OF HEGEMONY

First, then, what is hegemony? In the work of the Italian Marxist Gramsci, hegemony is the distinguishing characteristic of advanced capitalist, as opposed to pre- and semi-capitalist, societies. In the latter, state power and class domination are built upon coercion, whereas in advanced capitalist societies they are built upon a more sophisticated and resilient balance of coercion and consent. Hegemony is "the 'spontaneous' consent given by the great masses of the population to the general direction imposed on social life by the dominant fundamental group" (Gramsci, in Hoare and Nowell Smith 1971, 133). The "dominant fundamental group" is formed by the political and ideological articulation of ruling-class interests in a way that unites competing interests within the ruling class and justifies them as interests of the whole society.

In the early phases of the development of advanced capitalist states, and in the later development of peripheral capitalist states, a given "historic bloc" mobilizes a coalition of ruling-class fractions with a shared project for managing the future accumulation of capital, which is imposed upon the majority "subaltern" classes in that society. Domination is effected through coercion and the threat of coercion. Changes in such regimes of domination are effected either through "passive revolution," the introduction of changes from above without the mobilization of popular forces, and, therefore, without the possibility of the new historic bloc achieving substantial popular consent, or through a "war of movement," a revolutionary smashing of the state by popular movements. In these terms the development of peripheral capitalist states like Gramsci's Italy and the bulk of the Third World, is characterized by unstable, Caesarist regimes (Hoare and Nowell Smith 1971, 219 ff.), and by "transformist" strategies designed to co-opt the ideas and leadership of proto-revolutionary movements (58 ff.). In contrast to this typical experience of peripheral or early capitalist states, and also to the exceptional experience of states like the Soviet Union in which a revolutionary "war of movement" is effectively waged against the developing capitalist state, the advanced capitalist states have achieved a qualitatively different type of hegemonic order.

Hegemony is a situation in which class rule is maintained through the widespread consent of the majority classes, "an acceptance, not necessarily explicit, of the socio-political order or of certain vital aspects of that order" (Femia 1981, 37). In such situations classes actively participate in their own domination, and the use of coercion, "the armature of consent," is minimized and obscured. Gramsci uses the concept of hegemony to counterpose the political experience of East and West, arguing for the greater resilience of class rule, and therefore for a different socialist politics in the West. He also uses the concept to distinguish the historical genealogies of Western states like Britain, France, and the United States, where a genuine hegemony or organic unity has been built upon a thorough social revolution, from these of states like Italy, where capitalist transformation was imposed rather than internally generated, and where the new industrial bourgeoisie failed to achieve hegemony.

Gramsci's concept of hegemony is both flexible and historically concrete and escapes the rigidities imposed by the epistemological purism of much Marxism. He distinguishes "integral" or full hegemony from "decadent" and "minimal" hegemony, and sees integral hegemony as a rare condition, prevailing only "when the ruling class performs a progressive function in the productive process, when it really causes the entire society to move forward ..." (Femia 1981, 46–7). More generally his focus is upon the limits to hegemony, crises of hegemony, and the political strategies to be adopted in consequence. Hegemony is not simply a superstructural element of ideology or consciousness, isolated from the underlying causal influence of economic forces. Rather, hegemony involves an articulation of the interrelated forces of economics, politics, and ideology, none of which is a pure realm of reality rather than deception, material rather than subjective experience, or coercion rather than consent.

Hegemony is achieved by the political leadership of a class occupying a concrete position in the economy (Mouffe 1979). Hegemony is thus conceptualized as a *political* process in which a cohesive historic bloc is created among elements of a ruling class, and between that class and the general population. The political process is dialectically related to economic processes, and to associated cultural and social-psychological processes. The interrelationships are well captured by Adamson:

The central thrust is the suggestion that a class, as it develops itself historically, becomes more or less politically powerful not only because of its position within the economic structure but also because it is the carrier of certain values which, though certainly expressions of its experience in the world of work and everyday life, become detached as images or projections of its political outlook. Depending on the attractiveness of such images, the class will be able to attach itself to other political groups as joint power-seekers, potential power-shapers, and the social forces behind new cultural expressions. (Adamson 1980, 177)

Clearly this formulation speaks of the influences of values, images, and projections, but never in a way that abstracts these from their material context in economic and political relations. Gramsci's materialism does not involve the primary determination by economic factors, nor is there simply equal determination by economic and ideological factors. Instead it involves a dialectical, mutually reinforcing unity of these categories.

Gramsci points to the role of political leadership, and of "organic intellectuals," in disseminating the values of the ruling class but he does not simply picture a voluntarist creation of hegemony by the great men and minds of history. His "modern prince" derives from a Marxist reading of Machiavelli:

The active politician is a creator, an initiator; but he neither creates from nothing nor does he move in the turbid void of his own desires and dreams. He bases himself on effective reality, but what is this effective reality? Is it something static and immobile, or is it not rather a relation of forces in continuous motion and shift of equilibrium? If one applies one's will to the creation of a new equilibrium of forces among the forces which really exist and are operative ... one still moves on the terrain of effective reality, but does so in order to dominate and transcend it (or contribute to this). (Hoare and Nowell Smith 1971, 172)

Political leadership, in the creation of hegemonic (or counter-hegemonic) projects thus operates on the terrain of "effective reality," and is limited by it. Similarly, the organic intellectuals who produce the values and perspectives necessary for the ruling classes to exercise hegemonic leadership over subordinate groups are attached to concrete classes with definite economic interests. "Every social group, coming into existence on the original terrain of an essential function in the world of economic production, creates together with itself, organically, one or more strata of intellectuals which give it homogeneity and an awareness of its own function not only in the economic but also in the social and political fields" (Hoare and Nowell Smith 1971, 5). Gramsci's materialism is very definite, but it does not abstractly counterpose the subjective realm of ideology to the material realms of economic and political life, nor is ideology reified as a phenomenon that acts on mass consciousness in its own right. Ideology, for Gramsci, has its own social agents, and it is imposed upon subordinate classes in concrete institutions by acts of political leadership. Because ideology is constructed politically in the context of economic disequilibrium and conflictual class relations, it is always subject to change. Ideological change in response to changing material conditions, however, is no more certain than ideological domination that prevents the emergence and realization of popular conceptions of the possibility for change inherent in new material conditions. "It may be ruled out that immediate economic crises of themselves produce fundamental historical events; they can simply create a terrain more favourable to the dissemination of certain modes of thought, and certain ways of posing and resolving questions involving the entire subsequent development of national life" (Hoare and Nowell Smith 1971, 184).

However, economic crises *may*, if taken advantage of by effective organization and leadership, lead to a genuine "organic crisis," in which the ruling class ceases to lead and the masses are no longer led.

In every country the process is different, although the content is the same. And the content is the crisis of the ruling class's hegemony, which occurs either because the ruling class has failed in some major political undertaking for which it has requested, or forcibly extracted, the consent of the broad masses (war, for example), or because huge masses (especially of peasants and petit bourgeois intellectuals) have passed suddenly from a state of political passivity to a certain activity, and put forward demands which taken together, albeit not organically formulated, add up to a revolution. A "crisis of authority" is spoken of: this is precisely the crisis of hegemony, or general crisis of the State. (Hoare and Nowell Smith 1971, 210)

The sweep of Gramsci's conceptualization of hegemony is clear and impressive; it provides us with a powerful organizing principle for empirical inquiry into political history. This is evident, for example, in the work of Robert Cox (1987), which gives a comprehensive and historically concrete conceptualization of the development of liberal democratic states and changing patterns of world order based upon the hegemony of dominant capitalist states. Cox analyses the development of a liberal world order founded on the principles of free trade imperialism in the seventeenth and eighteenth centuries; the developing crisis facing capitalist states, and the world order in which they were hierarchically related, dating from the long world depression of 1873–96; the gradual construction of the national welfare state in the subsequent era of rival imperialisms from Otto von Bismark's social programs in the late nineteenth century, to the first *Beveridge Report* (1909) and the political and social reforms following the First World

War; the consolidation of the welfare state following the second *Beveridge Report* (1942) and other adaptations of the economic and social policy implications of Keynes's *General Theory of Employment, Interest and Money* (1936); the shift from the nationalist and protectionist welfare state to the neo-liberal state, making adjustments to the open world economy under the hegemonic direction of the United States after the Second World War, and the change from boom to crisis conditions in the mid-1970s, with unstable regimes reflecting differences in the balance of forces supporting either the hyperliberal, or neo-conservative projects undertaken by Margaret Thatcher and Ronald Reagan in Britain and the United States, or the state capitalist projects undertaken in countries like France, Japan, and Sweden.

We cannot reproduce or even survey the range of conceptual and historical argument that buttresses this analysis in only one, if one of the best, of the many works building on Gramsci's guidelines. What we propose instead is to provide a sketch of Canadian political history in these terms, a sketch that emphasizes the interrelated economic, political, and ideological aspects of changes in hegemonic regimes.

Canadian political history, like the history of any other capitalist state, can be viewed as a series of attempts, in the face of domestic and international economic crisis, to formulate a hegemonic national policy that secures national unity and economic growth. Each of these attempts can be seen as responding to and in turn generating specific class and regional conflicts.

The paradox of Canadian political development has been the simultaneous strength and fragility of the state – its expanding powers and intervention in the society and economy, accompanied by its continuing weakness relative to domestic class and regional supports, and to the power of international capital. In one sense hegemony has perhaps been less securely established in Canada than in other advanced capitalist states, where the solidarity and autonomy of a dominant, national capitalist class has been more marked; where cultural homogeneity and independence have been more entrenched; and where economic self-sufficiency and trading clout have been more apparent. On the other hand the lower expectations of Canadians, accustomed to their place in the world order, contribute a low-key durability to a less than "integral" hegemonic order, and the general logic of the dialectical development and undermining of hegemony is a useful guide to Canadian affairs, and to locating the specific political problems of the late 1970s, with which this book deals.

The next section illustrates this dialectical development. We take up successively the origins of the modern Canadian state and the first formulation of hegemonic rule under the National Policy after 1878; the collapse of this cycle of hegemony in the interwar era and the development of the postwar hegemonic "settlement" in terms of Keynesian welfare state policy; and, finally, the collapse of this settlement in the mid-1970s, and the partial and unsuccessful attempts to combat the intensifying crisis of hegemony through the last years of the Trudeau era. As suggested in our introduction, we make no pretense here to complete historical analysis and documentation. It is, nevertheless, important to lay out this historical context, since it is as much, and maybe more, the source of our interpretation of survey data as the more abstract theoretical arguments in which our data analysis is couched.

HEGEMONY AND CRISIS IN CANADIAN HISTORY

The National Policy

The Canadian state established in 1867 can be characterized as an attempt by indigenous capitalist interests to establish a hegemonic project for the economic development of a colonial society threatened by changes in the international and imperial system of which it was a subordinate part. Like all such hegemonic projects, this one was born in a situation of impending crisis and involved an attempt to universalize a particular ideology, in order to obtain consent for a project that reflected a rather narrow class interest.

The Canadian federation was conceived in 1867 as a strong state with central government powers sufficient to avoid the political paralysis of the parity and veto provisions of the Act of Union between Quebec and Ontario and to escape the presumed deficiencies of the residual state powers in the constitution of the United States, which had not long before emerged from traumatic civil war. The deterioration in diplomatic relations between the United States and Britain during and after that civil war and the implied threats to the security of the Canadian colonies were also precipitating causes of the agreement to the devolution of power to a stronger post-colonial state. Finally, Confederation was conceived as a mechanism for the promotion of economic growth, and an escape from the vulnerable position *vis-à-vis* British and American economic power following the loss of protected markets in Britain in the 1840s and 1850s, and the impending abrogation of the Reciprocity Treaty with the United States in terms of which Canadian industrialization had made considerable progress during the civil war (Stevenson 1979, chap. 2).

This defence of the strong state was not uncontested. Opposition to it was grounded in an indigenous reform tradition that, despite defeat in the rebellions of the 1830s and 1840s and relative weakness at the time of Confederation, would re-emerge in agrarian protest movements in the twentieth century. Nor was the Canadian ideological formula without internal contradictions, most obviously those having to do with opposing arguments that privileged free trade and the minimal, night-watchman state above protection by strong government. In the short run, however, Tory hegemony was jeopardized less by such threats than by scandal arising from the symbiotic relationships between government and business, by intense rivalries between the two commercial centres of Montreal and Toronto, and by the economic threat of the "great depression" beginning in 1873.

Deposed by the scandal in that year, John A. Macdonald was fortunate to have the political costs of the depression charged to the Liberals. Re-elected in 1878, he moved to buttress the Tory's hegemonic project of state-led economic growth through the formulation of the National Policy. This formula for national unity and economic growth combined economic protectionism and regional development: tariff protection for central Canadian manufacturing, the export of the wheat staple to generate the capital and income necessary for domestic manufacturing, and railway development to integrate the society from sea to shining sea by moving the staples to export and central Canadian manufactures to the staple-producing hinterlands (Craven and Traves 1979).

The class and ideological supports for this project are subjects of considerable argument. One highly influential, but disputed, view is that Confederation and the national policy reflected the "material position" of a dominant commercial fraction of Canadian capital, "big merchants, bankers and transportation entrepreneurs" (Naylor 1975, 18). Against the view that Canadian economic development suffered from a lack of indigenous entrepreneurship, R.T. Naylor argues that "the real problem was the stultification of indigenous industrial capital by the continued dominance of merchant capital, together with the historically rooted characteristics of American capitalism" (Naylor 1975, 24). Against this emphasis on commercial interests Vernon Fowke argues that the objectives of the National Policy were to join the commercial, financial, and manufacturing interests of the central Canadian provinces; and to help build rather than hinder an indigenous industrial bourgeoisie, but at the expense of the wheat-producing hinterland (Fowke 1957, 245). Other economic historians (Easterbrook and Aitken 1956) emphasize the autonomy of government decision makers who were constrained by the overriding objective of the National Policy to maintain Canadian sovereignty north of the American border, and by their dependence for that purpose on staples exports for overseas earnings, but otherwise independently shaped a national economy. Glen Williams rounds out this argument with an analysis of the national policy as a strategy of import substitution industrialization, designed to capture "primarily consumer-oriented sectors of the home market with a production process borrowed from foreign industrialists" (Williams 1983, 13). As such it appealed to the interests of Canadian industrial capital, who joined their support for the policy to that of finance capital, and who benefited from it even if state action was characterized by "a near monopoly of effort in the direction of resource export" (32).

As a hegemonic regime, the first National Policy combined the support of ruling-class fractions with the incorporation or marginalization of subordinate classes. Leo Panitch suggests that the emphasis on capital borrowing from the United States is explained not simply by the interests of capitalists, but also by the relations of production in Canadian industry. He argues that relatively high Canadian wages meant that Canadian industry was uncompetitive and in a weak position to resist the foreign competition introduced behind the tariff wall (Panitch 1981a, 16–20). Paul Craven and Tom Traves point out that Canadian labour supported Macdonald in his National Policy election, but that far from being unconditional, this support was secured by the Tory agreement to legitimize organized labour (in the Trade Union Act) and support the nine-hour day (Craven and Traves 1979, 17).

Apart from the farm sector, therefore, the National Policy achieved a substantial degree of support from all classes and class fractions. Opposition by farmers and lumbermen was significant, notably in Ontario, where the provincial government opposed high tariffs and supported free trade, eventually persuading the federal Liberals to adopt a policy of free trade with the United States (Stevenson 1979, 85). But the National Policy had become sufficiently effective as a hegemonic instrument that it was maintained even after 1896, when the Liberals came to power under Wilfrid Laurier. By that time the far-reaching changes effected by industrialization under the National Policy refocused the electoral and ideological positions of political parties competing for the urban vote. There was no difference in the two parties' responsiveness to big business, at either the federal or provincial level, and the end of the recession in the world economy was an additional impetus to growth, and further disincentive to dismantling the national policy (McNaught 1976, 188 ff.).

The success of the national policy as a formula for growth and prosperity was not, however, unproblematic. It brought about "geographical centralization of the economy with concomitant regional underdevelopment, and the integration of the country's industrial leadership into the established commercial and financial elite which had long dominated the Canadian economic and political system" (Traves 1979, 5). Mounting farmer protests, culminating in the 1910 "March on Ottawa," sought relief from the tariff and a reciprocity agreement with the United States. In order to forestall further political unrest, Laurier complied, only to be defeated on the free trade issue in the 1911 election by the opposition of a well-organized, solid business class and the inability to gain an alliance between a disorganized and politically marginal working class and the farmers (McNaught 1976, 198–203). Important though class divisions were to the outcome in this election, they were superimposed upon marked regional divisions, with Liberal support concentrated in the West and parts of Quebec and with Conservative victories elsewhere (Brodie and Jenson 1980, 199).

Electoral victory temporarily secured the National Policy, but the threats to the hegemony of the regime based on this policy were soon accentuated by economic crisis. In 1913 the wheat economy faltered and railway expansion collapsed. Despite a recovery led by war contracts, and despite the efficiency and rationalization of wartime regulation of the economy, the postwar economy fell into recession between 1920 and 1925. The associated political crisis of these times was evident first in the breakdown of party politics and the formation of the Union government of 1917. But this manoeuvre could not disguise the fact that "interregional, intersectoral, intra-industrial, and marked inter-class conflict prevailed on all fronts" (Traves 1979, 8). Escalating political protest was expressed in the 1917 Canadian Council of Agriculture's demand for a new national policy, the demand for "better terms" from the Maritime Rights Movement a few years later, the Winnipeg General Strike of 1919, and the dramatic rise of the Progressive party after 1920.

The Progressives captured all but two of the seats in the Prairie provinces in the 1921 federal election, but their effectiveness was limited by internal division and by co-optation by the dominant federal parties, especially after record production and profit levels were re-established after 1925 (Traves 1979, 7 ff.). The economic recovery, however, was short-lived, and the profound impact of the Great Depression began to be felt within four years. Despite the severity of the collapse, the call for a radical alternative to a failing capitalism was muted by the decline of the Progressives, the weakness of the Communist party of Canada and its proscription in 1931, the internal divisions within the trade union movement, and by the relatively localized, agrarian base of the newly formed (1933) social democratic Co-operative Commonwealth Federation (CCF).

Nevertheless the years of intermittent political unrest between the economic collapses of 1913 and 1929 indicated the exhaustion of the national policy under which hegemony was established in the newly independent Canada. A new hegemonic project was required, and formative efforts in that direction began during the Depression. Clearly but timidly, imitating initiatives taken in Britain and the United States, the new policy involved a settlement of the class conflicts of the pre-war era in the form of programs designed to ensure the security and welfare of labour *vis-à-vis* capital, through an enlarged state responsibility in the field of social welfare, an agricultural policy concerned with price supports and crop-failure legislation, and a full employment policy based on Keynesian principles (Fowke 1957, 247 ff.). Further, the new national policy aimed to settle the associated regional conflicts through the equalization of fiscal resources, economic development investments, and national standards of social welfare across the different regions and provinces of Canada. These settlements were to be achieved as the result of a new regime of accumulation in which the highly concentrated, oligopolistic industrial economy brought into being at the beginning of the century would be relieved of the problems of overproduction and underconsumption by new forms of state intervention and regulation designed to guarantee full employment and the stability of effective demand.

The Welfare State in Canada

The Keynesian welfare state, under which this hegemonic settlement of the conflicting interests of labour and capital was achieved following the Second World War, was materially institutionalized in a complex matrix of policies. These provided for the indirect macroeconomic regulation of the economy by fiscal and monetary instruments, rather than by direct state intervention in the economy; the recognition of trade union powers and a system of "free" collective bargaining as a restraint on the powers of capital in the otherwise "free" market economy, with corollary restraints on labour's right to strike; the state's absorption of the most significant costs of the reproduction of labour (health and education); and, finally, the creation of a social welfare safety net, to cover the minimum needs of the unemployed and unemployable and thereby to ensure aggregate demand and labour mobility.

The key to achieving hegemonic consent to this new national policy lay in the work of Keynes, which could be used to rationalize the consent of members of the capitalist class and state officials to the new regime of accumulation and to its associated structures of social policy and labour relations. This theoretical and ideological breakthrough did not, however, create the new structures. Especially in the areas of social policy and labour relations, the welfare state had been gradually forming in capitalist societies as the result of the political struggles in the preceding era of rival imperialisms (See Cox 1987, chap. 6). The rhythm and specific institutional character of this development differed depending on the nature of those struggles, and the institutional framework within which they took place. In Canada, as elsewhere, the escalating political and ideological coherence of opposition movements representing farmers and the urban working class was, as we have indicated, crucial in setting the stage for reform in the interwar period, but the emergence of a welfare state before the Second World War was slow. Even after the war the pace of the Canadian welfare state was slow relative to other advanced capitalist countries, the scope of welfare measures introduced was relatively restricted (cf. Heclo 1974, 112), and the application of strictly Keynesian policy more marked in the breach than the observance (Campbell 1987).

Canadian social policy makers were particularly reluctant to move from the classical liberal postulate that individual welfare was a private, rather than a state, responsibility taken care of by the work and savings of the able bodied, and by charity for the incompetent (Guest 1980, 1; Bryden 1974, 18–20). With relatively weak industrial expansion, and the concomitant weakness of organized labour (only 6 percent of the workforce in 1926), there was little to motivate the adoption in Canada of the Bismarkean or Fabian logics of state social welfare policy as a defence against working-class militancy and as a minimal guarantee of equality of opportunity in a democratic state. In the years before the Great Depression social welfare was limited to a handful of provincial programs, like those providing benefits to injured workers in Ontario and to widowed mothers in British Columbia.

The passage of the Old Age Pensions Act in 1927, however, marked the beginning of a long-term process of welfare state development similar to that in other developed capitalist countries. As in these other countries, the process reflected the pressures of class conflict in the state (cf. Shalev 1983; Korpi 1983), with the turnaround on pensions affected by the growing articulation of working-class power from the Winnipeg General Strike of 1919 to the electoral victories of Progressive, Independent, and Labour candidates in the 1925 federal election (Guest 1980, 75–7). Pension legislation was supplemented in 1930 by the first national unemployment relief act, a cost-shared arrangement for assistance through provincial work projects and direct relief (Manzer 1985, 56).

The reluctance of Canadian governments to move further in these directions except under extreme pressure (Bryden 1974, 70) and the minimal provisions of existing income security legislation was evident again in the Richard Bennett "New Deal." The response to massive unemployment in the 1935 On-to-Ottawa Trek and the Regina food riots added muscle to the intellectual critique of the capitalist order in the CCF's Regina Manifesto and to its growing support in public opinion. In the face of such pressure, and despite the counter-pressure of business opposition (Cuneo 1979; but see Finkel 1979, chap. 2 for a different view), legislative proposals were introduced to establish comprehensive programs of health and unemployment insurance, old age pensions, cost-shared social assistance and public works, and aid to farmers. The motivation for these initiatives was clearly conservative, concerned "to extend the power and the influence of the state, as in the direction of social reform, in so far as this may be necessary to protect and defend the essentials of the *status quo*" (H.M. Cassidy, quoted in Wilbur 1968, 32).

Prime Minister Bennett's "deathbed conversion" to social welfare policy did not save him, and the Canadian Employment and Social Insurance Act was struck down in 1937 as *ultra vires* of federal government jurisdiction by the Judicial Committee of the Privy Council. The new William Lyon

MacKenzie King government nevertheless maintained the focus of the New Deal proposals on containing labour unrest by initiating in 1937 and achieving in 1940 an Unemployment Insurance Act, made possible by constitutional amendment. The momentum behind the gradual adoption of the 1935 welfare package was maintained by the effects, real and anticipated, of the war economy. Rapid industrial expansion and the demonstrated efficacy of state management of the economy, family allowances for families of armed servicemen (Guest 1980, 105), the concern with health deficiencies among otherwise inductable recruits to the armed services (cf. Taylor 1978, 18), rapid increases in union membership during the war (Finkel 1979, 358), and the growing popularity of the CCF (Granatstein, 1975, 268), all added to the fear of postwar economic collapse and of political unrest in the absence of social welfare measures to "maintain the free-enterprise economy against assaults from the left" (Granatstein 1975, 250). This motivation was clearly felt by Leonard Marsh, the author of the much-read 1943 report *Social Security for Canada*, which he modelled on the 1942 report of his former mentor Lord Beveridge. Marsh's call for a comprehensive social security system, reinforced by a coherent employment policy, was operationalized in the Throne Speech of January 1944, which outlined a series of programs to promote employment, nutrition, and housing, and to protect against unemployment, misfortune, illness, and old age (Wolfe 1985, 54).

The theoretical transformation of liberal economic doctrine that would make such policy possible had in the meantime been communicated within the government by "new men" like Robert Bryce, a former student of Keynes, and by Professor W.A. Mackintosh, whose "schoolmasterish drill" gained cabinet approval for the 1945 *White Paper on Employment and Income* (Granatstein 1982, 153–68, 256–61). The White Paper stated that "the maintenance of a high and stable level of employment and income" was now a major aim of government policy, and that a Keynesian counter-cyclical economic strategy would be adopted to that end (Granatstein 1975, 277). This statement announced the emergence of the modern welfare state in Canada, and an ideological revolution in the understanding of social policy.

Whereas earlier social policy had been formulated on a limited, uncoordinated, and ad hoc basis, mostly as a reaction to pressures for change, the Canadian government now proposed to establish a comprehensive social welfare system that would institutionalize the government's, rather than the market's, ultimate responsibility for social welfare. This assault on the hitherto impregnable "market ethos" was justified by a critical ideological transition in the understanding of limited government as an economic agent of last resort. Interventionist government was now seen as a principal instrument of economic development and social progress, with social expenditures, previously viewed as a means of maintaining a surplus population, now seen as an engine of economic expansion and job creation, as well as the guarantor of social stability.

As with the Bennett New Deal, however, constitutional limitations and a resurgence of economic growth stalled the implementation of the postwar welfare state. The Family Allowance Act was passed in 1944, but the "Green Book" proposals to the 1945 Dominion-Provincial Conference on Reconstruction for implementing other aspects of the new social policy met with provincial government opposition. The comprehensive scheme was therefore translated into another phase of incremental and relatively uncoordinated change in the various fields of social policy.

In this new phase of implementation of the Keynesian welfare state, the determining influence of class conflict on the implementation of social policy is less significant than that of executive and bureaucratic politics. But the institutional complexities of federal politics could only delay, not halt, the expansion of the welfare state (Banting 1982), and class-based conflict over new policies was far from insignificant. Movement on labour relations legislation was more or less immediate, with the 1948 Industrial Relations and Disputes Investigations Act balancing recognition of unionization and the right to free collective bargaining with clear constraints on the right to strike. Pensions policy in 1950–51 reflected the marked conflict between business and labour leaders over the principal of universality, the Social Security Act providing selective, means-tested assistance to persons between sixty-five and sixty-nine, and the Old Age Assistance Act providing universal benefits to those over seventy (Bryden 1974, 117–24). The Unemployment Assistance Act of 1956, though not any substantial modification of existing legislation (Guest 1980, 147) was a reaction in part to growing unemployment following the recession of 1953–54, when unemployment reached 4.6 percent. The 1957 Hospital Insurance and Diagnostic Services Act was the last piece of the social policy matrix mapped out in 1945 that the still surviving postwar Liberal regime could implement before its defeat that year. The victory in this case of labour interests over those of private medical practitioners and hospital managements, supported by provincial governments, was perhaps as much assisted by the renewed onset of economic difficulties and unemployment (7.1 percent in 1957–58 following a worldwide recession) as it was by the success of the decade-old legislation of this kind under the social democratic government in Saskatchewan (Taylor 1978).

By the onset of the 1960s, therefore, and certainly by the time of the 1966 Medical Care Act, this second national policy had changed the face of Canadian society. This policy became very deeply embedded in the ideological perspectives of the general Canadian public, as we will show. Despite its continuing appeal, however, this second hegemonic regime showed signs of internal strain soon after its full implementation.

Towards Hegemonic Crisis

To understand how the hegemonic unity of the postwar settlement degenerated into the hegemonic crisis of recent years, it is useful to begin with a brief detour into theoretical arguments about the problems of the Keynesian welfare state. At the most general level, these problems have been expressed as the mutually contradictory commitments to accumulation and legitimation by the interventionist Keynesian welfare state (O'Connor 1973). The threats to the hegemony of the welfare state are expressed in terms of the antagonism between the dominant form of capitalist accumulation, the multinational, oligopolistic corporation, and the requirements of full employment and regional equity. According to James O'Connor, this antagonism produces a fiscal crisis generated by the growing "structural gap" between state expenditure and revenue.

So long as the postwar reconstruction of the global capitalist economy produced growth in a context of relative stability in the international economy (and, necessarily, in its politics), stability of commodity prices, and a reasonably predictable trade-off between inflation and unemployment, this gap could be contained. But unless the Keynesian strategy of increasing demand can be rapidly translated into increasing investment, failing economic growth leads to a fall in state revenue coupled with increased costs of social programs, and, given the welfare state's fixed commitments to social expenditures, a "fiscal crisis." And in the absence of effective Keynesian management, the political price of buying legitimacy with social expenditures is massive opposition to the alternative remedy of cutting expenditures so as to release supply-side rather than demand-side resources for accumulation.

In Offe's formulation the central contradiction of the welfare state originates in the welfare state's intervention to promote the conditions for profitable accumulation. This effort actually institutionalizes threats to profitability, because welfare state programs provide goods and services on a decommodified basis, in response to politically defined needs or rights. This inherent contradiction potentially accentuates, rather than mediates, class conflict by sharpening the antagonism between "the political reproduction demands of labour power and the private reproduction strategies of capital" (Offe 1984, 77). Further state policy making and administration is politically vulnerable because the state, unlike private firms operating in the market, "does not have unequivocal, uncontroversial, and operational cues as to what the goals of its productive state activities should be" (Offe 1984, 138).

These problems were first revealed in the ambiguous populism of the John Diefenbaker interlude, following the economic slow-down of 1957. Only nine years after the presentation of the *White Paper on Employment and Income*, which outlined the Keynesian strategy for economic management, the economic growth of the postwar period, which had in any event required little or no application of Keynesian technique (Campbell 1985, 70), came to an end in the recession of 1954. In this year of low growth, as in the earlier periods of increased unemployment and inflation preceding and during the Korean War, the Liberal government rejected Keynesian demand management in favour of monetarist control of inflation and a supply-side policy of encouraging unregulated foreign investment (Campbell 1987, 94–116). But after a brief boom in the export of raw materials, private investment peaked and unemployment grew again after 1957.

The political response that brought Diefenbaker and the Progressive Conservatives to power revealed the continued importance of class tensions within the hegemonic discourse of the Canadian welfare state, as well as the strong comingling of class and regional political oppositions. Where economic growth under the first national policy was based upon a protective economic nationalism, in the second national policy it was based upon commitments to the functional integration of the international capitalist world. The rapid Americanization of investment, production, and culture that followed in Canada, and the decay of "welfare liberalism" into "business liberalism," provoked a renewal of the regional and class divisions of the pre-war period.

Diefenbaker was no more able to satisfy his new coalition of disaffected regional and class constituencies than the preceding government. The rapid expansion in social expenditures, from $885 million in 1957 to $1,970 million in 1962, under the Diefenbaker government reflected continuing economic stagnation in that period, especially after the North American recession of 1961–62. The new prime minister's populist articulation of the interests of the "little man" in "social justice" (Newman 1963, 190–1) illustrated his sensitivity to the breakdown of "spontaneous consent" in these times of economic difficulty, but increasing social spending was no longer considered a means to economic recovery by a government that had explicitly rejected Keynesian policy. Instead the government resorted to a "miniaturized" national policy of subsidized economic development and make-work schemes in time of recession (Campbell 1983, 120 ff.). The financial considerations that constrained the Diefenbaker vision resulted in a combination of increasing social welfare payments with rising government deficits and debt servicing, and with political struggles over the restrictive monetary policy of the Bank of Canada (Newman 1963, chap. 15). This trajectory closely parallels later developments in the Trudeau era, but convenient political amnesia buried the point in Conservative contributions to the partisan debates of the next decade.

This early manifestation of the tendency toward fiscal crisis as a result of contradictory pressures for accumulation and legitimation in the welfare state was partially responsible for the political blunders and internecine conflicts that marked the end of the Diefenbaker government. These mistakes

gave a narrow victory to the new Liberal government, which had no fundamentally different vision of economic policy, but "had the good sense to return to office once the period of sluggishness had ended" (Campbell 1983,
144). Good luck gave momentum to the reform orientation of key organizers
of the Liberal party's electoral strategy to displace Diefenbaker, though internal struggles over economic policy between reformers and conservatives
in the new Liberal government became increasingly clear after 1963 (McCall
Newman 1982).

Lester B. Pearson chose as minister of finance Walter Gordon, author of
the 1957 Royal Commission on Canada's Economic Prospects, which had
provided the justification for Diefenbaker's unsuccessful attempts to regain
control of an economy dominated by United States investments. Gordon
pursued an interventionist strategy of counteracting sectoral and regional underdevelopment, and the associated problems of American ownership and
balance of payments. But the nationalist finance minister's sectoral development policies failed to stem the tide of foreign investment and control: between 1939 and 1967 the proportion of Canadian manufacturing assets that
were U.S. controlled rose from 32 to 57 percent and the equivalent proportions in mining and smelting rose from 38 to 65 percent (Laux and Molot
1988, 53). Despite his overriding commitment to a conservative, balanced-
budget management of the economy, Gordon's attempts at a relatively ag-
gressive interventionism succeeded only in irritating the Canadian business
community. Finally, his effort to stoke popular support for the Liberal government by a 1965 tax cut failed and Pearson did not reappoint him to his
third minority government.

The political and economic difficulties of the Liberal government forecast
the much-intensified problems of the 1970s. The Pearson government was
unable to gain effective control of the economy or, in the last years before the
coming to power of Trudeau, to control the escalating labour unrest and inflation (Campbell 1987, 157–65) that would be the key problems of the
1970s. The boom of 1962–66 delayed recognition of the underlying economic problems and allowed for the continuing development of the Canadian welfare state in response to regional and class dissatisfactions
associated with uneven economic development. Such dissatisfactions were
articulated by the more *dirigiste* and reformist Liberal government leading
the Quiet Revolution in Quebec after 1960 (McRoberts and Posgate 1976,
95), and by the development, within the NDP, of the "Waffle" movement's
more radical critique of liberalism. These political and ideological forces
shaped the continued development of social policy in a field of recognizably
intensified class conflict.

The 1965 Canada/Quebec Pension Plan reflected popular pressures for
pension reform and Quebec's 1963 proposals for a comprehensive pension
plan. The debate was marked, however, by sharp divisions between capital

and labour. The insurance industry and the Canadian Chamber of Commerce opposed the government proposals, while the Canadian Labour Congress supported them with a postcard-petition campaign (Bryden 1974, 161–2). The 1966 federal Medical Care Insurance Act likewise followed a more progressive Saskatchewan provincial government's initiatives, and the articulation of radically diverging interests on the part of labour and business (including the business-minded professionals) in the Saskatchewan doctors' strike (Badgeley and Wolfe 1967), with similar expressions of conflict of interest in the federal provincial negotiations preceding national medicare (Taylor 1978).

With the introduction of universal, taxation-based medical insurance the Canadian welfare state reached its zenith. Compared to the experience of other rich developed nations, except for the United States, however, the "complete" version of the Canadian welfare state was quite limited. Significant redistribution and gains for the poor and marginalized groups were achieved by old age pensions and unemployment and medical insurance, but in retrospect and in international context the limited nature of the Canadian welfare state is clear. Years of political struggle would be necessary before the concerns of native peoples and women received much attention, and Canada's partial welfare state never rejected assumptions about the justice of markets and private ownership, about the distinction between the deserving and undeserving poor, and about the possibility and importance of equalizing opportunity without changing the overall distribution of income or wealth (see, for example, the essays in Moscovitch and Drover 1981). Minimum wages and social assistance rates were unaffected by reforming zeal, lest reforms imperil the incentive to work – thus a new generation of single parents was consigned to poverty. Physician and hospital domination of the medical system was unaffected by the institution of an insurance program since there was no parallel reform to the structure of health care delivery, and health insurance funded fees for services by physicians. The structure of the taxation system was unaffected by minor reforms that succeeded only in shifting the burden of federal taxation increasingly from business to personal taxes; while provinces slowly increased their highly regressive sales taxes, excise taxes continued to be a major source of federal government revenue and municipalities remained dependent on property taxes.

The Trudeau Era: Organic Crisis and a Third National Policy

There was nothing automatic in the transition from the expansion to the contraction of the Canadian welfare state. The continued economic difficulties of the Pearson era did not simply escalate to the point of crisis in the Trudeau years, and the contradictions between accumulation and legitimation did not simply intensify so that the relationship between social welfare spending and economic policy in support of investment and employment changed suddenly from being functional to dysfunctional. The process of change was critically affected by political and ideological responses to economic circumstances, as much as by the "objective" circumstances themselves. In seeking to understand this process, we must be sensitive not only to the increasing economic instability and resulting threat to the material supports of the welfare state consensus, but also to the political and ideological variations on that theme composed by the central actors: capital, labour, and state.

Despite promises at the 1967 World's Fair (Expo 67) that the present if not the future belonged to Canada, and despite the euphoric Trudeaumania of the 1968 election, an interaction of unsteady economic environment, fiscal squeeze, social policy conflicts, and welfare state contraction was soon apparent. The unemployment rate, which had been halved between the retirements of Diefenbaker and Pearson, rose more or less consistently from 1967 to 1970, when it was again over 6 percent. Inflation, which in the Diefenbaker years had behaved more in keeping with Phillips curve expectations of an inverse correlation of unemployment and inflation, had risen rapidly from 1965 to 1967, and rose again after a slight decline in 1967–68 to 4.5 percent in 1969 (Employment and Immigration Canada, 1981, in Doern and Phidd 1983, 493). Industrial conflict also increased, peaking at eight million person-days lost in 1969, dropping again to less than half that in 1971, and then increasing again to that figure in 1972. Working-class militancy, expressed in terms of strikes, was relatively higher in Canada than in other advanced capitalist countries, averaging 812.7 working days lost through strikes per annum per 1000 workers employed, for the period 1971–80 (Rotstein 1984, 81).

As labour's militancy grew and as capital's ability to sustain economic growth was undercut in the 1970s, the partnership between labour and capital that had been critical to the hegemonic capacities of the postwar settlement began to erode. For capital, of course, the two phenomena were causally related: labour's wage increases pushed inflation, retarded productivity, and cut profitability and investment. The influence of this argument in government circles, and of the associated links between Keynesian demand management, welfare state expansion, and economic difficulty, were clear to Robert Bryce, the deputy minister of finance and one of the godfathers of welfare-Keynesianism in Canada:

There has been a structural element in the persistence of this particular price and cost inflation, engendered by the expectation that the business cycle has been cured at last, by the increased size and importance of the government sector, by the belief that governments are committed to the maintaining or restoring of full employment and by other factors, such as the continued world-wide prosperity ... the widespread belief that inflation will continue to find its expression and effect in demands for large wage increases by workers, and for high interest rates by lenders, and in a willingness on the part of business to pay both. (Bryce 1971, 230)

Under this influence, the government first attempted to gain a corporatist agreement on restraint measures to restore stability. The February 1969 National Conference on Price Stability convened by the newly established federal Prices and Incomes Commission failed to secure labour's participation (Wolfe 1977, 168), but business leaders agreed to voluntary measures to restrict profits, and inflation rates dropped to 3.3 and 2.9 percent in the next two years. Business support in this area increased its bargaining power with the Trudeau government, as reflected subsequently in the 1971 tax bill. Originally intended to implement many of the far-reaching proposals of the Carter Royal Commission on Tax Reform, the bill was eviscerated in parliamentary review; and the resulting new act "provides the first instance in which Trudeau's lip-service to social democratic ideals collapsed under pressure from the business community" (Campbell 1983, 159).

Restraint, price stability, and tax concessions to business did nothing, however, for unemployment or the poor. The extent of poverty in an affluent Canada achieved prominence as a result of the 1971 Report of the Special Senate Committee on Poverty, which called for a guaranteed annual income to combat the high tax burden of the poor, and the dissenting *Real Poverty Report* (Adams 1971), which attacked the tax system, corporate autonomy, and restrictions on collective bargaining as factors that institutionalized poverty. Faced with these pressures and an impending election, the government moved from restrictive to expansionary fiscal policies before the 1972 election: increased equalization payments to the provinces, increased capital expenditures, manpower training, summer employment programs for youth, reduced taxes on low income earners, and extended temporary employment programs (Wolfe 1977, 269–70). This alternation between restraint and expansion in response to "the changing sensitivity of the government to the competing pressures on it from business and labour" (Wolfe 1977, 269) in the first government of the Trudeau era was a forecast of the future.

The election of 1972 gave additional strength to labour, following the radical electoral campaign attack by the NDP on "corporate welfare," and the dependence of a new minority Trudeau government on that party's support. The government responded by increasing unemployment insurance benefits and expanding program coverage. UIC spending more than doubled from $891 to $1,869 million between 1971 and 1972 (Bergeron 1979, 21). The government was aware of the intensifying fiscal crisis, but was unable to move unilaterally in the direction of cost controls on social programs, and the Throne Speech of 1973 called for a comprehensive, federal-provincial review of the entire social welfare system. In the meantime the federal budget in the following month proceeded in an expansionary direction: a 5 percent reduction in the personal income tax rate, indexing of the basic personal tax exemption, increases in old-age pension benefits, the extension of contributory pensions to cover a wider range of earnings, plus a series of corporate tax cuts reflecting the pressures from the other side (Wolfe 1977, 272–3).

Business pressures continued as inflation increased from the 1971 low of 3.0 percent to 10.0 percent in 1974. Labour militancy likewise increased, both as a cause and effect of inflation, and the total number of strikes and lockouts rose from 598 in 1972 to 1218 in 1974 (Department of Labour 1975, table 1). Still constrained by its minority status, the government continued to act as if accumulation and legitimation could both be achieved, despite the loss of confidence in that proposition within government and business since the restraint initiatives of the first majority Trudeau government. Along with the implementation of budget promises effecting more generous pensions and old age assistance, Family Allowance payments were tripled in 1973, and the 1974 budget promised still further business tax cuts. The blind eye to economic disequilibrium could not, however, be long maintained. Though the Liberals regained a majority government in the 1974 election, against the threat by the PC opposition to confront inflation with wage controls, they were soon to demonstrate the shallowness of electoral commitment in the face of deepening economic crisis.

With no clear policy direction or mandate defined in the election, but no doubt affected by a sense that concessions to conflicting interests could not continue indefinitely, Trudeau called upon his senior bureaucrats to develop detailed policy priorities. The resulting Priorities Exercise of 1974–75 resulted in a "fashionable set of issues," which despite a single vague reference to national industrial and regional development barely focused upon economic growth and not at all on inflation, and "seemed to suggest that it might be possible to find some circuses to divert the citizenry from the issues of bread" (French 1984, 79). This strange exercise in ostrich planning was in part a result of the Department of Finance's monopoly over macroeconomic policy and that department's ideological commitment to a non-interventionist Keynesian "fine-tuning," which coupled indirect fiscal and monetary manipulation to a "reflex anti-interventionism, a confidence in the allocation of resources by the market, and a sense that these essentials must be protected at all costs" (French 1984, 31). This conflict of "planning systems" operationalized the underlying conflicts between legitimation and accumulation in the encompassing welfare state. Political policy priorities emphasized the welfare needs of the society, while economic policy emphasized the needs of the market and the demands of business. Mounting economic difficulties after the onset of the 1973–74 oil crisis forced a hard-headed confrontation with the underlying problem that economic policy was not working and that welfare programs were therefore imperilled.

Released from the shackles of minority status, the government reverted to its former policy of fiscal constraint. New quasi-corporatist attempts were made to construct a voluntary labour-business consensus "about what the various groups can safely take from the economy over the next few years" (Finance Minister John Turner, quoted in Wolfe 1977, 274). When labour remained obstinate in its refusal to be enticed into tripartite negotiations, the government responded to business pressures to cut its own contributions to inflation by limiting government salary increases and restricting social spending. The June 1975 budget included cuts to medicare contributions, Unemployment Insurance payments, and the Local Initiatives Programme; the elimination of the Opportunities for Youth program; and the rejection of the minister of Health and Welfare's recommendation for a commitment of $2 billion to finance a new federal income support and supplementation program. This spelled the end of the social security review initiated in 1973, as well as the Priorities Exercise of the following year. The latter was quietly buried in October 1975 when the Cabinet responded to still-mounting inflation and falling business confidence by introducing mandatory wage and price controls. Significantly, controls were for the most part supported by business but opposed by organized labour.

Although couched in the terms of John Kenneth Galbraith's (1967) call for more direct intervention to regulate monopolies no longer responsive to market pressures, this about-face did not reflect a coherent reorientation of policy. Rather, the next budget of May 1976 contained a combination of short-term Galbraithian controls, coupled to longer-term structural adjustments based on the postulates of Galbraith's monetarist opponents. Under the leadership of the Bank of Canada, the monetarists rapidly assumed the dominant position, especially when after an initial downturn following the imposition of controls inflation began to climb steeply, accompanied by sizeable increases in the unemployment rate and government debt (Doern and Phidd 1983, table 17-3; Rotstein 1984, table 4-2).

In August 1978 the government again moved precipitously. Following an international meeting of heads of Western governments, Trudeau announced, without prior Cabinet consultation but in keeping with the international monetarist consensus on the importance of controlling government debts, cuts in planned federal government expenditures of $2.5 billion. The sense of governmental impotence in the face of economic decline was clearly expressed in the pre-election budget speech later that year, when Finance Minister Jean Chrétien indicated that he was "sceptical about the search for a single grand industrial strategy," resorting instead to larding the tax system with incentives to private business (Doern and Phidd 1983, 250 and table 10-2).

The tilt towards business interests was further expressed in continued moves to restrain the powers of labour. The movement from voluntary restraint to coercion, clearly signalled by the imposition of wage controls in

1975, was further intensified by the increasing resort to coercive action against strikes. As Panitch and Swartz (1985, 320) note, "While in the first fifteen years after 1950 there were only six instances of back-to-work legislation in total, there were *forty-five* such instances in the following decade and a half, with half of these coming in 1975–79 alone." Although this partly reflected a new phenomenon of increased public sector unionization, it was to have serious consequences for the ability of the Liberals, as the "governing party" largely responsible for the postwar hegemonic settlement, to retain working-class support.

In the 1978 election the Liberals attempted to downplay the seriousness of their economic difficulties and divert attention from their attacks on working-class interests by focusing on problems of national unity, dramatized by the coming to power in 1976 of the *independentiste* Parti Québécois. Economic issues were uppermost in the minds of the electorate, however, and the Progressive Conservatives formed a minority government in 1979.

Apparently overestimating the extent to which electoral shifts represented a political realignment favouring neo-conservative attacks upon the welfare state, and lacking either the "discipline of power" or a coherent ideology, the new government was quickly defeated in the House of Commons and in the following election, after only twenty-seven weeks in office. The Progressive Conservative party's electoral promises, based on principles remarkably akin to those soon to be known as Reaganomics, had called for a "stimulative deficit," combining tax breaks and a promised reduction in the size of the civil service by 60,000 over three years with a large inventory of new spending programs (Simpson 1980, 58–61). Divisions within the Conservative party and conflicts between government ministers, the Bank of Canada, and the Department of Finance, however, modified these election promises. The result was a politically disastrous policy that combined a new tax on gasoline, designed to help balance a budget undermined by $1.5 billion worth of tax credits, including new deductions for mortgage interest and municipal taxes that would disproportionately benefit homeowners, with higher interest rates, imposed by the Bank in order to restrain inflation, attract foreign capital, and sustain the value of the Canadian dollar (Simpson 1980, chap. 8).

Trudeau and the Liberals returned in 1980 with what amounted to an outline of a third national policy, built around constitutional patriation and reform, and a new economic union forged through a national energy and industrial policy. Although introduced with considerably more force and pursued with more vigour in the first years after the return to power, neither of these elements of the third national policy was particularly new, and neither of them successfully displaced the political opposition that had kept them from becoming a more coherent national policy in earlier Trudeau governments.

Ever since he came to Ottawa in the late 1960s in order to combat the rising influence of nationalism in Quebec, issues of constitutional reform had been a priority of Trudeau's. The hallmarks of his constitutional policy, enunciated during his tenure as justice minister in Pearson's last government, and then in the constitutional negotiations with provincial premiers he initiated as prime minister, were the protection of French educational and language rights within an entrenched national charter of individual rights and freedoms. Patriation of the British North America Act, and the addition to it of a Charter of Rights and Freedoms, would, he argued, strengthen the Canadian nation by eliminating its vestigial colonial status; link the collective rights of the founding peoples of Canada, as well as the civil rights of individuals in a liberal state, to national institutions; and thereby erode the cultural distinctiveness of Canadian provincial communities in general, and the "tribalist" proclivities of the Québécois in particular (Trudeau 1968; Cairns 1991; Russell 1983).

These intentions were continuously frustrated: by Premier Robert Bourassa's last-minute withdrawal from a deal worked out in the Victoria conference in 1971; by the demand from other provincial premiers in addition to Bourassa for the expansion of the constitutional reform agenda to include a redivision of powers, rather than narrowly concentrating on patriation and an amending formula as the federal government proposed in 1975; and by the lack of progress in response to the 1978 report of the Pepin-Robarts Task Force on Canadian Unity, commissioned after the coming to power of the Parti Québécois. His unexpected return to power in 1980 gave Trudeau the chance to do battle with his arch-rival Premier René Lévesque in the referendum held on a proposition for Quebec's sovereignty with economic association in the rest of Canada, and victory in this battle required fulfilment of the promise of a constitutional reform safeguarding the rights of Quebeckers.

But Trudeau's victory was by no means decisive. The referendum was followed by the revitalization and stunning electoral return of the Parti Québécois in the 1981 provincial election. With Premier Lévesque reinstated as the champion of Quebec's constitutional prerogatives, an intense struggle for constitutional reform led to the ambiguous results of the 1982 Constitution Act, which "no one cheered" (Banting and Simeon 1983). Quebec refused to be a party to the final deal worked out with the other nine provinces and the price of those provinces' accommodation to the new constitution was purchased by allowing them to unilaterally exclude themselves from the application of the national Charter of Rights to their legislation.

In terms of economic policy, a third national policy was discerned early on by Donald V. Smiley (1976). He saw an emerging emphasis upon organized research and development activities, the rationalization of the secondary manufacturing sector, a greater finished goods component in trade based on natural resources, greater ownership and control of key, technologically advanced industrial sectors, encouraging industrial performance through trade liberalization, and decreasing levels of foreign investment. The sources of the new economic policy prescriptions, oddly enough, were neglected recommendations from the early Trudeau regime: the Gray Report (*Foreign Direct Investment in Canada*, 1972), the report of the Senate Special Committee on Science Policy (1972), and reports of the Science Council of Canada. Despite some moves in the prescribed direction, such as the establishment in the early 1970s of state corporations – including the Canada Development Corporation, the Export Development Bank, and Petro-Canada – to take a leading role in the development of high technology and resource industry development (Laux and Molot 1987, 57), the real articulation of this third national policy awaited the return to power in 1980.

The broad strategy of economic development, outlined in the government's 1980 *Statement on Economic Development in the 1980s* and in the Blair-Carr "Mega-projects" Task Force, emphasized coordinated public support for "the production of basic commodities, related manufactured products and high productivity, high technology manufactured goods" (Doern and Phidd 1983, 434 ff.). The centre-piece of this policy was the National Energy Program (NEP). "Interventionist, centralist, and nationalistic" (Pratt 1982, 37), this program aimed to establish 50 percent Canadian ownership in the oil industry, and to change pricing, taxing, and exploration incentives for petroleum so as to optimize the investment and growth possibilities of developing the most lucrative natural resource, and to salvage the fiscal problems of the national government.

Despite the nationalistic and statist flavour of the NEP, there is considerable debate as to how far the new national policy represented a more general break with earlier strategies of continental integration (see Mahon 1984, especially chap. 8). The establishment of the Canada Development Corporation in 1982 reaffirmed the earlier commitments of the 1977 Trudeau government to administer Crown corporations "on a sound commercial basis, to promote their efficiency and maximize the return on investment to the Canadian taxpayer," and its subsequent support for principles of private business management, and privatization where possible, in the management of state business, as developed in the 1979 Lambert Commission on Financial Management and Accountability (Laux and Molot 1987, 72–3, 131). Included in this perspective, of course, was a continued commitment to liberal trade policy, a constant since the Second World War.

No matter how "new," the third national policy had no opportunity to prove itself one way or another, before being cut short by "the seriously depressed economy, high interest rates, plummeting oil prices, increasing federal deficit," and an inadequate ideological defence rooted in concerns with enhancing federal visibility and national community (Doern and Phidd 1984,

445). The prospects of constitutionally protecting a national economic community were undermined by compromises in the course of constitutional diplomacy, and the effectively limited autonomy and capacity of the federal government was further revealed in the field of international diplomacy, as national energy policy and foreign investment review were progressively weakened to allay the protests of foreign capital and the U.S. government (Clarkson 1982). Finally, the sharp recession of 1981–82 put an end to the initiative.

Part of the failure of the third national policy was the absence of a coherent economic analysis of the problems of the national economy. Seen largely as a problem of adjustment to the demands for competitiveness and productivity in the international economy, the interventionism of the Trudeau national policy was based on the same economic analysis as that used by neo-conservative opponents calling for privatization and deregulation. Even had a much-improved economic diagnosis been adopted by the Trudeau government, it is not clear that the new national policy could have been sold to business and labour as the basis of a new hegemony at the brink of recession. Whether the recession could have been prevented through pursuit of an alternative to the monetarist policies that had dominated economic policy since 1978, and that had not fundamentally been called in question by the new national policy after 1980, is not clear. What is clear is that monetarist policy, even had it been more internally consistent in its application after 1975, could not stem the economic collapse of 1981–2. In that year unemployment peaked at 12.8 percent and business bankruptcies increased by 40.3 percent (Rotstein 1984, 17).

The other clear deficiency of this formative effort to redefine a national policy in the early 1980s relates to social and labour policy, the critical areas that define the state's appeals to subordinate classes, and in which inter-class alliances designed to adjust to the massively costly changes occurring in the world economy might be forged. Here the Trudeau vision was very nearly absent. Social policy and national standards in health, education, and welfare had been seriously undermined by budget constraints and provincial deviations from principles underlying federal social policy since the onset of economic crisis in 1974. And the 1980 national policy did not seriously confront this issue, except for initiatives resulting in the 1983 Canada Health Act (which penalized provinces allowing extra-billing and hospital user fees). The emphasis upon individual rights in constitutional reform was only partially balanced by the social emphasis on matters of language and culture. Bilingual and multicultural policy accelerated ethnic competition for resources, however, and a backlash was particularly observable in the Manitoba language disputes of the early 1980s. Finally, labour relations reforms were virtually disregarded as a means of mobilizing working-class support for the new policy regime. The major initiative here, the 1981 Industry and Labour Adjustment Program, concentrated on wage subsidies to business, thus enhancing the competitiveness of some branches of industry and groups of workers at the expense of others (Mahon 1984, 147). The almost complete isolation of the federal government from organized labour, stemming from the mid 1970s period of wage and price controls, continued throughout this period.

These deficiencies of the national policy formulated in 1980 meant that state mediation of ideological and political conflict was quite ineffective. Indeed the policy can be seen as directly stimulating such conflict. On the terrain of ideology, with which we are primarily concerned, this is especially the case. The emphasis upon a national economy *vis-à-vis* foreign investment, upon a national standard of civil rights and social welfare, and upon the greater centralization of political power required by these other emphases challenged classical, bourgeois commitments to limited government and the separation of state and civil society, and advanced a conception of political justice as the judicial protection of the rights of those underprivileged by the operation of the "free market." However, the third national policy had no effective national economic policy to counter the alienating effects on support for the government of these arguments within the Canadian capitalist class, and to make compensatory gains in support from non-ruling classes.

Lacking a coherent economic program, and avoiding questions of how the interests of a recognizable nationwide coalition of classes would be favoured in the zero-sum conditions of economic crisis, the ideological core of the national policy was the liberal invocation of individual freedom and opportunity, and the nationalist corollaries of national sovereignty and economic autonomy. These principles have a significant ideological resonance in any capitalist society, and may have had some success in fostering support for the third national policy across class lines. Such ideological appeals may have muted the expression of an historically weakly organized class consciousness, but they were less able to confront relatively strongly organized regional and provincial interests. Indeed the failure to explicitly invoke class politics in the formulation of the national policy may, as is cogently argued in a more general context (Cairns 1968), have reinforced rather than suppressed regional conflicts. Given the economic defects of the national policy, the emphasis on individual freedom and opportunity encouraged both the identification of regional inequalities and the claims of provincial governments to better defend individual freedoms and opportunities in regions where these were relatively denied. Further, the more substantive emphases of the national policy summarized in the last paragraph were easily translated as attacks, by a predatory central government, upon the economic resources and political powers of provincial governments that represented the interests of historically deprived sectors of the nation.

The combination of economic crisis and national policy thus intensified rather than reduced regional divisions at the same time that it undermined the ability of the government to hegemonically articulate the interests of a ruling class. The regional conflicts, so much emphasized in Canadian political commentary, became more and more obvious as the Liberal party was successively eliminated from government in all of the provinces, and as the federal Liberal party all but disappeared in western Canada. Less observed, but also evident, was an intensification of political and ideological conflict with clear-cut class dynamics.

Class conflict was marked by deteriorating relations between Trudeau's government and the labour movement towards the end of his time in office, as the movement from restraint to coercion in labour relations continued (Panitch and Swartz 1985) The opposition of organized labour to the Trudeau national policy can be gauged from the Canadian Labour Congress's 1980 report, *Battle of the Eighties: Trade Union Rights vs. Corporate Power*, which called for expanded emphasis on social policy and more state regulation and "positive public ownership" of the economy, along with greater controls on the regional distribution of investment and the introduction of technological change (Mahon 1984, 132 ff.).

The other side of the articulation of class conflict was represented by increasing business opposition to the government, funnelled through a succession of newly formed organizations – the Canadian Federation of Independent Business, the National Association of Business, the Conference Board of Canada, the Fraser Institute, the Business Council for National Issues, and others (Langille 1987). In a sense these organizations testified to the growing differentiation of the capitalist class, and the inability of the long-established organizations like the Canadian Manufacturers Association to represent the range of political interests of this class. Collectively, however, business was increasing united in a growing criticism of government policy. Except for a few organizations, like Gordon's think-tank, there was broad business support for a campaign to modify social and welfare policies developed during the national policy of the postwar era. Their common ideological line was to increase productivity and improve the investment climate with new policies that would cheapen labour and redistribute resources from social programs to business assistance.

The increasing intensity of this ideological class conflict was reflected in debate within the very institutions claimed to be immune to such activity – political parties and governments. Major debates over the ideological orientations of the federal parties took place in this period, even if they resulted in no great clarification of ideological differences between the parties. At the provincial level, party competition in the Western provinces, between the NDP and PC or Social Credit parties, was overtly ideological, and the nationalist movement in Quebec was embroiled in class and ideological issues. Most interestingly, perhaps, federal-provincial relations took on an increasingly ideological tone, as the federal and provincial governments argued questions like energy policy or medicare in terms of the proper defence of a truly capitalist society.

Finally, as in other advanced capitalist societies, some of the most obvious indications of ideological conflict in Canada are associated with the growth of what are called the "new social movements." Distinguished from "old" movements precisely by their lack of fit to the basic labour-capital division, these movements increasingly define the forms of debate in our political agenda, and they, rather than political parties or class organizations like unions and business associations, have increasingly become the focus of mass political participation. The interests of these new movements, including the feminist, environmentalist, civil libertarian, and peace movements, as well as the organizations of aboriginal peoples, are not easily placed in the context of traditional class or regional conflicts over social programs and the distribution of income and wealth. But this does not mean that the new social movements have no basis in the class structure, or that their political programs are completely independent of ideological and political forces rooted in older traditions of defending or criticizing capitalist society.

The development of the new social movements is best understood as a response to the contradictions of the welfare state. Many of them respond to the inadequacies of the state's provision of welfare in its regulation of civil society – in domains previously depoliticized as a result of their containment in the more autonomous jurisdiction of family, church, and market (Offe 1987). The ideological discourse is therefore infected by the class logic of defences of the welfare state. Although this politicization is motivated by anti-political, anti-state, and anti-growth sentiments that conflict with established political and ideological forces, the new social movements seek the support of unions, parties, and other established political organizations, and those organizations seek to build effective coalitions with them. Such interaction shapes but does not displace the classical ideological discourses of class division in capitalist society. Further, in its attempt to create a hegemonic order, the state plays an active role in relation to the new social movements. The organization of new social movements can be as much a direct and intended consequence of policy as an unintended consequence of the contradictions of the welfare state. Certainly, Canadian new social movements have been stimulated by various aspects of the Trudeau national policy: the early emphasis upon participation, and the establishment of citizen groups to monitor policy developments; the emphasis upon volunteer organizations as the beneficiaries of social and cultural programs under agencies like The Secretary of State; the emphasis in the constitutional debate upon civil liberties and minority group rights; and, in the waning days of the Trudeau regime, the commitment to peacemaking interventions in the revitalized cold war of the late 1970s and early 1980s.

In summary, rather than re-establishing hegemony in the face of the disintegration of the economic challenges to the Canadian welfare state, the third national policy intensified levels of political and ideological conflict. This book seeks to establish with much greater precision just how intense such conflict was, how it was structured in class and regional terms, and what this balance of forces implied for subsequent political developments in Canada.

CONCLUSIONS

No one living in Canada during the period discussed in this book would have needed telling that it was a time of political and economic trouble. And few would have considered it an exaggeration to speak of a time of "crisis," using the ordinary language meaning of a "moment of danger or suspense in politics or commerce" (*Concise Oxford Dictionary*). Most obviously the crisis was marked by an incapacity to sustain the economic growth that had characterized most of the quarter-century following the Second World War. The associated political crisis was marked by an incapacity to sustain public commitments to political parties and confidence in government, by intensifying intergovernmental conflict, by intra-governmental incapacities to formulate coherent public policy, and by escalating ideological conflict over the direction of government.

The response of the Canadian state to these unfolding crises was personified in that most enigmatic of national leaders, Pierre Trudeau. For a brief moment the Trudeaumania of 1968 disguised the political crisis of liberal democracy and suggested the peaceable kingdom might be immune from the troubles apparent in other Western countries that year. But the effects of worldwide crisis were soon felt with the same severity in Canada. With the exception of a brief interlude, Trudeau survived in power for sixteen years while most other leaders and national governments foundered. His survival was particularly remarkable because, despite the evident force of his intellect and personality, his personal appeal to public opinion was no more durable than that of other leaders, and his policies in response to crisis no more effective or less contradictory.

Trudeau's own career encapsulates the conflict and contradictions that threatened the postwar political and ideological settlement: anti-nationalist become Canadian patriot; internationalist transformed into economic nationalist; liberal champion of the autonomy of civil society and the free market become the godfather of state regulation and investment in culture, state control of wages and prices, and government overtures to business and labour to enter into "tripartite" corporatism; civil libertarian become warrior against internal insurrection and the "bleeding hearts" who lacked the will to confront it; high theoretician of balanced federalism transformed into the chief prosecutor of provincialism and intense advocate of national as opposed to provincial interests; and architect of expanded participation and rational decision making in government appearing as the aloof, autocratic leader, contemptuous of the public and its representatives.

An understanding of this leader and his party during increasingly troubled times is inconceivable without a sense of the emerging national policy they proclaimed. The key elements of this policy included national independence through patriation of the constitution, and internal readjustments in the balance of powers; the development of a bilingual and multicultural society as an antidote to ethnic and regional nationalism; the constitutional entrenchment of civil liberties, and associated increase in the powers of the courts, as a further means of redesigning national political culture; the development of a national economy through foreign investment review, a national energy policy, the expansion of crown corporations in areas of investment and production, and, finally, and least prominently because of the ravages of fiscal crisis and the accommodation to provincial constitutional prerogatives in these areas, the continuing identification of a national interest and federal government responsibility in social welfare – health, education, income maintenance, etcetera.

If a relatively coherent national policy agenda was defined in these terms during the last phase of the Trudeau era, it nevertheless failed as a hegemonic project, and it is the objective of this book to provide an explanation of why it failed. A full explanation, in terms of the conceptualization of hegemony we use, would have to go into a detailed discussion of the political economy of Canada, exploring the economic logic of crisis and restructuring in the 1970s and 1980s, and the limits and effects of political leadership and organization in mediating the conflicts surrounding such developments. For such a full explanation one will have to wait in Canada for the kind of systematic historical analysis that Colin Leys (1983) has applied to British politics, using the concepts of class struggle and the contradictory construction of hegemonic rule in a capitalist society.

In this book we confine our attention to the ideological facet of hegemony and hegemonic crisis, and ask, in light of the preceding outline of the economic and political manifestations of crisis and formative attempts to overcome it through new public policy in the period 1975–81, how ideological conflict was structured in this period, and how ideological conflicts influenced future attempts by governments to mobilize the consent of Canadians to the needs of capital, as capitalists in this country defined them. This concentration on ideology raises serious questions of theory and methodology, which we go into in the next chapters. Here we simply announce our assumption of the importance of ideology to the understanding of crisis and change in society, and expand upon the kinds of questions that we think are raised about the shape of ideological conflict in Canada during the specific period of crisis and change we discuss.

To return to the terminology of Gramsci quoted at the beginning of the chapter, the stagflation of the late 1970s presented an "immediate economic crisis" to the managers of the Canadian welfare state. The crisis conditions provided a "terrain more favourable to the dissemination of certain modes of thought," and the pre-eminent "active politician" of the time, Prime Minister Trudeau, moved to "transcend or dominate the shifting balance of forces" supporting or attacking elements of the imperilled welfare state. But like all good theory, Gramsci's terminology poses a problem that is not answered theoretically. A terrain favourable to revolution does not a revolution make, nor, short of revolution, does it determine shifts in the balance of forces contending for state power. If the crisis of the welfare state provoked a crisis of ideological understanding and justification, the particular character of economic and political problems in Canada did not determine any particular ideological response – any particular "modes of thought and ways of posing and resolving questions about the future of national economic life."

How then can we establish the dissemination of new versus old modes of thought, the limits of consent to Trudeau's new formative projects, and the construction of new ideological underpinnings for a new alliance of political forces committed to an alternative hegemonic strategy? How can we gauge the extent to which Trudeau "failed in [the] major political undertaking for which [he] requested ... the consent of the broad masses," and how can we understand the political changes by which his project of centralization, state regulation, and national autonomy was replaced by his successors' regime of decentralization, privatization, and international harmonization? Why did the shift involve more a "passive revolution" than a genuine "crisis of authority" in which "huge masses ... pass from a state of political passivity to a certain activity, and put forward demands which taken together ... add up to a revolution?" To what extent can the relative fragility of class rather than regional and other social cleavages account for the weaknesses of public commitment to Trudeau's national policy, for the intensity of competition between governments in Canada's federal system, and for vacillation in state policy during this period? Was this vacillation a normal pattern of "muddling through" in the art of the possible exercised by state officials incrementally arbitrating the conflicting interests of plural elites, or was the incoherence rooted in more intense ideological conflict among classes and their political representatives over the basic principles of the postwar settlement? To what extent can the Trudeau national policy be seen as the action of a relatively autonomous government trying to straddle a sharply defined conflict between those elites and the social classes they represent, and to what extent does such conflict account for the failures of the Trudeau national policy to remould a political consensus in Canada? Finally, how does the structure of ideological conflict, the relative solidarity and strength of different ideological forces, help account for the new directions of ideological and political alignment that follow the end of the Trudeau era in Canadian politics?

These are the questions raised by our retrospective appraisal of recent Canadian political history. Such questions demand more fine-grained attention to the actual content of the ideological perspectives of members of the general public and of the dominant groups in their society. Ideologies are generalized understandings or beliefs about how power relations are and ought to be organized in society, and they are a crucial factor in the mobilization and justification of support for new directions in politics and society. They are shaped by material conditions and by existing discourses tied to those material conditions, but the structure of ideological conflict is not a simple reflection of underlying economic problems.

The problems of stagflation and deficit financing in the late 1970s, for example, could be given radically different interpretations from differing political and ideological perspectives. Measurable declines in economic productivity and growth could be understood as identical results of diametrically opposing models, in which the exogenous variables and causal relationships are reversed as the result of differing ideological assumptions. Either Canada's involvement in the world economy produces problems for labour (as a result of a relatively low rate of research and development, capital investment in high-productivity sectors, adverse terms of trade between staple exports and finished imports, etc.) or Canadian labour produces problems for Canada's involvement in the world economy (as a result of intensifying wage demands, the costs of income security programs, etc.).

Empirical research is required, therefore, to understand what new modes of thought are articulated in a given historical situation. Our task is to discover empirically the balance of contending ideological perspectives in Canada during the period 1975–81, and to show how this balance is consistent with changes in political alignment and public policy. Although there are a variety of methods of analyzing the changing balance of ideological perspectives, we will argue that survey research is a particularly useful means of getting a fix on the kinds of questions raised by Gramsci's concept of hegemonic crisis – questions dealing with the balance of consent and dissent in the bosom of the state. Before we can discuss our own survey evidence in these terms, however, in the next couple of chapters we must contend with influential arguments that deny the importance that we attach to questions of ideology, and that question the utility that we ascribe to survey research.

2 Ideological Divisions in Capitalist Society: Competing Perspectives in Political Sociology

We have talked so far of ideology and ideological conflict as if the terms were unambiguous. In treating ideology as a component of Antonio Gramsci's conceptualization of hegemony, we have simply assumed that everyone knows what is meant by ideology. In a sense this is true. We think easily in conventional terms of ideology as referring to highly formalized belief systems about the meaning and purposes of politics, and about the justification and use of power. Ideological leanings to the "left," meaning a tendency to oppose the political status quo, calling for a more egalitarian distribution of power and for the mobilization of popular participation in projects to change the system, are contrasted with leanings to the "right," meaning a tendency to support the status quo, aristocratic or meritocratic inequalities, and orderly change following established institutional procedures or tradition.

More specifically we refer to conservatism, liberalism, and socialism, meaning ideological movements with well-identified roots in the European transition from feudal to modern capitalist states, historically clear organization in both classes and parties, and, despite argument and change over time, sufficient doctrinal coherence and continuity for one to identify clearly the ideological differences between them. These movements have defined major political cleavages between the left and right in most contemporary liberal democracies, for most of their histories as distinct nation-states, and the terms are part of the common discourse of political discussion.

For all this apparently straightforward understanding of the concept, there are serious difficulties in the use of ideology as an explanatory term in political analysis. This is especially true for the analysis of Canadian politics, which is conventionally supposed to be peculiarly devoid of ideological content and contestation. Canadian literary critics have argued that historical and geographical peculiarities have led to a lack of positive cultural identity and security that prevents Canadians from moving beyond the ambiguities and uncertainties of national identity to larger issues of quest and achievement, from themes of victims surviving in an unpredictable environment to themes of personal and political transcendence over the inert forces of nature and history (Frye 1971; Atwood 1972). Canadian political sociologists have emphasized the relatively undemocratic, elitist tradition of Canadian politics, in which the mass public is removed from political influence by elite manipulation of the vertical cleavages that have historically divided them by ethnicity, language, and religion, thereby restricting the articulation of horizontal cleavages that would cut across the society as a whole and develop nationwide, if conflicting, identities and ideologies (e.g., Porter 1965; Cairns 1968). Canadian political scientists have reinforced this perspective with evidence for the public's "moderate, widespread tolerance of and support for the way things are done" (Meisel 1974, 39); for the limiting effect of the Canadian party system and political culture on electoral politics "organized around leaders rather than around political principles and ideologies," and "appeals to narrow interests and proposals that amount to little more than short-term tinkering" (Clarke et al. 1984, 10). And Canadian journalists have celebrated the cultural pluralism of Canada, the elite tolerance of diversity and pragmatism in resolving political differences, and the progressive consensus, to the left of the Anglo-Saxon liberal tradition, that has made such accommodation possible (Gwyn 1985; Graham 1986).

As indicated in the last chapter, we believe that these arguments must be treated with caution in light of the historical record. They misstate or exaggerate both the extent and the organizing principles of the unity in Canadian political culture. They underestimate the historical resilience of ideological divisions, glossing over the historical conjunctures at which political uncertainty and conflict generate relatively clear ideological conflict over questions of public policy, with party politics attaining a visible level of ideological definition and intensity. Rather, they exaggerate an abstract conception of a unitary and socially progressive "liberalism" in Canada, which obscures the contradictory elements of the dominant ideological perspective in Canada, as well as its class content. The contradictions and the class base of this dominant ideology are interrelated phenomena in any historical era (whether that of the National Policy, the New Deal, or the present), which limit the progressive scope of politics in Canada. To be specific about the period with which this book is concerned, we have suggested that there were intensified ideological divisions about the justification of the welfare state, as a result of which the Canadian state took inconsistent and ineffective steps towards invigorating the national economy and social welfare system, before succumbing to the ideological offensive of a disaffected capitalist class bent on restructuring the economy at the expense of the welfare state.

But these arguments beg questions about the nature of ideology. One person's dominant ideology is another's un-ideological consensus in political culture. What appears to one as an ideological reconstruction of historical circumstances, appears to another as a pragmatic and rational acceptance of reality. Where one sees the importance of ideological discourse, another sees only the *ex post facto* rationalization of underlying material interests. Put bluntly, some see a phenomenon that others see not at all.

Three general difficulties in the use of the term ideology account for these disagreements. First, there is an important slippage and confusion in moving from the neutral, observational, everyday usage of the terms left, right, conservative, liberal, socialist, etcetera to the implicitly pejorative reference, in all major traditions of social science, to ideology as a species of irrational thought. This we might refer to as the problem of *defining* ideology. Second, there is the problem of understanding the relationship between the subjective realm of ideas and the objective or material realms of existence. How tight is the fit between traditional ideologies and historic class structures; how tight is the fit been economic change and ideological adaptation; how much of an independent causal significance can be assigned ideological phenomena in analyzing social change? This we might refer to as the problem of *theorizing* ideology. Finally, the political significance of ideology is analyzed in terms of arguments like those for the end of ideology or for hegemonic or dominant ideology, in which the problem is one of specifying the ideological content and the extent of ideological consensus entailed by the arguments. How complete, how progressive, how stable is a hegemonic ideology? This we might refer to as the problem of *empirical analysis*, although it is also, of course, essentially a theoretical problem.

In this chapter we work through a resolution of each of these problems, with the aim of justifying our emphasis on the importance of ideology in Canadian politics. We argue that these problems have been substantially resolved in the course of the development of an increasingly sophisticated Marxist approach to the understanding of ideology and politics in advanced capitalist societies, and we begin with a discussion of the general conceptualization of ideology in Marxist scholarship. This is followed by a brief review of the highly influential elaboration of a Marxist theory of ideology by the French philosopher Louis Althusser and his followers. Although this theorizing leads to interesting formulations of the relative autonomy of ideology and its potential significance in the shaping of classes, class struggle, and political change, the resistance to empirical research on the part of its major authors left them insisting upon essentially economistic arguments about the conservative functioning of a dominant ideology in the reproduction of capitalist hegemony.

Ironically the empirically richer tradition of non-Marxist political sociology arrives at a quite similar position, as we discuss in the third section. These logically similar arguments for the end of ideology in a consensual political culture were reasonably appropriate to the circumstances of the postwar, cold-war 1950s, especially in the case of the newly dominant world power, the United States, but also in the case of Canada, where they were adopted. The argument was undermined, however, by the ideological ferment created by the "new left" from the mid-1960s onwards, and the fourth section discusses the accommodation to these new historical developments in both liberal and Marxist political sociology.

The changes in liberal political sociology concentrated on the emergence of new values in the creation of a silent revolution in the politics of liberal democracy, while neo-Marxists conceptualized the same phenomena as a crisis of legitimation in such states, leading potentially to a more dramatic and revolutionary change. Both these lines of theoretical innovation were essentially optimistic readings of new cultural and ideological developments, with very limited attention to their socio-demographic and therefore political limits. The emergence in the 1970s and 1980s of the neo-conservative counter-revolution required, therefore, a substantial further revision of theoretical argument, as we show in the fifth section of this chapter.

With this latest revision neo-Marxists, leaning to some extent on the empirical research of liberal political sociologists, have provided for a conceptually rich elaboration of Gramsci's problematic of hegemony and hegemonic crisis that informs our subsequent analysis of ideological divisions in Canadian politics.

DEFINING IDEOLOGY

From its first conception in eighteenth-century France, ideology has been given widely varying and contradictory meanings. The most carefully developed use of the term as a critical concept in political analysis is to be found in the Marxist tradition, although serious vulgarizations of Marx contribute to the dismissal of Marxist scholarship on this topic.

The vulgar Marxist approach takes ideology to be the distorted interpretation of ruling-class interests as the universal interest of society. The end of ideology is possible only with the historical emergence of a society in which the increasingly vast majority have no independent source of power or survival, and who, while they collectively produce the means of social existence, have alienated the power over the allocation and enjoyment of this collective product to an increasingly tiny minority. The interests of this exploited class (the proletariat) are universal interests, because they entail a truly universal extension of rights and freedoms; and only this class can acquire such interests because, unlike all prior historical classes, it has no material experience of private rather than social power. That this is so is "hidden" from members of the class by their acceptance of an ideology in which private appropriation and individual rather than social existence is privileged and justified. The task of "scientific Marxism," then, is to demonstrate that such understandings are ideological distortions, in time to be rent asunder.

The obvious and basic problems with such a perspective are why, if all historically prior understandings of society and history have been ideological, Marxism should be uniquely immune in this respect, and why, if false consciousness has hitherto exercised a commanding hold upon the proletariat, its hold should be expected to decline. The typical defences against such lines of questioning entail either a recondite philosophical affirmation of the truths of Marxism because of their proper recognition of the dialectical unfolding within present historical structures of contradictory forces leading to their complete transformation, as in the work of Lukacs ([1923] 1971), or, alternatively, in the footsteps of Vladimir Lenin, an emphasis upon the historical effectiveness of Marxist praxis in which intellectual leadership of the proletariat transforms a purely trade-unionist consciousness into truly revolutionary perspectives and capabilities (see the discussion in Seliger 1977, especially 67–75 and 82–104).

Neither approach – philosophical or political – has achieved much plausibility in face of the continued resilience of capitalism, conservative working-class politics in Western Europe and North America, and the bankruptcy of Leninist political regimes. Contemporary Marxist theory in these societies has, therefore, been concerned with a redefinition of the problem of ideology in an attempt to bypass the dead ends of vulgar Marxism. At the heart of these new approaches to the problem is a reconsideration of the definition of ideology as false consciousness. Although the critical kernel of the concept remains the notion of the masking of power relations in systems of ideas that justify them, these systems of ideas are not purely false. They derive their vitality and longevity, in fact, from their grounding in material experience, and to the extent that a scientific analysis can uncover the ideological understandings of social experience, it uncovers not a totally different order of things, but a different logic of their organization.

The model here is Marx's analysis of commodity fetishism (see Geras 1972). In this analysis, commodities, which in reality embody values established in social relations of exploitation, are mystified as objects whose value is established through free exchange, and the ideological model of commodity exchange is fetishized into a model of all human relations. Human beings themselves are thus valued by their possession of commodities, but especially the key commodity "labour power," which they are "free" to sell for a price established by the market. The ideological model thus masks relations of exploitation that force the majority to sell their labour to the minority who own the means of production. The essence of the relations of exploitation concealed by the model is the process by which exchange values (prices) of commodities exceed the costs of the labour expended in producing them by an amount equal to the surplus value accruing to the minority that controls the means of production. The false perception is that the real value of commodities is not their use value, but their exchange value.

Four theorems are embodied in Marx's analysis of the fetishism of commodities: (1) that ideology hides, mystifies, or distorts a social reality; (2) that ideology represents objective social relations in the guise of subjective questions of individual choice, thereby accommodating individuals to their role in an order of domination; (3) that ideology infuses political relations with a mystical, affective attachment, providing a psychological identification with the ideological symbols that mask the exploitation of the majority of individuals in society; and (4) that ideology is, none the less, not simply a distortion, but a plausible representation of the appearance of things, the underlying reality requiring complicated scientific investigation.

To emphasize the last point, the key to Marx's analysis is not that there is no reality to commodity and exchange relations, or that these are merely determined by production relations. Although its inner logic *is* determined by the relations of production, the world of commodities and exchange has a material existence and a relatively autonomous effect upon other aspects of social experience. And, while the inner logic of contradiction and exploitation in this world of "free exchange" is invisible to orthodox economics, that social science is not purely ideological. Its data and statistical generalizations do, in fact, accurately describe a great deal of economic life in capitalist societies. Likewise, the data and findings of liberal political science are not purely an ideological reification of the extensive civil rights, limited but real electoral competition, and the primacy of bureaucratic and executive politics in the determination of public policy. While they conceal the class conflicts and class interests embedded in these processes, the processes they describe are substantially real, none the less.

For Marx, then, ideology refers to the use of ideas to mask or distort the relations of domination or exploitation between classes (Larrain 1979), so that individuals experience domination as a necessary and legitimate feature of society. Ideology, in this sense, includes formal theories of society, which as Marx argued against classical political economy misrepresent the true nature of society, as well as the informal ideas according to which individuals interpret and misinterpret their everyday world. Ideology does not, however, as in the caricature of vulgar Marxism, comprise all ideas whatsoever, nor is ideology simply a superstructural reflection of the base relations of production in which the interests of dominant classes are reproduced as universal in society. Ideology and non-ideological or counter-ideological ideas clearly play a relatively independent role in shaping classes, class relations, and historical change. Otherwise it is impossible to understand Marx's larger intellectual project: his concern with the problematic development of class "consciousness" – the distinction between a class as a category, existing "in itself," and class as a conscious historical agent existing "for itself" – and his concern for praxis as the effective combination of theory and action to bring about change in a world otherwise dominated by the constraining forces of ideology.

The fundamental issue in the Marxist definition of ideology is, therefore, well stated by Jorge Larrain (1979, 13 ff.), who asks whether ideology should be understood in the negative sense commonly labelled "false consciousness" or in the positive sense of "the expression of the world view of a class ... the opinions, theories and attitudes formed within a class in order to defend and promote its interests." We follow Goran Therborn (1980, vii) in saying that both views are correct. Therborn argues for a "dialectical" understanding of ideology: "Ideologies not only subject people to a given order. They also qualify [people] for conscious social action, including actions of gradual or revolutionary change." The problem, of course, is how to understand the dialectical unity of irrational and distorted, as opposed to rational and objectively accurate, perceptions in the make-up of ideologies, and the emergence and changing balance of opposing ideologies.

We shall define ideology as that aspect of consciousness that masks an underlying system of domination in social relations, and *an* ideology as a coherent tradition of intellectual thought that develops the concepts and arguments that make plausible an account of a society as a unified community uninfluenced by the contradictory interests of the dominating and the dominated. More loosely, we shall lump together as ideological perspectives all systematically formulated arguments about the justification or the deficiencies of a system of power relations. It might be better to distinguish between ideologies and counter-ideologies, but in making a radical break from the vulgar Marxist assumption of uniquely privileged critical perspective it is preferable, we think, to treat justificatory and critical ideologies as epistemologically identical. Some ideologies may have a greater rational purchase on reality than others, but, in order to survive for any length of time, all ideological traditions must have a sufficient grounding in the objective features of the social world they describe to make plausible the distortions and mystifications they entail. This reality component of all ideologies explains their popular appeal and functional effectiveness in the reproduction of a social order otherwise destabilized by internal contradictions and conflicts. A Marxist analysis of ideology, therefore, needs both to comprehend those features of ideological discourse that obscure relations of conflict, along with the material grounding of these distorting arguments, as well as to comprehend features of the discourse and its material context that are contradictory and give rise to counter-ideological consciousness and action.

This is no simple task, however. For all the theoretical sophistication of Marx's conceptualization of commodity fetishism, and its utility for a general theory of ideology, Marx did not himself apply it to the problems of mass political consciousness and political psychology. He was himself much more concerned with the formal expression of ideology in the pseudo-science of the bourgeois economists or, earlier in his career, in the philosophy of Hegel and the neo-Hegelians. This interest rarely extended to the study of ideology as practiced or expressed in everyday life and politics, although there are clearly concerns of this kind in works like *The Eighteenth Brumaire of Louis Napoleon*. More typically, Marx wrote of ideology in ways that have encouraged the vulgar translations referred to earlier, tending to see the objective interests of classes as inevitably leading to class struggle and thereby to the transformation of the mode of production, no matter what the temporary distortions of opposing interests in subjective, false consciousness. In vulgar Marxist formulations, ideology is merely a superstructural reflection of the determining relations of power and exploitation in the economic base. While these underlying economic relations are undisturbed by crisis, ideology makes domination legitimate and assists its reproduction through the continued motivation to labour and political deference on the part of subordinated classes. When economic crises develop, however, they determine a corresponding change in political relations and in the content of ideology required for their justification.

This mechanical and simplified model is based on the normal operation of dominant ideology: except in times of crisis, class rule is reproduced by the imposition of a uniform ideology. This line of argument is clearly inadequate, however, to the tasks of explaining the heterogeneity of ideological discourse, the complex interweaving within ideological perspectives of discourses rooted in different class and non-class situations, and the conflicts and changes in ideology that are not preceded by economic crisis or changes in the composition of the ruling class. We have to turn to the major contemporary contributors to a Marxist theory of ideology for a more adequate account of the nature of ideology, moving from the simple definition of ideology to a more sophisticated understanding of variable and contingent ideological perspectives as opposed to interests logically linked to determinate class positions, and to an understanding of the complexities of the relative autonomy of ideology in the determination of social change.

THEORIZING IDEOLOGY:
THE ALTHUSSERIAN BREAK

The most sustained attempt to salvage the critical heart of the Marxist theory of ideology – that is, the materialist determination of ideology – and at the same time to cope with these complexities is the theoretical argument initiated by Althusser (1969; 1971; 1977) and continued by Poulantzas (1973; 1974; 1975; 1980) and Therborn (1978; 1980). This attempt is flawed, however, by the epistemological isolation of ideology as a separate "instance" of the structure of a social formation, and by the essentially woolly notion of overdetermination. These formulations treat social change as interactively determined by the conjoint influences of class struggles rooted separately in the economy, in ideology, and in politics, with results attributable to no unique effect of the particular instances, but with the economic given a theoretical privilege as determinant "in the last instance." Since, however, in Althusser's poetic phrase, the "lonely hour of the last instance never comes," this theoretical privilege functions only to narrow Althusser's conceptualization of ideology to an economistic notion of dominant ideology, functionally related to the reproduction of capitalist social relations (Abercrombie et al. 1980).

Still, Althusser's attempt to move the Marxist conceptualization of ideology beyond the simplicities of false consciousness is often illuminating. It is to him that we owe the understanding of ideology in terms of Marx's analysis of fetishism. His polemical insistence upon the break between Marx's account of fetishism and his preceding analysis of alienation may hide the textual continuity between the two concepts, and reduce some of the richness of Marx's conception of the dialectical relationships between domination and mystification (Geras 1972), but he retains a highly sophisticated sense of the material and psychological grounding of ideology. It is worth understanding his basic argument.

For Althusser ideology is not reducible to a subjective false consciousness. Instead there is an objective core to its representation of social reality and its role as a functional prop of the social order it represents. "An ideology is a system (with its own logic and rigour) of representations (images, myths, ideas or concepts, depending on the case) endowed with an historical existence and role within a given society" (Althusser 1969, 231). The distinguishing feature of an ideology, as a system of ideas, is that it mystifies social relations; ideology is the mystified form in which people experience their relation to the world. "In ideology men do indeed express, not the relation between them and their conditions of existence, but *the way* they live the relation between them and their conditions of existence. In ideology the real relation is inevitably invested in the imaginary relation, a relation that *expresses a will* (conservative, reformist, or revolutionary), a hope or a nostalgia, rather than describing reality" (Althusser 1969, 233–4).

The emphasis here upon mystification as the formalization of subjective experience indicates the function that ideology serves in the reproduction of an objective order through the representation of society in ways with which individuals can identify. The argument is very clear in Althusser's depiction of the distinctive vocabulary and presuppositions of all ideological thought. A commentator puts the argument succinctly:

> We can start from the function ideology fulfils: that of adapting individuals so as to enable them to respond to the needs of society ... The category of the subject ... is uniquely fitted to the purpose of ideology since the complicity of the subject and object that underlies it gives the world a meaning *for the individual* that suppresses the mechanisms of exploitation and oppression at the heart of society and the meaninglessness and chaos which enables him to recognize himself in the world, to see it as a world in a sense created for him, in which there is a place for him. An assurance is offered that if he conforms with what is required of him by society, all will be well for him. (Callinicos 1976, 65)

Added to this argument about the psychological meaning of ideology is Althusser's insistence upon the material existence of ideology. In his conceptualization of the "ideological state apparatuses," he indicates that ideology exists not simply in the realm of ideas, but that it has a material existence institutionalized in the state. To reproduce the dominant mode of production, the state employs a combination of repression and ideology. These functions are fulfilled by the (Repressive) State Apparatus, which "functions incisively and predominantly by repression," and the Ideological State Apparatuses, which "function massively and predominantly by ideology" (Althusser 1971, 141). The odd discontinuity between the capitalized terms indicates that *the* State Apparatus, for which it is hardly necessary to add the parenthetical repressive, has a "unified and central organization under the leadership of the representatives of the classes in power executing the politics of the class struggle of the classes in power," (Althusser 1971, 142) while the Ideological State Apparatus*es* are plural and relatively autonomous entities (churches, schools, universities, trade unions, political parties, etc.), which allow for the isolated representation of special interests, reunifying them in the common discourse of the ideology of the ruling class.

Here it is evident that Althusser's conceptual innovations are constrained by the implicit economism he has tried so hard to dispel. The State Apparatus sounds like the executive committee of the bourgeoisie, while the Ideological State Apparatuses organize the compliance of subordinate classes through the imposition of a dominant ideology. There is no room in this conception for ideological struggle, or for the development, independently of the structure of class/state relations, of discourses that tend to undermine the dominant ideology. Though much more sophisticated in its conception of the psychological character and material institutionalization of ideology, Althusser's argument retains the essential logic of vulgar Marxism's functionalism and economism. This is not entirely so because Althusser does talk of the *classes* in power and the politics of the class struggle, and his theoretical reinterpretation of the para-political institutions of civil society is not trivial. But Althusser does not really link ideology to class struggle; he does not indicate how ruling classes rule, and how ideology is involved in the process, and more problems are raised than solved by his conceptualization of the state as having at the same time its own particular institutional location but extending also through all the institutions of society (cf. Miliband 1977, 54 ff.).

Althusser's great student, Nicos Poulantzas, relaxes the functionalism, to the extent that he conceives of class struggles as inscribed *within* the state, and as characterizing the structures and practices within each level of the social formation. His repetition of Althusser's emphasis upon a dominant ideology and of the unifying role of ideology that "refuses to allow a contradiction in it" is qualified by his conceptualization of the importance of "ideological ensembles and sub-ensembles," and, therefore, of ideological class struggle (1973, 195 ff.). He also relaxes the economism by arguing for the theoretically prior importance of ideology in the constitution of the "free individuals" necessary for capitalist economic relations. More generally, he attributes to ideology the function of "inserting agents into their practical activities" and, therefore, of playing a foundational role in the constitution of classes and, by extension, of the state.

Although he improves upon Althusser's economism, Poulantzas's conception of ideology moves too much towards a "politicist" emphasis uncharacteristic of Marxist theory. Poulantzas emphasizes the role of politics and ideology in shaping classes, class struggle, and state action, but he gives no detailed attention to the way in which ideology does this. Even though he explicitly disavows the view that ideologies can be viewed as number plates worn on the backs of social classes (1973, 202), his most extended analysis of a concrete ideological phenomenon (fascism in Poulantzas 1974) tends to do just this (Laclau 1977, 92 ff.).

Poulantzas's contribution is especially important in relation to the analysis of the state as a site of class struggle, and we discuss his views further when we consider the conceptualization of ideological divisions between classes, class fractions, and their organizational representatives in the public policy arena (chapter 7). But we must turn to the work of Therborn and Ernesto Laclau for the further development of the Althusserian perspective on ideology, for attempts to go beyond the conception of dominant ideology.

Therborn presents a sophisticated elaboration of Althusser's conceptualization of ideology as "lived experience," which sees ideology as allowing for subjugation and qualification in social relations (1980, 15 ff.). Individual identity, the meaning of ego and alter, is something not naturally given, but given in ideology. In this generalization of the psychological necessity of ideology, Therborn moves from the epistemologically constructed separate instances to the really separate realms of discursive practice and experience. On the basis of this recognition of the diversified realms of social experience, Therborn distinguishes between class and non-class ideologies, differentiating, for example, a feudal aristocrat's ideology from a proletarian's, a feminist's, or a racist's (1980, 66 ff.).

Therborn's detailed attempt to develop Althusser's principles of the materialist determination of ideology produces a useful conceptual advance in pointing to the material affirmations and sanctions necessary to the maintenance of an ideological position, but does nothing, as Therborn is quick to admit, to develop the point into a theoretical or empirical analysis of the nature of such affirmations and sanctions in contemporary capitalist society (1980, 31 ff.). The rather rigid attempt to defend a materialist position in terms of the independent and determining effects of the material matrix over the dependent matrices of ideological discourse moves in a contradictory direction from Therborn's general approach to the pervasive and determinant influences of ideology in social experience.

The internally contradictory, although insightful, perspectives of Althusser and his students suggest the need to move away from an overly epistemological and psychological emphasis in the conceptualization of ideology. The central ingredients in that emphasis – the demarcation of ideology from science, and the isolation of ideology as a separate level, along with the economic and political levels of social structure – are unhelpful. They exaggerate the homogeneity of a hegemonic ideology, leaving the identification of ideological divisions in society to entirely ad hoc, empirical investigation. Also they fail to resolve the question of how ideology is determined; a vaguely defined "relative autonomy" is combined in the case of Althusser and Therborn with strongly economist views and, in the case of Poulantzas, with strongly "politicist" views, in neither case with adequate justification. The Althusserian perspective, finally, offers little guidance as to how to go about studying the "complex concatenations of forces and voices" that describe "the operation of ideology in the organization, maintenance, and transformation of power in society," to use Therborn's pithy phrases (1980, 125, 1). The Althusserian school has produced a great deal of important refinement in our definition and conception of ideology, but little theoretical advance on Gramsci's rather vague theorizing of the ways in which ideology works to structure consent to domination, and to produce counter-hegemonic thought and action.

Perhaps the most interesting example of the limitations of the Althusserian perspective is in the early work of Laclau (1977). In his tentative theory of populism, Laclau uses the Althusserian conceptual system in an attempt to excise from it its economistic root. He adapts Althusser's concept of a social formation as an historically specific articulation of theoretically distinct modes of production; Poulantzas's concept of the people/power bloc contradiction as the dominant contradiction in concrete social formations; and the Althusserian concept of interpellation as the way in which ideology functions to insert individuals into historical structures as if they had an autonomous existence within them. Populism, according to Laclau, is an essentially ideological phenomenon, in which *different* classes have mobilized popular antagonisms in situations of hegemonic crisis. In order to properly understand the differences between left- and right-wing populisms, it is necessary to dispense with the conceptual equation of an ideology with a particular class interest, although it remains important to identify the class character of ideological movements. In Laclau's terms, "the class character of an ideology is given by its *form* and not by its *content*," and the form of an ideology is its "specific articulating principle" (1977, 160).

This complicated argument refers to the articulation of different class interests with popular antagonisms towards a particular dominant ideology and power bloc, when these latter antagonisms are expressed in the non-class terms of relatively continuous popular traditions. In these terms "it is possible to assert the class belonging of a movement or an ideology and, at the same time, to assert the non-class character of some of the interpellations that constitute it" (1977, 164). What gives populist movements and ideologies their distinctive form is the importance of a people/power bloc contradiction rather than a class contradiction in the development of political opposition to states in particular social formations, the results of which are to privilege the articulating principles of popular rather than class discourses in antagonism to the dominant ideology. Laclau sees populism as the generic form in which political realignments leading to major political transition occur in time of "general social crisis" (175).

In these terms Laclau converts distinctively Marxist arguments dealing with the nature and effect of class struggle into arguments dealing with the nature and effect of ideology. In his perspective, the motive force in history becomes "the people" mobilized by ideological interpellations, rather than classes in struggle. Particular ideologies and, therefore, social changes do have a class character, but this is not to be determined by observation of the concrete organization and activity of social classes. Rather, "the precondition for analyzing the class nature of an ideology is to conduct the inquiry through that which constitutes the distinctive unity of an ideological discourse" (1977, 99).

This essentially idealist preoccupation with discourse (illustrated in a much more extreme form in the later work of Laclau and Mouffe 1985) is, perhaps, not a surprising result of an attempt to confront the problems of Marxist economism from within the conceptual system of Althusser, itself rooted in strictly textual analysis and opposed to empirical and historical methods of analysis. There is, however, no substitute for empirical work to investigate the important issues raised by Laclau against vulgar Marxist formulations of dominant ideology: the class and non-class elements interwoven in ideological discourse; the ways in which classes are divided or unified by such discourse; and the extent to which a dominant ideology is confronted by the antagonism of the people, expressed in the terms of popular tradition.

These questions are at the heart of the Gramscian analysis of hegemony and hegemonic crisis, and the value of the Althusserians has been to re-emphasize their importance. Unfortunately, despite the now widespread agreement about the limitations of the Althusserian perspective, there are only a handful of Marxists or neo-Marxists who have found more compelling means of extending the work of Gramsci by inquiry into the character of ideological developments in advanced capitalist countries. Those who have, notably C.B. Macpherson, Jürgen Habermas, and Stuart Hall, have made very considerable contributions. But the importance of their work cannot be understood without setting it against the development of the much more voluminous body of work on the empirical characteristics of political culture in capitalist societies by non-Marxists.

In the absence of a body of empirical work in the tradition of Gramsci, Marxists have had to react to and reinterpret the empirical work of an opposing school. In this process the Marxist theory of ideology has, nevertheless, moved considerably beyond the epistemological culs-de-sac into which it was led by Althusser's objections to empiricism (see chapter 3). In order to show these new developments, we now discuss the interaction between Marxist and non-Marxist contributions to the empirical study of political culture and ideology.

NON-MARXIST PERSPECTIVES: PLURALISM AND THE END OF IDEOLOGY

As opposed to the Marxist insistence upon the importance of ideology in capitalist societies, the dominant political sociology of the liberal state essentially denies the importance of ideology in the political process. Ideas that are functional to the established liberal-capitalist state, that justify and sustain it, are seen to be rational and necessary. Rather than degrading them with the pejorative term "ideology," this theoretical tradition resorts to the more hygienic vocabulary of "political culture," "political supports," and "legitimacy" when speaking of such ideas, while the term "ideology" is reserved for the irrational, radical, and subversive ideas on the left or right of a spectrum of system-functional ideas.

Further, in place of Marxist conceptions of class-divided capitalist societies, ordered by states that articulate the hegemonic interests of the ruling capitalist class, the dominant political sociology views the political process in terms of the dispersal of political power, and dispenses with the notion of the state as the site of concentrated power in society. As in the market, so in the political system, rational outcomes result from the competition and bargaining of multiple groups in society, each pursuing its narrowly defined self-interest. Despite the obvious formal relationship of this political theory to the economic theory of capitalism in the tradition of Adam Smith, these rational outcomes are not seen to be exclusively the working of a guiding hand. Legislative, executive, and juridical functions of government are carried out by separate institutions with their own self-interest, and these institutions are embedded in the wider system of group interactions to which they respond by endorsing compromises that secure majority support among the affected groups.

Despite these evasions of the terminology and the problem at issue in this book, the dominant political sociology has to confront the same questions of how such a complicated system is given unity and stability, and the answers it provides are a useful foil to our investigation of the ways in which class power and hegemony are organized within the state, and of the ways in which that hegemony may be undermined. They also provide, as we have argued is true for all ideological perspectives, a partially correct analysis of the workings of capitalist society, and give us, therefore, an important set of empirical indicators to replicate and reinterpret in our own analysis.

Though nowhere systematically stated, we can reconstruct the main lines of the non-Marxist sociology of liberal democracy around six associated theses, that is, combinations of theory and empirical evidence. Two of these theses, relating to "the end of ideology" and to the "civic culture," have to do with what we refer to as popular ideology. Four additional theses, of "elite constraint," "elite liberalism," "elite integration," and "elite representativeness" elaborate the concept of pluralist democracy as a system of elite rule constrained by free electoral politics. We take up these latter four theses in chapter 9, when we get to questions of how the state operates to reproduce the hegemonic rule of capital, satisfying the requirements of accumulation and legitimation. For the moment we are concerned only with the first two theses concerning political ideas or political culture in liberal democracies.

While the thesis of the end of ideology is easily criticized in application to an era of ideological controversy in Western nations such as that discussed in this book, it had a "natural" plausibility in the capitalist states of the late 1950s and early 1960s, from which time it derives. And it is not simply an historical curiosity, no longer relevant to political theory and practice: there remain theorists and political actors very much committed to the central tenets of the end-of-ideology thesis. In the current era of the end of official socialism in the East and the relative incapacity of socialist movements in the West, the argument is reappearing in an even more extreme form as "the end of history" (Fukuyama 1989).

Simply put, the thesis of the end of ideology held that class cleavages in capitalist society after the Second World War were progressively attenuated and replace by a shared consensus on the values of economic growth and income redistribution financed by growth, and a corresponding consensus supporting state economic regulation to foster and stabilize economic growth and state welfare programs to redistribute the fruits of growth. Within this broad consensus, ideological division was virtually eliminated.

As Seymour Lipset put it: "The key domestic issue today is collective bargaining over differences in the division of the total product within the framework of a Keynesian welfare state, and such issues do not require or precipitate extremism on either side ... The ideological issues dividing left and right (have) been reduced to a little more or a little less government ownership and planning" (1960, 82, 441). Although all inequalities and injustices are not eliminated in this "good society in action," additional factors prevent the ideological mobilization of the marginalized.

Psychologically, the success of the welfare state encourages supportive rather than deviant politics. "Lack of tension and anxiety, generalized into a basic satisfaction with oneself and one's life (euphoria), tends to increase a person's interest and participation in the non-deviant areas of American politics. Euphoria tends to produce a greater trust in politicians, and greater interest and awareness of the political world. American politics tends, therefore, to express the needs and wishes of the more contented and satisfied citizens at every level" (Lane 1959, 157). In such a euphoric situation, "... the problem of politics is less to solve conflicts than to prevent them" (Lasswell, cited by Kariel), and "it is far less important to worry about the distribution of power and influence than to perfect the devices by which good feelings can be improved" (Kariel 1970, 145).

But politics cannot be entirely eliminated by technocratic administration and policy science. Although ideology is not needed to direct political regimes, there is need for a set of cultural "rules" and "values" to maintain the appearance and the reality of public constraint upon elite rule, without jeopardizing its basic efficiency. This is the basis of the thesis of the civic culture, which has much in common with the end-of-ideology thesis. Both theses have a clear derivation from the dominant sociological theory of Talcott Parsons, in which social order and the stability of social systems is rooted in a shared value system (Parsons, Bales, and Shils 1953; Parsons and Smelser 1956; Parsons 1951, 1977). In these terms the civic culture thesis states the cultural or value prerequisites for sustaining the polyarchic political system of elite rule.

The thesis holds that there must be a balance in the mass political culture between attitudes justifying active political participation and attitudes justifying political deference (Almond and Verba 1963). These almost contradictory positions specify the requirements of a system that is simultaneously democratic and elitist: it provides opportunities for the public selection of rulers, but restricts direct public participation in decision making. Political withdrawal, cynicism, alienation, and non-participation negate the active citizenship necessary to any notion of democratic society, but political activism, intensified levels of public demand, and direct political participation in the political process tend to overwhelm the capacity for efficiency in government and to produce ungovernability (cf. Almond and Verba 1963; Crozier, Huntington, and Watanuki 1975; Dahl 1970).

Polyarchic rule requires public trust *and* a sense of political efficacy or competence among citizens, but not too much of either. Trust in government, when it becomes the uncritical approval of authority rather than the balanced judgement of the performance of regimes, promotes tyranny not democracy, autocracy not polyarchy. Political efficacy, when it becomes the radical demand to have recognition of the individuals' preferences in all public choices rather than a sense of individual self-esteem and civic right balanced by tolerance of diverse interests and respect for democratic decisions, promotes anarchy not polyarchy (cf. Sniderman 1981).

This balance is precarious, however. The antinomies of the civic culture and of polyarchic governance make the political system vulnerable to shifts in the delicate balance of activism and apathy, of vigilance and deference. Alexis de Tocqueville's concern that the vitality and openness of America's democracy could be transformed into the tyranny of the majority is the classic statement of the problem (Tocqueville 1966). In the twentieth century McCarthyism and the phenomenon of the moral majority illustrate how real a problem this is in that country, and the elaboration of the American theory of polyarchy is very much a response to domestic and external threats of the emergence of fascist, anti-democratic popular movements in constitutional democracies. Pluralist political culture stands guard against the intrusions of ideological movements: the consensus on welfare state mechanisms of income security and redistribution and the acceptance of limited participation make politics a sideshow and assure the stability of democracy in economically dynamic capitalist states.

It is along such theoretical lines that mainstream political science has proceeded in Canada, at least in so far as it has been concerned with questions of political culture. We have, thus, a long tradition of electoral studies in which the paramount considerations have been questions of partisan identification, assessments of parties and leaders, and the psychological predispositions to reasoned political choice and participation. From the latter concern stems the detailed description of patterns of "political trust" and "political efficacy" (Simeon and Elkins 1974).

Because the underlying theoretical model of pluralism and brokerage politics insists upon the relevance only of changing, short-term issues, mostly manipulated by political elites in the context of electoral campaigns, there has been no need to go beyond this. A critical comment made over two decades ago is still largely accurate today: "A foreign observer reading the literature on Canadian voting would assume that issues play no part in

Canadian politics. Perhaps they are relatively unimportant, but we have no basis for saying so except our ignorance" (Elkins and Blake 1975, 323).

REVISIONS OF NON-MARXIST THEORIES OF IDEOLOGY

The orthodox, pluralist formulations of the nature of liberal democratic culture have never, however, been accepted without criticism, even within the confines of non-Marxist scholarship, and even before the current era when the critical assumption of economic growth and effectiveness has become so suspect. First, a number of British scholars challenged the American sociology of value integration and embourgeoisement (see Marshall 1964; Goldthorpe et al. 1969). Michael Mann (1970) and Frank Parkin (1971) analyzed the political consciousness of workers in terms of the variable but contradictory commitment to dominant and subordinate value systems. In their view, dominant values govern working-class understandings of abstract political issues, so that there is, for example, widespread attachment to the monarchy and support for foreign military adventures; but subordinate values govern the understandings of authority in everyday life, with widespread militancy in the workplace, support for trade unions, and community-based action.

Second, a number of American and Canadian scholars argued that the democratic pretensions and the scope of public welfare promoted by pluralist governments were flawed by the economic bias in the distribution of power (Schattschneider 1960; Porter 1965); that conflict was neither limited nor dysfunctional, especially since the roots of conflict lay in the nature of organization and the distribution of power rather than in economic class relations (Coser 1956; Dahrendorf 1959); and that the absence of a coherent public philosophy as opposed to the glorification of self-interest limited the technocratic competence of the pluralist state to produce welfare – that it made social planning impossible, reducing welfare policy to the indemnification of damages rather than the righting of wrongs (Lowi 1969), stimulating private wealth but public squalor (Galbraith 1958), and reducing private life to the defensive, fearful, and lonely struggles for consumer and status satisfaction (Riesman, Denney, and Glazer 1953; Slater 1976).

Compelling though much of this criticism was, it failed to move beyond a moral indictment of the liberal society towards a sociological conception of the social forces that might bring about change. The essential durability of the capitalist welfare state, despite its moral and aesthetic defects, was not questioned. The crisis of liberalism, if there was one, was not of revolutionary contradictions, but of "a nightmare of administrative boredom" (Lowi 1969) or other Weberian forebodings. This, it must be added, was not simply a limitation in non-Marxist scholarship of the times (cf. the popularity of Herbert Marcuse's gloomy account of the deadening impact of "one dimensional society" [1964]). A tradition of cultural criticism that assumes the universality of a dominant ideology that condemns capitalist society to decadence but not to transformation remained vibrant in both liberal and Marxist circles (cf. the influential work by Lasch 1979; Bellah et al. 1985; Berman 1981).

While these two streams of justificatory and critical political sociology continued more or less in isolation from each other for the first two decades after the Second World War, disagreeing on major issues but not on the essential stability of liberal capitalism nor on the existence of a powerful dominant ideology, the year 1968 represents a critical turning point in the development of political sociology. The impact of the political revolt of youth, and the intimations of new radical coalitions outside of the conventional framework of party politics in that year, prompted a re-examination of the theory and practice of the capitalist welfare state. The street warfare in Chicago and Paris, the treason of the clerks and students, the ideological ferment of anarchism, Trotskyism, Maoism, and the "green" movements for ecology and peace, and the militant irredentism of ethnic groups all combined to question the psychological and cultural foundations of the liberal capitalist state. The restraint upon political participation and ideological manipulation through the satisfaction of needs by economic growth and the inculcation of political trust and loyalty through webs of group interaction seemed to have failed in the face of a rising tide of political activism and ideological conflict. The politics of happiness had given way to the politics of disorder, and compensating shifts in political sociology were bound to follow.

THE RESPONSE TO THE NEW LEFT

The apparent embourgeoisement and conservatism of most working-class organizations – trade unions and established Communist parties – in the struggles of 1968 facilitated the characterization of this political disorder in normative and psychological terms divorced from the analysis of class struggle. The decline or stagnation of many labour union movements and the defeats of social democratic governments in the years following likewise contributed to a tendency to see ideological and political struggle as a product of changes and divisions in the "middle class," with a consequent emphasis upon psychological and political explanations. The tendency was most marked among liberal theorists, although it also affected the development of Western Marxism.

The work of Theodore Lowi, David Apter, and Ronald Inglehart is representative of the changes in liberal political sociology. Lowi recharacterized the political left and right as the opposition between organized and unorganized interests (Lowi 1969). Apter (1973) argued that the intensity of ideological oppositions reflected the corrosion of organization that resulted from high rates of mobility and marginalization of persons, and the progressive instrumentalization of values in a rapidly changing division of labour. He, like Lowi, reconceptualized divisions of left and right in ways divorced from their traditional identification with class divisions: "Occupants of nonfunctional roles or roles losing functional significance are susceptible to reactionary or conservative norms, whereas individuals that reject instrumental criteria are attracted to radical or revolutionary norms" (Apter 1973, 76).

Inglehart (1977) saw in the disorders of the time a "silent revolution," in which concerns with material consumption and scarcity were gradually displaced by post-material concerns for the quality of life, and class cleavages in political ideology were displaced by psychological and generational cleavages. The clamour of 1968 is thus reduced to a debate over materialism and post-materialism – a debate in which Marxism and mysticism are marginal alternatives, which does not threaten the survival of the capitalist welfare state, but shifts its direction from growth and consumption to stability, conservation, participation, and the inner fulfilment of human needs. These latter needs, following Abraham Maslow's (1954) theory of motivation, shift under the impact of prosperity from physiological and safety concerns to the "higher-order" needs for belongingness, esteem, and self-actualization.

The response to 1968 and its aftermath by scholars starting from a Marxist perspective was substantially different, as the work of Habermas and Macpherson reveals. In the dislocations of 1968 these scholars, and others like Marcuse, saw a cause for optimism, but an optimism very different from Inglehart's. For them the emerging ideological struggles of the time were directly tied to the long history of struggles exposing the fundamental contradictions of capitalism and its ideological justification in liberalism.

Macpherson's early work involved an important study of class and ideology in Alberta (1962a), but just as that work had little impact on the scholarly consensus about the irrelevance of ideology in this country, so his other major works scarcely touched the theoretical consciousness of Canadian political sociology. Relegated to the curricula of "political theory," these works are, nevertheless, perhaps *the* major contribution in English to an analysis of the nature of ideology in capitalist society. In a series of books, Macpherson shows the confusion and contradiction in successive attempts to ground a justification of the liberal capitalist state by reference to the ontological theorems of "possessive individualism" in Thomas Hobbes and John Locke, the differently reasoned defence of the inviolability of property and the negative content of freedom in the utilitarianism of Jeremy Bentham and John Stuart Mill, the Hegelianism of Thomas Hill Green, or the modern contractarianism of John Rawls and Robert Nozick (Macpherson 1962b; 1966; 1973; 1977; see also the commentary on Macpherson in Tucker 1980, on which our summary is heavily reliant).

None of these traditions of liberal thought, according to Macpherson, escape the central criticism of Marx that the juridical freedoms and equality of citizens in a liberal capitalist state are fundamentally limited or contradicted by the compulsion for a majority of citizens to sell their labour power as a commodity, and by the inequality in the market transfer of power resources (and, therefore, of freedom to develop one's capacities) effected by the private appropriation of the socially produced surplus in capitalist relations of production. As Macpherson argues, this inability to provide a coherent defence of the liberal capitalist state on the grounds of freedom, equality, and justice has meant a progressive historical expansion of the role of the state in regulating markets and producing public goods. Forced by political struggles over the unequal and worsening conditions of large sectors of the population in the distribution by free market forces of welfare opportunities and conditions, the expansion of the state has, nevertheless, been restrained by the ideological entrenchment of the central liberal commitments to possessive individualism. Macpherson sees in this expansion a gradual process towards the eventual suspension of the capitalist economy and to the establishment of a genuine democracy as the equally effective right of individuals to live as fully humanly as they may wish.

This optimistic projection is based upon Macpherson's argument that the expansion of state investment, regulation, and redistribution, though intended to facilitate the process of capital accumulation, is less and less constrained by the interests of the capitalist class. This class is often internally divided over appropriate policy and unable itself to formulate a collective program for sustained capital accumulation. In the absence of a coherent direction from the class with the greatest resources for influence, the state is rather influenced by the increasing propensity on the part of citizens to exercise their rights against the interests of capital. Macpherson points to the power of groups that have direct interests in state economic intervention, even where this may be "inefficient" for capital accumulation. Such groups include state personnel, welfare recipients, and organized labour in declining industries. In addition he points to a growing belief that unlimited economic expansion has a negative impact on the quality of life and to resulting demands for greater environmental protection by the state. This is part of the general tendency in conditions of greatly increased productivity for a shift in consciousness. Third, Macpherson points to signs of increasing experimentation with participatory democracy in local contexts, especially by organized workers in the workplace but also by community organizations, and the increasing political activism in relation to state policy that results. Finally, he suggests that the frequency of recessions of near crisis proportions is encouraging an awareness of the irrationality of the capitalist system that requires increasing consumption but produces inequalities that inhibit expansion of the purchasing power of the majority.

Macpherson's optimism is guarded by a recognition that the dynamics of the electoral and party system moderate the articulation of radical opposition to the status quo, and that the relative success of organized labour has moderated the perspective of working-class movements in capitalist states. He suggests, however, that working-class movements will gradually force more and more political regulation of market decisions. He argues that the contradictions between sound public policy and the interests of private enterprise will stimulate strikes by organized labour and riots, terrorism, and other modes of protest by the disadvantaged, which will turn liberal societies into conditions of near-anarchy until significant changes in property relations effectively alter the class nature of those societies.

In the context of the last decade, rather than that of two decades ago to which Macpherson's texts referred, many of these sociological predictions will seem dubious. It is not simply this hindsight, however, that suggests that Macpherson's investigations in the history of political thought are much more rigorous than his political sociology. He tends to grant a Hegelian inevitability to the logical resolution of contradictions in consciousness as an explanation for historical change, giving little or no attention to problems of the economic and political organization of historical actors. "Groups" that are in the avant-garde of the critique of liberalism and the capitalist state are, therefore, privileged as the bearers of the future. The historical contingency of political movements and mobilization is not given sufficient emphasis; the uneven pattern of economic growth, and the dynamics of growth and decline are not seriously examined; and the class character of the state is obscured in an essentially pluralist view of the state as responsive to different group pressures. Macpherson's Marxism lacks adequate attention to the nature of production, class structure, and state power (cf. the very critical Wood 1981 in reply to a defence of Macpherson in Panitch 1981b).

Whatever its deficiencies, however, Macpherson's work provides a lucid analysis of the content and contradictions of liberal ideology, and of some of the main forces leading toward the intensification of ideological struggle in capitalist societies. Macpherson's contribution is usefully supplemented by that of Habermas (1976), who appropriates the key concept of possessive individualism, but expands the conceptualization of the crisis of liberalism.

To begin with, Habermas establishes a clear theoretical separation between levels of crisis that avoids the simplistic emphasis on a crisis of political ideology as the major explanation for changes in capitalist society. Habermas describes four levels of crisis tendency, of which two – economic crisis and administrative crisis – have nothing intrinsically to do with ideology, but are necessary, if not sufficient, conditions of a general crisis of society, that is, a condition in which the general structure of the social system undergoes fundamental change. The additional levels of crisis, which must develop coterminously with the economic and administrative in order to produce fundamental social change, are crises of legitimation and motivation. In describing these latter terms Habermas makes a very important contribution to the analysis of ideological developments in capitalist society.

Like Macpherson, Habermas argues that a legitimation crisis is a consequence of the expansion of state activity, but the legitimation problem is one directly pertaining to the justification of government activity rather than a problem of controlling the activity of citizens (1976, 71). The expansion of the scope of government activity brings into question a whole range of cultural matters (education and child rearing, for example) that were formerly taken for granted – that is, their meaning and justification were assumed to be obvious when left in the sphere of private responsibility and religious instruction. Government intrusion in these matters raises questions about the meaning and justification of state planning, and also about the meaning and justification of these activities themselves. Government intrusion upon past traditions creates a scarcity of meaning and an increase in demand for value – that is, for demonstrations of the utility of government action: "Missing legitimation must be offset by rewards conforming to the system. A legitimation crisis arises as soon as the demands for such rewards rise faster than the available quantity of value, or when expectations arise that cannot be satisfied with such rewards" (1976, 73).

This notion of legitimation crisis leads Habermas into abstruse philosophical questions of meaning and authentic communication, which need not detain us. More important for our purposes is the link in the last sentence quoted from legitimation to motivation crisis, that is, the importance to Habermas's conception of a crisis in capitalism of expectations that cannot be satisfied with rewards conforming to the system and of the loss of motivational support for activity that cannot be so rewarded. The system-conforming expectations and motivations are summarized in Habermas's discussion of "syndromes of civil and familial-vocational privatism." Civil privatism refers to the limitation of political activity to the institutional opportunities for electoral participation and the limitation of that participation and further interest in politics to the performance of governments rather than any interest in the ideological principles of government. Familial-vocational privatism complements civil privatism by confining social horizons to the family, and by stimulating interests in consumption, leisure, and occupational achievement (1976, 74 ff.).

Providing that this culture of privatism is sufficiently well maintained, Habermas argues, legitimation needs do not necessarily result in a crisis of the capitalist system. He suggests, however, a number of threats to the maintenance of these syndromes of privatism (1976, 80–4): the philosophical "necessity" of natural law and religious justifications of the morality of individual differences in capitalist society, of the obligation to work, of deference to political authorities, etcetera, are eroded by the success of scientism.

"Practical questions no longer admit of truth; values are irrational," and "theories of technocracy and of elites, which assert the necessity of institutionalized civil privatism, are not immune to objections, because they too must claim to be theories." Further, the orientation to achievement, possessive individualism, and exchange value – "the components of bourgeois ideologies directly relevant to privatistic orientations" – are being undermined by social changes such as: the weakened connection between formal schooling and occupational success; the difficulty in many areas of the economy of making evaluation according to individually accountable achievement; weakening of the motivation to work by the equalization of the standard of living of lower-income workers and the "reserve army" outside of the labour process; the increasing proportion of collective commodities and socialized production in transportation, leisure, health care, education, etcetera "that increasingly discards the forms of differential demand and private appropriation" typical of the market allocation of consumable goods; the increasing proportion of the population "who do not reproduce their lives through income from labour ... and the spread of areas of activity in which abstract labour is replaced by concrete labour"; and the increasing relevance of leisure pursuits as compared to occupational concerns that "do not directly privilege those needs that can be satisfied momentarily."

Habermas thus provides a very rich conception of the ideological supports of capitalist society and of the processes leading to the undermining of those supports. He makes no clear identification, however, of the social forces behind legitimation and motivation crises. He clearly means to link the cultural and psychological threats confronting civil and familial privatism to the latent class struggle in capitalist society, but he makes no clear argument to that effect. Without such an argument, he is left to call for empirical research to clarify the nature and extent of legitimation and motivation crises in specific societies.

Empirical research is, indeed, necessary to clarify the extent to which the descriptive features of arguments like Macpherson's and Habermas's fit the current condition of Canada or other capitalist societies. Their arguments help to a considerable extent to operationalize the abstract conceptions of hegemony and hegemonic crisis, of ideology and ideological conflict, and to make possible an intelligent empirical assessment of the content and extent of threats to the hegemony of capitalist political order. There are, however, profound problems of an epistemological or methodological order in making the move to strictly empirical research. Habermas's throw-away call for empirical research on legitimation crisis is a gratuitous call for others to enter what the bulk of his other work insists is a profoundly problematic domain – the empirical assessment of theoretical knowledge of society.

In the absence of efforts to take up the challenge of systematic empirical research, and in the absence of any clear analysis by Macpherson and Habermas of the class dynamics of ideological conflict, there has been a tendency for some Marxists to pick up on the superficial indications of massive cultural dislocation and change divorced from class conflict after 1968, and to move to interpretations that explicitly renounce the relevance of traditional classes, especially the industrial working class, to contemporary social change, emphasizing new social movements rather than traditional class organizations as the agents of change, and seeing ideological conflict as operating in a radically autonomous realm of discourse and symbolic experience (cf. Gorz 1982; Touraine 1981; Baudrilliard 1981; Laclau and Mouffe 1985).

This tendency, following Michel Foucault, has become increasingly prolix and without empirical substance developing post-structuralist and post-modernist theories of discourse and new subject positions. Such developments nevertheless reflect complex developments in the real world of political and ideological struggle, not covered in the work of Macpherson and Habermas. This latter work was rooted in the experience of the 1960s and early 1970s, when the new left had not yet been challenged by the "new right," when political programs for dismantling rather than reforming the welfare state were not the order of the day, and when the new social movements had not yet so clearly replaced the organized movements of labour as the most vital oppositions to these latter developments. The new emphasis on discourse theory was a response to these far-reaching changes.

But the drift to discourse has not yet swamped the further development of a more conventional political sociology in the Marxist tradition, and we turn, in the final section of this chapter, to a review of approaches to the nature of political and ideological divisions in the era of welfare state crisis, and beyond.

IDEOLOGY AND CRISIS IN THE KEYNESIAN WELFARE STATE

The preliminary insights of Macpherson and Habermas were, ironically, more widely appropriated by liberal than by Marxist political sociologists. While erstwhile Marxists became cultural and psychological theorists, erstwhile liberals and pluralists became neo-conservative theorists of a crisis of legitimacy in the welfare state. The key to this historical irony is, of course, the extent of the economic crisis in world capitalism during the late 1970s, and the response to these new conditions in liberal political sociology can best be seen in the representative work of Daniel Bell.

One of the fathers of the end of ideology orthodoxy, Bell was writing by 1977 of a crisis of capitalism broadly comparable in scope to the European crisis of the 1930s. Central to this analysis is the view that "what has been singular about modern life is the emphasis on demand ... In a crucial sense, the modern era is defined as the shift in the character of economies – and in the nature of modern economic thinking – from supply to demand" (Bell 1977, 177). This shift reflects the emerging "cultural contradictions" of capitalism, and provokes a crisis of political confidence and stability (Bell 1976). A growing disjunction is said to have developed between a capitalist order based upon ideals of efficiency and self-denial, originating in the puritanism and Protestant ethic of the pre-modern period, and a new culture of self-gratification and self-indulgence, spawned by the rise of mass production and mass consumption in the modern era. Aggravating this contradiction, there has developed a growing disjunction between the glorification of plenty and individual self-gratification and the growth of the "public household" in which more and more collective goods and services are controlled by government, requiring more and more regulation of economic growth and social consumption to satisfy public as opposed to private needs. The welfare state stimulates expectations but is limited in its capacity to satisfy them: "The final irony is that with all the money being spent on social expenditures there is an evident sense that the quality of service is poor, that the social science knowledge to design a proper health system, or a housing environment, or a good educational curriculum, is inadequate, and that large proportions of these moneys are increasingly spent on administrative and bureaucratic costs" (Bell 1977, 120).

Nevertheless the welfare state is the key to the "revolution of rising entitlements," and in the absence of an effective ideological restraint upon demands for self-gratification, the governments of advanced capitalist states are faced with a double bind in which the demand for the provision of social, cultural, and welfare services outpaces its capacity to supply them. The demands for social services cannot be balanced against the requirements of state investments in production and accumulation.

Thus Bell appropriates the neo-Marxist concepts of a fiscal crisis (O'Connor 1973) and a crisis of administration (Habermas 1976), but strips them of their original connection, however indirect, to class conflict. Bell's fiscal crisis is a product not of the logic of capital accumulation and of the resulting problems of class conflict and its containment, but of purely cultural contradictions that stimulate psychological dispositions inappropriate to a stable political order. The problem of these dispositions is not simply that they cannot be satisfied, but that they directly impair the legitimacy of the state. In this way Bell appropriates also the neo-Marxist concept of legitimation crisis (Habermas 1976), but again this concept is stripped of its original connotations of contradiction between qualitatively different principles of legitimation. The differences between the Protestant ethic and the demands for consumer satisfaction are not specified as contradictory with the same theoretical precision as are the differences between orientations to positive rather than negative liberty in Macpherson's arguments, or the difference between orientations to exchange value as opposed to use value, commodified as opposed to non-commodified goods, in arguments by Habermas and his students (especially Claus Offe). For Bell the legitimation problem lies in the absence of principles to restrain the quantitative escalation of demand, not in the emergence of principles in qualitative opposition to capitalism: "The emerging system of state capitalism lacks the kind of philosophical legitimation that liberalism has provided ... The democratization of demands ... is subject to few constraints, or fewer than those represented by the limited credit available to individuals or firms that at some point would have to pay their debts, rather than 'postpone' them by increasing the public debt" (Bell 1977, 178).

The legitimation crisis, therefore, produces a problem of government, a paralysis and instability of regimes, but not a fundamental problem of the social order, with intimations of far-reaching change. It is not that Bell fails to consider the economic in his concentration on cultural variables; his concern with the economy is merely as a symptom of cultural contradiction, and there is no deep-structured logic of contradiction in the development of a capitalist economy and society. The economic problems after 1974 are thus centrally a question of demand-pushed inflation. The resulting pressures towards deflationary policy exacerbate the corporate fragmentation of society, producing a political crisis of public alienation from government and of unstable minority and coalition regimes (Bell 1977, 113). Deflation reduces confidence in the capacity of the state to respond to demands, and therefore intensifies competition for the allocation of the state budget and for exemption from the impact of deflationary economic policy (133). "The double bind of democracy wreaks its contradictory havoc in the simultaneous desire for more spending (for one's own projects) and lower taxes and less interference in one's life" (135).

The neo-conservative pessimism reflected in Bell's post-1974 analysis is in sharp contrast to the optimism of Inglehart's silent revolution. Where the latter envisages a "greening" of capitalist society, and a humanizing of liberalism, brought about by qualitatively new value orientations, the former sees only gloom in the results of new value-orientations, and calls for a conservative retreat to the old values of traditional liberalism. The key to this call is the assault on the welfare state – the reduction of state activity according to an undefined principle of "appropriate scale," with the greater centralization of some governmental functions and the greater decentralization of others, and the substitution of the market principle for much of the existing bureaucratic regulation of social programs (Bell 1977, 133–5).

The neo-conservative appropriation of the neo-Marxist identification of crises of fiscal management and legitimation is not, however, the only recognition in liberal political sociology of the utility of such concepts in application to the period after 1974. A prominent American liberal and critic of neo-conservatism in U.S. politics, Walter Dean Burnham, has, for example, confessed that while his earlier work pointed to serious problems in the American electoral analysis of the 1950s and 1960s, the system-wide crisis of political articulation, representation, and support was not visible to him because "the age, after all was of Gabriel Almond and Sidney Verba's *The Civic Culture*." In the 1970s, however, he adopted the logic of James O'Connor's (1973) analysis of the contradictions between accumulation and legitimation, identifying a crisis of political legitimacy as a result of the erosion of the traditional liberal conception of the primacy of individual liberty brought about by the expanded role of the public sector and the emergence of the corporate sector as the dominant form of social organization (Burnham 1982). In addition to this substitution of the power of organized interest groups for the powers of independent individuals, and the recasting of American democracy as the interaction of institutionalized powers rather than the exercise of popular choice, Burnham points like Bell to an erosion of the classic puritan and Victorian values on accumulation as the result of the elevation of hedonistic values in the modern mass-market economy, and their entrenchment in welfare state protections against unemployment and poverty. These cultural transformations wrought by economic and political changes are linked by Burnham to the decomposition of American political parties as the articulators and therefore mediators of contending political interests. This symptom of the legitimation crisis is reflected in the massive decline in party loyalty, voting turnout, and the associated loss of public interest and trust in politics.

The problem with Burnham's argument, as with Bell's, and indeed with the neo-Marxist theory on which they draw, is the theoretical and empirical imprecision of their conceptualization of legitimation crises. Critics quite properly focus on the ambiguities of measures of declining turnout and partisan identity as evidence of anything so serious as a legitimation crisis. More pointedly, one might focus on the absence of any systematic evidence of the value changes that are supposed to have resulted in the collapse of traditional liberalism as a legitimating system. What is the evidence for the new hedonism, and for the resistance in the mass public to the short-term restraint on gratification?

Partly the problem has to do with the overly abstract conception of liberalism and the conflicts between accumulation and legitimation. Partly it has to do with the ad hoc invocation of evidence of party and government instability as evidence of an untheorized crisis, that is, of a crisis that is tautologically defined as political instability, without serious analysis of the underlying logic of the stability of the economic and political system.

As a result, although there is some rhetorical force to the language of legitimation crisis, many of those who use the language add little or nothing to more straightforwardly empirical accounts of political dissatisfaction linked to short-term fluctuations in economic growth, as in the prominent account of Canadian politics as "decline and dissatisfaction" without ideological conflict or change (Clarke et al. 1984, chap. 1), or in Samuel Beer's (1982) more sophisticated account of the development of ideological conflicts in present day Britain, which dispenses with the notion of legitimation crisis and with an abstract conception of capitalist society, focusing rather on the more specific form of the postwar welfare state and its dialectical subversion as a result of the declining hold of cultural restraints on political deference and economic expectations.

Such work argues for a purely political crisis of inadequate support for a particular type of political system. For example, Clarke et al. begin with the crucial problem of the capacity of states to meet the needs of their citizens (1984, 7), and with the incapacity of the Canadian system of brokerage politics to produce "mandates for change that might relieve discontent" (1984, 27). Their analysis, however, does little to clarify the extent of dissatisfaction among Canadians, the manner in which it is linked to the incapacity of the party and electoral system to produce meaningful change, and the extent of the problem posed for the continued stability of the Canadian political system. Beer's analysis, similarly, derives much of its power from an argument about the collapse of the "collectivist" state as a result of its declining economic performance, but particularly because of the collapse of its cultural supports. The latter argument is, however, theoretically and empirically weak (see the review in Leys 1983), and Beer's conclusions about the open-ended possibilities of any of a large number of different ideological strategies determining the future of Britain fail to inspire confidence in the ability to go beyond empirical and *ex post facto* interpretations of politics.

A more adequate concept of political crisis is therefore necessary to come to grips with the realities of contemporary politics in capitalist societies. This requires a return to the Gramscian tradition in which hegemony is seen as an unstable unity of divided class forces, forged by political and ideological leadership in the context of historically specific economic conditions. Hegemonic crisis, from this perspective, is not as it tends to be in much Marxist political sociology, even as sophisticated as that of Habermas and Macpherson, a working out of simple contradictions that tend cumulatively and linearly to undermine the capitalist order. Crisis is, rather, a complex, theoretically indeterminate although not unintelligible, process of political and ideological struggle, in which the contending forces have to be conceptualized as creative social agents with class and non-class identities and interests, and in which the balance of forces has constantly to be empirically examined. There is no simple recipe for such analysis, but recent Marxist political sociology offers some important guidance.

Perhaps the most stimulating new work in this direction is that of Hall and his colleagues (Hall 1978; Hall and Jacques 1983). Hall describes a crisis of hegemony that has emerged progressively through a series of stages in which the postwar welfare state has been shaken by political struggles. These struggles are seen as intensifying as a direct result of the requirement for the welfare state increasingly to intervene in an unstable economy, "managing capital where capital could no longer successfully manage itself, and thereby *drawing the economic class struggle increasingly on to its own terrain*" (Hall 1978, 214). According to Hall and his colleagues, the contemporary conjuncture is characterized by the exhaustion of social democratic strategies of organizing consent, and the transition towards a more exceptional form of state based less on consent and more on coercion. The transition is described in a brilliant analysis of the escalation of the ideological significance of crisis from the discrete moral panics of the 1960s through " 'the mapping together' of moral panics into a *general panic* about social order" (222). The empirical content of this analysis is restricted to a subtle content analysis of mass media, and particularly to the phenomenon of street violence. But on this basis they forecast well before the coming to power of Margaret Thatcher the emergence of a repressive, neo-conservative state attempting an authoritarian-populist strategy for re-establishing hegemony.

In subsequent development of this argument about authoritarian populism, Hall is careful not to overstate either the extent to which the "great moving right show" has successfully built a counter-hegemonic strategy on the articulation of public needs for better housing or schooling, and for greater standards of living, than that made available by the stagnant social democracy it seeks to replace (Hall 1979). He insists upon a distinction between a popular and populist project, and the inherent difficulties of the latter, despite its partial ability to "harness to its support some popular discontents, neutralize the opposing forces, disaggregate the opposition and really incorporate *some* strategic elements of popular opinion into its own hegemonic project" (Hall 1979). He makes clear, therefore, the need to establish in much more systematic ways the exact nature of the relations of forces contending for a new resolution of the hegemonic crisis. He is also careful to acknowledge the limitations of his emphasis on the ideological manifestations of the crisis, and his awareness of the "decisive nucleus of economic activity" that Gramsci sees in any analysis of hegemony. He insists, nevertheless, on the utility of focusing analysis of the crisis of hegemony on questions of ideology, the most neglected dimension of the problem in Marxist analysis (Hall 1985, 120–1).

If Hall, despite his self-conscious disclaimers, tends to overstate the significance of purely ideological discourse in the construction of hegemony, and of the new right's formative actions in the contemporary era, the work of Offe (1984) offers a useful corrective. Although working in the tradition of his mentor Habermas, rather than explicitly in the tradition of Gramsci, Offe provides a rich conceptualization of the crisis of the Keynesian welfare state, of the changing fields of political and ideological struggle, and of the magnitude of the obstacles facing the construction of any new hegemonic project.

Offe begins with a basic argument about the contradictory nature of the Keynesian welfare state, according to which crisis tendencies result from "the fact that the dynamics of capitalist development seem to exhibit a constant tendency to *paralyse* the commodity form of value" (1984, 122). Although the Keynesian state itself is part of the problem, reinforcing the tendency towards decommodification under monopoly capital, it also seeks as a capitalist state to re-establish the primacy of market relations through "administrative recommodification," using a variety of regulations, financial incentives, public investments, and corporatist stabilization of market activities (1984, 125). But state recommodification policies amplify the contradictions between commodified and decommodified relations because they have "the empirical side effect of depriving capital of either capital or labour power or the freedom to use both in profitable ways"(126), because they "presuppose the growth of state-organized forms of production that are exempt from the commodity form" (127), and because they "result in the subversion of the syndrome of possessive individualism" required for the "functioning of the commodity form" (128). These contradictions are expressed in contemporary evidence that after its initial success the Keynesian welfare state can no longer manage stable economic growth or reproduce its ideological and class supports: "… the non-productive public sector has become an intolerable burden upon the private sector, leading to a chronic shortage of investment capital; the work ethic is in the process of being undermined, and the independent middle class is suffocated economically by high rates of taxation and inflation" (200).

The capacity of the Keynesian welfare state to contain "the democratic class struggle," as defined in the liberal political sociology of Seymour Lipset and others, is undermined by rising levels of demand and dissatisfaction on the part of those dependent upon state support or expectant of it, and by the declining ability of state institutions to add new demands to the policy agenda (Offe 1984, 164). This crisis of governability is handled, instead, by increasing resort to undemocratic, neo-corporatist arrangements for resolving policy issues. An associated crisis of political participation is marked by the retreat of citizens from established political institutions and by the progressive separation of state and mass politics.

Here Offe stresses the significance of new social movements in the "unmediated opposition between the individual and the state" (1984, 170). These new social movements for the causes of women, peace, and environmental conservation (to cite the most obvious ones) reflect the demands of those exposed to the threats to collective and individual identity that result from a constantly expanding involvement of the state in all spheres of production. This expansion has the ironic effect that "as *politics* move beyond the reach of the citizen, state *policies* move ever closer" (174).

The new social movements offer a major challenge to the hegemony of the Keynesian welfare state because they tend to "challenge the prevailing mode of production and the effects it has upon the physical and human substance of social life" (Offe 1984, 176). For precisely such reasons, they are not easily incorporated within traditional political parties that have programmatic identification with the welfare state, and that have held power within it. But political parties are bound to seek ways in which to gain support from those mobilized by these movements, and there are bound to arise new political and ideological forms in which the people/state antagonisms articulated by the new social movements are redefined as hegemonic projects. Offe indicates the plasticity of potential party/movement alliances, and he sounds a warning for those who attempt to read hegemonic appeals from the interactions between political parties and social movements.

The warning is contained in his insistence on the necessity, despite its contradictory character, of the welfare state to the continued development of capitalist societies: "The embarrassing secret of the welfare state is that, while its impact upon capitalist accumulation may well become destructive (as the conservative analysis so emphatically demonstrates), its abolition would be plainly disruptive (a fact that is systematically ignored by the conservative critics). The contradiction is that while capitalism cannot exist *with*, neither can it exist *without*, the welfare state" (1984, 153).

Although neo-conservative parties may well, as Hall has argued, have capitalized upon the anti-state sentiments in public opinion, Offe warns that there are limits to their ability to follow through on their own prescriptions for the privatization of the state. And although there may in many cases be a more natural alliance between the new social movements and socialist rather than neo-conservative parties, Offe is sceptical about the likelihood of such alliances (1984, 295). He points to two difficulties in theoretical arguments for such alliance.

First, with respect to psychological arguments that ground the attraction to social movements in the search for self-actualization, Offe points out that no convincing argument is made for the public, as opposed to private, realization of self-actualization. "The supposedly predominant need for self-actualization could equally lead to new and unconventional, but entirely *private*, life-styles and consumption patterns rather than to new *politics*" (Offe 1987, 84). Second, he points to the deficiencies in the related sociological argument about the "carriers" of the new politics, and the way in which their ideas are spread beyond their initially narrow social base. The argument is "contingent on the age cohort that experiences prosperity and security; it is unable to account for either the spread of the politics into strata that have not participated in these conditions, or the stability of such movements even after the generation that initiated them ceases to be active" (1987, 84).

Before the coming together of a new counter-hegemonic movement in radical opposition to the capitalist system *per se*, Offe's analysis suggests a continuation of the conflictual and disorderly politics that have so far characterized the Keynesian welfare state in decline. Despite our own sympathy for this cautious conclusion, there has been a growing consensus in both liberal and Marxist political sociology on the emergence of a qualitatively new, post-Keynesian or post-Fordist political economy, with an associated development of post-modernist ideology and politics. Although these developments are essentially beyond the time frame that concerns us in this book, they begin within that period, and some sensitivity to them ought properly to inform our analysis.

The essential elements in this new theoretical consensus about the changing political economy and culture of advanced capitalist societies can be summarized as follows. First, it is argued that there has emerged a new, global "regime of flexible accumulation" (Harvey 1989) that has radically transformed or "disorganized" (Lash and Urry 1987) the advanced national economies on which the Keynesian welfare state was based. The growth of world markets, the globalization of production and the division of labour, the acceleration in the international mobility of money and capital, and the dislocation of the advanced capitalist economies through processes of decentralization, deregulation, and de-industrialization have removed the material basis of the state-regulated welfare state.

Second, it is argued that these developments have radically transformed the class structure that gave rise to the welfare state "compromise." A new, "hour-glassed" stratification of an increasingly affluent professional and managerial middle class and an increasingly impoverished, casual, and non-unionized working class dominates (demographically and therefore politically) the traditional bourgeoisie and proletariat (Davis 1984).

Third, it is argued that the de-centring of the state and the proliferation of new identities entailed in such changes have fuelled the rise of new social movements, which share a radically democratic openness to the liberation of interests and identities not defined by capitalist production relations, and an opposition to conceptions of liberation grounded in the capture of the state (Magnusson and Walker 1988). Understood this way, the new social movements are critical social movements, "open, experimental, innovative, and oriented towards dialogue," as opposed to the traditional political movements of the left and right, "which claim a monopoly of the truth, and are closed to the possibility of change" (Magnusson 1990, 527).

Fourth, it is argued that the pace and substance of such changes have produced a post-modern sensibility marked by the experience of diversity, schizophrenia, decentralization, deconstruction, and distraction. The cultural interpretation of such experience is what defines post-modernism (Harvey 1989). The consensus breaks down, however, over just how to understand these new cultural interpretations. On the one hand, post-modernism is criticized as the ideology of late capitalism (Jameson 1991). On the other, post-modernism is celebrated as the discourse of radical democracy, open to the centrality of "difference" and "otherness," and rejecting any claims to "transcendental authority." On such grounds, or rather having no need of "grounds," a hegemonic project is made possible by "the creation of a chain of equivalence among the democratic demands found in a variety of movements – women, blacks, workers, gays and lesbians or environmentalists – around a radical democratic interpretation of the political principles of the liberal democratic regime" (Mouffe 1990, 63).

These arguments open up fascinating new questions, but they remain more the terrain of political theory than of political sociology. It seems fair to observe that a hegemonic project of radical democracy remains far from reality. The current politics of the social movements are characterized more by fragmentation than hegemonic solidarity, and the application of post-modernist theory by western intellectuals has more typically focused on fiction than on politics (Helvacioglu 1992).

Life may well imitate fiction, and fiction may well serve as a critical mirror to a changing social reality, but the claims made for the hegemonic appeals of post-modernism are exaggerated. For the present, and certainly for the recent past, we are better advised to expect empirical complexity, contradiction, and conflict in the ideological response to the decline of the welfare state.

SUMMARY

We have tried in this chapter to indicate, through a review of a very large literature, the interest and vitality of a theoretical perspective on ideology in capitalist societies. Although the critical heart of that perspective remains the Marxist conception of ideology as a mystification of the underlying relations of domination in society, the analysis of ideology has moved far beyond a vulgar notion of capitalist society as propped up by a dominant ideology in which the ruling ideas of a dominant class maintain the false consciousness of subordinate classes. Ideologies both distort and reflect material reality; they condition and are conditioned by the material experience of individuals and society; they mediate class struggle, but are themselves a terrain of class struggle.

The analytical precision and sophistication of Marxist analyses of ideology has been vastly improved over the past two decades, especially as the narrowly theoretical preoccupation characteristic of the Althusserian initiative has given way to a greater openness to empirical concerns, whether derived from the "findings" of liberal political sociology or generated by autonomous programs of research. This openness to empirical inquiry is associated with marked changes in advanced capitalist states since the Second World War, and with the obvious incapacity of past theoretical accounts to deal with the shifts from conformity and consensus in the 1950s to the new left of the 1960s, the counter-reformation of the right in the 1970s, and the vitality of post-modernist discourses of the 1980s and 1990s. As the result of this openness, we have in the work of scholars like Macpherson, Habermas, Hall, and Offe a rich conceptual outline of the basis and character of ideological conflict in contemporary capitalist societies.

At the same time, these accounts remain heavily theoretical and lacking in empirical precision. We gain from them a great deal of conceptual clarity in the understanding of the tendencies towards hegemonic crisis in the contemporary capitalist welfare states, but we cannot clearly describe the balance of forces shaping their future, let alone predict the shape of that future. In part these deficiencies reflect the enormity of the task, and perhaps the impossibility (and undesirability) of genuine prediction. They reflect also, however, the impoverished state of empirical research in Marxist political sociology, which is in turn a reflection of philosophical and political objections to what passes for empirical social inquiry. We turn in the next chapter to a consideration of these objections, and to contrary arguments for the utility of empirical methods typical in liberal social science as a means of further developing a Marxist understanding of the role of ideology in the politics of a capitalist society.

3 Class, Ideology, and Survey Research: Methods and Operational Approaches

In this chapter we move from the broad outline of a theory of ideology and ideological conflict in capitalist societies to the problem of substantiating the validity of this theory as an account of contemporary Canadian politics. There are difficult empirical problems in determining the exact content and extent of ideological conflicts that characterize political life in concrete societies. Even the best theory does not give a precise forecast of what we can expect to find in any society at any point in time. Theory is subject to a constant process of revision in light of changing historical circumstances. That is, there is a dialectical interchange between theoretical expectations and what to look for in the realm of concrete political life, on the one hand, and the incorporation of evidence that modifies those expectations, on the other. The problem is how to discipline the process of investigation and theoretical modification.

There is little in the way of Marxist research that is helpful in suggesting how to go about dealing with this problem when undertaking research on ideology. Contemporary contributions to the Marxist theory of the state and the associated reinterpretations of the nature of class structure and ideology in modern capitalist countries generally stop short of any systematic empirical analysis of ideology. Marxists have made major empirical contributions, but almost entirely in the study of what is usually termed "social structure," particularly in analysis of class structure rather than ideology. The analyses of ideology in Erik Olin Wright's extensive study of the American class structure (1985) and his later comparison of the United States, Sweden, and Japan (1996) are based on just one scale made up of six survey questions. The British participants in Wright's international project, Gordon Marshall et al. (1988), included an extensive battery of questions on ideology, but confined their crucial comparisons between classes to one scale.

There is, we believe, an unhelpful schizophrenia among the now quite considerable numbers of Marxists with an interest in empirical research: while the study of structure of all kinds – indexed by education, occupation, income, wealth, crime rates, strikes, spending by governments, rates of economic development, and so on – is thought to be quite appropriate, the study of ideology is regarded as best left to broad historical generalization or, at most, to qualitative research in which individuals' accounts of their situation can be appropriately contextualized. The most important exception is the tradition of empirical research in Britain, where there is also a much stronger dialogue between Marxist and non-Marxist researchers than in North America. While we have no argument against the conjunctural and qualitative analysis of ideology, Marxists' avoidance of broader-scale research on ideology has, in practice, left the field to scholars of quite different persuasions. One result of this prejudice is that the corpus of public opinion research disproportionately emphasizes electoral behaviour, and the narrow view of citizenship and the state embodied in the tradition of studies of the "civic culture," civil rights, and opinion on specific issues of interest to state elites.

It is not difficult to locate the political and intellectual perspectives that have encouraged some kinds of scholarship and not others, within the community of Marxist scholars. In the main, particular interpretations of classical texts and the development of survey research by scholars whose principle interests are methodological have fostered an antipathy to survey research on ideology. While one consequence of this tradition has been ignorance of the potential of survey methods, Marxists' lack of interest, we suspect, also reflects a desire to avoid bad news. In unrevolutionary times the study of great, past moments in the class struggle may seem more attractive than studying the opinions of workers who have repeatedly failed to support relatively reformist versions of social democracy, let alone revolution. A more extensive treatment of alternative Marxist perspectives on empirical research can be found in Pauline Marie Vaillancourt's (1986) *When Marxists Do Research*.

This is not to minimize the opposition to the kind of enterprise in which we are engaged. Some of the major figures in the development of contemporary Marxist theory have poured scorn on empirical research and in doing so have popularized an unhelpful confusion of the terms "empirical" and "empiricist." This has produced among many Marxists a prejudice against the methods and results of orthodox political sociology, and it has reinforced a prejudice among orthodox political sociologists that Marxist theory cannot generate serious empirical investigation, or that Marxists will not subject their theorizing to serious empirical challenge.

Obviously we believe that there is no adequate reason for such prejudice. Marxists need to acknowledge that the relative richness of their theory is undercut by relatively weak empirical supports, while orthodox political sociologists need to acknowledge that the relative richness of their empirical research is undercut by relatively weak theoretical supports. There is much to be gained from a marriage of Marxist theory and the empirical methods of orthodox political sociology. In order to defend that position, we have to indicate why we reject the strong arguments in the Marxist tradition against the methods of "empiricist" social science, and we have to indicate how we think such methods can be adapted to the investigation of class and ideology as these phenomena are conceptualized in Marxist theory.

We begin this chapter, therefore, with a discussion of problems associated with the empirical study of society and with a defence of the utility to Marxist analysis of methods common to liberal political sociology. We focus attention on the problems of public opinion research, since we believe that such research can be employed to resolve some of the empirical problems in arguments about the nature of ideology and hegemony in contemporary capitalist societies. In the second part of the chapter we describe how we have operationalized social class, power, and ideology so as to obtain measures of consent, dissent, and ideological class struggle in Canada, and gain insight into the ways in which such struggle is mediated through the access to, and control of, state power. We discuss sample surveys of the population and the complementary method of elite surveys as means to obtaining information on the structure of ideology and ideological conflict. From the point of view of the Marxist arguments with which we are concerned, the key problems here are the empirical identification of class divisions and the linkage between such divisions and associated measures of ideological division. The bulk of the second half of the chapter is therefore spent discussing an operational approach to the measurement of class divisions, before we proceed in the next chapter to the detailed investigation of ideology. This categorization of social classes is employed in following chapters to examine ideological differentiation; appendix A provides the detailed comparison of alternative Marxist operationalizations of social class.

PROBLEMS OF METHOD:
MARXISM VERSUS SOCIAL SCIENCE

Among contemporary Marxists, Louis Althusser and Nicos Poulantzas have been the most influential exponents of the antagonism to empiricism, and by extension to empirical research. Because of their influence on the contemporary study of ideology and the state, it is important to address their objections. This is not because we believe that Marxists' avoidance of the questions that we address and methods that we use reflects broad agreement with a precise philosophical stance. We have chosen to address the relatively extreme anti-empiricism of Althusser and Poulantzas because they theorize and exemplify what for most Marxists is a much less formalized view.

Following Althusser, Poulantzas aligns empiricism with the idealist principle of an identity of knowledge and thought. This principle is common, he argues (1973, 137–9, 145–6), to critics of bourgeois sociology like Antonio Gramsci and Gyorgy Lukacs, who employ a Hegelian or a Viconian assumption that knowledge of history is possible for the subjects of history because they make it, as well as to the proponents of bourgeois social science, who regard sense data received from the real world as evidence of that world, comprehensible to the subject who would but observe it. In contrast, the first principle of materialism is that theoretical knowledge of the real is radically distinct from the object of that knowledge, operating in terms incomprehensible to the ordinary subject/observer of the "information, notions, etc." used in ordinary discourse (Poulantzas 1973, 12). Knowledge of real, concrete objects is determined by theoretical work that operates in an autonomous realm of abstract concepts.

To continue the argument, in a materialist as opposed to empiricist perspective social reality is a complex totality, which must be grasped as such. The distinguishing marks of theoretical knowledge of social reality are, therefore, its grasp of the totality as opposed to any isolation or compartmentalization of social relations, its grasp of complexity as opposed to simplification (as, for example, in linear causality), and its capacity to stimulate an "open space" in which knowledge can be produced or developed rather than confined in the closed space of ideology (see the summary of Althusser's arguments in Callinicos 1976, 58). This line of argument entails a radical rejection of the tradition of Western philosophy that seeks to establish guarantees for knowledge: that is, criteria external to theory for the validity of theory. For Althusser the ultimate mark of the autonomy of theory is that "*theoretical practice* is ... its own criterion and contains in itself definite protocols with which to *validate* the quality of its product ..." (Callinicos 1976, 59). And this line of argument assumes the prior determination of scientific problems by the theoretical problematic in which science operates: "[Science] can only pour problems on the terrain and within the horizon of a definite theoretical structure, its problematic, and hence the absolute determination of *the forms in which all problems must be posed*, at any given moment in the science" (Callinicos 1976, 35).

Important elements of this argument are unobjectionable and consistent with developments outside of Marxism in the philosophy and history of science (e.g., Kuhn's [1962; 1970] discussion of paradigmatic revolutions). There is now general agreement that the meaning of "facts" depends upon theoretical assumptions and unobservables, and also that social reality cannot be understood simply in the form in which it appears to social actors at a particular point in time. The radical autonomy of theory postulated by Althusser has, however, tended to privilege philosophy as *the* theoretical practice, and to confine the development of a Marxist knowledge of society to the philosophic readings of Marxist classics. The core emphasis in the natural sciences upon methods of empirical observation is dismissed as a practice governed by the autonomous criteria developed in those terrains, and empirical research in the social sciences is equated with and dismissed as empiricism. The problems of an objective analysis of society and social change are thus reduced to a vague insistence upon the unity of theory and practice, allowing for the limitation that a Marxist theory of the dynamics of capitalist society is true only when it is made to be so by revolutionary praxis.

Without resorting to a spurious distinction between theoretical and empirical work, there is to our mind a clear requirement that knowledge of concrete social reality must be built upon disciplined observation of social phenomena. While systems of theoretical argument structure observation, there exists a concrete world of action, and that world exists, in the strong sense Poulantzas defines, outside of determinations by thought. Theoretical knowledge of society can and must be evaluated by reference to observations that reflect this independent world of action. The nature and interpretation of social observations or data are heavily influenced by theory, and there is no immaculate conception in knowledge of society. Still, a record of activity that is relatively independent of the theoretical interests and manipulation of the observer is a fundamental requirement of such knowledge.

The claims of the sciences to an objective knowledge of concrete reality are based on their ability to construct models of that reality. Models represent the relationships between concepts or "variables" conceptualized in theoretical argument about the underlying structural mechanisms that generate a pattern of observable outcomes in nature or society (Bhaskar 1978). The adequacy of the representation is concretely expressed in indications that the form of the relationships specified in a model captures the variation in observations of the real world being modelled (cf. Brodbeck 1968; Blalock 1968). Models are representations of theory, with a logical structure isomorphic to that of a theoretical argument. They have, therefore, no epistemological status independent of theory, but they are a means of reconstructing the abstract understandings of theory in ways that allow for empirical validation. Science involves the production of empirically satisfying models – satisfying in the dual sense of their logical affinity to a persuasive theoretical argument and in their empirical reflection of reality through independent observation.

This is not to claim any exact criteria of "proof" or "falsifiability," or any other guarantees of scientific knowledge, all of which fail in the "quest for certainty" (Dewey 1930; Lakatos and Musgrave 1974). It is, however, to deny that the autonomy of theory is such that it provides a self-sufficient grasp of reality. It is also to insist that although the criteria for the evaluation of scientific models are, *pace* Althusser, developed within scientific communities in which they have the status of belief or tradition, and are not reducible to empirical signals from the external world, they are nevertheless necessarily empirical, based on raw materials observed in the field of investigation. Finally, although there are important differences between natural and social phenomena, we believe that it is possible to acquire knowledge of society that is scientific in these general terms.

The problem of social science is how to model society without ideological distortion, given that *the* difference between natural and social phenomena is that the latter are constituted through self-conscious, meaningful interaction. Some have argued from this that theoretical or genuinely comparative generalizations about societies are impossible because of the *sui generis* character of different systems of meaning, and because explanation of meaningful action must begin from concepts that have the same meaning for observers and those committing the actions involved (Winch 1958; MacIntyre 1978, chaps. 19, 22). Theory that introduces concepts unintelligible to the actors in order to explain their action becomes ideology (MacIntyre 1978, chap. 3). But such arguments obscure the difficulty and importance of unconscious and habitual, unreasoned action, as well as the key importance of the unintended consequences of reasoned action in social life, and they lead to the politically anodyne interests of "phenomenological" sociology in the description of "everyday life."

Others, like Althusser, have rather emphasized that meaning and self-consciousness are limited by ideological distortions embedded in the institutional structures that define the acceptable meanings of things, and that theory becomes ideology when its models incorporate ideologically distorted conceptions of things. This is the crux of the Marxist objection to the liberal social sciences. Under the authority of science and objective knowledge, liberal social science presents a model of the operation of society that is a crystallization and formalization of the ideological assumptions explaining and justifying capitalist social arrangements; a model that is buttressed by empirical observations themselves derived from an ideologically structured conceptualization. Within orthodox political sociology, for example, the emphasis is on the individual and his or her goals and needs as the basic unit of society; the organization of society as a contractual and consensual response to the need for social cooperation in order to satisfy individual needs; and the state as the regulating or integrating subsystem of society, in which government plays an independent role in the arbitration of competitive interests in the allocation of social values. Liberal political sociology is "voluntarist" because it reduces social action to psychological processes and their integration within cultural or normative systems of valuation; it is conservative because it reduces explanation to the categories that make sense to the actors involved in social action, and therefore reifies existing categories in everyday discourse at the expense of categories that pose alternatives; and it is mystifying because its analysis is rooted in the assumptions and discourse of an ideology that masks social power in the disguise of individual choice and functional stratification. Of course, liberal political sociology is also explicitly anti-Marxist: its formation is tied closely to a rebuttal of the central theorems of Marxism, especially those describing the process of class reproduction and conflict, and to a critique of the political practice of Marxism in non-capitalist societies. In contrast to the political sociology and the politics of capitalism, which are portrayed as unideological, pragmatic, empirical, and rational, it is Marxism that is defined as ideology.

These arguments explain why Marxists have treated liberal political sociology with derision. But to move from such derision to a total avoidance of the content and method of liberal political sociology would be to adopt an attitude quite uncharacteristic of the work of Karl Marx himself, whose mature theory of capitalism is less a reinterpretation of Hegel than a reinterpretation of classical, bourgeois political economy. Although Hegel provides a fundamental point of departure for a problematic that questioned what political economy took for granted, the key to *Capital* lies in the posing of questions raised by the political economists, rather than pursuing a logic driven independently by philosophical inquiry. The mature theory of *Capital* deals with ambiguities in the conceptualization of value in classical political economy, in particular the questions of whether the exchange between capital and labour constituted an exception to the law of value, and whether the fact that capitals with different organic composition yield profits at the same rate contradicts the law of value (Callinicos 1976, 37).

As indicated in chapter 2, Marx's solution to these problems begins with a theory of fetishism, which is also a theory of ideology. This theory explains how classical political economy remains imprisoned by the categories according to which capitalism appears to work, categories that mystify the process of value appropriation and allow for the domination of the producers of value. But the success of this theory as mystification, and its contribution to the reproduction of capital, lies not in the magnitude of its distortion but in the extent to which it does accurately reflect aspects of the reality of everyday experience. It is in this light that we believe liberal political sociology ought to be read – not as mumbo-jumbo designed purely to mystify, but as a highly articulate and sophisticated explanation of political life that conforms in many respects to the reality it seeks to explain, although it fails to answer or even to pose more fundamental questions that give rise to this reality.

Of course invoking Marx's approach to classical political economy is not by itself a satisfactory rationale for the appropriation of the methods or data of liberal social science. In particular, it says nothing about the method of the social survey, which was basically unknown to Marx (despite Friedrich Engels's status as an innovator in the development of the method), and which is central to our analysis in this book. Also it says nothing about the general methodology of model building and quantitative analysis typical of much research in liberal political sociology, especially that dealing with public opinion data gathered through social surveys. We need to comment on arguments against these particular methods before moving from abstract methodological issues to the substantive, operational problems of adapting these methods to the conceptual requirements of Marxist theory.

THE SOCIAL SURVEY AND PUBLIC OPINION RESEARCH

The objections to public opinion data of the sample survey or opinion poll variety, for our purposes, can be reduced to three. The first objection is that "public opinion" is a misnomer, that what is conceived as public opinion has nothing to do with public activity or with genuine opinion. The second objection is that public opinion has no determinate relation to public behaviour, and therefore is of no consequence in the analysis of the real world of social action. The last objection is that the concept and use of public opinion, despite or because of these defects, is a device for organizing and manipulating political consent.

The preliminary objection to opinion poll data rests upon the ordinary language meaning of opinion. On the one hand, an opinion is a point of view, which implies that it reflects reasonable information about a matter and a comprehension of the argument between contending perspectives on the matter. In a connotation quite as common, however, opinion reflects the opposite of knowledge, "mere" opinion being simply the expression of feelings, bias, and other irrational motives. In these straightforward terms the objection to survey or poll data is that it degrades public opinion from reasoned argument in the context of social exchange and collective action – an obvious element in the operation and justification of democracy – to the artificial and manipulable production of gut responses by isolated individuals to questions whose logic is purposely concealed.

It is impossible to deny the artificiality of the polling procedures that have become a regular feature of the modern interference with privacy in the service of profit, or the dangers this imposes for the production of meaningless or erroneous response. The counters to this objection by proponents of survey methodology are, however, rarely understood by the critics. These responses reflect a "logic" of survey analysis that, far from a simple positivism, insists that the meaning of survey data is buried within the structure of responses to *sets of* questionnaire items. This logic requires: (1) that a theoretical argument specify the connotations of concepts and their logical interrelationship; (2) the development of a number of different questions ("items"), predicted on the basis of the theoretical argument to measure the *different* connotations of the underlying concept; and (3) the application of statistical techniques for constructing "error-reduced" measures of the base concepts from their multiple indicators, and for estimating the epistemic relationships between concepts (i.e., their relations in theory) on the basis of these measures. The relationship between concepts and individual survey questions designed to measure them *is* problematic, and even the most precise question is open to misinterpretation by respondents who are wrongly assumed to share the researchers' linguistic code. But these ambiguities, in the logic of survey research, are overcome by redundancy. By comparing the responses to a number of different questions it becomes possible both to gain assurance about the validity of the research and to arrive at substantive interpretations of ideology.

It is true that the opinions on any particular question asked in a social survey are artificially stimulated in response to a question of uncertain interest to the respondent, asked in a fashion that restricts the answers, and having no clear meaning in and of itself. At the same time, the methodology summarized above is designed to model meaningful concepts through the logical specification of the relationship between indicators of their various connotations. Factor analysis, for example, can be thought of as a statistical method applied to confirm a hypothesized argument linking a variety of statements to an underlying proposition. The fact that the concepts measured by such techniques are not known to the respondents to the social survey from which they are derived, and if known would not necessarily be given the exact interpretation given by the investigator, is no obstacle to the meaningfulness of measures of opinion, attitude, or ideological orientation derived this way. Obviously the meaning given the measures is a matter of debate, but this does not distinguish the analysis of surveys from, say, the analysis of historical accounts (i.e., "data") describing mass movements.

There is now a very substantial literature on the validity and reliability of attitudinal measurement (a good review is Converse and Presser 1987). Much of it deals with technical details, for example the consequences of offering different numbers of potential responses to a question and of varying the order in which they are presented, but it also addresses more basic issues. Of particular relevance to the present study are the results of the research, conducted by Howard Schuman and Stanley Presser (1979), dealing with what are known as open- and closed-ended questions in surveys. The findings in our study involve the analysis of closed-ended questions, that is, questions in which respondents are asked to choose among pre-defined answers. A legitimate question concerns whether, by asking respondents to choose among what we define as appropriate answers, we are not artificially imposing an order on potentially confused respondents and/or leading people with radical or unconventional views to choose from a narrow range of conventional alternatives. Schuman and Presser provide strong evidence that, generally, the opposite holds: the alternative responses to a question are not merely receptacles for opinions expressed by respondents reacting to a question, instead they convey additional information about the question. There are situations when open-ended questions are more appropriate, such as when asking respondents to choose from a very wide range of alternatives, but our emphasis on closed-ended items is appropriate for the kinds of issues we want to address (broader reviews of measurement issues and survey enterprise include Marsh 1982; Schwarz and Sudman 1996; and Ornstein 1998).

Whether or not Canadians have coherent opinions, or more precisely how many of them do, remains, none the less, an important question (and reason to be thankful that, while they provide more reliable responses, closed-ended questions do not make people with no, or incoherent, opinions appear to be interested and coherent). The discussion of ideological "constraint" in appendix B takes up this question in detail by examining the extent to which there are logically predicted (that is, what from our perspective are ideologically coherent) interrelationships between opinions. Phillip Converse (1964) and other political sociologists have attempted to demonstrate that there is little real meaning to most surveys of political attitudes in the mass public. Ironically, this demonstration does not lead Converse to question the meaningfulness of measuring public opinion in this way. The absence of coherent attitudes on questions of the justification of public policy is interpreted as evidence of "the end of ideology" and the isolation of politics from the mass public; only "elites," it then stands to reason, can be expected to have coherent answers to such questions. For obvious reasons we shall be concerned to argue against this position, showing that coherent positions on political questions and coherent structures of ideological orientation *can* be observed in public opinion data, and that there is no extreme break between elite rationality and mass irrationality in the consideration of political issues.

The second objection to public opinion data involves the absence of a connection between "opinion" and "action." This argument is strongly related to the third objection, that public opinion polling is a device for creating political consent. It is argued that there can be no such thing as meaningful opinion outside of the interaction of acting subjects whose opinions entail action in defence of them. Public opinion data denies the authenticity of acting subjects by creating "opinions" whose subjects are merely randomly situated, unrelated respondents to a questionnaire, unable to act or communicate together on any matter addressed to them. Public opinion data, on such arguments, are representative of a tradition in the social sciences for which "deeds and events are rare occurrences in everyday life and history," with statistical terms substituting for the "search for meaning in politics or significance in history" (Arendt 1965, 39). The extent of this reduction of meaning is evident in the journalistic fascination with polls as substitutes for genuine political events. Such is the influence of this general perspective, it is argued, that "the modern age – which began with such an unprecedented and promising outburst of human activity – may end in the deadliest, most sterile passivity history has ever known" (Arendt 1965, 295).

This existentialist objection brings out clearly a double problem with public opinion data. On the one hand, the very notion of public opinion is often associated with the assumption of a public consensus, against which deviations are mere errors. What is problematic here is not the absence of a connection between opinion and action, but the possibility that a connection may be made so that behaviour, like opinion, will be moulded in the "sterile passivity" of consensus. On the other hand, the more fundamental objection is that public opinion is an empty category of human experience, in which action is irrelevant. This leads to an opposite problem, not of the self-fulfilling prophecy in which what is described as a consensus of opinion becomes a unifying tendency in behaviour, but of the inability to explain social action by reference to public opinion.

The double attack on public opinion is neatly reformulated by Poulantzas. In the first place he describes the historical motivation for public opinion data in terms of the typical function of ideology to create a unity that mystifies conflict.

It is, in fact, in capitalist formations that the political category of public opinion and the related category of consent, first mentioned by the physiocrats, make an appearance ... Public opinion, which is necessary in the functioning of the capitalist state, and which is the modern form of political consent (consensus), cannot in fact function unless it manages to present itself and to be accepted in terms of "rational" scientific technique, i.e., in so far as it sets itself up and its principle in opposition to those which it designates and marks out as utopian. It thus designates as utopian any representation in which the class struggle is present in any form whatsoever. (Poulantzas 1973, 217–18)

Thus public opinion data are the pre-eminent form of the presentation of ideology; they describe a consensus on acceptable conduct in an artificially constructed realm of political options, and present majority opinion as the scientifically justified defence of the political status quo as against any utopian alternative. Here, then, is the objection that the *sui generis* character of public opinion data assists the ideological manipulation of a political defence for capitalism.

While there is much in this critique that is a valid representation of the normal practice of "scientific" polling and of the normal uses of public opinion data, the real issue is whether public opinion polling must, no matter in whose hands, conceal class conflict and ideological debate over political issues. This assertion rests upon the strongest form of the argument that public opinion data have no relationship to action. As Poulantzas expresses it: "The various ideologies and ideological sub-ensembles are only constituted in the course of an ideological class struggle, and must therefore be chiefly considered not as constituted conceptual ensembles, but rather as they are materialized in class practices ... This is, of course, the basic source of error of those abundant 'sociological investigations' that attempt to grasp the 'consciousness' of various social classes and fractions on the basis of their agents' answers to 'questions' " (1973, 290–1).

These arguments raise a number of problems. For example, "ideological class struggle" is not clearly defined. Obviously it is important to look at real organizations, and their real activity, for any comprehensive analysis of social change. Equally obviously there is no necessary relationship between such organizational activity and public opinion. Ideological perspectives are not acquired solely on the terrain of struggle (unless, for example, television and other mass media are tautologically and metaphorically interpreted purely as class weapons), and ideologies may be "materialized in class practices" other than organized conflict and struggle, unless, again tautologically, classes are present only in struggle. The whole problematic of hegemony, reviewed in the last chapter, loses any meaning if there is no possibility of an ideological unity across classes, and if ideology is only constituted in struggle how are we to account for such unity? Further, the unilinear causality implicit in the notion of struggle constituting ideologies, rather than ideological argument motivating struggle, is not defensible.

Poulantzas's objection to the voluntarist assumption that action is simply the product of individual consciousness and that class practices are the product of variation in individual consciousness is clear, but the language of class practices cannot be fully developed without a conception of individual motivation, and aggregate measures of individual motivation are plausible measures of class consciousness and of the limits to class action. Our belief in the possibilities of the latter uses of public opinion data reflects, we believe, the partial utility of Poulantzas's own insistence on the independence of ideology as a level of the social formation: ideology establishes a framework that structures class struggles and state policy to contain them. Ideology is not, therefore, coincident with class or state practice, just as attitude is not coincident with behaviour. One presumes a relation between the two, but there is always a problem of establishing the relevance of public opinion data to action, even when the data report answers to questions about likely behaviour (cf. Schuman and Johnson 1976).

Interpreting the relevance of patterns of public or elite opinion described in this book to the concrete history of mass political activity or elite policy making is difficult, but so is the interpretation (at least in the sense in which active prediction is involved) of the historical events that are the raw material of the conventional study of politics. Both surveys and traditional sources of information about politics rest upon theoretical interpretation, not upon necessary conclusions given by the empirical evidence. On many of the issues presented in our surveys, all or major sections of the respondents cannot or will not engage in direct action. A lack of visible action does not, however, imply the irrelevance of the opinion data to political analysis. Surveys like ours make it possible to examine issues for which the relevant political actions, like telephone calls, private correspondence, informal conversations, and even organized meetings, are not subject to scrutiny. Even where a good deal of such information can be labouriously collected by detailed case-study methods, it is impossible to imagine a sustained effort at systematic research of this kind sufficient to map the contours of ideological conflict among all politically significant actors.

How we understand political significance is, however, the nub of the problem. As estimated from sample surveys, "public opinion" gives equal weight to the opinions of all individuals in the population. Although this is in itself a reasonable perspective, when we are interested in the motivational basis for the political mobilization or demobilization of popular forces, it is clearly not an adequate perspective if our interest is in the motivational basis for state action – the balance of opinion and interest articulated by active social forces, and the independent opinions and interests of the managers of state apparatuses. First, it is clear that only a minority of the public is actively engaged in politics, and tolerably well informed about political issues (cf. Converse 1964; Neuman 1987). Second, it is clear that public opinion may be as much or more the effect of action by the politically active forces within and outside of the state, rather than the cause of such action (Noelle-Neumann 1984). Third, it is clear that sample surveys of conventional size produce very limited information about the most politically active and influential people (although, of course, their influence accurately reflects their significance as a proportion of the total population).

One conventional, and appropriate, means of addressing this problem is to compare sectors of the general population, focusing particularly on people with high education, who are most knowledgeable and interested in politics, and whose opinions are the most coherent and articulate. It will still be true, however, that the most influential people will not be present, even in a very large representative sample, in sufficient numbers to provide a basis for analysis. A full analysis of class and ideology must involve information supplementary to that generated by the sample survey and measures of public opinion. We need information about politically significant decision makers who appear in representative samples in only tiny numbers. In this book such information is obtained from surveys of the "elite" leadership of business, labour unions, political parties, and state bureaucracies. This appropriation of the methodology of elite surveys does not entail the theoretical alternative to class analysis with which the methodology is properly associated in orthodox, anti-Marxist sociology. Rather it endorses the appeals for an integration of the methodology of elite research and class theory made by a good many political sociologists seeking ways to advance the Marxist analysis of class and power. The general point of these appeals is well made by Anthony Giddens:

> Elites may be regarded as fundamental to the structuration of the upper class (in a class society); and … the "hierarchy" of elite groups is one principal medium whereby the translation of economic into political power, or the reverse, is effected. Hence to discern, in any given society, the existence of an "upper class" whose position is founded upon privileged access to property, should be considered not as the conclusion but the starting point of analysis of the system of power that pertains in that society. In order to demonstrate how this class is a *ruling* class, it is necessary to specify the modes in which its economic hegemony is translated into political domination; which means examining, among other things, processes of recruitment to elite positions in the major institutional spheres, the relations between economic, political and other elites, and the use of effective power to further definite class interests. (1973, xi)

Although these considerations go well beyond the confines of survey research, much of this agenda of class analysis is equally clearly open to survey research. If it is social agents, and particularly those in positions of influence, who give meaning to class and the legitimation of class power, then the investigation of those meanings and their distribution in society must be a central empirical requirement of political sociology. Such a perspective on the problems of class and power, amplified as we argue in this book by theoretical work in the tradition of Gramsci, makes for complementary rather than opposing concepts of political elite and ruling class (Bottomore 1966), and invites the application of the methodology of elite and public surveys to theoretical issues in class analysis.

The proof of any theoretical pudding is no doubt in the eating, dependent to a large extent upon standards of taste and judgement educated in a definite tradition. But in the same way that much of the fun and creative advance in gastronomy depends less upon the rigid adherence to tradition than upon the introduction of innovative cooking materials and methods, so it is with social research. Our task will be to convince those educated in theoretical arguments about the nature of hegemony in the politics of advanced capitalist societies that we can extend their understanding of these matters by modelling structures of class and ideology from the materials of survey research. Conversely, it will be to convince those educated in the methodology of survey research that these tools can be usefully applied to modelling theoretical arguments they have thus far supposed impenetrable or unsustainable by their preferred methods of empirical investigation.

The argument will depend of course on the plausibility of the empirical analysis in the following sections of the book. Before moving there, however, we summarize the general methodological assumptions and strategy that guide our analysis of the survey.

MODELS AND MEASUREMENT

In this book we undertake a *general* analysis of the relationship between the important features of the social structure of Canadian society and political ideology. Aside from social class these features of the social structure include regional divisions, gender, age, socio-economic differences in education, occupation, and income (which are related to, but not in our view reducible to, class differences), and cultural differences related to ethnicity and religion. While our interpretation of the findings reflects the theoretical perspective that we have elaborated in this and the previous two chapters, we see the following analysis as speaking to a larger research community concerned with understanding the political culture of Canadian society.

Our first concern, still, is to understand the relationship between class and political ideology. We want to establish that there is such a relationship and that its form reflects our theoretical understanding of the relationship between classes. We have taken care, however, that our analysis not become the kind of barren exercise in hypothesis testing that often characterizes contemporary social science. With the large samples at our disposal it would be relatively easy to fire several volleys of statistical tests at carefully selected dependent variables, and then claim to have established the usefulness of Marxist theory. Instead we have chosen to focus our interpretations on the *magnitudes* of differences between classes, that is on the common-sense interpretation of the survey findings. Tests of statistical significance will be employed primarily as a safeguard to prevent efforts to interpret patterns that could potentially represent random error; and for analysis of smaller subsets of the population, where the risk of over-interpretation of chance (i.e., "non-significant") findings is greater. Of course this is only possible because we have relatively large samples for analysis.

Our objection to conceiving our mission as an effort to demonstrate the "success" of class analysis reflects both our view of ideology and assessment of the findings of previous empirical research on ideology. We want to determine the extent of class polarization, but we also need to know what other factors pattern ideology, both in order to understand the alternative bases of polarization and to determine the relative balance between the simple absence of a relationship between class and ideology (i.e., hegemonic consensus) and the presence of *non*-class-based patterns of differentiation (i.e., ideological divisions based on the alternative discourses of non-class communities).

The idea that the distinctive histories, economies, and ethnic and linguistic compositions of regions, for example, should give rise to ideological differentiation is neither a fetish of liberal social science nor an instance of false consciousness. While regional differentiation in Canada has important class elements, there is a general tendency for Marxist analysis to underestimate the durability of regional and cultural divisions. More generally, it is fair to say that Marxists' persistent inability to appreciate the strength of national divisions suggests a theoretical deficiency, rather than a tendency to misread particular historical conjunctures. Whether this tendency is stronger or worse than its opposite (casting class in regional terms) is moot; to attempt to understand the nature of political ideology in Canada without a regional dimension flies in the face of strong empirical evidence. A similar case can be made for the value of examining gender and other aspects of the social structure.

All this empirical analysis, as the saying goes, is easier said than done. Even the most sophisticated and theoretically minded of our ideological allies can be forgiven, by this point, for wondering precisely what we mean by class and ideology and how the analysis of surveys addresses our theoretical concerns. Indeed we think that the absence of a significant body of empirical research on these problems reflects both the difficulty of operationalizing these concepts and premature closure brought about by negative findings that result from mistaken and oversimplified operationalizations. The operationalization of variables such as education and age is not completely unproblematic, but the problems posed by class and ideology are of a different magnitude.

Our research is based on a combination of surveys of representative samples of the Canadian population and surveys of elites. While there are questions about what constitutes the general population (for example, at what age should people qualify for inclusion), there simply is no commonly shared definition of the population of elites. The selection of a sample of elites reflects the researchers' theoretical views about what are and who represents the major interests in society. Whether the chief executives of a sample of the largest corporations (our choice) are the most appropriate representatives of the capitalist class is a matter of opinion; even the decision to include the capitalist class among the sectors represented in the elite sample reflects our model of the structure of contemporary capitalist societies. We provide a full description of the elite sample and the implicit model of the power structure it references after a discussion of class divisions in the general population.

Operationalizing the Concept of Social Class

Surely some of the attraction of class analysis – what major theorist has not tried her or his hand at it – lies in the ambiguity and difficulty of the concept. There is an enormous literature on the subject, if only because non-Marxists have felt as compelled to demonstrate that classes are irrelevant as Marxists have the reverse. Following the logic of our understanding of ideology, we need to review the major strategies, both Marxist and non-Marxist, for operationalizing the concept of class. While there is much we disagree with in the non-Marxist, and much of the Marxist, discussion of this topic, there is also much to be gleaned from this body of work.

In its common meaning, class refers to structured differences in the positions of members of society that affect individuals' life experience and opportunities. Marx and Max Weber agree that classes are defined in terms of relations to the ownership or control of the means of production. Marx, who never got to his intended theoretical treatment of class in his major work, conceived of the fundamental structure of societies as inhering in the relations of production: "it is always the direct relation between the owners of the conditions of production and the direct producers which reveals the innermost secret, the hidden foundation, of the entire social edifice." While the *Communist Manifesto* may be more categorical than we would like, Marx's fundamental insight was to see social change as rooted in the conflicts between owning and producing classes: "the history of all hitherto existing society is the history of the class struggle."

Weber opposes Marx in not assigning social class, as determined by the underlying mode of production, primacy in the determination of historical change and of the essential character of different societies. Weber agrees that property is a fundamental aspect of "class situations," but he thinks of class distinctions in terms of the production *and acquisition* of goods. We differ from Marx in attaching an independent significance to people's positions in the market, that is to their income and occupational status. Epistemologically, Weberian political sociology denies the feasibility of a general theory of history, and the possibility of laws of social change of the kind advanced by Marx; rather it moves in the direction of descriptively comprehending different "types" of society. Methodologically, the construction of these types is grounded in the logic of individual goals and actions, rather than in the society and its component classes united as a social whole by an underlying logic open to theoretical analysis. Substantively, Weberian analysis works from the effects of independent sources of power (class, status, and party), of potentially complex (rather than structurally limited) differences in these dimensions, and of the independent power of a rational-bureaucratic state (Weber's classic statement is the section "Class, Status, and Party" in Weber 1978, vol. 2, 926–40; for a good discussion of the differences between Marx and Weber, see Crompton and Gubbay 1978, 5 ff.).

There is a sophisticated conception of social change and of the constant tension between political order and social disorganization in Weber's theory. While the state is capable of disinterestedly arbitrating among divisions of interest, its capability is undermined by tendencies towards bureaucratism and militarism and by the threats to authority posed by the progressive "disenchantment" of the world. Weber, however, does not provide, as does Marx, a theoretical specification of the particular content of individual and group interests and of the nature of conflict between these social forces; nor does he conceive of historical crises in response to the balance of these conflicting social forces. It is this greater theoretical precision of the Marxist tradition that guides our development of the questions and concepts in this book, and of our understanding of Canadian politics.

Within the dominant, Weberian-influenced tradition of political sociology, most of the major empirical studies of the relationship between social class and politics define classes: (1) as occupational groups, often simply the dividing of manual and non-manual workers, which are identified as the "working" and "middle" class; (2) as a combination of education, occupation, income, and sometimes other variables, which are often termed "objective indicators" of class; or (3) in terms of individuals' perceptions of their own class positions. While research guided by these traditional conceptions of classes has provided important insights into the relationship between social class and politics, we chose instead a Marxist conceptualization of social classes that incorporates, first, the distinction between the owners of businesses and their employees and, second, the distinction between the business owners, managers, and supervisors who control the labour processes and workers who are subject to their control. These distinctions embody what we understand to be the fundamental features of the economic structure of capitalist society. Indeed the critical difference between this conceptualization and mainstream definitions of class is that the classes are specific to capitalist society, whereas differences in income, between manual and non-manual workers, etcetera are found in any differentiated society.

There is also an important difference in conceptualization of the causal relations between class and other social factors like ideology. In the Marxist conception, class has *causes* – the existence of class positions (and their elimination) reflects the economic structure; and particular individuals come to assume class positions as a result of inheritance and of the class-allocating function of educational institutions. Class also has *effects* – on working conditions, on income and the many things that are dependent on income such as the housing and communities in which people live, and, of course on political ideology. In mainstream analysis of class there is not the same distinction between the causes and effects of social class. The combination of education, occupation, and income mixes up what, in our terms, are causes and effects of social class, and the conventional treatment of ideas or culture as independent of class and as influenced by the multiple factors of power, wealth, and status obscures the underlying logic of ideology as mediating class relations.

In setting out to investigate the ideological character of social classes – as defined on the basis of Marxist theory – it is not our intention to argue that income, education, and other conventional indicators of social class have no effects on ideology or that it is inappropriate for us to examine such effects. At issue is their interpretation. It is unreasonable, for example, to expect that all manual industrial workers have the same ideology, despite the great variation in how much they are paid and the conditions in which they work. Material differentiation *within* social classes is, in part, responsible for the lack of ideological unanimity within classes. Our argument is not that ideological differences within classes do not exist, but that they are differences within and not between social classes.

Non-Marxist Concepts of Class

The precise definition of social classes has been the subject of prolonged, extensive, and inconclusive debate. In reviewing alternative approaches to social class in this and the next section, our goal is less to show that we have a superior strategy than to indicate why other approaches to class do not do what we want them to do. We think that the findings of our detailed analysis of class differences in ideology in chapter 5 justify the approach that we have taken, but they do not prove that Marxist conceptions of class are better than non-Marxist conception, or that our Marxist approach is better than other Marxist alternatives. In this and the next section our purpose is to provide some general background on measuring social class and, particularly in reviewing the non-Marxist schemes in this section, to indicate how empirical findings from these perspectives can remain visible to our Marxist perspective.

The most common non-Marxist approach to social class simply divides the employed population between the working and middle classes on the basis of the distinction between manual and non-manual work. Richard Hamilton (1972, 27–9, 64 [note 11], 152–4) takes this approach in his analysis of American political attitudes, though he notes (152) that a "small upper class or elite" is included with the middle class and he also overrides the manual/non-manual distinction in assigning foremen and self-employed manual workers to the non-manual category (228).

Hamilton's work raises another concern, about the "level" at which class is determined. Hamilton uses the occupation of the "head" of the household to define the social class of all individuals in the household (1972, 153); almost all his empirical analysis is restricted to husbands and wives in "intact" families in which the "head of the house," by which he means the husband, is employed or seeking work. He goes on, "essentially we have omitted the retired, the economically active single persons, the widows and widowers as well as the divorcees. We are also going to be working only with the nonfarm population" (1972, 189). In the 1964 data set these exclusions leave Hamilton (1972, 226) with only 972 out of the original sample of 1751. The sexist assumptions, not to mention arbitrariness, are starkly obvious with two decades' hindsight. In our own analysis we need to deal with the respondents who are not working for pay, and it is certainly not obvious how to proceed.

Many other studies, including important work on Britain by David Lockwood (1989), Michael Mann (1970), Frank Parkin (1971), Giddens (1973), and K. Roberts et al. (1978), offer convincing empirical evidence of ideological differences between manual and non-manual workers, with manual workers generally taking positions to the left of non-manual workers. The existence of these ideological differences is often used to justify focusing on the manual/non-manual difference as the key class distinction (especially in Britain, where the differences are greater than in the U.S. or Canada). Thus Roberts et al. (1978, 18) define classes as "collectivities with which individuals identify themselves in making the hierarchical environments they inhabit meaningful," and then argue (20–1) that "sociologists cannot too frequently stress that their working/middle class dichotomy is not dictating but, to a large extent, is merely following the public's own practice ... [M]ost manual workers describe themselves as 'working class' while the majority of white-collar employees assign themselves to a 'middle class.'"

While it is not a class distinction in the Marxist sense (manual workers working for the government, for example, are not doing productive labour; while, for at least some Marxists, some non-manual work is productive labour), this research provides strong grounds for arguing that the manual/non-manual division corresponds to important ideological differences. Still, this distinction is not sufficient. First, the "middle class" category conceals the differences among a number of distinct groups, including the owners and managers of large and small businesses, high-income professionals, and routine and poorly paid office and sales personnel. Because low-level non-manual workers are disproportionately women, the manual/non-manual model of class results in a middle class that is also disproportionately, and counter-intuitively, composed of women.

A second problem with the manual/non-manual definition of social class, which helps explain why in practice researchers often make arbitrary amendments to the scheme, concerns the difficulty of classifying some occupations in the manual/non-manual dichotomy. The problematic groups include farmers, who are mostly business proprietors doing largely manual work; supervisors of manual workers, who frequently spend some part of their time doing manual work but exercise supervisory authority; and technicians and "pink collar" workers, many of whom use equipment to carry out manual operations, but who are also responsible for the non-manual tasks of record keeping and control. This difficulty in deciding whether an occupational group is manual or non-manual and the resulting heterogeneity of the two classes partly reflects an obsolete historical generalization about the difference in the income, working conditions, and mobility of manual and non-manual workers (Hamilton 1972, 29). Until perhaps the beginning of the twentieth century, non-manual workers were a small and privileged minority of all workers. But non-manual jobs were eventually subject to the same pressures towards de-skilling and regimentation that transformed craft into factory production. Office automation could affect the jobs of clerical and sales workers in the same way that assembly-line production and factory automation threatened the jobs of manual workers. The decline in the status, pay, and working conditions of non-manual jobs was accompanied by a marked feminization of non-manual work. Women came increasingly to occupy the poorest paid non-manual jobs, as retail store clerks and clerical workers. Structural changes in capitalism thus undermine the justification for focusing on the manual/non-manual distinction as the pre-eminent class division. The final word concerning the ideological implications of the practice of defining all non-manual workers as the middle class goes to John Westergaard and Henrietta Resler (1975, 29): "Thus the common language of class covers up the most central feature of class ... the concentration of power and property in a very small section of the population on which the whole ramified structure of class inequality turns."

More complex occupational classifications avoid the most obvious shortcoming of the manual/non-manual model of class, the crude division of all occupations into only two categories, while still permitting an examination of the manual/non-manual division. In their study of British elections, David Butler and David Stokes (1974, chap. 4) argue that their six-category measure of occupation is the best single objective indicator of social class; and, in his study of class mobility, John Goldthorpe (1987, 39 ff.) makes a similar claim for his seven-category classification of occupations. James Davis (1982) employs a five-category occupational variable in his analysis of "class cultures," which is based on national surveys of the American population. Consistent with our arguments about the heterogeneity of the broad manual and non-manual categories, Butler and Stokes and Goldthorpe find significant differences among the occupational categories *within* the categories of manual and non-manual workers.

Defining social classes in terms of occupational categories remedies some of the empirical shortcomings of the manual/non-manual division. For example Peter Pineo, John Porter, and Hugh McRoberts (1977) developed a sixteen-category occupational classification of the approximately 500 occupations in the *Canadian Census Dictionary of Occupations* that differentiates manual from non-manual workers, managers from workers, farm from "urban" occupations, farm owners from farm labourers, and "semi-professionals" (such as teachers) and technicians from workers in the "new" manual occupations and from workers in "old" manual occupations. Manual and non-manual workers are also classified by level of skill (skilled, semi-skilled, unskilled) and managers by level of authority (high-level management, middle management, supervisors, and foremen/-women). From our point of view, the difficulty with this scheme is that it is based entirely on occupations. Thus, in the Pineo, Porter, and McRoberts scheme, the difference between "employed" and "self-employed" professionals depends on whether an occupation largely involves self-employment (contrasting, for example, lawyers and physicians with professors), irrespective of whether a given *individual* is self-employed. Interestingly, a now-standard classification for the analysis of occupational mobility, due to Robert Erikson, Goldthorpe, and Lucienne Portocarero (1979), separates manual and non-manual workers, levels of skill, and proprietors of small businesses from employees. Marshall et al. (1988) find that Goldthorpe's Weberian scheme explains more variation in their political index than a class scheme based on Wright's (first) class conception (180–1).

The second major approach to social class involves using multiple indicators. In *The American Voter*, Angus Campbell et al. (1960) define class as a combination of occupation, education, and income, which are taken as "objective" indicators of social class. At another point, though, they define class in terms of a Weberian dichotomy: "current evidence indicates that all societies are stratified into 'upper' and 'lower' layers as a result of unequal distribution of values and honours" (333). This multiple-indicator approach is exemplified in the U.S. election study by Norman Nie, Sidney Verba, and John Petrocik (1979) and in study of Americans' beliefs about inequality by James Kluegel and Eliot Smith (1985). Both refer to "socioeconomic status" and to "economic inequality" and neither includes an entry for "class" or "social class" in their index. This is particularly strange in the case of Kluegel and Smith, who examine the impact of workplace control on beliefs about stratification, measuring the latter in five categories that are much easier to think of in class terms: workers, who have no supervisory authority; first-line managers; middle managers; small-business owners, who have two or fewer employees; and large-business owners, who have three or more employees (1985, 248). Some reviews of research on political disaffection (Wright 1981, 37–9), political ideology (Monroe 1981, 166), and political participation (Milbrath 1981, 222) also do not distinguish social class from socio-economic status.

Nie, Verba, and Petrocik measure socio-economic status with a combination of education and occupation, which is divided into different categories in the northern and the southern states. Among northern white Protestants, the contrast is between "higher status wasps" (defined as the combination of respondents with at least a high school diploma and professional or high-white-collar occupations and all others with white-collar occupations who have at least some college education) and "middle and lower status wasps" (defined as respondents with all other combinations of education and occupation). For southern white Protestants, Nie, Verba, and Petrocik contrast "middle and upper" status respondents (defined as the combination of all people in professional and high-white-collar occupations, high school graduates in all other white-collar occupations, and people with some college education in blue-collar jobs) to "lower status" respondents (those with all other combinations of education and occupation). Four additional status groups, which are not further subdivided into classes, are defined to include white Protestants in the border states, Catholics, Jews, and Blacks. This sounds, and is, terribly complicated.

Whether or not the collection of objective indicators – education, occupation, and income – is referred to as social class or merely as socio-economic stratification, because the concept lacks theoretical grounding investigators feel free to make arbitrary modifications. More often, social class is treated in very loose way. For example in *Political Man*, Seymour Martin Lipset (1960, chap. 4) also employs a multidimensional definition of social classes. But he also refers to the working class, the lower class, the lower class*es*, and the middle class, without defining them or describing his understanding of the overall class structure.

In Canada, Harold Clarke et al.'s (1979) study of the 1974 Canadian federal election employs the same multidimensional concept of social class as the American studies on which it is modelled. Clarke et al. (1979, 108) use occupation, socio-economic status scores, and education as objective indicators of class. They conclude, "In summary, the analyses of the relationships between social class and vote indicate the weakness of socio-economic status as a politically relevant societal cleavage in Canada" (1979, 119). In his early study of social class in Canada, Porter (1965, 20) demonstrated the extent of unequal opportunity, though he regarded social classes as arbitrary statistical categories that are imposed on underlying continuous distributions of occupational status, income, and other variables. In the most recently published book-length study of a Canadian election (Johnston et al. 1992), interestingly, no serious effort is made to deal with the extent or nature of class differences, except for looking at farmers and trade-union members.

Studies that conceptualize class as a combination of variables embody the assumption that modern capitalist societies are differentiated, but not categorically. While the owners and managers of corporations might have unusually high incomes and occupational status, they are not identified as the occupants of distinct class positions. Analyses that employ education, occupation, income, and other variables as "objective indicators" of social class are actually studies of socio-economic status rather than studies of social class. Still, there is strong evidence that education, occupation, and income actually affect many aspects of life and, to some extent, these findings may be interpreted in terms of class differences. Some of these effects can be attributed to social class, since it is hard to imagine a sensible operationalization of the concept in which the resulting classes do not have unequal incomes. Indeed a number of empirical analyses have demonstrated the existence of such income differences (Wright 1979; Koo and Hong 1981; Ornstein 1983a, 1983c). The role of education, another common component of socio-economic operationalizations of social class, is different. It is appropriate to examine the effect of education on ideology both with and without controls for social class. Although a person's class *origins* influence her or his educational attainment, over and above the effect of parental social class, education also plays a major role in determining social class.

A third non-Marxist approach defines social classes in terms of subjective perceptions of class membership. An example is Mary and Robert Jackman's (1983) study. They conceive of classes as "social communities" and argue that Americans recognize five such communities: the poor, the working class, the middle class, the upper middle class, and the upper class. "Our view of classes as a graded series of status groups defined by economic interests ... puts an explicit emphasis on popular conceptions of class" (1983, 9). The Jackmans' work is concerned with the important question of understanding what leads individuals to identify themselves as belonging to a particular social class and with the implications of that sense of belongingness for other aspects of political ideology. They also employ education, occupation, and income as "objective" measures of social class, but their otherwise extremely interesting analysis of ideology does not isolate and examine class differences, as we understand them.

We have a lot to learn from these non-Marxist approaches to the definition of social classes. These conceptions of class in terms of manual/non-manual and of other socio-economic differences are much more than an effort to force society into liberal ideological categories. Not only do they represent divisions in society, in the public's as well as in the researchers' minds, but there is strong evidence that the divisions correspond to ideological differences. While we will want to interpret these cleavages in class terms, unless the situation in Canada at the time we conducted our research is extremely unusual, we should expect to find some ideological differences along these lines.

The efforts to understand whether and how people identify themselves in class terms are interesting, but less helpful to us. It doesn't make sense to think that other aspects of ideology, say perceptions of corporations and unions, depend on class self-identification because it requires the assumption that class, defined in this sense, is determined prior to the other aspects of ideology. One could, of course, imagine quite the opposite – that ideological orientations lead people to develop subjective class identifications and allegiances. Without long-term longitudinal survey data, these interrelations cannot be understood. In any event our interest in class primarily concerns the relationship between structural divisions and ideology.

Marxist Concepts of the Class Structure of Capitalist Society

Operationalizing social classes according to Marxist theory is a far more difficult task than our confident endorsement of Marxist theory so far might suggest. The difficulties arise from problems in Marxist theory itself and from the weaknesses of empirical work by Marxists dealing with the systematic description of class and class conflict. Fundamental to Marxist analysis are the theoretical categories used to understand the capitalist economy, particularly the theory of value and the relations to the production and expropriation of surplus value. Here are intermingled the thorny issues of the difference between productive and unproductive labour; the real nature and measurement of the exploitation of labour; the constantly changing and differentiated institutional regimes through which the basic wage-labour relation in capitalist society is regulated; and the survival and articulation of pre-capitalist production relations within the capitalist mode of production.

Marxist theory of the class structure begins with the concept of economic exploitation. In classical Marxism exploitation involves the purchase by capitalists of (the commodity) labour power from workers, and capitalists' consequent ability to command how and in what circumstances workers are employed. From this follows a general agreement among Marxist class theorists about three specific aspects of the class structure: (1) the capitalist class includes the owners and (whether or not they are major stockholders) the top managers of businesses; (2) the owners of small businesses constitute the petty bourgeoisie, which is a class distinct from the bourgeoisie proper (this is not quite the same as saying, as does Wright [1976], that simple commodity production by the petty bourgeoisie constitutes a mode of production distinct from capitalist production [see Scase 1982]); and (3) manual workers who produce goods (but not services) employed in private businesses and who do not supervise other employees are members of the working class. Beyond these three points, however, agreement among Marxist theorists breaks down. An empirical indication of the limits of the theoretical consensus is the fact that about 70 percent of the *employed* population (which in turn constitutes less than half the total population) cannot be assigned to any class on the basis of these three points. A neo-Weberian formulation that incorporates some of the concerns of the Marxist theorists may be found in Robert Robinson and Jonathan Kelley (1979). We will proceed with efforts to resolve these dilemmas in the broadly Marxist tradition.

While the theoretical shortcomings of the classical Marxist theory of class are inherent in its original formulation, the need to complete the theory has been accentuated by the consequences of the evolution of capitalist societies since Marx's time. The features of this evolution are of two kinds. First, there has been a dramatic increase in the proportion of wage earners who are not in the classical proletariat, defined as workers who create surplus value for capitalists by manufacturing commodities. These include: employees who create *non-material* commodities (services) for sale by private capitalists; employees of private capital whose jobs involve the sale (in Marxist terminology, the "circulation") rather than the production of commodities, either in the employ of producing capitalists or of merchants and financial institutions (who gain a share of the total surplus value by performing these specialized functions for producers as a whole); employees of governments, cooperatives, and charitable, professional, and other organizations that do not create surplus value (most of whom do not make commodities for sale, although employees in nationalized industries do).

The second kind of structural change that requires an extension of classical Marxist theory involves differentiation among individual workers, rather than a change in the composition of economic and state functions. While pay differences between workers, for example between skilled and unskilled workers, predate capitalism, the degree and complexity of these differences has increased dramatically. This reflects a number of factors: increased formal education ("human capital," to economists); the related growth of linkages between formal education and particular jobs; the development of bureaucratic job evaluation schemes; and increased differentiation in the pay, benefits, and working conditions of workers employed by different employers of different sizes, in different industries and located in different places (known as "segmentation"). In addition there has been a tendency for a job – defined as the set of tasks assigned to the individual worker – to include a combination of activities that cross the boundaries of Marxist economic categories, for example the diffusion of part-time supervisory responsibilities to many employees whose main job is to make or sell commodities (O'Connor 1975, 88 ff.).

Marxist scholars have attempted to resolve the theoretical deficiencies of orthodox Marxist treatments of class and to accommodate the complex changes in the occupational structure in a variety of ways. In seeking a theoretical framework to use in analyzing our surveys, we set two limits on what would be considered. The first reflects our view of the relationship between social action and class structure. Especially among Marxist labour and social historians, there is a view that classes are constituted in class action, in more traditional Marxist terminology that classes can only be classes *for* themselves: classes can only include people in a common economic-class position, but they become classes only in their self-organization, and in class struggle. The work of the eminent Marxist historian E.P. Thompson is seen to exemplify this approach. Whatever one makes of the trajectory of class action in Canadian history, this orientation leaves us *without* genuine classes at present, except perhaps for the capitalist class, or at least the well-organized segment of large corporations. Only intense projection of one's theoretical predispositions could discern the class structure from the recent decades' record of sporadic demonstrations, occasional strikes, and rare social democratic electoral victories. In any event our view is that classes are structural categories constituted from the economic relations of capitalism; common class positions provide a potential basis for class action, but action is not an appropriate criterion of class.

Our second theoretical limitation relates to the differentiation among workers. In this book, except for differentiation that reflects control of the work process itself, differences between workers are not treated as class differences. So educational credentials, occupational skills, rates of pay, and similar "indicators" are not taken as class criteria *per se*, despite their correlation with control of work. In revising his initial theory of class (about which more below), Wright (1985, 1976) makes such distinctions – arguing for what he calls an "exploitation-centred" theory of class, based on John Roemer's (1982) concept of exploitation. Wright's redefinition incorporates "organizational" assets, which take the form of managerial authority (operationally, managers are separated from supervisors), and "skill/credential" assets, which are measured by the skill and educational requirements of jobs. Phillipe van Parijs (1987) takes this one step further in arguing that employment itself, as opposed to unemployment, is also an asset defining a class position. Our quarrel is not with this use of organizational assets as a class criterion, since these derive from the relations of production (though we prefer a different terminology), but with the manner in which skills and credentials are used to define social classes. By using their organizational assets, classes of workers exploit *each other*. Even proletarians – employees who are paid wages for producing material commodities for profit, but who have no authority over other workers and do not determine their own conditions or pace of work – can still exploit other workers (see Meiksins 1989). We find this an unacceptable criterion of class because attributes of jobs that are entirely controlled by capital result in exploitation, which is the basis for class antagonism. Marshall et al. (1989) provide an extensive discussion of Wright's second, exploitation-centred theory of class, arguing that it is inferior to his first theory, on both theoretical and empirical grounds (see their chapter 3). They have a right to be upset about his change of heart, since Wright radically revised his views on social class *after* they had undertaken an extensive survey that employed a very large battery of questions in order to locate respondents in his initial categorization (see 45 ff.). The Canadian component of Wright's international project, directed by Wallace Clement and John Myles, was also conducted before Wright's change of theoretical heart and they chose to work with the earlier "domination-based" class typology (1994, xi).

To repeat our previous argument about the empirical analysis of class ideologies, we believe that it is necessary to assess the impact of, say, education on ideological differentiation, but not because education is an indicator of social class. Furthermore, differences in the education and pay of individuals who are in the same class are a potential obstacle to their ideological and political unity, but again, not because they are class criteria.

We return to the problem of defining social classes in structural terms, but in a manner that deals with the large proportion of workers whose positions are ambiguous in the context of what we have termed classical Marxist views of class. Three approaches to the class structure that meet the criteria we have set out are described in the sections below. There we describe the conceptual basis of the class theories put forward by Poulantzas (1973; 1975), Wright (1976, i.e., this "first" version of class theory); and Guglielmo Carchedi (1975a; 1975b; 1975c). These theorists were chosen because their work is generally acknowledged to be among the most important by contemporary Marxists (for example see Crompton and Gubbay 1978 and Marshall 1983, 264). We should say that, in focusing on these three theorists, we implicitly reject the position of some Marxist theorists (Johnson 1972; Becker 1973; Freedman 1975; and Loren 1977) that all employed workers, regardless of whether they produce value in the Marxist sense or supervise other workers, comprise a single working class. Extensive theoretical comparisons of alternative Marxist conceptualizations of the class structure may be found in Rosemary Crompton and Jon Gubbay (1978), Pat Walker (1979), Wright (1980a; 1980b), and Nicholas Abercrombie and John Urry (1983).

Each of the three views of the class structure has been operationalized using our 1981 Canadian population survey – that is, all employed respondents were assigned to the class categories defined in each of the three schemes. We then investigate the relative merits of the categorizations empirically by comparing the socio-economic characteristics of the various classes. We conclude that the conceptualization put forward by Wright is the most appropriate to our purpose and this is the one that is employed in our subsequent ideology. Details of the operationalization of the class categories and detailed comparisons between the three groupings are provided in appendix A.

Restricting the analysis of classes to employed respondents constitutes a significant limitation. Homemakers, retired persons, students, disabled people, and the unemployed are left out of the class schemes entirely. The examination of class differences in ideology below, therefore, is supplemented by an analysis that examines these additional categories and compares them to employed workers. This is not entirely satisfactory, though we have been unable to fashion a good alternative to it. The traditional practice is to assign to non-labour-force participants the closest social substitute for their class: for homemakers with partners, the class of their partners (which, in practice, involves assigning large numbers of women the class of their spouses); for students, the class of their fathers; for retired persons, the class of their occupation before retirement; and so on. We instead chose to conduct analysis that reveals the particular ideological character of the separate statuses of people who are not employed.

Poulantzas's Model of Class   Poulantzas (1975) restricts the working class to employees of privately – owned companies whose work is exclusively devoted to the production of manufactured goods and who have no supervisory authority. Among the groups outside the working class, on this basis, are clerical workers and the lowest level of factory inspectors; truck drivers, cashiers, and all other employees of wholesale and retail business; bank tellers and all other employees in finance; workers engaged in maintenance and repair and in transportation, even though they produce surplus value; all production workers employed in state-owned corporations, even if the state corporation competes with private industry, and pays for and organizes work in a similar way; and routine clerical staff in state bureaucracies, except for the top level of managers.

Poulantzas characterizes these non-proletarian employees in terms of their individualistic aspirations and values, in which respect he believes they are similar to the traditional petty bourgeoisie (of farmers, artisans, and shopkeepers). This similarity in aspirations and values leads Poulantzas to the conclusion that non-working-class wage earners constitute a "new petty bourgeoisie," which is said to be a fraction of the traditional petty bourgeoisie (rather than comprising an independent class in its own right). Poulantzas distinguishes between the petty bourgeoisie and bourgeoisie proper on the basis of the size of the businesses that they own.

Wright's (First) Model of Classes   Wright (1976) begins his analysis with a critique of Poulantzas that focuses on the small proportions of the population – far less than half of all employed people in contemporary western societies – who actually belong to the working class, and the implications of such a view for socialist movements. By excluding many workers who are poorly paid and have little job autonomy or prospect of promotion, Wright points out that Poulantzas reduces the working class to a small minority, in the neighbourhood of one-fifth of the employed labour force in advanced capitalist countries. Wright himself defines social classes in terms of the intersection of three variables: ownership of the means of production, "possession" of the means of production (that is, the right to decide the types and amounts of commodities produced), and control of labour power. In Wright's terms, members of the working class are non-owners of the means of production, non-possessors of the means of production, and non-controllers of the work process at their jobs. Members of the capitalist class are defined by their ownership of the means of production, possession of the means of production, and control over their own work process.

A distinctive feature of Wright's approach is that not all employed people belong to one of these theoretically pure social classes. The large part of the employed population, who occupy positions that are less "consistent" than those occupied by the working and capitalist classes, is assigned to a number of "contradictory locations." The contradictory location for "semi-autonomous employees," for example, includes employees who do control their own work process but do not own nor "possess" (i.e., have effective control over) the means of production. Typical semi-autonomous employees include professors, scientists in private industry, and some technicians and craft workers. Manual and non-manual low-level supervisors are assigned to a contradictory location because they control the labour process of other workers, but are themselves subject to tight discipline. Wright also distinguishes the class of petty bourgeoisie, who spend a significant amount of their time working alongside their employees, from the contradictory location for "small employers" and from the "bourgeoisie" itself. Two other contradictory locations include middle-level "managers" that do not own businesses and "technocrats," who are professionals with technical or scientific skills used to supervise complex business operations.

Wright's own implementation of his class theory makes no use of occupational information at all, since he is able to rely on precise data concerning management prerogatives, job autonomy, and supervision. In the absence of comparable data we have relied heavily on occupational information. In some circumstances a strong case can be made for the use of occupational data, thus our contradictory location for supervisors includes both individuals who say that is what they are, irrespective of what they say about how much time they spend supervising, how many people they supervise, and what degree of authority they have, *and* workers who say they do a certain minimum of supervision regardless of what occupation they give.

We think that there are some problems with Wright's approach. First, leaving a significant proportion of workers outside the class structure in "contradictory" locations is inherently unsatisfactory. Wright correctly identifies groups whose situation leaves them open to contradictory political polarization – some semi-autonomous employees are part of what is traditionally known as the aristocracy of labour, a group that has been drawn to conservative political views. In our view these employees are workers because they work for wages and do not own their means of production; they exert immediate control over their means of production, but they are only able to control the manner in which they work and must work to be paid. Furthermore, at a number of points Wright departs from the requirement that social classes are inherently categorical. While the divisions between supervisors and managers and between workers and semi-autonomous employees reflect genuine polarizations – and are worthy of study in our view – they are not class differences. To summarize, Wright identifies critical dimensions of the contemporary structure of class, but we think that some of his divisions *between* classes and contradictory locations are divisions *within* social classes.

Carchedi's Model of Classes   Carchedi's analysis of social classes is based on an expansion of the Marxist concepts of capitalist and worker to the *functions* of the "global capitalist" and "collective worker." Carchedi's original formulations are complex and obtuse, but good summaries may be found in Crompton and Gubbay 1978, 94–6, 154 ff. and Wright 1980, 356 ff. The "function of the collective worker" expands the role of the individual worker to encompass the communication and coordination that are necessary in the complex and coordinated production operations characteristic of the monopoly phase of capitalism. The functions of the global capitalist include the management of non-productive state activities and production in state-owned enterprises and the maintenance of social order, as well as the supervision of workers and management of private companies. Most actual jobs involve employees in some combination of the functions of the collective worker and global capitalist. Depending on which function predominates in a given work situation (which is to some extent independent of the person's occupation), a worker is assigned to working class or new middle class. Following this principle, most low-level clerical workers, whether employed by private industrial corporations, by private firms in the commercial and financial sectors, by state enterprises, or by government bureaucracies, perform the function of the collective worker and so are members of the working class. All supervisors, workers responsible for the ideological reproduction and control of capitalism, including teachers, workers involved directly in social control such as the police, and workers involved directly in the defence of private property such as guards, perform functions of the global capitalist and are assigned to the middle class. The petty bourgeoisie includes the owners of small businesses and independent farmers and commodity producers, while the capitalist class includes the owners and top managers of larger businesses.

Carchedi's scheme shares some of the characteristics of Poulantzas's and some of the characteristics of Wright's theory of class. Like Poulantzas, Carchedi is attentive to the social content of occupations. For example policemen are in the middle class (instead of the working class), despite their being employees who are paid to carry out routinized tasks, because they are involved in enforcing capitalist order. Like Wright, Carchedi assigns employees who produce no surplus value, including workers in some service industries and in occupations ancillary to production in privately owned manufacturing companies, to the working class.

The Social Composition of Wright's Social Classes

A more extensive discussion of how survey respondents were classified according to the three social class categorizations, along with the analysis of class differentiation according to the three schemes, may be found in appendix A, but a brief discussion of Wright's classification is in order here because it is employed extensively in chapters 5 and 6. Table 3-1 gives the social characteristics of the respondents who have been classified into each of Wright's seven categories. The relative proportions of employed persons in these categories, clearly, is critical. Just over half the population (of employed persons), 56 percent, are in the working class. An additional 8 percent are in the contradictory location for semi-autonomous employees, that is they are employees with a high degree of control over their own work process but without significant managerial authority. We think of them as a fraction of the working class. Also in the working class, in our view, are the 11 percent of employees who are supervisors and exercise authority over other workers, but who are without significant autonomy or control of their own workplace. Managers and technocrats, the category of workers most closely allied with capital, make up 7 percent of the population. Capitalists, who own or directly manage organizations with at least thirty employees, and small employers (who do the same for organizations with five to twenty-nine employees) make up, respectively, 2.8 and 3.5 percent of the sample. The petty bourgeoisie, consisting of "own account" workers or proprietors of very small businesses that are significantly dependent on their own labour, make up the remaining 12 percent of the sample.

Roughly speaking, then, the working class accounts for nearly three-quarters of all employees; but nearly a third of its members are, potentially, ideologically compromised because their autonomous working conditions shield them from social relations that embody class opposition or because they are enlisted in controlling the work process. The remainder of the population is split almost equally between the petty bourgeoisie and the owners, managers, and technocrats who control large enterprises. Of course the actual owners of larger business are a tiny minority.

Table 3-1 also shows the occupational composition of the seven categories, using conventional census definitions of occupation categories. Only managers and technocrats, who are drawn entirely from the occupational category of managers and professionals, and capitalists, three-quarters of whom are managers and professionals, are defined or largely definable in conventional occupational categories. Seven percent of the working class are managers and professionals, 46 percent are non-manual workers, 46 percent are manual workers, and 1 percent farmers; while the petty bourgeoisie consists of 10 percent managers and professionals, 38 percent are non-manual workers, 26 percent manual workers, and 26 percent farmers. As we understand them, then, social classes are not simply a reformulation of occupational categories.

Table 3-1
Characteristics of the Members of Wright's Social Class Categories

Social class	Occupation (percentage distribution)				Percent Women	Mean age	Education		Annual Pay (in $1000/yr)		Number of cases	Percentage distribution of classes
	Managers and professionals	Non-Manual workers	Manual workers	Farmers			Percent high school grads	Percent university grads	Mean	Standard deviation		
Capitalists	73	25	2	0	23	43.9	80	42	40.3	28.3	51	2.8
Small employers	25	41	19	15	31	39.9	59	21	27.8	18.2	64	3.5
Petty bourgeoisie	10	38	26	26	27	46.9	49	7	20.8	17.4	217	11.8
Managers and technocrats	100	0	0	0	25	41.8	89	29	26.2	13.0	128	7.0
Supervisors	9	56	34	1	38	38.6	70	15	20.6	11.1	200	10.9
Semi-autonomous employees	34	31	29	6	24	37.4	82	30	22.9	10.9	148	8.1
Working class	7	46	46	1	49	35.6	58	9	15.4	6.8	1025	55.9
Total	19	41	35	5	40	38.2	62	14	19.0	11.6	1833	100.0

While women constitute 40 percent of all the employed persons, they make up 49 percent of the working class. The next most feminized category is supervisors, who are 38 percent female (they are disproportionately non-manual supervisors of female clerical and sales workers). For the remaining class categories, which involve owning or managing an enterprise or professional skills, women make up an average of only about 25 percent of all the incumbents.

There are moderately large age differences between classes, with the working class the youngest (35.6 years, on average) and the petty bourgeoisie the oldest (46.9 years). Without longitudinal data it is impossible to determine the extent to which this pattern represents change in the class structure – the older age of the petty bourgeoisie and capitalist class representing a decline in their numbers and increasing difficulty of younger people gaining access – as opposed to mobility processes, so that the age pattern represents a pattern of mobility over the life cycle.

In terms of pay and education the classes fall into a predictable order, with the petty bourgeoisie the only anomalous category. As well as being disproportionally older, its members are rather poorly paid and poorly educated. Their average income is close to that of the supervisors, only about half have graduated from high school, and 7 percent have graduated from university. Capitalists' average income is nearly three times as high as workers' and the variance in their income is also much greater. Small employees and managers and technocrats are the best paid after them. There is relatively little difference in the mean incomes of the petty bourgeoisie, supervisors, and semi-autonomous workers, who all earn about one-third more than the average worker.

There is nothing astonishing here, which is good. Despite their theoretical complexity, our categories *should* correspond to our common-sense ideas of who is who and who gets what. The only surprising finding concerns the petty bourgeoisie, whose material state puts them in a situation hardly better than the workers who are likely to have less taxing jobs and more security. While traditional views of the sanctity of private property and enterprise may fit the class position of members of the petty bourgeoisie, they clearly do not reap the corresponding material rewards.

ELITES IN CLASS TERMS

As anyone who has taken an introductory political science course knows, "elites" may be defined conceptually and identified empirically in a variety of ways. For our survey the objective was simply to select the individuals who exercised the most power in a variety of different sectors of society. In the words of Giddens (1974, 4) we use the term elite or elite group "to designate those individuals who occupy formally defined positions of authority at the head of a social organization or institution." Reflecting our theoretical interests, we concentrated on the organizations of capital, labour, and the state. For example there is no religious sector in our elite sample, although we have included samples of lawyers, academics, and mass media executives because they are central to the communication and decision processes through which legitimation is maintained.

Even with this theoretical specification of the key social organizations or institutions, there remain difficulties in specifying the formally defined positions of authority. This could itself be the subject of a large study. Like many researchers in this situation before us, we selected a "positional sample," consisting of individuals in positions in organizations. Unlike social circles and networks of interpersonal relations, organizations and the important positions in them are easy to identify and study. While the selection of a positional sample may run the risk of overlooking important people who do not hold important positions, there is much less risk that the people actually selected will not be important decision makers. The decision to select the presidents of the largest Canadian corporations (systematically sampling from the *Financial Post* listing of the largest Canadian corporations) as corporate elites, for example, was not very likely to result in our interviewing a group of unimportant people. Whether or not the sample design makes sense, however, is always a function of the use to which it is put. As a comparison group to examine the ideological differences between corporate elites, elites from other sectors of society, and the general public, our strategy makes perfect sense. But we are unable to examine some kinds of differences within the corporate elite, since we have excluded the chairs of corporate boards, executives of corporations other than the president, and non-executive members of corporate boards.

A sample of the executives of small business – that is of businesses with fewer than 100 employees – was also included in the study, in order to determine whether the executives of large corporations were typical of business as a whole. Since there is no national listing of small business, we used a combination of two sub-samples to represent the universe, in both cases selecting the president of the company for interview. The first sub-sample of companies was selected from lists provided by the chambers of commerce or boards of trade of the twelve largest census metropolitan areas (CMAs); the number of selections in each CMA was proportional to its population. The second group was a random sample of manufacturing companies selected from *Scott's Directory of Manufacturing Firms* for 1980; and again the number of selections was proportional to the CMA population.

The elite lawyers in our analysis consisted of the senior partners from all Canadian law firms with twenty or more partners, as listed in the 1979 *Canadian Law List*. In the analysis we view these lawyers as a distinct sector of the capitalist class, responsible for arranging the relations between capital and the state and between capitalists. For this service, we shall see below, elite lawyers have incomes that are so high that they can only be explained in terms of their class position.

In selecting the state elites we made the conventional division between the three levels of government and between elected politicians and civil servants, whom we call bureaucrats. At the federal level the politicians were represented by a random sample of Members of Parliament, stratified by party to assure the parties would be present in proportion to their numbers in Parliament. At the provincial level the selected politicians were the cabinet ministers responsible for a preselected set of ministries. At the municipal level the selected politicians included the mayor and a random selection of the controllers (where they existed) or of the city councillors (where there were no controllers or other more senior representatives). For bureaucrats the sample consisted of deputy and assistant deputy ministers of the federal government, deputy ministers of the provincial governments of each province (in the same ministries selected for the sample of provincial politicians), and the heads of the major departments in the twelve largest cities.

Trade union leaders are taken as representatives of the working class, though the nature of this representation is clearly different than the representation of capital by corporate executives. In the sample, we included the presidents of the largest trade union locals, as listed in the *Directory of Labour Organizations*, the presidents of the provincial labour federations, the presidents of the labour councils in the twelve largest CMAs in Canada, and the top officials of the national labour organizations.

Finally, there are three other types of organizations or sectors of potential political influence, from which we obtained much smaller samples. From the farm sector we selected the national and provincial leaders of the main farm organizations – the Canadian Agricultural Association, the National Farmers Union, and (in some provinces) the Christian Farmers Association. To represent the mass media we selected the news editors of the major national radio and television stations and the major Canadian newspapers. Academics were represented by a representative sample of the membership of the Royal Society of Canada and of the presidents of the Learned Societies.

OPERATIONALIZING THE CONCEPT OF IDEOLOGY

In keeping with our argument that it is the particular uses of survey research and not the method itself that are responsible for the limitations on our understanding of political ideology, our efforts to measure ideology empirically are little different in form from those used in previous research on political attitudes. What distinguishes our effort is more the theoretical stance and breadth of the enterprise. No previous Canadian study of political attitudes broadly examines the fundamental issues of class and the state. Indeed very few academic studies in Canada address these issues at all. Surveys conducted by commercial firms and sponsored by political parties and agencies of government address some of these questions. But, with some notable exceptions such as Richard Johnston (1986), a combination of timidity and disinterest on the part of academic researchers and the reluctance or outright unwillingness of private firms to make their data accessible have prevented their being used to address these issues.

As we have argued at great length, we see conflicts between capital and labour, understood broadly, as the central problem facing contemporary capitalism. We understand the development of the welfare state as a means of coping with conflicts between labour and capital, although not simply. Two of the ways in which the role of the state is not simple are, first, that many of the functions of the capitalist state (although not the way that they are accomplished) are the functions of any state in a bureaucratic and technologically advanced society in the world market system and, second, that the regulation of capitalist society turns out to involve many issues whose immediate outcomes reflect a balance of class forces, but whose resolution is not ultimately tied to structural imperatives. Across advanced capitalist nations there is considerable variation in the solutions to conflicts involving the civil and economic rights of women and men, ethnic groups, regions, etcetera and to moral issues such as censorship and regulation of sexuality. Our approach to the conceptualization and measurement of ideology therefore makes a distinction between the central issues of relationships between state, capital, and labour, and more peripheral (if often politically more salient) issues.

Our measurement of ideology is based, first, upon a triangular conceptualization of power relations in capitalist society and upon questions about the justification or alteration of those power relations. The simple model underlying these measures of ideology can be described as in figure 3-1. These tripartite relations, and their associated dimensions of ideology (conceptions of economic regulation, labour relations, and social welfare), are the core elements in our theoretical understanding of hegemony and hegemonic crisis in a capitalist society. Hegemonic relations in such societies are constituted on the basis of ideological assumptions that the powers of state, labour, and capital are properly directed and adequately limited. Centrally important in this connection, however, are supplementary ideological assumptions that limit the scope of influence of the major power holders in society by privileging private and individual relations above the key political relations defined in figure 3-1, and that limit the scope of conflict in political relations. These additional ideological assumptions have to do with support for civil liberties, an emphasis upon production and economic growth as necessary to the good life, and conceptions of the quality of life largely defined by the private satisfactions of consumer activity and family relations.

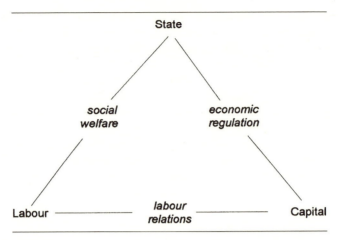

Figure 3-1
Components of ideology in relation to labour, capital, and the state

Using two extensive pre-tests, we developed a series of questionnaire items designed, in combination, to locate respondents in an ideological space defined by these relations between the state, capital, and labour. The precise wording of each of these items is given in the next chapter, where we examine their response distributions, so this section is confined to more general comments.

A multi-part question about the distribution of power represents our most direct effort to measure respondents' views about the power of contending class forces. In its most detailed version (in the 1977 survey) it asked about what changes there should be in the powers of eleven different groups "for the good of society"; these groups included capital (large corporations and small business), labour, and the state (taking the three levels of government separately), as well as newspapers, religious leaders, the medical profession, and farmers. Another multi-part question addressed these issues in terms of the effort "you think government should put into a number of areas." Among the objects rated were efforts in direct support of capital (effort towards "supporting the business community"), labour (in the form of unemployment insurance, workers' compensation, and creating more jobs), and a number of groups and social programs that were not defined strictly in class terms (the poor, retired people, daycare, etc.).

Afraid that, without any obvious constraint, our respondents would avoid making difficult choices (there was nothing in the question about government effort to prevent them from supporting efforts to assist both capital and labour or from supporting efforts to cut inflation and to create more jobs, etc.), we developed some questions that forced them to make choices in the form of evaluations of statements (using the Likert responses: strongly agree, agree, neither agree nor disagree, disagree, strongly disagree). Two examples of these statements, relating to redistribution and the labour movement respectively, are: "People with high incomes should pay a greater share of the total taxes than they do now"; and "During a strike, management should be prohibited by law from hiring workers to take the place of strikers."

In order to measure opinions about civil liberties and individual rights we developed a series of questions that dealt with the rights of the disabled, equal pay, protection of homosexuals from discrimination in employment, affirmative action, native self-government, film censorship, abolition of the War Measures Act, and civilian review of complaints against the police. Related to these issues are those involving the treatment of immigrants and linguistic rights. On these topics, opinions were measured using ratings of statements including the following: "People who come to live in Canada should try harder to be more like other Canadians"; and "People who do not speak English and move to Quebec should be able to find schooling for their children in English."

Finally, we devoted considerable effort to the measurement of personal satisfaction with the quality of life in the various domains of work and income, family and personal relations, and local and national politics. These efforts were predicated upon assumptions that satisfaction, especially with respect to market and family situation, served the ideological adjustment to the status quo. Although there is abundant evidence that, alone, dissatisfaction seldom leads to active efforts to produce change, we assume that there is an underlying relationship, and that it is worth investigating how such dissatisfaction is mobilized or articulated in political action, or mediated by other ideological and political forces producing political quiescence.

In order to determine just who is likely to engage in political action we asked a series of questions about a variety of forms of political activity, including working as a volunteer during a political campaign, working with others in the community to try to solve some community problems, spoken or written communication with an elected representative, signing a petition directed to some government agency, and attendance at a protest meeting or demonstration. In addition we were concerned about what constituted legitimate means of political action and therefore asked about the appropriateness of five different forms of political action: strikes; boycotts; legal and peaceful demonstrations like marches, rallies, and picketing; illegal but peaceful demonstrations like sit-ins; and violent protest demonstrations including actions such as fighting with the police and destroying property. Finally, the four-item measure of efficacy used in the national election study previous to our first survey (in 1974) was also included in the survey, partly to increase the number of points in the available series and partly because previous responses would provide a context for working with these data.

Many items were included in two or three of the surveys, both in order to examine the extent and dynamics of change over time and to give a continuing fix on our central concern with social and economic policy and labour relations. Other measures, such as number of items dealing with regional inequality, Quebec independence, and foreign ownership, dealt with major national policy debates. And still others were elaborations of the central themes of class conflict and the role of the state. We pre-tested a great many other items that, for lack of space and often lack of validity, were not used in the national surveys. For example an attempt to get respondents to differentiate the actions of occupants of top-level political positions from the actions of government as an institution failed utterly – reflecting what, at least in retrospect, appears to be the sensible belief that the institutions of government get the individual leaders they deserve.

The utility of these various measures of ideology is demonstrated, first, by their value as a means of describing, in ways congruent with our general conceptualization of hegemony, the overall structure of popular ideology in Canada. Second, in more technical terms, the utility of these measures of ideology is evaluated in terms of the requirement that responses to individual survey questions cohere in ways that make sense when analyzed using factor analysis and scaling techniques. Our data analysis in the following chapters therefore makes use of both individual questionnaire items and scales formed by combining the responses to two or more items.

In our analysis both individual items and multi-item scales have their uses. The conventional argument in favour of using scales is that the reliability of individual questions in surveys is quite low; error due to imprecision in the wording of an item, misunderstandings by respondents, and plain carelessness may account for more than half of the variance in a response. Note that this measurement error adds to and is independent of the sampling error (which is small for samples as large as ours). Multi-item scales achieve increased reliability by decreasing measurement error, since errors (if they are random) tend to cancel out when items are added. Because they contain less error, predictors of attitudes (such as social class) generally explain more of the variance in scales than in individual items; furthermore, with increased reliability it is possible to show that smaller differences between groups are statistically significant. While the samples in our study are large enough that statistical significance is rarely an issue in comparing the groups, in the regression analysis the greater reliability of multi-item scales is useful when there is a need to show that particular variables have significant effects when other variables are held constant.

Then why not carry out all the analysis on scales and forget the items entirely? The problem, of course, is that while they provide more precise measurement, scales eradicate the responses to the individual items. While questions about, say, whether corporations should be able to employ strike breakers and workers' representation on corporate boards may measure the same trait, Canadians' views of these specific issues are important. Furthermore while the measurement error in an individual item downwardly biases the estimate of its relationship to other variables, the frequency distribution is unbiased. As long as the question is free of bias, that is its wording does not favour one of the alternative responses, the measurement error has no impact on the estimate of the percentage of the population (or of a subgroup within the population) making some particular response. For characteristics of the Canadian public as a whole, our national samples are so large that sampling errors are within 2 percent of the population values, with 95 percent confidence. For subgroups of the population, such as class categories, the sampling errors are larger and, of course, statistical tests are employed to distinguish chance variations from real effects.

We would have liked to see our findings as a response to researchers who take seriously neo-Marxist ideas about class structure and who recognize standardized surveys as a legitimate, if not exclusive, way to look at political ideology. Where better to look than the surveys conducted as part of Wright's (1996, xxix) class project. Following the lead of his initial U.S. survey in 1978, surveys have been conducted in fourteen countries. Unfortunately only the most rudimentary comparisons are possible. First, disagreements over Wright's change from a domination- to an exploitation-based conceptualization of class led researchers in different directions. Wright (1996) employs no fewer than twelve categories to operationalize his exploitation-based typology. Clement and Myles (1994) stayed with Wright's first scheme, though their classification does not include the contradictory locations that feature so prominently in this approach – they have just four classes: the capitalist-executive class, old middle class, new middle class, and working class; while the British team (Marshall et al. 1989) deserted completely and adopted Goldthorpe's neo-Weberian scheme.

Equally important, the Wright-inspired projects have been aimed essentially at measuring characteristics of the class *structure*, rather than political ideology. Most of the surveys included just a handful of items dealing with politics. The studies that we reviewed – Wright deals with data from Japan, Sweden, and the U.S.; Marshall et al. with Britain; and Clement and Myles with Canada, Norway, Sweden, and the U.S. – focus on a single scale of attitudes toward class, made up of five or six items (but not the same items in the different studies!). Mainly, this inattention to the subtleties of ideology is a matter of research priorities, but we suspect that it also reflects a seriously limited version of politics. Our view of ideology is more complicated, and not only because we focus on relations among state, labour, and capital. Also, we look at the variables used by conventional researchers in political science. We have argued that their construction purposely ignores class issues, dividing the consideration of politics into measures relating to the civility, participation, and confidence in the state and its personnel on the one hand, and to voting on the other. But these aspects of ideology must still be investigated. However biased and "ideological" the focus on civic culture and voting, it reflects a real, though partial, description of the politics in which people live. It is significant that the Marxists who so strongly stress the relational character of class structures, and irreducibility of social classes to a simple hierarchy, think of ideology in precisely this unidimensional way.

In chapter 4 we explore the detailed distributions of public responses to individual items, in order to give a descriptively rich profile of ideological divisions in Canada. Chapter 5 is concerned with more complex models of the interrelationship between the measures of class and ideology analyzed in the previous chapter. There we develop multivariate statistical models, and readers may be concerned about the ways in which the assumptions of such models are potentially violated by characteristics of the survey data with which we test them, or by the ways in which the assumptions of the statistical models condition the kinds of statements we can make about the phenomena of class and ideology.

We do not propose to anticipate the full range of such objections, nor to prime the reader in the conventions of statistical analysis. Assuming that readers understand the basic logic of correlation between two measures, and of partial correlation between "intervening" variables, we hope simply to persuade them that models based upon such logic, and informed by prior theoretical specification of the measures, challenge their understanding of class and ideology in a capitalist society. Whether the challenge results in more refined defences of other understandings, or in the adoption of those we propose, is immaterial. Questions of the nature of political order will demand constant re-searching, no matter the calibre of our efforts in this book.

A BRIEF NOTE ON SAMPLING FOR THE NATIONAL POPULATION SURVEYS

Space, and we suspect most readers' interest, precludes full technical documentation on the surveys used in this book. Such detail may be found by consulting the technical documentation report developed for the Social Change in Canada Project (ISR, 1982). Here we confine ourselves to general observations.

In order to select a representative sample one requires a listing of the population (as, say, would normally be available for a survey of students at a university or employees of a corporation). In Canada, of course, there is no such listing, so it was necessary to substitute an aggregate listing, Statistics Canada's list of "enumeration areas" (EAs), which divide the inhabited territory of Canada into geographical units. Provided EAs are selected randomly, and individuals within the selected EA are also sampled randomly, one can obtain a representative sample of the population. Both the selection processes, of EAs and of individuals within EAs are quite complex. In order to ensure random selection within the selected EAs a list of all the dwellings is prepared and random selections made from this list. Within each selected dwelling, interviewers randomly select from the eligible respondents in each household.

This is a complex and expensive procedure. Often no one is home at a selected address and repeated visits were required to obtain an interview; a selected dwelling may have been subdivided or even demolished between the time when the listing of dwellings was conducted and the time of a visit to obtain an interview; the selected respondent in a household may be unable to speak English or French or may be too infirm to allow an interview; selected respondents may refuse to answer our questions; and so on. The complexity is even greater because we conducted a panel study – that is, where possible, we reinterviewed the same respondents in 1977, 1979, and 1981.

PART TWO

Public Ideology

4 Popular Ideology in Canada: The Contours of Public Opinion

We come now to a general analysis of the political ideology of Canadians, based on our 1977, 1979, and 1981 national surveys. In this chapter we describe the contours of public opinion on a variety of questions designed to describe Canadians' ideology broadly. Our questions deal with: state social programs, taxation, and related policies that make up what is usually termed the welfare state; the powers of business, labour, government, and other key institutions; civil liberties; political efficacy and participation; support for political institutions; and satisfaction with the quality of life. We want to draw a broad, multidimensional picture of ideology, reflecting our view that ideology involves the ways that people – all people – go about understanding and making their way in (an unequal and class-divided, "liberal democratic" capitalist) society. Differences between left and right are a major focus of our work, but ideology cannot be reduced to this single dimension of allegiance. Indeed the difficulty of reducing ideology to a single dimension helps to explain the durability of liberal democracy.

This is not say that we understand ideology as consisting of a huge and irreducible complexity in which nothing comes together. We use the triangular conception of ideology put forward in the last chapter, which involves the relations between capital, labour, and the state, to interpret the wide variety of questions in our surveys. We understand these three relations as describing the fundamental *structural* features of capitalist society; more generally the *range* of capitalist societies is conceived in terms of differences in these three relationships.

The clarity with which these relationships are revealed is problematic, however, especially in ideology, which tends to conceal them. An important challenge to the entire conception of ideology, at least as it is understood in terms of the broad public, concerns whether public opinion on the range of issues we address has the internal structure necessary to merit describing it as "political ideology." The question is whether *public opinion*, rather than the opinion of a small, politically engaged, and intellectually competent minority, has sufficient coherence to suggest the existence of general states of mind. In order to address this question, in appendix B we examine three aspects of the structure of political ideology: the levels of "constraint," or consistency about opinions on logically related issues, the temporal consistency of opinions, and the dimensionality of public opinion. Of course, that we have gone to the trouble to collect these opinions reflects the belief that the answers we get are more than random error or unthinking reactions to our jargon, but we need to address this concern empirically.

The description of public attitudes will answer a number of questions, raised in the first two chapters, about common characterizations of contemporary ideology. First, how much consensus is there among Canadians on political issues? Is there support for the orthodox view of an ideologically *un*divided political culture, consistent with theories of a "dominant" ideology (whether in Marxist or non-Marxist versions), which see political order as grounded in ideological consensus; or, alternatively, is there evidence of an unstable hegemony constructed on top of ideologically divided interests in society? Second, what is the class character of such consensus as may exist? Is it consistent with the "ruling ideas" that justified the postwar settlement of the class struggle in a Keynesian welfare state; is it "progressive" in its endorsement of "liberal" extensions of equality of opportunity as a condition of equal freedoms in society; or does it have a more complex character? Third, do the majority positions in Canadians' policy preferences reflect recent public policy, as theories of pluralism and brokerage politics suggest they should, and as the dominant institutionalist tradition of Canadian political science suggests by its rooting of political culture in the institutions and policies of Canadian government? Alternatively, is there a gap between public interests and public policy, with popular attitudes either more progressive or more reactionary than the drift of public policy? Fourth, to what extent is the ground of ideological controversy shifting from the old "materialist" issues of class struggle prior to the postwar settlement to the new issues of the empowerment and security of non-class collectivities? Fifth, and related to this last issue, to what extent is political acquiescence in the mass public maintained by the satisfactions of private life, or is privatized satisfaction breaking down and releasing political activism and protest in new social movements? All these questions, naturally, relate to the overriding question of this book: to what extent did the crisis tendencies of the late 1970s and early 1980s in Canada lead to problems of political order, as indicated by a changing pattern of consent to the basic values and institutions of the liberal capitalist state.

This and the next chapter have contrasting but complementary goals. In developing a characterization of contemporary ideology in this chapter, we search for areas of consensus and conflict *without* attempting to identify the social-structural basis of differences: the question is what can be said about the general ensemble of opinion. In the next chapter we look at the *relationship* between social structure and opinion, focusing particularly on class and regional divisions. The two chapters thus have the contrasting emphases of qualitative and quantitative research, with the former emphasizing broad themes and the logic of perception and allegiance and the latter emphasizing differences within the population.

THE STATE AND MATERIAL INEQUALITY: SOCIAL PROGRAMS AND REDISTRIBUTION

We begin with a discussion of the responses to a series of items from the survey dealing with government priorities. The larger issue addressed in this analysis is whether there is a broad public acceptance of the social programs, largely developed in the postwar period, that constitute the "welfare state." In terms of the triangle of relations between labour, capital, and the state, as noted, we understand social programs as an aspect of the relationship between labour and the state that strengthens the hand of labour in conflict with capital. Clearly, public attitudes towards these programs are relevant to current attacks on the universality of medicare, insurance against unemployment, and old-age pensions and decreased funding of housing, post-secondary education, and other areas.

The introduction to the survey question read as follows:

We would like to know how much effort you think government should put into a number of activities. Please choose the answer on this card which comes closest to your opinion about the effort that should be made in each area. Remember that putting more effort into one of these areas would require a shift of money away from other areas or an increase in taxes.

Five responses were presented to respondents on a card – much more effort, more effort, about the same effort, less effort, much less effort. When a respondent indicated that her or his opinion depended on the circumstances (for example, on what kind of effort was made to deal with a problem) or that she or he did not have a position, this was recorded by the interviewer, though there were no such responses on the card. More items were rated in the 1977 survey than in the 1979 or 1981 surveys. Table 4-1 gives the distributions of responses for a representative sample of the population. "No opinion" responses are included as a valid category in most of the tables in this chapter, to provide information on the different levels of knowledge of these questions. In most cases the "neither agree nor disagree," "depends," and "no opinion" responses are a small minority, so their inclusion does little to alter the figures for the other categories.

Table 4-1
Rating of the Amount of Effort "Government Should Put into a Number of Activities" for the Canadian Population in 1977, 1979, and 1981

Area of Government Effort	Year	Percentage Distribution of Responses							
		Much more effort	More effort	About the same effort	Less effort	Much less effort	Depends	Do not know	Total
Health and medical care	1977	13.3	32.9	49.4	2.6	.3	.5	.9	99.9
	1979	14.1	38.8	44.3	1.7	.3	.2	.7	100.1
	1981	12.1	36.9	47.9	1.9	.2	.4	.6	100.0
Protecting the rights of native people	1977	10.0	38.8	33.9	8.5	1.5	1.5	5.8	100.0
	1979	11.4	36.9	37.6	6.3	2.1	.6	5.2	100.1
	1981	9.8	35.2	39.1	8.7	2.0	.5	4.8	100.1
Providing assistance to the unemployed	1977	13.2	24.2	31.2	21.1	5.1	3.9	1.3	100.0
	1979	11.5	24.1	36.6	19.0	4.1	3.4	1.2	99.9
	1981	8.8	25.1	38.7	19.5	3.7	2.4	1.7	99.9
Supporting the business community	1977	4.9	27.4	43.0	14.3	2.4	2.2	5.9	100.1
	1979	5.5	30.9	45.2	9.8	2.0	1.3	5.3	100.0
	1981	5.6	29.3	45.8	12.2	2.2	.9	4.0	100.0
Promoting bilingualism	1977	8.6	23.7	27.3	21.9	14.3	1.5	2.7	100.0
	1979	8.0	20.0	30.3	24.0	15.0	.7	2.1	100.1
	1981	8.5	18.1	29.2	25.1	15.9	.6	2.5	99.9
Creating more jobs	1977	39.4	45.4	9.8	2.7	.8	1.2	.7	100.0

Table 4-1

Rating of the Amount of Effort "Government Should Put into a Number of Activities" for the Canadian Population in 1977, 1979, and 1981 (Continued)

Area of Government Effort	Year	Percentage Distribution of Responses							
		Much more effort	More effort	About the same effort	Less effort	Much less effort	Depends	Do not know	Total
Maintaining national unity	1977	28.5	40.1	22.1	4.1	1.4	1.3	2.5	99.9
Helping the poor	1977	23.1	40.3	28.5	3.3	.7	3.2	.8	99.9
	1979	17.1	41.8	33.5	2.8	.6	3.1	1.2	100.1
	1981	16.7	45.1	30.9	3.7	.5	2.0	1.1	100.0
Crime prevention	1977	27.5	41.6	27.7	1.0	.1	.5	1.5	99.9
	1979	23.0	44.4	29.7	.7	.3	.7	1.2	100.0
	1981	26.9	45.9	24.0	1.0	.5	.6	1.0	99.9
Building public housing	1977	13.9	33.8	36.6	9.4	1.6	1.8	2.9	100.0
Eliminating discrimination against women	1977	16.4	31.5	34.8	8.6	2.6	1.2	5.0	100.1
	1979	16.3	29.9	40.2	6.8	2.9	1.1	2.8	100.0
	1981	19.2	34.5	34.3	6.5	2.2	.7	2.6	100.0
Cutting inflation	1977	44.2	40.3	12.0	1.7	.4	.5	1.0	100.1
Eliminating pornography	1977	29.7	25.7	26.8	9.5	3.8	1.6	2.9	100.0

Table 4-1
Rating of the Amount of Effort "Government Should Put into a Number of Activities"
for the Canadian Population in 1977, 1979, and 1981 (Continued)

Area of Government Effort	Year	Percentage Distribution of Responses						
		Much more effort	More effort	About the same effort	Less effort	Much less effort	Depends	Do not know	Total
Protecting the environment	1977	30.0	46.5	20.1	1.4	.4	.3	1.2	99.9
	1979	24.0	44.9	27.7	1.3	.3	.1	1.7	100.0
	1981	24.5	46.0	26.2	1.6	.2	.1	1.3	99.9
Providing daycare	1977	11.4	33.5	32.8	9.0	3.2	1.5	8.6	100.0
Foreign aid	1977	3.5	13.5	46.4	21.7	7.3	2.2	5.4	100.0
Education	1977	18.2	35.5	38.8	4.5	.5	1.0	1.4	99.9
	1979	18.1	35.7	40.3	2.6	.6	1.0	1.6	99.9
	1981	18.5	35.9	41.4	2.2	.3	.3	1.4	100.0
National defense	1977	7.8	25.7	45.5	10.0	3.4	.9	6.8	100.1
Helping retired people	1977	26.5	43.7	26.9	.9	.0	.9	1.0	99.9
Workers' compensation	1977	13.2	28.2	45.6	3.4	.4	1.0	8.3	100.1
	1979	10.7	25.5	49.7	3.3	.7	1.0	9.2	100.1
	1981	11.5	25.0	50.1	3.8	1.0	.9	7.7	100.0
Decreasing regional inequality	1977	11.1	37.4	32.9	5.1	1.3	1.4	10.8	100.0

An initial examination of the table shows, first, high levels of support for government effort in almost every area and, second, great temporal stability. This stability may reflect the relatively stable economic conditions: unemployment rates were 8.3, 7.4, and 7.5 percent, respectively, in 1977, 1979, and 1981, the three years when the survey was conducted (Department of Finance 1984, 164), and the continuing growth in per capita real income was 0.9, 2.2, and 3.2 percent in the three survey years (141). Unfortunately our surveys did not extend as far as 1982, when unemployment increased from 7.5 to 11.0 percent following a serious economic recession.

Still, there is considerable variation in the evaluations of the different areas of government effort. In the light of the historically high levels of inflation and unemployment between 1977 and 1981, it is not surprising that public support for government effort is greatest for creating more jobs and cutting inflation – 80 percent of the population wanted more government effort towards these goals. Closely following these economic priorities were support for efforts to maintain national unity (rated only in 1977, the year after the election of the Parti Québécois government in Quebec), protecting the environment, crime prevention, and helping retired people. For only two of the listed items, government efforts to promote bilingualism and foreign aid, did the opponents of government effort outnumber the supporters of more government effort. It is significant that the strong support for national unity is not accompanied by any enthusiasm for bilingualism, which was one of the principle elements of Liberal party policies designed to bring about national unity in this era.

Although only one of the five top-rated areas of government effort involved a social program, public support for social programs is none the less very strong. There is unusually strong, temporally stable support for government effort to assist the poor: about 20 percent of the population favour much more effort, 40 percent favour more effort, and a further 30 percent favour about the same effort. Fewer than 5 percent of the respondents advocate much less or less effort to assist the poor, and about 5 percent say that their response depends on the form of efforts to help the poor, or take no position. While not as strong as support for government efforts to assist the poor, public support for efforts in the areas of education, building public housing, eliminating discrimination against women, protecting the rights of native people, workers' compensation, and daycare – all social welfare issues – and for eliminating pornography is at approximately the same level as for health and medical care.

Low in the public ratings are government efforts to support the business community and national defence, decrease regional inequality, provide foreign aid, and provide assistance to the unemployed. The low level of support for the unemployed and workers' compensation – for which about one-quarter of the population desire less or much less government assistance – compares to less than 5 percent taking this stand on assistance to the poor. More generally there is greater support for government efforts whose beneficiaries are defined in terms of the service involved, such as education, health care, daycare, and assistance to the retired, or that provide support to groups that are *not* defined in class terms (even if they might be predominantly of one social class) such as women and native people. Weak public support for efforts to assist the unemployed, the business community, and workers' compensation appears to reflect the perception of these efforts as benefiting special interests, as opposed to the general interest – in education and health care, for example. The reality, of course, is that the beneficiaries of education and other social programs are far from an even cross-section of the population.

While relatively small proportions of the population express no opinion about the appropriate level of government effort in each area, there is marked and interpretable variation across issues. Our respondents were most likely to say they had no opinion about the rights of native people, supporting the business community, daycare, foreign aid, national defence, and workers' compensation. The proportion of the population having no opinion about the efforts to eliminate discrimination against women falls from 5 percent in 1977 to about half that in 1979 and 1981 (a difference that is statistically significant). While there were some prominent exceptions, such as attitudes towards effort to assist the unemployed, public support tends to be lower in the areas of government effort about which there is the greater uncertainty.

Although the responses to these questions demonstrate strong public support for the key elements of the postwar welfare state, the relative ratings of the different areas of government effort appear to bear little relationship to government priorities at the time of the surveys or later. The strong support for health and medical care and education and very strong support for assistance to the poor remained high between 1977 and 1981, in contrast to the substantial federal government cutbacks in health and education transfers to the provinces, provincial social welfare payments that did not increase as rapidly as inflation, and a stable and highly unequal income distribution. Despite the relatively low level of public support for foreign aid and defence spending, there was increased spending in these areas in the years after the survey, although, interestingly, the 1989 federal budget brought massive cuts in both areas.

These disparities between public opinion and public policy suggest that, while ideological attachments to the broad policy commitments of the postwar settlement remained widespread during this period, governments did not meet public expectations for the satisfaction of those commitments. The combination of fiscal constraint and political pressures from the right led public policy in directions opposite to those endorsed by the majority of Canadians. These tendencies are not, however, equivalent to a crisis of legitimacy, let alone a crisis of political order. Two characteristics of public opinion, as we have so far described it, suggest this qualification.

First, immediate economic interests clearly take priority in the public ranking of public policy priorities. This finding is consistent with the evidence that economic problems are the most frequently mentioned in response to surveys asking respondents to name the most important problems faced by the country (Hamilton 1972, chap. 3; Johnston 1985, chap. 4). These findings suggest that the success of selling cutbacks to the public in the face of strong public commitment to social programs depends on convincing people that the continuation of social programs endangers the economic health of the country. The power of these appeals is heightened by the finding that the economic concerns that are translated into a lack of confidence in government are as likely to be impersonal estimates of national economic problems as they are to be reports of personal economic difficulty (Johnston 1985, 62–4).

People who are not in personal economic difficulty, but who nevertheless see serious economic problems as the priority political problem, are particularly likely to favour restraint policies that run counter to their commitment to social welfare programs. This argument is far from academic. The escalation of business attacks on social programs subsequent to the passage of the Free Trade legislation and the Conservative government's deficit-reduction efforts in the year following our survey involved just this combination of rhetoric about economic exigencies and cutbacks in social programs, in the context of the need for international competitiveness in a global economy.

A further caution against exaggerating the gap between public opinion and public policy concerns the nature of the question regarding public policy priorities. Responses to the question rating government effort in different areas may be influenced by the "ease" of positive responses; while the questions were preceded by the warning that "putting more effort into one of these areas would require a shift of money away from other areas or an increase in taxes," respondents were not actually forced to choose among competing alternatives in an environment where total resources were limited. Although support for government efforts, aid to injured workers, education, or support for the business community, etcetera has implications for the balance of class forces, respondents were not required to make explicit choices between competing interests. It is possible, therefore, to overemphasize the extent to which divisions in public opinion reflect class distinctions and to exaggerate the extent to which the gap between public opinion and public policy reflects a crisis in which government is no longer able to satisfy the commitments that made possible the mediation of divided class interests under the postwar settlement.

However, other data lend support to the picture already painted of support for the principles of the postwar settlement and of a gap between public opinion and public policy. The responses to the first two statements listed in table 4-2 add a strongly egalitarian element to our initial characterization of

Table 4-2
Responses to Statements Concerning Redistribution

Statement	Year	Percentage Distribution of Responses							
		Strongly agree	Agree	Neither agree nor disagree	Disagree	Strongly disagree	Depends	Do not know	Total
There is too much difference between rich and poor in this country	1977	19.4	43.1	16.9	16.0	1.3	.8	2.5	100.0
	1979	18.4	47.2	14.5	15.5	.9	1.0	2.5	100.0
	1981	18.2	48.2	14.3	15.6	.7	.4	2.5	99.9
People with high incomes should pay a greater share of the total taxes than they do now	1977	18.7	39.0	13.4	21.2	3.9	1.3	2.5	100.0
	1979	13.3	41.3	12.0	26.2	3.1	1.2	2.9	100.0
	1981	14.2	41.2	12.4	26.5	2.3	1.0	2.4	100.0
Unemployment is high these days because it is too easy to get welfare assistance	1977	25.8	40.7	8.6	16.6	5.3	1.2	1.7	99.9
	1979	13.0	46.4	9.8	23.0	3.9	1.2	2.7	100.0
	1981	16.9	48.6	10.4	19.6	2.3	.4	1.9	100.1
The government should provide jobs for Canadians who want to work but cannot find a job	1977	25.7	51.2	8.3	10.9	1.3	1.5	1.2	100.1
	1979	15.6	55.8	10.8	14.4	.9	1.4	1.0	99.9
	1981	17.0	52.3	10.4	16.6	1.2	.9	1.7	100.1
In provinces where they now exist rent controls should be abolished	1981	2.7	15.1	10.1	53.6	11.3	.8	6.4	100.0
Doctors should be prohibited from charging their patients more than the fee covered by medicare	1981	19.3	49.8	7.7	16.3	3.1	1.0	2.7	99.9

popular political ideology. A large majority of the population support changes to make the system of taxation more progressive and to decrease the gap between the rich and poor. Fully half the population agree and another fifth of the population strongly agree that there is too much difference between rich and poor in this country, while only 15 percent of the population disagree and another 1 percent strongly disagree; the remaining fifth take a neutral or no position. A similar question, which asks whether people with high incomes should pay a greater share of the taxes, elicits responses that are only marginally different. Except for a slight decline in support for a more redistributive taxation system between 1977 and 1979, there is little temporal change in the responses to these items.

More than two-thirds of the population agree or strongly agree with the radical proposition that government should provide jobs for Canadians who want to work but cannot find a job, while (depending on the year) between 12 and 19 percent disagree with the statement. Support for the government's acting as an employer of last resort declined moderately between 1977 and 1981. Still, there is remarkably strong public support for a principle that is clearly at variance with one of the central features of Canada's capitalist economy and with the policies of governments under the two major political parties. This is true elsewhere. In a 1980 national survey, for example, James Kluegel and Eliot Smith (1986, 153) found that 61 percent of Americans agreed that "The Federal government should guarantee a job to every person who wants to work" (it appears that non-respondents are excluded from the sample – the percentage of non-respondents is not given). Nicholas Abercrombie, Stephen Hill, and Bryan Turner (1980, 144 ff.) describe similar findings from a number of British studies and interpret them as evidence *against* the proposition that the social order of contemporary capitalism requires public support for an explicitly pro-capitalist "dominant ideology."

In light of the apparent willingness of Canadians to accept widespread government employment programs, the distribution of responses to the next item may come as a surprise. Support for the government's acting as an employer of last resort is combined with almost equally strong endorsement of the punitive view that unemployment is high these days because it is too easy to get welfare assistance. There is a temptation to interpret the responses to these two items as an indication of inconsistency in public opinion or, in Frank Parkin's (1971) terms, as involving a mixture of dominant and subordinate values. Examining similarly discordant combinations of attitudes obtained in a variety of American and British surveys, Michael Mann (1970, 426) characterizes working-class ideology as follows: "at the political level are rather confused values with surprisingly conservative biases." Our own interpretation of these findings is quite different: we interpret them as indicating a widespread public concern with inequality (and with the condition of the poor, as indicated in the question above), combined with a distrust of *both* the working class and big business. We will pursue this problem below.

If the last statement that we examined demonstrated deep suspicion of the unemployed, responses to the next item (again in table 4-2) suggest that there is little public support for the operation of free markets in essential services. Canadians generally disapprove of the removal of rent controls in provinces where they exist and approve of the statement that doctors should be prohibited from charging their patients more than the fee covered by medicare. These last two findings may help account for the tendency for some otherwise conservative provincial governments to control rents and for the all-party support for the Canada Health Act introduced by the Liberal party in 1984, which penalized provinces that allowed doctors to bill over the rates for medical services insured by the government health plans. The opposition to the removal of rent controls also offers some methodological comfort by demonstrating that the surveys do not elicit approval of just any statement put before the public.

The overwhelming support for the universal provision of essential social services funded through a progressive (in principle) income tax system; for measures to increase the progressiveness of the tax system in order to effect greater redistribution of income; for government employment programs for those who cannot find jobs in the regular labour market; and for the regulation of housing rental markets all confirm the conclusions from responses to the question about public policy priorities. At the time of our surveys a large majority of Canadians approved of the social welfare state's intervention in the "free" market to secure greater social justice.

This well-entrenched consensus on the principles of the social welfare state outdistanced the commitment of governments to these principles, at least as that commitment was established in social policy. Although governments moved some distance on the questions of housing and health policy to which our data refer, there was no appreciable movement on questions of employment or income redistribution. In the Allan MacEachen budget of 1982 the Pierre Trudeau government attempted to introduce measures for a progressive reform of the income tax, but was roundly defeated in this effort, and employment policy moved only on subsidies to private employers and to training programs for enhancing success in the job market.

These data establish the strength of popular commitment to the postwar settlement and demonstrate the "progressive" bias of Canadian political culture. In terms of our triangular model of ideology, Canadians see the relationship between labour and the state as involving significant support for health and social services and for the equalization of income by taxation, in contrast to market allocation. In principle, and as has been clear from consistent business opposition, such measures strengthen the hand of labour relative to capital (irrespective of one's judgement of how equal this relationship is). The significantly lower support for unemployment insurance relative, say, to medical care makes clear that the primary basis of public support for the welfare state is commitments to welfare and to the government's role in reducing inequalities produced in the labour market. That this affects the position of labour relative to capital is incidental, rather than being the public intention. More direct support for this comes in the next section, which deals more directly with the distribution of power in society and the powers and rights of organized labour.

POWER IN SOCIETY AND TRADE UNION RIGHTS

Because only a significant rearrangement of power is likely to alter the direction of government policy and reduce systematic conflicts between popular belief and government policy, it is necessary to examine public perceptions of the distribution of power in society. Our survey question confronted respondents with the assumption of conflicting interests in society, beginning as follows:

Some groups in Canada have more power than others to get the things they want. I am going to read you a list of groups and would like you to tell me if you think each one has too much power for the good of the country, too little power for the good of the country, or about the right amount of power.

As with the question about government effort, respondents are not faced with the problem of allocating a fixed amount of power among institutions, but could support an increase in the power of all or of none of the groups. The response distributions are in table 4-3.

Beginning with the two institutions most obviously associated with classes and class power, we find that there is a strong consensus that *both* large corporations and trade unions have too much power. One-fifth of the population say that large corporations have much too much power, and one-half say they have too much power; only one-fifth say corporations have about the right amount of power, and less than 3 percent say corporations have much too little or too little power. Very similar evaluations of corporate power have been obtained in surveys conducted in the U.S. (Hamilton 1972, 97), Britain (Abercrombie, Hill, and Turner 1984, 147), and Canada (Clement and Myles 1994, 97).

Public ratings of the power of trade unions are quite similar to the ratings of corporations, although the percentage believing trade unions had too *little* power is about 7 percent greater. Given that well over half the respondents rate both corporations and trade unions as too powerful, a large proportion of respondents must believe that *both* corporations and labour unions have too

Table 4-3
Ratings of the Power of Various Groups and Governments, by Year for the Canadian Population

		Percentage Distribution of Responses						
Institution	Year	Much too much power	Too much power	About the right amount of power	Too little power	Much too little power	Depends	Do not know	Total
Newspapers	1977	5.7	31.0	55.2	2.9	.3	1.0	4.0	100.1
The government of this province	1977	4.0	23.3	50.6	13.8	1.3	1.5	5.4	99.9
	1979	3.4	22.2	50.4	15.2	1.6	1.2	6.1	100.1
	1981	4.2	22.4	49.5	17.1	1.3	.9	4.6	100.0
Religious leaders	1977	2.7	14.2	58.1	15.7	2.2	1.6	5.6	100.1
Labour unions	1977	21.9	45.3	20.1	5.6	1.1	1.2	4.6	99.8
	1979	21.0	45.9	19.0	6.2	1.2	1.5	5.2	100.0
	1981	18.2	47.6	21.0	6.6	1.0	.7	4.8	99.9
Large corporations	1977	19.8	48.8	21.3	1.5	.2	1.2	7.3	100.1
	1979	17.9	50.8	20.0	2.2	.6	.8	7.8	100.1
	1981	18.0	51.2	21.2	2.2	.4	.6	6.3	99.9
The medical profession	1977	4.0	21.0	56.3	11.4	.9	1.2	5.4	100.2
	1981	4.0	19.0	54.9	15.7	1.5	.6	4.3	100.0

Table 4-3
Ratings of the Power of Various Groups and Governments, by Year for the Canadian Population (Continued)

		Percentage Distribution of Responses						
Institution	Year	Much too much power	Too much power	About the right amount of power	Too little power	Much too little power	Depends	Do not know	Total
Farmers	1977	.4	3.5	27.4	47.6	14.8	.7	5.6	100.0
The federal government	1977	8.4	30.6	45.7	6.9	.7	1.5	6.2	100.0
	1979	9.2	28.5	43.1	9.7	.9	1.6	7.0	100.0
	1981	14.9	32.3	36.8	9.6	.8	.8	4.9	100.1
The legal profession	1977	7.6	30.2	46.0	4.1	.5	2.2	9.5	100.1
Local governments	1977	1.8	13.1	57.6	19.3	1.5	1.1	5.6	100.0
Small businesses	1977	.6	1.6	27.9	53.1	10.2	.9	5.7	100.0

much power. While there is a temptation to conclude that these beliefs are simply inconsistent, such a conclusion depends critically on the assumption that conflict between large corporations and trade unions constitutes a fundamental line of conflict in society. The data suggest that, for a large proportion of the population, there is instead a quite different polarization between the powers of large institutions, including both the corporations and unions, and the power of individuals. This reasoning is supported by our finding that more than 60 percent of the population believe that farmers and small businesses have too little power.

Many Canadians also believe that the federal government, along with large corporations and trade unions, is too powerful. This is especially true in 1981. In that year 15 percent of the respondents indicated that the federal government had much too much power and another 32 percent believed it had too much power, while only 10 percent said it had too little or much too little power; 37 percent chose the "about the right amount of power" response. Ratings of the "government of this province" and local governments were nearly evenly split, with narrow majorities favouring the views that the provinces' powers were too great and local governments' too weak. This differentiation between levels of government lends further support to the suggestion that the big-small distinction is critical to public perceptions of power.

Finally, respondents who believed that the legal profession was too powerful outnumbered those who felt it had too little power by 38 to 5 percent, although the majority of the population rated the powers of the legal profession as about right or had no opinion. On the medical profession opinion was more evenly divided: respondents who believed the power of the medical profession was too great outnumbered the people who felt the medical profession should have more power, 25 to 12 percent in 1977 and 23 to 17 percent in 1981. The distribution of ratings of newspapers is similar to that of the legal profession, while approximately equal proportions rated religious leaders as too powerful and not powerful enough.

In this period a large proportion of the Canadian population felt that big institutions, corporate, labour, and governmental, had too much power, while local governments, small businesses, and farmers had too little power. These findings permit a further specification of the pattern we observed in responses to the questions about government effort and redistribution: the relative lack of sympathy for the unemployed, as compared to the poor and other marginal social groups, and the combination of support for income redistribution and job creation with the belief that unemployment is increased by the availability of social welfare.

In class terms the combination of views observed here can be characterized as petty bourgeois, since it combines a critique of big capital, the organized working class, *and* big government with support for enhancing the power of the business and farm-based elements of the petty bourgeoisie. Although the term "populist" also suggests itself as a characterization of these views, the pronounced and generalized antipathy to the working class suggests, at least, that we are dealing with a distinctly petty bourgeois version of populism. The historical resonance, here, is with the agrarian populism that developed in regions where and at times when the petty bourgeoisie was dominant.

These results suggest that it would be fruitful to examine the relationships between individuals' ratings of the different groups. Even if many respondents indicate that both corporations and trade unions are too powerful, it is still possible that individuals who believe that corporations are too powerful are *less* likely to say that trade unions are too powerful. If there exists a fundamental dimension of political ideology involving the extent to which a person is critical of large institutions, we should observe *positive* correlations between the evaluations of the powers of labour unions, large corporations, and the federal government; on the other hand, if a more appropriate model of this aspect of ideology involves support for *shifts* in the balance of power among unions, corporations, and government, we should observe at least one *negative* correlation among the ratings of the three.

For the 1981 survey, table 4-4 shows the relationship between assessments of the power of large corporations, trade unions, and the federal government. Eighty percent of the respondents who indicated large corporations were too powerful had the same view of trade unions, but only 62 percent of the respondents who rated corporations as having about the right amount of power or too little power thought trade unions were too powerful. Thus people who rate corporations as too powerful tend to have the same view of trade unions and, as table 4-4 also shows, of the federal government. The tendency is only moderate, though these findings are clearly incompatible with a model of public opinion that places individuals on a right-left continuum between support for corporations and support for trade unions.

As a model emphasizing the distinction between large and small institutions would suggest, there is a negative relationship between the evaluations of the power of farmers and small business, on the one side, and large corporations, trade unions, and the federal government, on the other. Sixty-nine percent of the respondents who believe that large corporations have too much power say that farmers have too *little* power, while 56 percent of those who say corporations have about the right amount of power say that farmers have too little power. Similar tendencies are found in the relationships between the other small and larger institutions. Underlining the conflict between big capital and labour and the petty bourgeoisie, the strongest antithesis marks the evaluations of small business and those of large corporations *and* trade unions, though even here the relationship is only moderately strong.

Table 4-4
Cross Tabulations of Assessments of the Power of Large Corporations, Trade Unions, and the Federal Government and between These Three Measures and Assessments of the Power of Farmers and Small Business, for 1981

		Evaluation of The Power of:								
		Large Corporations			Trade Unions			Federal Government		
Institution	Evaluation of power	(Much) too much	About right	(Much) too little	(Much) too much	About right	(Much) too little	(Much) too much	About right	(Much) too little
Large corporations	(Much) too much				79.8	62.3	61.5	82.7	69.0	69.0
	About right				19.2	36.1	27.6	16.3	28.9	27.6
	(Much) too little				1.0	1.6	10.9	1.0	2.2	3.3
	Total				100.0	100.0	100.0	100.0	100.0	100.0
Trade unions	(Much) too much	76.8	59.3	40.6				74.4	70.2	62.2
	About right	17.5	32.4	17.9				19.3	23.4	23.4
	(Much) too little	5.7	8.3	41.4				6.3	6.5	14.4
	Total	100.0	100.0	100.0				100.0	100.0	100.0
Federal government	(Much) too much	47.2	29.7	24.7	44.0	37.6	37.6			
	About right	45.2	60.5	60.0	48.7	53.4	45.3			
	(Much) too little	7.6	9.8	15.4	7.3	9.0	17.1			
	Total	100.0	100.0	100.0	100.0	100.0	100.0			

Table 4-4

Cross Tabulations of Assessments of the Power of Large Corporations, Trade Unions, and the Federal Government and between These Three Measures and Assessments of the Power of Farmers and Small Business, for 1981 (Continued)

| | | Evaluation of The Power of: | | | | | | | | |
| | | Large Corporations | | | Trade Unions | | | Federal Government | | |
Institution	Evaluation of power	(Much) too much	About right	(Much) too little	(Much) too much	About right	(Much) too little	(Much) too much	About right	(Much) too little
Farmers	(Much) too much	4.3	3.7	4.8	3.4	5.9	6.7	5.1	2.9	6.1
	About right	26.4	40.3	21.0	28.6	34.2	25.5	23.9	33.2	35.5
	(Much) too little	69.3	56.1	74.1	68.0	59.9	67.8	71.0	63.9	58.4
	Total	100.0	100.0	100.0	100.0	100.0	100.0	100.0	100.0	100.0
Small business	(Much) too much	2.7	1.2	2.9	2.1	2.6	4.5	3.5	1.7	1.2
	About right	26.4	41.6	20.4	26.0	44.6	26.2	22.8	36.3	34.2
	(Much) too little	70.8	57.2	76.7	71.9	52.8	69.2	73.8	62.0	64.6
	Total	100.0	100.0	100.0	100.0	100.0	100.0	100.0	100.0	100.0

A more extensive analysis of the ratings of all the institutions, as measured in the 1977 survey, reveals correlations of +.23 between the ratings of the power of large corporations and trade unions, and +.19 and +.09 between the ratings of the federal government and the corporations and unions, respectively (these correlations are based on scoring the five responses, ranging from much too much to much too little power, from 1 to 5). These findings are consistent with the 1981 data in table 4-4, and underline the weakness of the associations between the ratings of the various institutions. The correlation between ratings of the power of small business and the farmers is +.27, and those between small business and, respectively, large corporations and labour unions are −.09 and −.12 (the correlations between the ratings of the three levels of government, of course, have no bearing on the previous finding that there is a relatively widespread perception that the federal government, although not the provincial or local governments, is too powerful). The relationships between the ratings of newspapers and the legal profession suggest that they tend to be lumped in with the big institutions in popular evaluations of the distribution of power.

There is a widespread public perception that the powers of capital and labour are comparable. In addition to suggesting the petty bourgeois character of popular ideology, such a perception indicates the weakness of the Canadian trade union movement. Popular support for the postwar settlement is not grounded in terms of a perceived need for a changed balance between the powers of labour and capital. Rather it reflects a commitment to a limited form of social justice, through ameliorative state efforts to assist the "unfortunate," and to provide social goods and services. This reflects the relative weakness of the trade union movement in Canada, compared to other advanced capitalist nations, the U.S. and Japan excepted. Of course in contemporary Canada capital enjoys enormous advantages over labour, not only in terms of control over investment decisions and the work process, but also in terms of access to the state (especially at the federal level) and the ability to obtain state action favourable to its purposes. That most Canadians perceive capital and labour as equally too powerful does not alter the fact that a neutral stance in conflicts between capital and labour strongly favours the corporate sector.

The political weakness of the labour movement and the dilemmas it faces in achieving political power are apparent in these results. Also apparent is the ideological basis of the Liberal party's almost unbroken period of postwar rule and its success in holding off social democracy in the late 1960s and early 1970s. The Liberal party's support for social programs and its apparent neutrality in maintaining a status quo between capital and labour more successfully mirrors the ideological mindset of our respondents than the New Democratic Party's combination of support for social programs and identification with labour.

The responses to four additional statements about labour relations, in table 4-5, somewhat qualify this picture of how Canadians choose between the conflicting interests of labour and capital. In 1977 more than 90 percent of Canadians believed that "workers should have the right to refuse to work in conditions which they consider to be unsafe, until a government inspector assures them that conditions are safe." There is also strong endorsement for workers gaining seats on the boards of directors at their place of work: in 1981 more than two-thirds of the population approved of this measure, and only 14 percent were opposed. A majority also supported some protection of the right to strike, although there was very limited approval of extending such rights to all workers. In 1981, 53 percent of the population supported a ban on employers hiring strikebreakers, compared to 30 percent opposing a ban; the remainder had no opinion. With a similar question, Wallace Clement and John Myles (1994, 197) report 60 percent support for prohibiting strikebreakers in Canada, and 49, 51, and 82 percent support in the U.S., Norway, and Sweden, respectively. Fifty-six percent of the population, however, *opposed* teachers having the right to strike in 1977, compared to 24 percent opposed and 20 percent with no position (taking respondents with an opinion only, more than two-thirds opposed teachers' right to strike).

Though opposition to teachers' strikes was somewhat lower in the two later surveys, this finding significantly qualifies any conclusion of public support for the powers of labour and trade unions. Still, these responses to other questions suggest some modification of our initial evidence of the widespread belief that trade unions have too much power. If we examine public opinion in the context of the encroachments on the powers of trade unions discussed in chapter 1, Canadians generally take positions to the left of their governments. There was broad support in the 1970s and early 1980s for changes to labour legislation that would significantly improve the position of trade unions. For example the passage of anti-strikebreaking legislation (which at the time, and for the next decade, was law only in Quebec) would certainly shift the balance of power towards labour, especially in attempting to gain initial contracts and in disputes involving smaller companies or where the majority of workers are poorly paid, female, or unable to speak English or French. And, even if trade union leaders are ambivalent on the question, public support for the addition of employee representatives to corporate boards is clearly viewed as an invasion of management prerogatives by most Canadian corporate executives.

These findings have implications for what political tactics are most likely to be effective in attempts by the labour movement to effect change in the face of a generalized belief that its powers are too great, but with an accompanying sympathy over specific issues, such as legislation to prevent strikebreaking. The interest of business and political forces hostile to the labour movement lies in confining public debate to the rhetorical level at which it is

Table 4-5
Responses to Statements Concerning Labour Relations

Statement	Year	Agree	Strongly agree	Disagree	Neither agree nor disagree	Strongly disagree	Depends	Do not know	Total
				Percentage Distribution of Responses					
Workers should have the right to refuse to work in conditions that they consider to be unsafe, until a government inspector assures them that conditions are safe	1977	40.7	53.3	2.5	1.7	.2	.6	1.0	100.0
Teachers should not have the right to strike	1977	15.0	41.5	15.0	20.5	3.4	2.0	2.6	100.0
	1979	12.6	38.2	11.0	30.0	3.1	1.4	3.7	100.0
	1981	13.5	37.9	12.5	29.5	2.8	1.2	2.7	100.1
During a strike, management should be prohibited by law from hiring workers to take the place of strikers	1977	16.2	36.9	11.6	22.8	5.0	3.6	3.8	99.9
	1979	11.6	37.9	9.7	27.5	4.3	3.8	5.2	100.0
	1981	12.1	41.0	10.7	26.2	3.5	2.0	4.5	100.0
Workers should have positions on the board of directors of the organization for which they work	1977	10.8	54.2	12.6	11.0	3.3	2.8	5.3	100.0
	1979	9.7	59.0	8.7	12.7	1.5	2.2	6.2	100.0
	1981	8.4	59.4	10.8	12.6	1.6	1.3	5.8	99.9

possible to capitalize on public fears of "big labour." To the extent that the labour movement can refocus debate on specific issues, it is much more likely to attract public sympathy. It is also apparent that the widespread unionization of government workers had not, as yet, been accompanied by a public willingness to accord them the basic rights granted to private sector workers. Especially in light of the past decade's dramatic increase in the proportion of union members who are state employees, efforts to change public perceptions in this area will be critical to the ability of the labour movement to make some political progress.

These data reveal the mixture of dominant and subordinate values also found in the British studies of working-class consciousness. Because there are large majorities critical of the power of trade unions and supportive of particular measures affecting unions, as well as redistribution and social programs, a significant proportion of the population must have both dominant *and* subordinate values (a point taken up below in our analysis of the correlations among political attitudes). The particular combination of attitudes towards the distribution of power suggests that these apparently contradictory views may be understood as aspects of a consistent, petty bourgeois ideological perspective. While Gordon Marshall (1983) insists that only an ethnographic perspective can untangle the detailed structure of popular ideology, these results suggest lines of further investigation that are amenable to conventional survey approaches. Such investigation must clearly probe deeper into the ambiguities of attitudes towards the distribution of power in society.

Finally, we need to put these findings in the context of our triangular model of the relations between capital, labour, and the state. Commitments to the welfare aspects of the welfare state are unaccompanied by what we think of as parallel commitments to the rights of labour, relative to the power of capital. Support for no more than the status quo in labour-management relations in the private sector is accompanied by antipathy to public sector workers. More important however, given a free choice, citizens would rather diminish the powers of both capital and labour than change the balance between them.

RIGHTS ISSUES

Our conception of "rights issues" encompasses economic issues as well as the traditional concern for civil liberties. In terms of our triangle of relationships, civil liberties involve the state's relationship to both labour and capital, not simply the rules governing the rights and freedoms of unclassed individuals. We expand our concern in another way, as well, to community rights, particularly those of aboriginal peoples, immigrants, and the French and English communities in Canada.

For each of the issues listed in table 4-6 respondents were simply asked whether or not they supported each measure and the interviewer then coded

Table 4-6
Support for Civil Liberties Issues for the Canadian Population in 1981

Civil Liberties Issue	Percentage Distribution of Responses					
	No	No, with qualifi- cation	Yes, with qualifi- cation	Yes	No opinion	Total
Legislation to protect the rights of the disabled	1.4	1.6	10.2	82.5	4.3	100.0
The right of women to equal pay for work of equal value	2.2	1.4	6.6	87.9	2.0	100.1
Protection of homosexuals from discrimination in employment	26.2	5.8	16.6	39.2	12.2	100.0
Programs to favour the hiring and promotion of women and other minorities to make up for their lack of opportunities in the past	22.1	5.8	13.8	48.4	10.0	100.1
Granting native peoples lim- ited rights of self-government	25.4	5.4	16.2	39.8	13.2	100.0
Elimination of existing boards of censors	42.2	8.6	9.5	26.1	13.5	99.9
Abolition of the War Measures Act	42.5	7.3	6.8	24.4	19.0	100.0
Civilian review of complaints against the police	20.1	4.0	13.9	51.6	10.4	100.0

the responses into five categories: yes, no, yes with qualification, no with qualification, and no opinion. The respondent was not explicitly presented with the option of giving qualified approval to a measure, but was recorded as qualified when she or he spontaneously expressed some reservation, when approving or disapproving of a measure.

Considerably predating the federal and provincial legislation and regulation of the mid 1980s, there was virtually unanimous public support, more than 90 percent approval, for legislation to protect the rights of the disabled and the right of women to equal pay for work of equal value. The implementation of equal-pay legislation in the years subsequent to the survey is testimony to the extent that public opinion led, and perhaps encouraged, policy making in this area, despite strong business opposition. None of the remaining six measures received the very strong support accorded the rights of the disabled and equal pay. Not only was the public divided on these issues, but the proportion of "no opinion" responses was at least 10 percent in every case, suggesting considerable public uncertainty. Still, the responses to the remaining questions indicate a very liberal climate of opinion. For example protection of homosexuals from discrimination in employment was endorsed by 39 percent of the population and endorsed with qualification by another 17 percent, compared to 26 percent opposed and 6 percent opposed with qualification, and 12 percent with no opinion. In light of these responses the failure of the effort to include sexual preference among the protections offered by the federal Charter of Rights suggests that political elites are to the right of their constituents. Also in light of relatively little governmental action at the time, it is surprising that 48 percent of the population supported and another 14 percent supported with qualification the institution of "programmes to favour the hiring and promotion of women and other minorities to make up for their lack of opportunities in the past" – our effort at a non-technical description of affirmative action. About 30 percent of the population opposed the measure and another 10 percent had no opinion. Support for granting native peoples limited rights of self government was only very slightly weaker than support for affirmative action.

Responses to the last two items on censorship and police powers are much less clear-cut. A slim majority (51 percent) of the population *opposed* the elimination of censorship, compared to 36 percent favouring it and 14 percent with no opinion. This may explain the willingness of the Ontario government to fight an extended public relations and legal battle to preserve its censor board in the early 1980s. In light of the increasing concern about violence against women and children, which became manifest in the years just after our surveys, these results should not be understood simply as an "illiberal" response to the expansion of civil liberties. Still, they do reflect a tolerance of state intervention in civil society.

Similarly, concerning the War Measures Act, used to justify military intervention in Quebec in 1970, the *opponents* of abolition outnumbered its supporters nearly two to one. The salience of this issue was very low, however, as indicated by the nearly 20 percent of respondents without an opinion. Furthermore the evidence from these responses to questions of censorship and police powers is qualified by responses to a question concerning civilian review of complaints against the police. Fully 52 percent of the population supported civilian review of complaints and an additional 14 percent gave qualified support, compared to 20 percent opposing it, 4 percent opposing it with qualification, and 10 percent with no opinion. Such a measure has met bitter opposition from the police and most politicians across Canada, despite persistent accusations against the police in a number of major metropolitan areas, including Halifax, Montreal, Toronto, and Vancouver.

An obviously important aspect of civil liberties, especially in Canada, is the way that society deals with cultural diversity. The responses to a series of statements about immigrants to Canada and about language policy, in table 4-7, suggest widespread public ambivalence on such questions. On the one hand, there is overwhelming agreement with the statement that "The hard work of immigrants has done a lot to help this country" and disagreement with the statement that "Immigrants to this country aren't prepared to work as hard as people born in Canada." On the other hand, almost equal agreement is found for the statements that "People who come to live in Canada should try harder to be more like other Canadians" and that "Immigrants often bring discrimination on themselves by their own personal habits and attitudes." The notion that the failure of the police and courts to take a strong stand encourages discrimination is greeted with some bafflement: there are about equal levels of agreement and disagreement, but 12 percent of respondents have no opinion and another 21 percent say they neither agree nor disagree with the statement. Widespread public recognition of the role of immigrants in Canadian development is coupled with the ethnocentric belief that immigrants should assimilate culturally and are to blame for bringing discrimination on themselves.

It is impossible to think about civil rights in Canada without dealing with the status of French and English, although, as Paul Sniderman et. al. (1989) point out, linguistic issues involve the claims of communities as well as those of individuals. On these issues, the *average* opinions of Canadians are not very meaningful, because the potentially conflicting interests of Québécois and English Canadians and of anglophones and francophones are such that averages will not necessarily reflect the opinions of anyone. Table 4-8, therefore, distinguishes the four categories of respondents defined by the intersection of location and ethnicity. More extensive coverage was given linguistic issues in the 1977 survey, so this discussion focuses on the seven items included in that questionnaire. Three items were included in all three surveys and those results are also included in the table.

Five of the seven items deal with the availability of schooling and government services in the two official languages. First, we asked whether French-speaking Canadians outside of Quebec should be able to find schooling for their children in French. Agreeing or strongly agreeing to this proposition, in 1977, were 47 percent of people in English Canada who were not French, 82 percent of non-French Québécois, 86 percent of French people outside Quebec, and 90 percent of French Québécois. Compared to other items in the survey, large proportions (just over 20 percent of non-French outside Quebec!) gave ambiguous or neutral responses. Not surprisingly the distribution of responses to a question about French language services, termed the right of French speakers outside Quebec to be "able to communicate with their provincial government in French," is almost identical to those just described.

Table 4-7
Responses to Statements about Immigrants

Statement	Year	Percentage Distribution of Responses							
		Strongly agree	Agree	Neither agree nor disagree	Disagree	Strongly disagree	Depends	Do not know	Total
People who come to live in Canada should try harder to be more like other Canadians	1977	17.7	48.5	14.3	14.7	1.3	1.0	2.3	99.8
	1979	16.4	51.3	12.0	14.8	2.1	.9	2.5	100.0
	1981	17.4	48.8	13.3	16.6	1.7	.5	1.8	100.1
Immigrants are often discriminated against because the police and the courts are not prepared to take a strong stand against discrimination	1977	3.4	31.6	20.5	27.5	3.3	2.0	11.8	100.1
Immigrants to this country aren't prepared to work as hard as people born in Canada	1977	2.7	10.2	9.5	54.5	18.0	1.7	3.4	100.0
	1979	1.7	8.3	7.3	53.0	25.0	1.3	3.4	100.0
	1981	2.4	8.2	9.1	54.2	21.7	1.0	3.3	100.0
The hard work of immigrants has done a lot to help this country	1977	17.5	54.9	12.2	7.9	1.7	1.2	4.6	100.0
	1979	17.5	56.8	10.9	7.5	1.8	1.0	4.5	100.0
	1981	16.8	56.3	11.9	7.7	1.8	.4	5.1	100.0
Immigrants often bring discrimination on themselves by their own personal habits and attitudes	1977	9.5	54.4	15.0	11.5	1.7	2.2	5.7	100.0
	1979	9.0	52.8	13.9	13.6	1.8	2.1	6.7	99.9
	1981	9.0	52.0	14.8	15.6	1.9	1.0	5.6	99.9

Table 4-8

Responses to Statements Concerning Linguistic Rights, by Ethnicity, by Region, for 1977, 1979, and 1981

Item	Year/language	Location	Percentage Distribution of Responses								Number of cases
			Strongly agree	Agree	Neither agree nor disagree	Disagree	Strongly disagree	Depends	No opinion	Total	
French-speaking Canadians outside of Quebec should be able to find schooling for their children in French	**1977**										
	non-French	English Canada	4.0	43.3	10.3	29.6	6.4	2.5	3.7	100.0	2094
		Quebec	24.6	57.5	3.4	10.2	1.7	1.8	.7	100.0	212
	French	English Canada	32.1	54.3	3.3	4.9	3.5	1.6	.3	100.0	180
		Quebec	40.8	49.2	5.2	3.0	.6	.9	.4	100.0	690
	1979										
	non-French	English Canada	4.5	44.5	12.4	27.2	5.3	1.7	4.0	100.0	1951
		Quebec	31.3	54.4	4.4	4.2	1.3	2.5	1.9	100.0	220
	French	English Canada	22.5	55.8	6.3	7.9	.9	2.2	3.6	100.0	204
		Quebec	44.4	44.8	4.5	3.3	.7	.3	2.0	100.0	574
	1981										
	non-French	English Canada	4.2	46.1	11.5	28.5	3.8	1.7	4.1	100.0	1894
		Quebec	15.9	57.5	7.1	13.3	1.8	.8	3.6	100.0	186
	French	English Canada	34.3	51.7	4.9	4.6	1.2	2.1	1.2	100.0	149
		Quebec	40.1	46.5	4.8	4.9	.4	1.5	1.8	100.0	594

Table 4-8
Responses to Statements Concerning Linguistic Rights, by Ethnicity, by Region, for 1977, 1979, and 1981 (Continued)

Item	Year/ language	Location	Percentage Distribution of Responses								Number of cases
			Strongly agree	Agree	Neither agree nor disagree	Disagree	Strongly disagree	Depends	No opinion	Total	
French-speaking Canadians outside of Quebec should be able to communicate with their provincial government in French	1977										
	non-French	English Canada	2.8	41.6	9.7	34.0	6.1	1.2	4.4	100.0	2095
		Quebec	17.9	56.9	5.3	15.1	.4	1.5	2.9	100.0	212
	French	English Canada	22.2	61.1	6.1	7.8	3.4	2.5	.0	100.0	180
		Quebec	36.4	51.5	6.9	3.4	.8	.6	.5	100.0	690
English-speaking people who move to Quebec should be able to find schooling for their children in English	1977										
	non-French	English Canada	18.1	64.2	5.0	8.4	.6	1.7	2.1	100.0	2095
		Quebec	24.6	66.7	2.3	4.8	.8	.8	.0	100.0	212
	French	English Canada	39.4	53.4	2.5	2.7	.4	.9	.7	100.0	180
		Quebec	23.3	52.0	8.8	11.6	2.2	1.9	.2	100.0	690
	1979										
	non-French	English Canada	14.6	66.8	5.7	7.5	.9	1.1	3.3	100.0	1943
		Quebec	23.3	45.0	5.1	18.7	3.7	2.7	1.5	100.0	220
	French	English Canada	23.6	62.6	4.5	2.9	1.5	2.2	2.8	100.0	202
		Quebec	21.2	38.6	10.4	17.6	8.8	.9	2.5	100.0	574

Table 4-8
Responses to Statements Concerning Linguistic Rights, by Ethnicity, by Region, for 1977, 1979, and 1981 (Continued)

Item	Year/language	Location	Percentage Distribution of Responses								Number of cases
			Strongly agree	Agree	Neither agree nor disagree	Disagree	Strongly disagree	Depends	No opinion	Total	
	1981										
	non-French	English Canada	12.5	66.5	6.1	10.1	.5	1.3	3.1	100.0	1897
		Quebec	11.1	73.9	4.9	6.5	1.8	.0	1.9	100.0	186
	French	English Canada	20.1	46.2	11.4	13.5	4.6	2.7	1.4	100.0	149
		Quebec	14.8	42.1	12.4	19.9	7.1	1.0	2.7	100.0	594
	1977										
People who do not	non-French	English Canada	13.8	64.4	6.3	10.2	.7	.7	3.8	100.0	2094
speak English and		Quebec	15.9	62.7	6.1	10.4	1.6	.2	3.1	100.0	212
move to Quebec	French	English Canada	23.1	41.9	7.8	17.2	4.8	3.9	1.3	100.0	180
should be able to find		Quebec	7.5	29.7	11.2	30.3	17.1	2.9	1.3	100.0	689
schooling for their											
children in English											

Table 4-8
Responses to Statements Concerning Linguistic Rights, by Ethnicity, by Region, for 1977, 1979, and 1981 (Continued)

Item	Year/language	Location	Percentage Distribution of Responses								Number of cases
			Strongly agree	Agree	Neither agree nor disagree	Disagree	Strongly disagree	Depends	No opinion	Total	
	1977										
English-speaking people in Quebec should be able to communicate with the government of Quebec in English	non-French	English Canada	15.1	74.3	2.4	4.4	.3	.5	3.1	100.0	2094
		Quebec	18.2	69.8	4.4	6.4	.0	.2	1.0	100.0	212
	French	English Canada	34.7	52.5	3.3	5.5	1.3	2.1	.5	100.0	180
		Quebec	16.8	58.4	8.1	12.0	3.1	.8	.9	100.0	688
	1977										
French should be the language of work in all medium- and large-size businesses in Quebec	non-French	English Canada	1.2	18.1	13.9	47.9	10.3	2.1	6.6	100.0	2093
		Quebec	3.2	29.5	14.1	42.3	6.6	2.8	1.5	100.0	210
	French	English Canada	13.3	25.1	15.0	30.6	9.7	3.4	2.9	100.0	180
		Quebec	38.0	39.4	14.4	5.4	.8	1.5	.5	100.0	686
	1979										
	non-French	English Canada	.8	20.3	13.4	49.6	8.4	1.6	5.7	100.0	1943
		Quebec	21.2	37.8	13.4	14.5	9.8	2.0	1.1	100.0	220
	French	English Canada	5.2	22.8	21.8	35.1	7.0	2.8	5.2	100.0	203
		Quebec	40.1	40.1	10.3	6.5	1.1	.4	1.5	100.0	574

Table 4-8
Responses to Statements Concerning Linguistic Rights, by Ethnicity, by Region, for 1977, 1979, and 1981 (Continued)

Item	Year/language	Location	Percentage Distribution of Responses								Number of cases
			Strongly agree	Agree	Neither agree nor disagree	Disagree	Strongly disagree	Depends	No opinion	Total	
	1981										
	non-French	English Canada	.8	19.3	15.2	49.7	7.4	1.1	6.4	100.0	1898
		Quebec	3.7	29.3	15.1	43.3	2.5	1.7	4.3	100.0	186
	French	English Canada	22.6	30.9	15.2	20.5	8.3	.4	2.1	100.0	149
		Quebec	43.2	40.6	9.5	4.6	.8	.1	1.2	100.0	594
	1977										
The federal government in Ottawa is right to require that many senior government jobs be filled by people who speak both French and English	non-French	English Canada	7.7	59.3	6.1	17.0	4.7	1.7	3.5	100.0	2095
		Quebec	19.4	64.8	3.9	8.7	0.0	1.8	1.4	100.0	212
	French	English Canada	36.9	54.5	2.4	4.3	.3	1.0	.7	100.0	180
		Quebec	36.2	52.2	4.8	4.8	1.1	.3	.6	100.0	690

The next questions dealt with the corresponding rights of English speakers in Quebec to schooling and government services in that language. Strikingly, 82 percent of the respondents in English Canada who were not of French ethnicity agreed or strongly agreed that English-speaking Canadians who move to Quebec should be able to find schooling for their children in English. Support for this proposition was exceptionally strong among non-French Québécois and French people in English Canada, with 91 and 93 percent, respectively, supporting it. Furthermore 75 percent of French Québécois were also in favour. Again, support for the right to communicate in English with the Quebec provincial government was nearly identical.

This pattern of responses is amplified in evaluations of the statement that "People who do *not* speak English and move to Quebec should be able to find schooling for their children in English." Seventy-eight percent of non-French respondents in English Canada and in Quebec agreed or strongly agreed, as did 65 percent of French people in English Canada. But only 37 percent of French Québécois supported this proposition. The responses most clearly showed the gap between the English-Canadian views of language in terms of individual civil rights and French Canadians' conceptions of their rights as a community.

Public opinion on linguistic issues, it is apparent, *cannot* be understood simply in the context of individuals' positions on a continuum of tolerance or support for civil rights. The intellectual framework in which tolerance is normally understood as arising from the civilizing influences of education and participation (however peripheral) in the democratic process cannot account for the enormous differences in the opinions between the ethnic majorities in Quebec and English Canada. The differences in educational attainment, social class composition, and income of the four national/linguistic groups are far too small to explain their ideological difference here.

Conflicting national interests in matters of language policy are clearest where economic and cultural interests intersect. Asked whether French should be the language of work in all medium- and large-size businesses in Quebec, only 19 percent of English Canadians not of French descent agreed or strongly agreed, 58 percent disagreed, and 23 percent neither agreed nor disagreed, or had no definite opinion. In startling comparison, 77 percent of French Québécois agreed or strongly agreed with the proposition. In between, but closer to the position of the English-Canadian majority, with about 35 percent support, are the ethnic minorities in Quebec and English-Canada.

In contrast, differences in support for official bilingualism are relatively minor, suggesting the effectiveness of justifications in which the equal political rights of Canadian citizens outweighs the importance of restrictions on employment and mobility associated with the policy. Respondents were asked if they agreed with the statement "The federal government in Ottawa is right to require that many senior government jobs be filled by people who speak French and English." In 1977 fully 67 percent of English Canadians who were not French supported this proposition, compared to 22 percent opposed and 13 percent with a neutral or no opinion. Support for this proposition from the other three groups was overwhelming.

Differences in attitudes towards the language of government and schooling and the language of work are suggestive of the complicated relationship between civil rights and liberties and the requirements of a market economy. Setting linguistic issues in the context of capital's freedom to define its own conditions of production and in the context of equality of employment opportunity helps make intelligible the ambivalence of English-Canadian attitudes towards French. Support for bilingual government services and for schooling in the language of choice is not extended to support for linguistic rights in the workplace. Similarly attitudes towards immigrants reveal a public ambivalence that turns on the centrality and "freedom" of the economy. Immigrants' economic contributions gain an acknowledgement and respect not granted their cultural autonomy. The hegemonic consensus in popular ideology on these as on other questions is based more on our approval of the requirements of the free market than on the liberties of free citizens and the rights of autonomous communities.

POLITICAL CULTURE

We now examine Canadians' attitudes towards politics and government, including measures of political efficacy, participation, attitudes on federal-provincial conflicts, and support for different forms of political protest. These attitudes, which are central to the orthodox study of political participation and "civic culture" in liberal democracies, are the subject of extensive previous research. They have been measured in the federal election studies conducted by John Meisel (1973) and by Harold Clarke and his colleagues (1979, 1984). Richard Johnston (1986) has also presented a detailed analysis of commercial public opinion surveys of support for governments and political leadership. The central aspect of political culture, in the theoretical approach built around it, is the relationship between the "public" and the state. The public is commonly differentiated, often in terms of education and sophistication, but not in terms of class; educated people, for example, are commonly seen to have an advantage that, implicitly, is what they deserve for their better understanding of society and their responsibilities. Thus the separate relations between the state and labour and between the state and capital are subsumed into one and advantage is tied to status but not class. While, obviously, we do not subscribe to this theoretical view, the concepts and measures developed in the context of "political culture" seem to us to identify important aspects of politics, ideology, hegemony, and class relations.

At a number of points in our analysis we point to contrasts between public opinion and public policy and the implications of such contrasts for problems of hegemony and the decline of consensual support for government. It is necessary, however, to distinguish support for particular governments from support for the *system* of government, and to bear in mind the more complex arguments that lie behind combinations of positive and negative opinions. The obvious question is whether the divergence between public opinion and public policy is reflected in negative judgements of politics and government, and to what extent such judgements pose problems for the hegemonic stability of the liberal democratic state.

Table 4-9 provides evidence of widespread cynicism about government. In each year of our surveys, more than 70 percent of the population agreed or strongly agreed that "Generally, those elected to Parliament soon lose touch with the people;" about 65 percent agreed or strongly agreed that "Sometimes politics and government seem so complicated that a person like me can't really understand what's going on"; and 60 percent agreed or strongly agreed that "I don't think the government cares what people like me think." There was also majority agreement with the statement "People like me don't have any say about what the government does." Even if the wording of these items encourages respondents to agree, these responses indicate a strong alienation from government.

There is no apparent trend in the responses to these questions between 1977 and 1981. Such slight changes as occur are in different directions, and cannot support the conclusion that there was a crisis of support. Political alienation was palpable, but not exacerbated during this period. Over a longer time span, however, there has been a more clear-cut increase in the alienated response to these questions. The averages for the positive responses in table 4-9 are about 20 percent *higher* than those obtained by Clarke et al. (1979, 32) in their 1974 election survey, and these were higher than those obtained by Meisel in the 1965 and 1968 election surveys.

Although the difficulties of the late Trudeau regime were not therefore related to any dramatic changes in the extent of public support for the regime in its last years, and although the increased attacks on the role of government by big business in these years were not on this evidence prompted by a swing in public opinion, the climate of public support for the regime clearly deteriorated over the longer run and was not helpful to government's capacity to re-establish a hegemonic order in the face of serious economic difficulties. Still, one must be careful in the interpretation of these data. Alienated responses may be quite rational confessions of individuals' very limited ability to affect the highly complex process of public policy formation in modern government, rather than a more fundamental critique of the system of government. Further, they may reflect a temporary fluctuation in alienation from a particular government (in this case the government of Trudeau) rather than

Table 4-9
Responses to Statements about Political Efficacy

Statement	Year	Strongly agree	Agree	Disagree	Strongly disagree	No opinion	Total
							Percentage Distribution of Responses
Generally, those elected to	1977	15.3	56.2	20.9	2.7	4.9	100.0
Parliament soon lose touch	1979	14.5	53.7	24.6	2.3	4.8	99.9
with the people	1981	15.5	56.6	23.2	1.2	3.5	100.0
I don't think the government	1977	13.0	45.5	34.5	3.6	3.4	100.0
cares much what people like	1979	11.9	48.2	32.4	3.5	3.9	99.9
me think	1981	14.4	48.1	32.8	2.1	2.6	100.0
Sometimes politics and	1977	16.9	49.0	25.5	6.2	2.4	100.0
government seem so compli-	1979	16.8	51.5	24.4	5.5	1.8	100.0
cated that a person like me	1981	19.0	45.9	28.9	5.0	1.3	100.1
can't really understand what's going on							
People like me don't have	1977	12.2	39.9	36.6	8.0	3.3	100.0
any say about what the	1979	13.3	41.3	35.3	7.2	3.0	100.1
government does	1981	15.1	38.7	38.6	6.0	1.6	100.0

from the system of government. We can disentangle these alternatives to some extent by looking at attitudes towards participation in the political system and at more explicit questions of satisfaction with government.

Table 4-10 shows how often Canadians engaged in a number of different forms of political participation over the previous five years, though these estimates are subject to a positive "social desirability" bias and should be taken as *upper* bounds. Sample surveys are known, for example, to overestimate the proportion of people voting (as measured exactly by the number voting). So there is likely a tendency for respondents to exaggerate their levels of political participation, although this bias is to some extent countered by a tendency for people to forget about instances of participation. The highest levels of participation were recorded for three forms of participation: having "worked with others in your community to try to solve some community problems"; having "signed a petition directed to some government agency"; and having "spoken or written to an elected representative of yours." About one-third of the population reported having participated in each of these activities at least once in the previous five years. For two other forms of participation, having "been a volunteer worker during a political campaign" and having "attended a protest meeting or demonstration supporting something you believed in," the incidence of participation was only about half as great.

Table 4-10
Involvement in Politics for the Canadian Population

			Frequency of Involvement (percentage distribution of responses)				
	Year	Never	Once or twice	3 to 5 times	6 or more times	Do not know	Total
Been a volunteer worker during	1977	84.8	11.7	3.2	.3	.0	100.0
a political campaign	1979	84.5	10.9	2.6	2.0	.1	100.1
	1981	84.1	10.4	3.6	1.7	.2	100.0
Worked with others in your	1977	69.0	20.9	9.9	.2	.0	100.0
community to try to solve some	1979	64.8	19.6	5.7	9.7	.3	100.1
community problems	1981	67.5	18.3	6.3	7.6	.3	100.0
Spoken or written to an elected	1977	68.9	22.8	8.1	.2	.0	100.0
representative of yours	1979	69.4	19.5	4.9	6.0	.2	100.0
	1981	68.8	20.2	5.5	5.3	.2	100.0
Signed a petition directed to	1979	62.9	28.8	5.6	2.4	.3	100.0
some government agency	1981	58.9	31.8	6.5	2.2	.6	100.0
Attended a protest meeting or	1979	81.5	13.5	3.1	1.6	.2	99.9
demonstration supporting	1981	82.2	12.7	3.0	1.9	.2	100.0
something you believe in							

There is no absolute standard of political participation with which these responses may be compared. If we take the top category, indicating a person participated in the activity six or more times in the past five years, or just over once a year, and assume that working in a political campaign or attending a protest meeting or demonstration indicated a relatively active form of political participation, then only about 2 percent of the adult population can be said to be politically active. Even lowering the standard of active participation to three or more times *in five years* only increases the estimate of the percentage of politically active people to about 5. By any reasonable standard, half the population is completely inactive politically. These ratings reveal a society in which the level of political involvement is low and in which politics, even defined in terms of relatively informal community action, is remote from the lives of most people.

Again although such conclusions run counter to the expectations of a democratic society, this lack of popular political participation does not in itself mean a crisis of legitimacy. Low mass involvement is logically consistent with a deep-seated alienation from the political system and from current governments, with satisfaction with the system but not with the government,

Table 4-11
Justification of "Protests which Might Be Used to Get the Government to Change Its Policies"
for the Canadian Population

Form of Protest Activity	Year	How Often Is Tactic Justified? (percentage distribution of responses)				
		Often justified	Sometimes justified	Never justified	Do not know	Total
Strikes	1977	10.0	63.5	23.4	3.0	99.9
	1979	8.6	68.5	18.6	4.2	99.9
	1981	10.0	68.7	17.5	3.8	100.0
Boycotts	1977	13.6	52.7	26.7	7.0	100.0
	1979	14.8	57.5	19.9	7.8	100.0
	1981	13.3	56.2	22.0	8.5	100.0
Legal and peaceful demonstra-	1977	18.7	54.7	22.6	4.0	100.0
tions, like marches, rallies, and	1979	18.5	57.2	19.0	5.4	100.1
picketing	1981	18.8	56.7	19.7	4.7	99.9
Illegal but peaceful demonstra-	1977	6.4	36.9	51.1	5.6	100.0
tions like sit-ins	1979	5.6	38.1	48.9	7.4	100.0
	1981	6.1	36.8	49.6	7.5	100.0
Violent protest demonstrations						
including actions such as fighting	1977	2.0	8.2	87.1	2.7	100.0
with the police and destroying	1979	2.7	6.8	88.0	2.5	100.0
property	1981	2.2	5.4	89.9	2.6	100.1

or with satisfaction with both. One way of more directly assessing the extent
of alienation from the system is by reference to data in table 4-11 on attitudes towards modes of protest against government.

The question dealing with protests begins:

We would like to know how you feel about different kinds of protests which might be
used to get the government to change its policies. What about strikes, do you think
they can often be justified, that they can sometimes be justified, or that strikes are
never justified to change government policy?

Approximately one-fifth of the population would *never* condone protests involving strikes, boycotts, or "legal but peaceful demonstrations" – all perfectly legal means of extra-parliamentary protest; about three-fifths believed
protests of these types are sometimes justified, and the remaining fifth believed that they are often justified. About one-half of the population believed
that non-violent civil disobedience, which we described as "illegal but

peaceful demonstrations like sit-ins," is never justified, about 35 percent believed it is sometimes justified, and only just over five percent believed protest of this sort is often justified. Finally, for nine-tenths of the population "violent protest demonstrations including actions such as fighting with the police and destroying property" were never justified. There is virtually no change in public views about forms of political protest in the period between 1977 and 1981.

Obviously, high levels of political alienation are not for the most part accompanied by beliefs in the legitimacy of militant political protest designed to achieve political change. How, then, is one to account for this lack of rejection of the political system, when, as our earlier evidence suggests, there is deep-seated disaffection with particular governments, and a lack of correspondence between public opinion and public policy? Have we exaggerated these negative evaluations of government, or is the underlying political support for the system rooted in something other than satisfaction with the performance of governments, as the brokerage model suggests? One way to address this question is by asking explicitly about satisfaction with government. Table 4-12 provides such information from a question in which respondents were asked to indicate satisfaction, using an eleven-point scale shown to them on a card, which was labeled "completely dissatisfied" and "completely satisfied" at its two ends. The ratings of the three levels of government were substantially lower than the ratings of the neighbourhoods and cities in which people live, of "life in Canada," and of a variety of personal aspects of personal life including peoples' financial situations, their jobs, their marriages and "your life as a whole."

The percentage of people who were satisfied (which we defined, somewhat arbitrarily, as giving a rating of eight or more on the eleven-point scale) with the federal government decreased from about 30 percent to 26 percent to 23 percent between the 1977 and 1979 and 1981 surveys. In each year satisfaction with the government of the province in which the respondent lived was greater than satisfaction with the federal government. Rather than declining, provincial government satisfaction increased from 32 to 36 percent between 1977 and 1981. The highest level of satisfaction was reserved for local governments. In 1981 just over 41 percent gave the governments of their cities (or towns or counties) ratings of eight or more on the eleven-point scale; only 14 percent gave a rating of four or less; the remaining 44 percent choose one of the middle categories.

Compare Canadians' rating of government with their rating of the places where people live. Canadians overwhelmingly approve of the neighbourhoods in which they live, perhaps because they move out of neighbourhoods they do not like. In each survey more than 40 percent gave their neighbourhoods a score of ten or eleven, another 30 percent or more gave a fairly positive score of eight or nine. Only about 5 percent scored their neighbourhoods

Table 4-12
Ratings, on an Eleven-point Scale from Completely Dissatisfied to Completely Satisfied,
of the Three Levels of Government, Communities, and Aspects of Personal Life

Item	Year	Rating on Eleven-Point Scale (percentage distribution of responses)					
		1–2	3–4	5–7	8–9	10–11	Total
Federal government	1977	8.5	15.3	45.9	23.6	6.7	100.0
	1979	10.3	18.0	45.2	19.1	7.4	100.0
	1981	13.6	17.4	46.3	16.9	5.8	100.0
The government of this province	1977	9.3	14.8	43.5	25.3	7.2	100.1
	1979	8.3	11.1	43.0	27.2	10.5	100.1
	1981	5.7	11.7	46.5	27.0	9.1	100.0
The government of this city (town/county)	1977	6.5	9.6	40.4	30.5	13.1	100.1
	1979	5.8	9.3	39.9	30.5	14.6	100.1
	1981	5.8	8.3	44.3	30.7	10.8	100.1
Life in Canada today	1977	1.0	3.8	25.7	47.2	22.3	100.0
	1979	.8	2.9	24.9	42.8	28.5	99.9
	1981	.8	3.4	28.8	42.5	24.5	100.0
This city (town/county)	1977	2.3	4.3	17.3	34.2	41.9	100.0
	1979	1.7	3.0	16.6	37.6	41.2	100.1
	1981	1.6	2.7	20.8	40.7	34.3	100.1
This neighbourhood	1977	2.0	3.5	18.6	31.6	44.3	100.0
	1979	1.6	3.5	16.6	32.8	45.5	100.0
	1981	1.2	3.2	17.5	37.4	40.7	100.0
Your financial situation	1977	5.9	9.7	31.2	34.2	19.1	100.1
	1979	3.6	7.3	31.4	40.0	17.7	100.0
	1981	4.0	9.2	36.1	35.2	15.5	100.0
Job	1977	2.6	3.7	19.3	43.0	31.3	99.9
	1979	2.1	2.9	21.6	44.5	29.0	100.1
	1981	2.3	3.6	26.9	45.2	22.0	100.0
Your marriage	1977	1.0	2.2	8.9	27.8	60.1	100.0
	1979	2.3	2.6	11.1	31.2	52.8	100.0
	1981	.7	1.7	11.9	33.7	52.1	100.1
Your life as a whole	1977	.8	1.7	17.4	44.9	35.3	100.1
	1979	1.0	2.0	14.2	45.7	37.1	100.0
	1981	.6	2.0	19.1	47.8	30.5	100.0

below five on the eleven-point scale. Ratings of the city, town, or country where the respondent lived were nearly as positive as the ratings of neighbourhoods, and ratings of "life in Canada today" were also overwhelmingly positive: in 1981 less than 5 percent chose a rating below five on the scale, 29 percent chose a middle category, 42.5 percent chose an eight or nine, and 24.5 percent gave a rating of ten or eleven.

A second standard of comparison for the satisfaction ratings of the three levels of government is provided by assessments of a number of domains of personal life. Marriages were given overwhelmingly positive ratings, perhaps because of the tendency for people to leave marriages that they find intolerable. "Your life as a whole" and employment situations were given highly positive ratings and even ratings of their "financial situations" were substantially more positive than ratings of the most favoured, local level of government. Thus the negative views of government manifest in the previously discussed items do not reflect a general scepticism about life.

Overall life satisfaction is fairly strongly correlated (Pearson correlations about .4) with ratings of respondents' reported satisfaction with their jobs, spouses, and financial situation; moderately correlated with ratings of neighbourhoods, cities, and life in this country (around .32); but only weakly correlated with satisfaction with government (.14 for ratings of the federal government, slightly more for the provincial and local governments). Thus dissatisfactions with government have relatively little influence on people's general view of their situation in life. Put the other way, peoples' evaluation of the quality of their individual lives has little to do with their evaluation of government. There is evidence of a statistically significant, although rather small, decline in the perceived quality of life in these years, accompanied by mounting economic difficulties; but these developments have little political effect, if our analysis is correct. The correlational evidence shows that declining support for the federal government in this period was not a consequence of declining satisfaction with the quality of life.

Partly, this may be a consequence of the timing of surveys, which as we have pointed out earlier took place in periods of real, if limited, growth of the Canadian economy, just before or after periods of stagnation or recession. The lack of relationship may, therefore, be a consequence of volatile assessments of the quality of life, moving in synchronization with the economy, and a more resilient evaluation of government that remains low even in periods of improvement as a result of memories of past failures. Partly, the lack of relationship may be due to psychological pressures on individuals to give positive responses to aspects of their lives that they think reflect their own initiative and ability, pressures that do not influence assessments of matters not tied in this way to self-esteem.

The lack of relationship between perceptions of individual and collective (at least at the national level) well-being is so great, however, that it invites different interpretations. One such interpretation, common to orthodox liberal sociology, is that "pocket-book voting" on the basis of one's personal economic situation is less common than voting on the basis of broader assessments of the state of the national economy. Another, not inconsistent necessarily with the former argument, derives from the basic Marxist view that there is a necessary separation of politics and economics in capitalist society. On the basis of the evidence presented here and a more extensive regression analysis of the factors affecting confidence in government and support for political protests (reported in Stevenson and Ornstein 1982), three points summarize our understanding of these issues.

First, we find no sense of a level of political demands in Canadian public opinion that is easily interpreted as an indication of a crisis in the political system. Public opinion is deeply conservative with respect to the justification of political protests, support for existing government policies, and the distribution of political power. This is accompanied, though, by marked dissatisfaction with political regimes, indicated by the dissatisfaction with the federal and provincial governments. Such dissatisfaction focuses primarily upon inadequate performance in economic policy, and is not translated into a more substantial critique of the political system.

Second, we find no evidence that critical responses to government or demands for political change are motivated by subjective perceptions of the quality of life. Those perceptions are in general so positively skewed in Canada that they appear to reinforce a psychological identity with the political system rather than any motivation to political opposition. In any event, we find no statistical evidence that satisfaction with the quality of life inhibits or that dissatisfaction stimulates political responses.

Third, our analysis suggests no reversal of the historic depoliticization of the mass public in capitalist society. The "attentive public" – those participating in political activity and having a sense of political efficacy – remains small in proportion to the total population. The range of political demands is thereby quantitatively and qualitatively restricted – quantitatively, by the low rate of public involvement, and, qualitatively, by the conservative identification with a system that is seen to recognize the worth of those who participate and by the apolitical concentration on the needs of family life and security on the part of that greater number who do not.

CONCLUSIONS

We began this analysis with strong evidence of public commitment to the welfare state, both in terms of support for general welfare expenditures, health care, education, and so on, and in terms of support for particular disadvantaged groups, including the poor, the aged, and women. Further analysis also showed evidence of strongly egalitarian elements in popular ideology, in the form of support for redistribution of income, the rights of minorities, and affirmative action. The high degree of support for the government's providing jobs for the unemployed, for rent control, for prohibiting extra billing, and for affirmative action in hiring clearly break with the belief that markets can be counted on to produce the fairest distribution of goods. There is strong evidence, therefore, of a progressive liberalism, consistent with the basic principles of the postwar settlement, and confirming the general consensus among students of Canadian politics about the character of this country's political culture.

Although we have also described the widespread satisfaction of Canadians with their manifold experience of everyday life in civil society, our results should not be interpreted as support for the theoretical view that a dominant ideology and adherence to a set of common values is the basis for an unproblematic political order in Canada. Not only is the strong support for social programs a "subordinate" value in opposition to the "dominant" value placed on the free market, but major corporate and governmental institutions arouse widespread public opposition and cynicism. It might be objected that our surveys have failed to tap deep underlying beliefs about the legitimacy of private profit, the market system, the opportunity structure, etcetera, and that had we done so we would have found stronger evidence for a dominant ideology. To counter this objection we can cite a variety of studies, carefully reviewed by Abercrombie, Hill, and Turner (1980, chap. 5), which document, as we do, a contradictory mix of dominant and subordinate values. Kluegel et al. (1995, 182) refer to this as "split consciousness," which they describe as a mixture of dominant ideology and "challenging beliefs" that are said to arise from the everyday experience of social inequality. They provide additional empirical evidence from surveys conducted as part of the International Social Justice Project (see Kluegel, Mason, and Wegener 1995).

We have also pointed to the recurrent tendency for trends in public policy in the era we discuss to run counter to majority public opinion. These discrepancies between public policy and public opinion also suggest problems for political order. They cannot be explained by the argument that popular tastes have simply run ahead of, and in the future will prompt, corrective government action. For example the distribution of income has remained remarkably stable since the Second World War. If anything, the 1980s have seen a retreat from efforts towards redistribution, the percentage of families defined as poor because they spend 58.5 percent or more on food, shelter, and clothing rising from 12.2 percent to 14.5 percent between 1980 and 1984, although later falling to 13.1 percent (Cook 1987). Nor can these discrepancies be explained by arguments that the political process is not very precise in translating public opinion into policy – that would explain the presence of differences between public opinion and policy, but not the general tendency for government policies to be to the right of popular opinion. It is more plausible to argue that the public does not take into account the inherent limitations of government, that there are simply not enough resources to meet public demands. But a number of our questions involve the *redistribution* of resources and not their magnitude – for example the distribution of the tax burden – or non-economic issues – for example civil rights protection for homosexuals. A much more reasonable interpretation of these findings, explored further in part three of this book, is that the power of big business, the limitations business places on the state, and the structure of the state itself thwart public opinion.

Mingled with the subordinate values in popular ideology to which we have referred are, however, less progressive beliefs – dominant values in Parkin's terminology, with a strongly individualist rather than collective welfare bias, and with a tendency to favour dominant over subordinate classes. Aid to the poor, as such, receives more support than aid to the unemployed and workers' compensation, despite the fact that unemployment is a major cause of poverty. The availability of social welfare is also widely believed to increase unemployment. Predominantly egalitarian beliefs are also combined with a generally populist orientation to political power. Big business, labour unions, and the federal government are all seen as too powerful, while there is support for increasing the power of two petty bourgeois groups, small business and farmers.

There is, however, an ambiguous quality to opinions on the distribution of power, for there is evidence of widespread support for measures that would strengthen trade unions, even if the trade union movement as a whole is seen to be too powerful. Similarly there is an ambiguous attitude towards the power of the state. While governments are believed to have become too powerful, there is very strong support for the network of government programs that comprise the Canadian version of the welfare state and that have done the most to account for the growth of government. These ambiguities in popular political ideology are further evident in our description of attitudes towards civil liberties. Generally progressive views on civil liberties issues are qualified by a measure of prejudice towards immigrants and minority language rights, and by a tendency to endorse the state's right to censorship and extraordinary police powers.

Such ambiguities clearly qualify the celebration of Canadian political culture as especially progressive, and as the result of a coherent evolution from liberalism to social democracy. The continuing support for elements of the postwar settlement in popular ideology ran counter to the welfare state retrenchments in government policy during the period we discuss. Popular ideology was more progressive in these respects than public policy. On the other hand the reverse can be said with respect to language and immigration policy. The coherence of both popular ideology and public policy, and the fit between them, is simply not what is predicted by a brokerage conception of

Canadian politics. While it may be true that elections involve the major parties in competition for the ideological centre, this competition does not result in public policies that represent majority public opinion. What is required, as John Shiry (1976) suggests, is a model of politics that emphasizes the low salience of public opinion and political culture. Nevertheless in some instances, such as pay equity, public opinion leads policy making and public opinion is not irrelevant to political analysis. Rather, we have to inquire into the failure of the political system to respond effectively to public opinion, and to ask what it implies for the maintenance of political order.

In this connection our analysis shows widespread public alienation from politics, but again a complex mix of oppositional and supportive responses to government and the political system. The lack of feelings of political efficacy, the low rates of political participation, and the pervasive dissatisfaction with the national government among Canadians in this period can be conceived of as additional elements of what Parkin defines as the subordinate value system. On this basis we can contrast the evidence of alienation with the more supportive attitudes towards the political system. Political order can then be seen, with Parkin, as a result of this balance of opposition and allegiance, more generally of a contradictory consciousness made up of "rather confused values and surprisingly conservative biases" (Mann 1970, 436).

An alternative explanation is that the political alienation we have described is a natural response to the numerous differences between public opinion and public policy, but the cynicism and opposition to politics thus engendered do not develop into political protest because of the coercive constraints of life in capitalist society – the constraints of having to make a living in a society of limited opportunity and mobility, of limited sources of information from media and parties dominated by minority financial interests, and of state police and legal restrictions on political activism. In this light Abercrombie, Hill, and Turner's emphasis on the oppositional and radical nature of popular ideology provides a good characterization of our data on Canadian attitudes towards government and the political system.

That we question the dominant ideology thesis is not grounds for discarding the concept of hegemony. Popular ideology in Canada is not simply supportive of a political system that produces the goods because it is either confused or consensual, but it is also not simply oppositional and radical. There is a progressive bias to popular ideology that favours the maintenance and extension of the postwar welfare state. In this respect popular ideology is "conservative" in support of the institutional basis upon which hegemony has been constructed in the past, but it is also deeply cynical and angry about the failures of governments to deliver the goods in periods of economic difficulty like the one we describe. This anger is expressed to some extent in a petty bourgeois antagonism to "big" institutions presumed to control the state, to some extent in privatized withdrawal from a political process over which individuals have no control, into the private life of family and friends, where they do have some control, and to some extent in the ideological artic- ulation of the conflicting interests that divide classes, races, genders, and other social movements.

Only in terms of these social movements can we can speak of genuinely oppositional and radical elements in popular ideology, although progressive commitments to redistributive and civil libertarian principles of the welfare state become oppositional in the context of government's increasing with- drawal from those principles. We have little evidence in this chapter, how- ever, that such opposition was very threatening. Certainly it was not radical, if by radical we mean a commitment to active and even violent protest. Canadian politics in this era, therefore, was a product of strong, but in an his- torical sense residual, attachments to a hegemonic formula previously devel- oped for the institutional accommodation of conflicting interests, a reflection of cynicism and political alienation in the face of failures by government to follow that formula, and the emergence of ideological differences over the defense of the welfare state.

To talk of the emergence of ideological differences is to broach other top- ics. To begin with this begs a prior question about the coherence of popular ideology, that is the extent of ideological constraint in Canadian public opin- ion, which is discussed in appendix B. And it raises questions about the so- cial bases of the political forces articulating different ideological positions. Those questions are discussed in the next two chapters on the relationships between popular ideology, social class, and political parties, and in part three of the book, which deals with the articulation of ideological conflict by elites active in the public policy process.

5 Class, Region, and Ideology in Canada: The Structure of Ideological Divisions

In the last chapter we began to show how the character of popular ideology in Canada can be understood in terms of the language of class and hegemony. We have argued that bourgeois hegemony in modern capitalist societies has been materially rooted in the development of the welfare state, and we have shown that this hegemony is subjectively grounded in the Canadian public's support for civil liberties and social welfare programs. We have also argued that this consensus in public opinion has a fundamentally petty bourgeois character: favouring individual "freedom" from the state, cynical about the representative character of the state, and critical of the power of all large corporate institutions, while nevertheless committed to an extensive welfare state.

The ideological consensus in Canada, as we interpret it, is built upon conceptions of civil liberty that emphasize the mobility and opportunity of individuals in free markets, rather than the rights of groups and communities to equitable conditions of life, and upon conceptions of social welfare that emphasize limited state corrections to market failure or inequity, rather than a major redistribution of power and wealth among social classes. The crucial evidence for these interpretations is the relatively limited support in public opinion for affirmative action, as opposed to civil liberties, programs that legislate against discrimination in employment markets, and the very weak support for measures to increase the powers of labour *vis-à-vis* capital.

These arguments suggest the very firm foundation of Canadian politics in hegemonic commitments to the capitalist welfare state. But, at the same time, we have emphasized the difficulties for the continued reproduction of this hegemony. Most obvious is the difficulty posed by the failure to realize the economic growth necessary for the material reproduction of the welfare state. Insufficient growth creates a gap between the material reality and the subjective expectations of the welfare state, and this can be expected to erode the ideological consensus we describe. By the end of the Trudeau era, this divergence could only be contained by large government deficits, and ideological cleavages undercutting the dominant consensus were apparent in this period when fiscal crisis imperilled the Canadian welfare state. Our analysis of constraint gives evidence that there were reasonably well-defined, ideologically constrained, left-right cleavages in Canadian public opinion, defining different conceptions of the proper direction of state policy.

Our analyses of these tendencies and divisions in Canadian public opinion have suggested the utility of a theoretical perspective that emphasizes the dialectical interplay between the reproduction of hegemony and its dislocation in ideological conflict. But, in order to make our argument more persuasive, we have to establish that the divisions in public opinion described in the last chapter are rooted in social class, rather than being simple differences of opinion about the pace and direction of desirable social change, cutting across the major socio-economic divisions in the social structure, and having as a result no great political significance. Here we confront the two major contrary themes in the liberal, political sociology of Canada. The first states, simply, that there are no politically significant class divisions in Canadian political culture. The second, by way of explaining the first, states that *the* politically salient divisions in Canadian political culture are regional divisions, and that the vertical divisions of region unite horizontally separated social classes, thereby preventing the emergence of class cleavages in the national political community.

In this chapter we will argue that the importance of regionalism in Canadian political culture has been exaggerated, and that there *are* significant class divisions on key questions in popular ideology. The chapter begins with a review of arguments for the regional rather than class cleavages in Canadian political culture. We proceed thereafter to examine the extent of regional differences in responses to measures of ideology derived from our 1981 survey. Following this regional analysis we consider the ideological differences between social classes, using Erik Olin Wright's characterization of the class structure, which was set out in detail in chapter 3. We will also examine ideological differences *within* social classes, focusing on the distinctions between manual and non-manual workers, between workers with some supervisory authority and those with none, and between workers who are paid different amounts. The chapter concludes with a multiple regression analysis designed to show whether regional differences in ideology reflect the differing class compositions of the regions. The regression will also provide estimates of the relative effect on ideological divisions of class, region, and a variety of other variables, including age, gender, education, language, and religion. Using our 1979 survey, Geraldine Pratt (1987) provides an interesting examination of the impact of home ownership on political values.

CLASS, REGIONALISM, AND CANADIAN POLITICAL CULTURE

The near universality of agreement on the importance of regionalism in Canadian political life does not rest upon a corresponding degree of agreement or clarity in theoretical explanations and empirical descriptions of the phenomenon. There are three relatively distinct theoretical approaches to the problem of understanding regionalism in Canada. The first, best characterized as an institutionalist approach, marries the assumptions in liberal political sociology about the lack of organization in public ideology to an understanding of the institutionally specific character of Canadian politics. The second, a "political economy" approach, marries the assumptions of neo-Marxist theories of uneven capitalist development to an understanding of the specific character of dependent development in Canada. For the most part, neither of these approaches touches directly on the question of political culture or ideology, instead assuming that the shape of mass political culture is irrelevant or a foregone conclusion. The third approach, which is best characterized as an evolutionary approach, is a hybrid of institutionalist and political economy arguments. This last approach is the only one specifically developed to examine the character of Canadian political culture, but it has produced only limited empirical evidence in support of the significance of regional political cultures.

The institutionalist approach to regionalism in Canadian politics emphasizes the conflicting interests of governments in the Canadian federal system as the critical determinant of regionalism. This claim rests mainly on the history of federal-provincial conflict, large and persistent provincial differences in federal electoral support, structural differences in the provincial as opposed to federal party systems in the same provinces, and survey data showing Canadians' strong attachments to the places where they live, as well as their stronger attachments to provincial rather than national government (Elkins and Simeon 1980, 20). All of these differences may be implicitly related to differences in the values and interests of individuals living in different regions, but the institutionalist approach tends to argue for the irrelevance of mass culture to the explanation of Canadian regionalism. From this perspective it is elite rather than popular political culture that determines regional cleavages in Canada. There is little need to probe the content of mass political consciousness, since the extent of public competence to judge questions determined in the isolated realm of executive federalism is very limited, and public opinion on such questions is manipulated by the elites to whom members of the public defer (Shiry 1976; Smiley 1976). Regionalism in political culture results, therefore, from regional elite mobilization of public sentiments (sub-national identity, allegiance to sub-national governments, perceptions of deprivation *vis-à-vis* other regions) that favour the entrenching and extension of power in regional institutions directed by those elites. A national political culture reflects the contrasting sentiments mobilized by national elites, and the balance of regionalism and nationalism reflects the intensity of conflict between regional and national institutions (governments, primarily, but other institutions as well).

The major alternatives to such politicist explanations of Canadian regionalism are economist explanations based on versions of staples and dependency theory. These approaches to the problem emphasize uneven economic development as the critical determinant of regionalism. Although they suggest, therefore, a potentially more far-ranging content to regional differences in popular political ideology, and a greater importance of popular reactions to unequal economic conditions, the economistic biases of such approaches have meant that politics and ideology are treated simply as a logical expression of differences in economic well-being and needs, requiring no detailed investigation. Wallace Clement (1978) argues that regional inequality is a product of the coincidence between a corporate hierarchy, which is dominated by the multinationals and national corporations, and a class hierarchy, which is dominated by economic elites who choose to live in the major metropolitan centres. Carl Cuneo (1978) places more emphasis on the origins of regionalism in regional differences in class structure, wage levels, and supplies and types of labour power and on the role of migration between regions. Although the structure of social classes and the disproportionate power of multinational and monopolistic elements of the capitalist class are central to both these perspectives on regionalism, Clement and Cuneo do not attempt to explicate an articulation between these economic forces and local political and ideological structures. Elisabeth Gidengil's (1989) effort to develop a theory linking class, region, and voting (but not ideology more generally) is considered in the next chapter.

Neither of these major theoretical approaches to the explanation of regionalism in Canadian politics leads to a well-developed model of regional ideology. Not surprisingly, therefore, there is a lack of theoretical argument in most accounts of regionalism in Canadian political culture and ideology, which tend to be largely descriptive and untheoretical, although they refer to institutionalist or political economy arguments. For example in an entire volume devoted to regionalism, Mildred Schwartz (1974, 165) ventures no theoretical statement beyond the argument that "if regions differ politically, it is because social, economic, and political conditions specific to them have led to different adaptations of the party system." Surprisingly, Schwartz does not attempt to specify *which* social, economic, and political conditions are responsible for regional differentiation. Roger Gibbins's (1982, 178 ff.)

discussion of the differences among the five major regions is also largely descriptive, although it is tied to the institutional explanation for regionalism as a consequence of federal structure and intergovernmental conflicts of interest, and makes important correctives of the normally vaguely defined boundaries of regions as well as of the assumed scope of regional differences. Ralph Matthews (1983, 84 ff.) argues that dependency theory provides a framework for understanding regional differences in political culture, but he does not address the question of just how dependency theory accounts for the ideological divisions among regions. This omission is significant in light of the apparently different effects of dependency in the party politics of the eastern and the western provinces. Further, the content of regionalism in popular political culture remains heavily tied to identity, as in the institutionalist arguments. Matthews (1983, 17) defines regionalism as "a sense of 'identification' or 'consciousness of kind' which the inhabitants of a particular region feel for that region and/or for their fellow inhabitants of that region." Against Bernard Blishen and Tom Atkinson's (1981) conclusion from our data that the absence of significant differences in measures of personal values demonstrates the absence of significant regional differences in the Canadian value structure, he argues "a similarity in some attitudes and values does not imply a similarity in the intensity of attitudes towards a region or in the nature of regional identity" (Matthews 1983, 26). But differences in regional identity do not imply anything about the shape of common values or ideological cleavages across regions, nor do they imply, as Matthews with so many others assumes, the greater importance of vertical, regional differences, as opposed to horizontal, national consensus or cleavages, to Canadian politics.

These deficiencies in the empirical identification of regional differences in Canadian political culture result primarily from the failure in both the institutionalist and the political economy approaches to develop an adequate account of the social forces shaping popular political consciousness. Because these approaches do not explicitly conceptualize the relationship between class and region, they cannot provide the basis for a coherent theorization or prediction of the relative significance of class and regional cleavages in political ideology, except by assumption or ad hoc empirical evidence. In contrast the evolutionary approach does attempt to theorize regionalism in terms of the changing class structure of societies or communities at different stages of economic development, and the differences in political interests and consciousness that result.

The evolutionary approach was first developed by John Wilson, and later elaborated by Richard Simeon and his colleagues. Beginning with a series of observations about the evolution of party structures, Wilson examined the links between party structures and economic development and divided the provinces into three developmental categories. Because of their truncated economic development, the Atlantic provinces are said not to have evolved beyond their "pre-industrial" two-party structures; Quebec, Ontario, Manitoba, and British Columbia are "transitional" because one of the two traditional parties (in all cases the Liberal party) changed to accommodate the development of the working class following the industrialization of these provinces; only Alberta and Saskatchewan have party systems characteristic of "developed" regions, because (as of the time Wilson was writing) in those two provinces one of the two traditional parties had been supplanted by a social democratic party. Wilson (1974, 453–5) describes the evolution of party systems as follows: "What happens to the pre-industrial party system is that as the structure of the society changes, … as it industrializes, so it becomes clear that the older party system is inadequate. With the development of industrial society a new interest appears which was not previously of any consequence – namely a wage-earning class – and as its cohesiveness grows through the organization of the trade unions, cooperative societies, and the like it becomes necessary for the party system to adjust to accommodate its demands." This developmental sequence has implications for the patterns of party support: in the "undeveloped" provinces voting is said to follow religious and ethnic lines, while in the "developed" provinces voting is said to follow class lines.

There are a number of flaws in Wilson's approach, despite the importance of his recognition that there are complex relationships between class and region, rather than a simple dominance of the latter over the former. Dependency theorists have made a strong case for the argument that underdeveloped regions are not retarded in their development but, instead, *have been underdeveloped* by the powerful economic interests in core regions (Acheson 1972; Forbes 1979; Veltmeyer 1979; Matthews 1983; for a fine critical review of the arguments see Brodie 1990, 48–50). The historical evidence of the development of underdevelopment undermines Wilson's assumption that the provinces are all at some stage of evolution between farm- and fisheries-based economies and full-scale industrialization. Wilson's contention that resource-dependent Saskatchewan and British Columbia are in the most developed economic category while Atlantic Canada is underdeveloped poses another problem. In Saskatchewan (and to a lesser extent British Columbia) the industrial working class is proportionately small; it is certainly not the predominant class. But Wilson (1974, 460) argues that a predominant working class is a prerequisite for the emergence of a two-party system with one social democratic party. To escape this difficulty with his theory Wilson simply transforms Saskatchewan farmers into proletarians with the implausible argument that farmers are only "nominally independent producers" because, like the working class, farmers "are inescapably dependent for their well-being on the will of others who are outside their control."

While Wilson's arguments concerning the content of regional political cultures have not been seriously explored, our data analysis will indicate a number of problems in this connection. Specifically, we object to Wilson's conception of Quebec as a province "comme les autres," straddling the middle of the developmental continuum with provinces having developed economies but no strong social democratic party. Even an ad hoc correction for the rise to power of the Parti Québécois after the appearance of Wilson's work, on the assumption that it was in part a social democratic party, would not account satisfactorily for the quite distinctive political culture of Quebec, as we describe it. Further, our data for other provinces cannot be squared with the provincial differences in the degree of left-wing ideological orientation predicted by Wilson's expectation of a leftward shift in political debate as the condition of the rise to power of social democratic parties. The political cultures of the Atlantic provinces are in aggregate more left leaning, not less so, and Western provinces in which social democratic parties have come to power are less, not more, left leaning than other provinces.

The attractiveness of evolutionary social theory has seldom suffered, however, for want of substantial empirical confirmation. And so it has been with the evolutionary approach to Canadian regionalism, which has been further refined in the work of Simeon and his colleagues. Simeon and David Elkins (1974) began by combining Wilson's theory with Gabriel Almond and Sidney Verba's (1963) conception of the evolutionary development of political culture. They argue that distinct political cultures correspond to the three evolutionary steps in the development of party structures identified by Wilson. The most primitive, pre-industrial political system is characterized by Almond and Verba's "subject" political culture, the industrializing, transitional political system is characterized by a "participant" culture, and the mature, fully developed political system by a "civic" culture. Using this conceptual framework and data from the 1965 and 1968 national election studies, Simeon and Elkins analyzed the provincial political cultures using three measures of citizens' relationships to the state: political efficacy, a measure of citizens' confidence in their ability to affect government; trust in government, a measure of whether citizens believe their government will act correctly, even in the absence of pressure from the citizenry; and political participation, a measure of actual involvement in politics.

Because their conclusion that the Canadian provinces have distinct political cultures is so striking, Simeon and Elkins's work has attracted a great deal of attention. We believe, however, that a number of problems seriously undermine this conclusion. Especially notable is their lack of attention to the relationship between social class and ideology, so important in Wilson's original formulation. Simeon and Elkins are concerned only with whether the interprovincial differences "survive" controls for social class. Within these limitations they characterize the interprovincial differences in the three key measures of political culture as "very strong ... Variations in political efficacy and political trust were especially marked" (Elkins and Simeon 1980, 68).

But on the basis of the means and standard deviations of the measures reported in their tables, the provincial differences explain 8.3 percent of the variance in efficacy, 2.5 percent of the variance in political trust, and 0.7 percent of the variance in political participation. Furthermore, because the correlation between efficacy and trust is quite high (the gamma is .49 for the cross-tabulation of the dichotomized variables), it is likely that the interprovincial variation in trust largely reflects differences in efficacy. Even if these differences were of major theoretical significance, and it is not clear that they are, this would be very limited evidence upon which to hang any forceful conclusion about the significance of regional political cultures in Canada, let alone about the inhibiting effects of regionalism on class cleavages in Canada.

This argument tends to disappear entirely from focus in the latest elaborations of the developmental approach, which suggests the integration of regional communities over time. In their analysis of provincial variation in policy preferences, Simeon and Donald Blake (1980, 78–80) argue that a "developmental model" predicts an historical tendency towards regional convergence, and the data on public policy preferences rather than political trust and efficacy are indeed consistent with such a conclusion. The regional differences in such preferences are less remarkable than the class differences across the nation. Ironically this purely empiricist approach by mainstream political scientists concedes too much to the opposing paradigm of class forces, losing sight of the institutionalist focus on interprovincial conflict over public policy. Strikingly absent from Simeon and Blake's work is a framework for dealing with the resurgence of regional conflicts in the 1970s and early 1980s. Although their work documents important regional differences in public policy attitudes, such as attitudes towards social welfare, they provide no discussion of the *direction* of these ideological differences between the provinces, and no rationale to account for the regional differences.

We are left, therefore, with very major weaknesses in our understanding of the conventionally assumed significance of regionalism, and insignificance of class cleavages, in Canadian political culture. Simply put, it is not clear how theoretically to weight the differences in identity but similarities in hegemonic value orientations across regions, or how to weight the unity of identity as opposed to ideological cleavages within regions, nor is it clear empirically what the relative weights of these phenomena are. The arguments for the predominance of regionalism in Canadian political culture proceed from a descriptively rich account of geographically uneven economic development, intergovernmental conflict, and provincial party-electoral system differences, to a descriptively much poorer (at least more ad hoc) account of differences in regional political culture, and thence to the logically unrelated conclusion that these regional phenomena are *the*, or at least *a*, primary determinant of political life in Canada. Most important, there is no concern with the possibly hidden relationships between class and region, such that differences in the political structure produce differences in the articulation of class conflict in different regions, or that regional and class cleavages exist in an historically changeable balance, with the latter never completely mute as a result of the former, and in some conjunctures the predominant influence on political affairs.

Our own approach will be theoretically eclectic, accepting the fundamental importance of uneven development, and associated differences in the social relations of production, as in the political economy approach, but accepting also the crucial mediating influence of political institutions, as in the institutionalist approach. Unlike the developmental approach, we make no functionalist connection between economic development, the emergence of distinct patterns of ideology, and particular types of political institution. Rather we emphasize the relative autonomy of ideology and politics, and the disjuncture between popular ideology and political institutions in different regions of Canada. Nor do we accept the functionalist logic of integration, which sees a gradual evolution of a national value consensus reflecting national policy developments across regional communities, preferring theoretical arguments for the contradictory development of hegemonic tendencies toward integration and counter-hegemonic tendencies towards class conflict in the national political community. Finally, rather than adopting an economist logic of the emergence of class politics, as found in the political economy or developmental approaches to class and region in Canadian politics, we will argue that attributes of political institutions (such as the organizational strength of existing parties) have greater effects on the shaping of class conflict within the political system than do economic developments or shifts in political ideology (cf. Przeworski 1985; Brodie and Jenson 1988). We accept the burden of John Shiry's (1976) argument that, because existing political forces attempt to restrict the range of political choice available to the public, parties do not automatically arise in order to represent significant bodies of public opinion. This is precisely the point of C.B. Macpherson's (1977, 89) characterization of party systems as the political counterpart of economic oligopolies. In these terms parties exercise their oligopoly power to prevent the emergence of new competitors, although they do not always succeed in doing so. One has to look to their failures of organization and strategy in order to understand the rise of new, non-oligopolistic parties and governments at various times and in different provinces.

The contradictory effects of uneven development and economic inequality create differences between regional political cultures, but not differences that can be simply predicted from the level of development. In some peripheral regions the combination of high levels of unemployment, low education, and conservative government serve to reduce workers' bargaining power while increasing the government's dependence on corporations. Those governments thus tend to support employers' efforts to keep wages low and unions out, a classic example being the Nova Scotia government's passage of labour legislation designed to prevent unionization at the Michelin tire plants. Regional dependency therefore fuels popular resistance to outside domination and legitimates claims for compensation from the central regions, while reinforcing corporate and government efforts to dominate a population whose poverty makes them extraordinarily dependent on capital and the state. Robert Brym's (1979) account of the history of "third" parties in Atlantic Canada shows how the economic oppression that gives rise to political resistance and the establishment of alternatives to the traditional parties becomes a liability in the context of long-term efforts to alter fundamental political and economic structures. Thus parts of the underdeveloped periphery may exhibit relatively left-wing popular ideology *and* traditional, conservative political structures. This duality is brought home in the contrast between Rex Lucas's (1971) portrait of single-industry towns, which emphasizes their social and political domination by corporations, and Stuart Jamieson's (1968) documentation of the intensity of class struggles in the same places.

In other peripheral regions the coupling of economic difficulties with institutionalized, class-oriented political parties may produce greater levels of class cleavage on ideological questions, as Blake (1985) suggests for British Columbia's provincial politics. This polarization may lead, however, to the greater aggregate concentration of public opinion on the right of the ideological spectrum (as opposed to Wilson's predictions), because of the strategic alliances made by right-wing parties between the classes of the bourgeoisie, the traditional petty bourgeoisie (in commerce and agriculture), and the new petty bourgeoisie in the expanding categories of white collar employment in state and service-industry employment. The urban, industrial working class in these regions may, that is, be more left wing than comparable sectors of the population in other regions, but yet be dominated ideologically and politically by other classes.

We expect the balance of forces to be quite different still in the metropolitan core where higher wages and the greater strength of trade unions strengthen social democratic parties but also encourage the adoption of an economist ideological perspective. Again, however, the strength of class cleavages and the aggregate central tendency of popular ideology in these central regions will vary as a result of institutional factors, most obviously in the case of the ascendance of the Quebec state and its temporary control by a nationalist and not clearly social democratic political party.

No doubt the different political traditions and cultures in the various provinces limit the development of an integrated national political community and the associated salience of horizontal political cleavages defining political conflict across regions of the country. But this limit is far from absolute and there are powerful countervailing forces at work to limit regional differences in political culture. A national, capitalist economy and a national state and capitalist institutions serve to unify Canadians' social and political experience. National and multinational corporations tend to homogenize the social relations of production and the marketplace. In particular the growth of capitalist production and of large corporations tends to reduce the economic and therefore the political significance of the independent commodity producers, whose claims played a critical role in the regional conflicts of the past. Furthermore governments, federal and provincial, tend to homogenize the essential relations between citizens and the state. As Simeon and Robert Miller (1980) have indicated, there is a remarkable uniformity in the spending policies of the ten provincial governments. Thus, despite the complex development of federal-provincial fiscal sharing and intergovernmental political diplomacy, the welfare state has been reasonably uniformly imposed upon the society as a whole. This homogeneity of material experience leads to a corresponding hegemony of ideological commitments justifying the political economy of the welfare state, just as the associated contradictions and inconsistencies in the social relations of production lead to corresponding tendencies towards counter-hegemonic conflict.

Our view of regional political culture may thus be characterized as follows. Instead of deriving the nature of regional political culture from the uneven situations of regions in a national economic context, we look to the balance of class forces *within* regions as the economic determinant of ideology. Whether the resulting class differences find expression in the party system depends, then, on the institutional character of local party systems. These systems may successfully resist conforming to the ideological divisions and, in so doing, effectively suppress the expression of class interests.

In attempting to describe the dialectical balance of these contrasting processes as they are reflected in the shape of public opinion and popular ideology, we have suggested (Ornstein, Stevenson, and Williams 1980) that it is useful to consider an architectural layering of the political culture in three levels. The most basic of these levels consists of fundamental *ideological* orientations related to the proper uses of political power and the ends of public policy. The second level consists of attitudes towards the *political process* by which ideological interests are translated into political action – that is attitudes towards political participation, political efficacy, trust in government, and political protest. The third level consists of attitudes towards actual *political institutions*, governments and parties. Simultaneously, we conceptualize political relations in terms of the three relations among capital, labour, and the state.

Class conflict, we argue, is most apparent at the most abstract level of the political culture. Fundamental ideological orientations at this level are, in contrast to the conventional wisdom, a terrain of significant class cleavage in Canada. Because they relate to the uses of state power, and because in Canada there are important regional differences in the economic and political resources of the provincial governments, these ideological orientations are also, however, regionally distinctive. Nevertheless we argue that regionalism in the political culture is not, at this most basic level, a more significant phenomenon than class conflict. The reasons why this substratum of class conflict has been concealed from theoretical and empirical analysis relate to the structure of political attitudes on more concrete questions of political participation and identification with political institutions. At these more concrete levels there are, first, significant class differences in attitudes towards political participation, the effects of which (it has been demonstrated in studies of many nations) limit the political participation and representation of working-class interests in politics. Second, significant regional differences in attitudes towards political institutions further limit the articulation of class conflict, and reflect how, in the absence of such class conflict, the political agenda is set by the conflicting interests of competing fractions of capital, and competing governments aligned with different business interests in regionally distinct economies.

We leave to the next chapter the key question of the ways in which the party system operates to limit the articulation of class conflict, but the rest of this chapter examines empirical evidence for the complex balance of regional and class differences in popular ideology we have just outlined. We begin with a discussion of regional differences, moving thereafter to an examination of class differences, and the interrelationship of class, region, and other factors, in the structure of popular ideology.

REGIONALISM AND POLITICAL IDEOLOGY

In order to investigate the empirical differences in political ideology across Canada's regions, we must specify how regions are defined. Some of the existing research employs five regions: Atlantic Canada, British Columbia, Ontario, the Prairies, and Quebec (Schwartz 1974; Simeon and Blake 1980; Gibbins 1982, 184 ff.). A concern with governmental structures has led other political scientists to focus on the ten provinces instead (Wilson 1974). Empirical studies by Simeon and Elkins (1974), Ornstein, Stevenson, and Williams (1980), and Gibbins (1982) lend support to the argument for dealing separately with each of the provinces by demonstrating that there is as much variation within the Atlantic and Prairie regions as there is variation between the five regions of Canada. These findings throw serious doubt on the credibility of regional comparisons that employ Prairie or Atlantic composites.

Confining our attention to the ten provinces (or nine, considering the very small number of interviews from Prince Edward Island) limits the scope of our analysis. A more complete study of regionalism would add the Yukon and Northwest Territories, as well as examining differences between major regions within the provinces and territories. While our comparisons between the provinces reflect a constraint imposed by our data, this choice can be defended on the grounds that provincial state institutions have served to reinforce and create provincial societies, even when the provincial boundaries did not correspond to natural physical or cultural boundaries. While the differences between French and English Québécois and between the French living outside Quebec and other English Canadians are discussed in our analysis, we feel it is inappropriate, *pace* Simeon and Elkins, to designate these divisions as "regions."

Table 5-1 gives the survey items and scales on which this analysis is based. Note that the left-right index, our most general measure of a respondent's ideological position, contains a number of items also found in the "welfare effort" and "support for redistribution" scales. As a result there are some similarities in the results of analyzing the three scales.

The extent of regional variation in each of the measures of political ideology is shown by the two figures given for the percentage of variance explained by region in right-hand columns of table 5-2. In each column the first figure gives the variance between all the provinces, while the second figure measures the variation between the provinces of English Canada. For most of the items and scales it is immediately apparent that the variation between the English-Canadian provinces is smaller than the equivalent variation when Quebec is included. With Quebec excluded the ideological variation between the provinces of English Canada is generally quite small; indeed for many of the variables there is negligible variation within English Canada. Only for two items, measuring respondents' views of whether their province has been treated fairly by the federal government and their support for a shift in the powers of the two levels of government, is there strong variation within English Canada. Within English Canada it is significant that the substantial variation in these two indicators of public opinion about intergovernmental relationships is *not* accompanied by (and therefore could not be caused by) differences in policy priorities. With or without Quebec there is negligible interprovincial variation in political efficacy and participation, our measures of two of the three variables (there is no measure of political trust in our survey) that form the cornerstone of Simeon and Elkins's analysis of regional variation in political culture.

With Quebec excluded the extent of interprovincial variation is far too small to indicate the presence of distinct regional political cultures. While there is strong evidence of interprovincial rivalry and resentment of the federal government, differences in the key elements of political ideology are almost entirely lacking. For nearly every item and scale there are, however, substantial differences between Québécois and English Canadians. The data make a strong case for the proposition that there are two political cultures, or more appropriately two *nations*, in Canada – Quebec and English Canada.

Table 5-1
Definitions of Measures of Political Ideology

Variable Name	Description of Variable	Scoring Procedure

Government effort for:
health
unemployed
the poor
	Rating of government effort for
	"health and medical care"
	"providing assistance to the unemployed"
	"helping the poor"
		much more effort = 2;
		more effort = 1;
		about the same
		effort = 0
		less = −1;
		much less = −2

Cutbacks	"Pressures to reduce government deficits have led recently to a variety of measures to cut back expenditures on social services. Do you think governments in Canada have cut back too much on social expenditures, that these cuts have been justified but there should be no further cuts, or that further cuts should be made in social expenditures?"	too much = 1; no more = 0 more cuts = −1
Support for social programs index	Scale of support for "government effort" for health and medical care, protecting native rights, assisting the unemployed, helping the poor, eliminating discrimination against women, protecting the environment, education, and workers' compensation (the items are averaged; Cronbach's alpha = .820)	"effort" scores above
Redistribute taxes	"People with high incomes should pay a greater share of the total taxes than than they do now."	strongly agree = 2; agree = 1; neither agree nor disagree = 0 disagree = −1 strongly disagree = −2
Blame unemployed	"Unemployment is high these days because it is too easy to get welfare assistance."	
Rent control	"In provinces where they now exist, rent controls should be abolished."	
Redistribution index	Scale made up of responses to the statements listed above for the "redistribute taxes" and "blame unemployed," and the responses to the statements "There is too much of a difference between rich and poor in this country" and "The government should provide jobs for Canadians who want to work but cannot find a job."	standardized scale
Foreign investment	"What do you think has been the result of foreign investment in Canada?"	very good effects = 2 mostly good effects = 1 about equally good and bad = 0 mostly bad effects = −1 very bad effects = −2

Table 5-1
Definitions of Measures of Political Ideology (Continued)

Variable Name	Description of Variable	Scoring Procedure
Corporate power	Rating of power of large corporations	much too much = 2;
Union power	Rating of power of labour unions	too much power = 1
		about right = 0
		too little power = −1
		much too little = −2
Outlaw strikebreaking	"During a strike, management should be prohibited by law from hiring workers to take the place of strikers."	"agreement" scores above
Outlaw teachers strike	"Teachers should not have the right to strike."	"agreement" scores above
Labour index	Scale made up of responses to the two statements listed above for the "strike-breaking" and "teachers strike" and the responses to the statement: "Workers should have positions on the board of directors of the organizations for which they work."	standardized scale
Left-right index	General index created from 14 items measuring government effort for social programs, French schooling, affirmative action, redistribution, and labour (Cronbach's alpha = .744)	standardized scale
Fairness of federal government	"Do you think that this province is fairly treated by the government in Ottawa?"	All of the time = 4 most of the time = 3 some of the time = 2 none of the time = 1
Provincial power	"In the future should the provincial governments have more power, the federal government have more power, or should things stay as they are?"	provincial more = 1 Federal more = −1 same = 0
Attention to Quebec	"What about Quebec, do you think the federal government has given Quebec too little attention, too much attention, or about the right amount of attention in recent years?"	too much = 1 about right = 0 too little = −1
French schooling	"French-speaking Canadians outside of Quebec should be able to find schooling for their children in French."	"agreement" scores above
Homosexual rights	"Protection for homosexuals from discrimination in employment"	yes = 2 yes, with qualification = 1
Censorship	"Elimination of existing boards of censors"	no, with qualification = −1 no = −2

Table 5-1
Definitions of Measures of Political Ideology (Continued)

Variable Name	Description of Variable	Scoring Procedure
Police review	"Civilian review of complaints against the police"	as above
Affirmative action	"Programs to favour the hiring and promotion of women and other minorities to make up for their lack of opportunities in the past"	as above
Sex discrimination	Rating of effort for "eliminating discrimination against women"	"effort" scores above
Civil liberties index	Scale made up of the items on "homosexual rights," "censorship," "police review," "affirmative action," and ratings of "legislation to protect the rights of the disabled," "the right of women to equal pay for work of equal value," "granting native peoples limited rights to self-government," and "abolition of the War Measures Act"	standardized scale
Immigrants should assimilate	"People who come to live in Canada should try harder to be more like other Canadians."	"agreement" scores above
Blame immigrants	"Immigrants often bring discrimination on themselves by their own personal habits and attitudes."	"agreement" scores above
Immigrant index	Scale made up of responses to the statements listed above for the "immigrants should assimilate" and "blame immigrants" and the responses to the statements: "Immigrants to this country aren't prepared to work as hard as people born in Canada," and "The hard work of immigrants has done a lot to help this country."	standardized scale
Efficacy index	Leduc's four-item efficacy scale (alpha = .575)	standardized scale
Participation index	Five-item scale measuring volunteer work in political campaigns, work on community problems, having spoken or written to elected politicians, signing of petition, and attending a protest meeting or demonstration (alpha = .668)	standardized scale

Table 5-1
Definitions of Measures of Political Ideology (Continued)

Variable Name	Description of Variable	Scoring Procedure
Protest index	Five-item scale concerning support for the legitimacy of strike to change government policy, boycotts, legal and peaceful demonstrations, illegal but peaceful demonstrations, violent demonstrations; items scored 1 for never justified, 2 for sometimes justified, 3 for often justified	standardized scale
Inconsistency index	Extent of inconsistency among a variety of political attitude measures	standardized scale

The amount of regional differentiation is a function of the dimension of ideology being considered. The top panel of table 5-2 refers to social programs. Although there is little variation in support for health and medical care, support for government effort to assist the unemployed displays moderate regional differences, with the highest levels of support in Quebec and Atlantic Canada, the lowest levels in the West, and Ontario in between. A rather similar, but weaker, pattern obtains for the question about government effort to assist the poor. There is virtually no provincial variation in responses to the question about whether cutbacks in social services have proceeded too far, except that Newfoundlanders are more likely and Prince Edward Islanders less likely to believe cutbacks have proceeded too far (in both those provinces, however, the number of interviews was very small). Within English Canada there is little variation in opinions about social programs, except that Nova Scotians are to the left and Manitobans to the right of people in the other provinces.

Because it was made up of a number of different items and so eliminates idiosyncratic responses to individual issues, the scale of support for social welfare allows more precise analysis than the single items just described. Again Québécois are on the left, .39 standard deviations above the national mean, followed closely by the people of Newfoundland and New Brunswick, whose mean scores are, respectively, .24 and .13 standard deviations above the national mean. For this scale the difference in means between Quebec and English Canada as a whole is approximately half a standard deviation. Paradoxically, despite their entrenched social democratic parties and, according to Wilson's typology, more "modern" political systems, Westerners are apparently *less* left wing than the people of other provinces.

The next items in table 5-2 refer to policy issues that have a more direct bearing on inequality than the changes in the general level of social programs just considered. For the item dealing with the distribution of the tax

Table 5-2
Means of Measures of Political Ideology by Province

Measure of Political Ideology	PQ	NF	PEI	NS	NB	ON	MB	SK	AB	BC	with Quebec	without Quebec
				Mean for Province							Percentage of Variance Explained	
Government effort for health (%)	53	46	27	42	51	47	48	62	49	50	1.1	.6
Government effort for unemployed (%)	48	49	40	39	52	31	27	21	24	27	4.6	2.2
Government effort for the poor (%)	72	82	55	62	70	58	60	62	59	63	3.2	1.6
Cutbacks too great (%)	22	37	11	18	23	22	21	19	20	23	.9	1.2
Social programs index, mean	.39	.24	-.35	-.11	.13	-.15	-.28	-.40	-.15	-.11	6.4	1.3
Redistribute taxes (%)	66	53	57	65	56	54	41	58	51	50	3.6	.4
Blame unemployed (%)	62	53	59	67	75	70	74	70	68	52	.5	.6
Abolish rent control (%)	21	14	13	24	25	20	12	18	18	16	.6	.7
Redistribution index, mean	.46	.15	.16	.24	.15	-.20	-.11	-.12	-.33	-.28	9.1	2.0
Favour foreign investment (%)	41	33	29	48	38	42	37	40	53	36	1.6	1.4
Corporate power too great (%)	69	68	74	78	73	78	73	73	77	76	.3	.5
Union power too great (%)	73	53	66	62	66	68	69	65	73	78	1.5	1.6
Outlaw strikebreaking (%)	71	69	49	62	54	54	42	39	41	55	5.6	1.6
Outlaw teachers strike (%)	60	35	53	40	47	58	46	40	49	44	4.3	2.1
Labour index, mean	.46	-.09	.02	-.02	-.24	-.11	-.26	-.32	-.30	-.24	8.2	.9
Left-right index, mean	.67	.21	-.27	-.05	.22	-.26.	-.35	-.50	-.30	-.28	17.6	2.4

Table 5-2
Means of Measures of Political Ideology by Province (Continued)

Measure of Political Ideology	Mean for Province										Percentage of Variance Explained	
	PQ	NF	PEI	NS	NB	ON	MB	SK	AB	BC	with Quebec	without Quebec
Federal government fair to own province (%)	42	12	62	33	42	64	37	20	27	33	9.2	12.3
More provincial power (%)	56	58	20	43	33	22	39	51	53	46	8.5	7.7
Too much attention to Quebec (%)	11	63	67	68	57	58	84	81	65	69	30.5	2.5
Support French schools (%)	89	73	63	67	72	58	42	53	51	44	18.6	3.2
Support gay rights (%)	77	55	28	62	60	60	44	64	55	63	3.7	1.2
Eliminate censorship (%)	50	46	36	31	39	40	33	30	32	43	1.6	.7
Civilian review of police (%)	78	75	63	61	70	72	59	73	78	75	1.4	1.4
Support affirmative action (%)	88	65	81	72	67	62	62	50	66	59	6.3	.7
Effort against sex discrimination (%)	67	53	43	47	52	54	50	47	55	47	3.0	.3
Civil liberties index, mean	.39	-.03	-.11	-.10	-.24	-.14	-.23	-.30	-.24	.00	6.0	.7
Immigrants should assimilate	82	44	67	75	64	63	65	57	61	63	3.9	.9
Blame immigrants	63	64	55	69	52	67	57	57	72	74	1.2	1.4
Immigrants index, mean	.46	-.09	.02	-.02	-.24	-.11	-.26	-.32	-.30	-.24	8.2	.5

Table 5-2
Means of Measures of Political Ideology by Province (Continued)

Measure of Political Ideology	Mean for Province										Percentage of Variance Explained	
	PQ	NF	PEI	NS	NB	ON	MB	SK	AB	BC	with Quebec	without Quebec
Efficacy index, mean	.00	-.03	-.23	-.11	-.11	.04	-.08	-.09	-.04	.05	.3	.4
Participation index, mean	-.03	-.11	.00	-.15	-.12	.02	-.25	.24	.08	.12	.9	1.3
Protest index, mean	.04	-.04	-.27	-.02	-.23	.01	-.18	-.06	.02	.05	.5	.6
Inconsistency index, mean	.07	-.27	-.32	-.13	.10	.02	-.20	-.08	-.07	.03	.7	.8
Number of cases	778	56	17	122	84	1086	160	91	227	308		
Standard error, assuming simple random sampling, for:												
percentages near 50%	1.8	6.7	12.1	4.5	5.5	1.5	4.0	5.2	3.3	2.8		
percentages near 35% or 65%	1.7	6.4	11.6	4.3	5.2	1.4	3.8	5.0	3.2	2.7		
percentages near 20% or 80%	1.4	5.3	9.7	3.6	4.4	1.2	3.2	4.2	2.7	2.3		
means of standardized variables	.036	.134	.243	.091	.109	.030	.079	.105	.066	.057		

burden, Québécois are, again, to the left of all the other provinces, but there is very little variation in evaluations of whether social welfare increases unemployment and the responses to the rent control question. In light of the high levels of support for social programs, it is noteworthy that more than half the respondents in every province believe that the availability of welfare increases unemployment. Still, no more than one-quarter of the population in any province would abolish rent controls in provinces where they exist. The means of a scale incorporating these and some other items conform to the following pattern: Quebec is on the left; Atlantic Canada occupies an intermediate position; and Manitoba and Saskatchewan, Ontario, and British Columbia and Alberta (in that order) are on the right. These differences are precisely the opposite of what Wilson's theory would suggest.

The strongest support for foreign investment is found in Alberta, a province characterized by very high foreign investment in the dominant, resource industries. People in Quebec and Atlantic Canada, the provinces with the most unemployment at the time, might have been expected to greet foreign investment as a solution to unemployment, but are not particularly sanguine about its role. The general lack of provincial variation in support for foreign investment suggests that this issue is not simply tied to regional variation in other aspects of ideology or to economic differences between provinces.

The next two items involve ratings of the power of corporations and trade unions, which were introduced in the last chapter. These ratings also exhibit little interprovincial variation. Ratings of institutions, recall from the last chapter, bear little relationship to the patterns of support for social welfare programs and redistribution. We interpreted this as indicating that Canadians' views about equality and deservingness are poorly articulated with their views of some of the major institutions whose structure and powers ultimately shape the system of inequality. Consistent with the weakness of the individual-level relationship, the people of Atlantic Canada are more likely to support social welfare programs, but are no more critical of corporations or favourable to trade unions. This demonstrates the limits of regional differentiation, and perhaps the dependency of Atlantic Canada on the large corporations that have invested there.

Two less rhetorical questions about labour relations exhibit somewhat larger interprovincial differences. About 70 percent of Québécois and Newfoundlanders would outlaw the hiring of strikebreakers, compared to just over 50 percent in the other provinces and around 40 percent in Manitoba, Saskatchewan, and Alberta, despite the presence of strong New Democratic Parties in two of these provinces. Surprisingly, Québécois, who are strongly opposed to strikebreaking, are the most likely to favour outlawing teacher strikes, suggesting that their support for trade unions is mixed with resentment of teachers and other state employees. Aggregating these items into a scale of support for labour results in a pattern like that observed in the scale of attitudes towards redistribution, with Quebec on the left, followed by the Atlantic Canada and Ontario, and the West on the right.

The pattern of interprovincial differences in the left-right index is quite similar to that for the other indices, which is not surprising given that they use some of the same items. The mean scores for Quebec and English Canada on this standardized scale differ by about one standard deviation, a large difference. The political climate of Quebec is obviously much to the left of all other provinces. With Quebec excluded, the interprovincial differences are quite small; the explained variance drops from 17.6 percent to 2.4 percent. The mean values for the provinces again suggest a split between Atlantic Canada, on the left, and the rest of English Canada. This pattern is, of course, absolutely contrary to the conventional political wisdom, which tends to view Atlantic Canada as a political backwater dominated by party allegiances and patronage that have long disappeared in the rest of Canada.

Large interprovincial differences are found for the four items dealing with federal-provincial issues. The proportion of respondents believing their province is treated fairly by the federal government all or most of the time ranges from 12 percent for Newfoundland to 64 percent for Ontario. High levels of dissatisfaction are also found in Saskatchewan, where only 20 percent of the respondents believe the federal government has been fair to their province, in Alberta (27 percent), in Nova Scotia and British Columbia (33 percent), and in Manitoba (37 percent). Support for increasing the power of the provinces relative to the federal government closely parallels the ratings of the fairness of the federal government. Only 20 percent of Prince Edward Islanders and 22 percent of Ontarians wanted to increase provincial powers, compared to more than half of the residents of Quebec, Newfoundland, Saskatchewan, and Alberta. The nature of alienation from the federal system in the Maritime and Western provinces of English Canada is closely tied to perceptions of an exploiting "Central Canada," which includes Quebec. But, these perceptions have no confirmation in the perceptions of Québécois themselves, a majority of whom (if not so large a majority as in the other peripheral provinces) did not feel they are fairly treated by the federal government; a majority of Québécois (larger than in any other province but Newfoundland) wanted increased provincial powers *vis-à-vis* the federal government.

The lack of awareness that Québécois share their grievances with the peripheral provinces of English Canada is not just a matter of ignorance. The non-Québécois also see their grievances as resulting in part from the responsiveness of the federal government to the demands of Quebec. In every province of English Canada, at least 55 percent of the population believed that the federal government has "paid too much attention" to Quebec. Manitoba and Saskatchewan, where more than 80 percent of the people take this view, differed from the other provinces of English Canada, where the majority support for this proposition is much lower. This might be interpreted as scapegoating, and suggests that federal-provincial conflict is complicated by elements of ethnic prejudice. While this is no doubt true to some extent, it should not be exaggerated. Our data on attitudes towards linguistic rights suggest that substantial majorities in all except the Western provinces (and even there minorities only in Manitoba and B.C.) favour the extension of French language rights in English Canada. Support for French schooling is far stronger in Atlantic Canada than in Ontario or the West, although in no province did less than 40 percent of the respondents agree that French speaking Canadians outside of Quebec should be able to find schooling for their children in French. Manitoba is unique in combining weak support for the French language with the presence of a large French minority and an historical tradition that legitimizes the position of French. This combination was clearly a recipe for the clashes over language that took place in that province shortly after our surveys were completed.

The next three items in table 5-2 deal with civil liberties issues: protection of homosexuals from discrimination in employment, elimination of existing boards of censors, and civilian review of complaints against the police. Québécois were the most likely to support each measure, but otherwise there is little in the way of systematic interprovincial differences. Within English Canada, the previously observed interprovincial differences in support for social programs and the trade unions within English Canada are not translated into more general support for civil liberties.

Québécois also gave the strongest support to affirmative action, defined in the questionnaire as "programmes to favour the hiring and promotion of women and other minorities to make up for their lack of opportunities in the past." Fully 88 percent of Québécois approved of affirmative action. Otherwise there is little interprovincial variation except that support for affirmative action was stronger in Prince Edward Island and weaker in Saskatchewan than in the other provinces of English Canada. One-half or more of the respondents in every province supported affirmative action, so the population was significantly to the left of most of the governments of the time on this issue. A more general question concerning effort to decrease discrimination against women also finds the strongest support in Quebec and little variation among the English Canadian provinces.

The consistent tendency observed so far for Québécois to concentrate on the left of the ideological questions breaks down to some extent on questions relating to immigrants. The statement that immigrants should become more like other Canadians received the strongest support in Quebec, where fully 82 percent agreed or strongly agreed with it. In the provinces of English Canada the corresponding figures range from 44 to 75 percent. A second statement blaming immigrants for bringing discrimination on themselves, however, shows little interprovincial variation. A scale measuring assimilationist attitudes towards immigrants also serves largely to separate Quebec from English Canada. These differences likely reflect the continuing conflicts in Quebec over the language of schooling for immigrant children and the perceived threat to French culture of immigrants choosing to learn the English language, rather than any greater ethnocentrism in relation to immigrants on the part of Québécois as opposed to English Canadians. Again such data emphasize the distinctive political problems and political culture of Quebec.

As we noted above, the interprovincial differences in political efficacy, participation, and support for the legitimacy of protest serve to test the claims of Wilson (1974) and Simeon and Elkin (1974) concerning the existence of regional political cultures. All three measures combine individual items in order to achieve higher reliability. Table 5-2 indicates that interprovincial variation is small, whether or not Quebec is included. Not one province differs significantly from the national mean for the measure of efficacy; Saskatchewan and British Columbia are above and Manitoba is below the national mean for participation; and only New Brunswick is different from (and below) the national mean in support for protest. These very small interprovincial differences provide no grounds for differentiating the provinces according to the dimensions specified in "civic culture" approaches to Canadian political culture.

The variable that we label "inconsistency" measures the degrees of similarity in each respondent's opinions about the items that enter into the calculation of the left-right index discussed above. The items used for this measure had been shown, by means of a factor analysis, to be highly intercorrelated and therefore appropriate measures of an overarching left-right dimension of political ideology. Inconsistency in individuals' responses to these items is high for people who have a mixture of left- and right-wing views; individuals who chose the right-wing alternative for every item (or the left-wing alternative for every item) score zero on the scale. The measure of inconsistency in political attitudes also demonstrates little provincial variation. Thus although Québécois are more likely to hold left-wing views, the extent of internal consistency of their views is no greater than that found in the other provinces.

Independent of the interprovincial differences in the percentages and mean scores of the political ideology measures there may be differences in the variances in measures of political ideology. A province that exhibits larger variances would have a wider spectrum of opinion, suggesting a lower than average level of political consensus. If major shifts in electoral support are indicative of widespread ideological conflict, we should expect that Quebec and three of the Western provinces, Manitoba, Saskatchewan, and British Columbia, should exhibit the largest variation in ideology. In using the survey results to address this question, we employ the scales rather than the individual items, for responses to the items are truncated by the limited range of options presented. Table 5-3 gives the standard deviations of the scales, and shows little interprovincial variation.

Table 5-3
Standard Deviations of Selected Measures of Political Ideology by Province

Measure of Political Ideology	Province									
	PQ	NF	PEI	NS	NB	ON	MB	SK	AB	BC
Social programs	1.01	.98	.66	1.03	1.17	.92	.90	.80	1.03	.98
Redistribution	.94	.92	.86	.79	.90	.97	1.05	.85	.97	.96
Left-right index	.88	1.01	.83	1.00	1.05	.92	.81	.74	.87	.94
Labour	1.01	.74	.94	.92	1.00	.93	.98	.77	.97	.99
Civil liberties	.87	1.03	.96	1.06	1.13	1.01	1.14	1.03	.90	.96
Immigration	1.01	.87	1.10	.70	1.01	.92	1.08	.93	.88	.90
Efficacy	1.10	.77	1.08	1.09	1.18	.91	1.07	.83	.99	.98
Protest	1.04	.86	1.03	.89	1.01	1.03	.86	.81	.92	1.00

For the social programs scale and left-right index, there is somewhat more *intra*-provincial conflict in New Brunswick and somewhat less conflict in Prince Edward Island, Manitoba, and Saskatchewan, compared to the other provinces. On the left-right index, Quebec exhibits somewhat less internal conflict than the other provinces. These results bear little relation to a common-sense analysis of provincial politics. Judging from these data, Quebec and the Western provinces, with their apparently more ideologically based political systems, do not exhibit greater ideological variation. Common-sense evaluations of the extensiveness of political conflict, based on the conduct of provincial elections and party politics, appear, therefore, to reflect factors other than simple differences in the extent of ideological dissent among their provincial electorates.

These results underline the fact that the relationship between public opinion measured in sample surveys and political conflicts portrayed in the mass media is not straightforward. First, the public as a whole must be distinguished from the non-representative minority of the population who actively participate in electoral politics. Second, the development of political conflict requires the presence of and polarization between specific groups, such as social classes, income, or ethnic groups, rather than a high level of political polarization in the population as a whole. Third, as Brym (1979) argues, the nature of the provincial party structures and the political systems also determine whether ideological conflicts are expressed in electoral politics, expressed in extra-parliamentary politics, or not expressed at all. Of course the provincial political structures, in turn, reflect the historical distribution of power in the province and therefore the class structure of the province.

If our analysis provides no direct explanation of the dynamics of political conflict in particular provincial political systems of Canada, it nevertheless provides straightforward answers to a number of the questions posed in the theoretical discussion of regionalism. First, the ideological difference

between Quebec and English Canada is much greater than the internal variation within English Canada. Any characterization of regional political cultures in Canada must begin with an acknowledgement of the difference
between the two nations. Second, the extent of ideological differentiation in
English Canada is very small. This is a powerful argument against the proposition that the provinces are characterized by distinct political cultures. The
relatively weak interprovincial differences suggest that the readily apparent
conflicts in federal-provincial politics reflect institutional factors, such as different party and governmental structures and the constitutionally determined
competition for economic and political autonomy between the different levels
of government, rather than fundamental ideological differences. Third, such
ideological differentiation as does exist does not confirm the pattern predicted
by the most carefully elaborated theoretical argument on this topic.

"Political culture" variables have been the subject of an extensive effort by
conventional political science to produce a framework for comparative studies of politics, and to apply that framework to the explanation of Canadian
politics. But the measures of political participation and efficacy central to
that framework also exhibit very little interprovincial variation in Canada;
even Quebec is near the mean for Canada. This finding strikes at the heart of
attempts by Wilson and by Simeon and Elkins to deal with provincial differences in the "civic culture" framework. Of course the differences that they
found in the 1965 and 1968 survey data may have dissipated in the decade
between the collection of those data and our own, but our analysis shows that
the civic culture framework misunderstands even such limited ideological
differentiation of the provinces as can be detected in the transitional period
from 1977 to 1981.

Any attempt to characterize the political orientations of the provinces of
English Canada on the basis of these survey data would place Atlantic Canada
(perhaps excluding Prince Edward Island) on the left, Ontario in the centre,
and the Western provinces on the right. Within Atlantic Canada, Newfoundland is on the left, followed by Nova Scotia. In the West, Manitoba and
Saskatchewan are to the right of British Columbia and Alberta, which seems
entirely at variance with an account of the postwar electoral history of those
provinces. This characterization seems out of keeping with any common-
sense map of political ideology: Westerners, with their social democratic parties and (sometimes) governments fall clearly to the right of Atlantic Canada,
with its entrenched bourgeois parties. There is a startling disjuncture between
provincial party systems and voting patterns, on the one hand, and the profile
of political ideology shown by these data, on the other hand. While we cannot
say anything about the past, at the time of our surveys the presence of social
democratic parties did not reflect greater support for social democratic policies. Conversely, the entrenched two-party systems of Atlantic Canada did
not reflect more conservative public policy preferences.

These results call into question the proposition that provincial party systems and governments reflect an underlying distribution in provincial political culture or ideology. Our findings, therefore, support the arguments by Shiry (1976), Brym (1979), and Janine Brodie and Jane Jenson (1988) that parties do not spring into existence to represent the contours of public opinion and that we have more to learn from historical studies of the balance of class forces and the development of political institutions than from efforts to link these social forces and political structures to value systems or the climate of public opinion in each province.

While we will argue for the importance of class cleavages in ideology, we should indicate in advance that we do not mean by "importance" anything so strong as "determining influence." The underlying relationship between class and political ideology that we establish in the next section is mediated (filtered, accentuated, attenuated, displaced, or even eliminated) in the institutional arrangements that govern political action. Those arrangements bias recruitment to political activism and leadership, so that the balance of ideologically defined interests represented in those forums of the state where public policy decisions are made may be very different from the balance in the society at large. This mediation is highly complex, and even contradictory. In subsequent chapters we will describe two contrasting political "circuits," those of electoral and elite/organized class politics. In the first, the party system works to minimize the articulation of class cleavages and the ideological expression of class interests. In the second, the leadership of the major interest groups in society, representing business, the professions, organized labour, and so on, express the opposing ideological orientations of classes in a more clear-cut fashion than is the case in the general public. For the moment, however, we are interested in the null hypothesis, assumed in conventional Canadian political studies, that there is no relationship in the society at large between class and political interests.

CLASS DIFFERENCES IN POLITICAL IDEOLOGY?

In this section we examine class cleavages in ideology, using Wright's typology of social class (see the description in chapter 3). As we interpret it, at the first level the concept of class involves a fundamental conflict between capital and labour (crudely, between private employ*ers* and employ*ees*). But modern capitalism, perhaps any capitalism, requires a richer and more complex analysis of social class. We address five aspects of this complexity. First, we look at the effect of differences in business ownership rather than control, and in the size of businesses, as influencing the solidarity or factional division of the capitalist class. Second, we look at differences in authority and individual autonomy, and the "inconsistent" class locations, in order to address the arguments about the inconsistency of working-class ideology and the new class theorists' prediction that there are different class bases for traditional materialist demands and for demands related to quality of life issues. Third, we examine differences between manual and non-manual workers to evaluate the adequacy of arguments for the overriding importance of this distinction. Fourth, we examine the influence of differences in supervisory authority and rates of pay on working-class consciousness. Finally, we examine the ideological perspectives of a number of groups outside of the paid labour force, including the unemployed, homemakers, retired people, students, and people who are ill or disabled.

Table 5-4 shows the extent of class differences in political ideology, comparing the respondents in the seven class categories defined according to Wright's scheme and using the items and scales for which regional comparisons are made in table 5-2. There are indeed systematic and fairly sizeable class differences in political ideology. The largest explained variance is obtained for the left-right index, presumably because it is more reliable than the other scales and the individual items. For the left-right index 7.1 percent of the variance is explained by class, compared to 17.6 percent explained by province when Quebec is included, but only 2.4 percent when Quebec is excluded. More generally, for the items and scales dealing with social programs, redistribution, corporations, and labour, the magnitudes of the class differences are substantially larger than the regional differences within English Canada but somewhat smaller than the differences among all the provinces. Although the effect of class on the other items is small, it is notably and predictably smaller than the corresponding regional effects only on questions concerned with federal-provincial relations. On questions more closely tied to the distribution of power between classes, questions of political efficacy, political participation, and protest, the effect of class is substantially larger than the negligible regional effect.

The variable strength of the class and regional effects across different items is always intelligible, as in the cases of the participation, protest, and efficacy items just discussed. For example the disproportionately larger class than regional differences in support for more government effort on health care reflect the greater need for health care among lower income groups and the redistributive effects of government health insurance in favour of the poor (Evans 1984, 90–1). Also the more pronounced class differences in agreement that cutbacks in social spending have been too severe reflect the greater impact of social spending cuts on the working class whose private resources cannot compensate for the reduced accessibility to higher education, cultural activity, or lost consumption standards as a result of cuts to unemployment insurance, old age pension, or other income security programs. The substantially larger class differences in attitudes to rent control reflect the obvious class interests of the property owners and tenants.

Table 5-4
Means of Measures of Political Ideology by Social Class

Measure of Political Ideology	Mean for Class							Percentage of variance explained
	Capitalist class	Small employers	Petty bourgeoisie	Managers and technocrats	Supervisors	Semi-autonomous employees	Working class	
Government effort for health*	23	39	36	37	45	40	55	3.4
Government effort for unemployed*	14	23	31	30	23	20	37	2.4
Government effort for the poor*	52	48	55	65	64	53	69	2.6
Cutbacks too great*	8	19	12	21	18	17	23	3.1
Social programs index, mean	−.50	−.37	−.36	−.26	.00	−.22	.14	4.7
Redistribute taxes*	20	39	54	55	64	46	58	3.1
Blame unemployed*	58	79	72	65	73	53	65	1.4
Abolish rent control*	31	26	29	24	22	27	14	3.1
Redistribution index, mean	−.90	−.52	−.19	−.32	−.11	−.38	.10	5.4
Favour foreign investment*	70	67	44	54	44	49	40	2.7
Corporate power too great*	55	80	78	74	74	74	75	.9
Union power too great*	80	96	79	86	68	66	64	5.7
Outlaw strikebreaking*	18	30	49	47	47	47	64	5.9
Outlaw teachers strike*	54	64	55	65	54	44	49	.9
Labour index, mean	−.66	−.41	−.32	−.23	−.13	−.14	.06	3.4
Left-right index, mean	−.78	−.48	−.34	−.36	−.10	−.39	.14	7.1
Fed government fair to own province*	53	54	38	48	58	50	45	.9
More provincial power*	27	39	51	30	34	34	42	4.2
Too much attention to Quebec*	42	51	58	58	56	54	46	1.2
Support French schools*	52	45	61	67	62	57	67	1.2
Support gay rights*	50	75	54	64	74	59	68	1.9
Eliminate censorship*	45	45	42	52	49	49	43	.5
Civilian review of police*	72	59	70	65	82	73	75	1.4
Support affirmative action*	49	64	63	61	60	54	72	2.8
Effort against sex discrimination*	35	58	37	52	54	52	59	2.4
Civil liberties index, mean	−.47	−.19	−.15	−.28	.13	−.10	.08	2.2
Immigrants should assimilate*	57	62	71	66	55	55	66	.9
Blame immigrants*	52	76	67	63	66	58	66	.3
Immigration index, mean	−.47	−.13	−.03	−.22	−.21	−.27	.00	1.6
Efficacy index, mean	.59	.29	−.05	.41	.13	.40	−.05	3.6
Participation index, mean	.09	.44	.28	.40	−.01	.22	−.04	2.6
Protest index, mean	−.17	.07	−.26	.01	.15	.15	.16	2.2
Inconsistency index, mean	.02	.13	.02	−.03	.29	.08	.01	.8
Number of cases	51	64	217	128	200	148	1025	

* Percent agreeing or strongly agreeing

Compared to this consistent pattern in attitudes towards social policy, attitudes towards labour relations issues are less clearly structured. Although the class differences are relatively larger than the regional differences for most of these items, there is little class differentiation in assessments of the power of corporations, and there is more provincial than class variation in views of whether teachers should be allowed to strike. Generally speaking the working class approves and the capitalist class disapproves of the powers of unions inasmuch as they have generally defended the political interests of the one against the other. On the other hand there are clear limits to working-class support for the powers of unions, with marked opposition to public sector unionization, particularly in Quebec where public sector union militance was most pronounced in these years. Further, there is no sharp conflict in attitudes towards the dominant fraction of the ruling class; monopoly capital or the dominant corporations are viewed with relative approval by the relatively more organized and privileged fractions of the working class, and they are opposed by fractions of capital and the petty bourgeoisie operating in more competitive sectors of the economy.

Taken together these results amplify arguments made in the last chapter. Superimposed on a substantial consensus in favour of the social policy commitments of the postwar settlement is a definite division among classes over the scope and content of social policy. In a period like the one we discuss, when the economic supports of the social welfare state are in doubt, class divisions may become politically salient. In such times the dialectical balance between conflict and integration that characterizes the hegemony of the welfare state may shift more in the direction of conflict. At the same time the weakness and lower salience in public ideology of those aspects of the postwar settlement that relate to the adjustment of powers between capital and labour mean that the perception of a conflict of interest over social policy is not easily translated into a corresponding clarity of identification of the reasons for this conflict of interest, or into an effective capacity to organize the interests of the working class on these issues.

This interpretation may be criticized as exaggerating the importance of the proportions of variance in the measures of ideology explained by class position. An alternative estimate of the magnitude of ideological class conflict that may be more persuasive is based upon inspection of the actual differences between the capitalist and working-class respondents. Unlike measures of explained variance, such comparisons are unaffected by the highly unequal distribution of respondents among class categories. The ideological differences between capital and labour, summarized in table 5-4, are clearly comparable to what have generally been regarded as the overriding effects of region on Canadian political culture. For the left-right index, the difference between the means of the capitalist and working classes is .94 standard deviations (taking the difference between −.78 and .14, in the table). Pooling the capitalist class and small employers (which contain relatively few respondents) the difference drops to .75 standard deviations. In comparison there is a difference of .91 standard deviations in the mean scores of left-right index between Quebec and English Canada; among the nine provinces of English Canada, the range of mean scores is .72 standard deviations and if the three outlying provinces (Newfoundland, New Brunswick, and Saskatchewan) are disregarded, the range drops to .3 standard deviations. For the item dealing with the redistribution of taxation, the difference between the capitalist and working classes is 38 percent, compared to a Quebec–English Canada difference of 13 percent and a range among the provinces of English Canada of 14 percent.

Because the capitalist and working classes are at the right and left of the political spectrum for almost all these items and scales, the difference between them provides an appropriate estimate of the *range* of opinion. For the scales measuring support for social programs, redistribution of income, and labour and the left-right index, this range of mean scores for the class categories is between two-thirds and one standard deviation; for items for which the percentage differences are relevant the range is between 20 and 50 percent.

In light of the widespread assumption that Canadian politics is largely devoid of class, these are striking results. Thus the strong regional differences in party structure and support, and in some aspects of political culture, do not prevent a limited expression of class interest in ideology. The limitations on class divisions in ideology are, furthermore, as much a function of the complexity of the class structure, and the consequent heterogeneity of "interests" defined by class position, as they are of regional divisions, and we should therefore examine in greater detail the differences in ideological orientation by class category.

Considering the differences in the measures of both class and ideology, we are pleased to report that our findings are consistent with Clement and John Myles's (1994, 102 ff.) findings about their measures of pro-labour and anti-business attitudes. In both cases, of course, they find their "capitalist-executive" and working classes on the right and left, respectively. As with our labour index, they find a gradient of opinion for the labour index, with the old middle class (of self-employed persons with no more than two employees) closer to the capitalist-executive class and the new middle class (the – in our opinion unlikely – combination of non-executives with some authority in the workplace *or* some policy-setting authority) on the left. The anti-business index, however, results in a polarization that pits the capitalist-executive class against all three other classes, much like the pattern for our "corporate power" item. Interestingly, for the pro-labour scale Clement and Myles find that Canada, the U.S., and Norway are quite similar, but there is greater class polarization in Sweden. For the anti-business measure there is less polarization in the U.S., about the same in Canada and Norway, and more in Sweden;

in Sweden only, they find that the old middle class is similar to the capitalist-executive class.

Wright presents a similar global comparison for a single "class conscious-ness" index made up of five items dealing with corporations benefiting their owners at the expense of workers, strikebreakers, income inequality, the power of corporations, and the ability of non-management employees to run a business (1996, 410–11). For the U.S. he finds a polarization between the capitalists and expert managers on the right and the skilled and "nonskilled" non-managers (we call them workers) and nonskilled supervisors on the left. Skilled supervisors and the petty bourgeoisie are more left wing, while skilled and nonskilled managers and expert supervisors more right wing; in the middle of the range are the small employers and expert non-managers. This is interesting and not does not appear inconsistent with our findings, but the differences between this and our class schemes preclude a more serious comparison. Of course we have every reason to believe that Wright would have found distinctive patterns for the different items he combined in one scale. Furthermore the variation among the five items suggests that the scale will not likely be much more reliable than the individual items (he does not present a reliability estimate). Like Myles and Clement, Wright (419 ff.) finds similar class oppositions in the U.S. and Sweden, except there is greater polarization in Sweden. In Japan, on the other hand, Wright finds much less class polarization and a remarkable alliance of the petty bourgeoi-sie and the traditional working class on the left.

Finally, there are the results of the British study (Marshall et al. 1989). They report that their preferred class typology, the one developed by John Goldthorpe and his colleagues, accounts for 12 percent of the variation in their class consciousness index, compared to only 8 or 9 percent for Wright's scheme (1989, 180). Unfortunately they do not provide a comparison of the differences among Wright's class categories. This would be illuminating, by identifying attitudinal variation that cannot be explained in Marxist terms. Equally important, it would provide assurance that the difference in ex-plained variation found by Marshall et al. is not the result of differences in the distributions of the Marxist and Weberian schemes. All else equal, a cat-egorization with more equal numbers of respondents in the different catego-ries will explain more variance than if their numbers are highly unequal. As it happens, the two classifications differ in just this way: in their operational-ization of Wright's (second) class scheme, 42.9 percent of the population are in the "proletariat," another 14.4 percent are "semi-credentialed" workers; while none of the other ten classes includes more than 8 percent of the cases. In any event, Marshall et al. find that the right and left of the political spec-trum, respectively, are occupied by the upper section of the "service class," which includes "higher grade professionals, administrators and officials, managers in large establishments and large proprietors" (22), and by manual workers, irrespective of their level of skill. Then closer to the right are the lower level of "service class" and the "small proprietors" and closer to the left are the (combination of) lower-grade technicians and supervisors of manual workers. On the ideological fence are the "routine non-manual employees" and "personal service workers." The scale used in this analysis, note, contains very disparate items, including "subjective class identification, the perception of persisting and gross class inequalities, support for market principles, support for incomes policies which favoured the lower paid, for tax increases in order to increase welfare benefits and for taxes on profitable companies in order to maintain and create jobs" (180).

These comparisons provide the comforting reassurance that the patterns we observed, of limited but systematic class conflict, resemble those obtained in similar studies, though there is significant international variation. But differences in the class categorizations of the different studies make precise comparisons impossible: genuine comparative research requires the exact comparisons like those provided by Wright and by Clement and Myles. Finally, these studies show how restricting the analysis of ideology to a simple scale does more than just hide the details; it obscures important, interesting aspects of political ideology.

THE PATTERN OF
CLASS DIFFERENCES IN IDEOLOGY

Because there are a number of class categories, very different patterns of inter-class difference in ideology could give rise to the same explained variances. That the capitalist and working class are the right and left ends of the ideological spectrum makes sense in theoretical terms, but it is important to examine the positions of the intermediate categories. While the precise pattern of class differences is a function of the item or scale being considered, the left-right index gives a good idea of the modal differences. For this index, recall, the mean scores of the capitalist class and working-class respondents differ by .9 of a standard deviation. About one-quarter of a standard deviation to the left of the capitalist class are the small employers and about one-quarter of a standard deviation to the right of the working class are the supervisors. Near the middle of the political spectrum (but slightly closer to the capitalist class) are the petty bourgeoisie, managers and technocrats, and semi-autonomous employees.

At least after the fact, deviations from this modal pattern can be interpreted in common-sense terms. On foreign investment, for example, the capitalist class and small employers exhibit similar high levels of approval, while the petty bourgeoisie and all the other class groups are nearly evenly split on the benefits of foreign investment. For small-business proprietors fear of increased competition of (mainly larger) foreign investors appears to outweigh the sanctity of the free movement of capital. Resentment of big business is also apparent in the finding that both small employers and the petty bourgeoisie are as likely as respondents from the non-business-owning classes to believe that large corporations are too powerful.

Many of the contradictory patterns observed in our initial examination of the overall distributions of public opinion also characterize the ideology of individual classes. For example while there are large class differences in the items dealing with the power of trade unions and the hiring of strikebreakers, there are negligible class differences in views of teachers' right to strike. And while there are large class differences in opinions of the power of trade unions, no such differences appear in opinions of the power of large corporations. On average, members of the working class are clearly to the left of all the other classes. This class is also characterized by a very high degree of internal variation and by a large body of opinion that does not support policies that are, prima facie, in its interest. For example 64 percent of workers believe that trade unions have too much power, 49 percent would outlaw strikes by teachers, only 37 percent believe the government should do more to assist the unemployed, and 65 percent blame welfare for creating unemployment.

Members of the capitalist class take very conservative positions on these issues and seem to display less internal variation than we observe for the working class. For example just 8 percent of the capitalists believe that social program cutbacks have been too great, 20 percent believe the taxation system should be more redistributive, and 18 percent would outlaw strikebreaking. That only 31 percent of the capitalists support the abolition of rent controls and 52 percent support greater efforts to assist the poor suggests, however, that many capitalists temper their views with a pragmatic concern to moderate social conflict and ensure economic stability by maintaining aggregate demand.

More than the other class categories, petty bourgeois respondents exhibit a combination of right- and left-wing sympathies. They give unusually weak support to social programs and foreign investment, but unusually strong support to income redistribution. Perhaps because they have the most to fear from unionization of their own businesses, small employers are more likely than either the capitalists or petty bourgeoisie to believe that trade unions are too powerful and to oppose teachers having the right to strike. Because of its vulnerability to competition and relatively low levels of income (see appendix A) the petty bourgeoisie is often said to be especially prone to appeals from the far right. But, in this survey, members of the petty bourgeoisie almost always took positions significantly to the left of the capitalist class and usually to the left of the small employers.

In general terms the class differences in ideology correspond to a classical conception of class interest, with the working class taking the most left-wing positions, and the owners of business the most right-wing. The "new class" theorists' belief that the strongest support for state intervention comes from those outside the working class, whose status and prosperity are tied to the growth of the state, receives little support from the results. Our examination of the manual/non-manual divisions within classes, below, will address the new class arguments more directly.

There is considerable ideological variation among the groups commonly lumped into the "middle class," which we have differentiated according to our interpretation of Wright's schema of social class. Supervisors, the lowest level of managers, are ideologically very similar to the working class, while the managers and technocrats are most similar to the business-owning groups. The semi-autonomous workers are much more ambivalent and they tend to be polarized in the direction of capital on some issues and towards the working class on others, although the first tendency appears to be stronger. While the experiences of supervising workers and of managing a business (including both supervision *and* making decisions about what is produced) have conservatizing influences, the experience of managing appears to have a stronger influence on ideology. These patterns of ideological differences suggest that the class differences are not reducible to underlying effects of education and income, the former a "cause" and the latter a consequence of class difference. For example despite its members' low incomes (see appendix A) the petty bourgeoisie is generally on the political right. This issue is taken up directly in the regression analysis below, which includes statistical controls for education, income, and a number of other variables.

We have so far confined our discussion to opinions about social programs, redistribution, and other issues with a fairly direct bearing on class relations. The remaining variables in table 5-4 are less strongly linked to traditional conceptions of left and right, but the nature and extent of class differences in the responses have an important bearing on the nature of class ideologies. The items dealing with regionalism and language address the question of whether regional conflicts have a class dimension or whether they pit the entire class structures of provinces against each other. Examination of the civil liberties issues will test Seymour Martin Lipset's contention that the working class combines egalitarian views on economic issues with authoritarian views of civil liberties. Examination of the political efficacy, political participation, and inconsistency scales tests the hypothesis that there are class biases in the capacity for political organization and influence, which work to the advantage of capital.

Support for provincial powers is strongest in the petty bourgeoisie and weakest among the capitalist class, managers, and technocrats, while the working class and the other groups take intermediate positions. Not surprisingly there are similar but much weaker patterns of class differences in evaluations of whether the federal government treats the respondent's province fairly and in support for more provincial power. Presumably the strong provincial loyalties of the petty bourgeoisie reflect the importance of provincial government support for the local markets in which they do business, and the dependence of many in this class on state employment. Support for French schooling is strongest in the working class and among managers and techno- crats and weakest among the capitalists and small employers. To the extent that opinions about French-language schooling reflect ethnic intolerance, the working class is *less* authoritarian than other classes although we should not make too much of these very small class differences in support for French- language schooling; the issue is not, to a significant extent, a class issue.

The class differences in the civil liberties items are also not large (recol- lect that the regional differences within English Canada were negligible and the difference between Quebec and English Canada was large only for the affirmative action issue). On all four items and on the composite index of support for civil liberties, the working class takes positions on the liberal side of the scale. An inspection of the mean scores on the civil liberties index shows that the working class and supervisors are on the left, the capitalist class is on the right, and the remaining groups take intermediate positions. Once again the supervisors' attitudes place them much closer to the working class than to the managers and business owners who supervise and plan the operation of businesses. Despite the relatively low levels of education in the petty bourgeoisie, its members do not take distinctively right-wing positions. While the economic cast of some of the items may be responsible for the relatively right-wing stand of capitalist class members, even on the non- economic issues of gay rights and film censorship, the business-owning groups do not take especially liberal stands. More important than any class differences in these data, however, is the lack of support for Lipset's charac- terization of the working class as authoritarian. Both absolutely and relative to other classes, the working class is neither homophobic nor a strong supporter of police activities being exempt from civilian review. On non- economic aspects of civil liberties there is little in the way of class differ- ences, while on economic aspects the working class is clearly on the left.

The two items and the scale dealing with immigrants show very little class differentiation. Although the mean for the working class is the middle of the range of opinion for the two separate items, assimilationist sentiment is clearly strongest in the working class and petty bourgeoisie and weakest in the capitalist class, which does support Lipset's arguments, taking assimila- tionist sentiment as an indicator of authoritarianism.

The class differences in the political culture variables are also not large: class explains 3.6 percent of the variation in efficacy, 2.6 percent in partici- pation, and 2.2 percent in protest, compared to less than 1 percent explained by region, even with Quebec included. Of course efficacy and participation are two of the three key indicators used by Simeon and Elkins (1974) in their argument that there are regional political cultures in Canada. On this basis, however, we have stronger grounds for arguing that there are class than regional political cultures. Political efficacy is lowest in the petty bourgeoisie and working class and also relatively low for supervisors. The middle class groups, capitalists, and small employers score relatively high on political efficacy. Generally the class differences in political efficacy, which measures the belief that one can affect the political system, are similar to the pattern of differences in political participation. There are important exceptions to this relationship. While working-class and petty bourgeois respondents were equally pessimistic about the likelihood they will succeed in effecting change, the petty bourgeoisie had a much higher rate of political participation. Members of the capitalist class, on the other hand, were highly efficacious but had relatively low rates of political participation.

The strongest support for protest was found among the supervisors, semi-autonomous employees, and the working class, while the lowest level of support for protest was found among the capitalist class and petty bourgeoisie: there is a dichotomy between business owners and non-owners. That business owners have more confidence in the system of electoral politics suggests that, compared to the non-owning classes, they are better served by it. Again contrary to the thesis of working-class authoritarianism, if one measure of anti-authoritarianism is the willingness to challenge authority, it is not the working class but the capitalist class and owners of small business who are more authoritarian.

Except for the suggestion that the supervisors are somewhat more inconsistent than the other groups, there is almost no class difference in the measure of political inconsistency. The working class and capitalist class, which define the left and right of the political spectrum, prove to be no more consistent than the other classes. Note that mean inconsistency scores of the two class categories with the lowest levels of education, the working class and petty bourgeoisie, are almost identical to the means for the best-educated groups, the capitalist class, managers, and small employers. This finding strikes still another blow against the argument that the working class is less competent to engage in rational political decision making than other classes and the implication that low levels of working class participation in the political system prevent their authoritarian leanings from damaging the political system.

Also bearing on the ability of a social class to influence the political process is the extent of internal ideological variation. Even if, on average, the individuals in different classes do not differ in their ideological consistency, there may be large differences in the extent of ideological variation between the individuals within each class. Presumably, an unusually high level of internal variation would make it more difficult for the social class to mobilize politically. To examine these differences, table 5-5 compares the standard deviations of eight ideology scales (it does not make sense to consider variation in the inconsistency scores).

Table 5-5
Standard Deviations of Selected Measures of Political Ideology by Social Class

Measure of Political Ideology				Social Class			
	Capit-alist class	Small employ-ers	Petty bourg-eoisie	Man-agers and techno-crats	Super-visors	Semi-autono-mous employ-ees	Working class
Social programs	1.16	.92	1.02	.83	.91	.96	.98
Redistribution	1.02	1.11	1.05	.96	.98	1.04	.97
Left-right index	.96	.82	.96	.89	.94	.94	.97
Labour	.94	.88	.97	.87	.99	.91	.98
Civil liberties	1.34	.88	1.00	1.12	1.06	1.03	.95
Immigration	.81	1.08	1.19	.99	.91	.93	.96
Efficacy	1.13	.95	1.06	.95	.94	.81	.99
Protest	.96	1.01	.98	.85	.93	.99	.96

There is only the slightest suggestion of class differences here. There are higher than average levels of ideological variation within the capitalist class and petty bourgeoisie. The working class, which, compared to other social classes, is low on both efficacy and participation, is *not* more internally divided ideologically and (as the comparison of means of the inconsistency index indicated) its individual members are no more likely to take inconsistent positions. All of this suggests that the political weaknesses of the working class are not the result of its being more divided internally than other classes – as a result of ethnic heterogeneity, differences between manual and non-manual workers, differences between men and women, pay differentials, and so on. But we need to turn to a more systematic investigation of such divisions within classes.

IDEOLOGICAL DIFFERENCES *WITHIN* SOCIAL CLASSES

In this section we investigate the effects of differences within classes on the ideological divisions among classes. We focus, first, on differences among persons in regular paid employment associated with manual and non-manual work, supervisory authority, and pay differentials. We move then to consider the differences in ideology associated with positions outside of regular paid employment.

The manual/non-manual division is taken by many scholars to be the only or the most important class division in advanced capitalist society. The class differences we have observed so far suggest that we should also find substantial differences in a simple comparison of manual and non-manual workers. After all, the three business-owning classes and the contradictory location for managers and technocrats, whose positions are clearly on the conservative side, consist very largely of non-manual workers. Indeed it is common to classify business proprietors in the non-manual ranks regardless of whether they do manual work.

Our own approach to social classes treats the manual/non-manual distinction as one of a number of potential sources of ideological variation within classes. The respondents classified as supervisors, semi-autonomous employees, and workers all include some manual and some non-manual workers. We also examine the effects of supervision and pay, though constructing these class categories required us to decide how much supervision should result in the reclassification of members of the working class and semi-autonomous workers into the category of supervisors. The petty bourgeoisie is somewhat different, for it includes a mixture of "own-account" workers, who have no employees, and small business owners who have one to four employees. Thus a comparison of supervisors to non-supervisors within the petty bourgeoisie compares the own-account workers to small employers. Within the four class categories, respondents who reported that they did *any* supervision were compared with respondents who did none.

The measure of pay in the analysis compares each individual's pay to the mean for his or her class category *in units of standard deviations* (also measured within his or her class category). It is appropriate to deal with pay differences within social classes, because class is a cause of pay rates and not the reverse; people in different social classes have different levels of pay, as a consequence of their class positions. Because these new variables measure differences within social classes, the results are independent of our previous findings about class differences. We will provide comparisons of the magnitudes of internal differences in social classes to the class differences.

Table 5-6 shows that the ideological differences between manual and non-manual workers differs radically among the four class categories containing significant numbers of each. There are very large differences between manual and non-manual semi-autonomous employees and moderately large differences for the working class and supervisors, but only negligible differences between the manual and non-manual sectors of the petty bourgeoisie. Thus, in terms of ideology, the effect of business ownership takes precedence over the effect of the manual/non-manual difference. For the three classes in which there was a manual/non-manual difference, the manual workers took positions to the left of their non-manual counterparts, as found in many other studies. The extent of manual/non-manual differences was also a function of the particular measure of ideology examined, with larger differences appearing for variables that exhibited larger interclass differences.

Table 5-6
Means of Political Ideology Scales by Class and Manual versus Non-manual Workers

					Social Class						
			Petty bourgeoisie		Managers and technocrats	Supervisors		Semi-autonomous employees		Working class	
Measure of Political Ideology	Capitalist class	Small employers	Non-manual	Manual		Non-manual	Manual	Non-manual	Manual	Non-manual	Manual
Social programs	-.50	-.37	-.31	-.37	-.26	.03	-.04	-.30	-.07	.03	.28
Redistribution	-.90	-.52	-.22	-.16	-.32	-.26	.17	-.61	.08	.01	.23
Left-right index	-.78	-.48	-.33	-.35	-.36	-.14	-.03	-.53	-.11	.00	.31
Labour	-.66	-.41	-.26	-.36	-.23	-.21	.02	-.20	-.02	.01	.10
Civil liberties	-.47	-.19	-.02	-.28	-.28	.12	.13	.00	-.32	.07	.10
Immigration	-.47	-.13	-.03	-.02	-.22	-.32	-.02	-.41	.00	-.13	.17
Efficacy	.59	.29	-.13	-.01	.41	.22	-.03	.54	.12	.06	-.17
Participation	.09	.44	.33	.20	.40	.09	-.18	.24	.17	.03	-.12
Protest	-.17	.07	-.31	-.19	.01	.06	.31	.26	-.05	.20	.11
Inconsistency	.02	.13	.07	-.08	-.03	.46	-.01	.12	.00	.05	-.05
Number of cases	51	64	108	109	128	129	71	96	52	551	474

Non-manual members of the working class were somewhat more conservative than their manual counterparts. For the measures of support for social programs and redistribution and the left-right index, the difference was about one-quarter of a standard deviation, but the differences in support for labour and for civil liberties were negligible. Manual workers were less tolerant of immigrants and less well integrated into the political system, with lower levels of both efficacy and political participation. Dividing the working class in this way produces a category of manual workers who are to the left of all other classes and a category of non-manual workers whose views overlap those of supervisors and manual semi-autonomous workers. Despite these internal differences, however, non-manual workers remain clearly to the left of all three categories of business owners, managers and technocrats, and non-manual supervisors and semi-autonomous workers. Thus the manual/non-manual division corresponds to a fairly significant ideological difference within the working class, but does not disrupt the general ideological alignment of classes.

Despite their craft skills and control over their work, *manual* semi-autonomous workers were ideologically similar to non-manual members of the working class. In contrast the *non-manual* semi-autonomous employees were very conservative: they exhibited levels of support for social programs and redistribution close to those of the small employers. Non-manual semi-autonomous workers were also very negative in attitudes towards immigrants and had very high levels of political efficacy and willingness to support extra-parliamentary protest. For the index measuring support for redistribution, the difference between manual and non-manual semi-autonomous employees was more than half a standard deviation and for three other scales the difference was more than .4 of a standard deviation. The extreme ideological heterogeneity of semi-autonomous employees leads us to question its usefulness as a category. It proves to contain an odd mixture of skilled workers with quite left-wing ideology and highly educated, well-paid non-supervisory workers with views quite close to those of the managers and small employers. Marshall et al. (1988, chap. 3) raise similar concerns about the wide variation among semi-autonomous workers.

Supervisors in manual occupations were ideologically similar to the manual semi-autonomous employees and non-manual members of the working class, while supervisors in non-manual occupations took positions just to the left of the managers and technocrats. Non-manual supervisors were much less supportive of redistribution, less assimilationist in their views of immigrants, more efficacious, more likely to participate in politics, more supportive of protest, and more *inconsistent* in their views. Within what we have defined as classes there are systematic differences between manual and non-manual workers, with the former generally on the left.

At the left of the political spectrum are manual members of the working class, in line with traditional class theory. There follows a grouping of non-manual members of the working class, manual supervisors, and manual semi-autonomous employees; and to their right are the non-manual supervisors. Finally, the non-manual semi-autonomous employees resemble the managers in some respects and the small employers in others. In any event the non-manual semi-autonomous employees fall within that part of the ideological spectrum defined by the three categories of business owners and the managers and technocrats. The combination of right-wing ideology, high political efficacy, and support for protest among non-manual semi-autonomous employees and non-manual supervisors has interesting implications for the understanding of working-class consciousness. In these positions there exists a degree of militant opposition to the general interests of the working class that limits the solidarity of that class. In addition it is in these positions, if anywhere, that anything like "working class authoritarianism" is localized. This evidence tends therefore to counter the original specification of the authoritarian outlook of the traditional working class, and the implications of more recent theories of the more humanitarian social concerns of the new middle class.

We now turn briefly to the effects of supervision and pay differences within classes. Table 5-7 includes two rows for each of the dependent variables: the first row shows the effects of the class variables alone and the second, discussed in the next section of this chapter, shows those effects controlled for region and a number of other variables. The values in the table show the effects of these two sources of variation within classes and the manual/non-manual distinction – the effect of each variable is net of the other two (regression being used to separate the effects).

One important question is whether the manual/non-manual differences just discussed are significantly reduced by controlling for the amount of supervision involved in the respondent's job and her or his pay – that is whether they reflect underlying differences in these variables. The table shows that manual/non-manual differences are completely unaffected by controls for the amount of supervision and rate of pay. Generally the impact of supervision is smaller than the manual/non-manual difference. There are only isolated effects: for example, compared to members of the working class who do no supervision, workers who did some supervision were significantly less supportive of trade unions; and petty bourgeois supervisors were more favourable on civil liberties issues and less assimilationist in their views of immigrants. Because the effects are small and unsystematic, they add little to our general analysis of the effects of social class on political ideology.

Each standard deviation of pay corresponds to a difference of about one-sixth of a standard deviation (rightward) on the left-right scale. Higher pay *lowers* support for social programs and redistribution and increases political efficacy and support for protest. This makes sense – within social classes,

Table 5-7
Means of Political Attitude Indexes, by Class/Status Group, Relative to the Working Class, for Employed People

Measure of Political Ideology	Control variables	Mean for Class, Relative to Working Class						Manual, Relative to Non-Manual				Some Supervision			Rate of pay (standardized within social classes)
		Capitalist class	Small employers	Petty bourgeoisie	Managers and technocrats	Supervisors	Semi-autonomous employees	Petty bourgeoisie	Semi-autonomous employees	Supervisors	Working class	Petty bourgeoisie	Semi-autonomous employees	Working class	
Social programs	None	-66*	-53*	-53*	-42*	-16+	-34*	-5	16	-4	29*	-13	-30	2	-15*
	All	-51*	-44*	-48*	-39*	-12	-27*	4	23	-9	24*	-12	-31	8	-12*
Redistribution	None	-98*	-60*	-29*	-40*	-12	-36*	7	60*	46*	27*	-13	10	-16+	-14*
	All	-67*	-55*	-28*	-34*	-10	-19+	8	50*	35+	15+	-7	14	-3	-7+
Left-right index	None	-92*	-61*	-48*	-49*	-21*	-46*	1	35+	13	33*	-5	-19	-14+	-15*
	All	-65*	-54*	-42*	-48*	-17+	-33*	15	40*	11	28*	-1	-15	3	-9*
Labour	None	-68*	-42*	-32*	-24+	-10	-13	-8	16	24	8	4	9	-26*	-2
	All	-38*	-34*	-27*	-14	-5	8	-6	8	14	-2	13	14	-12	6+
Civil liberties	None	-58*	-28+	-18+	-38*	3	-26*	-24	-37+	2	4	48*	4	7	-7*
	All	-38+	-17	-4	-33*	3	-22+	-3	-26	9	6	47*	9	18*	-5

* significant at .01
+ significant at .05

Table 5-7
Means of Political Attitude Indexes, by Class/Status Group, Relative to the Working Class, for Employed People (Continued)

Measure of Political Ideology	Control variables	Mean for Class, Relative to Working Class						Manual, Relative to Non-Manual				Some Supervision			Rate of pay (standardized within social classes)
		Capitalist class	Small employers	Petty bourgeoisie	Managers and technocrats	Supervisors	Semi-autonomous employees	Petty bourgeoisie	Semi-autonomous employees	Supervisors	Working class	Petty bourgeoisie	Semi-autonomous employees	Working class	
Immigration	None	-49*	-15	-9	-24+	-19+	-23+	1	38+	30+	31+	-30+	-7	1	-5+
	All	-16	-7	-11	-6	-13	1	0	16	10	15+	-30+	5	14+	3
Efficacy	None	66*	35*	4	48*	15	40*	11	-36+	-28	-27*	20	26	-5	16*
	All	37+	20	7	23+	6	17	31+	-14	-10	-11	11	17	-3	5
Participation	None	-34+	-9	-41*	-15	2	-5	15	-31	24	-9	8	-4	3	-1
	All	-34+	-1	-15	-15	4	-8	29+	-5	36+	1	6	-15	-2	-2
Protest	None	10	46*	30*	41*	-4	22+	-14	-1	-30	-18*	5	28	20*	14*
	All	-18	38*	27*	17	-14	6	-4	23	-22	-6	1	18	20*	4

* significant at .01
+ significant at .05

Table 5-8
Analysis of Variance for Regression of Political Ideology Scales on All Variables

		Percentage of Variance Explained (Adjusted for degrees of freedom)						
		Quebec versus English-Canada	Province	Class	Class, super-vision, manual/non-manual	Province class	Province, class, demo-graphic	Province, class, demo-graphic, religion
Social programs	Population	5.6	6.1	3.3		8.8	12.0	12.2
	Employed	4.4	5.2	4.3	7.6	12.3	13.1	13.2
Redistribution	Population	7.7	8.8	5.0		13.1	19.5	19.9
	Employed	6.5	7.6	5.1	9.1	15.0	18.2	18.5
Left-right index	Population	16.2	17.4	5.6		21.7	26.9	27.8
	Employed	14.6	15.7	6.7	10.7	24.3	26.6	27.4
Labour	Population	7.6	7.9	3.7		11.1	13.7	13.7
	Employed	6.9	7.3	3.0	3.9	9.8	12.7	12.6
Civil liberties	Population	5.7	5.7	1.6		6.9	8.8	11.1
	Employed	5.9	6.4	1.8	2.8	9.0	11.2	14.6
Immigration	Population	8.5	8.5	2.7		11.2	18.8	19.6
	Employed	8.9	9.0	1.2	3.1	11.8	17.6	18.2
Efficacy	Population	.0	.0	4.0		3.9	12.6	13.0
	Employed	.1	.0	3.3	6.9	7.1	13.9	14.3
Participation	Population	.0	.6	2.7		3.4	10.7	11.4
	Employed	.0	.8	2.3	5.1	5.9	10.8	11.4
Protest	Population	.1	.2	8.3		8.3	17.4	18.3
	Employed	.1	.4	1.8	1.9	2.3	12.3	13.6

higher levels of income decrease support for policies that assist poorer people. Significantly, pay has little effect on support for labour. Table 5-8 shows that distinguishing manual from non-manual workers and including additional measures dealing with supervision and pay substantially increases our ability to predict political ideology. For example the explained variance (adjusted for degrees of freedom) in the left-right index increases from 6.7 percent to 10.7 percent; and the corresponding figures for political efficacy are 3.3 percent and 6.9 percent. Although the *magnitudes* of these differences *within* classes are smaller than the previously observed difference *between* classes, the within-class differences produce relatively large increases in the explained variance.

GROUPS OUTSIDE THE PAID LABOUR FORCE

About the ideology of respondents outside the labour force, we do not have very definite expectations. The social relations of production that we believe are the cause of class differences in ideology affect people outside the work force indirectly. Homemakers, for example, are largely the spouses of employed people who are distributed throughout the class structure. While the research on labour force participation shows that the spouses of homemakers are not a representative cross-section of the work force, the disproportionalities are not so great as to push homemakers strongly in some ideological direction. Retired people are also likely to be distributed over the entire ideological spectrum, since retirement affects all social classes. Students, whose ideology is likely to reflect the class positions of their parents, resemble homemakers in their relation to the class structure. The two remaining categories, for people who are unemployed and people who are ill and disabled, are rather different: higher levels of unemployment of the working class and its dependent economic position suggest the political views of the unemployed should resemble those of the working class, while the people who are ill or disabled are likely to be very dependent on the state and therefore to strongly support social programs.

Treating the occupants of these categories in terms of their relationship to the class structure disregards the other ways in which they are distinctive. Students and the retired, for example, are highly concentrated in the low and high age groups, respectively, and homemakers are largely female. It is therefore necessary to determine whether particular ideological positions simply reflect their distinctive age and gender composition. The mean scores of the ten ideology scales for the non-labour-force participants are given in table 5-9.

Except for the protest scale, for which the differences among the groups explain 7.2 percent of the variance, these variances are quite small – none exceeds 2.2 percent. The large value for the protest scale is clearly due to the high level of support for extra-parliamentary protest, .89 standard deviations above the mean, among students and the very low level of support, .52 standard deviations below the mean, for retired people. These differences are age related.

The survey responses of the unemployed and the manual working class (see table 5-6) are very similar, even though unemployed people are drawn from a variety of different occupations. The implication is that being unemployed leads people to more left-wing positions. Homemakers' ideological positions are somewhere between those of non-manual and manual workers, except their

Table 5-9
Means of Political Ideology Scales by Labour Force Status

			Status				
	Employers					Percent of
Measure of	and		House-		Ill,	variance
Political Ideology	workers	Unemployed	workers	Retired	Students	disabled	explained
Social programs	−.02	.29	.04	−.15	.04	.43	.8
Redistribution	−.07	.29	.13	.12	−.24	.61	1.8
Left-right index	−.06	.33	.13	−.07	−.01	.64	1.6
Labour	−.08	.19	.22	.02	−.27	.40	2.0
Civil liberties	−.01	.23	.02	−.19	.19	.02	.6
Immigrants	−.08	.28	.16	.22	−.37	.25	2.2
Efficacy	.07	−.21	−.17	−.18	.42	−.35	2.1
Participation	.07	−.19	−.19	−.10	.22	−.15	1.5
Protest	.09	.15	−.28	−.52	.89	−.09	7.2
Consistency	.05	.00	−.09	−.10	−.07	−.18	.4
Number of Cases	1833	99	603	236	106	43	

support for protest is lower. Retired people do not differ markedly from the mean for the population, except that their support for protest is very low. The ideological positions of students differ from the population in a complex way. While students are near the average in support for social programs, they are about one-quarter of a standard deviation below the mean in support for redistribution and for labour. They also differ from the population average in their high efficacy and political participation and very strong support for extra-parliamentary protest. That the political activism of students is coupled with mainstream views of society suggests that the political action of students is not likely to make a distinctive mark. If anything our evidence describes, in this period, a distinctively right-wing student activism, as illustrated, for example, in studies of Progressive Conservative party leadership conventions (Martin, Gregg, and Perlin 1983). Finally, people with disabilities are very left wing in their support for social programs, redistribution, and labour, but have low levels of efficacy and participation. In the next section we will explore the extent to which these differences are the result of income, gender, age, and other variables.

COMBINING REGIONAL, SOCIAL CLASS,
AND SOCIO-DEMOGRAPHIC VARIABLES

Thus far we have dealt with the effects of province and social class on political ideology separately. It is therefore possible that some of what we have described as provincial differences in ideology might reflect underlying differences in the class compositions of the provinces, such as the concentrations of farm owners on the Prairies or of industrial workers in Ontario. This section begins with an analysis designed to determine what, if any, modifications to our previous discussions of the effects on ideology of province and class are required by an analysis that includes both variables simultaneously. We then examine the effects of a number of additional variables that figure prominently in orthodox political sociology, including age, gender, education, family income, religion and religiosity, and the differences between people of French ethnicity and other ethnic groups in Quebec and English Canada. We refer to these as "socio-demographic" variables. Finally, we redirect our attention to province and class and determine how their effects are altered by statistical controls for the socio-demographic variables.

In order to determine whether the effects of province and class are independent it is only necessary to compare the sum of the variances explained by province and class alone with the variance explained when the measures of political ideology are regressed on province and class simultaneously. If their effects are completely independent, the sum of the variances explained by province and class individually will equal the variance explained by province and class together; conversely, if the effect of province is entirely reducible to class differences between provinces or vice versa, the combined variance will equal the larger of the variances explained by province and class separately.

As table 5-8 indicates, these results are straightforward. For all of the measures of political ideology and whether the entire sample or the sub-sample of the employed is considered, the effects of province and social class on political ideology are almost entirely independent. For example using the entire sample, province explains 6.1 percent of the variance in support for social programs, class explains 3.3 percent of the variance, and the two variables combined explain 8.8 percent of the variance; in the corresponding analysis using the sub-sample of the employed, the corresponding figures are 5.2, 7.6, and 12.3 percent of the variance.

These results argue strongly against attempts to reduce regional differences in ideology to the effects of class, and vice versa. While individual provinces may have distinctive class structures, our conjecture that this might account for interprovincial differences in political ideology is clearly not sustained. Most important, the major regional difference that we observe, between Quebec and English Canada, has very little to do with the effects of class. The synthesis of our separate analyses of region and class thus requires little more than their addition.

EFFECTS OF THE
SOCIO-DEMOGRAPHIC VARIABLES

Our measures of the socio-demographic variables are mostly self-explanatory, but some explanation is required. In order to address arguments in the literature that stress the effect of educational credentials, educational attainment is measured with three variables: the number of years of education and two dummy variables identifying the high school and university graduates. In addition to a direct measure of family income in thousands of dollars, two dummy variables were used to distinguish the respondents who refused to state their family income or who said their families had no income in the previous year (an unlikely event) from respondents who answered the question. (For respondents who refused to give their income, family income was set to the mean for the population.) Religiosity was measured on a scale from 0 to 5, which signify, respectively, no church attendance and attendance more frequently than once a week.

Table 5-8 (referring back) shows how much socio-demographic variables increase our ability to predict political ideology, beyond the effects of province and class. Because religion and religiosity are often said to have a strong impact on Canadian politics – at least on the basis of the election studies (Irvine 1974; Clarke et al. 1979, 100 ff.) – their contributions to the explained variances for each of our measures of ideology (net of all other variables) is given separately. The effect of the socio-demographic measures varies dramatically according to which measure of ideology is considered. The strongest effects are for the variables that are only *weakly* related to class and province, including political efficacy, participation, and support for protest. Also, the socio-demographic variables generally had stronger effects in analysis of the entire sample than on the sub-sample of the employed, presumably because the measures of manual/non-manual differences, supervision, and rate of pay are included only in the analysis based on the employed. The effects of religion and religiosity are generally quite small.

In the analysis for the entire sample, for example, province and class together explain 3.9 percent of the variance in political efficacy and the addition of the socio-demographic variables raises this substantially to 12.6 percent; for the sub-sample of the employed the increase is less dramatic, from 6.9 to 13.9 percent. Adding religion and the measure of religious observance to the regression equation raises the explained variances by only 0.4 percent. The impact of the socio-demographic variables is somewhat smaller for the index of support for redistribution; the explained variances without and with the socio-demographic variables are, respectively, 13.1 and 19.9 percent for the entire sample and 15.0 and 18.5 percent for the employed. Again, the additional variance explained by religion and religiosity is quite small – 0.4 and 0.3 percent in the two analyses, respectively. While the socio-demographic variables have larger effects on the consistency than either province or class, the total explained variances remain small. Even including measures of years of education and high school and university graduation, which is generally believed to be a strong predictor of ideological constraint (but see our findings above), all the variables explain only 2.7 percent for the entire sample and 4.2 percent for the employed.

To provide a more detailed picture of the specific effects on ideology of particular divisions within classes, we examine the regression coefficients in tables 5-10 and 5-11, which respectively give the differences among class and status groups and the effects of age, gender, education, and other "demographic" variables. The coefficients are taken from regression equations that include statistical controls for province and class. To improve the appearance of this table all the coefficients have been multiplied by 100 (so decimal points can be omitted, except for the income variable). Thus, for example, if one of the regression coefficients for the effect of gender is 14, then the difference between women and men is 0.14 standard deviations.

Age

The strongest effect of age on political ideology is the dramatic decline in support for extra-parliamentary protest as age increases. Holding all the other variables constant, support for protest falls by nearly one-fifth of a standard deviation for each decade of age (as indicated by the coefficient of −18). Thus the average difference between twenty- and sixty-year olds would be nearly three-quarters of a standard deviation. As age increases, support for social programs and civil liberties declines somewhat, and political participation increases. Age does not, however, affect support for redistribution, the left-right index, or labour. Also, while political participation increases with age, political efficacy was unaffected.

Older people are more politically conservative, but in a very specific way. The most important effect of age is to lower support for extra-parliamentary protest; by comparison there is a weaker and more limited tendency for older respondents to take more conservative positions on policy issues. An inspection of detailed tabulations showed that the effects of age are roughly linear, so there is no evidence that the cohort that came of age in the late 1960s is particularly unusual as suggested by theorists of the "post-materialist, silent revolution."

Gender

Gender had little impact on the measures of ideology employed in this study. Women were stronger supporters of civil liberties (which included the item dealing with affirmative action), had lower levels of efficacy and participation, and were marginally more inconsistent in their responses. But none of these significant effects is strong. The largest gender difference, for the participation index, amounts to only one-fifth of a standard deviation. Given the traditional stress on women's support for social programs, it is surprising that gender had no significant effects on that scale, on support for redistribution, or on labour. While the statistical controls for province, class, education, and the other socio-demographic variables might have hidden from view large differences in the ideology of women and men, no such effect was found. For example in the entire sample the differences between the mean scores of women and men for the social welfare, redistribution, and labour indexes were, respectively, .05, .06, and .11 standard deviations (for the sub-sample of employed workers, the differences were comparable in magnitude).

That we found little difference between women and men is not unusual. As Marianne Githens (1983) argues in her review of research in this area, "several of the more recent studies of political socialization have found gender differences to be insignificant, minor or relatively limited" (476). In a comparative study of the U.S. and eight European nations, Ronald Inglehart (1977, 90–1, 228–9) observes rather small gender differences in voting behaviour and value priorities. On the basis of comparisons between some Western European nations and the U.S. and comparisons between age groups, Inglehart argues that while women traditionally took more conservative positions, industrialization leads to a decline in the political differences between women and men. To the limited extent to which there are differences between men and women, our evidence shows that women are less, not more, conservative than men, and the differences are *least* marked for questions of social policy (closest to "household" and "maternal" interests) as compared to questions of redistribution and labour relations. Further, it is not an abstract modernization through industrialization that has eliminated many of the differences in the political consciousness of men and women, but concrete political reforms eliminating the institutional exclusion of women from power and freedom in the public realm. Sylvia Bashevkin (1983) has shown with our data the significant differences in gender comparisons between cohorts of men and women defined by the timing of key political reforms. Women in English Canada, socialized in the post – First World War era of franchise reform and "progressivism," are more likely to identify with the NDP and to espouse left-wing ideological principles than women socialized in the late 1940s and 1950s; women in Quebec are similarly influenced in their party commitments and ideology by the granting of the suffrage in the postwar era, and women socialized in the recent period of feminist mobilization are likewise ideologically to the left of other women, and of men in the same cohort.

The absence of significant gender differences in ideology is particularly interesting in light of the finding that the great postwar increase in women's labour force participation has done little to alter women's almost exclusive responsibility for the care of children. The traditional view of sex role theorists is that women's roles in the family are the underlying cause of psychological differences between women and men. Our findings suggest that the continuing differences in the political positions and activities of women reflect material differences in power and privilege, rather than underlying psychological differences or a distinctive women's political culture (see Kopinak 1987 for a more extensive analysis of gender differences with these data).

Table 5-10
Means of Political Attitude Scales, by Class/Status Group, Relative to the Working Class, without and with Controls for Province and Socio-demographic Variables

Measure of Political Ideology	Control variables	Mean for Class/Status Group, Relative to Working Class										
		Capitalist class	Small employers	Petty bourgeoisie	Managers and technocrats	Supervisors	Semi-autonomous employees	Unemployed	Domestic workers	Retired	Students	Ill, disabled
Social programs	None	-65*	-51*	-50*	-41*	-14	-36*	15	-11+	-29*	-11	27
	All	-31+	-35*	-39*	-30*	-6	-23*	0	-17+	-10	-26*	16
Redistribution	None	-100*	-62*	-29*	-42*	-21*	-47*	19	3	2	-34*	52*
	All	-53*	-46*	-28*	-27*	-12	-20+	3	-10	-10	-28*	-29+
Left-right index	None	-93*	-63*	-48*	-51*	-24*	-53*	18	-1	-21*	-15	49*
	All	-47*	-45*	-38*	-40*	-14*	-32*	-1	-14+	-9	-26*	28+
Labour	None	-73*	-47*	-38*	-29*	-19+	-20+	13	16	-4	-33*	34+
	All	-46*	-41*	-33*	-19+	-11	0	4	7	-10	-30*	20
Civil liberties	None	-57*	-27+	-23*	-37*	5	-19+	15	-6	-26*	11	-6
	All	-32+	-11	-7	-28*	7	-11	3	-4	-4	-3	-15
Immigration	None	-48*	-13	-3	-22+	-21*	-27*	28*	16*	21*	-38*	25
	All	-14	-2	-7	-3	-11	1	9	3	4	-31*	6

Table 5-10
Means of Political Attitude Scales, by Class/Status Group, Relative to the Working Class, without and with Controls for Province and Socio-demographic Variables (Continued)

		Mean for Class/Status Group, Relative to Working Class										
Measure of Political Ideology	Control variables	Capitalist class	Small employers	Petty bourgeoisie	Managers and technocrats	Super-visors	Semi-autono-mous employees	Unem-ployed	Domestic workers	Retired	Students	Ill, disabled
Efficacy	None	63*	33*	-1	45*	17+	44*	-17	-13+	-14	47*	-31+
	All	27	16	2	19+	5	15	-6	8	2	34*	-18
Participation	None	13	49*	32*	44*	3	25*	-15	-15*	-6	25+	-11
	All	-26	36*	29*	16	-8	0	-7	1	-6	15	-2
Protest	None	-36+	-11	-44*	-17	-3	-2	-3	-46*	-70*	72*	-26

* significant at .01
+ significant at .05

Table 5-11

Regression Coefficients for the Effects of Socio-demographic Variables on Political Attitude Scales, with Controls for Province and Class/Status Group

Measure of Political Ideology	Sample	Age in decades	Gender	Education			Family Income			English in Quebec	French in English Canada	Religion			Catholic by religiosity interaction
				In Years	High school graduate	University graduate	In thousands	None	Missing			Catholic	None	Religiosity	
Social programs	Population	−7*	1	0	−16*	0	−5*	8	−14+	10	27*	10	10	−1	2
	Employed	−3	−1	0	−16+	3	−2+	33	−11	14	9	12	16	0	1
Redistribution	Population	0	2	−3*	−15*	−5	−6*	−24*	−26*	−29*	11	9	1	−3	4
	Employed	2	3	−3*	−7	7	−4*	−67*	−22+	−26+	18	11	0	−1	3
Left-right index	Population	−1*	5	−1	−19*	7	−6*	−3	−21*	−3	50*	18*	11	−2	3
	Employed	0	8	−1	−15+	16+	−3*	−2	−15	3	41*	23*	21+	0	1
Labour	Population	0	3	−3*	−7	7	−2*	−12	−25*	−19+	14	4	−2	1	1
	Employed	1	9	−4*	−7	8	−4*	−45*	−20+	−15	34*	1	−6	1	−1
Civil liberties	Population	−4*	9+	0	6	15+	−4*	2	−6	−12	23+	26*	24*	−8*	−1
	Employed	−3	8	0	17+	8	−3*	7	10	−19	25	31*	51*	−7*	−1

Table 5-11

Regression Coefficients for the Effects of Socio-demographic Variables on Political Attitude Scales, with Controls for Province and Class/Status Group (Continued)

Measure of Political Ideology	Sample	Age in decades	Gender	Education			Family Income			English in Quebec	French in English Canada	Religion			Catholic by religiosity interaction
				In Years	High school graduate	University graduate	In thousands	None	Missing			Catholic	None	Religiosity	
Immigration	Population	2	1	-3*	-19*	-40*	.1	7	4	-46*	47*	-8	-22*	-4*	-1
	Employed	2	8	-3*	-20*	-33*	.1	-9	0	-50*	27+	3	-22+	-2	-4
Efficacy	Population	2	-14*	5*	24*	23*	.2*	5	-9	-7	-6	17*	5	3	-2
	Employed	2	-12+	6*	13	18*	.2	-9	2	-11	3	15	1	0	1
Participation	Population	4*	-19*	5*	13+	31*	.1	-2	-7	-8	-12	-6	22*	4*	3
	Employed	5*	-17*	4*	19*	24*	-.1	-26	-2	-20	-16	-8	25+	2	5
Protest	Population	-18*	-7	1	10+	25*	-.1	0	-12	16	-20+	15+	40*	0	-2
	Employed	-18*	-4	2+	10	23*	-.2	-19	-1	20	-9	16+	45*	-1	-1

* significant at .01
+ significant at .05

Education

Even with all the other variables held constant, education affects almost all aspects of political ideology. Higher levels of education are associated with increased political efficacy and participation and lowered assimilationist views of immigrants. For the efficacy, participation, and immigration scales, the differences between the mean scores for a person with, say, nine years of schooling (and therefore a non-high school graduate) and a university graduate (with a total of sixteen years of schooling) were, respectively, .82, .79, and .80 standard deviations. Education also had a number of smaller effects (whose magnitudes are about half those of the three variables just mentioned): increasing education raised support for civil liberties and extra-parliamentary protest, but lowered support for social programs, redistribution, and labour.

All three measures of education – years of attainment and high school and university graduation – had statistically significant effects on ideology. High school graduation had small effects on all the variables (in the same direction as years of education), while university graduation affected the measures of efficacy, participation, and support for protest but not support for social programs, redistribution, and labour. On support for civil liberties, the effect of increased education is positive, but very weak. An inspection of the correlations between education and the various indexes shows that the statistical controls for the other variables lower the impact of education by about one-third. It is, nevertheless, significant that these unique effects of education are found when social class and family income are held constant. While in the past there has been a tendency to avoid class analysis and to ascribe class differences to the effects of education and income, our findings should serve as a caution against compensating for past biases by focusing exclusively on class and avoiding an examination of the effects of education.

These findings are consistent with the numerous previous findings of Lipset (1960), Almond and Verba (1963), and Lester Milbrath (1981) that more-educated people are more involved in the political process and more tolerant of extra-parliamentary politics and ethnic diversity. Unfortunately, the likely effect of this heightened participation is to increase the support for social policies that will *increase* inequality and cut back social programs. In the context of a political science community primarily concerned with levels of tolerance, the avoidance of extremism of right or left, legitimacy, and participation in electoral politics, rising levels of education have been seen as a positive aspect of the modernization process. What emerges from our broader analysis of ideology is evidence that people with more education are less critical of existing, unequal class relations.

Family Income

Not surprisingly, higher income is associated with *lower* support for social programs, redistribution, labour, and civil liberties. Unlike education, however, higher income is not associated with increased efficacy, participation, or tolerance of immigrants. Compared to respondents who reported low, but non-zero, levels of family income, respondents who said they had no income were more opposed to redistribution, less supportive of labour, and more *inconsistent* (this last result suggests that individuals who [implausibly] say their family income is zero also give more erratic answers to questions about politics). The tendency for respondents who would not disclose their income or said they had no income to take more conservative opinions on redistribution and labour suggests that they tend to be upper-middle-income people, though it is possible that the willingness to disclose one's income in an interview taps some aspect of personality that is not reducible to income.

These findings about the relationship between income and ideology – which control for social class – demonstrate the importance of income divisions within classes. Without the imposition of statistical controls for other variables (mainly education and social class) the effect of income on support for social programs and redistribution would be about 50 percent larger while the effect of income on support for labour and political efficacy would be about three times larger. In a society so heavily organized around the consumption of commodities, it should not be surprising that family income, the simplest measure of the power to consume, should be related to ideology and that people with more income should be less likely to want to rearrange the distribution of resources. The regression shows that class cannot be subsumed by education and income. There are fairly large income differences *within* social classes, related to gender, sector of employment, and occupation, and the unique ideological differences attributable to differential location in the "wage nexus" represent a significant limitation on the development of class consciousness and class conflict.

French-English Differences

We restrict our analysis of "ethnic" and "cultural" differences to the two minorities whose constitutional role is the most important: non-French Canadians in Quebec and French Canadians in English Canada. We consider two opposite conjectures. First, because members of these two minorities depend on the state to protect their linguistic rights, they may also support other aspects of state intervention; alternatively, the superior status of non-French (or at least English) Québécois and the inferior status of the French outside Quebec might cause these minorities to diverge politically.

The second conjecture is clearly more correct: the nature of minority-majority differences are quite different in Quebec and English Canada. While the non-French in Quebec give *less* support to redistribution, labour, civil liberties, and immigrant rights than French Québécois, the French in English Canada are *more* supportive of redistribution, labour, and immigrants than other English Canadians. Thus the non-French in Quebec tend to be more like other English Canadians and the French in English Canada tend to be more like French Québécois. Because these differences are not as large as the differences between Quebec and English Canada as a whole, the ideological position of these minorities is intermediate between that of the provinces where they live and that of their own ethnic majority.

Religion and Religiosity

Finally, we turn to the effects of religion and religiosity. The three categories of religion employed in this analysis include Catholics, respondents who say they have no religion, and a residual group including people of all other religions. The third category includes largely Protestants. While religion has been shown to have strong effects on party preference, there has been little research on its effects on other aspects of political ideology. There are a small number of statistically significant effects. Compared to non-Catholics, Catholics were generally more left wing, more supportive of civil liberties and protest, and higher in efficacy, while respondents with no religion gave greater support to civil liberties, immigrants, and extra-parliamentary protest and had higher levels of political participation. Increased religiosity *decreased* support for civil liberties and immigrants. Examination of the effects of the interaction term shows that there is no detectable difference in the effects of religiosity on Catholics and non-Catholics.

Summary

Of the variables considered in this section, it is apparent that only family income and education have substantial effects on the full range of measures of ideology. Gender has virtually no effects at all and the impact of age is large only for the measure of support for extra-parliamentary protest. Although religion is usually included among the three most important factors affecting Canadian politics, our data suggest that the ideological effects of religion are largely confined to the area of parliamentary politics. Second, the magnitudes of the effects of the socio-demographic variables, in absolute terms and especially relative to the effects of province and social class, are somewhat greater for variables measuring individuals' relationships to and beliefs about the nature of the political system, as opposed to their policy views. Partly in response to the history of neglect of social class we have stressed the impact of social class on political ideology and, in this section, emphasized that class differences "survive" statistical controls for the socio-demographic variables. The results in this section also show, however, that education and income have effects on ideology that are not reducible to social class.

PROVINCIAL AND CLASS DIFFERENCES IN IDEOLOGY: THE EFFECTS OF CONTROLLING FOR SOCIO-DEMOGRAPHIC VARIABLES

Having found that the socio-demographic variables affect our measures of political ideology when province and social class are taken into account, it is appropriate to consider the effects of the socio-demographic variables on our initial analyses of the effects of province and social class (whose effects were shown above to be largely independent of each other). Controlling for the socio-demographic variables in table 5-12 has very little effect on the provincial differences; the only result is to slightly decrease the difference between Quebec and English Canada – a change due entirely to the concentration of Catholics in Quebec. On the left-right index, for example, the mean score for Quebec is .93. Controlling for the effects of class and socio-demographic variables other than religion, the mean for Quebec is .94 standard deviations; controlling for religion and religiosity, in addition, lowers the Quebec-Ontario difference to .80. This change is relatively small in light of the fact that the mean scores for the nine provinces of English Canada range between −.16 and .50.

Given the fairly strong educational and income differences of the social class categories that were discussed in the previous chapter, it is not surprising that controls for these variables affect the class means. Beginning with the analysis for the employed in table 5-12, we find that the controls for the socio-demographic variables alter the class differences in a number of ways. First, the ideological distinctiveness of the capitalist class is somewhat reduced: for the social program, redistribution, labour, and left-right measures the controls reduce the difference between capitalists' responses and those of other classes. Even with these controls, however, the average position of the capitalist class respondents is to the right of all the other class categories. For the measures of support for civil liberties, views of immigrants, and support for extra-parliamentary protest the controls reduce the liberalism of the capitalists, relative to the other class categories; and the high level of efficacy is also reduced by the controls.

Taking account of the socio-demographic variables affects the responses of small employers and semi-autonomous workers in a manner similar to but weaker than we observed for the capitalists. The weak tendency for workers with some supervisory authority to take more conservative positions on the redistribution, left-right, and labour scales almost completely disappears

Table 5-12
Means of Political Attitude Scales, by Province, Relative to Ontario, without and
with Controls for Class/Status Group and Socio-demographic Variables

Measure of Political Ideology	Control variables	Mean for Province, Relative to Ontario								
		PQ	NF	PEI	NS	NB	MB	SK	AB	BC
Social Programs	Population									
	None	54*	39*	−21	4	27+	−13	−26+	0	4
	Class	52*	38*	−18	6	30*	−9	−25	4	5
	Class, demographic	51*	40*	−19	7	17	−10	−21+	6	8
	Class, demographic, religion	43	40*	−20	7	19	−9	−21+	7	7
	Employed									
	None	47*	47*	−12	−10	23	−24+	−33+	3	4
	Class	47*	52*	−14	−10	27	−17	−29+	16	14
	Class, demographic	45*	54*	−15	−7	23	−19	−26	16	13
	Class, demographic, religion	37*	53*	−18	−8	25	−18	−27+	17	12
Redistribution	Population									
	None	66*	34*	44	35*	34*	9	8	−13	−8
	Class	64*	32+	39	33*	35*	9	8	−10	−10
	Class, demographic	69*	34*	37	35*	31*	7	15	−5	−4
	Class, demographic, religion	59*	34*	36	34*	33*	10	14	−4	−3
	Employed									
	None	59*	20	44	27+	33+	−3	17	−25*	−17+
	Class	57*	21	31	25+	38+	1	18	−14	−10
	Class, demographic	63*	23	26	27+	32+	0	20	−12	−10
	Class, demographic, religion	53*	21	21	26+	33+	1	19	−11	−9
Left-right index	Population									
	None	93*	47*	−1	22+	48*	−9	−24+	−4	−2
	Class	91*	46*	1	22+	50*	−7	−24+	0	2
	Class, demographic	94*	50*	−1	24*	31*	−6	−16	−4	4
	Class, demographic, religion	80*	50*	2	24*	34*	3	−16	6	4
	Employed									
	None	85*	44*	3	7	42*	−22	−28+	−11	−4
	Class	83*	48*	6	6	47*	−15	−25+	3	4
	Class, demographic	88*	52*	−8	10	33+	−15	−20	4	5
	Class, demographic, religion	75*	50*	−12	9	36*	−14	−21	6	4
Labour	Population									
	None	57*	2	9	13	−13	−15	−21+	−19*	−13+
	Class	55*	1	6	11	−14	−17+	−22+	−18+	−14+
	Class, demographic	58*	2	5	13	−17	−18+	−16	−15+	−10
	Class, demographic, religion	54*	1	3	12	−16	−17+	−16	−14+	−8

Table 5-12
Means of Political Attitude Scales, by Province, Relative to Ontario, without and
with Controls for Class/Status Group and Socio-demographic Variables (Continued)

Measure of Political Ideology	Control variables	Mean for Province, Relative to Ontario								
		PQ	NF	PEI	NS	NB	MB	SK	AB	BC
	Employed									
	None	52*	1	−19	9	12	−25+	−17	−22+	−16+
	Class	50*	2	−20	12	−7	−24+	−14	−16	−15
	Class, demographic	55*	5	−24	15	−13	−24+	−10	−15	−15
	Class, demographic, religion	54*	4	−25	14	−14	−24+	−10	−14	−13
Civil liberties	Population									
	None	53*	11	4	3	−10	−19	−17	−10	14+
	Class	52*	10	6	5	−10	−17	−18	−8	15+
	Class, demographic	55*	11	7	6	−22	−5	−16	−7	15+
	Class, demographic, religion	44*	15	14	9	−16	−2	−18	−7	9
	Employed									
	None	54*	−4	44	−2	−20	−6	−36*	−18+	16
	Class	54*	−7	36	1	−19	−2	−36+	−15	18
	Class, demographic	60*	−8	44	4	−35	1	−37*	−15	14
	Class, demographic, religion	46*	−6	50	7	−27	2	−40*	−14	4
Immigration	Population									
	None	67*	9	24	−18	14	−4	−7	6	5
	Class	66*	6	16	−23+	13	−7	−8	7	2
	Class, demographic	73*	8	12	−19+	6	−9	−2	11	9
	Class, demographic, religion	79*	10	17	−19+	7	−9	−3	8	8
	Employed									
	None	67*	15	57	−31*	0	−3	0	−1	2
	Class	68*	18	51	−34*	3	−2	1.	5	5
	Class, demographic	76*	23	52	−31*	4	−3	7	6	6
	Class, demographic, religion	78*	24	58	−30+	6	−3	7	5	7

* significant at .01

+ significant at .05

when education and income are taken into account. An examination of the regression coefficients for the socio-demographic variables suggests that these
alterations in the effects of class reflect class differences in income and educational attainment. More generally, controls for the socio-demographic variables reduce the values of almost all the coefficients for the immigration and
efficacy scales (thus diminishing the class differentiation), suggesting that for
these variables class was acting as a surrogate for education and income.

The introduction of controls for the socio-demographic variables to the analysis based on the entire sample adds two observations to what was just observed for the sub-sample of the employed. First, the controls dramatically *decreased* the group differences in support for extra-parliamentary protest, presumably because of the strong effect of age on this scale. Second, the controls decreased the tendency for people who are unemployed, ill, or disabled to take a relatively left-wing position in responses to the items dealing with redistribution, presumably because of the (positive) effect of income on support for redistribution.

CONCLUSION

We do not propose to summarize all of the findings in this detailed chapter on the relationship between class, region, and ideology in Canada. It is necessary, however, to put the findings in the context of this book's broad inquiry into the nature of politics in Canada in the late 1970s and early 1980s. Four points can be made, each substantiating the general argument in the book about the relevance of looking at questions of class and hegemony in order to understand Canadian politics in this period.

First, one must emphasize the extent to which the continuing hegemonic appeal of principles underlying the liberal welfare state limits ideological conflict in the mass public. As we indicated in chapter 4, public support for social welfare programs and for civil liberties in Canada is very widespread, and the evidence in this chapter shows that divisions of opinion on these subjects are not tightly tied to the different situations of individuals in the social structure. Only about 13 percent of the variance in attitudes towards social policy and civil liberties is explained by complex multivariate models incorporating measures of region, class, socio-economic status, and religion. The same is true for attitudes towards labour relations, another key component of the postwar settlement, around which hegemony was constructed in the modern era. Here, however, the relative lack of fit between ideological divisions and structural differences is not so much a function of the extent of positive support for bolstering the powers of labour *vis-à-vis* capital. Hegemonic agreement on this principle is far from well-established, and yet disagreements over particular proposals for the organization of labour relations do not reflect or reinforce regional, class, or other social cleavages.

Second, one must qualify this first observation by noting that there is a greater structural coherence to ideological divisions over questions of income redistribution, and that there is a well-structured, underlying, left-right division of ideological orientation in the mass public that is reasonably well accounted for by differences in social position. Twenty percent of the variance in our index of attitudes towards income redistribution was explained by the multivariate regression, as was close to 30 percent of the variance in the left-right index. The hegemonic discourse of the liberal welfare state does not, therefore, obliterate ideological conflict. On matters not directly addressed by the postwar settlement, income redistribution as opposed to income maintenance, conflict is more endemic, and it is evident that to the extent that arguments are made linking positions across the issues of social welfare, labour relations, civil liberties, and income redistribution, these arguments divide ideologically "left" and "right" segments of the mass public, concentrated in particular areas of the country and the class structure.

Third, on the central question of the predominant influence of regionalism in the political culture, the evidence in this chapter suggests a substantial qualification of the conventional wisdom in Canadian political studies. Regional differences in Canadian political culture largely reflect the differences between French Quebec and English Canada outside of Quebec. This *is* a regional division of great significance in Canadian politics. It is not reducible to differences in the class structures of regions, although it does no doubt reflect the pronounced interaction of class and ethnicity in the historical ethnic stratification of Quebec society. Questions of regionalism, or, more to the point, of nationality *do*, therefore, reduce the salience of class in the political discourse of Canadians. It is not the case, however, as is so widely assumed, that class divisions are minuscule and insignificant in comparison to the divisions of region. As compared to differences in provincial background, differences in class position together with intra-class divisions in the extent of supervision and manual work explain more variance in measures of support for social programs, and income redistribution. Class has less impact on the left-right index than provincial background, but still accounts for somewhat more than one-third of the total variance explained. On questions of political efficacy, political participation, and protest, provincial background explains nothing, while class situation explains about one-half of the total variance explained. Even on questions of labour relations, civil liberties, and immigration, where the explanatory contribution of class situation is weakest, it remains about one-half as great as that of provincial background.

Fourth, although intra-class differences of social status exercise a significant moderating effect on the extent of ideological class divisions, these latter differences, normally given emphasis along with region in Canadian political sociology, have a minor effect on basic ideological orientations in comparison to class situation, although they have an equal or slightly larger effect on questions of political efficacy, participation, and protest.

The concepts of class and hegemony do, therefore, clarify the nature of popular ideology in Canada. The standard accounts of the overriding significance of regionalism in Canadian political culture disguise the importance to the development of that political culture of class conflict and its mediation through the state's hegemonic projects. Orthodox political science and political sociology is, in this sense, ideological, masking the underlying conflicts within the bosom of the state. Like all ideology, however, this one has significant support in the "real world." In this case the reality of the insignificance of class in Canadian politics stems largely from the insulation of electoral and party politics from class and ideological cleavages of the kind discussed in this chapter. This brings us to the subject of the next chapter.

6 Party and Ideology in Canada: The Mediation of Conflict

In the last chapter we argued that the way in which Canadians think about fundamental political issues is influenced by their location in the class and social structure, as well as by the regions in which they live. In this chapter we will argue that the Canadian federation and the national political party system serve to moderate the articulation of class conflict and class consciousness, and to magnify the articulation of regional/provincial interests and divisions. This mediation of class conflict is most clearly expressed in the minimal differentiation in the national political parties' attractiveness to different social classes. While these "catch-all," brokerage parties do not develop ideologically distinct party programs and policies, their supporters still tend to read those programs and policies as supporting their own class interests (see Brodie 1988, 4 ff. for a nice review of brokerage theories). Party support is more related to a party's relative strength in, and presumed identification with, different regions of the country, the personal appeal of leaders, and short-term, ad hoc issues raised in election campaigns.

These are the general conclusions of the literature on Canadian voting and party identification, and we will not quarrel with them. Nevertheless, despite the absence of coherent appeals by parties to different classes, and despite the muting of the ideological class conflict that would otherwise be expected on the basis of our results in previous chapters, we will argue that ideological discourse rooted in the different experiences of social classes is not irrelevant to Canadian party politics. Although not as pronounced as in other Western countries, there are limited but significant differences in the attractiveness of different parties to segments of different social classes, and there is a greater ideological differentiation of the national parties than is conventionally assumed in Canadian political studies. A fine review of research on voting in Canada is Elisabeth Gidengil (1992).

These qualifications to existing scholarship do not, however, alter the fundamental facts of the *limited* differentiation of Canada's national political parties on the basis of the class and ideological orientations of their partisans. At most they press for further reflection on the meaning of these facts. Given the evidence of "objective" class conflict in labour relations, and of "subjective" ideological class division in public opinion, why are divisions of class and ideology not reflected in party politics? This question is the focus of attention in the introduction and conclusion to this chapter.

THEORETICAL ISSUES

Students of Canadian politics are all but unanimous in saying that social class has little or no impact on federal party politics, or at least that differences of social class have little influence on voting behaviour in a country where regional cleavages are magnified. The exceptional character of Canadian politics in this regard was pointed out by Robert Alford (1963), who showed that Canadians' voting choices were less influenced by social class than in other Anglo-Saxon democracies. He surmised that this was because regional and religious identities provided alternative bases of solidarity, citing a variety of historical factors, including the regional, ethnic, and religious cleavages that crossed class boundaries, the lack of institutional relations between organized labour and a political party (at least at the time when Canadian unions developed significant strength), and the escape hatch offered to dissatisfied workers by the availability of frontier land for settlement.

Nearly two decades later the major study of Canadian voting came to essentially the same conclusions about the impact of mutually reinforcing provincial, ethnic, and religious cleavages and the comparative weakness of cross-cutting class, age, and gender cleavages. Harold Clarke et al. (1979, 93 ff.) distanced themselves from Alford only in rejecting his expectation that Canadian exceptionality would in time disappear:

In summary, the analyses of the relationships between social class and vote indicate the weakness of socio-economic status as a politically relevant societal cleavage in Canada ... More generally, these findings, taken in conjunction with data demonstrating the continuing existence of relationships between region, religion, ethnicity, and voting, and the relatively high levels of regional consciousness among younger voters, do not support the developmental model espoused by Alford and others. If processes of industrialization and urbanization do generate forces tending to increase the significance of social class while diminishing the political relevance of regional, religious, and ethnic characteristics, such forces have yet to make their effects apparent in any large-scale fashion in Canada. (1979, 119)

Despite this agreement over a very long period of intensive investigation, there remain two basic difficulties in the orthodox understanding of the relationship between class and party politics, one empirical and one theoretical.

To begin with the basic empirical point about the relative significance of regional and religious, as opposed to class, differences in party and electoral choices, the more general argument can be made that even provincial and religious cleavages are quite weak. Also, the point about class would be stronger if the studies on which they were based had utilized a more adequate conceptualization and operationalization of class. Almost all studies of electoral politics have employed the manual/non-manual dichotomy (e.g., Alford 1963; Fletcher and Forbes 1990; Gidengil 1989), a small number of occupational categories (e.g., Pammett 1987), or some combination of education, income, and occupation, the three traditional measures of socio-economic status (e.g., Clarke et al. 1979; Lambert et al. 1987; Lambert and Curtis 1993).

Although our analysis improves on past studies in defining social class in a more theoretically consistent manner, this does not lead us to revise previous conclusions about the effects of class, relative to regional and other individual differences, on party choice. The effect of region on party support, which is seen as the major class-*dis*organizing factor, is weak, though larger than the effects of other factors. Except in the case of identification with the Progressive Conservative party, region accounts for less than half of the total variance explained in our models. For the Conservatives, our measures explain more of the variation than for the other parties, and region accounts for 10 of the only 15 percent of total variation explained. By comparison, in chapter 5 we explained twice as much of the variation in our left-right index of ideological orientation with a similarly elaborate multivariate model.

It is the weak structure of political party attachments in Canada that needs emphasis rather than the relative strength of region in explaining those attachments. Such an emphasis redirects attention to the problem of *changes* in party attachments, rather than to the orthodox conception of party identifications as stable and stabilizing elements in the political culture (Stevenson 1987). It directs attention, also, to the analysis of electoral *campaigns*, the major emphasis of the 1988 and 1993 National Election Surveys (Johnston et al. 1992). Indeed if Richard Johnston et al. are representative of the present generation of quantitative electoral researchers, concern about social class and other aspects of socio-economic difference has virtually vanished from the intellectual agenda.

Given our previous finding that there is a fairly strong relationship between class and political ideology (especially when items are combined as in our left-right scale), an obvious corollary of the low degree of class differentiation in support for the Canadian federal parties is the argument that policy issues have little impact on party choices, though there is relatively little Canadian empirical research on the question of "issue voting" and less on the associated question of the extent to which political party attachments are the result of the match between a party's and an individual supporter's stands on issues. In a study of Ontario voters in the 1968 election, Lynn McDonald (1969) found that the effect of political attitudes on voting was not strong and the attitudes that did predict voting related to group membership. John Zipp (1978) found that there were differences in the political attitudes of Liberal and NDP supporters, on the one hand, and supporters of the Progressive Conservatives and Social Credit parties, on the other hand. But Zipp was *un*able to separate Liberal from NDP supporters on the basis of attitudinal differences. Clarke et al. (1979, chap. 8) are equivocal on this point: they argue that issues have some impact on party support, but only for Canadians with high levels of interest in politics who do not have a strong pre-existing attachment to one of the parties. Unfortunately the persuasiveness of Clarke et al.'s findings is undermined by the absence of direct measures of voters' policy positions in their survey. Instead Clarke et al. rely on voters' reports of the similarity between their views and those of the various parties and on individuals' assessments of whether their votes are affected by the issues. Voters' misperceptions of the party positions and their wishful thinking about the importance of policy in their voting judgements all tend to inflate Clarke et al.'s estimates of the extent of policy voting.

An issue not addressed in Clarke et al.'s (or our own) analysis is the possibility of *reciprocal* causation between voters' policy preferences and their party choices. If party allegiances lead voters to support particular policies, in addition to or instead of voters choosing their parties because of their ideology, regression analysis, in which party support is the *dependent* variable, will yield biased estimates. For a summary of debate on the appropriateness of nonrecursive and recursive models of voting and a summary of recent empirical studies see Herbert Asher (1983). The "classic" analysis of U.S. election data using a simultaneous equation model is Gregory Markus and Philip Converse (1979) and the only Canadian study is Keith Archer (1987). Archer's analysis is based on the Clarke et al. survey and he too uses "respondent's perceptions of the party closest to them on the issue[s] most important to them" (1987, 557) as a predictor of party identification and vote. Whatever the answer to the difficult questions about the relationship between party support and ideology, using respondents' own, idiosyncratic views of their closeness to the parties is quite dubious.

Our analysis of the relationship between voting and political ideology, based on extensive measures of non-party-related political attitudes, has potentially the most to contribute to the study of Canadian party and electoral politics. Still we will not argue for a dramatic reformulation of the conventional wisdom about the relative absence of ideological differentiation among supporters of the different Canadian national parties. We will argue that there were significant if not very marked ideological differences between NDP, Liberal, and Progressive Conservative party supporters in the declining years of the Pierre Trudeau regime. These ideological differences are consistent with the greater salience of questions of government intervention in the economy, the dramatization in debates over constitutional change of issues of civil liberties, and the growing conflict over measures aimed at reducing the powers of labour and cutting back on the costs of the social welfare programs inscribed in the postwar settlement.

For a great many students of Canadian political sociology the answer to the problem of the lack of class ties to political parties lies in the lack of class identification by Canadians. With John Porter (1965, 3), they argue that Canadians have a classless image of their own society. This assumption is empirically supported by survey evidence on the extent of class identification among Canadians. For 1979 the National Election Study and our Quality of Life survey yield exactly the same estimate, that 58 percent of the adult Canadian population do not think of themselves as belonging to a distinct social class, and subjective class identities have little effect on party identification. Using National Election Study data, John Pammett (1987, table 9) shows that NDP voting is substantially higher among *non-manual*, but not manual, workers who identify themselves as "working class."

Analysis of our data show that party identification is more strongly related to subjective class identification than to "objective" measures of social class. Combining spontaneous and forced responses to the subjective class identification question, over 50 percent of NDP partisans saw themselves as working class, compared to fewer than 30 percent of Progressive Conservative and fewer still of Liberal partisans. Further, middle-class identification among members of the working class exerted a strong pull away from the NDP towards the Liberals: over 50 percent of middle-class-identifying members of the working class were Liberals, and less than 10 percent were NDP supporters. But this lack of class identification, and the concomitant weakening of class affiliations with political parties, needs to be explained. Orthodox political sociology, following Porter, points to the internal differentiation and mobility characteristic of social classes and to a model of Canadian parties as parts of a benign brokerage system. In this model it is "the politics of moderation and brokerage politics which minimize differences, restrain fissiparous tendencies and thus, over time knit together the diverse interests of a polity weak in integration" (Cairns 1968, 63).

Characterizations of Canadian politics in such terms can be found in the classical works of Canadian political science (e.g., Underhill 1960, 168; Dawson 1963, 466–72; Mallory 1971, 25), although many, like Alan Cairns, adopt the more critical perspective of Porter's classic contribution to Canadian political sociology. From this perspective the brokering of national interests is conducted by elites, whose narrow base of recruitment and high degree of social integration biases political action towards the maintenance of a highly unequal society. The development of class conflict that might otherwise be expected in such a society is prevented, according to Porter, by the disintegration of classes and the disappearance of class consciousness in modern societies generally, and by the peculiar vitality of regional divisions and conflicts in Canadian society.

Porter's conception of the relationship between class and region is, however, ambiguous. His argument, as emphasized by Cairns, is that the integrative functions of the elite brokerage system are undermined by the perpetuation of regionalism, and the stability of the national political system would be enhanced by a greater measure of political organization and identification along the vertical divisions of class as opposed to the horizontal divisions of region (Cairns 1968). The problem with this appeal to the more progressive consequences of a politics organized around class, as opposed to regional, issues is that if classes disintegrate in the process of modernization, it is mere wishful thinking to call for a politics that places greater emphasis upon class issues. Even if they do not entirely disintegrate, it remains a purely voluntarist exhortation bypassing the need to explain why classes are not the basis of greater political organization and identity, and why elites, otherwise conceived of as the rational brokers of multiple group interests in a modern society, perpetuate the pre-modern, irrational attachments to region.

One resolution of this ambiguity is provided by Rick Ogmundson (1975a; 1975b; 1980), who argues that the lack of class voting reflects elite control of the major parties and their interest in avoiding appeals to class. "The parties have more influence on the voters than vice versa, and the apparent classlessness of our politics can best be explained, not by public opinion, but by the skill of the 'bourgeois' parties in manipulating the situation ..." (1980, 47). Ogmundson argues that in these circumstances the apparent lack of class consciousness in party identification and voting reflects voters' misperceptions of the political choices offered by the different parties. Many working-class supporters of the Liberals and Progressive Conservatives believe that these parties pursue the class interest of the working class. More generally, on the basis of national survey data, Ogmundson is able to show that voters are confused about the interests pursued by each of the parties. In a later publication Ogmundson and M. Ng (1982) find that, if voters' beliefs about what class interests are represented by each of the parties are taken into account, Canada has as high a level of class voting as Britain (which is often used as an example of a country with a very high level of class voting). Ronald Lambert et al. (1987) and Lambert and James Curtis (1993) employ a similar strategy in analyzing what they label "subjective class voting": "We created two *party class orientation* variables by asking respondents to rate each of the federal parties and each of the provincial parties in their respective provinces on the seven-point 'for the lower social classes' vs. 'for the higher social classes' scale; and then we assigned the appropriate rating given by each person to the parties for which he or she reported voting at each level" (1987, 530). The finding that people vote in what they think is their class interest provides an *interpretation* of the lack of relationship between class and party support, but the argument that class voting in Canada is little different from other nations, *except that Canadians are confused about what the parties stand for*, mistakes the psychologically comforting notion that people vote in what they think is their interest for party attachments rooted in material conditions. Analysis of this perceived class voting may be a reasonable adjunct to, but is not, as Ogmundson suggests, a substitute for, analysis of the relationship between class and party support.

That the Canadian national parties avoid substantive issues that might excite class-conscious choices between them is widely agreed. For example, John Wilson (1983, 173) argues: "... Canadian political parties – including, in more recent years, even the New Democratic party – have nonetheless assiduously sought to avoid any kind of conflict which might divide the nation in an ideological way." Whether this reflects a conscious manipulation of the electorate by "bourgeois" parties is not, however, obvious. In order to argue that the moderation and similarity of party platforms is anything more than the natural consequence of oligopolistic competition for votes (Downs 1957), it is necessary to establish the ruling class position of the party leadership, their self-conscious anticipation of working-class opposition to ruling class interests, and the careful manipulation of issues in electoral campaigns to counteract such developments. Above all, the argument assumes a manipulation of a relatively self-conscious working class, and it is necessary to establish that ruling class manipulations divert working-class voters from greater support for the NDP – which is generally perceived as offering a more left-wing alternative to the two major parties.

Despite its centrality to his argument, Ogmundson has surprisingly little to say about the elites who are said to control the two major parties. He notes, somewhat lamely: "When one considers the elite structure as a whole, a host of other explanatory influences on party behaviour emerge. Factors such as class origins and elite interlocks are commonly mentioned ... It seems clear enough that a plausible case can be made for the idea that all these variables have some influence on party behaviour" (1980, 51–2). His reliance on public opinion data also prevents Ogmundson from undertaking the historical analysis necessary to establish the manipulation of the electorate. Janine Brodie and Jane Jenson (1988) have gone some way towards providing such historical evidence, particularly in documenting the co-optation of third-party reform proposals, and the self-conscious efforts made by the major federal political parties to focus debate away from class issues. The difficulty with this line of argument is that it avoids dealing with the historical dominance of the Liberal and Progressive Conservative parties, and the weakness of the social democratic NPD, in class terms.

Of course the two major parties' traditional ability to frame their appeals in terms of overriding national interests reflects the interest of the dominant class. But this is not an unusual electoral strategy – even parties with much stronger and more direct ties to national capitalist classes, such as the U.S. Republican and British Conservative parties, claim to represent the common national interests of their countries, often on the basis of the argument that they are the only parties capable of encouraging the economic growth needed to increase the overall standard of living. What distinguishes Canada is not the major parties' efforts to make their appeals in non-class terms, but their remarkable success in accomplishing that aim. Not only have the two major parties avoided conflict over class issues, they have also succeeded in preventing the growth of the NDP beyond about 20 percent of the total vote.

The lack of class differences in party support most obviously reflects the political weakness of the working class, which has the most to lose from a party alignment that avoids class issues. It could be argued that the NDP's appeals to class are very limited and that this reflects the hold of middle-class people and trade union leaders over the party apparatus. But then we have to ask why a militant working class is not more successful in challenging the leadership of the NDP. If conservative political elites control the NDP, this is either a manifestation of the weakness of the working class or a reflection of its actual political ideology. Our elite survey findings (in chapter 9) actually show that trade union leaders have political positions far to the left of the working class as a whole (though perhaps not to the left of some militants), which undermines the premise that a conservative elite in the NDP misrepresents its constituency. Particularly on questions relating to labour relations, our data in the previous chapter speak to the weakness, rather than the strength, of working-class consciousness in Canada.

In attempting to rescue the Canadian working class from the ignominy of low class consciousness, Ogmundson protests too much. It is scarcely credible that, except for the tight elite control of the Progressive Conservative and Liberal parties, the Canadian and British working classes would exhibit the same degree of class consciousness. While Ogmundson deals with voters' "errors" in assessing the class character of the parties by introducing statistical controls that eliminate them, it is more reasonable to understand voters' misperceptions as indicative of a lack of class consciousness.

Another attempt to rescue the working class is Gidengil's (1989) effort to show that, once region – defined in terms of dependency – is taken into account, there are significant class differences in voting. Unfortunately the nature of these differences varies radically: in the "depressed periphery" and "industrial periphery" working-class people are most likely to vote *Conservative*; in the "centre," "secondary centres," and "vulnerable periphery" they are most likely to vote *NDP*; and in the "advantaged periphery" they are most likely to vote *Liberal* (see 583)! Furthermore language also affects the relationship between social class and vote, and again "This impact differs depending upon the type of region. In the industrial periphery, being franco-phone made it significantly *less* likely that working class respondents would vote Liberal ..." (585). From all of this Gidengil argues that social class af-fects voting, but that this relationship is distorted by the "socially fragment-ing effects of dependency." The generality of her findings, however, is undermined by her decision to restrict her sample to "respondents whose self-perceived class membership was consistent with their objective occupa-tional status (dichotomized as manual versus non-manual)," in order to min-imize the difficulties in measuring class. This could easily have biased her analysis. Not only are some occupations (such as nursing and technician) difficult to classify as manual or non-manual, but because women are con-centrated in non-manual jobs whose incumbents are included in the analysis only if they identify themselves as middle class, the working class must be predominantly male, thus confounding the effects of sex and class (sex is not included as a variable in her analysis). In any event it is difficult to see how one could interpret a pattern of party support in which working-class attach-ment to the NDP is inconsistent across regions, and in three out of six regions weaker than Conservative or Liberal support, as indicative of strong working-class consciousness. We question the advisability of dividing the major economic regions of Canada entirely on the basis of local economic structures. Quebec, for example, is divided among regions, so its distinc-tiveness is manifest only in terms of language. It is one thing to argue that economic factors might affect political alignments, quite another to overlook cultural divisions as important as that between Quebec and English Canada.

All this leaves us in what may seem an inconsistent and compromised po-sition. While reaffirming our view that studies of electoral politics are inher-ently biased in the direction of minimizing class differences, we also believe that the weakness of the relationship between social class and party support *at the national level* is an important indicator of the low level of class polar-ization and of the powerlessness of the working class – which, because of its economic position and numerical strength, has the most to gain by more overt emphasis on class issues. Weakness is not, however, non-existence. There are important indications of class consciousness both in the kinds of survey evidence we have presented in the last chapter, and in the high level of strikes and lockouts that, at least in the 1970s, expressed a significant de-gree of class consciousness and class conflict. What we have to investigate is why this class consciousness and conflict is not reflected in the political party system.

Functionally speaking, the political party system works to channel conflict into a manageable agenda for legislative action, and the rules of the electoral system put a premium on parties' abilities to construct the broadest coa-litions around the centre of public opinion. The success with which these mediating tendencies contain or obscure class conflict is a function not of the public's erroneous identification of parties with class interests, nor of the elite's manipulation of such error, but of the success with which parties create a relatively hegemonic discourse out of the materials given in ideological class struggle. Survey research on voting or party attachments can chart only the state or dynamics of these mediating influences. The explanation for them must be based upon historically detailed investigation of the particular policies and programs articulated by parties and party-based governments. Although we offer no such historical detail, the argument in this chapter will point in that direction.

MEASUREMENT OF FEDERAL PARTY IDENTIFICATION

A preliminary question, before examining our data, concerns the measurement of federal party identification. Previous researchers have employed a variety of different strategies. The simplest, used by Clarke et al. (1979) and by Alfred Hunter (1982), involves assigning scores to each of the party preferences, thus allowing a single regression analysis to measure the effects of any variables on voting. Clarke et al. (130) assumed the parties were equidistant on a linear scale, in the following order from left to right: NDP, Liberal, Progressive Conservative, and Social Credit. Using survey respondents' perceptions of the positions of the parties, Hunter (1982, 29) assigned the parties' positions on a seven-point rating scale anchored at its ends with the labels "for the working class" and "for the middle class." These scores were as follows: Liberals 3.6, Progressive Conservatives 3.8, Social Credit 3.9, Creditistes 5.2, and NDP 5.3. While each party is assigned a different score, the scores effectively divide the parties into only two categories – one containing the Liberals, Progressive Conservatives, and Social Credit (all with scores between 3.6 and 3.9), and the other containing the Creditistes and NDP (with scores of 5.2 and 5.3). With these scores, what appears to be a regression analysis of voting across the ideological spectrum is effectively no more than a comparison between just two supposedly distinct groups of voters.

Whatever scores are employed, this analytical strategy has serious shortcomings. Clarke et al.'s version of such scoring makes arbitrary assumptions about the positions of the political parties. Even accepting the proposition that the Progressive Conservative party is significantly to the right of the Liberals, there is no empirical support whatever for the assumption that this difference is of the same magnitude as the Liberal-NDP difference. Hunter's alternative raises as many problems. Given Ogmundson's findings that Canadians have confused and wildly differing views of the relative positions of the parties, it doesn't make much sense to use mean ratings of the parties in creating scores.

The basic problem with assigning scores to the parties is that the differences among three or more weakly ordered categories are reduced to a single dimension. In the process some patterns of party support become undetectable. For example suppose that, as an alternative to the NDP, more conservative working class people tend to vote Liberal, while more conservative members of other classes tend to vote Progressive Conservative. Because the Liberals and Conservatives have nearly identical scores in Hunter's analysis, the difference between Liberal and Progressive Conservative party supporters is undetectable. Another problem with this analysis strategy is that the fairly large numbers of respondents who state no party preference must be eliminated from the analysis, potentially giving rise to sample selection bias in estimates of the effects of social class and other variables.

Attempts to dichotomize party preferences run into exactly the same problem as using linear scores. Thus Irvine and H. Gold's (1980) analysis, which only differentiates between Liberal party supporters and all others, is unable to detect differences among the disparate combination of Progressive Conservative, NDP, Social Credit, and Creditiste voters. Though we would be hard-pressed to find support for the notion that the supporters of these four different parties are alike in class composition or other attributes, Irvine and Gold's analysis cannot detect any such differences.

Our own approach, which was used in most of the analysis by Clarke et al., is simply to differentiate the supporters of the three major parties. We also examine the potentially important differences between people who say they support one of the political parties and those who state no party preference. This allows us to retain in the analysis respondents who do not support any party. Because their numbers were very small, we decided against conducting separate analyses of the supporters of parties other than the three major parties. Compared to the 1244 Liberal party identifiers, 774 Progressive Conservative identifiers, and 365 NDP identifiers in our 1981 survey, only 47 respondents chose Social Credit and another 71 chose some other party. In our tables, the reader should note that the percentages of respondents who are reported as supporting any party (in the top rows) are not equal to the total of Liberal, Progressive Conservative, and NDP supporters (reported below). This is because the Social Credit and other party supporters are not included in the total respondents reporting any party preference, but are included in the counts of supporters of the three major parties.

In order to estimate levels of party support, we employ ordinary least squares (OLS) regression with dummy variables for party identification. Because the percentages in the different categories of party support are not near zero or one hundred, the regression coefficients would not differ markedly from the corresponding (but more difficult to interpret) logistic regression results. The binary dependent variable does lower the explained variances in OLS analysis, though this is not a problem in comparing the impact of different groups of *independent* variables. For a more detailed, essentially similar, justification of this strategy, see Johnston et al. (1992, 261–2).

Our questions about party identification are taken from the 1974 federal election study. To reduce the number of respondents giving no party preference, a series of questions was used. The initial question reads, "Thinking of *Federal* politics, do you usually think of yourself as a Liberal, Conservative, N.D.P., Social Credit, or what?" Respondents who said they were "independent," had no party identification, or said they did not know were then asked, "Still thinking of Federal politics, do you think of yourself as being a little closer to one of the parties than the others?" And those responding positively to this question were asked, "Which party is that?" Respondents who still had not mentioned any party were then asked, "If a federal election were held today, which party's candidate do you think you would favour?" In order to maximize the number of respondents for which federal party identification was available, all three of these questions were used to define the variable. Using the two last options, for people leaning towards a party or who did not feel closer to a party but stated an electoral preference, added only marginally to the number of people making any selection. For the Liberal party, 1181 identifiers were located by the initial question, an additional 61 were added by the second question, and only 2 were added by the third question. The corresponding numbers for the Progressive Conservative party were 730, 40, and 4, and for the NDP they were 332, 31, and 2.

Although there are very large interprovincial differences in federal party support, the following analysis employs region only as a control variable. We are interested in the variance explained by region and whether controlling for region affects the impact of other variables. Because regional differences are discussed in detail in almost every analysis of national data, there is little our own research can add. Using our 1979 survey data, Janine Brodie (1985) has shown that *within-party* regional differences in the attitudes towards selected policy issues of Liberal and Progressive Conservative party supporters are as important as the differences between parties and regions: "both parties, in short, house regional policy cleavages" (80). Federal party support is, therefore, differently motivated in different regions of the country. Our analysis in this chapter confirms this general observation by showing that provincial differences in party support are virtually unaffected by controls for social class, the socio-demographic variables, *and political ideology*. Thus although we have demonstrated the presence of large provincial differences in political ideology, those differences do not account for party support, nor do the differences in class or ideology relative to local provincial identities and interests. Of course, this finding lends support to interpretations of federal party support that focus heavily on institutional factors, as we have just argued.

ANALYSIS OF FEDERAL PARTY
IDENTIFICATION

We begin by examining the effect of class differences in party support, as shown in table 6-1. These differences are not very large. Taking first the proportion of respondents who support any party, there are three slightly outlying groups. Capitalists and small employers were *more* likely and the unemployed *less* likely than other groups to choose some party. Presumably this reflects business owners' greater confidence in the party system and unemployed workers' lesser confidence. The high levels of support for any party of small employers and the lower levels of support for any party by people who are unemployed are associated, respectively, with unusually high (62 percent) and low (25 percent) levels of support for the Liberal party. Otherwise the proportion of respondents in the various class and status groups that supported the Liberal party varies only between 37 and 47 percent. Support for the Progressive Conservative party is strongest among the capitalist class members and petty bourgeoisie, and weakest among the unemployed, students, and the ill and disabled – but, once region is held constant, the variation in levels of support is only from 21 to 33 percent. Finally, support for the NDP reflects a division between the business owners, including the capitalists, small employers, and petty bourgeoisie (only 1, 4, and 7 percent of whom support the NDP), and all the other class and status categories (for whom the level varies between 11 and 18 percent).

Except for the low level of NDP support among business owners, and the apparent disaffection with the Liberals and party system in general of the unemployed, there is remarkably little class differentiation in party support. There are virtually no differences among the major categories of employed workers. Support for the Liberal party was voiced by 43 percent of the managers and technocrats, 47 percent of supervisors, 41 percent of semi-autonomous workers, and 43 percent of the working class – these differences are small and could be random. The differences in support for the Progressive Conservatives are of approximately the same magnitude and support for the NDP is in the very narrow range of 13 to 15 percent.

Now observe the great similarity between the first row of each of the four panels in table 6-1, which gives the class distribution of party support, and the second row of each panel, which gives the class distribution adjusted for region, which is measured as the ten provinces. The lack of significant change indicates that, while province may have a strong effect on party support (see the figures for explained variance in table 6-4, discussed below), the class differences in party support are independent of region and could not arise from the regional differences in class structure.

Table 6-1
Percentage Distribution of Federal Party Identification by Class/Status Group

Federal Party Identification and Control Variables	Class/Status Group											
	Capitalist class	Small employers	Petty bourgeoisie	Managers and technocrats	Supervisors	Semi-autonomous employees	Working class	Unemployed	Domestic workers	Retired	Students	Ill, disabled
SUPPORT ANY PARTY												
None	93	92	83	87	88	88	85	75	86	81	82	82
Province	90	92	83	87	88	88	84	76	86	81	83	83
Above + socio-demographic	84	89	82	83	88	85	85	80	87	81	85	84
Above + ideology	84	89	82	83	88	84	85	80	87	81	84	85
LIBERAL												
None	45	62	40	43	47	41	43	25	46	37	38	42
Province	48	62	40	43	47	41	43	25	46	37	38	42
Above + socio-demographic	45	57	39	40	46	36	44	30	42	35	42	42
Above + ideology	44	57	38	39	46	36	44	31	45	36	44	44

Table 6-1
Percentage Distribution of Federal Party Identification by Class/Status Group (Continued)

Federal Party Identification and Control Variables	Class/Status Group											
	Capitalist class	Small employers	Petty bourgeoisie	Managers and technocrats	Supervisors	Semi-autonomous employees	Working class	Unemployed	Domestic workers	Retired	Students	Ill, disabled
PROGRESSIVE CONSERVATIVE												
None	38	26	35	28	25	32	24	22	26	32	17	20
Province	33	27	32	27	25	30	24	26	26	31	21	24
Above + socio-demographic	29	27	31	26	26	32	25	29	24	27	24	25
Above + ideology	27	25	30	25	26	31	26	30	24	27	24	27
NDP												
None	1	4	7	15	15	15	13	15	11	11	18	14
Province	1	4	7	16	15	14	14	16	11	9	20	14
Above + socio-demographic	1	4	8	15	14	13	12	13	15	14	15	14
Above + ideology	5	7	11	18	14	15	12	13	16	15	15	14

As we observed for political ideology, table 6-2 shows that there are some manual/non-manual differences within social classes in the patterns of party support. Of course voting studies have traditionally taken the manual/non-manual distinction as the most important (and sometimes the only) way in which social class affects party support. What distinguishes our results is the evidence that the direction and magnitudes of the manual/non-manual differences are a shown to be a function of social class. NDP support is much greater among manual than non-manual supervisors – 24 percent versus 10 percent – and among manual than non-manual semi-autonomous employees – 21 percent versus 12 percent.

Comparing manual and non-manual members of the working class, however, there is little difference in the patterns of party support. If anything (but the effect is not significant), NDP support is stronger and Progressive Conservative party support weaker among *non-manual* members of the working class. For the semi-autonomous employees, but not the supervisors, the greater NDP support among manual workers is accompanied by decreased Progressive Conservative support and, for both semi-autonomous employees and supervisors, the manual/non-manual differences in Liberal party support are negligible. Within the petty bourgeoisie, non-manual proprietors are slightly more likely than manual proprietors to support the Liberals and NDP and less likely to support the Progressive Conservatives, but these differences do not reach statistical significance.

It is interesting to compare these findings to the differences in the political ideology scales discussed in chapter 5. The stronger NDP support among manual supervisors and manual semi-autonomous employees is consistent with these groups' much greater support for social programs and redistribution, compared to their non-manual counterparts. Within the working class, however, manual workers' high levels of support for social programs and redistribution are *not* translated into correspondingly high levels of NDP support. NDP support is as strong among the managers and technocrats, whose views on policy issues are far to the right of the working class, as it is among workers. Of course these non-supervisory, manual workers are the core of the traditional working class, together with non-manual workers in routine jobs who constitute the fastest-growing (and largely female) sector of new workers. In the absence of an assurance that it can successfully appeal to these key sectors of the working class, the NDP's attempts to adopt more radical positions run the serious risk of alienating its supporters in the more privileged sectors of the population. These risks are accentuated by the low levels of political participation and efficacy of manual workers.

While the class differences in party support are interesting and their *direction* is consistent with what we have observed for the ideological measures, the *magnitudes* of these differences should not be exaggerated. As measured using Erik Olin Wright's categories in table 6-1, for employed people social

Table 6-2

Percentage Distribution of Federal Party Identification by Class and Manual Versus Non-manual Workers

| | | | Social Class | | | | | | | | | |
| Federal Party Identification | Capitalist class | Small employers | Petty bourgeoisie | | Managers and technocrats | Supervisors | | Semi-autonomous employees | | Working class | |
			Non-manual	Manual		Non-manual	Manual	Non-manual	Manual	Non-manual	Manual
Support any party	92	92	86	80	87	85	92	88	87	87	81
Liberal	45	62	40	32	43	48	43	36	40	43	44
Progressive Conservative	38	26	32	38	28	26	23	36	25	26	21
NDP	1	4	9	6	15	10	24	12	21	15	11

class explains just 0.6, 0.7, and 0.7 percent in support for the Liberals, Progressive Conservatives, and NDP respectively. Distinguishing the manual from non-manual differences within social classes raises these figures to 0.6, 1.3, and 1.2 percent, respectively. These very small percentages reflect the low degree of class differentiation in party support shown in the previous tables. Even allowing for the tendency for regression with binary variables to result in low explained variances, the explanatory power of class is small (for an extensive discussion of this point see Brym et al. 1989).

A more detailed look at the relationship between class and party support is provided by an analysis that examines the effects of supervision and of pay differences within social classes, shown in table 6-3. The addition of these variables modifies our earlier arguments to only a minor extent. Like the manual/non-manual differences just described, the effect of supervision on party support is a function of social class: members of the petty bourgeoisie who have one or more employees (as indicated by their doing some supervision) are more likely to support the Liberal party; semi-autonomous employees with some supervisory authority are marginally more likely to support the NDP and less likely to support the Liberal party; and workers with supervisory authority are less likely to support the Liberals and more likely to support the Progressive Conservatives. Most of these effects, however, do not reach statistical significance. Finally, the analysis suggests that, within class categories, higher levels of pay increase support for the Liberals and Conservatives and decrease NDP support.

Especially compared to the very large provincial differences in party support, the magnitudes of the class differences in party support should not be exaggerated. As table 6-4 indicates, the class and status categories defined for the entire population explain no more than 0.9 percent of the variance in any of the four party identification variables and the addition of the detailed information on manual versus non-manual occupations, supervision, and rate of pay differences raises this figure to a maximum of 1.3 percent. Province alone explains 6.4, 9.7, and 3.6 percent of variance in Liberal, Progressive Conservative, and NDP support, respectively. The addition of other socio-demographic variables to the regression analysis increases the predictive power of our analysis between 0.6 and 3.7 percent, with the larger increases in predicting Liberal and Progressive Conservative party support and for the analysis based on the entire population. The other socio-demographic variables generally have more influence on party support than social class. Further increases in the explained variance, ranging from 0.5 to 4.2 percent, are achieved by introducing the measures of political ideology, with the largest increase for NDP support. Thus, to a greater extent than for the other parties, NDP supporters are drawn to their party by their ideological convictions, rather than their structural location in society. For NDP support, but not for Liberal or Progressive Conservative party support, the impact of ideological

Table 6-3
Regression Coefficients for Class Variables from Analysis of Federal Party Identification, Relative to the Working Class

Federal Party Identification	Control variables	Mean for Class, Relative to Working Class						Manual, Relative to Non-Manual				Some Supervision			Rate of pay (standardized within social classes)
		Capitalist class	Small employers	Petty bourgeoisie	Managers and technocrats	Supervisors	Semi-autonomous employees	Petty bourgeoisie	Semi-autonomous employees	Supervisors	Working class	Petty bourgeoisie	Semi-autonomous employees	Working class	
Support any party	None	8	8	-1	3	5	3	-6	8	8	-7*	8	4	2	3*
	All	0	5	0	-1	5	2	-5	2	11+	-3	8	1	0	1
Liberal	None	3	19*	-5	0	3	-5	-6	5	-6	0	10	-6	-7+	1
	All	4	14+	-3	-2	3	-6	-1	2	-3	1	11	-3	-2	2
Progressive Conservative	None	13+	2	10*	3	-1	6	5	-9	-4	-5*	-2	0	8+	2+
	All	3	2	7	0	0	6	2	-4	-1	0	-3	-6	2	1
NDP	None	-12+	-10+	-6+	1	3	3	-3	9	13*	-3	1	6	3	-1
	All	-13+	-9+	-4	3	3	2	-5	9	12+	-4	1	5	2	-1

* significant at .01
+ significant at .05

Table 6-4
Analysis of Variance for Regression from Analysis of Federal Party Identification

			Percentage of Variance Explained (Adjusted for Degrees of Freedom)				
Federal Party Identification	Sample	Class	Class, super-vision, manual/ non-manual	Province	Province, class	Province, class, demo-graphic, religion	Province, class, demo-graphic, religion, ideology
Support any party	Population	.3		.8	1.1	3.1	3.6
	Employed	.1	1.0	1.0	2.1	4.4	5.6
Liberal	Population	.9		6.4	7.2	10.8	11.5
	Employed	.6	.6	5.2	5.4	7.9	8.4
Progressive Conservative	Population	.6		9.7	9.8	13.5	14.7
	Employed	.7	1.3	9.4	9.5	11.9	13.9
NDP	Population	.5		3.6	4.3	6.4	9.3
	Employed	.7	1.2	3.4	4.6	5.2	9.4

variables is comparable to regional effects. With both the structural and ideological variables in the regression model, the variances explained, for the different parties, ranges from 8.4 to 13.9 percent for the employed population and from 9.3 to 14.7 percent for the entire population.

These results are very similar to those obtained by Clarke et al. (1979, 126), who explained 10, 11, and 5 percent of the variance in Liberal, Conservative, and NDP support, respectively. We have included many more variables in our analysis, but gained no explanatory power. Of course it is possible that there were changes in the patterns of party support between 1974 and 1981 and there may be differences in voting behaviour, predicted by Clarke et al., and party identification, considered here. Unfortunately we cannot make precise comparisons of our regression analysis with other researchers. This is mainly due to the unusual way that we have defined social class, but there are two other methodological difficulties. Most disappointingly, the results of Clarke et al.'s regression analysis (1979, 126) are reported entirely in terms of correlation coefficients and *standardized* regression coefficients, neither of which is meaningful when dealing with dichotomous variables. And, rather than treating each of the provinces separately, Clarke et al. define the Prairies and Atlantic Canada as two "regions," despite the large differences in party support within regions (and especially between Alberta and the other two Prairie provinces).

It also is worth examining the specific effects on party identification, as measured by the regression coefficients. For each decade of age, support for the Liberal party increases by 1 percent, support for the Progressive Conservative party increases by 2 percent, and support for the NDP falls by 2 percent. Very similar age effects were found in John Meisel's (1973, 11) analysis of the 1968 election and in Clarke et al.'s (1979, 120) analysis of the 1974 election. The stability of the relationship between age and party support suggests that there are systematic changes of party support with age instead of a series of age cohorts with distinctive patterns of support.

Consistent with our findings about the lack of gender differences in ideology, gender had no significant effects on federal party support. Controls for province, class, or any other variables had negligible impact on the gender differences. These small effects are in the same direction of those observed by Clarke et al. (1979, 126), who found that women were more likely than men to support the Liberal party and less likely to support the NDP. Meisel (1973, 12) also obtained similar results.

The three variables measuring education have small, mostly insignificant effects. High school graduates are more likely than non-graduates to support the Liberal party and less likely to support the NDP, while Progressive Conservative party support is unaffected; university graduates gave less support than non-graduates to the Progressive Conservative party and more to the Liberals and NDP. More income is associated with small increases in the likelihood of supporting any party and tends to lower Progressive Conservative party support. Respondents who reported they had no income or refused to divulge it were much less likely than average to report that they supported any party (and there were correspondingly low levels of support for all three parties). These effects are of more methodological than substantive interest: it is not surprising that respondents who would not report their incomes would be more reluctant to reveal their party preferences.

As past research has also shown, party identification has a much stronger relationship to English-French differences and religion than to education or income. In Quebec, French respondents were about 20 percent more likely than non-French respondents to support the Liberal party. In English Canada, French respondents were about 20 percent more likely to support the Liberals and 15 percent less likely to support the Progressive Conservatives than other English Canadians.

Even controlling for province and French/non-French differences, religion has fairly strong effects on party identification, using our trichotomous measure of religion: the respondents who gave some religious affiliation are divided into Catholics and non-Catholics (termed "Protestants" for convenience, but also including all other religions besides Catholicism), and the third category includes respondents who named no religious affiliation (termed atheists for convenience). Compared to Protestants, Catholics and atheists are less likely to have supported any party; Catholics were less likely to support the Progressive Conservatives and atheists were more likely to support the Liberals and NDP and less likely to support the Progressive Conservatives. These findings are quite similar to those obtained by Clarke et al. (1979, 126) and Meisel (1972, 3). Table 6-5 also shows that religiosity has some impact on party identification. The likelihood of supporting any party and of supporting the Liberal party increases with church attendance for Catholics, but not for Protestants.

Table 6-6 shows the effects of the six measures of political ideology on party identification, *after* controlling for the influences of province, class, and the socio-demographic variables. Taken as a group the six measures of ideology have the strongest effect on NDP identification, which is increased by high levels of support for social programs, redistribution, extra-parliamentary protest, and civil liberties. While these four effects are in the expected direction, it is significant that support for labour (and also the measure of attitudes towards immigrants) has no effect on NDP support, despite the structural links between the NDP and the labour movement. Conservative party support is negatively related to support for social programs and redistribution and positively related to having assimilationist or negative views of immigrants. Finally, Liberal party support is negatively related to support for redistribution and extra-parliamentary protest; the net effect is to increase the explained variance by less than 1 percent. Thus supporters of the NDP are clearly more ideologically distinct than the supporters of the other major parties, but even for the NDP the impact of ideology is only moderately strong.

A look back at table 6-1 shows that the impact of successively adding controls to the class differences in party identification is remarkably limited. Controlling for province has minor effects on the patterns of Progressive Conservative party support, lowering the high level of support in the capitalist class and petty bourgeoisie and raising the low level of support among the students and ill and disabled, while leaving unaffected the patterns of Liberal party and NDP support and the proportions supporting any party. The addition of the socio-demographic variables then raises NDP support and lowers Liberal and Progressive Conservative party support among the retired and does exactly the opposite for students – presumably because some of the distinctiveness of the retired and students is related to age, which is one of the socio-demographic variables.

CONCLUSIONS

This analysis does not challenge the scholarly consensus on the nature of federal party support in Canada. Our more theoretically consistent treatment of social class and our introduction of a greater variety of socio-demographic variables and independent measures of political ideology have not enabled

Table 6-5
Regression Coefficients for Socio-demographic Variables from Analysis of Federal Party Identification, Holding Constant Province and Social Class

Federal Party Identification	Sample	Age in decades	Gender	Education			Family Income			English in Quebec	French in English Canada	Religion			Catholic by religiosity interaction
				In Years	High school graduate	University graduate	In thousands	None	Missing			Catholic	None	Religiosity	
Support any party	Population	1	-1	1+	0	2	.1+	-2	-11*	6	3	-10*	-10*	-1	3*
	Employed	1	1	1	0	-2	.1*	-21*	-8+	6	2	-7+	-12*	-1	2*
Liberal	Population	1*	2	0	6	5	.0	-4	-5	19*	20*	5	-5	-1	4*
	Employed	1	4	0	4	1	.1	-17*	3	22*	16+	0	-10+	-2	5*
Progressive Conservative	Population	2*	2	1*	-2	-6	-.1	5	-5	-4	-13*	-13*	-16*	1	-1
	Employed	1	2	1	0	-5	.1	-1	-10	-4	-16*	-6	-12*	0	1
NDP	Population	-2*	-2	0	-6*	2	-.1	-6*	-3	1	-5	-2	-12*	0	0
	Employed	-2+	-3	0	-4	3	.0	-5	-3	-1	-1	-2	7+	0	0

* significant at .01
+ significant at .05

Table 6-6
Regression Coefficients for Measures of Political Ideology, from Regression Analysis
of Federal Party Identification, Holding Constant Province, Social Class, and
Socio-demographic Variables

Federal Party Identification	Sample	Regression Coefficient					
		Support for social programs	Support for redist-ribution	Support for labour	Assimilat-ionist views of immigrants	Support for protest	Support for civil liberties
Support any party	Population	−2.1*	−1.9+	.6	1.7+	.9	1.9+
	Employed	−2.8*	−1.7	.5	3.0*	.3	2.7*
Liberal	Population	.2	−3.4*	1.6	−.5	−4.3*	.4
	Employed	.4	−3.1+	.1	1.0	−3.8*	−.6
Progressive Conservative	Population	−3.9*	−2.7*	−.4	2.1+	.6	−.3
	Employed	−5.0*	−2.8+	−.7	3.1*	−.6	.4
NDP	Population	1.8+	3.1*	−.2	.3	3.6*	1.9*
	Employed	2.0+	3.4*	−.5	−.5	3.2*	3.5*

* significant at .01
+ significant at .05

us to predict party identification more accurately than previous studies. The patterns of party support that we observe at the end of the Trudeau era are similar to Meisel's (1972) observations for the 1968 election that introduced it. Meisel's description of the NDP, for example, could as well describe our results: "it attracts a larger proportion of skilled than unskilled workers, its vote does not vary with age or education" (47). And the lack of differentiation between the two larger parties remained as obvious after a decade of serious political and economic instability as it did before it.

Still, our results make some useful additions to the existing research. We have demonstrated that the effects on party support of the distinction between manual and non-manual workers is a function of social class: specifically, the difference is much larger for more privileged wage workers. Simply dividing the workforce into manual and non-manual categories is therefore likely to provide misleading results about patterns of party support. Furthermore, business owners have distinct patterns of party support, which are not the same as for managers with whom they are grouped in conventional studies of party support. In addition to such refinements of the nature of class distinctions in party support, we have shown, as previous studies could not for want of adequate data, that the NDP is, as one would expect, a more ideologically distinctive party than its brokerage party opponents, although ideology plays only a very minor role overall in Canadians' identification with political parties.

Such marginal qualifications to previous analysis of party identification hardly call for a reappraisal of the character of Canadian party politics. As we argued at the beginning of this chapter, our results confirm the relevance of the emphasis in orthodox political science of specific institutional and historical developments as explanations for the differently based appeals of federal parties in different regions, and for the brokered alliances within and across regions of electoral blocs that are heterogeneous in both class and ideological terms.

There remain, nevertheless, important questions about how to interpret such institutional developments. Prediction is not explanation, and our understanding of party politics requires a theoretical interpretation of the statistical relationships predicting differences in party identification. Orthodox political sociology explains Canadian party politics in terms of the absence of class consciousness and the absence of ideological constraint or rationality among members of the mass public; the greater salience of local/provincial and personal/personality issues; the manipulation by political elites of these short-term issues to mobilize electoral support; and the relative weakness and instability of partisan identities in a brokerage party system that creates no enduring national communities of interest, no coherent political mandates for government, and, despite the long history of Liberal party dominance through the era discussed in this book, no brake against large swings in the electoral fortunes of the different parties (see Stevenson 1987). Revisionist and critical responses to such orthodoxy argue not against the observed lack of class and ideological coherence in Canadian party politics, but against the interpretation that such observation indicates the irrelevance of class and ideology.

We wish to make such an argument, though we depart from the two best alternatives available in the work of Brodie and Jenson (1988), and Ogmundson (1976; 1980; Ogmundson and Ng 1982). For Brodie and Jenson the major Canadian parties rule class issues off the electoral agenda, thereby making it impossible for members of the public to respond on the basis of the fit between different party platforms and their opposing class interests. In these circumstances the system produces a lack of class consciousness and class-motivated political action. Ogmundson goes further, arguing that members of the public are not, in fact, lacking in class motivation; that they identify with political parties that they think best represent their class interests, but because the party system is managed by elites to deflect class conflict, they have no reliable guide to party choice and make essentially irrational decisions about which parties best represent their interests.

In our view the problem with the Brodie and Jenson argument is that it allows for the mechanical obliteration of class interests by elite manipulation, and for a conclusion that is too close to the orthodox assumption of the irrelevance of class and ideology to Canadian party politics. The problem with Ogmundson's argument is that it strains too much to recapture a relevance for class, by making a strength of an obvious weakness. We believe, first, that one has to accept the obvious weakness of class consciousness and of class or ideological bases to party identification, but that such acceptance need not entail the obliteration and irrelevance of class in mass politics. We believe, second, that one has to devise a concept of the institutional mediation of class politics that goes beyond the mechanical and always efficient elite manipulation of the mass public.

With respect to the first issue of the relevance of class to Canadian party politics, we have noted the limited but nevertheless interesting qualifications in our analysis of the absence of class and ideological differences in party support. This sense of the very limited but significant role of class and ideology in shaping Canadian party politics can be amplified in a number of ways. First, as we have noted elsewhere (Stevenson 1987), *shifts* in individual party identification in the era covered by our surveys show a perhaps greater, though still minor, influence of class and ideology. Analysis of changes in the party identification of individuals we surveyed in 1977, 1979, and 1981 reveals that before the massive electoral swing of 1984 there were interesting class and ideological dynamics to changing party alignments. There was a consolidation of Liberal party support among homemakers and among semi- and unskilled workers who presumably identified with the emphasis on civil rights and welfare issues in the post-1980 national policy, and a corresponding consolidation of support for the opposition Progressive Conservative party among more privileged classes who it could be argued were disproportionately responsible for meeting the costs of those policies. Ideology also shaped changing party alignments. Left-wing voters were more likely to shift support among parties, all of which presumably failed to satisfy their concerns, but they tended to confine their choices to the Liberals and NDP, while more right-wing voters predominated among those shifting towards the Progressive Conservatives.

A different but complementary body of evidence on the importance of ideology to party politics is that contained in surveys of party activists. Against the assumption of a conspiratorial avoidance of class-dividing issues among party elites, such evidence shows that Liberal and Progressive Conservative party elites attending the leadership conventions prior to the 1984 election were ideologically distinctive, and that within parties ideological differences had a significant if slight influence on the outcomes of leadership contests (cf. Stevenson 1987; Blake 1988; Johnston 1988).

If such evidence suggests a non-trivial effect of class and ideology in electoral and party politics, it is nevertheless an effect that is relatively minor in comparison to other influences on party identification and voting in the complex mediation of class conflict in Canadian party politics. In order to understand this mediation in ways that move beyond the mechanical and conspiratorial manipulation of the public by elites, we have to understand the disjunction between the analysis in this and preceding chapters. To be consistent with the results of our previous analysis of class differences in political ideology we should have found much larger differences in party support than were observed. Even single items dealing with social programs, redistribution, and labour relations exhibited much larger class differences than we find in party support – despite the items' low levels of reliability and focus on specific issues with which the respondent may have little familiarity, especially in comparison with party identification. Why this inconsistency?

It is not conceivable to us that elites in all parties manipulate the electoral and policy agenda in ways that simply prevent ideologically divisive issues from entering election campaigns. An alternative approach to the understanding of the mediation of class conflict has to move in two directions, one having to do with analysis of political parties *per se*, but the other moving more far afield into the wider institutional structures of the state.

With respect to political parties *per se*, our analysis of public ideology suggests that parties cannot simply manipulate out of existence the class divisions on public policy issues that we have described, but that they *do* succeed in mediating, that is in reducing, the salience of these divisions. This cannot be the result of simply avoiding class issues, since the issues we have shown to be class-divided cannot and have not been avoided in party and electoral politics. The dominant ideological perspectives of party activists are different in the different parties, and ideological divisions within parties reflect regional differences in the ideological perspectives of the general public. Nor can the mediation of ideological divisions be simply the result of the manipulation of the more salient, non-class factors in party identification – attachments to language/religion and region. Region and language are said to obscure class differences in party support, but regional differences in ideology coexist with class differences in ideology, and the fact that regional but not class cleavages arise in party support must reflect a process by which parties and governments respond to the ideological interests of the mass public that is more complex than the simple articulation of non-class interests.

We have evidence of widespread support for the social programs and redistributional policies that have been championed by the NDP (but adopted by Liberal governments); on the whole, the public is ideologically closer to the NDP than to the Liberals or Conservatives. But this closeness is not translated into majority support for the NDP; nor do patterns of party support reflect the divisions in public opinion on issues that generate significant class division. Only to a very limited extent are NDP supporters ideologically distinctive. In order to understand this mediation of class conflict, we have to examine the specific institutional developments that account, for example, for the continuing hold of the Liberal and Progressive Conservative parties in Quebec and Atlantic Canada – despite the fact that the people of these provinces are more ideologically sympathetic to the NDP than the people of Ontario and the Western provinces.

We need to pay greater attention therefore to the institutional developments by which different parties come to dominate in different regions and at different historical time periods by articulating the dominant ideological tendencies in public discourse, by appropriating the ideological perspectives on key issues of classes formerly aligned with other parties, and by a complex process of monitoring and in turn shaping public opinion. But even if we succeed by such means in obtaining a more sophisticated picture of the way in which parties act as agents of social control, as mediators of class conflict in Canada, we will have an incomplete picture of the ways in which social control, order, or hegemony are created and maintained. Parties exist to form governments, and it is in the wider institutional realm of the state, a realm centred in the institutions of government, that the response to class divisions is most clearly shaped. The appeals and promises of parties are directly related to the performance of governments, and the extent to which class divisions are removed from party politics is a function of the extent to which governments mediate class-divided interests in the formulation of public policy.

Orthodox political sociology, buoyed by the absence of class divisions in party politics, can assume that governments are in the hands of elected members of political parties that have no class base, and that public policy formulation is an essentially technical business constrained by the availability of resources and the competition for them among functionally divided elites. Because we argue that class divisions are not insignificant, nor made irrelevant in the process of party politics, we believe it is important to move beyond the analysis of public opinion and party politics that so dominates orthodox political sociology, and to take up questions about the articulation and mediation of class and ideological divisions by those influential or actively involved in the public policy process. In the rest of this book, therefore, we move deeper into the bosom of the state – from the surface measures of the overall pulse of public affection and disaffection, to more internal measures of the flows of influence and information that determine which parts of the body politic get what, when, and how.

PART THREE

Elite Ideology

7 State Power and Elite Ideology

In this and the next three chapters we address a series of questions about how power is organized and used in the formulation of public policy. Canadian politics, according to our analysis thus far, is not driven in any simple way by the motor forces of class and the conflicting interests of classes. Our findings of the relative weakness of the relationships between divisions of class and ideology among Canadians and the even weaker links between these divisions and attachments to political parties confirm the scholarly consensus, as does our confirming evidence of marked regional divisions in attachments to political parties and government institutions. Weakness is not, however, the same thing as the absence of a relationship, and we have emphasized a number of ways in which the contours of class and ideology give a definite shape to the Canadian political landscape.

These underlying divisions over the proper direction of government and public policy pose potential problems for political order, as does the pronounced public discontent with the overall performance of government and the organization of power within the society. Does the high degree of public alienation and dissatisfaction with public affairs strain the capacity of the state to govern, having no popular mandate to decide among competing claims? Alternatively, does the relatively high degree of satisfaction that Canadians experience in their private lives drive people away from and compensate for the dissatisfactions of public life, thereby leaving the state relatively free to govern? And whatever the constraints of public opinion, how is the state given order and direction; whose ideas and interests underlie public policy? Referring to the national policy debates of the Pierre Trudeau era that are the focus of this book, why did the Canadian state enter upon apparently innovative and conflictual policy shifts; at whose behest and prompting, if any, were government officials acting in the redefinition of public policy? Were such shifts in policy incremental adjustments to mobilized and active social groups, or did they more narrowly represent the interests of politicians and bureaucrats acting for "reasons of state?"

In raising these questions we bridge the three concerns of this book – class, ideology, and the state – arriving at the most contentious issues in political theory: how does, and how should, the state represent or lead society? In this chapter we review a variety of theoretical approaches to such questions derived from the dominant pluralist understanding of the liberal democratic state, and a number of Marxist alternatives. Theories of the state are essentially "macro" theories of the organization of societies, and none of them can be satisfactorily tested by reference to micro data on the characteristics of individuals alone. Further, none of these theories is primarily concerned with questions of ideology, though they all entail assumptions or hypotheses about the character of popular ideology or political culture, and about the structure of interests and interest representation within governments. Nevertheless these arguments can be fruitfully examined, as we will try to show, using survey data on the political perspectives of elite decision makers in the major organizations of society, especially government, business, and labour organizations.

THE PLURALIST ORTHODOXY

Pluralist theory represents the most widely accepted account of contemporary Western politics. It serves also as a buttress of liberal ideology, legitimizing the highly unequal distribution of resources and power with the nostrum that anyone can speak up and be heard. By focusing on the idea that anything could happen, rather than on the enormous differences in the likelihood of different political outcomes, pluralism legitimizes the distribution of power. The discussion of pluralism here necessarily involves an amalgam of classic statements (such as Dahl 1961; 1963; 1971; 1982; 1989; Lindblom 1977).

Pluralist theory and analysis of the workings of liberal democratic states conceives of such states as ruled by minorit*ies*, rather than *a* minority, that is by elites who represent the many – plural – interest groups in society, rather than by a homogeneous elite or ruling class. This form of oligarchy (rule by the few) is checked by a limited form of democracy (rule by the many) as the result of institutional arrangements for the free and open political association and participation of the adult population, taken advantage of in the multiple memberships of individuals in voluntary associations, trade union or other occupational interest groups, and political parties, as well as their involvement in periodic elections.

Polyarchic rule, as these theorists like to call it in distinction from democratic or oligarchic rule, is sustained by the weakness of ideological divisions and the strength of a unifying consensus in the mass political culture, together with the apolitical character of the mass public, which prevents the overloading of the state with public demand. The state or political system (the latter term is preferred in this tradition in order to get away from the connotations of domination and coercion associated with the "state") is conceived as an arena for the accommodation and adjudication of interests articulated by the elite leaders of multiple organizations in society.

Pluralism, as the simple sense of the word implies, refers to the existence of numerous, different interests in society. In pluralist theory modern societies are characterized by the proliferation of increasingly differentiated organizations, with individuals pursuing their diverse interests through multiple organizational affiliations. Where there are competitive interests among diverse organizations, the elite leaders of those organizations bargain for compromise solutions. Generally, however, conflicts of interest in such societies are moderated by the cross-cutting rather than overlapping structure of group affiliation, so that individuals in conflict in one sphere of social activity (e.g., workers vs managers in a firm) are allied with some of their opponents in other conflict situations (e.g., members of ethnic associations contesting exclusionary membership in a social club). The weaknesses of political ideology in the mass public, and the public's general political isolation as the result of the deferral to elites of most political activity, are functional to the stability of the state as a system of bargaining amongst elites.

This formulation begs questions of organization: of how the public interest is defined, how coherence in public decision making is achieved in the adjudication of a multitude of competing interests, and how stability and legitimacy is achieved when elites drawn from more privileged backgrounds or occupying more privileged positions make decisions with only minimal direction from the much less privileged majority. In this context organization is generally admitted to involve the "mobilization of bias," in Elmer Schattschneider's felicitous phrase (1960), but such bias is not generally seen as dysfunctional or inherently contradictory to the promise and performance of liberal democracy. Also, organizational interests conflict, as pluralists readily admit, and if such conflicts of interest require political regulation, that regulation cannot be presumed to be automatic.

The response to these problems in pluralist theory is that such regulation is provided in advanced industrial societies through the institutions of liberal democracy. As a theory of democracy, pluralism refers to political arrangements for the accommodation of diverse interests, for the sustenance of diversity as the result of the different interests pursued by individuals and groups in a free society, and for limiting the state's powers to impose a tyranny of either minority or majority on the freedom of choice in society. The classical meaning of democracy as popular rule, the rule of the majority, is altered in pluralist theory to mean elite rule subject to popular accountability – the rule of the few in the interest of the majority. Liberal democracy, that is, is a form of state in which the rule of political elites is subject to institutional checks on their capacity to act in the interest of a minority of citizens. These checks provide for periodic accountability in popular elections, and for the freedom of organization and lobbying by interest groups between elections.

Liberal democracies require certain institutionalized practices in order to provide this accountability: the constitutional grant of executive powers to elected officials; the provision of free and fair elections; a universal suffrage, and right to run for office; and the guarantee of basic civil liberties such as freedom of expression, freedom of information, and freedom of association. But even when these provisions are satisfied, liberal democracies remain, as pluralists emphasize, a far cry from popular rule. As the major theorist in this tradition argues, the development of such provisions in existing liberal democracies "unquestionably falls well short of achieving the democratic process" but "if citizen control over collective decisions is more anaemic than the robust control they would exercise if the dream of participatory democracy were ever realized, the capacity of citizens to exercise a veto over the re-election and policies of elected officials is a powerful and frequently exercised means of preventing officials from imposing policies objectionable to many citizens" (Dahl 1989, 223).

The interesting theoretical question is not whether or not, or how often, liberal democracy provides for the popular electoral veto of governments, but why in highly pluralistic societies, assuming the impossibility of deriving a coherent social welfare function from diverse individual preferences (Arrow 1963), there is stable government and coherent public policy at all. Here pluralist theory argues for some general limitation on the extent of societal division and conflict: minimal levels of sub-cultural pluralism or special "consociational" arrangements for the accommodation of sharply divided cultural communities (Lijphart 1977), and the support of processes of elite accommodation and popular accountability among elites and the general public.

These arguments touch on questions of ideology, but they are only very vaguely articulated by pluralist theorists (e.g., Dahl 1989, 260–3). Essentially, pluralists argue that elite accommodation in liberal democratic societies requires the *absence* of strong ideological divisions in the mass public – particularly the absence of divisions aligned with structural divisions, such as regional and class lines – and limited popular political mobilization and participation. These conditions facilitate bargaining among the elites who represent the diverse organizations to which members of the mass public are most attached. Political elites, legislative and executive, are less representatives or delegates of public constituencies than they are trustees of the public interest, whose day-to-day interpretation of that role depends upon information and consultation with the lobbies of organized interests in society (Presthus 1973; 1974).

But still the question is posed of how any stable and coherent accommodation of diverse interests is possible. Two general arguments are made in pluralist theory, having to do with elite integration and elite liberalism. The first addresses the capacity of elites to act in concert, the second the capacity of elites in so doing to respond to public interests. The two arguments are buttressed by a third having to do with elite rationality – the greater capacity of elites, as compared to the mass public, to deal with complex and sophisticated questions of public policy. All of these arguments deal with questions of elite ideology.

The central logic of the theory of elite integration is elaborated by Claude Ake (1967), with numerous authors giving additional specifications about the central importance of a consensus among elites on the "rules of the game." This consensus is built around support for the procedural requirements and civil liberties without which no genuine system of periodic electoral alternation in the pattern and personnel of the regime could be said to exist, and without which no plausible claim could be made for the fair representation of interests in authoritative decisions about competing claims for state action. The argument here is very straightforward. Liberal democracies require support for liberal democracy, and because liberal democracies are based upon elite rule, the elites must be committed to the essential liberal principles of freedom of association and political participation. Where elite integration is not built around a commitment to the institutions of liberal democracy, one may find relatively stable, authoritarian, but not democratic regimes. Support for this argument is produced by comparative analysis of the attitudes and behaviour of political elites in states with varying records of stable democracy, reproducing the logic of Gabriel Almond and Sidney Verba's (1963) analysis of the requirements for stable democracy in mass political culture (cf. Putnam 1973; 1976; O'Donnell, Schmitter, and Whitehead 1986).

The argument for elite integration is somewhat tautological: in order for elite rule to be democratic, elites must adhere to rules of democracy; in liberal democracies, therefore, elites are liberals. However, there are a variety of more interesting arguments about the scope and content of elite liberalism.

The theory of elite rationality is designed to explain the ability of elites to manage or organize a potentially unstable system of plural interest groups. The argument is quite simple again. Not only are elites integrated in their commitment to liberal democratic principles, but they can manage the aggregation and mediation of the diverse interests they represent because of their greater political sophistication and intelligence as compared to members of the mass public. Empirical support for such arguments was first laid out in Phillip Converse's empirical description of the narrow limits of ideological constraint in the mass public of such societies (1964), and in Herbert McClosky, Paul Hoffmann, and Rosemary O'Hara's analysis of the greater clarity of ideological divisions amongst party elites as compared to their support groups in the general public (1960). This argument, already dealt with in chapter 3, holds that there is a much greater intellectual sophistication in the capacity of the elite as opposed to members of the general public to reason about political problems. Elites not only hold more consistent ideological world-views – making, for example, the connection between economic and political liberalism, as suggested below – they can organize arguments over practical policy issues in terms of general ideological principles.

Together these arguments converge in a theory of elite liberalism, according to which elites are more liberal than members of the mass public. This argument holds that elite liberalism results from the experience in bargaining and compromise of the leaders of the core groups and institutions in a pluralist society. Their direct involvement in the day-to-day experience with the bargaining and compromise involved in interest group politics embeds in elites a greater understanding of, and commitment to, the procedural/ juridical principles that make it work than is possible within the public at large. Members of the general public not involved in decision making are concerned primarily with the performance and not the procedures of the system. They are concerned, therefore, primarily with a tolerable range of material welfare and mobility, rather than with more philosophical and procedural commitments that allow those benefits to be obtained and enjoyed. At the extreme, the masses have a "fear of freedom" that leads easily to populist or proto-fascist manipulation unless elites provide the necessary bulwark to liberal democracy (Fromm 1941; Lipset 1960).

Another, essentially opposite, argument holds that the mass public is fundamentally supportive rather than fearful of freedom, but is not correspondingly supportive of the equality of condition that would promote true liberties (Lane 1962). Here it is argued that elites have had the greater commitment to economic as opposed to political liberalism, and have led the support for equality of opportunity as guaranteed by social service programs in health, education, and welfare (cf. Heclo 1974; Heidenheimer, Heclo, and Adams 1975). According to both arguments, though, the public has confused commitments to liberalism, while elites hold consistently liberal positions, decide practical policy issues in ways consistent with those principles, and produce, therefore, a consistent and rational tradition of public policy that re-produces the liberal democratic state.

The argument that elites are more concerned with economic equality is on its face difficult to make. Why should elites support the interests of the least privileged, when they themselves are from disproportionately privileged backgrounds, when electoral systems are biased in favour of the representation of more privileged interests, and especially when the majority of the public oppose improving the position of the least privileged? Pluralists explain the counter-intuitive outcome in essentially functionalist arguments. Stable democracies require that elites know what the public wants, that elites agree with public priorities, and that elites devote effort to and are effective at dealing with these priorities (Verba and Nie 1972, 302). This requirement is met in at least three ways in pluralist theory.

First, where electoral systems operate in such a way as to reflect cleavages on questions of economic power and distribution, with relatively strong electoral representation of the less privileged classes, and with relatively pronounced ideological conflict over questions of the distribution of wealth, political elites, like members of the public, will be ideologically divided on these questions, and in some circumstances the electoral victory of working-class parties and their allies may bring about the direct representation of those interests by a majority of the political elites in government. But this is not the typical outcome, and given the bias of electoral systems (cf. Schattschneider 1960; Przeworski 1985; Przweorski and Sprague 1986) there will typically be an over-representation of upper-class interests in the political elite.

Where such over-representation produces relatively pronounced political and ideological conflict within the political elite, because it represents a divided and conflictual society, a second means of meeting the requirement for elite responsiveness to the interests of the relatively deprived is that bureaucratic elites formulate progressive compromises in the "public service" (cf. Heclo 1974; Aberbach, Putnam, and Rockman 1981). In this argument it is not the elite as a whole that is ideologically committed to economic justice, but the bureaucracy that frames public policy to adjust to the balance of ideological divisions in society. Finally, where direct representation of the deprived within the political elite is relatively weak or non-existent, a third means of ensuring the sensitivity of government to their interests may be the vitality of extra-parliamentary interest groups and social movements articulating those interests, and the disproportionate influence of such groups and movements on the public policy process (Verba and Nie 1972, 204).

Taken together, these arguments in the pluralist theory of the state suggest a number of questions for our analysis of elite ideology. How different are the ideological perspectives of elites and members of the mass public? Are elite ideological perspectives more sophisticated and better organized? Are they more strongly committed to civil liberties? Are they more responsive to the need for economic redistribution in order to satisfy the broadest public interest? Are politicians more representative of the general public than other elites, and are bureaucrats more middle of the road? Are elites outside of government closely tied to the state elites, and does the closeness of such ties promote a commonality of outlook on questions of ideology and public policy? Does it make sense, in general, to talk of a unified elite ideology or political culture as a key to the politics of liberal democracies like Canada?

The empirical evidence from our surveys of elites relevant to the pluralist theory of elite liberalism is presented in the next chapter. We shall argue that *none* of these expectations from pluralist theory can be well substantiated for Canada in the recent period, and that such theory gives very little help in understanding the policy shifts of the Trudeau era. Before taking up that discussion, we review alternative theoretical perspectives that indicate why such arguments are likely to be difficult to support empirically, and that suggest alternative questions about the structure of elite ideology taken up in later chapters.

LIBERAL CRITIQUES OF PLURALISM

Radical Pluralism

Coherent though the pluralist theory of the capitalist state may be, and dominant though it may still be in the academic study of politics, it has never been without challenge, even from essentially liberal perspectives. Three lines of revision are noteworthy within the liberal tradition, variously dealing with the inequalities of power in pluralist societies, with corporatism, and with pluralist stagnation. These revisions may cast more light on the questions we pose about the explanation for the shifts in Canadian public policy during the Trudeau era.

A first line of revision, "radical pluralism," reincorporates much of the argument of elite theory that the orthodox pluralists had originally sought to dismiss, and an important part of an argument in Marxism rejected by both classical elite theorists and orthodox pluralists. Although classical elite theory, as formulated by Gaetano Mosca and Robert Michels, might have been supposed to have been damaged beyond recovery by its association with fascism, it was, in the context of the anti-Marxism of the Cold War, a major source of inspiration for new attempts to understand the nature of the liberal democratic state. The hard-headed insistence on the conflict between elite power and democracy, which the original elite theorists used to deny the possibilities of democracy in modern society, was recovered by a new generation of elite theorists who used it to question the claims of liberal democracy. Despite agreeing with their classical forebears about the empirical reality of elite and undemocratic rule in liberal democracies, this new generation rejected the inevitability of elite rule and, far from pessimistic about the prospects of democracy in modern society, they vigorously advocated its desirability and possibility.

As applied to the U.S. by Charles Wright Mills (1956) and to Canada by John Porter (1965), the new brand of elite theory announced a radical critique of liberal democracy and its defence in pluralist theory, emphasizing the upper-class bias of elite recruitment and the elite's pursuit of its own interests, instead of its representation of contending groups. There is no argument with the empirical basis of pluralists' description of multiple elites. Despite its title, Mills's *The Power Elite* (1956) described privileged elite*s*, in business, the state, and the military, and Porter's analysis extends to judicial, academic, and mass media elites. But the argument with pluralism turns on the concentration and coordination of elite power, and its isolation from public interests. These theorists draw attention to the narrowness of the social base of recruitment to elite positions, and the resulting narrowness of ideological interest and a close mutuality of interest among elites that is at variance with the public interest. The radical content of their position lies in their advocacy of a much more extensive democracy than that allowed for in pluralist theory, and in their exposure of the undemocratic bias of elite power. They and those who followed them in this tradition are therefore most appropriately called radical pluralists.

The social background analysis of the power elite that is key to these arguments can in fact easily be read as revealing something akin to the Marxist notion of a ruling class. By reference to the class and educational background of those who hold office at the commanding heights of society, it is argued that political and business elites are tied closely by social background and, by inference, ideological agreement, which makes public policy an instrument of the business elite, or that business elites have the resources to shape public opinion and public policy preferences, or at the limit to veto initiatives that contradict their interest. Analysts like Ralph Miliband (1969) and his Canadian successors (Clement 1975; Olsen 1980) have in fact used the methodology and findings of elite analysis to support a Marxist account of the state as the instrument of the capitalist class.

However, the radical pluralists retain their theoretical distance from Marxism in emphasizing the sources of power in institutional, organizational leadership positions, rather than in class positions tied to the mode of production; the centrality of institutional rather than class interests in the logic of policy formation; the dominance of elite power in relation to the mass public; the manipulation of parties and other mass organizations; and the irrelevance, therefore, of political action and consciousness from below the "command" positions of the major institutions of society. As opposed to Marxists, the radical pluralists see the balance between pluralist dispersal as opposed to the elitist concentration of power, between the democratic responsiveness of governments to diverse constituencies and the undemocratic bias towards the minority interests of business, as simply a matter of empirical contingency.

Thus Porter, in an introduction to the work of his still more radical student, writes:

The power of economic, political, bureaucratic, military and other institutions tend to be separated because they perform different tasks for a society and, in so doing, become specialized, and hence there is always a tendency for power also to be separated. At the same time the overall coordinating and guidance needs of the society require interaction between the various elite groups. It therefore becomes a matter of empirical investigation to discover the extent to which these coordinating and guidance needs lead to an aggrandizement of power, to the creation of what might be called a power elite. (Clement 1975, xiv)

For others, like Charles Lindblom (1977), and more recently even Robert Dahl (1985), the bias of liberal democracies in favour of business elites is a structural consequence of the inequalities of power in capitalist societies and will persist until "economic democracy" puts power over the management of economic enterprise in the hands of the majority of those who work in them. This economic restructuring, however, is contingent on the voluntarist reorientation of individual moral perspectives, and cannot be predicted.

These latter arguments nevertheless begin to approximate arguments in structural Marxism, as we will discuss below. Still, radical pluralists have not been moved by their empirical observations of the unequal structure of power to rethink their theory of the state in liberal democracy. Rather, they stick to the simplifications of instrumentalism or the vagaries of pluralist accommodation, painting a static picture of the operation of the capitalist state in equilibrium that supposes an unrealistically smooth process of agreement and conciliation in the normal political process. Such a perspective cannot easily comprehend the crises of party instability, ideological conflict, and political protest in capitalist countries since the late 1960s.

Radical pluralists locate the structural limits to state action at "a level of generality which is unable to explain particular national patterns of policy," and empirical case-studies of policy tend to "attribute differences in policy and policy-making to the culturally specific attitudes or aptitudes of national elites," leaving "explanations for particular policies which do not fully capture the structural factors which may lie behind cultural accounts of the national patterns of policy" (Hall 1986, 23). In the Canadian case, they have not even produced the empirical information on the "attitudes or aptitudes" of elites necessary to investigate their major argument. Porter's, Dennis Olsen's, or Wallace Clement's exclusive methodological concentration on class background tells us only of the preponderance, perhaps increasing significance, of upper-class background in the Canadian business elite, with a much more middle-class-dominated state elite. There is actually no empirical evidence, however, about the ideological socialization of the state elites – that is about how state elites come to acquire the views of a particular social class, or even about the implied unity of the ideological outlooks of the two sectors.

Nevertheless the central question raised by the radical pluralists, the question of the "closure" of elites, remains important for our purposes. Chapter 10 is devoted to examining the extent to which Canadian elites are united by their class backgrounds, and the extent to which the class background of elites is linked to their ideological perspective on public policy questions. Our analysis in that chapter suggests that there is more openness and mobility in recruitment to elite positions in Canada than research in this tradition has previously shown, and that there is *no* significant link between the class background and ideological perspective of elites.

Corporatism

For further insight into the nature of state power and the maintenance of political order in contemporary capitalist societies, we turn to a second brand of "critical" liberal political sociology, developed in response to the deficiencies of orthodox pluralism – the theory of corporatism. Like the radical pluralists, contemporary theorists of corporatism revive a much more ancient tradition of social theory. In this case they build on Hegelian and traditional Catholic political philosophy according to which there are natural, functionally divided collectivities or corporate entities within society, which have to be organically knit together in the state so as to ensure harmonious and fruitful cooperation.

Without subscribing to the hierarchical, undemocratic prescriptive content of philosophical corporatism, theorists of corporatism in liberal democracies argue that the state in such societies plays a dominant role in limiting, licensing, and even creating corporate organizations that are "granted a deliberate representational monopoly ... in exchange for observing certain controls on their selection of leaders and articulation of demands and supports" (Schmitter 1979). In place of pluralist assumptions of the free expression of multiple group interests, the corporatist view is that the major role in policy making is taken by organizations representing functional interests – chiefly capital and labour – and that these interests and the groups representing them are limited and selected *by the state* to participate cooperatively in the making of public policy through quasi-public or public institutions.

Canadian proponents of this line of argument include Robert Presthus (1973), K.J. Rea and J.T. McCleod (1976), and Koula Mellos (1978). Presthus argued that corporatism has been a prominent aspect of French Canadian political culture, and that "in English Canada, corporatism has been an unquestioned latent assumption" (1973, 26). This reflects the influence of Tory and socialist fragments in the political culture, each of which promotes the ideological basis of corporatism: "an organic view of society in which collective aspirations are seen as prior to those of any discrete individual group, including the state" (25). But it is unclear how corporatism differs from pluralism for Presthus, whose analysis of interest group politics in Canada concludes that "the claim of virtually all major articulate groups are equally legitimate and should be honoured," and that there is "a relatively uncontrolled expansion of (government) activities without much qualitative differentiation among the competing claims of major social interests" (348–9).

With much greater respect for the theoretical point of corporatist theory, Rea and McCleod argue that Canadian elites manifest corporatist behaviour in the face of crisis: "When our elites perceive that they are threatened by external enemies, free trade, foreign competition, foreign investment, class diversions or inflation, the orthodox Canadian response is an organic corporatist response to seek the cooperation of various groups; to eschew market norms of liberal competition; to rally round the concept of a unique Canadian community (1976, 339–40)." In a similar fashion Mellos sees an increasingly dominant corporatism in the Canadian business elite's response to the developing crises of monopoly capitalism in Canada. On the basis of her reading of public statements by prominent businessmen and a small number of interviews, Mellos divines a "highly integrated rapport" between capital, the state, and organized labour, which, in advanced capitalism, must cooperate in defining "an economic policy of expansion." The major elements of the ideological justification for such cooperation include the view that profits serve "the collectivity as reinvestments in the expansionary programmes of economic growth and development" (1978, 845), the acceptance of economic planning, the replacement of beliefs in the virtues of competition by justifications of monopoly, the acceptance of state intervention in the economy, and the belief in the benevolence of science and technology.

Although theorists of corporatism draw attention to important developments in the politics of liberal democracies that contradict the assumptions of orthodox pluralism, they overstate the implications of an abstract model. Corporatist tendencies, the institutionalization of extra-parliamentary and public service policy making, and the balance of specific interests in policy consultation and administration vary substantially across different countries, and over time in the same countries. Even when most completely established, corporatist arrangements do not completely eliminate the traditional forms of interest group representation through electoral and parliamentary arrangements, and even when dominant, corporatist structures have a limited character in the modern capitalist state (Panitch 1980, 173). In Canada, and during the Trudeau era specifically, there have certainly been corporatist initiatives, but state-sponsored collaboration between business and labour leaders has occupied a more prominent place in political theory than in practice (Panitch 1979, 85). For at least the last two decades corporatist initiatives have been met by steady resistance from labour leaders, and, however strong the corporatist commitments of the pre-war Prime Minister William Lyon Mackenzie King, there is no evidence of deep attachments to such principles on the part of subsequent political leaders. This lack of interest, of course, was combined with policies – particularly wage controls in the Trudeau era and free trade, social policy, and foreign investment in the Brian Mulroney years – that were anathema to labour.

It is worth investigating, nevertheless, just how great the support for or obstacles to corporatist initiatives may have been in the Trudeau era, and we are able to do so in part by examining the extent of agreement or otherwise among labour, business, and government elites on questions of labour relations, state involvement in the economy, and the direction of social welfare policy. To anticipate our analysis in chapter 9, we show a very marked conflict between business and labour elites on all questions of public policy that makes corporatist solutions to the pressing problems of the 1980s inconceivable, even if they had seemed more enticing a decade earlier.

Pluralist Stagnation

The final revisionist response to orthodox pluralist accounts of the politics of liberal democracies, and potentially the most insightful from our point of view, is the theory of pluralist stagnation. One of the earliest indications of this line of theorizing was the work of Theodore Lowi (1969) on the political difficulties of the United States following the mid-1960s, in which he developed an insightful critique of pluralism, then at the height of its intellectual dominance.

Lowi argues that the political theory of pluralism superimposed upon an essentially correct sociological description of the origin and character of differentiated sources of power an essentially ideological theory of the political process. This ideology involves a celebration of process rather than substance – that is the means rather than the ends of democratic government – and the consequences of this ideological bias in pluralist political theory, Lowi argues, have been the absence of a coherent public philosophy and glorification of individual and group self-interest. In turn this bias has led to the reinforcement of inequities built into the economic stratification of political resources; the transformation of traditional ideological positions on the right and left into the simple opposition of organized and unorganized interests; the incapacity of government in these circumstances to give meaningful definition to the notion of social welfare or to find a basis for genuine planning and reform; the reduction, therefore, of welfare policies to the indemnification of damages rather than the righting of wrongs; and the institutionalization of privilege by regulatory policy that delegates state power to established interests, and by redistributive policy that protects the powerful by subsidies and guarantees in a system of "permanent receivership."

In these terms Lowi's argument fills in the political explanation for the complementary indictments of economists and sociologists who saw American society producing the stimulation of private wealth but public squalor (Galbraith 1958); the reduction of private life to the defensive, fearful, and lonely struggles for consumer and status satisfaction (Riesman, Glazer, and Denney 1953; Slater 1976); and the overloading and paralysis of the state by the unbridled competition of special interests, and its capture by the interests of "big" organizations, whose power it subsidizes and reproduces, despite the fact that by so doing it further depletes a declining stock of legitimacy amongst other groups in society, and further erodes the economic base from which to manage welfare subsidies of any kind (Bell 1976). Thus Lowi turns pluralist theory upside down, accepting its premises, but deriving from them a coherent explanation for a weak state with incoherent and ineffective policy.

Although published before the Ronald Reagan presidency, Lowi's analysis provides a useful point of departure for explaining the capture of a weak state by a movement organizing single-issue constituencies around an ideological program that emphasized the restoration of national power and a militarily strong but socially reduced state. For our purposes, however, it provides little clear direction for the understanding of elite ideology. It suggests that state elites have little or no ideological moorings, and that they are captive, in some instrumental sense, of large, organized interests. In this way Lowi does not do more than the radical pluralists, although the logic of his argument is distinctive.

More interesting for our purposes is Samuel Beer's work on British politics (1982). His analysis of the stagnation of pluralism and its vulnerability to radical and undemocratic movements is similar to Lowi's, but Beer emphasizes the importance in these conditions of ideological cleavages in mass and elite politics. Writing after the coming to power of the Margaret Thatcher government, Beer has the advantage of working with hindsight and his argument is much more explicit about the collapse of welfare state liberalism. Also, given the quite different politics of Britain and the United States, Beer incorporates the insights of the corporatist revision of pluralist theory, and sees ideological cleavages flowing from the breakdown of the neo-corporatist welfare state, as opposed to Lowi's starting point in the pluralist emphasis upon individual and group differentiation or competition. In these terms Beer provides a good deal more substantive clarification of the patterns of ideological discord that result from pluralist stagnation.

He describes the development of a collectivist rather than an individualist society in Britain, resting upon a settlement of the mutual interests of capital and labour in the postwar era, institutionalized in the formal involvement of those bodies in political parties and the policy process, and in a common ideological commitment to a shared distribution of the fruits of economic growth and a shared responsibility for the economic costs of economic decline and recovery. Despite the explicit emphasis upon an ideologically substantive rather than empty arrangement, Beer's collectivist state is, like Lowi's receivership state, dominated by large, organized interests. However, the nature of the corporatist system in Britain leads Beer to a rather different understanding of the breakdown of the collectivist ideological consensus and political practice of the postwar welfare state.

The British state is undermined not because as a pluralist state it lacks a coherent public philosophy; for Beer the collectivist principles of the capitalist welfare state initially formulated by the British Labour party and later adopted by the Conservative party were such a coherent philosophy. Rather, the consensual commitment to these principles has been dialectically undermined by a number of interacting tendencies. First, there has been the breakdown of the basic ideological props of a polyarchy – that is a decline in the distinctively British political culture of deference, and in the more general civic culture of trust and efficacy. This degeneration of the key ideological supports of the political process has, according to Beer, led to, or reinforced, the degeneration of the basic structures of the British political system: the decomposition of classes, their de-alignment in an increasingly unstable party system, and the disorderly scramble for benefits and subsidies by plural groups no longer unified by class and collective interests organized by party and state.

These developments produced a pluralist disorder similar to what Lowi describes. Out of this malaise emerged a new tendency toward ideological and political conflict, with neo-liberal or neo-conservative forces replacing the postwar Tory collectivism, with a major conflict within the Labour party over a renewed commitment to democratic socialism rather than to the parliamentary social democracy of the collectivist era, and with a new populist definition of the "middle ground" in terms of decentralization, participation, and the quality of life by the Liberals and Social Democrats.

Perhaps the key point of the theory of pluralist stagnation lies in this latter clear-cut identification of the greatly expanded relevance of ideological contestation within capitalist states, and of the lines along which new ideological positions are drawn up. Against the theorems of elite integration in the standard theory of polyarchy, the theory of pluralist stagnation predicts radically less inter-elite agreement on ideological questions. In Lowi's version there is simply an ideological confusion, a high degree of disaffection with the capacity of the system to produce welfare, and an integration of state and big organizations in their mutual commitment to existing distributions of the state's subsidies. In his version, that is, one expects at best a difference between elites involved in big advantaged organizations and small disadvantaged ones, but these differences may have little ideological coherence. In Beer's version, however, the ideological confusion has clearly articulated contours, with established political elites still committed to collectivist ideals, but other elites moving among the various new positions on the ideological spectrum from neo-liberal to more radical social democracy.

With Beer, therefore, we arrive at a refinement of liberal theory that leads out of the empty and abstract conceptions of pluralism. Where in these conceptions the state responds mutely to the multiple, independent forces bearing upon it, in Beer's conceptualization the state has more of the autonomy and muscle attributed to it by corporatist theory. Where in the former conceptions politics is a silent whirl of smoothly regulated competition, Beer lets in the clamour of ideological contestation. His empirical mapping of the alternative ideological positions that have emerged is particularly useful, and we make use of it in chapter 9, where we develop a typology of alternative elite ideologies. This structure of ideological discourse remains, however, relatively unexplained. No matter how sophisticated and accurate Beer's mapping of the salient lines of contestation, it is not clear why the corporatist consensus is so effectively undermined (his idealist explanation for the causal primacy of the erosion of the culture of deference is particularly thin), nor how the new lines of ideological division affect politics rather than political parties, especially in countries where parties are not as clearly defined ideologically as in Britain. In order to discover more about the potential answers to such questions, and to find a way of posing the questions more sharply for our subsequent empirical analysis of Canadian data, we must investigate recent contributions to the Marxist theory of the state.

MARXIST THEORY

Political analysis within the Marxist paradigm, like that within its pluralist counter, has over time moved from a perspective that essentially denies the significance of ideology to one in which it is progressively amplified. This movement in Marxist theory, and the theorization of the nature and significance of ideology in capitalist states, is at the heart of the debate between what we shall call instrumentalists and structuralists, bearing in mind that a rigid dichotomy does not reflect the considerable differences among different authors who share the same perspective nor the considerable blurring and merging of perspectives that has come about as a result of the cumulative theoretical work in this area.

Before exploring these different perspectives, we should indicate the common starting point of Marxist theories of the state – the view that the state in capitalist societies plays a key role in support of the accumulation of capital, by providing an appropriate legal and financial system, by providing for the appropriate supply of labour through immigration, education, training, health, and other services, and by restraining class conflict by means of adjudication or repression of conflicting interests. The state is "necessary" because the accumulation process requires the regulation of relations between capital and labour and the regulation of the relations between capitalists.

Beyond these very broad generalizations, however, there is no consensus among Marxist theorists as to just how the state fosters the accumulation process. Differences arise over two, interrelated issues: the autonomy of the state, and the importance of political and ideological, rather than strictly economic, determinants of state action. In the instrumentalist tradition there is a relatively direct correspondence between the structure and actions of the state and the imperatives of the process of capital accumulation. The state acts as an instrument of the capitalist class, on its behalf if not directly at its behest. This latter nuance is perhaps better captured by the characterization of this perspective as "functionalist" rather than instrumentalist (Alford and Friedland 1985, 272 ff.). In any event, this tradition emphasizes the dependence, rather than autonomy, of the state on the requirements of the capitalist economy. These requirements provide economistic explanations for state activity.

In contrast the structuralist tradition grants a great deal of autonomy to the state, either because the opposition of other classes prevents the capitalist class from taking full control of the state or because the short-sighted and competitive pursuit of profit prevents capitalists from introducing the reforms and regulations necessary for the long-term health of the accumulation process. Some degree of state autonomy is therefore necessary to regulate class conflict and to establish the hegemony of the capitalist class as a whole. The role of ideology, and of voluntarist rather than economist explanations, is more significant in this tradition of Marxist theory. This perspective has, therefore, a more obvious affinity to our interest in the empirical analysis of elite ideology, but both perspectives are of interest to us since they suggest alternative models of the distribution of elite ideological perspectives.

Instrumental Marxism

In the instrumentalist tradition the state is an instrument of the ruling class, or of its dominant "fraction" or "fractions," acting in accordance with their interests in the capitalist economy. In Karl Marx's famous formulation in the preface to *A Contribution to the Critique of Political Economy*, the whole complex of institutional, juridical, and ideological superstructures that comprise the state is determined by the specific form of the relations of production. These institutions change as the relations of production change, and as the interests and needs of the dominant class change.

Although it is nowhere any longer so crudely stated, this instrumental and economically determined perspective on the state remains an important tendency in Marxist scholarship. And in this current of economist Marxism the importance of a theory of the state *per se* is minimal, given the reflective properties of the political and ideological. Appearances of ideological divisions, or contestation over policy within the bourgeoisie, then reflect relatively inconsequential disputes over the best rationalizations of a common interest, or the competition for short-run advantage in a system whose long-run stability and cohesion is the common and overriding commitment of the class. If the state does seem to act against the expressed interests of capitalists, it does so because it is acting in their long-term rather than short-term interests. Similarly if the state seems to act to moderate the exploitation of workers, it does so not in any concession to the interests of the working class, but to entrench its false consciousness by the artful presentation of subsidies to capital as social welfare, and the mystification of the co-optation of workers' political organizations in institutionalized labour relations and tripartite consultation as social democracy.

There are two major currents within instrumentalist Marxist theories of the state: a "radical," Anglo-Saxon tradition most often identified with Miliband (1969), but having its roots in much earlier muckraking studies such as Gustavus Myers's *History of Canadian Wealth* (1914); and the "state monopoly capitalist tradition," developed largely by the various national sections of the Third International. The radical variant of instrumental Marxism is less completely theorized than the state monopoly capitalist version, and does not situate the state in the context of an explicit theorization of the capitalist economy. This variant of instrumentalism, as we have discussed earlier in this chapter, owes as much to elite theory as to Marxism, and authors like Miliband tend to substitute an empirical political sociology for the more definite political economy of the state monopoly capitalist theorists. A leading Canadian exponent of this approach (Clement 1975, 126) typifies the difference, referring to large corporations in terms of "concentration" and their domination of the economy, rather than to their emergence in a distinct phase of the capitalist economy, governed by certain economic constraints. Similarly Clement illustrates the political/sociological and functionalist emphasis in his characterization of the connection of state and capital:

often capitalists are not capable, alone, of responding to such society-wide problems as unemployment or inflation. This is where the state becomes critical in a liberal democracy. It is responsible for the *common* affairs of the capitalist class. These include providing workers' compensation, unemployment insurance, pensions, health care, availability of education, and so forth. None of these costs could be borne by individual capitalists, yet they are demands which must be met. It may even appear that they are met against the will of the particular capitalists through the pressure exerted by labour or consumers' groups, and indeed, they are important gains fought for by these groups. Fundamentally, however, they are concessions that sustain the prevailing system and do not interfere with the rights of private property. (Clement 1983, 122)

The typical analysis produced in this perspective focuses upon the *social* and *political* basis of capitalist domination: the social backgrounds of state and business elites, the web of organizations connecting the two, and their interpersonal connections. From empirical descriptions of this kind, instrumentalist conclusions are drawn about the flow of influence and the ideological hegemony sustaining the power of capital. Typical is Leo Panitch's generalization in his famous early text on the Canadian state:

a particularly striking characteristic of the Canadian state [is] its very close personal ties to the bourgeoisie. Whatever the merits of Poulantzas' contention that the most efficient state is that with the least direct ties to the dominant class, it is a rather academic point in Canada. [Here there is] "a confraternity of power" of such dimensions as to permit the clear employment of the term "ruling class" in the political as well as the economic sense ... It suggests, above all, an ideological hegemony emanating from both the bourgeoisie and the state which is awesome, which is reflected in the sheer pervasiveness of the view that the national interest and business interests are one, and which certainly ensures the smooth functioning of the relationship between the state and the capitalist class. (1977, 11, 13)

Instrumental analysis of this kind has an attractive purity of logic and a substantial critical purchase on the hidden dynamics of political life. This is so even if the abstractions "state," "class," and "hegemony" have only metaphysical weight in such formulations, and cannot comprehend or dispose of the rich empirical descriptions of the intra-class heterogeneity of attitudes, or the complexity of inter-class coalitions in competitive party systems, addressed in non-Marxist sociology. Still one should not be tempted for these reasons to throw out the theoretical baby with the bath water.

Despite the overlap between this work and that of the elite theorists, Marxist instrumentalists have a more precise theoretical rationale for the causes and content of the ideological unity of the capitalist class and the state. The functional requirements of assuring social overhead supports to capital accumulation, and of organizing the social order necessary for such accumulation through ideological manipulation and coercion, bind the state to capital. There are a number of questions raised by this instrumental perspective, especially as modified by work in the state capitalist tradition, that deserve attention.

In an extensive and interesting review of state monopoly capitalist approaches to the nature of capitalism and the capitalist state, Bob Jessop (1982, chap. 2) shows both the dramatic changes in this paradigm during its long development within the Third International, and the considerable variation among current versions of the theory. These variations aside, analysis in this tradition assumes that present-day capitalism represents a distinct "monopoly" phase of capitalism in which the competition between capitalists no longer determines the amount and nature of economic growth. While monopolies progressively increase their domination of the economy, some sectors of the economy remain competitive, but the state serves the needs of monopoly capital. The principle contradiction is between monopoly capital and *all* other classes and class fractions, including the working class. The strategic implication is that the successful advance of socialism requires an "anti-monopoly alliance" among all the opponents of monopoly.

The impact of such thinking is to loosen up the notion of class, to place implicitly more emphasis on ideological and political action, to invite attention to the autonomous role of the state in preventing the articulation of the "dominant contradiction" by formulating a counteracting hegemonic project, and to call attention to the global context in which monopoly capitalist development takes place, and the implications of this for the autonomy of the state in international relations. Not all of these implications are clear necessarily to instrumentalists, whose paradigm obscures the question of the autonomy of the state. But Miliband, for example, argued in his more recent work (following Skocpol in Evans, Ruechmeyer, and Skocpol 1985 rather than any version of state monopoly capitalist theory, to be sure) that state autonomy is particularly pronounced in foreign affairs, where the system of inter-state relations places limits on the freedom of the capitalist and other classes in individual societies. And others working in this tradition have focused attention on divisions within the capitalist class, as suggested by the state monopoly school.

We will ask therefore just how much state and other elites differ on questions of international relations as compared to domestic issues. Also in the context of international relations, we will follow up the most common Canadian extension of the looser conception of the unity of the capitalist class; that is the extent of divisions or agreement among representatives of national and foreign capital. More to the point of state monopoly capitalist theory, we will ask about the extent of division among big and small business. In this connection we will explore the typical argument relating to support and opposition to the welfare state.

As stated most clearly in James O'Connor's (1973) analysis of American capitalism of the 1960s and 1970s, the argument is that monopolistic firms receive significant benefits from social programs that "reproduce" the working class, and, as a result of a capacity to administer prices, they can afford to pass on the costs of their contributions to these programs. Companies in the competitive sector, by contrast, enjoy the same benefits, but competition prevents them from pricing their products at sufficiently high levels to pay for improved social programs. The result is a political split, with the monopolistic corporations supporting social programs and generally taking a more liberal position in opposition to capitalists in the competitive sector. By a different means, therefore, the argument arrives at a version of the pluralist argument for "elite liberalism," with the elite managers of large corporations and the state being more liberal than other elements in society.

Our results will show that even this more qualified argument is in need of critical modification. And for all the interest of questions like these, the instrumentalist tradition does little to open up analysis of the state. Apart from the exceptions granted in relation to foreign affairs, the state remains a blunt instrument wielded by the capitalist class or its dominant fractions. Such a rigid formulation is vulnerable to any indication of differences between state and capitalist elites, and especially vulnerable to the large differences we will show. In order to gain insight into such divisions, we have to move to the structuralist perspective, and to the question of the autonomy of the state.

Structuralist Marxism

The key element in structuralist versions of the Marxist theory of the state is an argument that political and ideological structures have a relatively autonomous existence, independent of economic structures. This is true, it is argued, precisely because the contradictory and conflictual character of economic relations under capitalism requires relatively independent agencies to create social order. Theoretical argument in this tradition has proceeded from a rather rigid view of an autonomous state, which inverts the instrumentalists' view of a monolithic state acting in the interests of capital by having a monolithic state determine the interests of capital. We will discuss the work of Fred Block as representative of this argument. A more sophisticated understanding of the state sees class conflict and contradictions embedded within the state, but persists with a rather rigid view of the functional necessity of order, the overriding hegemony of capital, and the structural unity of the state. Nicos Poulantzas's earlier work illustrates this second position. A third tendency within this tradition moves towards a much more radical decentring of the state, with a much more explicit and empirical investigation of ideological and political movements and cleavages as determinants of public policy and political order. The later Poulantzas illustrates this tendency. Finally, there have been attempts, particularly by authors in the German "capital logic" school, to rescue this last tendency from the purely contingent and empirical reference to political and social movements, by deriving the explanation for the conflicts and cleavages within the state from the contradictory structure of economic and political relations.

Block (1977) argues that the action of the capitalist state is the outcome of a conflict among three sets of agents – the capitalist class, the managers of the state apparatus, and the working class. Within this conflict the state intervenes with a relative autonomy from both classes to secure the interests of capital. Its action, though serving the interests of capitalists, cannot be identified with their interests. "Rationalization occurs 'behind the backs' of each set of actors so that rationality cannot be seen as a function of the consciousness of any particular group" (8). Two questions immediately arise. If it is not a direct instrumental connection to the consciousness of the capitalist class, what is it that makes the state act in favour of the capitalist class? And in what sense is this action "rational" rather than simply "rationalization."

Block is clearer in answer to the first than to the second question, but in both cases he verges on an exaggerated, absolutist depiction of the homogeneity, functional autonomy, and rationality of the state.

Block argues that concrete structural mechanisms serve to make the state work in the interests of capital. On the one hand, capitalist interest groups' pressure on and lobbying of state agencies and the recruitment of businessmen into government service reduce the likelihood that the state managers will act against the general interest of capital, as does the constraining influence of bourgeois cultural hegemony. On the other hand, state managers are motivated to pursue policies in the interest of capital because the state's capacities to finance its activities through taxation and borrowing and to sustain public support depend upon the aggregate level of economic activity, which are determined by the private investment decisions of capitalists. "State managers have a direct interest in using their power to facilitate investment, since their own continued power rests on a healthy economy" (1977, 12–15).

But these are instrumentalist arguments, and the structuralist argument for the autonomy of the state rests upon the *in*capacity of the capitalist class to formulate and realize its own class interest. Thus Block begins from an axiomatic limitation of the class consciousness of capitalists. Instead of pursuing the interests of their class, capitalists are governed by their narrow self-interest in profitability, which is not an adequate guide to policy. The influence of capitalists on state policy is thus expressed primarily in terms of the veto or constraint imposed by the threat of or an actual decline in the level of "business confidence," resulting in a fiscal crisis as tax revenue declines and demands upon social programs increase. State managers, however, are "capable of intervening in the economy on the basis of a more general rationality" (1977, 20), which allows them to choose policies that increase the overall levels of economic activity and profits, and, in the face of class struggle, to choose reforms that extend the state's role in economy and society, thereby increasing the rationality of capitalism.

Here Block's argument invokes a mystified concept of the rationality of the state, reminiscent of the Hegelian concept of the state as the rational agent of social progress, sitting astride the battle of classes, which are conscious only of their limited self-interests (cf. Avineri 1972). Block allows that "state managers can make all kinds of mistakes"; that they "have no special knowledge of what is necessary to make capitalism more rational; and that they grope toward effective action as best they can within existing political constraints and with available economic theories" (1977, 25–6) He nevertheless follows these qualifications with the assertion that "the more power the state possesses to intervene in the capitalist economy, the greater the likelihood that effective actions can be taken to facilitate investment."

By these arguments Block arrives at quite radical conclusions about the autonomy and rationality of the state. In opposition to the mechanical rationality of the instrumentalist account of the state as the executive committee of a class-conscious bourgeoisie, Block suggests a more complex, cybernetic rationality in which the state responds to the balance of class forces and class struggle according to some unspecified but still rational program. This begs the question of how the program is devised, and why and to what extent it is rational. It is necessary in this connection to introduce the categories of politics and ideology that Block avoids. His opening criticism of instrumentalism, that "it neglects the ideological role of the state" (1977, 8), is as relevant to his own argument, and we need to incorporate this latter concept as it has been developed in the work of Poulantzas and the capital logic theorists.

Poulantzas, much more structuralist in his style of argument than Block, makes clear that the state is not an agency directing the ideological orchestration of class relations in a self-conscious fashion. Rather the state is *the* field of the class struggle, and has class relations inscribed within its structures (1973, 27). "The state that is destined to reproduce class divisions cannot really be a monolithic, fissureless bloc, but is itself, by every virtue of its structure ... divided" (1976, 75). The state reflects the class struggle on the terrain of ideology, incorporating within its apparatuses the ideological positions articulated in the broader society by the leaders of business, the professions, the media, parties, and unions. The formulation and justification of state policy reflect, therefore, unstable compromises of divergent class positions (1978, 164).

The ideological role of the state in the construction of hegemony is, therefore, never simply and rationally fulfilled in the way that Block's formulation suggests. What is involved, rather, is a complex and contradictory process *within* the state to formulate programs and policy that articulate a "world-view," or a "national consensus" out of conflicting social interests and in the *absence* of a clearly "rational" path. The empirical content of this notion of the ideological role of the state remains vague, though one can say that Poulantzas's concept of class struggle as inscribed within the state is clearly inconsistent with Block's extreme views of the disorganization of the capitalist class and of the homogeneity of the state. Poulantzas's early work, however, gives very little guidance as to how to understand the process by which the state responds to class struggle. His vagueness here allows him to insist upon the hegemony of the dominant class or its dominant faction, but this insistence is a rabbit of empirical assertion pulled from a theoretical hat of imposing shape but concealing a large interior hole.

In his later work (1980) Poulantzas came to a much more empirically grounded sense of the fluidity of class relations, the importance of non-class forces and social movements, the divisions within the state, and the instability of state power and hegemonic rule: "Rather than facing a corps of state functionaries and personnel united and cemented around a univocal political will, we are dealing with fiefs, clans and factions: a multiplicity of diversified micro-policies. However coherent each one of these may appear in isolation they are nevertheless mutually contradictory; and the policy of the State essentially consists in the outcome of their collision, rather than in the (more or less successful) application of the global state apex" (Poulantzas 1980, 135–6). Without pretending to complete this theoretical argument, it seems reasonable to envisage the state as a field of ideological class struggle in the following terms.

First, despite the weaknesses of working-class consciousness in the society at large, union movements are recognized as a party to state-regulated labour relations, and, although they may for that reason be considered part of the "ideological state apparatus," they nevertheless represent working-class interests within the state in a more or less coherent way. At the purely ideological level, as opposed to questions of political tactics and concrete policy interests, union leaders may be presumed to be relatively unified and to articulate positions to the left of the public ideological spectrum.

Second, the other pole of the ideological class struggle can be presumed to be articulated in a relatively cohesive and coherent manner by leading representatives of the capitalist class, and by ideological organizations devoted to the articulation of capitalist class interests. The proliferation of organizations like the Canadian Manufacturers' Association, The Canadian Federation of Independent Business, the Business Council on National Issues, the Fraser Institute, The Gordon Foundation, etcetera, all speak to the highly developed state of political organization by business interests (Langille 1987). Further, the density of interlocking directorates connecting large Canadian firms (Clement 1977; Ornstein 1976; Carroll, Fox, and Ornstein 1982) provides for a high degree of shared communication and political discussion among representatives of capital.

The extent of cohesion in the capitalist class is a major issue, however, and we cannot dispose of it simply by saying that we expect less division than Block. Poulantzas and other structuralists emphasize the fractionalization of the capitalist class, and suggest the need to investigate the extent of division among fractions of "big" capital, as well as among big, medium, and small capitalists. The latter divisions between "monopoly" and "competitive" sectors are made much of by state monopoly capital theory, and by authors like O'Connor. Structuralists like Poulantzas dissociate themselves from the instrumentalist logic tying the state to the dominant fraction, although they seem to retain the same empirical posture with regard to the dominance of finance capital and the potentially progressive role of competitive capital in popular alliances. The empirical, contingent influence of monopoly capital is, nevertheless, clearly theorized as a political question of the organization of the power bloc, rather than as a necessary derivative of the development of capitalist production.

In these terms we can envisage ideological divisions between the oligopolistic corporate sector and small or medium business in relation to major ideological questions like economic regulation, labour relations, social welfare, and civil liberties. The general logic for such divisions lies in the greater ability of oligopolies to pass on increased costs attributable say to increased wage settlements, social welfare program co-payments, or affirmative action or gender-equity employment codes. But the general theory of the capacity of monopolies to extract above-average profits, which underlies such arguments, is questionable (Semmler 1982), and it is not clear empirically that there is an association linking size, technological development, and concentration of firms with higher wage structures and greater profitability (Hodson and Kaufman 1982).

Third, in the middle of the ideological continuum are the state managers who have to respond to the intensity of the opposing ideological expressions of capital and labour, and the practical political proposals to which they give rise. The ideological class struggle is not, however, simply inscribed *on* the state as a function of the balance of contending forces *à la* Block. It is also inscribed *within* the state, *à la* Poulantzas, inasmuch as state managers themselves represent different positions on the ideological spectrum. The lexicon of this inscription is, however, difficult to understand beyond simple empirical description. A couple of a priori theoretical predictions can, nevertheless, be suggested.

Rianne Mahon, for example, follows Poulantzas's lead about different social forces being differentially represented in different agencies of the state to the extent of envisaging the agency representation of different positions. She begins by amplifying Poulantzas's notion of the way in which the state produces the hegemony of the dominant class in terms of a pattern of unequal representation. The unity of the state is ultimately based on the long-term interests of the hegemonic fraction of the capitalist class, for her the owners of staples-producing business in Canada. The inequalities as between the power bloc and the subordinate classes and various members of the power bloc and the hegemonic fraction are expressed in the quality (or functions) of their respective representatives. Thus the dominant classes and fractions that belong to the power bloc are likely to have a more positive role – able to negotiate concessions that enhance the ability of those they represent to perform their leading role in the economic and social spheres. Conversely the representatives of subordinate social forces are likely to have a more limited mandate – for example to extract "concessions" limited to the sphere of consumption rather than production (1977, 170–1).

In this light Mahon envisages definite differences among state agencies in power and ideology, which mirror and reinforce the balance of social forces. Concretely, in Canada, she sees the Department of Finance as the seat of power of the hegemonic fraction of the capitalist class, "ensuring that those who 'represent' non-hegemonic forces basically accept the development philosophy that serves the fundamental interest of the hegemonic fraction"

(1977, 176). Other somewhat less important agencies, like External Affairs and Industry, Trade and Commerce, also represent capitalist interests, while still lower-ranking agencies like Labour, Health and Welfare, and Indian Affairs give greater representation to subordinate classes.

The geometric precision of Mahon's translation of the structured dominance of different class positions within the state is too functionally elegant and requires too great a degree of purposive rationality in hiring, socialization, promotion, etcetera within state agencies to be credible. Still, we need to inquire into the nature of the ideological bias of the state: how evenly distributed are different ideological positions among state actors, and in what ideological commitments does the unity and specificity of the state reside? Is it in the statistical preponderance of the perspectives of monopoly capital among all state actors? Is it rather, borrowing from pluralist theory discussed earlier, a function of a bureaucratic/executive conservatism that concentrates ideological conformity in the effective agencies of government, no matter the party in power, leaving to the formal opposition, backbenchers, and non-parliamentary elites the representation of other interests? Or is the whole question of the ideological unity and bias of the state mis-posed? Are we perhaps better advised to pursue the much more radical appropriation of pluralist logic and findings by other Marxists who counterpose to the strict functionalism of Block, or the more qualified functionalism of Poulantzas and Mahon, a vision of the state as reproducing rather than overriding the incoherence of the class structure, and being driven by the balance of plural social forces as established through the underlying process of capitalist development?

Here there are two related positions formulated by the German state-derivation theorists on the one hand, and by Claus Offe on the other. As a representative of the first school, Fred Hirsh emphasizes the complex fractionalization of classes produced in the process of capitalist development, and the necessity of a complex, even chaotic organization within the state for it to be able to function as "the guarantor of the domination of the bourgeoisie ... In order to secure the political domination of the bourgeoisie and keep class conflict latent, the state must maintain links with the proletariat and with other classes and strata not to be counted as part of the bourgeoisie" (Hirsch 1978, 100). The state is required, therefore, to stand apart from the anarchy of competition, which characterizes relations between the different elements of capital, but it must also fully represent contending capitals as well as the other classes (cf. Altvater 1978).

From this double contradiction – having under monopoly conditions to consider the competing individual capitals, and at the same time having to secure the political domination of the bourgeoisie as a class ... results the segmented and fragmented organizational structure of the political-administrative apparatus, the constant attempts

> to develop a coordinating "system policy" and their regular failure. Under these conditions the question of the state apparatus's "capacity to manage" or of the ability of administrative interventions to reach their target can strictly speaking, relate only to individual parts of the total apparatus ... (Hirsch 1978, 101)

This is a position different from Poulantzas's mostly in emphasis – incoherence and internal contradictions more strongly registered than the unity and coherence of the capitalist state. The logic of contradiction is further very like that of Mahon's – essentially instrumental, relying on the representation in different agencies of different class fractions. Offe, who is more eclectic in his theoretical inspiration, reaches essentially the same conclusions, but by a more persuasive logic that gives an important independent weight to substantive questions of ideology.

Offe describes a structuralist logic of contradiction in advanced capitalist societies, which is linked to abstract systems theory as much as to Marxism. In this logic capitalist society is composed of three interacting subsystems related to socialization, production and exchange, and the overarching regulatory functions of government. The latter state subsystem in late capitalist societies has developed in response to needs for crisis management arising from the self-paralysing tendencies of the other two subsystems. The growth of the welfare state in this way involves the autonomization of the state system and the relocation of the central contradictions of the society from the economy to the state. These contradictions have generally to do with the impossible demand placed upon the state to maintain and expand commodification (private, exchange relations) and decommodification (state interventions that restrict the private exchange system). Because of this contradiction, public policy has a tendency to undermine as it seeks to prop up the capitalist system as a whole. There is, as a result a systematic tendency, Offe argues, towards a "crisis of crisis management," (1984, chap. 1) typified by fiscal deficits, failures of administrative rationality, and the erosion of mass loyalty.

Offe develops this conception of the crisis of the modern capitalist state (which owes much, obviously, to Habermas 1976) by detailed attention to the necessary incoherence of the public policy process, and the lines of political struggle that ensue. Of particular interest to us is his indication of conflict between capital and the state, and of conflicts within the state over the coordination and rationalization of social policy. In the latter area, to begin with, Offe hypothesizes that the dynamics of policy innovation "do not 'serve' the needs or exigencies of any particular group or class, but instead react to the internal structural problems of the welfare state apparatus."

> Those actors (in the ministries, parliaments and political parties) who are responsible for social policy institutions and innovations within the state apparatus actually do

find themselves constantly faced with the dilemma that many legally and politically sanctioned demands and guarantees remain unreconciled to exigencies and capacities of the budgetary, financial and labour-market policy of the capitalist economy. They are brought into conflict with this policy by uncontrollable environmental factors. The initiatives to innovate in matters of social policy are chronologically and substantively tailored to the specific parameters of this dilemma. (1984, 105)

Offe adds that all measures of innovation or rationalization have " 'external effects' upon the level of wealth and power resources of social groups," so that conflicts within the state are reflected in political conflict external to it, "which in turn pose fresh consistency problems within the state apparatus and which may possibly require actual repeal of the innovations" (107).

This argument of Offe emphasizes concrete policy variables and interrelationships as the proximate explanations of political conflict in advanced capitalist societies. In these terms political conflict is endemic, but the lines of conflict are highly fluid rather than structured and aggregated in the pattern of classical class analysis. Ideological divisions, however, are of secondary concern to Offe, except as they are defined narrowly as the rationalization of policy interests. Following this emphasis, the key analytic focus for understanding political change in the contemporary capitalist state is on concrete policy positions rather than generalized ideology. From the point of view of our empirical analysis in this book, therefore, Offe leads us to expect a greater clarity of oppositions between elites or sectors of the general public on concrete questions of policy rather than abstract ideological principle. This follows particularly from his indication that the welfare state has undermined without replacing the traditional defence of capitalist society, thereby refocusing political conflict on questions of policy.

To the extent that exchange relationships are no longer "naturally" given, but are created and maintained through visible political and administrative state strategies, the actual exchange value of any unit of labour or capital on the market can be seen as determined as much through *political* measures as through *individual* management of one's property and resources. These individual resources thus come to be seen as something resulting from, and contingent upon, political measures. Considerations such as whether or not individuals can sell their labour power, and how much they receive for it, increasingly become – at the level of normative orientation and actors' self-understanding – a matter of adequate or inadequate state policies in such areas as education, vocational training and regional economic development. For owners of capital, similarly, market success depends less upon such factors as the willingness to take risks, inventiveness and the ability to anticipate changes in demand, and more upon state policies in such areas as taxation, tariffs, research and development, and infrastructure investment. (1984, 128–9)

This argument tends, as we say, to focus the analysis of political conflict upon concrete policy questions, and to emphasize the internal incoherence and divisions of classes on such questions. Offe nevertheless retains a more general concern with class and ideological tensions. These tensions are evident in the increasing clarity of the right- and left-wing critiques of the welfare state. The right argues that the burden of the welfare state is to impose a disincentive to investment and a disincentive to work, and articulates neo-*laissez-faire* or monetarist arguments for a dismantling of the system. The left argues that the welfare state is ineffective and inefficient and repressive, and that it produces an ideological false consciousness in the working class. The left calls instead for an expansion of workers' rights, decentralization, and self-management as the only basis for a genuine conception of social security. Offe argues, however, that these ideological oppositions are weakly supported (primarily by members of the old [right] and new [left] middle classes) and that "typically, both of these alternative models have no more than a very marginal role to play as long as they fail to form alliances with one of the principal classes, respectively, and the political forces representing them" (1984, 158).

Although such alliances "are immensely difficult to form and sustain," Offe expects "such struggles for new alliances to occupy the stage of social policy and welfare state reform in the years to come" (1984, 158). On this basis, clearly, the ideological alignments of classes and class fragments is an important subject of investigation, although there may be less rapid changes and less clarity of structure at this underlying level in which changes in the matrix of social power occur (160–1) than at the more immediately perceived level "at which the agenda of politics and the relative priority of issues and solutions is determined, and the desirability of alliances and compromises is conditioned" (159). The importance of looking at both levels of ideology and policy orientation is, nevertheless, clear.

SUMMARY

With Offe a circle of alternative theoretical approaches to the ways in which state and society are ideologically linked is completed. Work in the Marxist tradition comes back to an understanding of the autonomy of the state, and the significance of the policy process, that differs very little in these respects from work in liberal political sociology. Peter Evans, Dietrich Ruechemeyer, and Theda Skocpol's criticism of neo-Marxists for having "retained deeply embedded society-centred assumptions, not allowing themselves to doubt that, at base, states are inherently shaped by classes or class struggles and function to preserve and expand modes of production" (1985, 9) seems hardly to have comprehended the theoretical developments we have discussed. *Bringing the State Back In*, as in their title, is surely descriptive of these developments. The critics are correct to underline the continued emphasis of neo-Marxists on making some linkage between changes in state action and changes in the economy and class relations, but the neo-Marxists realize as well as their critics that the extent to which state policy reflects class relations "depends on the capacities classes have for achieving consciousness, organization, and representation. Directly or indirectly, the structures and activities of states profoundly condition such class capacities" (Evans, Ruechemeyer, and Skocpol 1985, 25).

Whether or not they would be so happy with the blunt conclusion that "the classical wisdom of Marxian political sociology must be turned, if not on its head, then certainly on its side," (1985, 25) neo-Marxists have moved in this direction. Indeed the most vital area of current neo-Marxist research is in the "regulation theory school," which has moved increasingly to detailed empirical work on comparative public policy developments. After an initial phase in which the emphasis was on an essentially economic understanding of the historical transitions in "regimes of accumulation" within the unfolding development of the capitalist mode of production (cf. Aglietta 1979; 1985; 1987; Lipietz 1985; 1987), there is increasing emphasis on research that uncovers the historical detail and variability in "modes of regulation." Largely unconcerned with a formal theory of the state, regulation theory was not influential in the conception of our research, because of its simultaneous or later development. However, new developments in regulation theory led in the direction of a retroactive synthesis with Marxist theories of the state (cf. Jessop 1991), a synthesis of important post-structuralist developments in "discourse theory" (cf. Jenson 1986), and empirically sophisticated comparative public policy research (cf. Jessop 1989; Drache and Gertler 1991), all of which complement the effort in this book.

Nevertheless it must be said that part of the difficulty in appreciating the shift in Marxian political sociology, and the convergence in many respects of neo-Marxist and neo-Weberian approaches to politics in advanced capitalist democracies, is still the relative absence of empirical political research in the Marxist tradition, and particularly the absence of work whose focus is on the ideological consciousness of classes and class fractions, their representation in the public policy process, and their response to public policy initiatives. In the following chapters we try to make some contribution in this direction. Before doing so, however, we summarize the theoretical arguments reviewed in this chapter, which suggest quite different expectations about what we will find in such empirical analysis.

For summary purposes, alternative approaches to questions about the structure of power and ideology in the state can be conceptualized in the "compass rose" described in figure 7-1. The north-south axis in the figure distinguishes instrumentalism from corporatism as opposite poles of a continuum defined by the extent of state autonomy. The east-west axis distin-

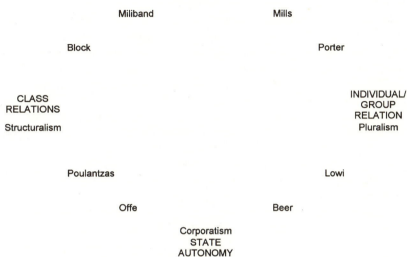

FUNCTIONAL
DEPENDENCY
Instrumentalism

Miliband   Mills

Block   Porter

CLASS   INDIVIDUAL/
RELATIONS   GROUP
                                                    RELATION
Structuralism   Pluralism

Poulantzas   Lowi

Offe   Beer

Corporatism
STATE
AUTONOMY

Figure 7-1
Ideological formulae mapped by state autonomy and class determination

guishes pluralism from structuralism as opposite poles of another continuum defining the extent to which society is structured by indeterminate and heterogenous social groups, or the primacy of a limited number of relatively closed classes or class fragments with interests fixed by their location in the system of production. Moving around the rose one obtains a variety of different modifications of the pure positions, the implications of which for the study of ideology can be summarized briefly.

Pluralists see society as composed of multiple groups competing for power resources to pursue their heterogeneous interests. The state in such a society is a partially autonomous umpire of this competition, with its own interests in maintaining its power and stability, the durability of its settlements, and the welfare of its clients. While it has a measure of autonomy in its pursuit of these interests, the state is also dependent upon the balance of power in society, so that public policy endorses the parallelogram of forces acting upon it in respect of any policy issue. Interest is here conceptually narrowly distinguished from ideology, the latter essentially a psychological failure to rationally pursue the marginal satisfaction and improvement of one's socially given interests and potential.

On the other hand, the pluralist system requires legitimation in order to preserve its delicate and quasi-anarchic balance of competition and inequality.

For these purposes it is argued that there has developed a civic culture, uniting elites and the mass public in a commitment to civil liberties, an acceptance of conflict and bargaining, and the legitimacy of elite settlements of such conflict. Further, it is argued that the pluralist society and the liberal democratic state pursue a liberal and egalitarian direction, rather than entrenching and endorsing the privileges and inequalities of the market, because elites have a greater commitment to economic and political liberalism than does the mass public, recognizing the necessity of compromise and openness as a *sine qua non* for the continuity and legitimacy of a pluralist government. Additionally, pluralists argue that there is in stable polyarchies a substantial measure of elite integration in these terms, but also clear divisions on concrete policy matters between elites representing different social groups, and an institutional division within the state among politicians who tend to represent the broad lines of conflict between social groups and classes in society, and civil servants who seek to minimize conflict and rationalize public policy in the general public interest.

Moving to the north-east of figure 7-1, we confront elitist counters to pluralism typified by the work of Porter and Mills. Porter is clearly more inclined to see the integration or closure of elites as an empirically variable attribute of advanced industrial states: "the degree to which their functional separateness and institutional specialization becomes mitigated because of the over-all coordination and planning of a complex society, should I think remain a problem to investigate rather than be subject to premature theoretical closure" (introduction to Clement 1975). Nevertheless he emphasizes the narrowness of recruitment to elite positions, and the coincidence of elites' interests in maintaining power and privilege in these highly stratified societies. Like Mills he sees the state as very closely tied to the economically powerful, state policy as essentially the implementation and protection of the interests of the economically privileged, a coincidence of ideological agreement and common class background among the elite managers of the major social institutions, and an associated cohesion derived from the close personal contact and interaction among elites. Finally, the persistence of elite dominance is understood in terms of the influence of a dominant ideology that effectively subordinates the underprivileged masses to a vision, portrayed in the mass media agencies controlled by the power elite, of risk- and productivity-rewarded achievement and mobility, the material variety and riches of market society. Mills, of course, also emphasized the role of seeming threats to these benefits from cold war enemies.

To the south of the ideological compass we have depicted in figure 7-1 is the theoretical perspective of corporatism that paints a similar picture of the homogeneity of the power structure and of a dominant ideology, but explains this in terms of the organizing autonomy of the state, rather than in terms of the latter's dependency upon the economically powerful. Beer's dialectical *rapprochement* between corporatism and pluralism sees the undermining of the unity of the dominant ideology as a result of socio-psychological and intellectual changes incurred in the process of modernization, and the undermining of state-organized power elites as a result of economic crises induced by the demands unleashed by plural and isolated social groups no longer disciplined by a dominant ideology.

In the western segment of figure 7-1 are a variety of Marxist parallels to the various alternatives in liberal political sociology just described. For our purpose these differ essentially in the precision they provide to the content of ideological cohesion or division predicted within and between elites in state and society. More than that they provide a logic of explanation for political change and crisis that is either largely absent in liberal theory, or else relies exclusively upon voluntarist, psychological formulae of the motivation and discipline of individuals. Where instrumentalism in the liberal political sociology of the power elite has no serious theory of change, Marxist instrumentalism at least implies the disintegration of power structures because of the innate opposition of classes, and because of the potential power of the dominated classes "in themselves." Similarly, where liberal theorists like Lowi, Bell, or Beer understand recent changes in liberal democratic states as a result of normative, cultural changes that are empirically poorly measured, their Marxist counterparts are able to reinterpret such changes as concretely grounded not in the motivational dispositions of individuals, but in the contradictions and limits of the liberal democratic state's regulation of a capitalist economy. In these ways the understanding of social change is removed from a logic simply of generational and evolutionary conversion to new cultural perspectives, to a more determinate logic of the conflicting interests of classes or class fractions capable of opposing old or initiating new social arrangements.

These latter remarks will indicate our preference for Marxist theory, but they should also forewarn the reader that such preferences are derived essentially from paradigmatic or theoretical positions. Although these positions entail empirical findings, their validity cannot be definitively demonstrated by empirical tests. As we have tried to suggest, there are empirically substantially parallel portraits of capitalist states in the different traditions of liberal and Marxist political sociology. No amount of empirical detail will conclusively demonstrate the validity of these contending theoretical perspectives.

One cannot, that is, simply take "bearings" on the Canadian state, and fix thereby its location on the theoretical compass described in figure 7-1. We have neither the firmly calibrated instruments for observing state-society relations and ideology, nor the tightly specified critical hypotheses or tests that would demonstrate unequivocally the greater fit of data on the Canadian situation to one theoretical position rather than another. Still, as we have pointed out in this chapter, the alternative theoretical approaches suggest quite different expectations about the structure of elite ideology and opinion on a variety of public policy issues, the differences between elite and public opinion, and the divisions within and between elite groups. We propose to examine these expectations with concrete survey data, and by this means to indicate the relative virtues of Marxist versus non-Marxist theory, and within Marxism, of structuralist approaches that emphasize the autonomy of the state and the critical importance of ideological and policy initiatives within the state.

8 Ideology and Representation: Elite and Public Attitudes

From its earliest uses the concept of public opinion has implied the influence on political rulers of the wishes of their subjects. In the metaphor of the seventeenth century, the state was king, but public opinion was "queen of the world" (see Gunn 1982). Then, as now, however, "opinion" was distinguished from "interest." Opinion referred vaguely to the voices of the people in general, but interest, in Gunn's words, "was the political buzz-word of the late seventeenth century," referring to "the designs of individuals or corporate bodies. Opinion might thus rule the world, but in the restricted realm of politics, its viceroy was interest" (4). The same presumption of the actual and desirable influence of public opinion informs public opinion polling, just as the presumption of the greater political relevance of interests rather than opinion informs most contemporary theories of politics.

Whether public opinion influences those in power and whether interests, relative to the contours of public opinion, are served by political power are questions of as major importance to twentieth- as to seventeenth-century political analysts. Were elite and public opinion identical, one would safely celebrate the coronation of the latter as queen of the world; but it requires no argument to persuade even the most royalist of Canadians that this seventeenth-century monarchical imagery is fanciful. In everyday language we talk of power and the state, thereby implying the capacity of some individuals, groups, or institutions to enforce or otherwise realize interests that are not universally shared, and we take for granted that the state and elites within it can and do exercise power in this sense. Power is, none the less, a complex relation, subject to constraint and deflation. It may grow out of the barrel of a gun, but at the limit power and force are mutually exclusive – one cannot get a dead person to do anything – and every power relation, every state, depends upon some capacity to engender and sustain some measure of support and acquiescence from the powerless. How this complex relation is described varies greatly for different theories of the state, as discussed in the previous chapter, and it varies for different actually existing capitalist societies. The role of ideas, opinion, or ideology in defining that relation is only one element in a complex of economic and political factors, but this chapter focuses upon the ideological factor in power relations, concentrating on the relationship between elite and public opinion.

In previous chapters we observed that at the time of our surveys the drift of Canadian public policy was out of phase with the public's ideological consensus on welfare-state commitments. The obvious explanations for such a dissociation of state action and the expression of public interest would be elite ignorance of, indifference to, or opposition to public opinion. Such a dissociation would be a plausible consequence of the class bias in the background of elites, as emphasized in the instrumentalist Marxist tradition, or of the class nature of the state and politics of capitalist societies, as emphasized in other forms of Marxist analysis. Some elite-theory approaches, such as corporatism (whether or not inflected with Marxism), can also accommodate, if not predict, significant conflicts between elites and the general public. Even pluralist theory admits that some constituencies are better able than others to organize and attain their policy goals. Still, finding that there were strong cleavages between elites and the general public would severely undermine the standard pluralist model, with its emphasis on the notion of a community of competing interest groups in which, there being agreement on "rules of the game" that are at least not manifestly unfair, struggles over competing policies involve "players" of relatively equal strength. In these terms Marxist approaches differ in that they privilege the interest of capital, and the conflict between the interests of capital and labour.

The theoretical ground covered in the previous chapter relates more directly to ideological conflict between elite groups than to the nature of elite-mass differences. Questions about the structure of elite ideology will be examined in the next two chapters. Chapter 9 examines the differences between elites in detail and chapter 10 examines them in the context of the social background of elites. This chapter concentrates on ideological differences between elites and the mass public, or, to use the vocabulary introduced above, the differences between elite interests and public opinion.

SOME PREVIOUS STUDIES

Direct comparisons between the ideological outlooks of members of the general public and the elites who occupy the command positions in the major institutions of contemporary society are relatively rare in contemporary political analysis. There are three important surveys of Americans that buttress the very general theoretical arguments about elites and power in Western democracies. The first and best known is Samuel Stouffer's *Communism, Conformity, and Civil Liberties*, which was published in 1955. A replication of the Stouffer study was conducted in 1973, and is reported in Clyde Nunn, Harry Crockett, and J. Allen Williams's *Tolerance for Nonconformity*. A much more sophisticated study is Herbert McCloskey and Alida Brill's *Dimensions of Tolerance: What Americans Believe about Civil Liberties* (1983). McCloskey also conducted an earlier study along the same lines in 1964, which included surveys of the general public and of delegates and alternate delegates to the Republican and Democratic party national conventions. A recent Canadian study by Paul Sniderman et al. (1996) deals with public and elite opinion on issues raised by the Charter of Rights.

Stouffer's landmark 1954 survey showed that "civic leaders" – defined as the leaders of important community organizations of cities with populations between 10,000 and 150,000 – were more willing than members of the general public to tolerate communists, atheist, socialists, and "a man whose loyalty has been questioned before a Congressional committee but who swears under oath he has never been a communist." In Stouffer's study tolerance was defined in a variety of different ways, including allowing the person in question to keep his or her job and the freedom to make a speech in the community. Using a multi-item Guttman scale divided into three categories (at apparently arbitrary points), Stouffer (1955, 51) reported that 19 percent of the general population were "less tolerant," 50 percent were "in between," and 31 percent were "more tolerant." In comparison only 5 percent of civic elites were "less tolerant," 29 percent were "in between," and 66 percent were "more tolerant." About twenty years later Nunn, Crockett, and Williams (1973, 51) reported that the percentage of "more tolerant" members of the public had increased from 31 to 55 percent and of the community leaders from 66 to 83 percent.

Both Stouffer's original study and the 1973 replication demonstrated a strong correlation between political tolerance and education: college graduates identified from a representative sample of the population were, on average, as tolerant as community leaders. This suggests that the observed elite-mass differences in tolerance reflect differences in the characteristics of individual elites and the public, such as in their levels of education, rather than structural or institutional factors. There is also some exaggeration in both studies' characterization of "community leaders," as a whole, as highly tolerant, given the considerable variation between the different types of community leaders. Nunn, Crockett, and Williams find that the attitudes of the presidents of labour unions and of patriotic organizations were very similar to those of the public, while civic officials, bar association presidents, and newspaper publishers were almost entirely in the "most tolerant" category.

Stouffer's definition of tolerance, in terms of the freedom of speech and due process accorded a variety of liberal and left-wing political forces quaintly termed "radicals and other types of nonconformists" (1955, 26), reflects the political climate of the McCarthy era in the U.S. But, of course, this narrowness – a pre-eminent concern with the way the game is played rather than what the game is about – is the norm in a long tradition of studies of "political culture," of which Gabriel Almond and Sidney Verba's *The Civic Culture* is the most prominent example. In concentrating on the tolerance of dissent, Stouffer ignores the structural mechanisms that prevent the expression of the full range of public opinion, such as the concentrated ownership of the media, the unequal distribution of income and wealth, sex, racial, and ethnic inequality, and so on.

To their credit, McCloskey and Brill's much broader and more methodologically sophisticated study of tolerance addresses these structural issues. Remarkably, considering the two and one-half decades intervening between Stouffer's and McCloskey and Brill's studies, their findings are very similar. Again, there is no difference in support for civil liberties between their elites and members of the general public with university degrees (1983, 249). Also there are large differences among sectors of their elite sample. The police, school administrators, and "private officials" (their euphemism for managers and business executives) showed relatively low support for civil liberties, while judges and lawyers, the press, school teachers and college professors, and administrators gave relatively high support. In enlarging the scope of the concept of tolerance, however, McCloskey and Brill come upon some findings that they have difficulty explaining:

Whereas elites and the mass public diverge sharply on the application of such traditional rights as freedom of speech, press, religion, and due process, they differ to a lesser degree on such emerging issues as equal or preferential job opportunities for minorities and women, abortion, homosexual rights, civil disobedience, prisoner rights, open admission to universities, birth control for teenagers, the right to die, crimes without victims, the rights of children and the aged, and freedom of life-style.

The explanation for these results, we believe, rests principally on the fact that norms have not yet crystallized around these issues ... To a far greater extent then [*sic*], say freedom of the press, they are surrounded by controversy, and not enough time has passed to permit a consensus to emerge. Nor do these issues enjoy the sanction of historical experience and tradition. They are rarely (or never) mentioned in the major historical documents in which our more familiar liberties have been set down, and they are not likely to be the subject of oratory and praise in the speeches of politicians and other community leaders. (If anything, many of them are avoided as being vexing and too controversial.) One day, perhaps, some of these issues will be resolved to the point of attaining widely approved status. At present, however, they remain signs of a growing change in attitudes among certain groups in the society, but they cannot be regarded as established libertarian norms. (1983, 272–3)

Confronted with the unexpected finding of much smaller differences between the elites and the mass, they avoid the obvious conclusion that the "newer" issues are not the same as the "older" civil liberties issues. These new issues, of course, reflect the new political agenda of the 1960s and the underlying realization that tolerance (and equality before the law) is quite compatible with the continuation of class, gender, and racial inequality. Of course, these new issues are *not* too recent to have been incorporated into norms, rather they are longstanding economic and moral issues that are much more likely to be the subject of class, sex, and racial conflict. McCloskey and Brill's findings can be interpreted in the context of the conflicting interests of various elite groups, social classes, and class fractions, but the concept of interest is outside the scope of "social learning theory," which McCloskey and Brill use to explain the patterns of difference in support for traditional civil liberties:

[T]here is nothing mysterious about the process by which the elites of a society come to learn civil liberties and other democratic norms. They are not "resocialized" or transformed; rather, they experience a greater measure of social learning than do individuals who, for whatever reason, have had little opportunity to participate actively in the public affairs of the community or nation. (1983: 238)

Why should elites be more libertarian than the mass public: Part of the answer is that the norms of the American political culture are predominantly libertarian, and access to those norms is, for various reasons, greater among the elites that among the members of the general public. Freedom and its constituent elements, it seems plain enough, are among the most venerated of American values. (1983, 240)

Alongside their unwillingness to admit the concept of interest is an unwillingness to deal with social structure. McCloskey and Brill conceive of elites as "members of society who engage in the kinds and levels of activities that almost any citizen might engage in if he or she chose" (1983, 237), not as members of particular social classes or strata. Temperamental differences, not the systematic effects of the social structure on political participation, explain why some people are more interested and involved in politics and so more tolerant.

Rather than a uniform difference between liberal elites and less tolerant masses, different aspects of the ideological universe are characterized by different degrees of elite-mass consensus and conflict. Even in the context of studies of political tolerance, broadening the focus of earlier studies changes the findings of the research. For example in his study of American elites (but not the general public) conducted in 1971–72, Barton asked whether

"Supreme Court decisions of the 1960s have imposed excessive restriction on the police." Fifteen percent of the leaders of "conservative organizations," 31 percent of business owners and executives, and 31 percent of Republican politicians and officials disagreed, while 45 percent of civil servants, 55 percent of Democratic party politicians, 63 percent of labour union leaders, 70 percent of mass media executives and professionals, 77 percent of "minority organization" leaders, and 86 percent of "Liberal organization" leaders agreed (Barton 1974, 519). There were even larger differences among elite groups in responses to the statement that "practices of the FBI and military intelligence in recent years have not threatened civil liberties." Barton remarks that this pattern of responses is very similar to the inter-elite differences that he observes for economic issues. In the context of such large differences between elite groups, analysis of differences between "the" elite and the public are not very meaningful. At least, Barton's results suggest significant restrictions to the conclusions of the traditional studies of tolerance. The validity of social learning theory is certainly limited to issues relating to freedom of speech, and in terms of its applicability to lower-level community leaders.

Besides our project, the only other serious study of the opinions of Canadian elites is the 1987 survey by Sniderman et al. (1996). Their central interest was in civil liberties and constitutional issues, particularly in relation to the adoption of the Canadian Charter of Rights, as seen through the theoretical perspective of "democratic elitism," the label they give to the ideas about elite liberalism and tolerance popularized by Stouffer and McCloskey. Fortunately Sniderman and his colleagues also asked their elites, and a comparison sample of the Canadian public, a number of questions about broader social and political issues.

The breadth of Sniderman et al.'s analysis, however, is sharply limited by their sample, which consists of "decision makers in the civil liberties area ... selected to represent the legislative, executive and judicial branches of government" (1996, 260). The legislative and executive "components" of the elite were defined, respectively, as members of the federal and provincial parliaments, and a combination of federal officials from the Ministries of the Solicitor General and Justice and their provincial equivalents and crown attorneys from across the country. Since the researchers did not think that they could or should interview judges, they used a sample of senior lawyers as a surrogate. While practicing senior lawyers constitute the pool from which almost all judges are appointed, this sampling method overlooks the dramatically *unequal* chances of gaining a judicial appointment, which must be a function of a lawyer's temperament, competence, and political views. A sample of police was also interviewed, but these results are only included in some of the articles and not in the summary volume.

In an early analysis of their questions about civil liberties, Joseph Fletcher summarizes results that are consistent with the American orthodoxy: "... in

Canada, as elsewhere, individuals drawn from elite groups are more supportive of individual rights and freedoms than are the public at large ... nearly
88% of the decision makers as compared to just over 60% of the citizens are
in favour of free speech for radicals and extremists. These data are consistent
with the theory of democratic elitism suggesting that decision makers have
more thoroughly assimilated democratic norms than the average citizen"
(1989, 229). So far, so good – but Fletcher also finds that decision makers
are *more* likely than citizens, by a margin of 66.5 versus 50.6 percent, to support wire-tapping. Moreover there is considerable variation between the elite
groups, ranging from 83 percent support by police and 77 percent support by
crown attorneys, down to 66 and 61 percent of ministry officials and lawyers. Among politicians of the four parties, however, support for wire-
tapping varies between 38 and 80 percent! Significantly isolated from the
mainstream Progressive Conservative and Liberal politicians, NDP and PQ
legislators both give about 40 percent support to wire-tapping. Intent on res-
cuing the theory of democratic elitism from this embarrassing finding,
Fletcher argues that elite support for wire-tapping is no more than another
aspect of their sophistication, which gives elites "greater knowledge of existing arrangements [for servicing wire-taps] and the safeguards built into
them." In our view Fletcher's findings actually cast doubt on the theory of
democratic elitism. Not only are elite views of wire-tapping an embarrassing
exception to the general argument, but the extent of variation between elite
groups throws into doubt the usefulness of the elite-citizenry axis as a principle for understanding political ideology.

In later articles (Fletcher, Russell, and Sniderman 1991) and the volume
describing their entire project (Sniderman et al. 1996), the shortcomings of
democratic elitism feature prominently: "The thesis of democratic elitism
presupposes that the decisive contest is between elite and mass public, *ignor-
ing the party system*. The electoral system, however, operates to provide a
choice between, not an average across, competing sets of elites. And the fallacy of democratic elitism consists exactly in its indifference to *which partisan elites* prevail" (1996, 51, emphasis added). Indeed the exploration of
further aspects of their surveys shows this exactly. To questions about redistribution, the survey reveals a wide gap between the Progressive Conservative
and Liberal politicians on the right and the NDP and Bloc Québécois politicians on the left. Almost always the legal and administrative elites are close to
the political right; the position of the public falls in between, just where depending on the issue, though inter-elite conflict is greatest for questions that
place rights in distributional terms. Affirmative action for women is supported
or given qualified support by 21, 41, 73, and 65 percent of the Progressive
Conservative, Liberal, NDP, and Bloc Québécois politicians respectively,
along with 22 and 31 percent of the legal and administrative elites respectively (and 32 percent of the public). Though there is considerable variation in

the extent of difference between elites, the right-left ordering of the groups is generally preserved, with the legal and administrative elites tending to be closer to midway between the political right and left than the example shows.

Now what to make of this evidence of elite dissent? "Conflicts over democratic rights," Sniderman et al. argue, reflect "the inherent contestability of democratic values" (1996, 237). Conflict over the right to protest, for example, is viewed in terms of the relative preferences for liberty and order. What this comes down to is "the distinctive commitments of political elites, organized into political parties competing for political power" (242), which are rooted in *shared values*. Sniderman and his colleagues, however, do not connect these values to anything about the social and economic structure, so the conflicting values that result in their elites disagreeing on major political questions simply hang as the pennants of competing teams. Elites have values, but not *interests*. This unwillingness to acknowledge structural conflict is even more apparent in relation to the national question, where their constitutionalism swings them back to the model of elite liberalism and distrust of the citizenry: "... the constitutional crisis is at its most critical point a crisis driven by the unwillingness of people who speak one language to get along with those who speak a different one ... If pluralist democracy is not secure in a country like Canada, in what country is it secure? In the end, the lesson to draw may be that ordinary citizens are always susceptible to the irrational passions of group identity and rivalry" (255). Because of their exclusive focus on civil and political rights, Sniderman et al. cannot account for economically based cleavages or for conflict between national communities – except by observing their organization in political parties. They take no notice of more than twenty years of impassioned (and voluminous!) debate over the state and the nature of order in developed capitalist societies, not to mention a burgeoning literature on modern nationalism.

METHODOLOGICAL ISSUES

Our analysis of elite-mass differences focuses on power and inequality, rather than on the traditional civil liberties issues that are the focus of the classic American studies. Our elite is also quite different from the community leaders in relatively small American cities (with populations between 10 and 150 thousand) who are the focus of the studies by Stouffer and McCloskey and Brill, and also from Sniderman et al.'s decision-making elite in the area of civil liberties. Although our sample includes elites in cities and provinces as well as at the national level, our respondents are generally much more influential – and presumably better informed and connected with other prominent decision makers – than the respondents in these studies.

As McCloskey and Brill (1983, 237) observe, any description of the aggregate structure of elite opinion is problematic because of the difficulty in defining precisely the population of elites. Indeed the sample design strategy employed in this and many other elite studies, which first identifies institutional sectors then elites within each sector, reflects the difficulty of implementing a sample based on a more general definition of elite status to be applied in widely varying institutional settings. Within each sector it is much easier to argue that a sample provides an adequate representation of elites. The key problem is raised by the process of combining the sectoral samples in order to measure views of *the* elite. Any such combination of different groups carries with it the assumption that the relative sizes of the sectoral samples correspond to the relative influence of those elites in the public policy process (or that weights could be introduced to into the statistical analysis to make the sample correspond to the population of elites in sectoral composition).

Whether combining sectoral samples is problematic is partly an empirical question. When there is consensus among the different sectors, we can make the claims that our respondents are properly thought of as decision-making elites and that the results of this process of combining would be *un*affected by the proportions of elites in the various sectoral samples. In order to minimize the risk of incorrectly assuming that the sectoral groups are similar, in this chapter we compare the public survey to all the elites and to three significant subgroups: business, combining big business, medium business, and lawyers; the state elite, combining politicians and bureaucrats at all three levels of government; and trade union leaders.

SURVEY RESULTS

To begin with we can examine the extent of elite sensitivity to public opinion by reference to the data in table 8-1. The first two columns of this table show comparable evaluations by members of the general public and elites of the quality of life in different domains of their everyday lives. Note, however, that the public ratings of housing, the standard of living, and education refer to individuals' perceptions of *their own* situations, while the elite ratings refer, more generally, to "the quality of housing in Canada," "the standard of living in Canada," and the "system of education." In designing these items we were primarily concerned with the impact of elite perceptions of *public* concerns on their views of social policy. Because of these differences in the questions addressed to the public and elites the response distributions of elites can be expected to exhibit less variation, since the elite responses refer to their perceptions of the *average* condition of housing, etcetera. For the other aspects of life in Canada rated by the public and elites, including "the quality of life in Canada," the system of medical and health care, and the three levels of government, the public and elite survey items are identical.

Table 8-1
Elite and Public Perceptions of the Quality of Life in Canada

| | Percentage Distribution of Responses* | | | | | | Mean rating | |
| | Elite | | | Public | | | | |
Domain	Low	Medium	High	Low	Medium	High	Elite	Public
Quality of life in Canada	15	74	11	20	55	25	7.8	7.9
Housing	36	58	6	17	57	26	6.8	8.1
Standard of living	19	69	12	34	50	16	7.7	7.2
Medical and health care+	11	63	26	12	44	44	8.4	8.8
Education+				39	47	14		7.1
Primary and secondary	53	42	5				6.2	
Post secondary	37	58	5				6.9	
City government	49	46	5	44	45	11	6.4	6.4
Provincial government	43	52	5	47	44	9	6.5	6.6
Federal government	70	29	1	63	31	6	5.0	5.6

* The 11-point scale, with 1 labelled "completely dissatisfied" and 11 labelled "completely satisfied" is trichotomized with 1 to 6 in the low category, 7, 8 and 9 in the middle category, and 10 and 11 in the high category.
+ 1977 data for the public

In general, elites and the general public have very similar perceptions of the quality of life in Canada. On a scale of satisfaction where 1 stands for "completely *dis*satisfied" and 11 stands for "completely satisfied," the mean ratings of the quality of life in Canada are 7.8 for the elites and 7.9 for the public. The differences between the mean ratings of the various areas are generally larger than the differences between the public's and elites' evaluations of each area. Generally there is less variation in the ratings of elites, suggesting their evaluations reflect more of a consensus. In some senses, of course, the elites are more homogeneous so that, for example, the range in education among elites is much smaller than the range in the population.

The largest discrepancy between elite and public ratings is in the area of housing: while 17 percent of the public rate the quality of *their own* housing as at or below the mid-point of the scale, 36 percent of the elite respondents give this unsatisfactory rating of the quality of housing in Canada. The difference is a bit difficult to interpret, because an overall evaluation of housing might reflect assessment of whether *any* significant portion of the population live in unacceptably poor housing, and this is not the same as asking what *percentage* live in such housing. Elites give *slightly* higher ratings of the standard of living in Canada than the public give of their own, individual standards of living. The elites also give lower ratings of the quality of education, especially of primary and secondary education, while the public give higher ratings of the federal government and the quality of medical and health care facilities. Elites and the public are about equally satisfied with local and provincial governments.

Relative to the other domains, elites and the public are relatively unlikely to report dissatisfaction with the standard of living, medical care, and the quality of life in general. Dissatisfaction with government, and especially with the federal government, in 1981 was relatively high. Fully 70 percent of the elite respondents and 63 percent of the public rate the federal government at or below the mid-point of the scale, while the corresponding figures for the "quality of life in Canada" are only 15 and 20 percent. Although opinion about the "government of this city" and the "government of this province" is not quite so negative, it is still much below the ratings of other areas of life. Elites and the public, therefore, have very similar personal evaluations of problems in everyday life, and elites take a somewhat more critical position on the quality of public programs and governmental performance. Both elites and the general public are happier with the state of their own lives and of the state of Canada than with the Canadian state – or at least with its government.

Similarities in the perceptions of the quality of life need not, of course, correspond to similarities in priorities for public policy. Table 8-2 gives the elite and public responses to a multi-part question about the effort, relative to the current effort, that government should devote to different policy areas. Measuring the relative priorities of various elements of public policy by the proportion saying that government should devote much more effort to a given issue, the public order of priorities is listed as in table 8-2. Three general observations may be made about this table. First, there is a strong correspondence in the priorities of public and elite. The variation in the ratings of the policy areas is considerably greater than the differences between the public and elite ratings of each area. There is a very broad range, about 50 percent, in the proportions of elite and public respondents favouring more government effort in the highest- and lowest-rated areas. Fully 85 percent of the public and 84 percent of the elites support more or much more government effort to control inflation, compared to only 18 percent of the public who favour more foreign aid and 28 percent of the elites favouring more effort to assist the unemployed. The largest elite-public difference, over government effort to eliminate pornography, has the public giving 20 percent more support than the elites, but in most of the areas the elite-public differences are much smaller. Thus in a broad sense there is indeed a general correspondence between the public policy agendas of elites and the public.

Table 8-2
Public and Elite Ratings of the Amount of Effort Government Should Put into a
Number of Government Activities

Government Activity	Amount of Effort	Public	All Elites	Capital	State	Labour
Health and medical care	More or much more	49	32	17	27	76
	About the same	48	63	74	68	23
	Less or much less	2	5	9	4	0
Protecting the rights of native people	More or much more	45	49	31	50	76
	About the same	39	36	43	40	19
	Less or much less	11	13	23	10	4
Providing assistance to the unemployed	More or much more	34	28	12	29	67
	About the same	39	43	37	51	27
	Less or much less	23	28	49	19	5
Supporting the business community	More or much more	35	29	32	31	17
	About the same	46	41	37	46	36
	Less or much less	14	28	28	23	46
Promoting bilingualism	More or much more	27	29	22	32	35
	About the same	29	31	28	34	34
	Less or much less	41	38	48	32	30
Creating more jobs*	More or much more	85	69	52	73	94
	About the same	10	17	21	19	4
	Less or much less	3	11	24	8	1
Maintaining national unity*	More or much more	69	62	63	67	63
	About the same	22	24	24	21	25
	Less or much less	6	11	12	10	12
Helping the poor	More or much more	62	58	40	63	83
	About the same	31	36	49	33	16
	Less or much less	4	4	8	2	1
Crime prevention	More or much more	73	64	61	63	73
	About the same	24	34	37	36	24
	Less or much less	2	2	2	1	2
Building public housing*	More or much more	48	38	25	36	76
	About the same	37	37	38	44	19
	Less or much less	11	23	36	20	4
Eliminating discrimination against women	More or much more	54	54	41	56	83
	About the same	34	37	45	39	14
	Less or much less	9	8	12	5	3

Table 8-2
Public and Elite Ratings of the Amount of Effort Government Should Put into a
Number of Government Activities (Continued)

Government Activity	Amount of Effort	Public	All Elites	Capital	State	Labour
Cutting inflation*	More or much more	85	85	88	84	86
	About the same	12	10	6	12	11
	Less or much less	2	3	4	2	3
Eliminating pornography*	More or much more	55	35	31	38	36
	About the same	27	40	42	42	35
	Less or much less	13	22	22	18	17
Protecting the environment	More or much more	71	59	43	61	80
	About the same	26	35	45	36	20
	Less or much less	2	6	12	3	0
Providing daycare*	More or much more	45	46	33	45	77
	About the same	33	38	40	43	18
	Less or much less	12	14	22	10	4
Foreign aid*	More or much more	17	35	24	40	37
	About the same	46	43	43	43	45
	Less or much less	29	22	32	15	17
Education	More or much more	54	40	35	33	66
	About the same	41	54	55	61	31
	Less or much less	3	6	8	7	2
National defense*	More or much more	34	35	43	36	26
	About the same	46	42	44	41	35
	Less or much less	13	22	12	22	37
Helping retired people*	More or much more	70	56	92	51	86
	About the same	27	38	42	45	12
	Less or much less	1	4	6	3	2
Workers' compensation	More or much more	37	20	7	18	61
	About the same	50	67	73	73	37
	Less or much less	5	9	17	6	1
Decreasing regional inequality*	More or much more	49	45	27	51	74
	About the same	33	36	42	34	23
	Less or much less	6	16	26	14	1

* Public opinion data for 1977

The differences between the elites and the public, however, are sufficiently systematic to require a qualification of this conclusion about elite-public consensus. Across the full range of policy issues elites are significantly more conservative. Only in the area of foreign aid do the elites give substantially more support than the general public to government effort; and elites also give somewhat more support to cutting inflation. The public is substantially more supportive of government effort in the areas of health and medical care, creating more jobs, crime prevention, eliminating pornography, protecting the environment, education, helping retired people, and workers' compensation, and somewhat more supportive of government effort in providing assistance to the unemployed, supporting the business community, maintaining national unity, building public housing, and decreasing regional inequality. Generally the elite-public differences suggest a greater public concern with social programs. Still, as their relatively high levels of support for crime prevention, eliminating pornography, and protecting the environment indicate, public concern is not limited to social programs; and, as the public support for the business community indicates, the public appears to be more supportive of government intervention generally than concerned particularly with redistribution and social programs.

Another point concerns the overall support for government effort to address the entire range of social concerns. Since respondents were cautioned that "putting more effort into one of these areas would require a shift of money from other areas or an increase in taxes," our surveys suggest that fiscal conservatism is a significantly more entrenched feature of elite than public ideology. Even though elites differ little from members of the public in their overall ranking of government priorities, they are consistently less likely to see government as having room to move beyond the status quo. This point is amplified by looking at the proportions calling for less effort in different policy fields. In sixteen of the twenty-one different policy fields support for government effort is greater in the public than among the elites. Elites are more likely, that is, than the general public to call for a redistribution of government resources, rather than for an extension of government commitments.

This fiscal conservatism has, on the one hand, a relevance to the hypothesis of the greater ideological constraint of elites. Elite ideology has embedded in it a sense of constraint, in the literal sense of a need to moderate demands for greater government effort by reference to a budget constraint. Public appeals for greater government effort, in comparison, look more like the unconstrained expression of needs consistent with theories of the overloaded state, unless one presumes a willingness on the part of members of the public to raise taxes in order to meet the costs of greater government effort. The evidence for this greater constraint in elite ideology also reveals, however, a clear substantive bias, which is relevant to our larger interest in understanding the consequences of biases in elite representation of public opinion.

Elites are proportionately much more likely than the general public to call for a reduction in commitments to public housing, workers' compensation, job creation, and regional equalization, all of which are areas in which state intervention constrains the actions of business. Elite opposition to government intervention is, interestingly, applied as equally to measures favouring business as to measures favouring disadvantaged areas or sectors of the labour force. Proportionately more elites (28 percent) than members of the public (14 percent) call for less effort in government assistance to the business community. This suggests, therefore, a coherent ideological opposition to state regulation of the market underlying elite attitudes towards government priorities. This ideology is by no means universal among elites, but it explains most of the differences between elites and the general public shown in table 8-2.

As we noted above it is difficult to make strong claims that our measure of elite opinion is the opinion of a real elite, in the sense of a stratum of individuals who, as a group, rule. At a more empirical level any comparisons of elites and the public must be sharply qualified if there prove to be structural divisions within our samples of elites that correspond to sharply differing responses to the questions in our survey. For example consider the fairly large difference in elite and public support for government effort in the area of health and medical care: 49 percent of the public support much more or more government effort, compared to 32 percent of the elite respondents. As table 8-2 indicates, 76 percent of the elite labour respondents, 27 percent of the elite state respondents, and 17 percent of the elite business respondents support much more or more government effort in this area. Less striking than the 17 percent gap between the aggregate elite and public responses, therefore, is the 59 percent difference between the business and labour elite respondents and the 49 percent gap between the state and labour elite respondents.

More generally, one can imagine a variety of different patterns of elite and public opinion, ranging from a combination of consensus among major elite sectors and elite-public consensus (as on issues of bilingualism and government effort to maintain national unity) to major conflicts among elite sectors combined with the public taking an entirely different position. Because our next chapter is devoted to an extensive analysis of inter-elite conflicts, in this chapter our treatment of the subject is brief and intended only to establish the relationship between elite and public opinion. While a great variety of alignments of elite and public opinion could exist, the overwhelming tendency is for capital and labour to define the right and left of the political spectrum and for the state elites and the general public to occupy a position somewhere between capital and labour – just where depending on the particular issue. A typical example is provided by the ratings of government effort to create more jobs: more or much more effort is supported by 94 percent of the labour elites, 85 percent of the general public, 73 percent of the state elites, and 52 percent of business elites. Of course these groups could be thinking about very different means of creating jobs.

The various areas of government involvement can be distinguished according to the level of elite dissent and, in areas in which there is significant inter-elite conflict, public opinion can be characterized according to whether it comes closest to the distribution for capitalist, state, or labour elites. There is relatively little inter-elite conflict over bilingualism, crime prevention, cutting inflation, eliminating pornography, protecting the environment, and foreign aid – and for each of these areas the distribution of public opinion is quite close to those of the elites. In the remaining areas of government involvement in which there is significant inter-elite conflict, fifteen of the twenty-one areas rated, the distribution of public opinion is closest to that of the state elites, to the left of the capitalist elites, and to the right of the labour elites. In no area does public opinion fall to the left of the labour elites or to the right of capitalist elites. There is greater public than state elite support for government effort in the areas of health and medical care, providing assistance to the unemployed, creating more jobs, building public housing, protecting the environment, education, helping retired people, and workers' compensation; and there is very slightly less public than state elite support for protecting the rights of native people, helping the poor, and promoting bilingualism, while support for foreign aid is much greater in the elite. On these questions about government priorities, there is a greater ideological gap between the state elites and capital than between the state elites and labour. The relatively strong public commitment to social programs is apparent in these results. More generally, these data demonstrate the difficulty faced by right-wing provincial and national governments in selling fiscal restraint, as illustrated by the Brian Mulroney government's failed effort in 1985 to limit old age pensions.

These results resist summary in the terms of the debate about elite liberalism. There is so much inter-elite conflict that a comparison between *the* elite and the public is not meaningful. In the areas that bear most directly on civil liberties, public opinion tends to be closer to that of the state elites than to the business *or* the labour elites. It is interesting that in the area of eliminating pornography, for which we have only a reading of public opinion from 1977, the public shows more concern than any of the elite groups. Since 1977, and especially from the early 1980s, we have seen a great deal of governmental activity in this area. Whether concern about pornography is a sign of intolerance has, of course, been the subject of extensive public debate in recent years.

The findings in table 8-3, which provide a comparison between public and elite opinion on a number of items bearing more directly on civil liberties and social inequality, further undermine the case for elite liberalism in Canada. Concerning legislation to protect the disabled, equal pay for equal work, and affirmative action the distribution of public opinion is slightly more liberal than that of the elites, taken as a group. For example "programmes to

Table 8-3
Support for Civil Liberties Issues for the Canadian Population in 1981

			*Percentage Distribution of Responses*			
			With qualification				
Civil Liberties Issue	*Group*	*No*	*No*	*Yes*	*Yes*	*No opinion*	*Total*
Legislation to protect the	Public	1	2	10	83	4	100
rights of the disabled	All elites	14	4	12	68	2	100
	Capital	20	6	15	56	3	100
	State	14	3	12	70	1	100
	Labour	3	2	5	89	1	100
The right of women to	Public	2	1	7	88	2	100
equal pay	All elites	9	2	8	80	1	100
	Capital	13	4	11	71	1	100
	State	9	1	7	82	1	100
	Labour	1	1	4	94	0	100
Protection of homosexuals	Public	26	6	17	39	12	100
from discrimination in	All elites	29	6	14	47	3	100
employment	Capital	39	8	16	34	3	100
	State	30	7	11	50	2	100
	Labour	13	3	11	70	3	100
Programs to favour the	Public	22	6	14	48	10	100
hiring and promotion of	All elites	38	8	12	40	2	100
women and other minorities	Capital	52	9	11	26	2	100
to make up for their lack of	State	33	8	12	46	1	100
opportunities in the past	Labour	19	4	16	60	1	100
Granting native peoples	Public	26	5	16	40	13	100
limited rights of	All elites	35	5	11	46	3	100
self-government	Capital	43	6	10	37	4	100
	State	32	6	11	49	2	100
	Labour	24	7	13	55	1	100
Elimination of existing	Public	42	9	10	26	13	100
boards of censor	All elites	45	7	8	34	6	100
	Capital	49	7	8	31	5	100
	State	48	8	8	31	5	100
	Labour	34	4	12	44	6	100
Abolition of the	Public	43	7	7	24	19	100
War Measures Act	All elites	59	8	5	25	3	100
	Capital	70	8	3	16	3	100
	State	59	10	5	23	3	100
	Labour	32	6	9	51	2	100

Table 8-3
Support for Civil Liberties Issues for the Canadian Population in 1981 (Continued)

Civil Liberties Issue	Group	No	With qualification		Yes	No opinion	Total
			No	Yes			
Civilian review of	Public	20	4	14	52	10	100
complaints against the	All elites	17	4	12	65	2	100
police	Capital	25	5	14	54	2	100
	State	15	4	10	69	2	100
	Labour	11	1	14	73	1	100

Percentage Distribution of Responses

favour the hiring and promotion of women and other minorities to make up for their lack of opportunities in the past," our précis of affirmative action, gain the support of 48 percent of the public, compared to 40 percent of the elites; however, 10 percent of the public, but only 2 percent of elites, have no opinion. Concerning the rights of homosexuals, native self government, eliminating existing boards of censorship, and the War Measures Act the public is either slightly more conservative or about the same as the elites, depending on how the missing data are treated. On all these items, members of the public are more likely to say they have no opinion, indicating relatively high levels of unfamiliarity with the issues. On five of the eight items, at least 10 percent of the public do not express an opinion. Omitting the non-respondents from the total would eliminate the elite-public differences for three of the four items in which the elites are more liberal. On that fourth item, which concerns censorship, the public is clearly more conservative.

As with the items dealing with government effort, the high degree of inter-elite conflict further qualifies any statement that might be made about elite liberalism. Affirmative action, for example, is supported by 26 percent of business elites, 46 percent of state elites, and 60 percent of labour elites, differences that are very much larger than the 8 percent gap between elites and the public. On most issues the trade union leaders are much more liberal than the business elites, with differences of 25 percent or more for the items dealing with the rights of homosexuals, affirmative action, and abolition of the War Measures Act. Again the tendency is for the public and the state elites to take positions between the left and right staked out by the labour and business elites.

Whatever the nature of the public-elite differences, we should stress that the responses of the public and of elites were quite liberal and in many areas placed members of the public in a position favouring more liberal legislation than existed at the time, or even now. Civilian review of complaints by police, for example, has only been implemented in a few jurisdictions and often in a form that gives the police the initial rights to investigate complaints. Even in areas such as equal pay and the rights of the disabled, where there has been significant government action, that action took place well after our surveys were conducted.

The results in table 8-4 show that elites are systematically less likely than members of the general public to support statements inditing the extent of inequality in Canadian society and calling for redistributive action. Although a majority 66 percent of the public agree that "there is too much difference between the rich and poor in this country," less than half, 46 percent, of the elites agree; furthermore 43 percent of the elites as compared with only 17 percent of the public disagree or strongly disagree with the statement. The results are similar for questions dealing with measures to remedy social inequalities. The statement that "In provinces where they now exist, rent controls should be abolished" gained the support of only 18 percent of the public, compared to 43 percent of the elites; though there is also extreme conflict between elites with 12 percent of labour elites, 44 percent of state elites, and 63 percent of business elites supporting the abolition of rent controls. A minority of the elite respondents, but a majority of the public, agree that governments should act as an employer of last resort (33 versus 69 percent support) and that there should be more redistributive taxation (29 versus 55 percent).

Responses to the statement that "unemployment is high these days because it is too easy to get welfare assistance" are an exception to the general pattern of elite-public differences. Half of the elites, but only 22 percent of the public, *dis*agree with this statement. The greater liberalism of the public is thus combined with attitudes that leave the public open to right-wing appeals that lay the problems of society at the door of the morally unfit, who take unfair advantage of the society. There is an inclination to regard this as an issue of constraint: elites, but not members of the general public, understand the need for social programs as responses to structural problems rather than to problems of individual immorality. However, as we observed in our previous analysis of public political ideology, even if we assess public opinion as having a distorting moralistic bent, there is no logical *in*consistency between supporting social programs and believing that some people take unfair advantage of them.

Moving from social welfare issues to labour relations, our data again suggest the greater entrenchment of business ideology among elites. On labour issues, however, there is far less ideological consensus in either elite circles or the general public. Of the various components of the postwar settlement in capitalist countries, the recognition and extension of the political rights of labour has been the least well established ideologically. Of course opinions on

Table 8-4
Responses to Statements Concerning Redistribution and Labour Relations

| | | | | | | | | | Percentage Distribution of Responses |
Statement	Group	Strongly agree	Agree	Neither agree nor disagree	Disagree	Strongly disagree	Depends	Do not know	Total
There is too much difference between rich and poor in this country	Public	18	48	14	16	1	0	3	100
	All elites	8	38	9	40	3	1	1	100
	Capital	0	24	11	56	5	2	2	100
	State	8	43	10	35	2	1	1	100
	Labour	25	58	5	12	0	0	0	100
People with high incomes should pay a greater share of the total taxes than they do now	Public	14	41	13	26	2	1	3	100
	All elites	4	25	8	52	9	1	1	100
	Capital	1	8	6	69	15	1	0	100
	State	4	29	10	50	6	1	0	100
	Labour	15	51	7	24	2	1	0	100
Unemployment is high these days because it is too easy to get welfare assistance	Public	17	49	10	20	2	1	1	100
	All elites	4	40	10	38	7	1	0	100
	Capital	7	56	12	22	1	1	1	100
	State	1	36	9	46	7	0	1	100
	Labour	1	17	5	54	22	1	0	100
The government should provide jobs for Canadians who want to work but cannot find a job	Public	17	52	10	17	1	1	2	100
	All elites	3	30	11	49	4	2	1	100
	Capital	2	24	6	61	5	1	1	100
	State	1	26	14	50	4	4	1	100
	Labour	11	49	2	24	1	2	1	100

Table 8-4
Responses to Statements Concerning Redistribution and Labour Relations (Continued)

Statement	Group	Percentage Distribution of Responses							
		Strongly agree	Agree	Neither agree nor disagree	Disagree	Strongly disagree	Depends	Do not know	Total
In provinces where they now exist rent controls should be abolished	Public	3	15	10	54	11	1	6	100
	All elites	6	37	9	38	5	2	3	100
	Capital	11	52	9	22	1	2	3	100
	State	4	39	8	40	3	2	4	100
	Labour	1	11	5	60	22	0	1	100
During a strike, management should be prohibited by law from hiring workers to take the place of strikers	Public	12	41	11	26	4	2	4	100
	All elites	11	29	6	39	11	2	2	100
	Capital	1	21	7	49	19	2	1	100
	State	3	36	6	43	8	3	1	100
	Labour	66	28	1	4	0	1	0	100
Workers should have positions on the board of directors of the organization for which they work	Public	8	59	11	13	2	1	6	100
	All elites	4	40	16	31	6	2	1	100
	Capital	1	19	16	48	13	2	1	100
	State	4	52	15	23	3	2	1	100
	Labour	14	45	22	16	1	1	1	100

the rights and powers of labour are the most difficult to reconcile with theoretical and ideological understandings of capitalism as a system in which labour and capital are related in a market of free exchange rather than in political relations of exploitation. By contrast, commitments to the regulation of the economy on anti-monopoly grounds, and because of the need to provide infrastructure requirements as public goods or public utilities, are more easily argued from traditional capitalist or liberal perspectives. The same is true for commitments to social welfare programs as reproducing a minimal capacity for participation in the market, or for ameliorating the social harm of short-term market disequilibria.

Although both elites and members of the general public are seriously divided over labour rights, there is significantly greater elite *opposition* to the expansion of labour's participation in the internal decision making of organizations and to the curtailment of management rights in the face of strikes. More than two-thirds of the general public support the addition of representatives of workers to the boards of directors of the organizations in which they work. Less than half of the elites support that idea, and proportionately twice as many elites as members of the general public oppose it. Fifty-three percent of the general public support measures to prevent management from hiring scab labour in the event of strikes, compared to the 40 percent of elites supporting such measures. Of course there is enormous conflict between elites. Anti-scab legislation is supported by 94 percent of labour elites, 39 percent of state elites, and 22 percent of business elites.

Finding that the questions in table 8-5 evoke serious inter-elite conflict somewhat tempers our conclusion that the public is generally more liberal than the elites on these items. When it comes to the relative powers of social classes, the public is generally to the left of the state elites and much closer to the labour elites than we found for the previous measures. For example on the issue of increasing the redistributiveness of the system of taxation, 55 percent of the public agree or strongly agree, compared to 66 percent of the labour elites, 33 percent of the state elites, and a mere 9 percent of the capitalist elites. These striking results show a far greater degree of public than general elite support for equalizing the distribution of resources in society.

There is one dimension in which the hypothesis of elite liberalism is confirmed by the data in tables 8-2 and 8-4. Elites appear to be more likely than non-elites to endorse procedural and institutional limitations to the exercise of state authority. That is, elites may have a more juridical or constitutional sense of liberalism than the public, if we emphasize the lower level of support among elites for government efforts to eliminate crime or pornography, and the greater elite support in table 8-5 for the elimination of existing boards of censors and for civilian review of complaints against the police.

Table 8-5
Correlations among Items Measuring Political Ideology, for the Elites above the Diagonal and for the Public below the Diagonal

	a	b	c	d	e	f	g	h	i	j	k	l	m	Standard deviation
a Health care	...	.39	.02	.39	.07	.29	.33	.18	.24	.07	.30	.30	-.24	.70
b Assistance to unemployed	.27	...	.02	.49	.07	.35	.27	.23	.28	.06	.34	.42	-.37	.94
c Support for business	.10	.18	...	.01	.10	-.03	.04	-.08	.03	-.12	-.17	-.12	.18	.93
d Helping poor	.29	.39	.13	...	.20	.40	.28	.23	.28	.05	.31	.46	-.30	.78
e Crime prevention	.24	.16	.16	.27	...	.12	.18	-.03	.02	-.07	.07	.06	.10	.77
f Elimination of discrimination against women	.23	.26	.12	.31	.33	...	.28	.29	.35	.11	.30	.35	-.26	.89
g Protecting the environment	.15	.08	.08	.18	.21	.28	...	.19	.21	.07	.19	.26	-.14	.86
h Protecting homosexual rights	.04	.12	.01	.15	.00	.21	.13	...	.25	.20	.22	.28	-.22	1.32
i Affirmative action	.15	.21	.07	.20	.19	.31	.11	.15	...	.06	.29	.32	-.16	1.36
j Eliminating boards of censors	.06	.10	.04	.08	-.05	.05	.03	.17	.06	...	.04	.06	-.19	1.38
k Prohibit strikebreaking	.19	.20	-.04	.18	.08	.18	.11	.12	.17	.08	...	.37	-.33	1.27
l Rich and poor too unequal	.21	.24	-.01	.25	.11	.18	.06	.09	.18	.10	.23	...	-.49	1.11
m Welfare increases un employment	.02	-.21	.04	-.11	.10	-.06	-.04	-.12	-.02	-.06	-.11	.03	...	1.10
Standard deviation	.73	.98	.84	.80	.78	.94	.77	1.29	1.26	1.33	1.13	.98	1.06	

Defined in terms of the negative freedom from state limitations on action, liberalism is more entrenched among elites than the general public. This commitment to negative liberties is consistent, certainly, with the underlying logic of business liberalism, that is the doctrine of the limited state, which we have argued is an underlying organizing principle in elite attitudes not specifically tied to questions of civil liberties. Authoritarian tendencies within the mass public on such questions are not, however, sufficiently marked to support hypotheses of working-class authoritarianism, or a generalized view of elite liberalism. When liberalism is defined in terms of positive freedoms – the rights of women or the disabled, or the issues of labour rights and greater equality of condition – members of the general public are more liberal than elites in Canada.

The discrepancies between governmental policies and public opinion are much better explained in terms of arguments about the organization of elite, and particularly of business ideology, than in terms of our findings about public policy priorities. Fundamental ideological conflicts are stimulated by questions that raise directly the "factual" perception of injustice in society and the responsibility for correcting it. As a result the data reveal a greater degree of conflict within the mass public than is apparent from the general consensus in support of the status quo or greater commitments in public policy; and the differences between elite and public are more dramatic than in reference to public policy priorities or to the extension or contraction of government expenditures in different policy fields. Assuming, however, a strong relationship between calls for more effort in social policy areas and these ideological orientations towards stratification and redistributive policy, we can ground elite reluctance to give more priority to social policy, and the associated elite approval of cutbacks in social policy, in their relatively right-wing ideological consensus.

Our emphasis on the hypothesis of the dominance of business ideology among Canadian elites as a rival to the conventional and dominant hypothesis in political sociology of elite liberalism invites another look at the question of ideological constraint. At a number of points in the analysis above, the concept of ideological constraint has figured as a possible explanation of the results. *Pace* the arguments of liberal political sociology, perhaps elites are more ideologically constrained than non-elites and, by implication, have more rational views of public policy than members of the mass public. The next section addresses this concern.

PUBLIC AND ELITE LEVELS OF IDEOLOGICAL CONSTRAINT

If, in a general sense, elites are no more liberal than the public, what remains of the moral justification for elite liberalism is the argument that elites have a greater interest in and a wiser view of public policy. Similarly, if elites are much more conservative than the public on issues of social welfare and income redistribution, it may be that they better understand the logical relationships between capital accumulation and the costs of social legitimation (to use the vocabulary of neo-Marxist theory rather than that of business ideology). The arguments about elite constraint make just such points, crediting only a small proportion of the general public with even a minimal understanding of political issues. We have addressed this issue at some length in our previous discussion of public political ideology and concluded that there was good evidence to refute the claims about the lack of significant ideological constraint in the general public. Whether or not there is a meaningful difference in constraint between the public and elites is a somewhat different issue.

We will consider three types of evidence in making this comparison: levels of non-response to questions in our surveys, the correlations between individual questionnaire items, and the correlations between scales made up of these questions. At first glance the last two analyses appear to be redundant. Finding higher correlations in the responses to individual items among elite than public respondents would appear to demand the same pattern for the correlations between scales. If the inter-item correlations are *uniformly* greater in one group than another, this is the case, but if only the *average* inter-item correlation is greater then the inter-scale correlations could exhibit a different pattern of relationships. What follows from this statistical argument is the possibility that a group that gives more consistent responses to closely related questions could exhibit weaker-than-average relations between more general dimensions of ideology.

As tables 8-3 and 8-4 show, there are large public-elite differences in levels of non-response. These differences are especially large for the questions dealing with civil liberties. Ten percent of the public take no position on civilian review of complaints against the police and on affirmative action, and nearly 10 percent give no response to the question about the War Measures Act. Our interpretation of these differences may be challenged by the observation that, because there is no valid ambivalent response, the "no opinion" category contains a mixture of respondents who have mixed feelings and respondents who have no opinion at all. Such an objection cannot be raised about the items in table 8-4, which are formulated so as to separate ambivalent respondents, who should choose the "neither agree nor disagree" response or say their position "depends" (on some further specification of the statement), from respondents giving no answer. Generally, members of the general public are more likely to be ambivalent or to say they don't know and less likely than elites to choose the "depends" response. The nature of these differences is, however, highly dependent on the issue in question. Contrary to the general pattern, for example, elites are more likely than members of the public to say they neither agree nor disagree with the relatively straightforward proposition that workers should have positions on the boards of the organizations for which they work. In spite of this variation, it should be apparent that these differences in the proportions of non-respondents clearly suggest the elite respondents have a greater awareness and understanding of particular public policy issues than members of the general public.

Table 8-5 gives the correlations among a number of individual questionnaire items for the public and elites, along with the standard deviations of the items, which are included because there is a likelihood of observing higher correlations when there is more variation in the pair of items being correlated. Thus the presence of a very high degree of polarization between the component groups of the elite sample could be mistaken for a high degree of ideological constraint. In the event, there is actually only a weak tendency for the elite sample to exhibit more variation than the public for most of the items, and there is little difference between the standard deviations observed for the two groups.

The first group of seven items in table 8-5 deals with government effort and provides strong evidence of greater elite constraint. Among the five items in which greater government effort is consistent with liberal views – health care, assistance to the unemployed, helping the poor, eliminating discrimination against women, and protecting the environment – the elite correlations are typically about .1 greater than the corresponding measures for the general public, which is a considerable difference. The correlations between the items dealing with efforts to support the business community and to prevent crime with the five items measuring support for government effort in the social policy related areas are higher for the general public than for the elites. To a greater degree than the elites, the public views government intervention in a unitary fashion with support for *all* different kinds of government activity being correlated, whereas elites think more in terms of what kind of government effort is appropriate. Consistent results are obtained for the other two groups of items in the table. The correlation between support for government effort to help the poor and the belief that social welfare increases unemployment is −.11 in the general public and −.30 in the elite sample. There is, however, considerable variation among the items. For example there is virtually no public-elite difference in the correlations between views of censorship and the other items.

Finally, table 8-6 gives the intercorrelations among four *scales* measuring support for social programs, redistribution, labour, and civil liberties (which are constructed somewhat differently in the elite and public). The striking finding is that the elite intercorrelations are not uniformly larger than the corresponding statistics computed for the general public. Consider first the correlation between the scales measuring support for social programs and

Table 8-6
Correlations among Scales Measuring Political Ideology, for the Public above the Diagonal and for the Elites below the Diagonal

	Social programs	Redistribution	Labour	Civil liberties
Support for social programs	...	.352	.488	.533
Support for redistribution	.386	...	.543	.250
Support for labour	.230	.375	...	.350
Support for civil liberties	.324	.241	.160	...

support for redistribution, for which the public and elite values are, respectively, .352 and .386, and the correlation between support for social programs and for labour, for which the public and elite correlations are .488 and .230. Instead of our finding, as for the individual survey items, that the intercorrelations between scales measured for the elite sample are uniformly greater than for the general public, their relative magnitudes are a function of the particular scales involved. For the correlation between the scales measuring support for redistribution and civil liberties there is almost no difference between the elites and public, while the correlations between support for labour and support for redistribution and civil liberties are also greater for the public.

CONCLUSIONS

Our findings do little to justify the fear of public opinion and public power that so characterizes the thinking of elite theorists, especially in the American tradition that began with the authoritarian personality studies. The Canadian public is generally quite liberal on civil liberties issues and very liberal on economic issues. Whether or not there are differences between Canadian and American public opinion on these issues cannot be said, because of the absence of sufficient measurement and sample comparability. The similarity between our findings and those of Allen Barton's elite study and the dissimilarity between our findings and the results of other studies of American community leaders clearly argue the need for greater clarity in defining precisely what "elites" the public is to be compared to. Further, it is apparent that whether the elites are top-level, national decision makers or lower-level "community leaders," there are substantial differences among *sectors* of the elite. On the substantive side it is apparent that once we move beyond the simplest conception of tolerance, it becomes important to separate civil liberties issues from questions about the fundamental differences in the power of social classes, the role of the state, and so on.

The emphasis on a narrowly defined political tolerance, on the one hand, and the issue of elite-mass differences in constraint, on the other hand, must be seen for what it is – a partisan theoretical position that legitimizes a social order in which an emphasis on civil liberties and tolerance, combined with elite rationality, becomes an alternative to a more widely conceived democracy. Our findings in this chapter speak to the poverty of elite liberalism and the inadequacy of the elite representation of public interests in a wider conception of democracy. They suggest the need for a closer look at more critical theories of the liberal democratic state, and for a more refined analysis of the conflict among elites that such theories anticipate.

9 Elite Divisions and Class Rule

Many of the simplified understandings of the relationship between elite and mass ideology, it is apparent from the previous chapter, cannot hold. If elites are more committed to the values sustaining liberal democracy in some respects, and this is debatable, it is only in the context of their weak commitments to the structural changes, such as affirmative action, the redistribution of income, and enlarged social programs, required to correct the biases built into Western democratic politics. Equally important, the analysis suggests serious limits to the conception of a generalized elite, as distinct from mass, ideology. Over most issues there are such large conflicts between elite sectors that there is no one elite position. With capital on the right, labour on the left, and the state elites somewhere in between, we discovered ideological divisions corresponding roughly to the divided class interests and the interests of a relatively autonomous state in Marxist theory. In this chapter we turn from a general discussion of elite ideology and elite-mass differences to a closer examination of the ideological divisions between structurally differentiated sectors of the elite and to a more refined examination of the character of elite ideology.

In the elite interviews it was possible to ask and get answers to important, but to the general public obscure, questions about public policy, such as the takeover of the provincial potash industry by the government of Saskatchewan. In this chapter these questions are used to draw a more detailed picture of elite ideology that differentiates between respondents' potentially more rhetorical views on political and economic philosophy and their opinions on specific policy questions. We employ scales obtained by combining the responses to different questions to get a more precise fix on elite ideology. Also we expand our focus from the basic ideological divisions between capitalist, state, and labour elites, differentiating within the state and business elites and expanding the analysis to include mass media elites, academic elites, and farm organization leaders. As we explained in chapter 3, the state elite is divided into six groups, separating elected politicians from bureaucrats and distinguishing the three levels of government. Capital is divided into three groups: executives of large corporations (referred to in the following discussion as "corporate executives"), proprietors of small- and medium-sized businesses (referred to as "business owners"), and lawyers.

The distinctions between bureaucrats and politicians and between the levels of government are universal, functional divisions in contemporary capitalist states. There are built-in conflicts along these lines, reflecting politicians' need to get elected and re-elected, bureaucrats' accumulation of expertise and concerns about continuity across political regimes, and the particular, Canadian division of powers in the federation. There are likely to be still other structural divisions, particularly between government departments responsible for the economy, whose chief concern is to encourage growth, and departments responsible for social programs. In our theoretical orientation the state is characterized by a distinct ideology and it attempts, no matter how imperfectly, to establish a hegemonic order, mediating social conflict. Though the opinions of individuals in elite positions in politics and the civil service will naturally vary, our finding that there were large, systematic differences between politicians and bureaucrats would throw into serious doubt the concept of the state that motivates this research. While we can no more expect perfect agreement between the state elite groups than between all the individuals in each group, there should be much less variation between politicians and bureaucrats and between the levels of government than between the state elites and either capital or labour.

The interviews with business elites can be used to address a long-standing argument about what are variously termed "monopoly" and "competitive" sectors of capital, "big" and "small" business, and the "core" and "periphery." Big business is often portrayed as more liberal than small business, for example in James O'Connor's 1973 classic *The Fiscal Crisis of the State*, on the grounds that their market power allows large corporations to pass the burden of higher taxes and wages on to their customers. Smaller, competitive-sector businesses are said to be unable to pass on such higher costs, and their concerns about high wages are compounded by union challenges to the status and power of individualistic entrepreneurs. Aside from the issue of unions, however, it is possible to formulate an economically based counterargument to the view that smaller business is more right wing: social programs that provide universal benefits, such as medical care and pensions, relieve businesses of the cost of providing them, which may work to the advantage of poorer businesses that would otherwise have to provide these benefits themselves. A third line of argument suggests that there should be no systematic ideological differences between big and small business because, in the context of globalized conflict between capital and labour, the class positions of different sectors of capital do not differ substantially. It is also possible to argue that while in the past there were important sectoral divisions within the capitalist class, in recent times increased foreign competition and changes in technology have removed the traditional advantages of domestic monopolies and oligopolies.

Lawyers are not often included in studies of business elites, presumably because they act for capital, regulating the relations between corporations and between corporations and the state, but are not, in their own right, owners of substantial businesses. But this is precisely why they are especially interesting in a study of ideology. The legal elites in our sample actually have a lot in common with the business executives. As the senior partners of the largest Canadian law firms, our respondents have personal stakes in medium-sized businesses in a highly professionalized and to some extent oligopolistic sector. Furthermore in terms of income level the lawyers selected for our sample are in the same class as the top executives of the very largest corporations (see the figures in table 10-4), and the lawyers are wealthier! We expect their ideological views to reflect this class position. Still, compared to corporate executives, lawyers might be expected to have more liberal views on civil liberties issues, though not necessarily on affirmative action and more structurally based attacks on inequality. Whatever the merits of the alternative arguments about their *relative* positions, the differences between corporate executives, business owners, and lawyers should be smaller than the difference between capitalist and state elites. This question is somewhat rhetorical. While there are likely to be interesting differences between the groups, given the relatively extreme right-wing positions of business elite in the last chapter, which *combined* the three business groups that are compared in this chapter, none of these groups could have markedly left-wing opinions.

The elite academics, mass media executives, and farm organization leaders are all subject to conflicting influences. The academics are heirs to a tradition of critical thinking, but are now employees (often unionized) of large, state-funded bureaucratic organizations; the mass media executives may be subject to pressures from a relatively civil-libertarian professional community, but they are also the beneficiaries of an oligopolized industry that has enjoyed substantial regulatory protection from foreign competition; and, while farmers are almost entirely independent businesspeople, state intervention is critical to producers of export commodities and of the many commodities covered by marketing boards. These conflicting forces suggest that the ideology of academics, mass media elites, and agricultural leaders is likely to be closer to that of the state elites than either capital or labour. Particularly interesting will be their attitudes towards trade unions. While for the capitalist, labour, and state elites there would be a strong alignment between, say, support for social programs and support for trade unions, this is less likely to be true here. The mass media executives may be strongly supportive of state intervention because of the protection from foreign competition provided by the state (and some are employed by crown corporations), but as managers they are likely to oppose increasing the power of unions. Likewise many farmers are employers and many academics believe that the presence of trade unions on their campuses compromises the independence of the universities.

In the long-standing debate over the ideology of intellectuals, which Robert Brym (1980) summarizes, a key question is whether intellectuals tend to have a distinct ideology by virtue of their profession or position in society. Brym argues that it is not the functional role of intellectuals, but the particular historical circumstances – the prevailing balance of class forces in society at large and intellectuals' own economic and social position – that shape their ideology. While there is no large-scale published study of Canadian academics, there are two, now somewhat dated, American (1969 and 1972 surveys are described in Lipset and Ladd 1975) and British (a 1966 survey reported in Halsey and Trow 1971) studies. Both show academics to be more left wing than the general public, but not by a wide margin. At least in the U.S., academic liberalism is manifest more by the avoidance of extreme conservatism than by support for radical left-wing politics. Seymour Lipset and Everett Ladd (1975, 26) report the following distributions of *self-described* political orientations for a national sample of American faculty and of the general public: "left," 5 percent for the academics versus 4 percent for the general public; "liberal," 41 percent versus 16 percent; "middle-of-the-road," 27 percent versus 38 percent; "moderately conservative," 25 percent versus 32 percent; and "strongly conservative," 3 percent versus 10 percent. To the extent that academics are concerned with their corporate interest, they are very likely to focus their interest on the state, which employs them and funds their research. The membership of the Royal Society of Canada, from which half the academic elite sample was selected, is very heavily weighted towards the (we assume more conservative) biological and physical sciences. This suggests that Canadian academic elites should be expected to favour state intervention, but not to assume strongly pro-labour or pro-capitalist positions.

We begin with a discussion of the differences between the elite groups in four areas of social policy: social programs, economic policy, labour relations, and civil liberties. In light of the striking and consistent findings about the general right-left polarization of business, state, and labour in the last chapter, our intention is less to enlarge the scope of our argument about this ideological polarization than to clothe the abstraction with the substance of contemporary politics. Less important than the quite predictable relative positions of capital, state, and labour elites is the question of whether there is substantial support, say, for a guaranteed annual income, in *any* of the elite groups. Thus our aim is to develop an account of the ideology of the major elite groups that combines an analysis of their relative positions with an effort to locate their ideologies on the terrain of the contemporary political debates that defined the transitional period of the early 1980s.

The second section of this chapter extends the discussion to additional aspects of ideology, including medicare, foreign policy, and the federal-provincial division of power. While our theoretical inclinations push us towards privileging class-related aspects of ideology, contemporary governments must deal with many issues whose relation to class politics is ambiguous. The object of our inquiry, therefore, is to establish connections between different aspects of ideology and specifically to gauge the extent to which class aspects of ideology are overarching. For greater statistical precision the analysis is based on multi-item scales.

The third section of this chapter condenses the discussion of elite positions on discrete issues into an analysis of the major contending ideologies in contemporary capitalism. To what extent, say, do state elites articulate an ideology that is "social democratic," in the sense of seeing a role for the state beyond providing social programs to compensate for inequalities produced by a market economy, for example by state investments in industry? And what about trade union leaders? While they are obviously to the left of the capitalist and state elites, is there anything about labour elites' ideology that is consistent with the characterizations of Canadian politics that refer to the relations between elites in terms of "elite accommodation," "corporatism," and "tripartitism," with the implied ideological incorporation of labour elites? To answer these questions we set out a model of contemporary ideologies and to establish an empirical procedure to interpret the survey responses in terms of the model. We do so by triangulating between what we conceive to be the three central ideological dimensions in contemporary ideology, relating to state welfare policies, state intervention in the economy, and labour relations (see our discussion in chapter 3).

The last section of this chapter deals with party politics. Of course the distributions of party support are interesting to us, particularly in the context of the ideological orientations of the elite groups. Because the two "bourgeois" political parties, the Progressive Conservatives and Liberals, are less ideologically identified than the NDP, and because they have majority support in every group besides the trade union leaders, we will focus on the differences between their supporters. A key question is whether, when our surveys were conducted, before the ascendancy of the business-dominated Conservative party that characterized the Brian Mulroney governments, the Liberal and

Conservative parties had drawn the allegiance of ideologically defined camps of elites. We first determine whether the more conservative elite groups had distinct patterns of party allegiance. The problem, though, is that the observed connection between elite groups and political parties might involve less in the way of ideological adherence than organizational opportunism and historical factors. For example more conservative farm leaders might be drawn to the Progressive Conservative party, while local political elites with the same orientations might choose the Liberal party. To address this issue we use the three-dimensional model of elite ideology to examine whether the political divisions *within* elite groups correspond to party allegiances. The question is not whether (say) the generally more conservative business elites are more likely than other elite groups to support the Progressive Conservative party, but whether *within the business elite* more conservative individuals support the PCs, while more liberal individuals are Liberal party supporters.

A SURVEY OF ELITE IDEOLOGY IN FOUR AREAS

Aspects of Social Welfare

As the last chapter suggests, on a broad variety of social welfare issues elite opinion is marked by wide differences between the state elites, business, and labour in the survey. We asked them, "Do you think governments in Canada have cut back too much on social expenditures, that these cuts have been justified but there should be no further cuts, or that further cuts should be made?" As shown in table 9-1, 71 percent of the corporate executives, 54 percent of the business owners, and 47 percent of the lawyers endorsed further cuts, and just 1 percent of the executives said that the cuts had gone too far. Most of the state elites felt that the social welfare cutbacks already carried out were justified, but opposed further cuts, though the number supporting further cutbacks was much greater than the number opposed to cutbacks that had already taken place. At all three levels of government civil servants were much more supportive of cutbacks than the politicians, but there was relatively little variation between the levels of government. Again, the trade union leaders were quite isolated: 58 percent believed that cutbacks had gone too far and only 8 percent favoured further cutbacks. Similar patterns of response are found for questions dealing with income distribution. Unqualified support for a guaranteed annual income, for example, was voiced by about 15 percent of the business respondents, about 45 percent of the state elites, and 71 percent of the labour leaders.

Elite responses to the general questions about social programs contrast with their answers to more specific questions about health and medical care. Asked

Table 9-I
Opinion on Social Welfare Issues by Group

Group	View of cutbacks by government in social programs			Support for guaranteed annual income				Government effort for health and medical care			There is too much difference between rich and poor (percent)	Number of Cases
	Too great	No more	More cuts	Yes	Yes, qualified	No, qualified	No	More	Same	Less		
CAPITAL												
Corporate executives	1	28	71	10	17	9	65	12	79	9	22	217
Business owners	4	42	54	12	10	9	69	29	64	7	31	80
Lawyers	6	47	47	16	8	4	71	19	74	7	32	53
STATE												
Politicians												
federal	30	37	33	42	12	5	40	46	49	5	55	57
provincial	26	40	34	46	12	5	37	32	66	2	57	59
municipal	19	50	31	40	5	7	48	36	62	2	45	46
Bureaucrats												
federal	15	45	40	41	16	2	41	17	82	1	53	81
provincial	13	52	35	39	14	7	40	14	78	8	50	108
municipal	10	57	33	46	19	5	30	37	61	2	51	43
Trade unionists	58	34	8	71	15	3	11	76	24	0	83	139
Mass media executives	10	51	39	44	12	2	42	47	47	6	47	51
Academics	17	50	33	32	14	4	50	32	63	6	48	73
Farm leaders	22	61	17	40	10	25	25	45	55	0	65	20

whether government spending in this area should be increased, be decreased, or remain unchanged, the relative positions of the elite groups are the same, but their substantive positions were much more supportive of the welfare state. An overwhelming majority of respondents in each of the three business groups – between 64 and 79 percent – supported the status quo ("about the same effort"); and among those who did not support the status quo, the supporters of more expenditures outnumbered those endorsing further cutbacks. As table 8-2 shows, the combination of strong support for cutbacks of social programs as a whole with pragmatic support for the status quo on existing programs is not the accidental result of our having chosen to deal with health and medical care. Similar results are observed for the questions about support for education, workers' compensation, or other social programs.

Business owners and lawyers prove somewhat more supportive of social programs than corporate executives, but the variation among the business groups is not sufficient to overlap the range of positions of the six state groups. Nor are the differences between the business groups very consistent. Corporate executives are more likely to favour cutbacks than business owners and lawyers. These findings are clearly inconsistent with the argument that because of its greater ability to pay for state expenditures and need for a healthy and well-trained workforce, "monopoly" capital will be more supportive of this aspect of the welfare state.

Despite the theoretical arguments that suggest systematic differences between politicians and bureaucrats and between levels of government, there are only small differences in their responses to the questions about social welfare. These differences among the state groups are especially small in comparison to the large gap between the state and business and between the state and labour. Municipal politicians appear to be slightly more conservative than the five other groups and, for all three levels of government, the politicians are marginally more liberal on welfare issues than the bureaucrats. These patterns are not very consistent over the range of questions in the survey. A more sophisticated analysis based on scales, in the next section, is required to tell us whether there are underlying, systematic disagreements.

On these issues academics are close to the state elites. For example 48 percent of the academics agreed that there is too much of a difference between rich and poor in Canada, compared to between 45 and 57 percent for the six state groups; and 33 percent of the academics, close to the average for the six state groups, wanted more cutbacks in social programs. The mass media executives are on the conservative side of the range of opinion defined by the six state elite groups; 39 percent of them, for example, supported further cutbacks in social programs, compared to between 31 and 40 percent for the six state groups, 71 percent of the corporate executives, and 8 percent of the trade unionists. The farm organization leaders generally fall on the liberal side of the range of the six state groups.

It is possible to differentiate between the survey questions as well as between the elite groups. Generally speaking there is more inter-elite conflict over the general formulations than over more specific policy issues. Wholesale business support for the rhetoric of cutbacks and justification of existing inequalities, for example, is combined with only weak support for cutbacks in specific areas. The right-wing ideological commitments of business leaders coexist with quite pragmatic views about what should or can be done with specific, existing social programs (which, of course, address real needs and have the support of strong constituencies).

Government Economic Policies

Consistent with our previous results, and as shown in table 9-2, direct government investment in industry, and the particular example of the Saskatchewan government's nationalization of a part of the potash industry, evokes very strong opposition from the corporate executives and lawyers. The business owners also opposed government investment and the potash takeover by a strong majority, but not quite so strongly. The state elites were quite divided on the potash takeover, with a complex pattern of differences among six groups. Stronger support for the potash takeover was found among the federal political and bureaucratic elites and the provincial bureaucratic elite. Only the trade union leaders, however, gave strong support to the takeover.

Only the municipal bureaucrats, and then by just a small margin, gave majority support to the use of wage controls to combat inflation. Most strongly opposed to such controls were the corporate executives, followed by the trade unionists! Business owners and the lawyers were also strongly opposed to controls. Wage controls thus evoke an interesting conflict between state elites pursuing interventionist policies that enhance their own power against the power of *both* business and labour. This axis of conflict is not general, however; all the other items exhibit the characteristic right-left polarization between capital and labour, with the state intermediate. These data demonstrate the consistency of state "mediation" of capital-labour conflict, rather than the corporatist accommodation of conflict within the state through an elite consensus on incomes policy.

The corporate executives and lawyers were the strongest supporters of the use of tight money policies to combat inflation; more than 80 percent of each group approved. The business owners, 68 percent of whom approved of tight money, are in the range of opinion voiced by the various state groups, between 54 and 71 percent of which approved of tight money. To this policy, however, there was strong labour opposition. "Monetarism," as an ideological alternative to the Keynesian social welfare state compromise or mediation of capital-labour conflicts, was therefore a relatively powerful factor uniting the state and capital in Canada by the early 1980s. However, the de-

Table 9-2
Policies to Combat Inflation and Government Investments in Industry, by Group

Group	Approve of wage controls to combat inflation			Approve of tight money to combat inflation			Approve of government investments in industry			Approve of Saskatchewan government potash takeover		
	Yes	Neither	No	Yes	Neither	No	Yes	Neither	No	Yes	Neither	No
CAPITAL												
Corporate executives	9	4	87	84	8	8	6	6	88	7	6	87
Business owners	29	9	62	68	15	17	22	11	67	12	18	70
Lawyers	21	7	72	84	10	6	17	2	81	14	10	76
STATE												
Politicians												
federal	13	12	75	67	11	22	46	7	47	40	11	49
provincial	36	8	56	54	11	35	42	6	52	34	12	54
municipal	47	13	40	55	17	28	33	13	54	31	9	60
Bureaucrats												
federal	28	18	54	71	9	20	45	10	45	44	23	33
provincial	30	18	52	66	16	18	44	7	49	44	18	38
municipal	37	12	51	74	16	10	42	23	35	33	16	51
Trade unionists	19	4	77	30	18	52	67	12	21	73	10	17
Mass media executives	29	8	63	57	28	25	25	12	63	35	12	53
Academics	35	18	47	52	29	19	51	8	41	52	21	27
Farm leaders	45	10	45	45	20	35	70	0	30	65	0	35

fects of this alternative as a hegemonic approach are indicated by the strong opposition of labour elites.

Not surprisingly the corporate executives and lawyers were extremely favourable to foreign investment and *un*favourable to foreign investment review. As shown in table 9-3, just 31 percent of corporate executives approved of the Foreign Investment Review Act (FIRA), 57 percent disapproved, and 13 percent were neither in favour nor opposed. In comparison, 68 percent of the business owners, between 50 and 79 percent of the various state elite groups, and 93 percent of the labour union leaders approved of FIRA. Economic self-interest explains the executive support for foreign investment and also the business owners' support for FIRA, which may have offered them some protection from competition. Assessments of the overall impact of foreign investment on the Canadian economy follow a similar pattern. Again there is strong evidence of ideological conflict between capital and the state elites, which is difficult to reconcile with the view that a broad ideological consensus – even if labour is excluded – governs the formation of policy. That the Mulroney government subsequently abolished FIRA and substantially shifted government policy in favour of foreign investment is, at once, testimony to the dramatic increase in the influence of large corporations on government policy and evidence that the relationship between capital and the state remains problematic. However, the historical shifts in the political influence of big business, in this and other areas, show that influence must be fought for; it is not a manifestation of the structure of advanced capitalism.

At the time of our survey, free trade between Canada and the U.S. occupied a far less prominent position in the political arena than after the completion of the MacDonald Commission report and the Mulroney government's successful effort to reach a free trade agreement after the 1984 election. The various elite groups had relatively *un*differentiated views on this topic in the early 1980s and there was less consensus within the capitalist and state sectors than would develop subsequently. Still, 60 percent of corporate executives, 66 percent of the business owners, and 57 percent of the lawyers approved of free trade; and the trade unionists were nearly evenly split. Among the state elites support for free trade was strongest among the local-level bureaucrats and weakest among the federal politicians and bureaucrats and provincial bureaucrats. The corporate executives were nearly evenly split over the continental energy pact, while the business owners and lawyers favoured it by large majorities.

While fairly similar to the pattern of responses to the issue of free trade, it is apparent that negotiation of a continental energy pact, which would presumably involve some Canadian guarantees to supply energy to the U.S., raised distinctive problems for our respondents. The generally continentalist business executives were quite evenly split on the issue, so business support for the energy pact was considerably weaker than their support for free trade.

Table 9-3
Opinion on Foreign Investment and Economic Relationships with the U.S., by Group

Group	Assessment of overall effect of foreign investment on the Canadian economy				Approve of passage of FIRA			Approve of negotiation of continental energy pact			Approve of free trade between U.S. and Canada		
	Mostly good	Some good	Mixed	Some/ mostly bad	Yes	Neither	No	Yes	Neither	No	Yes	Neither	No
CAPITAL													
Corporate executives	59	31	8	2	31	13	57	47	12	41	60	13	27
Business owners	46	28	16	10	68	10	22	71	10	19	66	7	27
Lawyers	60	27	11	2	42	6	52	61	10	29	57	16	27
STATE													
Politicians													
federal	28	31	23	18	70	4	26	31	5	64	37	20	43
provincial	38	25	20	17	50	11	39	49	13	38	51	16	33
municipal	27	38	22	13	71	3	26	55	9	36	50	14	36
Bureaucrats													
federal	25	33	26	16	78	8	14	26	9	65	41	13	46
provincial	33	39	24	12	66	16	18	43	14	43	37	20	43
municipal	24	40	24	12	79	14	7	67	9	24	64	14	22
Trade unionists	11	22	34	33	93	3	4	59	6	35	47	10	43
Mass media executives	29	31	29	11	82	10	8	47	6	46	54	15	31
Academics	30	22	33	15	86	9	5	42	6	52	47	15	38
Farm leaders	0	20	35	45	94	6	0	48	11	41	21	11	68

The trade unionists, however, gave stronger support to the energy pact (59 percent in favour) than to free trade (47 percent in favour).

As with our questions about social programs, table 9-3 gives evidence of very large group differences on the broad issue of whether foreign investment has benefited the economy and much smaller differences over specific policy issues. In addition, there are major changes in the relative positions of the groups. While the labour leaders were the most pessimistic about the effect of foreign investment on the Canadian economy, they were relatively supportive of free trade and evenly split over a continental energy pact. Of course subsequent to our survey a strong business-labour polarization over free trade developed. While corporate support for free trade increased, there was a much more striking shift in the labour movement, which was deeply divided on the issue at the time of our survey, but strongly opposed the Free Trade Agreement. Previous to free trade's taking centre stage and becoming the focus of a federal election campaign, the ambivalence of labour leaders on this issue stood in sharp contrast to their polarization towards the left on other issues. As attention came to focus on the issue, the labour leaders' positions on free trade came into alignment with their relatively pessimistic views of the past effects of foreign investment and their positions on social programs and other issues.

Academics' views on economic policies closely resembled those of the state elites, even on the questions dealing with foreign investment. Debates over hiring foreign academics had apparently done little to raise academic elites' concern about the dangers of foreign economic domination. The farm leaders were most distinctive in their views on the economy: they proved to be the most nationalistic of all the elite groups. Nearly half the farm leaders believed that foreign investment had had some or mostly bad effects on the development of the Canadian economy and 68 percent opposed free trade with the U.S. (only 21 percent were in favour and 11 percent were ambivalent). This strong nationalism suggests that farmers saw the state not only as protecting their place in the Canadian economy, but also as protection from foreign, often subsidized, competition. Media executives were also strongly supportive of FIRA. Not surprisingly, media executives gave the strongest support (68 percent approval) to abolition of censor boards – a stand reflecting both their professional and economic self-interest. Their critical stand on the police, though, suggests their position does reflect a broader commitment to civil liberties. Media elites' support for FIRA likely reflects the high degree of protection that the mass media have had from foreign takeover, as well as the need to define a distinct national cultural terrain that is theirs.

Labour Relations

As shown in table 9-4, the trade unionists are dramatically isolated from the state elites and capital on labour relations issues. A ban on strikebreaking by

Table 9-4
Opinion on Labour Union Issues, by Group

Group	Prohibit hiring of strikebreakers			Legislation should be used to decrease the power of unions			Prohibit postal workers from striking			Employees should be represented on corporate boards		
	Agree	Neutral	Disagree	Agree	Neutral	Disagree	Agree	Neutral	Disagree	Agree	Neutral	Disagree
CAPITAL												
Corporate executives	26	7	67	51	25	24	70	5	25	13	18	69
Business owners	8	10	82	69	18	13	79	5	16	38	14	48
Lawyers	29	8	63	42	23	35	78	10	12	29	16	55
STATE												
Politicians												
federal	32	13	55	42	14	44	54	2	44	79	12	9
provincial	38	7	55	37	19	44	52	15	33	54	15	31
municipal	51	2	47	51	13	36	49	9	42	48	4	48
Bureaucrats												
federal	38	6	56	40	18	42	40	5	55	60	22	18
provincial	37	7	56	46	21	33	54	6	40	53	18	29
municipal	59	2	39	56	21	23	51	12	37	55	17	28
Trade unionists	94	2	4	6	0	94	13	4	83	60	22	18
Mass media executives	28	12	60	44	16	40	51	4	45	55	11	34
Academics	41	6	53	52	10	38	46	13	41	62	14	24
Farm leaders	45	5	50	42	0	58	30	5	65	60	15	25

corporations, for example, was supported by 26 percent of the corporate executives, 8 percent of the business owners, and 29 percent of the lawyers, compared to between 32 and 59 percent for the six categories of state respondents, and 94 percent of the labour leaders. The pattern of responses to these labour relations items is quite uniform: trade unionists are isolated on the left; state elites are significantly to the left of business, but closer to business than labour. Within the capitalist sector, business owners are considerably to the right of corporate executives and lawyers.

The state elites and labour leaders took similar positions on workers' representation on corporate boards, with about 60 percent approving. While the business owners were relatively sympathetic to worker representation, business opponents of the measure still outnumbered its supporters. Of course, even without an exemption of smaller businesses from any legislation, business owners would not be much affected by a law calling for worker representatives on their boards, since the boards of smaller businesses usually have a nominal role and often consist entirely of the business owners and related family.

More than two-thirds of the corporate executives opposed worker representation on corporate boards and more than half of the remainder were neutral, rather than approving. Thus corporate executives' more liberal responses (at least compared to the business owners) to most of the items bearing directly on the bargaining power of unions, combine with a more conservative position on the issue of board representation. This might reflect an allegiance to the structures of traditional labour-management relations, but it probably has more to do with not wanting to share power. On the other hand, the labour leaders' support for board representation is a surprising contrast to the Canadian labour movement's expressed lack of interest in co-management. Perhaps the lack of labour movement enthusiasm for co-management reflects as much an assessment of the continuing hostility to any reform on the part of business as it does a radical opposition to attempts to co-opt labour. In any event these findings make sense of the absence of any serious effort on the part of state elites to broker a co-optive incorporation of labour into the policy process. At that time corporatism had very little ideological support in Canada as a means of salvaging the Keynesian welfare state.

The academic elites were divided on these issues. A majority opposed a ban on strikebreaking, by a margin of 53 to 41 percent, with 6 percent taking no position; and 52 percented support legislation to decrease the power of unions. At least at the elite level, the increasing unionization of universities was accompanied by no more than lukewarm commitment to the larger goals of the trade union movement. This can be seen in the virtual absence of university unions from the collective leadership, including both local labour councils and the central organizations, of the union movement. Mass media executives responded to these questions more like

Table 9-5
Percent Supporting* Four Policies Regarding Civil Liberties, by Group

Group	Legislation to protect homosexuals from job discrimination	Elimination of existing provincial boards of censors	Abolition of the War Measures Act	Civilian review of complaints against the police
CAPITAL				
Corporate executives	53	44	21	71
Business owners	51	38	17	69
Lawyers	40	28	17	66
STATE				
Politicians				
federal	61	47	47	77
provincial	44	30	35	82
municipal	64	33	30	70
Bureaucrats				
federal	70	55	28	80
provincial	61	38	24	84
municipal	65	35	10	84
Trade unionists	84	60	61	87
Mass media executives	72	68	44	94
Academics	80	49	31	78
Farm leaders	65	15	40	65

* Including qualified approval, as stated spontaneously by the respondent

state elites than executives, though they opposed prohibiting strikebreakers by a two-to-one margin. The agricultural organization leaders held similar positions. Despite representing a constituency of small-business people, some of whom employed farm workers, the agricultural leaders views' were nothing like the right-wing positions of the business owners. Of course, even relative to the business owners, most farmers have very small businesses.

Civil Liberties Issues

Compared to the issues just discussed, there was relatively little inter-elite conflict over civil liberties issues, summarized in table 9-5. Surprisingly, in view of the small number of cities in which there is civilian review of complaints against the police, at least two-thirds of the respondents in each group approved of this measure. Only the lawyers and provincial civil servants did not give majority support to protecting the civil rights of homosexuals. Only about one-third of the business and state elites supported the elimination of movie censorship. Abolition of the War Measures Act received the least overall support (only the labour leaders gave it majority support) and it generated the most inter-elite conflict.

Academics were more likely than any of the state elites to favour protecting the civil rights of homosexuals, but their opinions on film censorship (49 percent favoured its abolition), abolition of the War Measures Act, and civilian review of complaints against the police were close to those of the state elites. Farm leaders gave responses near those of the state elites for the items dealing with discrimination against homosexuals and the War Measures Act, but they were notably conservative on issues of censorship (only 15 percent would eliminate censorship) and civilian review of complaints against the police. While media executives were on the conservative side of the range of opinion defined by the six state elite groups, on two questions they were more civil libertarian than state elites. They were the most likely to favour elimination of boards of censors and civilian review of complaints against the police.

Although conflict over civil liberties is generally much weaker than for other policy domains, the relative positions of the groups are not different from what was observed in the other, more plainly class-divided domains. The labour leaders took the most liberal positions – business on the right and the state elites in between. Interestingly, on these issues, the lawyers were more conservative than the two other business groups: only 40 percent approved of legislated protection from job discrimination of homosexuals and 28 percent supported the elimination of existing boards of censors. The differences among the state elite groups were again quite small and the relative positions of the six groups varied somewhat according to the issue. For example while provincial politicians were the least likely of the six state elites to support legislation to protect homosexuals and the elimination of censorship, they were near the average of the state groups in their support for abolition of the War Measures Act and for civilian review of complaints against the police. The federal politicians and bureaucrats were marginally more liberal than their provincial and local counterparts. The relative positions of the politicians and bureaucrats varied according to the issue. There may be some systematic patterns of differences among the six state elite groups, but they are so small that only a only a statistical analysis based on multi-item scales will provide sufficient precision to detect them. There is indeed a "liberal" ideological consensus among elites on questions of civil liberties, but consensus is limited to those issues, and there is sharply structured conflict on the issues of social welfare, economic policy, and labour relations.

Summary and Discussion

The political terrain mapped by these data has the labour leaders located on the left, business on the right, and the state elites somewhere in between, precisely where being a function of what is at stake. There are systematic differences between the three sectors of capital and between the six state groups, but these differences are only moderately large, relative to the enormous ideological gap between capital and labour. Returning to the conceptualizations of relations between capital and the state discussed in chapter 7, we can see that the pervasive conflicts between capital, the state elites, and labour suggest that policy making involves the resolution of genuine conflicts corresponding to the economic and political interests of the parties. While there is obviously elite agreement on the "rules of the game," in the sense that none would likely favour a military insurrection as the medium of social change, the ideologies of the elite groups certainly cannot be characterized in terms of global consensus. Our findings are not compatible with pluralist theories of elite liberalism, corporatism, or economist versions of Marxist theories of the state, either state monopoly capitalist or instrumentalist. It may be – or at least one cannot imagine a means of disproving – that an overarching consensus in support of the fundamental principles of capitalism underlies the expressed opinions of business, the state, and even labour leaders, but the concrete formation of social policies is riven with conflict.

By defining the ideological terrain sufficiently narrowly, particularly in the direction of attitudes on some "civil liberties" issues, one could at least approach finding an ideological common ground. But it should be apparent from our data that there is widespread conflict over issues affecting the fundamental powers of social classes. Nor does it seem possible to sustain a weaker version of corporatism in which consensus is the necessary response to crisis. It is especially ironic that K.J. Rea and J.T. McCleod (1976) should describe free trade as the sort of external threat that would arouse from Canadians an "organic corporatist" response. Even narrowing the circle of consensus by excluding the trade union leadership does not explain the substantial ideological gap between business and the state on policy issues and the implausibility even of a limited business-state corporatism.

As explanations of our findings we are left, therefore, with radical pluralist and neo-Marxist theories, which explain inter-elite conflict in terms of the associated divisions of labour and differences in interests. These theoretical approaches share a perception of conflictual relations within the state, although pluralists tend to emphasize the contribution of conflict and conflict resolution to systemic stability, while Marxists emphasize tendencies towards instability. Why not favour a pluralist interpretation of these data, which would account for the inter-elite differences without dragging in the heavy theoretical baggage of class conflict that comes with Marxist accounts? We acknowledge that this difference between pluralism and Marxism cannot be resolved by our data, but there is a strong reason to favour the Marxist interpretation. Simply put, Marxism provides a surer guide to the actual ideological positions of the parties. Marxist approaches explain political conflicts in terms of the structure of conflicting group interests, which are rooted in production relations, and contradictory tendencies in the dynamic development of the economy. In our view this is theoretically superior to pluralist accounts in which conflicting *interests* are placed in the institutions of state and civil society, but no theoretical explanation is given to account for the extent and content of the salient political conflicts in a given place and time.

With reference to arguments in Marxist theories of the capitalist state, our results address Fred Block's contention that corporate elites cannot be regarded as "class conscious" in the sense of being able to formulate a viable political project of capitalist rule. In relation to the other elite positions, the positions of corporate elites reflected in responses to our questionnaire are not only consistently right wing, but potentially politically destabilizing. They are strongly opposed to increasing the power of trade unions, relatively opposed to the co-optation of labour, "middle of the road" on civil rights issues, right wing on social welfare issues posed in a general way, but supportive of the status quo on specific programs, pro-foreign investment and continentalist, fiscally conservative, and opposed to state investment in business. On these grounds it is hard to argue that the Canadian capitalist class lacks class consciousness. Even without the advantage of hindsight, it can be seen that in the early 1980s Canadian capital had a pervasive ideology, which would be predicted to give rise to policies distinctly to the right of those pursued by the state at the time.

The important conflicts between capital and the state require us to take seriously the semi-autonomy of the state, though not to disregard the relative influences of capital and labour. Our findings suggest that there is a state interest – in opposition to the demands of labour *and* capital – that involves the pursuit of the state's institutional interests, but still embodies the domination of capital and its protection; but we differentiate this from immediate rule by capital. Supporting our argument that there is such a defined state interest is the absence of strong ideological differences between elected politicians and civil servants. Our data give very weak support to Joel Aberbach, Robert Putnam, and Bert Rockman's (1981) contention that bureaucrats stabilize a political system that, if controlled by elected politicians, would be prone to erratic policy shifts. Since bureaucrats and politicians are not divided over key issues, bureaucratic control can only produce more consistent, but not ideologically distinct, policy. Finally, the lack of systematic cleavages between the levels of government suggests that the conflicts that do exist involve disputes over their turf, rather than overarching differences of principle.

The relatively small ideological differences between corporate executives, business owners, and lawyers confirm our understanding, from the last chapter, in which the three groups were lumped together, that business ideology overwhelmingly reflects class interest. In addition, however, there are consistent differences. Compared to corporate executives, business owners were less opposed to government investment and more critical of foreign investment, more anti-union but less conservative on social welfare issues than the corporate executives. Business owners are more antagonistic to the working class, but more supportive of state programs that reproduce the working class and of state intervention in the economy. These findings are incompatible with conceptions of the capitalist class that emphasize the liberalism of the largest corporations – linking their high degree of economy security, assured by market control, to a willingness to pay for social programs to buy social peace and provide highly skilled workers. Whether or not such a golden age of corporate domination existed in the past, by the time of our surveys the oil shock of the mid-1970s and increased global competition had destroyed the economic basis for corporate liberalism.

The elite academics in our sample merit no reputation for radicalism. Their ideology closely resembles that of the state elites on whom they are financially dependent. While we expected that any academic radicalism might be weaker on issues involving the power of labour, in no area of ideology do the academics take particularly radical positions. Academics may not deserve the reputation of being anti-establishment, but the academic elite is not particularly conservative. In the context of generalized conflict between the business, labour, and state elites, the academics are quite liberal, favouring social programs and civil liberties, but not particularly supportive of redistribution or the labour movement. This assessment is quite consistent with Lipset and Ladd's characterization of American academic opinion ten years earlier. Their ideological profile suggests that elite academics are "organic intellectuals" to use Antonio Gramsci's term – the articulators and defenders of the ruling ideas that shape a state's hegemony.

Despite the corporate domination of the mass media in Canada, our surveys show that mass media executives are consistently more liberal than the corporate executives and business owners. Of course this may reflect the ideological difference between top executives and proprietors of business and the less powerful managers who are represented in our mass media sample. Like the academics the mass media elites are closest to the state elites in ideology. This differentiates the mass media from the corporate elites, but only from the extreme right can this be construed as anti-establishment thinking.

While they speak for a constituency composed almost entirely of small-business owners, except for their conservative views on censorship and the police, the farm leaders have nothing in common with the ideology of business elites. The farm organization leaders are somewhat to the left of the state elites in their views of social programs, redistribution, and labour rights, – though not nearly as far left as the trade union leaders.

BROAD ASPECTS OF POLITICAL IDEOLOGY

Thus far we have focused on what appeared and empirically were shown to be class-related aspects of political ideology, including a variety of specific social welfare, economic, and labour relations issues. These aspects of ideology alone, however, are not sufficient to constitute a formula for dealing with the great variety of policy questions that engage advanced capitalist society. Nations must manage their external relationships with other countries and the internal relations between their regions and levels of governments.

In order to provide a more general picture of elite ideology, we constructed scales by summing the responses to individual survey items that had been shown, using factor analysis, to measure a single underlying dimension. The items contributing to each of the scales are given in appendix C. Three of the scales derive mainly from the items discussed in the last section; they measure support for the welfare state, support for state economic intervention, and support for trade unions (in tables 9-1, 9-2, and 9-4, respectively) – these are what we conceive to be the core dimensions of ideology. The scale of support for civil liberties also is mainly constructed from items just discussed (in table 9-5). Four additional scales measure support for socialized medicine, critical views of foreign investment, support for left-wing foreign policy, and support for the powers of the federal government relative to the provincial governments. In order to facilitate comparisons between the scales they are calibrated in the same way: the mean score of all the state elites (i.e., combining the six subgroups together) is set to zero, so the positions of the other elite groups are relative to the position of the state elites. Each scale is also standardized so that the standard deviation for the state elites is equal to 100. Table 9-6 gives the mean score on each scale for the thirteen elite sectors. At the right of each row in the table is the percentage of variance in the scale explained by group membership; larger values of the explained variance indicate greater degrees of *dis*agreement among the elite groups.

Table 9-6 shows the broad left-right polarization that characterizes elite opinion on the welfare state, state economic intervention, and trade unions just seen in the last section. In each case the corporate executives are about one hundred points (i.e., one standard deviation of the scale) on the right side of the state elites and the trade union leaders are at least as far on the other side of the scale. The polarization is greatest for support for trade unions, where the group difference explains 43.2 percent of the variance. The range of opinion among the six state groups is very limited, with no strong or consistent tendencies characterizing the relative positions of bureaucrats and politicians or the three levels of government. Farm leaders are somewhat to the left of the state elites and mass media executives somewhat to the right.

A partial exception to this left-right polarization of ideology is the measure of support for civil rights, which deals with affirmative action and aid to minorities.

Table 9-6
Means of Various Political Attitude Scales, by Group

Ideology Measure	Business			Politicians			Civil Servants			Labour	Mass media executives	Acad-emics	Farm leaders	Percent variance explained by group
	Corp-orate	Owners	Law-yers	Fed-eral	Prov-incial	Munic-ipal	Fed-eral	Prov-incial	Munic-ipal					
Support for the welfare state	-93	-69	-76	19	13	-4	-18	0	-6	140	-18	12	34	36.0
Support for state economic intervention	-122	-38	-94	0	-27	0	12	-3	25	103	-32	21	54	35.9
Support for trade unions	-97	-133	-60	17	-3	2	15	-14	-14	173	-39	-1	19	43.2
Support socialized medicine	-73	-20	-79	-3	-20	-15	11	5	13	92	-10	33	38	24.5
Civil liberties	-49	-21	-96	22	-19	3	13	-6	-17	59	10	12	18	13.6
Critical of foreign investment	-102	-54	-90	16	-20	-19	15	-11	30	71	-27	27	42	28.1
Support left-wing foreign policy	-73	-40	-62	-4	-4	-11	1	12	-9	98	-8	16	31	25.6
Increase power of federal relative to provincial governments	0	51	-16	28	-46	12	31	-29	29	75	8	56	39	8.7

As noted in our previous discussion of table 9-1, the alignment of the groups on this scale is the same as for opinion on the welfare state though with less inter-group polarization. Because the positions on civil rights issues of both the corporate executives and labour leaders are less extreme positions than for the three central dimensions of ideology, the elite-sector differences account for only 14 percent of the variance in this scale – around half the variance for the measures relating to the welfare state, state economic intervention, and labour relations.

Medical care is one policy area in which more general ideological orientations must be translated into positions on complex policy questions. The measure of support for socialized medicine is made up of questions dealing with physicians' right to extra-bill for medical service covered by provincial health plans, government supporting group practices with salaried physicians and paramedical personnel, replacing health care premiums with (more progressive) income tax revenues, and paying salaries to all medical personnel. By the middle of the 1980s these questions more clearly involved the trade-off between higher-cost market-driven medical care and lower-cost but ideologically more left-wing socialized medicine. At the time of our surveys, when the cost implications of free-market medicine were not so clear and the fiscal stringency not so acute, the ideological aspects of the delivery of medical care were clearly primary. With 24.5 percent of the variance in this measure explained by elite sector, and from the pattern of mean scores in table 9-6, policy preferences in this area replicate the directly class-based aspects of ideology. Again there are only minor divisions within the state. The difference between the means of the groups giving the strongest and weakest support (the provincial politicians and municipal bureaucrats, respectively) is only thirty-three points (or one-third of a standard deviation). As with the measure of state economic intervention, there is a considerable gap between big capital, corporate executives and lawyers, and medium-size and small business. A logical explanation is that smaller employers would rather have tax revenues pay for medical care than have to provide it as a benefit to their workers, though it might also reflect their somewhat less conservative views (except, of course, on labour issues).

Two scales deal with Canada's international relations. One dealing with foreign investment includes questions like those in table 9-3 and the other measures support for more left-wing foreign policy, using questions about resisting the spread of communism, international economic relations, foreign aid, and South Africa. On these dimensions the relative positions of the elite groups are closely aligned with their positions on social welfare and the other scales described above. The variation between the groups is slightly smaller – 28.1 percent for foreign investment and 25.6 percent for foreign policy – because the gap between capital and labour is not as large as for the other scales.

If the class position of the elites guides their responses to questions about foreign investment and foreign policy, the same is not true of the relative powers of the federal and provincial governments. While it is not surprising that the federal and provincial politicians and civil servants should be at odds, the alignment of the other groups is more surprising. First, while municipal governments are responsible to provincial governments, their political leaders and civil servants tend to favour the federal over the provincial governments. By a considerable margin the labour leaders are the most strongly federalist group, followed by the academics, business owners, and farm leaders. The corporate executives and lawyers are divided on this issue, demonstrating that at the time of our survey business had no uniform strategy, effectively favouring the status quo.

Taking all eight scales, a comparison of the mean scores for the six state groups indicates little in the way of a consistent left-right polarization or, for that matter, of generalized conflicts between the levels of government and between politicians and bureaucrats. On social programs there is a significant difference between more supportive politicians and less supportive bureaucrats, but no difference between the levels of government. Opinions on foreign investment and government investment in industry exhibit a quite different pattern: the federal politicians and bureaucrats are significantly more nationalistic and interventionist than the provincial politicians and bureaucrats. But at the municipal level the politicians were more conservative than the bureaucrats. Beyond these differences, and the conflict between federal and provincial elites over the division of powers, there are few differences among the state elites.

Table 9-6 reveals significant differences between the corporate executives and business owners, though this conflict takes place on a distinctly right-of-centre ideological terrain. This confirms the impressions from the last section, that corporate executives are *more conservative* than their counterparts in smaller businesses. Corporate executives are much more strongly opposed to state investments in industry and much less critical of foreign investment than business owners. And there is also substantially less opposition to socialized medicine among the business owners. Of course, the business owners are even more virulently anti-union than the business executives.

The correlations among the various dimensions of ideology constitute a more direct measure of relations between different aspects of ideology. In table 9-7 the correlations below the diagonal apply to the entire elite sample, and above the diagonal are the correlations for the capitalist, state, and labour elites, separately. The correlations for the entire sample exhibit a simple pattern. The highest correlations, ranging between .59 and .70, are between the measures relating to the welfare state, government economic intervention, socialized medicine, foreign investment, and foreign policy. Slightly smaller are the correlations measuring the relationship between these five variables and support for trade unions. Considerably weaker – the range is .39 to .51 – but nevertheless still strong are the correlations between support for affirmative ac-

Table 9-7
Correlations between Various Political Attitude Scales, for the Entire Elite Sample below the Diagonal and Separately for Capitalist, State, and Labour Elites above the Diagonal

		a	b	c	d	e	f	g	h	Elite Sector
			.48	.26	.38	.38	.38	.10	.49	Capital
a	Welfare state	...	.63	.48	.47	.56	.56	.15	.62	State .
			.56	.47	.48	.58	.50	.12	.68	Labour
				.18	.38	.52	.62	.24	.55	Capital
b	Government economic	.70	...	.41	.45	.56	.64	.29	.56	State
	intervention			.53	.35	.62	.62	.25	.59	Labour
					.11	.06	.15	.01	.21	Capital
c	Trade unions	.64	.57	...	.34	.43	.40	.04	.52	State
					.41	.41	.42	.09	.42	Labour
						.24	.22	.19	.28	Capital
d	Civil liberties	.51	.51	.39	...	.40	.41	.09	.41	State
						.29	.22	.08	.43	Labour
							.38	.25	.41	Capital
e	Socialized medicine	.64	.66	.51	.41	...	.53	.20	.49	State
							.49	.13	.59	Labour
								.16	.47	Capital
f	Critical of foreign	.61	.72	.51	.40	.59	...	.21	.53	State
	investment							.07	.55	Labour
									.13	Capital
g	Support more left-wing	.70	.66	.59	.43	.61	.63	...	.12	State
	foreign policy								.00	Labour
										Capital
h	Increase the power of	.16	.29	.11	.14	.24	.21	.17	...	State
	federal government									Labour

tion and these six variables. By far the weakest are the correlations involving the federal versus provincial powers, which range from .11 to .29.

With the exception of the measure of support for labour, the larger correlations involve the aspects of ideology characterized by *greater* inter-elite conflict, as measured by the explained variances in the analysis above. That the correlations between the labour dimension and the other scales are lower suggests that labour issues are a less important source of ideological orientation than views of the welfare state and government economic intervention. This is likely because policies towards the welfare state, and particularly questions about the cost and efficacy of social programs and state economic intervention, were more the subject of contention at the time of the survey. That support for socialized medicine and foreign investment should be tightly tied to views of welfare state and economic intervention is not surprising. The strong relationship between foreign policy and these dimensions indicate that respondents' views of the Canadian state, as a welfare state and an economic regulator, correspond to their views of international issues. There is a weak positive relationship between favouring the federal government over the provincial governments and progressive views on other issues.

The next question is whether the ideological map just drawn applies equally to the *internal* divisions within capital, labour, and the state, both in terms of the average strength of the relationships between the dimensions of ideology and in terms of the pattern. Generally we should expect the correlations computed separately for sectoral groups should be somewhat smaller than the correlations for the entire sample, because the range of variation within the groups is smaller (decreasing the reliability of the dimensions as indicators of internal differentiation within those groups). In table 9-7 there are important differences between the patterns of correlations in the three groups. For the capitalist elites the highest correlations are between the measures relating to state economic intervention, socialized medicine, foreign investment, and foreign policy; support for the welfare state is not quite as central and weaker still are the relationships between these dimensions and the measures dealing with federal-provincial powers, civil liberties, and trade union powers. Thus, central to ideological disputes among capitalist elites are debates over the economic role of the state. That support for socialized medicine is more tightly related to the central ideological ensemble than more general views of the welfare state reflects ideologically charged contention over the state regulation of medicine. The very weak correlation between views of labour and the other measures suggests that labour-relations issues are too unimportant to constitute a major source of ideological cleavage within capital, perhaps because labour is seen to pose relatively little threat to capital, compared to the encroachments by the state.

The state and labour elites exhibit similar patterns of correlations, which strongly resemble those of the sample as a whole (for the state elites this is partly because they constitute a large proportion of the total sample). For the state and labour elites the five most highly correlated measures relate to the welfare state, state economic intervention, socialized medicine, foreign investment, and foreign policy. The *two* critical roles of the state, in social programs and regulation of the economy, are both central. This compares with the slightly greater importance of the economic issues to business elites. For state and labour elites, as for capitalists, views of foreign policy are tied tightly to their views of Canadian society and economy.

These correlations indicate a fundamental similarity in the way that three major elites structure their ideological views. There are differences in emphasis, but no more. State intervention in the form of the social programs that compensate for inequities produced by market relations and state regulation and investment occupy central stage in the organization of elite ideology. Views of the fundamental conflict between labour and capital evoke widely different allegiances, but these have little to do with other political/ ideological alignments. One possibility is that at the time of the survey labour relations were in such an ossified state that opinions on this issue were not often mobilized in elites' global understandings of politics. Indeed, relative to the ongoing withdrawal of the federal government from social programs and the rapid acceleration of state intervention in the economy in the late 1970s, labour relations have changed very slowly.

The analysis of these additional dimensions of ideology lends support to our theoretical focus on the relations between capital, labour, and the state, as indicated by measures of support for the welfare state, state intervention in the economy, and labour relations. These dimensions provoke the sharpest division between elites and, with relatively minor and interpretable variations, are consistent with elite differences over foreign policy, socialized medicine, affirmative action, and foreign investment. Federal-provincial relations are clearly not part of this ideological universe, and must be seen as quintessentially political in the sense that they strongly invoke the institutional interests of governments and territorial allegiances of the population but have little or no ideological significance.

MODELS OF IDEOLOGY IN CONTEMPORARY CAPITALISM

So far, in our discussion of ideology, we have referred mainly to the broad distinction between left and right. While, as the last section demonstrates, this approach serves us well, existing ideologies are more complex than a single left-right continuum. As the variation between nations and over the past four decades demonstrates, even in the restricted context of postwar, "advanced" capitalism, there is no single hegemonic capitalist ideological order. The theoretical question that we must address, therefore, is how to characterize alternative ideological positions in a manner that is both theoretically adequate and empirically practical, using our survey data.

We approach this problem by triangulating between separate measures of respondents' opinions of social welfare policy, state regulation of the economy and direct investment, and the power of trade unions. In these terms social democratic capitalism combines support for the welfare state with heavy state involvement in the economy and a strong trade union movement. Conversely, the neo-conservative project – for example see Bill Schwarz's "The Thatcher Years" (1987), or Kim Moody's "Reagan, the Business Agenda and the Collapse of Labour" (1987) – combines state withdrawal from the social programs and economic regulation that are integral to the Keynesian welfare state with efforts to weaken the labour movement. The ideological formulae may not be a consistent guide to policy, however. So Ronald Reagan's attack on the state and commitments to *laissez-faire* were accompanied by increased military expenditures and a huge budgetary deficit, which did affect the economy.

Other existing capitalist ideologies, of course, are mostly somewhere in between these left and right ideal types. Until the late 1980s – and so including the time when our elite surveys were conducted – the terrain of postwar Canadian politics did not stretch nearly as far as even these ideological poles. On the right, especially at the federal level, Canadian neo-conservatism traditionally lacked the vigour of its British and American counterparts, while on the left, the NDP – especially the NDP in power provincially or in prospect federally – offered a tepid version of social democracy. Jane Jenson argues that this restricted ideological terrain reflects the particular "Fordist" settlement of the conflict between capital and labour in postwar Canada:

[While, generally,] Fordism was a form of capitalism constructed after 1945 in all of the advanced capitalist countries, including those – like the USA, Japan and Canada – where spending on the KWS was not as high, neo-corporatism did not develop, or the discourse and organization of politics was based less on a partisan cleavage between labour and capital. ... The fordist paradigm in Canada was not organized around class-based collective identities. The class compromise which did provide the institutionalization of fordism did not depend upon partisan politics ... [it was] not social-democratised ... and the collective identities which the paradigm mobilised were not class-based. (Jenson 1989, 3, 8)

Indeed traditional Canadian conservatism has been closer to the "red Tory" tradition, combining limited support for the welfare state with market-oriented economic polices and opposition to labour. The opposite pole of bourgeois Canadian party politics, represented by the left of the Liberal party, combined greater support for social programs – in the form of unemployment insurance and medicare – and stronger economic interventionism – in the form of FIRA, the establishment of the Canada Development Corporation and PetroCanada, and the National Energy Policy – with continuing opposition to labour, in the form of routinized intervention in labour disputes and regulation of trade union rights, untempered by any effort to bring labour into the policy process. Even during the relative social peace of the 1950s and early 1960s, labour's gains were restricted to the elementary rights of a dues check-off (the Rand formula) and recognition of state employees' collective bargaining rights (although in light of later developments, it is doubtful that this was foreseen to involve genuine rights to strike). Between these limited extremes, "mainstream" bourgeois party politics involved little more than an effort to make minor adjustments to the postwar settlement.

The terrain that we have described provides the appropriate interpretive context for our 1977 and 1981 elite surveys, but it is long past. The rise of the federal Reform Party, the elections of the Ralph Klein and Mike Harris governments in Alberta and Ontario, the post-Mulroney disintegration and rightward swing of the federal Conservative party, and the ascendancy of the business wing of the federal Liberal party – these mark a dramatic shift in the range of ideological alignments in Canada. Jenson's argument can be taken a step further: institutionalized without explicit class-based identities and bargaining, there was little structural impediment to the last decade's shift away from the postwar settlement, or to the corresponding shift to the right in contending ideological formulae. Of course that similar changes have taken place in many other countries, though always in particular, "special" circumstances, suggests the impact of more general, transnational forces.

Figure 9-1 locates some of these alternative ideological formulae in terms of three dimensions: support for the welfare state, support for direct government regulation of the economy, and support for the labour movement. Thus, for example, we distinguish between neo-conservatism and classical liberalism in terms of support for the welfare state: both are antagonistic to government intervention in the economy and to labour. "Trudeau liberalism," in these terms, adds to classical liberal support for the welfare state, and gives limited support for some kinds of economic intervention (in natural resources, particularly). In contrast with "classical social democracy," which involves a forceful combination of support for the welfare state, economic regulation, and labour, the NDP combines strong support for the welfare state with more timid forms of economic intervention and support for labour.

As in the last section, the empirical coordinates to this typology come from multi-item scales. The scale of support for the welfare state was constructed by adding the responses to eleven items, six of which involved the evaluation of the following statements on a scale between strongly disagree (scored 1) to strongly agree (scored 5):

(1) There is too much of a difference between rich and poor in this country.
(2) Unemployment is high these days because it is too easy to get welfare assistance. [reversed in scoring]
(3) The government should provide jobs for Canadians who want to work but cannot find a job.
(4) People with high incomes should pay a greater share of the total taxes than they do now.
(5) Children who grow up in poor homes have much less chance to get ahead than children who grow up in more prosperous circumstances.
(6) In provinces where they now exist, rent controls should be abolished. [reversed in scoring]

Ideological Formula	Support for the Welfare State	Support for Economic Regulation	Support for the Labour Movement
Neo-conservatism	antagonism	antagonism	antagonism
Classical liberalism	limited	antagonism	antagonism
Red Toryism	limited	limited	antagonism
the "Canadian postwar settlement"	limited	very limited	very limited
Trudeau liberalism	moderate support	limited	very limited/ indifference
"Canadian" social democracy	strong	some	some
Swedish social democracy	strong	some	strong
"Classical" social democracy	strong	strong	strong

Figure 9-1
Alternative ideological formulae

The other five items in the scale involve ratings on a five-point scale, between much less effort and much more effort, of the amount of effort the government should put into providing assistance to the unemployed, helping the poor, building public housing, eliminating discrimination against women, and workers' compensation.

The items included in the measure of labour relations included:

(1) During a strike, management should be prohibited by law from hiring workers to take the place of strikers.
(2) Trade unions that are attempting to organize a bargaining unit should have the right to a list of names and addresses of the employees.
(3) Postal workers should not have the right to strike.
(4) Employees should be represented on the boards of the companies for which they work.
(5) Workmen's compensation payments should be increased to the level where they provide injured workers with the same income they had before being injured.
(6) [support for] legislation to decrease the power of trade unions [as a means of combatting inflation].

And the statements rated to measure support for government regulation of the economy included:

(1) Passage of the Foreign Investment Review Act.
(2) Establishment of the Canada Development Corporation.

(3) Sponsorship of crown corporations in critical industries to compete with foreign firms, such as PetroCan.
(4) Takeover of some, but not all, of the multinational oil companies by crown corporations.
(5) Nationalization of the Canadian operations of large multinational oil companies.
(6) The Saskatchewan government's takeover of a major part of the potash industry.
(7) Nationalization of Bell Canada.

To aid in comparing the three scales, which are made up of different numbers of questions, the scale scores are computed as the average of the various items. Each item was measured on a five-point scale (with the categories scored 1 to 5) so the scale scores also vary between 1 and 5. To achieve a 1 or a 5 on the scale, a respondent would have had to answer with consistent, extreme responses to every item in the scale (on the scale measuring support for the welfare state, she or he would have had to strongly disagree or strongly agree with all eleven statements). Since it is likely that the distinction between strongly agreeing and agreeing with one of these statements, and between someone strongly disagreeing and disagreeing, is partly a matter of verbal style, rather than ideological position, we discounted this distinction in dividing the scales' scores into five substantive categories denoting strongly and moderately conservative positions, support for the status quo, and strongly and moderately progressive positions. Note that, while similar to three of the indicators employed in the last section, these scales are not constructed in exactly the same way. Table 9-8 shows the results of comparing the élite groups on the three scales.

For the elites as a whole, the means of the three scales are very close to the middle (within one-fifth of a standard deviation of the scale midpoint) of the political spectrum. Of course this reflects the choice of items to be included in each scale, although it was not our intention to construct the scales out of items to which the responses would be distributed uniformly around the middle of the ideological spectrum. On the other hand, the process of obtaining the items is not random. The questions that we asked were purposely designed to evoke disagreement in the elite population under study since items that produce very little disagreement contribute little to the goal of differentiating the elites into ideological camps.

Clearly there is much less disagreement over the welfare state than over economic regulation and trade unions. Only 3 percent of the elites took a strongly conservative position on the welfare state, compared to 18 and 16 percent, respectively, who took strongly conservative positions on government regulation and labour. Support for the status quo on social welfare is correspondingly high: 42.0 percent of the sample have mean scores

Table 9-8

Scale Scores Measuring Support for the Welfare State, Support for Direct Government Involvement in the Economy, and Support for the Labour Movement, by Group

Group	Conservative		Support the Status Quo	Progressive		Total	Mean	Standard deviation	Number of cases
	Strong	Moderate		Moderate	Strong				
SUPPORT FOR THE WELFARE STATE									
CAPITAL									
Corporate executives	8	37	44	10	1	100	2.74	.38	217
Business owners	6	24	60	8	3	100	2.87	.42	80
Lawyers	10	31	46	10	4	100	2.83	.46	53
STATE									
Federal politicians	2	12	42	23	21	100	3.30	.59	57
Provincial politicians	0	12	45	26	17	100	3.28	.53	59
Local politicians	0	19	42	21	19	100	3.19	.61	46
Federal bureaucrats	0	14	55	26	5	100	3.12	.40	81
Provincial bureaucrats	0	14	44	28	14	100	3.21	.47	108
Local bureaucrats	0	7	54	33	7	100	3.18	.40	43
Trade unionists	0	1	13	28	58	100	3.91	.53	139
Mass media executives	8	6	45	28	14	100	3.17	.57	51
Academics	1	14	45	19	22	100	3.27	.55	73
Farm leaders	0	20	20	30	30	100	3.38	.57	20
Total	3	18	42	20	16	100	3.17	.60	1042

Table 9-8

Scale Scores Measuring Support for the Welfare State, Support for Direct Government Involvement in the Economy, and Support for the Labour Movement, by Group (Continued)

Group	Conservative		Support the Status Quo	Progressive		Total	Mean	Standard deviation	Number of cases
	Strong	Moderate		Moderate	Strong				
SUPPORT FOR DIRECT GOVERNMENT INVOLVEMENT IN THE ECONOMY									
CAPITAL									
Corporate executives	46	24	21	6	3	100	2.40	.64	217
Business owners	15	14	43	18	10	100	2.97	.64	80
Lawyers	36	19	25	15	6	100	2.59	.72	53
STATE									
Federal politicians	21	9	17	14	40	100	3.22	.87	57
Provincial politicians	15	20	31	10	24	100	3.04	.79	59
Local politicians	9	21	23	16	30	100	3.22	.81	46
Federal bureaucrats	5	6	33	36	20	100	3.31	.54	81
Provincial bureaucrats	9	11	34	26	20	100	3.21	.59	108
Local bureaucrats	0	12	26	29	33	100	3.40	.48	43
Trade unionists	0	4	8	17	70	100	3.93	.55	139
Mass media executives	18	14	24	31	14	100	3.01	.71	51
Academics	8	11	18	26	37	100	3.37	.69	73
Farm leaders	0	5	20	35	40	100	3.60	.43	20
Total	18	14	24	19	25	100	3.10	.81	1042

Table 9-8

Scale Scores Measuring Support for the Welfare State, Support for Direct Government Involvement in the Economy, and Support for the Labour Movement, by Group (Continued)

Group	Conservative		Support the Status Quo	Progressive		Total	Mean	Standard deviation	Number of cases
	Strong	Moderate		Moderate	Strong				
SUPPORT FOR THE LABOUR MOVEMENT									
CAPITAL									
Corporate executives	31	37	19	12	1	100	2.54	.57	217
Business owners	49	29	16	5	1	100	2.32	.59	80
Lawyers	13	36	32	19	0	100	2.76	.58	53
STATE									
Federal politicians	7	16	27	29	21	100	3.23	.67	57
Provincial politicians	5	25	28	28	13	100	3.11	.61	59
Local politicians	16	7	32	21	25	100	3.15	.76	46
Federal bureaucrats	3	22	25	35	15	100	3.22	.55	81
Provincial bureaucrats	9	21	33	24	13	100	3.04	.57	108
Local bureaucrats	2	28	30	37	2	100	3.04	.50	43
Trade unionists	1	1	2	15	81	100	4.17	.58	139
Mass media executives	18	20	31	18	14	100	2.89	.74	51
Academics	12	15	25	36	12	100	3.12	.73	73
Farm leaders	10	20	10	35	25	100	3.25	.74	20
Total	16	22	22	21	19	100	3.05	.81	1042

within-one third of a point of the middle of the scale, compared to just over a fifth for the two other scales. In the elite population as a whole there is little support for a fundamentalist effort to destroy the welfare state. Omitting advocates of the status quo, there is considerably more support for enhancing rather than for reducing the welfare state (by 36 to 21 percent), while for the other two dimensions, opinion is nearly evenly divided between the right and the left. Government regulation, for example, is strongly opposed by 18 percent of the elites, moderately opposed by 14 percent, moderately favoured by 19, and strongly favoured by 25 percent.

Naturally the scale of support for the welfare state reveals the same relative alignment of elite groups that emerged in the discussion of individual items above. The business elites are on the right, with the business owners slightly more progressive than the corporate executives and lawyers; the labour leaders are isolated on the left; and the state elites occupy the middle ground. The politicians took somewhat more progressive positions than the civil servants (the difference is just shy of significance at .05 with a two-tailed test), but there are no systematic differences among the levels of government. The mass media elites and academics are close to the politicians, while the farm organization leaders are to the left of the state elites but not nearly as progressive as the labour leaders.

Table 9-8 reveals an ideological terrain characterized by an almost complete absence of overlap in the positions of capital and labour, even concerning the welfare state, over which we have shown there is significantly less overall conflict than over government involvement in the economy or over the labour movement. Only 10 percent of corporate executives took a progressive position on the welfare state – and of those only one-half of 1 percent, or one respondent in the sample of 217 – took a strongly progressive position, compared to 28 percent of the labour leaders who are moderately progressive and 58 percent who are strongly progressive. Still, just less than half of the corporate executives expressed moderately or strongly conservative views of the welfare state, and four-fifths of those are only moderately conservative. The proportion of business elites who took progressive positions is about the same for each of the three ideological dimensions – in the neighbourhood of 10 percent – but there is much less support for the status quo and correspondingly more support for conservative positions on the economy and labour than on the welfare state. Nearly half the corporate executives took strongly conservative positions on government involvement in the economy and a third were strongly conservative on labour issues. Business elites are divided in their views of the welfare state, but almost uniformly opposed to state intervention in the economy and labour. Four-fifths of the corporate elites either support the status quo or are moderately conservative on social welfare, with marginally greater support for the status quo. At the time of this survey radical neo-conservatism represented a small minority position. Within capital, the chief division was between a red Tory position and conservative, but not fundamentalist, right-wing politics.

Trade unionists are more strongly polarized to the left than are business elites to the right. Eighty-one percent of the trade unionists took strongly progressive positions on labour issues and 70 percent took strongly progressive positions on government regulation of the economy. The trade union leaders took the combination of positions that we have associated with classical social democracy. Their views are considerably to the left of the policies advocated by the federal NDP and the elected provincial NDP governments. Although empirically there is some overlap in the positions of capital and labour, in practical terms the polarization between them is virtually complete.

The state elites occupy an ideological middle ground between capital and labour, though the substance of their positions varies over the three dimensions. With regard to the welfare state, there is a minority (averaging about 15 percent of each group) with moderately conservative views, but only one respondent in nearly 400 was strongly conservative. The largest proportions of state elites – about 45 percent of the politicians and 55 percent of the bureaucrats – supported the status quo. The politicians are slightly to the left of the civil servants, but only at the federal level is this difference of any size (and there the bureaucrats are more supportive of the status quo but not more likely to take conservative positions). We can summarize by saying that the state elites are strongly supportive of the existing, limited Canadian welfare state, and that there is significant support for moderate increases in the breadth and cost of state social programs. More important than the comparatively small difference in the averages, inspection of the *distributions* of opinion and the standard deviations (in the right-hand column of table 9-8) indicates that there is more internal conflict *among* the politicians than among the bureaucrats. At the federal and local levels the politicians are more likely to have conservative *and* progressive opinions than the bureaucrats.

In an atmosphere of almost complete polarization between capital and labour, the state elites also occupy the middle ground in terms of support for government involvement in the economy. Still, in the context of the radical moves away from government intervention in the subsequent years, including the privatization of Crown corporations and virtual elimination of foreign investment screening, the position of the state elites seems very progressive, with nearly half taking moderately or strongly progressive positions. The differences between bureaucrats and politicians are small relative to the gap between capital and labour, but there are systematic and interesting differences between them. The bureaucrats are more favourable than politicians to state involvement in the economy and there is substantial internal disagreement among the politicians. At the federal level, 21 percent of politicians take a strongly conservative position and 40 percent take a strongly progressive position on state involvement, while 33 percent of the bureaucrats support the status quo, 36 percent are moderately progressive and 20 percent are strongly progressive.

Implementation of the labour relations policies supported by the state elites would bring some gains for trade unions, but would not approach the structural reforms that would make them a significantly stronger political force in Canadian society. State elites' responses to the questions about trade unions revealed an alignment similar to that obtained for social welfare, in that the politicians have very slightly more progressive views of unions than the bureaucrats, and similar to state intervention in that there is more internal disagreement among politicians. The pattern is most pronounced at the local level, where 16 percent of the politicians are strongly conservative and 25 percent are strongly progressive, while the bureaucrats are split almost evenly between the three centre categories for moderately conservative and progressive views and support for the status quo.

The more precise measurement available with these scales provides evidence, unavailable from the analysis of individual survey questions in the previous section, in support of Aberbach, Putnam, and Rockman's (1981) prediction that bureaucrats act as a stabilizing influence on elected politicians, whose views are more varied and less supportive of the status quo, and for Rianne Mahon's arguments about internal divisions of the state. This pattern is much more pronounced for state intervention in the economy than for labour relations or social welfare issues. As Nicos Poulantzas argues, the state is the site of significant ideological contestation, though it is also true that the state occupies a middle ground between capital and labour.

Returning to the more general problem of understanding the ideology of state elites in the context of the ideological packages that frame contemporary political debate, the wide variation between and within the elite groups demonstrates the presence of a number of competing camps. At the time of our survey, there was very little support among Canadian elites for a hard-line neo-conservative, Thatcher-Reagan formula. However, between 20 and 30 percent of the state elites combined moderate opposition to the welfare state with stronger opposition to state intervention and the labour movement. On the opposite end of the spectrum there was some support, including perhaps 15 percent of state elites, for a strongly social democratic package. Another 15 percent or so supported what might be termed the English-Canadian tradition of social democracy, which ties strong support for state intervention in the economy with support for trade unions. The largest ideological camp among state elites, however, is closer to status quo politics than to any of these positions. It combines support for minor to moderate extensions of the welfare state with limited support for state intervention in the economy – along the lines of the pre-Mulroney FIRA, the establishment of the Canada

Development Corporation and PetroCan – with mildly progressive views of trade unions.

This analysis brings together the fragmented findings of our earlier analysis of the responses of corporate executives, business owners, and lawyers to individual survey questions. In support for the welfare state the corporate executives and lawyers are slightly more conservative than the business owners – about 10 percent fewer business owners adopt strongly or moderately conservative positions. In terms of government involvement in the economy, big business and the lawyers are again far to the right of the business owners – only 15 percent of the business owners take strongly conservative positions, compared to 36 percent of the lawyers and 46 percent of the corporate executives. The direction of this difference is reversed, however, when it comes to the labour movement: 49 percent of the business owners take strongly conservative positions on labour issues, compared to 31 percent of business owners and only 13 percent of lawyers. This liberalism of lawyers is entirely relative; half the lawyers take positions to the right of the status quo, about one-third support the status quo, and only a fifth are even moderately progressive. Putting into law the views of the most liberal of the three business groups would result in a weakening of the already weak position of the labour movement.

It is difficult to square these findings with the idea that "corporate liberalism" is a significant contributor to social reform. In none of the three sectors of capital is there significant support for reformism of any kind, and the differences between them involve differentiation of an extremely conservative political terrain. For example while the corporate executives have slightly more liberal views of trade unions than the business owners – in conformity with the argument that the largest corporations have to some extent learned to live with unions – the large corporations still view trade union power as anathema: a third hold positions that are so conservative that their practical implementation would involve an outright attack on unions; another third might be described as moderately *anti*-union; and most of the remainder do no more than support the status quo. Even the more pragmatic lawyers' position is to the right of the status quo.

The differences among the three business groups reflect their economic interests. Since their corporations are most directly threatened, corporate executives have the most extreme views about direct state involvement in the economy. The small business owners are the most threatened by unionization. The pattern of support for the welfare state is not what would be suggested by the view that big business is better able to afford extensive social programs, which their small competitors view as an intolerable burden. The mildly greater opposition to social programs from big business suggests that this argument is not correct.

Consistent with our previous analysis of the responses to individual items, the mass media executives and academics are close to the state elites and the farm organization leaders are somewhat to the left of the state elites, but not nearly as far left as the trade union leaders. There is some variation in the relative positions of these elite groups on the three dimensions of ideology. The mass media elites, for example, take relatively more conservative positions on state intervention in the economy and the labour movement than on the welfare state, perhaps reflecting their concerns as a highly monopolized and regulated industry. Relative to the state elites, the academics are slightly more favourable to state intervention in the economy than to the welfare state and the labour movement.

In terms of ideological categories, it is apparent that varieties of liberal ideology predominate here. In terms of their broad mix of ideologies, the mass media elites are more like the politicians than the civil servants. Among the mass media elites there is significant support for the broad range of liberal positions between red Toryism and weaker forms of social democracy; there is only a very small neo-conservative minority and a slightly larger, strongly social democratic minority. The academics are mildly more progressive; perhaps a third support a moderate social democratic platform, and the remainder are scattered among the more liberal positions, but there is no support at all for the extreme right. At least one-quarter of the farm leaders are strong social democrats, and most of the remainder support a weaker version of social democracy or a relatively interventionist liberalism. With the exception of labour, the farm organization leaders are the strongest supporters of state intervention in the economy, which is certainly consistent with the populist history of Canadian farm organizations.

ELITE IDEOLOGY AND THE PARTY SYSTEM

In our analysis of public opinion in chapter 6, we stressed the discontinuities between party support and political principles. The existing political parties, we argued, monopolized the political terrain and shifted the centre of gravity of political debate to the right – in the context of mass alienation and very low levels of political participation. There are two questions about the role of the party system that we want to ask now. The first is whether the strong ideological differences in elite policy preferences are reflected in party allegiances, again basing the comparison on the structurally defined elite groups. Our main concern is with the Liberal and Progressive Conservative parties, rather than with the NDP. Subsequent to our surveys it is readily apparent that the Conservative party was chosen as the political vehicle of big business. The only question is how far advanced this alignment was in the pre-Mulroney era. In any longer historical context, of course, one would be hard pressed to argue that there were not two "bourgeois" parties – in the literal sense. This raises a second question. To what extent are there ideological differences between, say, the business-people who support different parties? Is particularly right-wing business opinion – one can see from the analysis so far that this is a only a matter of degree – linked to support for the Conservative rather than the Liberal party? In other words, our concern is with the connection between ideology and party support *within*, rather than between, elite sectors. Similarly, we want to examine the relationship between ideology and party support among state elites and trade union leaders, though it seems highly unlikely that NDP supporters would not be more left wing than unionists who supported the two other parties. The answers to these questions may be found in table 9-10, but first we compare the party allegiances of the elite groups in table 9-9. Note that the federal and provincial politicians are left out of table 9-9, because for them any difference between our sample and the distribution of party allegiances in the Parliament and provincial governments is purely a function of our sampling procedure.

Corporate executives supported the Conservative party over the Liberals by a two-to-one ratio. The lawyers were 41 percent Conservative and 47 percent Liberal, and small business was 45 percent Conservative and 51 percent Liberal. Only 2 of the more than 200 corporate executives, and not one of the business owners, supported the NDP. About 15 percent of the state elites in each of the four groups (i.e., excepting the federal and provincial politicians) supported the NDP. Except for provincial civil servants, support for the Liberals was stronger than for the Conservative party. For example 44 percent of the federal civil servants supported the Liberals, compared to 20 percent for the Conservatives and 13 percent for the NDP. Not surprisingly, two-thirds of the trade unionists supported the NDP, one-quarter supported the Liberals, and 10 percent supported the Conservatives. Comparison of the party allegiances of the business, state, and labour elites, and the correlation of these profiles with the ideological differences observed above, is consistent with the argument that the Progressive Conservatives represent a political ideology that is significantly to the right of the Liberals. The gap in party allegiance between the business and labour respondents is roughly comparable to the differences over the policy questions.

Not surprisingly in light of their opinions in the substantive areas discussed at the beginning of this chapter, 41 percent of the academics were Liberal party supporters, 28 percent were Conservatives, and 23 percent were NDP supporters (an additional 7 percent supported no party). The mass media executives gave equal support to the Liberals and Conservatives, but little to the NDP. This too is consistent with the "middle of the road" ideological views of these groups. More interesting are agricultural leaders, who gave relatively equal support to the NDP and Conservatives, but little to the Liberals. While the farm leaders' high level of NDP support corresponds to their relatively left-wing policy positions, their support for the Conservatives over the Liberals appears to represent regional and institutional factors.

Turning to the question of whether the party divisions represent ideological differences within sectors, it is apparent in table 9-10 that business supporters of the Liberal party are significantly more progressive than sup-

Table 9-9
Federal Political Party Support, by Group

Group	Liberal	Progressive Conservative, Social Credit	NDP	Other party	No party	Total
		Federal Party Support (percentage distribution)				
CAPITAL						
Corporate executives	31	62	1	2	4	100
Business owners	51	45	0	1	3	100
Lawyers	41	47	4	4	4	100
STATE						
Politicians						
Municipal	57	20	16	0	7	100
Bureaucrats						
Federal	44	20	13	1	22	100
Provincial	22	44	11	1	22	100
Municipal	55	33	16	0	8	100
Trade unionists	23	10	62	2	3	100
Mass media executives	34	32	12	4	18	100
Academics	41	28	23	1	7	100
Farm leaders	10	37	43	0	10	100

porters of the Progressive Conservatives. This is true for all three dimensions of ideology, but the strongest difference, by far, relates to support for state economic intervention. In 1981, the heyday of the National Energy Policy and a number of other prominent federal and provincial economic initiatives, 54 percent of the Progressive Conservative supporters took a strongly conservative position on state economic intervention, and only 3 percent were even moderately progressive; among Liberal party supporters, only 12 percent were strongly conservative and 31 percent were moderately or strongly progressive. In terms of the welfare state, the difference is in the same direction, but not as strong: 52 percent of Progressive Conservative supporters took strongly or moderately conservative positions and 5 percent took strongly or moderately progressive positions; for Liberal party supporters the corresponding figures are 29 and 16 percent. Surprisingly, while the difference is quite small, the Progressive Conservative party supporters were more sympathetic to labour than the Liberals. This is indicative of the insig-

Table 9-10
Three Measures of Political Ideology by Federal Party Identification, by Group

Group	Capital		State				Labour	
	PC	Liberal	PC	Liberal	NDP	None	PC/Lib	NDP
WELFARE STATE								
Strongly conservative	11	6	1	0	0	0	0	0
Moderately conservative	41	23	24	7	4	10	2	0
Support status quo	43	55	54	54	4	51	31	4
Moderately progressive	5	13	16	31	41	31	44	19
Strongly progressive	0	3	5	8	51	8	23	77
Total	100	100	100	100	100	100	100	100
STATE ECONOMIC INTERVENTION								
Strongly conservative	54	12	24	3	0	3	0	0
Moderately conservative	24	19	22	5	0	15	11	1
Support status quo	19	39	39	20	8	33	18	3
Moderately progressive	1	22	9	36	15	23	27	9
Strongly progressive	2	8	6	34	77	26	44	87
Total	100	100	100	100	100	100	100	100
LABOUR								
Strongly conservative	30	36	10	8	0	3	0	0
Moderately conservative	32	37	28	17	4	21	5	0
Support status quo	19	20	36	32	6	24	7	0
Moderately progressive	18	7	24	36	23	32	25	8
Strongly progressive	1	0	2	6	66	21	63	92
Total	100	100	100	100	100	100	100	100
Number of Cases	189	129	115	103	45	39	44	80

nificance of labour issues to business and their rather weak attachment to the key questions of the time. The character of Conservative party supporters in business at this time suggests that the party was less a gathering place for opponents of the welfare state than for extreme opponents of direct state intervention in the economy.

Among the state elites there are also large differences between the supporters of the different political parties, in all three ideological dimensions. Across these dimensions the largest ideological difference is between NDP supporters and all others. NDP supporters' ideological isolation is greatest for the measure of support for labour, for which 66 percent of NDP supporters among state elites took a strongly progressive position, compared to a minuscule 2 and 6 percent for the Conservative and Liberal supporters, respectively. For the state elites, 46 percent of Conservative supporters took strongly or moderately conservative positions on state economic intervention, versus 8 percent of the Liberal party supporters and *none* of the NDP supporters. Seventy-seven percent of the state elites who supported the NDP are strongly progressive about state economic intervention, versus 34 percent of Liberal party supporters, 26 percent of those with no party preference, and 6 percent of Progressive Conservative supporters.

On the measure of support for the welfare state, Conservative party supporters hewed to the status quo (54 percent took a middle position, 25 percent were more conservative, and 21 are more progressive); half the Liberal party supporters also opted for the status quo, but among those who did not a very strong majority was moderately progressive. NDP supporters in the state elites were dramatically more supportive of the welfare state: 51 percent are strongly progressive on this dimension, compared to 5 and 8 percent of the Conservative and Liberal party supporters, respectively, and the difference is even larger for the measure of support for labour.

Finally, the two-thirds of labour leaders who supported the NDP are considerably to the left of the Liberal and Conservative party supporters. For example nearly 90 percent of the labour leaders who support the NDP are strongly progressive in their views of state economic intervention, compared to only about half of the Progressive Conservative and Liberal party supporters.

Whatever the ideological confusions about political parties in the general public, ideology and party support are strongly linked for the elites. At this time party allegiance was more strongly tied to views of state economic intervention than to views of the welfare state; and for views on labour relations issues the connection was still weaker. In part this reflected the continuing strength of the consensus around social programs – medicare, pensions, unemployment insurance, and so on – which constitute the Canadian version of the welfare state, and the historical weakness in Canada of attachments to the labour relations components of the postwar settlement. From these results it is not difficult to discern why the ascendancy of the Conservative party nationally and, within the Conservatives, the ascendancy of individuals strongly linked to capital, would have resulted in the dismantling of the National Energy Policy and foreign investment review, in the privatization of state enterprises and, ultimately, in Free Trade.

CONCLUSIONS

To a much greater extent than in the general public, the ideas of elites reflect their places in capitalist society. It is natural to see these places largely in terms of the locations of elite groups in the capitalist *economy*, though ideologies are not completely reducible to economics. That contending ideologies are not pure or simple reflections of interests is clear from our finding that corporate executives are so strongly opposed to socialized medicine, even though the economic burden of medical costs would be *higher* (as they are in the United States) if medicine were organized entirely along market lines.

The findings of this chapter have added significant detail to, but do not fundamentally change, the conclusion of the previous chapter, that the political spectrum is defined by a pervasive left-right polarization, bounded by the views of business and labour, and that opinions of state elites fall somewhere between these boundaries, just where depending on the issue. There is not simply conflict between right and left: the polarized positions of capital and labour involve more-or-less complete disagreement over public policy. On the fundamental issue of distribution, for example, more than 80 percent of labour leaders felt that there was too much difference between rich and poor, compared to 22 percent of corporate executives. These findings rule out a number of theoretical approaches to the state and organization of developed capitalism. Versions of pluralism that emphasize elite consensus and accommodation, corporatist theories (even if, in recognition of the Canadian context, labour is left out of the equation), and, on the Marxist side, instrumentalist theories of the state simply cannot be bent to accommodate these findings.

As viable theoretical explanations of our findings we are left with varieties of pluralism that emphasize competing interests, stagnation, and dysfunction, instead of consensus and democratic competition, and with varieties of Marxism that embed the state in ongoing class-based conflict between capital and labour. Compared to Theodore Lowi and Samuel Beer, with their emphases on the Reagan-Thatcher era deflation of the state and its capture by organized interests, the Canadian state elites show a healthy ideological independence, not to mention strong support for the key policies of the Canadian welfare state. While the radical pluralists correctly point to the extent and importance of ideological conflict, the Marxist tradition insists on the class basis of these conflicts. The ideological difference between capital and labour, shown in our surveys, is too deep to be defined in terms of alternative strategies for managing an ongoing society and economy, or of particular groups capturing bigger shares of a pie guarded by a weak state. Rather, the visions of capital and labour involve enormous changes in the balance of class forces, with the state elites holding a genuinely different, intermediate position.

Corporate executives, our survey shows, take a neo-conservative view of their economic interests. At a time of already considerable cutbacks, nearly three-quarters of corporate executives supported further reductions in government social expenditures and 84 percent approved of "tight money" policies to combat inflation (with the inevitable increase in unemployment). Trade union leaders, for their part, are much more consistently left wing than the most militant sectors of the class they represent. The average views of state elites vary between support for the status quo and for moderately *pro-gressive* changes in policy. As suggested by structuralist Marxists, there is evidence of significant internal conflict among state elites, conflict that is preponderantly within the different levels of government and within the ranks of politicians and bureaucrats, rather than between these sectors.

We found evidence of considerable internal conflict between state elites, particularly regarding state intervention in the economy, and to a significant but lesser extent regarding labour issues and the welfare state. Our findings are consistent with Aberbach, Putnam, and Rockman's (1981) argument that a greater degree of ideological consensus among bureaucrats dampens the conflicts between politicians. Federal-provincial-municipal conflicts were rather minor and unsystematic. At the time of our survey there is no evidence that federal politicians and civil servants would play a leading role in preserving the welfare state by invoking "national standards." Indeed subsequent events showed the systematic reduction in federal funds to be as much a threat to social programs as the poverty or indifference of provincial governments.

With hindsight it is also possible to see the beginnings of the ideological polarization that characterizes the Mulroney years and to see strong business support for free trade, opposition to FIRA, etcetera that became government policy. Even among the business elites, however, opposition to the welfare state was, at the time, more relative than absolute. Missing from their views at this time was the bedrock opposition to the postwar settlement, which increasingly came to dominate business ideology, as well as the federal and many provincial governments.

There are strong links between general formulations of ideology, opinions on policy issues, *and the political parties*. If the institutional structures of party politics serve more to contain than to voice political conflicts in the mass public, this is not because they follow the lead of these elites. Not only are there large differences in the party allegiances of the different elite groups, but ideological differences *within* the state, business, and labour elites are reflected in party support. Generally speaking it is appropriate to consider the Progressive Conservative party, the Liberal party, and the NDP (in that order) as defining a right-left spectrum. Party politics thus makes sense to elites in a way that it does not to ordinary citizens.

Our conceptualization of ideology in terms of the three relations between capital, labour, and the state, which in policy terms involve the welfare state, state intervention in the economy, and labour relations, is successful in defining a political terrain into which other elements of ideology can be mapped. The significant omission, in this regard, is opinion on the division of powers between the federal and provincial governments. The very mild tendency for more progressive elites to favour the federal government is almost entirely the result of the strong federal allegiances of the labour elites, who are by far the most left-wing group. Federal-provincial conflict is thus what it appears to be, struggle over territory, rather than a mask for class-related conflict.

Even the reader who finds this detailed analysis of elite ideology persuasive, by this point is likely to be wondering what this all has to do with the master concept of ideology, which we have claimed motivates our analysis. We can address this concern with three arguments. First, conflicts between left and right, which express market relations in class society, are central to the structure of elite ideology. This is not to say that ideology is reducible to this dimension, both because of the complexity of technologically advanced capitalist societies and because the highly confrontational alignment that we see in Canada represents only one of a range of solutions to the ideological equation of developed capitalism. Second, that there is a hegemonic order in Canadian capitalism is not the same as saying that there is an ideological consensus. The fundamental link in the hegemonic order is the state. The ideology of state elites is closest to the public, and there is much less variation within the public than there is between capital and labour. This is not to say that the state, or the current ensemble of social and economic policies, is midway between capital and labour or that it represents an even-handed compromise. The class character of policies must be assessed on material grounds. Third, there is *a* state, which displays considerably ideological coherence, despite the structural complexities, and whose semi-autonomy must be taken seriously. The conflicts between sectors of capital, though not negligible, are small relative to the ideological division between capital and labour.

10 Social Background, Careers, and Elite Ideology in Canada

The ideological positions of business, labour, and state elites, we have argued, broadly reflect their structural positions in capitalist society. In its ideological commitment to the relatively conservative Canadian version of the welfare state – in which market domination is mitigated by state programs – the state acts independently, but within constraints. This is what we understand by "semi-autonomy," and why the state is not the instrument of capital. There is, however, an alternative, somewhat weaker instrumentalist version that ties ideology to the social origins of elites. This theme is prominent in some Marxist accounts as well as in what might be termed "radical" analysis. Now, obviously, the state and business elites have different ideological positions. The implication of this version of instrumentalism is that business and state elites have different social origins. Perhaps the state elites' middle-of-the-road positions and opposition to major reform reflect their privileged but not plutocratic origins.

For the instrumentalist argument to be plausible, we require two kinds of evidence: that there is selective recruitment to elites on the basis of their social backgrounds *and* that social background – presumably the combination of class origins, education, and career paths – affects elite political ideology. This influence of background on ideology *cannot* be reducible to the impact of elite position. In the terminology of causal modeling, instrumentalist theory requires that social background have a "direct" effect on elites' ideological positions. If background only has an "indirect" effect on ideology, so that elites from different sectors come from different backgrounds, but background has no independent effect on ideology, then the instrumentalist argument fails and structuralist arguments gain plausibility.

There is a strong individualist cast to this version of instrumentalism, in that ideology is seen to arise from the individuals, or more particularly from the networks of individual relations in society. Ideological conflicts, then, arise from inequalities in these networks rather than directly from the conflicting interests of people – collectively classes – in structurally distinct positions in capitalist society. Besides addressing arguments about the nature of the state and the genesis of ideological difference, analysis of the social background and careers of elite individuals provides insight into the inter- and intra-generational mobility processes that reflect inequality of opportunity in Canadian society and into the social processes that influence recruitment into elite positions. Sociologists interested in "status attainment" processes have shown that parental education and occupation are forms of privilege transmitted between generations and thus contribute to inequality of opportunity. But much less is known about the inheritance of property, which is potentially quite different from the "cultural capital" involved in the translation of high levels of parental education into high position.

In research based on representative samples of the Canadian population, such as the extensive study by Monica Boyd et al. (1985), members of elite groups are not present in numbers sufficient to permit investigation of their particular experience. Generally we can expect to find a lower degree of occupational mobility into elite positions than into higher-level (say, managerial and professional) occupations as a whole. Indeed societies in which the recruitment to the non-elite occupations is governed by relatively egalitarian opportunity structures may still be ruled by exclusive elites. As long as there is a significant amount of family ownership of large corporations, normal processes of mobility can be bypassed in the recruitment of corporate elites.

This chapter begins with a review of the previous research on the social origins of Canadian elites, then proceeds to an examination of the backgrounds of our respondents. Regression analysis is then employed to determine the impact of social and career background on ideology, testing the instrumentalist and radical pluralist arguments.

RECRUITMENT OF ELITES IN CANADA

In *The Vertical Mosaic*, his pioneering study of elites and stratification, John Porter (1965, 292) showed that, except for leaders of the trade union movement, members of the various Canadian elite groups were recruited from disproportionately privileged social backgrounds. Especially notable was the corporate elite, no more than 5 percent of whose members he found to have working-class backgrounds. From this Porter concluded that the talent of people from less-privileged backgrounds was being wasted and that expanding the system of higher education provided the best means of widening the recruitment base of Canadian elites. In retrospect Porter's emphasis on higher education seems very much a product of his time. Higher education in

Canada was expanding very rapidly in the 1960s and many of Porter's generation of sociologists – the first of any size in Canada – had their own lives transformed by attending university.

Two replications of Porter's studies – of the corporate elite by Wallace Clement (1975) and of the political and bureaucratic elites by Dennis Olsen (1980) – have shown that there was remarkably little change in the distributions of elites' social backgrounds in the twenty years after 1951. In a study of the social backgrounds of political party officials, Allan Kornberg, Joel Smith, and Harold Clarke (1979, 41) also demonstrated the characteristic pattern of recruitment from higher-income and -occupational groups – although, as might be expected from the lower exclusivity of the groups they studied, the party officials were much less distinctive than the elites studied by Porter, Clement, and Olsen.

The findings of studies of social background are heavily dependent on two aspects of the methodology employed: the definition of the elite population and the measurement of social background. Porter's study is the natural point of comparison for our own and later work, so it is appropriate to describe in more detail and to comment on his findings and methodology and how that affects comparisons between our findings and his. The most important difference involves the corporate elite, which Porter defined as the *directors* of 158 "dominant" non-financial corporations, the major banks, and some merchandisers. Porter meticulously documented the combination of quantitative and qualitative criteria that he used to determine the dominant corporations (in his appendix 2). Some of his judgements seem a bit arbitrary. For example while they qualified as dominant corporations according to the size criterion, "The printing and publishing industry was excluded because the power of these firms does not lie so much in their use of economic resources as their ability to influence opinion" (1965, 572) It is not likely, however, that Porter's decisions could have produced a significant distortion of his results.

In the present study the sample of capitalists is made up of the chief executives of the largest Canadian corporations, rather than directors. Compared to the members of boards, whose positions may reflect inherited ownership of significant stockholdings, it seems less likely that executives would have inherited their positions. Therefore the tendency is for our sample to yield lower estimates of the inheritance of positions.

Further problems in making these comparisons result from the high incidence of missing data in Porter's records and from his exclusion of the foreign-born from his analysis of class background. Defined initially as the directors of dominant corporations, Porter's corporate elite included 985 individuals, but for 225 of these "the information was considered insufficient to warrant … inclusion in the analysis" (1965, 274); a further 149 individuals were excluded because they were foreign born and therefore could not be traced through Canadian bibliographic sources. Porter was aware of the potential for bias due to the missing data, pointing out that the missing data related to less powerful members of the elite and therefore introduced an upward bias in measuring the class background of the corporate elite (274). Individuals whose backgrounds could not be determined from "Who's Who" and "Canadian biographical dictionaries or their forerunners as far back as 1896" (274, note) were likely to have come from poorer backgrounds than those whose predecessors were included in one or more of these publications. The effect of eliminating foreign-born corporate elites can be estimated from a comparison of the career patterns of the foreign- and Canadian-born elites, which may be recalculated from Porter's table 27 (275). These data strongly imply that Canadian-born elites are more likely to have come from privileged backgrounds: 19 percent had backgrounds in engineering or science, 17 percent had careers in family firms, 18 percent were lawyers, and 12 percent were "unclassified" because their careers could not be identified with one of the above, major avenues of access to the corporate elite. In comparison, 35 percent of the foreign-born had engineering or science backgrounds and 29 percent were unclassified, while only 7 percent had careers in family firms and none was a lawyer.

A final difficulty concerns Porter's assumption that all the university graduates in his sample were of at least middle-class background. The problem is that the tiny proportion of working-class people who become members of the corporate elite are those most likely to defy the great (but still small compared to the chance of entering the elite) odds against attending university. Unfortunately, university graduates are lumped in with individuals whose fathers were in middle-class occupations (in Porter's table 27, 292) so it is not possible to determine the impact of Porter's decision to assign them to the middle class. The decision to treat university graduates as having middle-class backgrounds also renders suspect comparisons between Porter's results and the replications carried about by Clement and Olsen, since the proportion of Canadians attending university increased considerably in the approximately twenty years between these studies.

For the labour, political, and bureaucratic elites there is less difference between Porter's and our sample. Porter's political elite included all federal Cabinet ministers, provincial premiers, justices of the Supreme Court of Canada, presidents of the Exchequer Court, and provincial chief justices who were in office between 1940 and 1960. Our political elites included members of Parliament who were not in the Cabinet, provincial cabinet members, and the mayors and councillors of major cities, all of whom were of significantly lower status than the groups included by Porter. Porter's bureaucratic elite included "federal public servants of the rank of deputy minister or equivalent, associate and assistant deputy minister or the equivalents, directors of the branches in the more important departments, and senior executives of Crown corporations" holding office during 1953. This sample is lower in rank than our federal bureaucratic elite. Our trade union sample is roughly comparable to Porter's, which included the senior officers of unions with more than 10,000 members, presidents and secretaries of the provincial federations and of the larger local labour councils, Canadian Labour Congress (CLC) executive council members and senior officials, plus some others. Assuming that class restrictions on recruitment increase with the exclusiveness of the group being considered and that there have been no changes in the patterns of recruitment since Porter's day, these methodological biases should result in our study showing that politicians have less privileged backgrounds, that bureaucrats have more privileged backgrounds, and that labour leaders have about the same backgrounds – all this assuming that there is no change over time.

Whatever the limitations of Porter's samples and indicators, he cannot have been mistaken in finding an extraordinary degree of inheritance in the Canadian corporate elite in 1951. Unfortunately the combination of the differences in defining the population and limitations of Porter's data permit only general comparisons between our capitalist respondents and his economic elite. For the other elite groups there is less of a difficulty, although the differences between samples encourage caution in making comparisons. For convenience, table 10-1 gives the backgrounds of the major elite groups, as reported by Porter, Clement, and Olsen.

AGE, ETHNICITY, RELIGION, BIRTHPLACE, AND LANGUAGE OF ELITES

Table 10-2 shows that our elite respondents are very largely middle-aged or older men. There are virtually no women. The lawyers stand out as the oldest group; 42 percent of them were sixty-five or older. This does not reflect the age distribution of the legal profession, but rather our decision to sample the senior partners of law firms, who frequently did not retire until an advanced age. The high mean age of the academics reflects our decision to select half the academic sample from the membership of the Royal Society of Canada, to which election is relatively late in most academics' careers. Still, it is natural that the elite would be older in professions marked by a high degree of age stratification – that is those in which high positions are gained only after long service. There is relatively little difference in the age distributions of the various state elites, the agricultural leaders, and trade union leaders: approximately 25 percent are thirty-five to forty-four years of age, 40 percent are forty-five to fifty-four, and 25 percent are fifty-five to sixty-four; only about 5 percent are under thirty-five and over sixty-five. The corporate elites are somewhat older: 13 percent are under forty-five, 37 percent are forty-five to fifty-four, and 51 percent are fifty-five or older. The local-level bureaucrats are somewhat older than the other five state groups, presumably reflecting internal recruitment processes heavily dependent on seniority. The mass media executives tend to be somewhat younger than the other groups.

Table 10-1

Social Backgrounds of Canadian Elites, as Determined by Porter, Clement, and Olsen

Background Variable	English Canadian Corporate Elite		Political Elite		Bureaucratic Elite		Labour Elite
	Porter 1951	Clement 1972	Porter 1940–60	Olsen 1961–73	Porter 1953	Olsen 1973	Porter 1958
Class Indicator							
UPPER CLASS					18	10	
Father in economic elite	22	29					
Father in other elite group	2	2					
Total			16	15			
Wife from elite family	7	6					
Father in substantial business	7	10					
Total			8	7			
MIDDLE OR HIGHER CLASS							
Attended private school	12	12	15	21			
MIDDLE							
Father in middle-class occupation and/or attended university	32	35	51	48	69	75	
POSSIBLY LOWER THAN MIDDLE CLASS	18	6	10	9	13	15	About 90
Total	100	100	100	100	100	100	
ETHNIC GROUP							
British	92	86	75	68	85	5	
French	7	8	22	24	13	24	
All others	1	5	3	8	2	11	
Total	100	100	100	100	100	100	
Attended University	58	81	86	84	79	92	8

* Because selection of the labour elite was done separately for Quebec and English Canada, the representation of ethnic groups is a function of the necessarily arbitrary sample selection procedures and do not reflect meaningful population.

Table 10-2
Cultural Background by Elite Sector, and for Canadian Population and for Men Aged 45–64

| | Capitalists | | | Mass media executives | Elected Officials | | | Bureaucrats | | | Academics | Agriculture leaders | Trade union officials | Canadian Population | |
	Big business	Small business	Lawyers		Federal	Provincial	Municipal	Federal	Provincial	Municipal				Total	Men aged 45–64
AGE															
Under 35 (%)	1	5	6	17	7	2	2	0	2	2	0	5	5	41	–
35–44	12	23	4	29	26	33	28	20	29	7	12	20	30	18	–
45–54	37	37	15	31	37	39	37	57	42	40	29	32	28	16	54
55–64	45	24	34	21	21	26	23	22	27	49	41	26	33	13	46
65 or older	6	11	42	2	9	0	9	1	1	2	18	11	4	12	–
ETHNICITY															
British (%)	65	50	62	66	57	73	51	57	73	51	51	58	53	47	53
French	9	9	15	18	17	3	21	23	10	14	16	5	22	30	24
Other	26	41	23	16	26	23	28	20	17	35	33	37	25	23	23
RELIGION															
Catholic (%)	20	19	21	29	26	20	44	31	23	28	23	25	38	48	43
Establishment Protestant	31	28	21	12	21	33	26	27	32	38	18	40	21	30	35
Jewish	1	19	6	2	2	3	2	4	0	3	4	0	1	1	1
All others	39	26	45	29	41	33	15	27	31	30	30	35	26	14	16
None	8	9	8	27	7	10	9	11	14	12	26	0	21	7	5
FOREIGN BORN (%)	23	33	9	17	14	3	9	17	12	30	41	15	15	20	22
MOTHER TONGUE															
English (%)	85	75	83	80	76	90	80	74	89	81	69	65	74	57	61
French	9	8	13	17	16	3	16	22	10	14	14	10	19	28	23
Other	6	18	4	4	9	7	5	4	1	5	18	25	7	15	16
Number of Cases	222	80	53	52	58	60	44	81	111	43	73	20	140	2948	425

In terms of age and sex these elites are not at all typical of the population. They are almost entirely male and considerably older than the population as a whole, even, say, excluding people under thirty-five and over sixty-five. In order to provide a comparison between elites and the population that "adjusts" (approximately, given the differences between the groups) for age and sex, in the following discussion, the elites will be compared to the forty-five- to sixty-four-year-old men, as well as to the entire population.

Porter showed that in 1951 the English "charter group" dominated the corporate world: 92 percent of the corporate elites were of British descent, only 7 percent were French, and just 1 percent were from other backgrounds. By 1972 Clement found that (for a similarly defined corporate elite) the proportions were 86.2 percent British, 8.4 percent French, and 5.4 percent "other". In our survey the corporate elites were 65 percent British, 9 percent French, and 26 percent of other groups. The corresponding figures for the Canadian population as a whole were 47, 30, and 23 percent. While our data show that the British continue to be over-represented at the highest level of business, their advantage is now entirely at the cost of the French, since the other ethnic groups are now present in similar proportions to their representation in the population. Of course, this "other" group is very heterogeneous and its composition reflects inequality among the non-charter groups; there are no native or black Canadians in the sample. Still, our evidence suggests that the domination of big business by the British ethnic group that Porter observed and that had changed only slightly by 1972 has been broken, although not to the advantage of French Canadians, who made only marginal gains in the thirty years between 1952 and 1981.

As we have noted it is not entirely appropriate to compare our sample to the samples of directors selected by Porter and Clement. To the extent that the directors represent inherited ownership of corporations, we can expect a conservative bias towards the ethnic groups that have dominated the corporate sector in the past. Still, evidence about the *ownership* of corporations strengthens the argument about the increased representation of non-charter groups in the highest ranks of business. Dwight Hamilton and Paul Mac-Names's (1996) list of the fifty greatest fortunes includes five Jewish families and several others that are not British, French, or Jewish. A similar analysis of the ethnic backgrounds of wealthy families by Alfred Hunter (1986, 157) indicates that, of the 184 families with wealth of $20 million or more in 1975, 55 percent were English, 7 percent were French, and 38 percent had other origins.

Except that the French are present in greater numbers, 15 versus 9 percent, the lawyers resemble the corporate executives in ethnic composition. This difference reflects the concentration of corporate head offices in Toronto, which is not to say that it is a methodological artifact, since the definition of the samples – which are drawn from lists of the largest corporations and the largest law firms – is completely unrelated to region. Non-charter ethnic groups are even better represented among business owners in our sample. While the small proportion of French Canadians in this group in part reflects the sample design, that 41 percent of these executives are neither British nor French – compared to 23 percent in the population as a whole – is evidence of very significant mobility.

In terms of ethnicity there is considerable variation among the six groups of state elites, with the primary differentiation between levels of government rather than between elected officials and bureaucrats. At the federal level the bureaucrats are 57 percent British, 17 percent French, and 26 percent from other ethnic groups. So there is at most a minor tendency for the French to be under-represented. At the municipal level the French are somewhat under-represented and the "others" over-represented among the bureaucrats, while there is little difference between the general population and elected officials. At the provincial level there is clear evidence of differences in the power of ethnic groups. Although the low response rate among politicians in Quebec considerably reduces their representation in our survey, that only 3 percent of the provincial elected officials are French also reflects the virtual absence of French people from the ministries of provincial governments outside of Quebec. In addition only 10 percent of the top-level provincial bureaucrats are French Canadian, compared to 73 percent who are British and 17 percent of "other" groups. Within the state and the corporate elites there is evidence that French Canadians have been less successful than the non-charter ethnic groups in overcoming the historical domination of the British.

Except among municipal officials and trade union leaders, Catholics are under-represented among the elites. While 48 percent of the Canadian population and 43 percent of forty-five- to sixty-four-year-old men describe themselves as Catholics, only about 20 percent of the three business groups and about 25 percent of each of the state elites (except for municipal politicians) are Catholic. Comparisons with the previous reported differences in ethnic background demonstrate that some, but not all, of these religious differences are accounted for by the strong tendency for French Canadians to be Catholic. There are also significant inter-elite differences in the proportions of the groups that report that they have no religion, which amount to 7 and 5 percent, respectively, of the general population and men aged forty-five to sixty-four. Significantly greater proportions of the mass media executives, academics, and trade unionists (27, 26, and 21 percent respectively) report no religion. About 1 percent of the Canadian population is Jewish, compared to between 2 and 4 percent of most of the elite groups, 6 percent of the lawyers, and 19 percent of the small-business executives.

Elites also differ from the Canadian population in terms of the division between "establishment" (Anglicans, Presbyterians, and United Church members) and "other" Protestants (with whom are included the very small numbers of respondents reporting a religion other than Catholic, Protestant, or Jewish). While the population is divided at the ratio of about two to one between the "establishment" and "other" Protestants, the elites are divided about equally between the two groups, although there is also considerable variation among the elite groups as well. The corporate executives, for example, are 31 percent "establishment" Protestants and 39 percent "others." This marks a change as well from the traditional patterns and suggests that, as well as a decline in the prominence of the British groups in the elite, the British members of the elite are now drawn from less-traditional backgrounds.

About one in five Canadian adults is an immigrant and, while most of the elite groups do not differ markedly from this proportion, there is considerable inter-elite variation. That 41 percent of the academics are born outside Canada reflects the well-documented recruitment of enormous numbers of foreign, mostly American and British, faculty members in the 1960s. The large proportion of people born outside Canada among small-business executives (33 percent) is consistent with other studies of immigrants, while the low representation of the foreign-born among the top-level lawyers (9 percent) presumably results from a combination of class and culturally specific recruitment into law school, hiring patterns of the large law firms in our sample, and the advanced age of their senior partners. Less expected, however, are the findings that 30 percent of the municipal civil servants, but only 12 percent of provincial civil servants, 9 percent of municipal elected officials, and 3 percent of provincial elected officials are foreign born. The suggestion that provincial and municipal political elites are representative of established ethnic groups leaves open the question of why municipal bureaucrats should differ. Perhaps that reflects the immigration of planners and city managers from countries where there is stronger professional training in these fields.

These differences in the proportions of foreign born are somewhat modified by the data on mother tongue, which was defined in our survey as "the language you first learned to speak as a child and still understand." About 15 percent of the Canadian population, or three-quarters of the proportion of adults who are immigrants, have neither English nor French as their mother tongue. In most of the elite groups, however, people born outside Canada considerably outnumber those whose native language is not English. Therefore the immigrants in the elite samples did not, as a general rule, face the language difficulties experienced by most immigrants to Canada. For example only 5 percent of the municipal bureaucrats did not have English or French as their mother tongue, compared to the 30 percent born outside Canada; the corresponding figures for corporate executives are 6 percent and 23 percent.

These findings are consistent with the evidence that the French remain significantly under-represented in most of the elite groups while the representation of "other" ethnic groups approximates their proportions in the population. Of course there is also considerable variation between the elite groups: the corporate executives, business owners, and lawyers differ from each other, and different factors affect the representation of ethnic, religious, immigrant, and language groups in the three levels of government and among politicians and bureaucrats. These findings demonstrate the success of the federal government's bilingualism policy and the contrasting failure, in the absence of formal policies, of rhetorical commitment to effect redress of the historical under-representation of French Canadians in big business and the provincial governments.

THE CLASS BACKGROUND OF CANADIAN ELITES

As table 10-3 shows, only the parents of trade union officials had levels of education and worked in occupations that in any way resembled the general population. Six percent of the fathers and 3 percent of the mothers of union leaders were university graduates, while for the population the corresponding figures are 7 and 4 percent respectively. Furthermore only 7 percent of the fathers of trade unionists were professionals or managers (versus 8 percent for the population), but their fathers were more likely than the population to have been in skilled non-manual and manual occupations (26 and 31 percent in these groups, respectively, versus 13 and 21 percent for the population). The developed left-wing ideology of the trade unionists is far to the left of the skilled manual workers who are the most left-leaning group in the general population, and is therefore not a direct result of the trade union leaders' distinctive class backgrounds, though they could account for the ideological difference between the labour leaders and other elites, whose backgrounds are far more privileged.

A second, less privileged group is the farm organization leadership. Their parents had extremely low levels of formal education: 89 percent of their fathers had no high school at all and 95 percent of the farm leaders' fathers were also farmers! What is critical here is the inheritance by the (entirely male in our sample) farm leaders of a combination of property and profession from their parents – rather than the inheritance of low or high status. These findings, of course, are entirely consistent with the results of studies of the population that show that there is virtually no mobility into farm occupations (though, of course, there are extremely high levels of mobility out).

Although there is considerable variation among them, examination of the parental education and occupations of all the other elite groups indicates their unusually privileged backgrounds. Most exclusive were the backgrounds of lawyers, a remarkable 54 percent of whose fathers were university graduates, which is of course very close to the percentage of their fathers who were lawyers. A further indication of lawyers' privileged class backgrounds is the finding that their mothers were unusually well educated

Table 10-3
Class Background by Elite Sector, and for Canadian Population and for Men Aged 45–64

| | Capitalists | | | Mass media exec-utives | Elected Officials | | | Bureaucrats | | | Acad-emics | Agri-culture leaders | Trade union offic-ials | Canadian Population | |
	Big bus-iness	Small bus-iness	Law-yers		Fed-eral	Prov-incial	Muni-cipal	Fed-eral	Prov-incial	Muni-cipal				Total	Men aged 45–64
FATHER'S EDUCATION															
No high school (%)	31	45	14	29	44	51	38	28	36	33	34	89	59	56	63
Some high school	16	17	10	8	13	22	20	14	20	18	13	0	20	18	17
High school grad	30	25	23	39	29	15	35	30	32	39	13	5	15	19	15
University grad	24	13	54	24	15	13	8	29	11	10	40	5	6	7	5
MOTHER'S EDUCATION															
No high school (%)	21	32	8	18	29	33	35	14	26	25	32	56	52	49	61
Some high school	18	21	12	10	15	22	30	24	20	33	15	11	22	23	20
High school grad	50	37	70	57	47	42	33	51	50	43	45	33	23	25	15
University grad	11	9	10	15	9	4	3	11	4	0	8	0	3	4	4
FATHER'S OCCUPATION[+]															
Professionals and managers	37	36	62	32	26	14	23	35	16	21	37	0	7	8	8
Skilled															
non-manual	25	21	30	32	0	1	25	26	7	21	20	0	26	5	13
manual	7	11	2	8	15	17	14	8	13	23	14	0	31	20	21
Semi-, Unskilled															
non-manual	7	4	4	14	15	5	2	6	6	16	7	0	7	18	4
manual, farm	8	9	0	10	11	14	16	5	18	7	11	5	20	28	26
Farmers	16	19	2	4	33	49	20	20	40	12	10	95	36	21	28

Table 10-3
Class Background by Elite Sector, and for Canadian Population and for Men Aged 45-64 (Continued)

| | Capitalists | | | Mass media exec-utives | Elected Officials | | | Bureaucrats | | | Acad-emics | Agri-culture leaders | Trade union offic-ials | Canadian Population | |
	Big bus-iness	Small bus-iness	Law-yers		Fed-eral	Prov-incial	Muni-cipal	Fed-eral	Prov-incial	Muni-cipal				Total	Men aged 45-64
BUSINESS OWNER (%)	39	61	59	31	43	57	44	46	40	30	31	95	33	39	41
FOR OWNERS ONLY															
NUMBER OF EMPLOYEES															
None (%)	18	4	29	38	42	46	6	37	25	17	40	58	47	88	88
1-9	42	40	32	38	33	42	6	42	50	67	40	37	47	→	→
10-99	21	48	26	24	24	12	6	16	2	16	20	5	5	11	7
100 or more	19	8	13	0	1	0	2	5	5	0	0	0	1	1	5

+ Based on Porter-Pineo classification of Statistics Canada four-digit occupational categories into "unit groups" and including middle-level managers, supervisors, and semi-professionals in the "skilled non-manual" category and technicians and supervisors in the "skilled manual" category.

(especially considering that 42 percent of the lawyers were over the age of sixty-five) – 10 percent graduated from university and 80 percent graduated from high school. About three-fifths of the fathers of the lawyers were professionals or managers and another 32 percent had skilled non-manual jobs; and 59 percent owned businesses, about half of which had ten or more employees. In total only 8 percent of the lawyers' fathers did not have professional, managerial, or skilled non-manual jobs. Because of the relatively advanced age of the lawyers, their fathers' occupations refer to a time before the widespread feminization of white-collar work, when this work was largely the domain of well-educated men.

While not nearly to the same extent as the lawyers, corporate executives also have unusually privileged backgrounds: 24 percent of their fathers had graduated from university; 37 percent had professional or managerial occupations; 39 percent owned businesses; 16 percent owned businesses with 10 or more employees; and 8 percent owned businesses with 100 or more employees. Relative to the general population, the mothers of corporate executives were three times more likely to have graduated from university; their fathers four times more likely to have graduated from university, been in professional or managerial occupations, or to have owned businesses with 10 or more employees; and their fathers were more than ten times as likely to have owned businesses with 100 or more employees.

We should recognize, but not exaggerate, the exclusiveness of the backgrounds from which the executives are recruited. About one-third of the fathers of the executives did not attend or graduate from high school, one-third were in semi- or unskilled jobs or were farmers, and 60 percent did not own a business. Men from privileged backgrounds enjoy huge advantages in the competition for elite positions, but the (seeming) converse does not hold: the corporate elites are *not* dominated by men with plutocratic backgrounds. Because these conclusions are the opposite of those reached by Porter and Clement it is worth considering why we differ.

As of 1972, Clement (1975, 192) found that 59 percent of the Canadian-born members of the corporate elite came from "upper class" families and 35 percent came from "middle class" families, while only 6 percent came from working-class families. The comparable figures for 1951 from Porter (1965, 292) are 50, 32, and 18 percent. Remarkably, there was a trend towards *less* egalitarian elite recruitment in the twenty-one years between these studies. The most obvious reason why our figures should be so different from Clement's and Porter's involves the definitions of the samples. To the extent that the boards of dominant corporations are made up of people who have inherited significant stockholdings or of people from an exclusive social circle, they are more likely to be made up of people from more privileged backgrounds than the executives of corporations, who are hired as managers. A second possibility is that social mobility into the top ranks of the capitalist class increased significantly in the nine years between Clement's and this study – the data on the ethnic backgrounds from three separate studies that is cited above suggest this is possible. Finally, there are differences in the measurement of class background that could account for some of the difference between our studies.

It is likely that all three factors had some effect. More important, our results give a quite different impression of big business than that provided by Clement, who in the rarefied social origins of Canadian capitalists finds one of the causes of the high level of foreign ownership and weakness of Canadian capital. At the time of our study the corporate executives were disproportionately recruited from more-privileged families, even if they were not the children of the previous generation of capitalists.

Compared to the corporate executives, the business owners are more likely to have fathers who were also the owners of businesses, but less likely to have parents with very high levels of education. Three-fifths of the fathers of small-business owners also owned businesses and 13 percent were university graduates (the corresponding figures for the top executives were 39 percent and 24 percent). More than half these businesses had ten or more employees. Obviously, business owners are better able than corporate executives to pass business directly on to their children. The fathers of business owners were likely to own businesses that were worth passing to their children – on average they had forty employees – but not so large that professional managers would have displaced family owners.

Again compared to the population, the state elites had privileged backgrounds, although there is significant variation between the levels of government, and between federal politicians and civil servants. Within the state, federal officials were recruited from the most privileged backgrounds, followed by the city and then the provincial officials. About 10 percent of the mothers of federal politicians and bureaucrats were university graduates, compared to 4 percent or less for the city and provincial elites. Where the state elites differ most from the three business groups is in terms of the proportion whose fathers owned businesses. Sixteen, 32, and 23 percent of the fathers of corporate executives, business owners, and lawyers, respectively, owned businesses with ten or more employees, compared to 11 percent of the federal politicians, 9 percent of the federal bureaucrats, and 6 percent or less of the provincial and municipal politicians and bureaucrats. In terms of parental occupation and education the most privileged of the state groups – the federal bureaucrats – is the equal of the corporate executives, but the other five state groups are from less-privileged backgrounds. More than one-quarter of their fathers and 11 percent of their mothers are university graduates and 35 percent of their fathers were professionals or managers. Compared to their bureaucratic counterparts, the Members of Parliament who make up the federal politicians are from less-privileged backgrounds: 9 percent of their mothers and 15 percent of their fathers are university graduates and 26 percent of their fathers were professionals, managers, or skilled non-manual employees; the corresponding figures for bureaucrats are 11, 29, and 61 percent.

The provincial state elites, especially the politicians, are drawn from considerably different and somewhat less-privileged backgrounds than the city elites, with the major difference in parental characteristics involving farm backgrounds: 49 percent of provincial politicians and 40 percent of provincial bureaucrats have fathers who were farmers, compared to 20 and 12 percent for the two corresponding city elites. This compares to 21 percent of the population as a whole and 28 percent of the men between forty-five and sixty-four whose fathers were farmers. This difference reflects a sample design in which each province is represented equally – thus over-representing (compared to the Canadian population) regions of the country that are heavily dependent on agriculture.

The education levels and careers of the elite groups are described in table 10-4. Again there are radical differences among the groups. Aside from the lawyers and academics, whose high levels of education involve occupational qualifications, the federal and provincial bureaucrats are the best educated: nearly one-third have professional degrees or doctorates, another third have master's degrees, one-quarter have undergraduate degrees, and just one-twelfth are not university graduates. Only 15 percent of the farmers and 23 percent of the trade union leaders are university graduates and 40 percent and 27 percent of the two groups, respectively, are not high school graduates; these two groups are only somewhat better educated than the population at large. All the other elite groups are much better educated than the agriculture and trade union leaders. Compared to the 23 percent of trade unionists with undergraduate university degrees, 84 percent of the corporate executives, two-thirds of the federal and provincial politicians and city bureaucrats, but only about 50 percent of the small-business and mass media executives and city politicians have undergraduate degrees.

The evidence on career experience in table 10-4 is rather crude, showing only whether or not each respondent was ever an elected official, full-time government employee, full-time university employee, and full-time employee of a private firm or crown corporation. Still, there are important differences among the elite groups. First, few of the elites have ever held elective office (excluding from the calculation, of course, the elected officials who are included in the sample). Except for the lawyers and agricultural leaders (for whom the samples are very small), 9 and 11 percent of whom have held office, respectively, no more than 5 percent – that is, one in twenty – of any group have held elective office.

Since about one in five Canadians is employed by government, it is not surprising that fairly large proportions of the elites have been full-time government employees at some time in their lives. Again, there are large group differences. About 15 percent of the corporate executives and business owners had worked for government, compared to 21 percent of the lawyers, 30, 47, and 27 percent of the federal, provincial, and city officials respectively, 27 percent of the academics, 5 percent of the farmers, and 28 percent of the trade unionists. Interestingly, relatively large proportions of federal and provincial elective officials and bureaucrats have taught in universities: 21 percent of the federal bureaucrats, 17 percent of the provincial bureaucrats, 14 percent of the federal elected officials, and 12 percent of the provincial elected officials – compared to no more than 5 percent of the other groups. Finally, only one-quarter of the elected officials and 40 percent of the bureaucrats report that they have *ever* worked full time for a private sector or crown corporation. Thus the elected officials are drawn heavily from government and from self-employment (which would, of course, include the large number of lawyers). The top levels of government bureaucracy consist mainly of career civil servants whose experiences are entirely within government. Porter (1965, 436) found that about one-half of the bureaucratic elite, slightly more than we find, were career civil servants. Generally these findings suggest a fairly low degree of movement between the elite sectors, although mobility from business to high-level bureaucratic careers is relatively high.

Finally, table 10-4 shows the income and wealth of the various groups. The trade union and agriculture leaders and civic officials, about one-third of whom earned under $30,000 in 1980, are far below the other groups – although considerably above the Canadian population. Only 14 percent of the trade union leaders earned $50,000 or more. The elected officials did not have particularly high incomes, either: 41 percent of the federal officials, 65 percent of the provincial officials, and 39 percent of the municipal officials earned $50,000 or more. The incomes of the bureaucrats, at all three levels, were strongly concentrated in the $50–69,000 range. The highest earners were the lawyers, 81 percent of whom earned $100,000 or more, and the business executives, 71 percent of whom earned $100,000 or more. Of course the distribution of wealth is strongly correlated with income, except for the poor but wealthy farmers whose land, machinery, and buildings are large assets that produce relatively little income. While not to the same extent, the politicians also have high levels of wealth relative to their incomes, suggesting that they previously enjoyed much higher levels of income, which have been reduced by their taking office.

These data underline the enormous differences in the life experiences of the various elite groups. In terms of their standards of living, the trade union leaders are not much different from ordinary workers in skilled, unionized jobs. With the possible exception of the city officials, the state elites have comfortably upper-middle-class incomes. The lawyers and business executives have an extremely high standard of living. In terms of social background and careers, the elites differ markedly from the Canadian population as a whole and there are also very large differences between the elite groups. At one extreme the corporate executives and lawyers are disproportionately recruited

Table 10-4
Social Background by Elite Sector and Social Class in the Population and for Men Aged 45–64

	Capitalists			Mass media exec-utives	Elected Officials			Bureaucrats			Acad-emics	Agri-culture leaders	Trade union offic-ials	Canadian Population	
	Big bus-iness	Small bus-iness	Law-yers		Fed-eral	Prov-incial	Muni-cipal	Fed-eral	Prov-incial	Muni-cipal				Total	Men aged 45–64
EDUCATION															
Not high school grad	3	13	0	8	7	14	7	0	0	0	0	40	27	46	55
High school grad	13	33	0	42	16	24	43	8	8	33	0	45	49	44	32
Undergrad degree	44	35	2	29	19	19	23	25	29	26	4	15	12	7	8
M.A.	18	9	2	15	21	17	14	36	32	33	7	0	9	2	2
Professional degree, Ph.D.	22	11	96	6	37	27	14	31	31	9	89	0	2	1	3
CAREER (percent ever being)															
Elected official	5	3	9	2	–	–	–	4	3	5	0	11	3	–	–
Full-time government employee	15	13	21	16	30	47	27	–	–	–	27	5	28	–	–
Full-time university employee	5	3	2	2	14	12	7	21	17	7	–	0	4	–	–
Full-time private firm/crown corporation employee	–	–		28	23	19	38	37	42	65	44	25	–	–	–

Table 10-4

Social Background by Elite Sector and Social Class in the Population and for Men Aged 45–64 (Continued)

| | Capitalists | | | Mass media executives | Elected Officials | | | Bureaucrats | | | Academics | Agriculture leaders | Trade union officials | Canadian Population | |
	Big business	Small business	Lawyers		Federal	Provincial	Municipal	Federal	Provincial	Municipal				Total	Men aged 45–64
ANNUAL INCOME ($1000)															
under 30	0	7	0	2	0	0	31	0	0	0	7	32	37	90	69
30–49	1	30	0	32	59	35	31	4	16	19	36	26	50	8	23
50–69	18	20	4	54	28	50	31	84	78	63	49	21	12	2	5
70–99	11	9	11	10	0	5	5	12	5	19	6	16	1	1	2
100–199	36	26	46	0	10	8	3	0	2	0	3	5	1	0	1
200 or more	35	9	39	2	3	2	0	0	0	0	0	0	0	0	0
NET WORTH ($1000)															
under 100	3	5	2	27	26	21	24	13	21	5	20	11	52	—	—
100–199	11	1	5	39	19	29	19	47	31	38	27	16	28	—	—
200–499	34	32	25	31	24	33	33	33	36	53	49	32	17	—	—
500–999	25	15	16	4	11	9	12	5	10	5	1	32	3	—	—
1,000 or more	28	37	52	0	20	9	12	3	2	0	3	11	0	—	—

from very privileged backgrounds, while the trade union and agriculture leaders differ significantly but not dramatically from the population. The different social background variables give somewhat varying indications of the strength of the relationship between parental background and elite status. By the standards of mobility studies of national populations, these relationships are very strong. On the other hand it is clear that access to the top ranks of the largest corporations and the state is not in significant measure inherited. To put it another way, even the corporate executives, who come from the most privileged backgrounds, are much more highly placed than their fathers. The elites may not be self-perpetuating, but our results still are not a very encouraging indicator of the degree of equality of opportunity in Canadian society.

The extent of class bias in the recruitment to elite positions (other than in labour and agriculture, of course) has understandably encouraged an instrumental interpretation of politics and policy making. Furthermore, there is a strong correlation between the class backgrounds of the elite groups and their positions on the political spectrum. So while our data do not support the strongest formulations of instrumentalist Marxism and radical pluralism, particularly the notion that the state elites are predominantly from extremely privileged and corporate backgrounds, it is still possible that the ideological positions of the elite groups derive from their dramatically different class and social backgrounds.

SOCIAL BACKGROUND AND IDEOLOGICAL DIFFERENCES BETWEEN ELITE GROUPS

To our knowledge, Canadian social scientists have not addressed the more general question of what, if any, relationship there is between social background and elite action. Porter offers only the most general comment, though he suggests that the nature of this relationship was self-evident and consistent with his understanding of the Canadian political process:

Frequency of interaction, homogeneity in social background, and class continuity all lead to common outlook and common attitudes and values about the social system and the place of corporate enterprise in it. The fact that the corporate elite hold important positions beyond the corporate world means that they are in a position to make their ideology pervade the entire society until it becomes identified with the common good. If they are forced at times to accept changes like labour legislation or health insurance it is not because of an opposing social movement based on class conflict, but because other elites, such as the political, are at work seeking to consolidate their power. (1965, 305–6)

Clement (1975) makes an ambitious attempt to link the social background of the Canadian business elite to the character of Canadian capitalism, and particularly to the very high level of foreign ownership of Canadian business. Following R.T. Naylor (1972), he argues that the inability of Canadian capitalists to maintain Canadian control of manufacturing and resource industries partly reflected the social conservatism and inbreeding of the dominant, "mercantile" element of indigenous capital. Clement's argument, in part, rests on showing that the directors and executives of Canadian-controlled corporations have more exclusive family backgrounds than their "comprador" counterparts who control foreign-owned corporations in Canada and who control American corporations (in the U.S.). Interestingly, while other elements of their argument have come under sustained attack from a variety of directions (for a summary see Brym 1985, 7 ff.), Naylor's and Clement's analysis of the social background of the corporate elite has largely been spared criticism.

There is no reason to be sanguine about the prospects of discovering powerful influences of social backgrounds on elite ideology – or at least of discovering influences net of the effect of position. While there is good reason to predict class bias in recruitment patterns, sectoral differences in ideology in previous research suggest that the impact of social background is entirely spent on the recruitment process. John Higley Desley Deacon, and Don Smart summarize the findings of previous studies in a number of different nations as follows: "... the hypothesis that elites' attitudes on political issues are systematically related to their social backgrounds has been invalidated by upwards of a dozen studies in different countries ... there is little evidence for or against the assumption that elites' more basic beliefs and orientations are formed early in life and retained throughout it. Moreover, there is strong evidence to show that elites' values and attitudes are strongly affected by their career experiences and sector locations" (1979, 74).

While this structural emphasis serves as an important corrective to the individualism implicit in much elite analysis, the study of elite backgrounds and careers is not incompatible with a more institutional framework. Moshe Czudnowski suggests a conjunctural approach to consideration of the influence of social background on political elites:

Where social stratification is relatively rigid and social change relatively slow, the social background of ruling elites is still a valid predictor of policies and political outcomes ... In increasingly pluralistic societies, where mobility and change are relatively high, the social background of decision-makers becomes a diminishing indicator of political affiliation and attitudes. Political parties tend to recruit a more heterogeneous membership which eventually translates into a more heterogeneous leadership. Under the impact of social and economic crises, however, ideologies and party platforms reclaim their predominance and reflect social differences or cleavages, even if only temporarily. (1982, 5–6)

The period beginning with the 1973 "oil shock" through to the present would seem to qualify as one of continuing social and economic crises of the kind to which Czudnowski refers, suggesting that we should find that the social backgrounds of state elites affects their ideology.

There is obviously a correlation between the major ideological differences between elite groups and their background characteristics. Big business and labour define, respectively, the right and left poles of the ideological spectrum and the most and least privileged social backgrounds, while the state elites are intermediate in both respects. Although the analysis done so far does not indicate the strength of the relationship, to some extent, therefore, social background must influence political ideology. The larger question, however, is whether social background affects ideology *after accounting for structural differences*. At issue is whether the influence of social background is confined to the recruitment of individuals to elite positions or whether it also accounts for some of the ideological variation within the groups.

To address these questions a number of measures of political ideology are regressed on indicators of social background and a set of variables comparing the groups. In order to limit its complexity, this analysis is limited to six dependent variables: the three key measures of political ideology, support for civil liberties, support (measured with dummy variables) for the (combination of) the federal Progressive Conservative and Social Credit parties, and support for the federal NDP. The regression analysis is reported in three tables: table 10-5 gives the analysis of variance for the regression; tables 10-6 and 10-7, respectively, give the regression coefficients for the differences between elite sectors and (combined) the background and career variables.

The first row of table 10-5 shows that, altogether, parental education, father's occupation and social class, language and ethnicity, religion, age, level of education, career, and region explain between 9.2 and 23.5 percent of the variance in the various measures of ideology. Social background thus has a very strong impact on ideology, although its effect is not as large as the difference between elite groups, which explains between 12.4 and 42.6 percent of the variance in these variables. Of course, because there are strong correlations between the background variables and elite group, which reflect the recruitment processes just discussed, the combined effect of background variables and elite group is not nearly as large as the sum of their individual effects. For example background variables explain 23.5 percent of the variance in the measure of support for the welfare state, elite group alone explains 35.1 percent, but together they explain 40.6 percent of the variance. Thus the "unique" effect of the background and career variables – the proportion of the variance that could not be accounted for by elite group alone – amounts to 5.5 percent (i.e., 40.6 – 35.1 percent) of the variance, compared to 17.1 percent of the variance that is uniquely attributable to group differences. Social background and career variables have a strong "indirect" effect on support for the welfare state that is transmitted through the elite group, but the "direct" effect of social background and career on political ideology is quite weak. The relationships between social background, elite group, and the other five measures of political ideology are quite similar.

Table 10-5
Analysis of Variance for the Regression of Political Ideology Scales on Elite Sector and Social Background

Group of Independent Variables	Variance Explained (adjusted for degrees of freedom)					
	Support welfare state	State economic inter-vention	Power of labour	Civil liberties	Support federal PCs or Social Credit	Support federal NDP
TOTAL EFFECTS						
Background and career variables and region	.235	.232	.226	.092	.174	.214
Elite group	.351	.352	.426	.124	.166	.280
All variables	.406	.422	.473	.151	.259	.385
INCREMENTAL EFFECTS						
Parents' education, father's occupation, language, and ethnicity, religion, age	.134	.137	.109	.063	.130	.090
Level of education	.036	.029	.026	.017	.003	.050
Career	.052	.047	.074	.017	.009	.021
Region	.014	.019	.014	.002	.032	.074
Elite group	.170	.190	.248	.059	.085	.165
UNIQUE EFFECTS*						
Parents' education	.000	.001	.001	.000	.001	.000
Father's occupation, class	.004	.004	.003	.002	.003	.005
Language, ethnicity	.005	.004	.004	.008	.005	.001
Religion	.018	.017	.011	.006	.028	.024
Age	.000	.000	.009	.000	.000	.003
Level of education	.002	.003	.000	.004	.000	.004
Career	.004	.002	.003	.005	.004	.008
Region	.018	.027	.020	.009	.047	.074
Elite group	.171	.190	.247	.059	.090	.172

* not adjusted for degrees of freedom

Before considering the effects of the background variables, which are shown in table 10-6, it is useful to examine summary measures of their overall impact. The second panel of table 10-5 gives the incremental effects of the various groups of variables, when they are entered in the temporal order of their impact on individuals. For example parents' education, father's occupation, language, ethnicity, religion, and age – taken as a group – explain 13.4 percent of the variance in support for the welfare state, education explains a further 3.6 percent of the variance, career experience an additional 5.2 percent, region an additional 1.4 percent, and finally, elite group adds 17.0 percent of the variance. The other

Table 10-6
Group Differences in the Mean Scores on Political Ideology Scales by Elite Group, with and without Controls for Social Background

Political Ideology	Adjusted for social background?	Difference from State Elites					Differences between State Elites			Differences within Business	
		All business	Mass media	Agriculture	Academic	Labour	Federal versus provincial level	Federal versus municipal level	Civil servants versus Politicians	Big versus small business	Big business versus lawyers
Support welfare state	No	-.40	-.02	.17	.06	.70	-.07	.05	-.09	-.09	-.04
	Yes	-.39	-.10	.10	.01	.64	.03	.01	-.09	-.04	-.08
State economic intervention	No	-.58	-.22	.37	.14	.70	.20	-.15	.14	-.64	.14
	Yes	-.58	-.29	.25	.05	.65	.28	-.29	.17	-.55	.07
Power of labour	No	-.60	-.24	.11	-.01	1.05	.12	.08	-.06	-.55	-.44
	Yes	-.57	-.36	.14	-.08	1.03	.15	-.06	-.04	-.54	.50
Support civil liberties	No	-.55	.10	.17	.11	.59	.21	.13	-.02	-.67	.77
	Yes	-.51	-.04	.07	.13	.43	.25	.12	.06	-.55	.63
Support federal Conservatives/ Social Credit	No	.15	-.06	-.02	-.07	-.25	-.44	.20	-.26	.10	.10
	Yes	.08	-.05	.02	-.05	-.20	-.49	.31	-.23	.03	.15
Support federal NDP	No	-.15	-.05	.17	.07	.45	-.02	.11	-.15	.02	-.02
	Yes	-.15	-.12	.21	.07	.45	.03	.01	-.07	.09	-.12

Table 10-7

Regression of Political Ideology Scales on Background and Career Variables, Controlling for Elite Group

Independent Variable	Regression Coefficient					
	Dependent Variable				Support federal	
	Support welfare state	Economic inter-vention	Power of labour	Support civil liberties	PC/Social Credit	Support federal NDP
LANGUAGE AND ETHNICITY (relative to British origin, native English speakers)						
Native language French		.17+			.37+	
English language, French ethnicity						
Native language not French or English	.13+	.17+	.20+		−.16*	
English language, non-English and non-French						
RELIGION (relative to none)						
Catholic	−.17*		−.27*		−.10+	−.16*
Jewish			−.25			−.12
Establishment Protestant	−.26*	−.22*	−.22*	−.19	−.21*	−.16*
Other Protestant and all others	−.24*	−.24*	−.22*	−.23+	−.24*	−.18*
AGE (in decades)			−.09*			−.02
FATHER'S OCCUPATION (relative to skilled manual)						
Professional, managerial						.07+
Non-manual						
Semi- and unskilled manual						
Farmer						
FATHER OWNED A BUSINESS						.10
Size of father's business					−.09	
RESPONDENT'S EDUCATION						
In years	−.02	−.02				−.02+
University graduate (dummy)	.12*	.15+				
Ever full-time employee of private firm		−.09				−.05*
Ever full-time civil servant				.20+	−.07	
Ever full-time university teacher						
REGION (relative to Ontario)						
Atlantic	.14+					
Quebec					−.21*	
Manitoba						−.08
Saskatchewan	.40*	.54*	.40*	.43+	−.43*	.54*
Alberta						
British Columbia			−.27*	−.26*	.10+	

* significant at .01; + significant at .05; figures with no sign are significant at .10; all other coefficients are omitted.
Mother's and father's education and a dummy variable indicating whether the respondent's father owned a business and the size of father's business are in the equations but had no significant effects.

two key ideological dimensions exhibit quite similar patterns. While support for civil liberties depends somewhat less on career experience, support for the Conservative (and Social Credit) party depends more heavily on region, and support for the NDP depends more strongly on level of education and region.

Education, career experience, and region have significant effects on elite attitudes, over and above the effect of previous background, although the combined effect of the various social background measures is always greater. Support for the Progressive Conservative party, however, is very little affected by education and career but is affected by region, which has little impact on the other variables. Interestingly, even after controlling for all the other variables, regional differences explain more of the differences in party support than in the more abstractly ideological measures. This is consistent with our previous analysis of ideological differences in the general public.

Table 10-6 shows the ideological differences between the elite groups, with and without adjustment for social background differences. The inter-elite differences are here presented in the form of "contrasts," which compare the state elites as a whole to the other major groups, compare the three levels of government, compare politicians to bureaucrats, and compare the three business groups. The inter-sectoral differences have been examined in considerable detail in the last chapter and the object of this analysis is to determine whether taking account of social background and career variables substantially reduces these differences – which would be the case if the instrumentalist hypothesis, that recruitment into elites helps account for their ideological orientation, is correct. In fact controlling on background and career variables has negligible effects on the differences between sectors, contrary to the instrumentalist argument.

The significant effects of social background and career on political ideology, controlling for group membership, are shown in table 10-7 (to highlight the significant effects in this large table, regression coefficients that are not significantly different from zero at the .1 level are left out of the table). In order to minimize type I error, that is reporting the results of random variation as findings, the following discussion refers only to variables that significantly affect at least two of the six measures of political ideology.

The first thing to observe in table 10-7 is that there are not many significant effects, as might be expected from the analysis of variance (in table 10-5), which indicates that once sector is taken into account, social background and career history have relatively little impact on ideology. There are a number of effects worth noting. First, elites whose native language is neither French nor English are somewhat more liberal (by an average of about one-fifth of a standard deviation) in their views of the welfare state, state economic intervention, and labour and less likely to vote Progressive Conservative or Social Credit than the reference group of British-origin, native

English speakers. French-language speakers are more likely than members of the reference group to support social programs and civil liberties.

Despite the major differences in family background between the elite groups the measures of family background have little impact on political ideology, once the other variables are held constant. Mother's and father's education had no significant effects and measures of father's occupation, whether he owned a business, and the size of the business each affected only one of the variables. However strong the impact of parental background on individual's education and on which sector they belong to, these variables have no long-term ideological consequence. The effect of education, measured by two variables – years of education and a dummy variable identifying university graduates – was also weak and ambiguous. More education is weakly associated with more conservative ideology, but university graduates are more liberal than non-graduates. Age had weak effects, in the same direction as for the general population; older respondents were less supportive of civil liberties and less likely to support the NDP. The range of age in the elites is much smaller than in the population large, which tends to diminish its impact on ideology.

Variables describing the respondents' previous careers, before taking up their positions at the time of the interview, affect ideology. Respondents who had previously been employed in the private sector (excluding, of course, respondents presently in such positions) were more opposed to state economic intervention and less likely to support the NDP; government employment (for respondents who were not civil servants at the time of the interview) was associated with slightly stronger support for state economic intervention and a disinclination to vote Progressive Conservative or Social Credit; while a background in university teaching (except for the present academic elite) had no effect on any of the measures of ideology.

Net of all these other variables there were two regional effects. Elites from Saskatchewan were substantially more left wing on all the ideological measures and the opposite was true for elites from British Columbia. In Saskatchewan, of course, this is the result of there being an NDP government in power at the time of our interviews and the relative absence of business elites from that province. Interestingly, Quebec respondents were ideologically indistinguishable from English Canadian elites.

The most consistent effect, surprisingly, was for religion – respondents who said they had no religion were more liberal (by between one-quarter and half a standard deviation), than Catholics, establishment (i.e. Anglican, Presbyterian, and United Church) Protestants, and other Protestants (with whom are included the very small number of people with some religion who are not Catholic, Protestant, or Jewish). There appear to be no differences between Catholics and Protestants, though there are too few Jewish respondents to say much about their position. A caution is in order regarding the interpretation of these findings about the relationship between religion and political ideology.

As measured here, religion is not a background variable, since individuals with no religion may have come from very religious households and subsequently turned away from religion. Furthermore we do not know whether respondents who say they adhere to a religion are at all active.

CONCLUSIONS

While the extent of inequality appears less extreme than in Porter's day, Canadian business and state elites continue to be recruited from disproportionately privileged backgrounds. In striking contrast, the backgrounds of trade union and agricultural organization leaders differ to only a small degree from those of the workers and farmers that they represent. Still, even the backgrounds of the capitalists and lawyers, who are clearly the most privileged, are not sufficiently elevated to suggest that direct inheritance is responsible for the patterns we observe.

Despite this evidence of the relatively successful transmission of privilege across generations, the different social locations from which the elites are drawn are not reducible to a single hierarchy. The federal bureaucrats, for example, tend to be recruited from highly educated families, but their fathers are much less likely to have owned substantial businesses than the fathers of executives. Compared to all the other groups, the corporate executives were substantially more likely to have come from families with substantial businesses, although only a tiny minority come from backgrounds in any way comparable to the positions, at the heads of the largest Canadian corporations, in which we interviewed them. The executives are also distinctive in that the representation of French Canadians remains very low despite the presence of significant numbers of executives of neither British nor French ethnicity. The differences in the social backgrounds of the state elites are also considerable. Generally, the federal bureaucrats and politicians come from more urban, better-educated, and more-privileged backgrounds, especially in comparison to their provincial counterparts.

Once the sectoral positions of individual elite respondents are taken into account, social background has very weak effects on ideology – a finding that is consistent with previous studies in other countries. This makes sense. Elites are recruited from among individuals with long experience in a corporation, government, trade union, university, or other organization, and this involves the selection of individuals who will represent the needs of those organizations. These will be individuals whose personal views are compatible with those needs. A democratization of the recruitment processes would decrease hereditary privilege, but would not affect the conflicting interests that give rise to ideological conflict.

Our findings caution against individualistic interpretations of the ideological conflicts among capital, labour, and the state, and are not compatible with an instrumental interpretation of the ideological differences between elites. Instrumentalist Marxism and radical pluralism correctly draw attention to the class bias in the recruitment of elites (as do sociological accounts of the mobility process) and to the ideological character of elites, but the direct relationship between social background and ideology required by these theories is not found in our surveys.

We have located the ideologies of the different elites in the context of the class structure of contemporary capitalism, though we require a more general logic than that of allegiance to *one's own* class. *Pace* Hegel we do not see the state elites as representatives of a universal class, or any other class. The ideology of state elites, however, is bound up in *the* class contradiction of capitalism. Elite recruitment is not responsible for this ideological alignment. Instead, more general social processes are at work. While the data at our disposal do not permit us to describe these processes in detail, the social processes that, at once, propagate inequality across generations and fill elite positions with able and dedicated individuals involve at least the following: inequalities built into the social networks of society; links between the networks and institutions such as universities and corporations; and the critical role of families in social mobility. The central point of this analysis, however, is that elite ideology cannot be understood in these terms; and the corollary is that equalizing opportunity, whether by diminishing the impact of family background, by education, or by mandated equity programs will not change the ideological differences among elites. These are tied to their structural role in the social relations of production in labour, capital, and the state.

PART FOUR

11 Conclusions

In this book we have pursued three objectives. At the simplest level we have used a unique body of surveys to describe the shape of Canada's political culture at a decisive moment in its history. These surveys describe the attitudes on a great variety of political issues of members of the general public and of elite decision makers in the leading institutions of government and society. In purely descriptive terms, our surveys provide a unique account of the contours of public opinion and of the perspectives of Canadians influential in the public policy process during a period marked by the onset of protracted economic and political instability.

This descriptive project has a related methodological objective: to use survey data to investigate competing theoretical perspectives on the workings of a liberal democratic state. Broadly speaking, we have sought to evaluate the relative merits of opposing accounts of the ways in which liberal democratic states are sustained or undermined by consensus and divisions in political culture. This has entailed a conceptual focus to our design of survey questions, which not only tap straightforward feelings about concrete public issues, but relate also to underlying theoretical arguments about the nature of conflict and consensus in societies like Canada. We have designed and interpreted our survey questions in terms of theoretical conceptualizations of class and ideological division, the political and ideological components of hegemonic projects and counter-hegemonic forces and the relative salience and satisfactions of public and private life.

This points to our third objective, which has been to give a theoretically plausible, but also historically concrete, understanding of Canadian politics at a particular conjuncture. The research project on which this book is based was conceived as an effort to try to understand the clear signals of rapid political change after 1968 – the date of the coming to power of Prime Minister Pierre Trudeau in Canada. Much more significantly, it was also the date of political rebellions in many liberal democracies, and the date of the high-water mark of the Vietnam War (the Tet offensive), which delivered such a heavy blow to the international dominance of the United States and the stability of the international economy over which it presided.

Our project and this book were conceived as a study of the interplay of politics, economics, and ideology in Canada at this time of threat to the international hegemony of the United States, and to the domestic political regimes in other developed western countries. With hindsight it is now much more clear than it was when we designed the project that the instability we sought to understand marked a shift in Canada from one form of political order to another: from the postwar order of a quasi-protectionist, quasi-corporatist, and government-regulated political economy of the Keynesian welfare state to a neo-liberal order of free trade, deregulation, down-sized government and cutbacks in social policy, attacks on labour unions, and the market deregulation of politics and society.

The late 1970s, when we began to collect the data examined in this book, mark the conclusion, more properly the exhaustion, of the Keynesian project in Canada. The early 1980s, when our surveys were completed, marked its last hurrah: a final attempt by the last of the Trudeau governments to reinvigorate the Keynesian welfare state, or at least certain of its elements. But that attempt was followed rapidly by economic recession and overwhelming political defeat by another party and leader committed over the next decade to the introduction of the new political order. The objective of this chapter is, therefore, to discuss the implications of our findings for understanding the political changes after 1980 as a breakdown of a previously established hegemonic project, and the initiation, however tentative and unsuccessful, of a new project to establish economic growth and political stability.

In this chapter we first discuss the structure of public opinion and ideology as we have described it in Canada at the end of the Trudeau regime. We summarize an interpretation of Canadian political culture at this conjuncture as reflecting crisis tendencies in the hegemonic order of the post–second World War welfare state. Second, we discuss the structure of elite ideology and alignments in public policy debates as a key to understanding the politics of the late-Trudeau era. We discuss the relevance of these findings for the relative autonomy of liberal democratic states to create political order and economic growth in capitalist societies. Finally, we discuss the implications of our historically contingent descriptions of public and elite opinion at the end of the Trudeau regime for a retroactive understanding of subsequent political developments that mark the failure of that regime, the end of the postwar welfare state, and the shift to the new politics of the Brian Mulroney era and beyond.

IDEOLOGY AND POLITICAL CULTURE:
POLITICS IN THE MASS PUBLIC

Using surveys to examine relatively abstruse theoretical arguments not normally subjected to such procedures has entailed a particular emphasis upon the concept of ideology as a guide to the production and analysis of opinion data. The data we have produced and analyzed result from a conception of ideologies as class-interested or class-relevant perspectives on the central issues dividing political forces in a capitalist society. These issues have been conceived of as relations between capital and labour (questions of labour relations), relations between capital and the state (questions of economic regulation), and relations between labour and the state (questions of social welfare).

This concept of ideology is further tied to a conceptualization of hegemony as an economic, political, and ideological order that is sustained predominantly by the consent of non-governing classes. Central to such an order in a capitalist society are agreements on these three generic problems of ordering capitalist relations. Equally fundamental, and a fourth general rubric in terms of which we have designed our surveys, is a conception of a liberal society grounded in civil liberty: the freedom of the individual *vis-à-vis* the state, and the separation of the private realm of freedom in markets, families, and civil associations from the public realm of authority backed by coercion. Concretely, and in relation to the specific historical conjuncture in which we worked, the institutional arrangements of the Canadian postwar welfare state had established a relatively successful hegemonic order, embodying a particular configuration of policy in the areas of labour relations, economic regulation, and social welfare, and a firm commitment to capitalist market relations and the civil liberties appropriate to them.

The ideological discourse supporting the welfare state in Canada during the early 1980s, however, was characterized by particular limitations. There *was* strong support for social expenditures on health care, education, and so on, and for particular disadvantaged groups, including the poor, the aged, and women. Beyond this there was evidence of strongly egalitarian elements in popular ideology, in the form of support for redistribution of income, the rights of minorities, and affirmative action. Moreover public support for social democratic policies extended to positions that represent a clear break from beliefs in the sanctity of markets, including majority support for the government's providing jobs for the unemployed, for rent control, for prohibiting extra-billing by physicians, and for affirmative action in employment.

Closer examination of our surveys, however, indicates that support for a thoroughgoing welfare state along social democratic lines was undercut by contradictory arguments in support of a much more limited state- and market-regulated order. Support for programs that were not identified in class terms, such as education, medical care, and daycare, and for non-class groups like the poor, women, and native peoples was much stronger than for the unemployed or for workers' compensation. The ambiguity of this orientation to social policy is underlined by our evidence of marked public antipathy to organized labour and to causes identified with the self-assertion of class rights. Many Canadians believed that the availability of social welfare increases unemployment. Moreover the demands of organized labour and business were lumped together, as reflecting special interests. Predominantly egalitarian beliefs combined with a populist orientation to political power in which big business *and* labour unions *and* the federal government were all seen as too powerful, while the classical embodiments of the petty bourgeoisie, small business and farmers, were seen as deserving more power. Even these opinions about the distribution of power were ambiguous and contradictory. Generalized antipathy to unions was coupled with widespread support for some concrete policies that would strengthen trade unions; not to mention the inconsistency between the belief that governments are too powerful and support for the network of government programs that comprised the Canadian version of a limited welfare state.

The same ambivalence is found in Canadians' generally progressive views on civil liberties issues, which are qualified by a measure of prejudice towards immigrants and opposition to minority language rights, and by a tendency to endorse the state's right to censorship and extraordinary police powers. These and other ambiguities in public opinion reflect not a lack of ideological "constraint," but a particular theoretical problem. Just as populism can be seen to resolve the conflicts between left and right by stepping outside an implicit, unidimensional paradigm of political ideology, the combination of civil libertarianism with ethnocentrism and support for censorship is not purely illogical. A liberal state may be defended as guaranteeing economic and political liberties to members of a political community defined in ethnically and morally exclusive rather than pluralistic terms.

More to the point, from our theoretical vantage point, the ideological inconsistency and contradiction is *perfectly consistent* with the contradictory character of a capitalist welfare state, which has at the same time to reproduce market relations and market inequalities while promoting state welfare and the equality of citizenship. Such contradictory pressures are reflected in the ambiguous, if not hypocritical, utterances of politicians who want to "downsize" governments while preserving the welfare state as a "sacred trust."

The Canadian welfare state has been characterized by a full measure of this ambiguity throughout its development. If the early 1970s mark the conclusion or exhaustion of the Keynesian project in Canada, that project was always marked by extreme pragmatism and represents one of the more conservative versions of a postwar welfare state in advanced capitalist societies. While potentially saleable as a populist enterprise, and arguably stolen from the official social democrats, medicare, old-age pensions, and other social programs, were not put forward as such. Also, more radical causes, even those with historical roots in Canada such as efforts to control monopolies, have never been seriously on the national agenda: witness the abject failure of attempts to strengthen competition legislation in the Trudeau era. Nor were managerial and corporatist elements of the welfare state well developed in Canada. In the Trudeau era even the sporadic efforts to develop corporatist advisory bodies sputtered out with the withdrawal of labour following the 1976 imposition of wage and price controls. Job training, another important focus of many European welfare states (some not even particularly social democratic in orientation), was never given much emphasis, despite the virtual withdrawal of employers from providing training in the highly skilled manual trades. Even medicare, which is often portrayed as the cornerstone of the Canadian welfare state, was instituted only very late in the development of this welfare state, and then only in the limited form of a government health insurance scheme to pay for the private provision of medical care on a fee-for-service basis. Medicare dramatically improved accessibility to medical care, but it bought the consent of physicians by substantially increasing their already high incomes and allowing hospitals, under the control of the medical profession, to become richer and more central to the delivery of care. This failure to reform health care delivery laid the foundation for the eventual fiscal crisis, which unfolded in the 1980s.

The slow and limited development of the Canadian welfare state, of course, reflects the political and ideological character of its principal agent, the Liberal party of Canada. At the level of party politics Canadian Keynesianism was driven by the Liberal party's cross-class constituency, by a paternalistic concern to serve that constituency within particular economic and ideological limits, supporting a continentalist and anti-nationalist economic and foreign policy, and by the implementation of welfare policy by well-educated bureaucratic career elites from middle-class, though not wealthy backgrounds. Occasionally, threats from social movements and the parliamentary left have been sufficient to accelerate these processes, but not – except in rare instances at the provincial level – by taking control of the political environment. More successful have been populist counters from the right – under Diefenbaker in a nationalist guise, under Mulroney in a more internationalist guise, but in both cases with an even less coherent perspective than the Liberal party's on a principled defense of the welfare state.

The fragility of political support for the Canadian welfare state in the two establishment political parties also reflects its having been instituted without the concrete representation of its working class beneficiaries. The very poor were not even beneficiaries, witness the absence of reform to social assistance; and, by the mid-1980s, food banks operated as private charities had to step in to address the needs of the very poor. This weakness is perhaps best symbolized by the identity of the only labour "representative" in the Senate, Edward Lawson, from the Teamsters Union, who was regarded as a pariah in the mainstream labour movement and whose union was not a member of the Canadian Labour Congress.

There is one other important weakness of the hegemonic order in Canada. By the time of our surveys skepticism about the state, and especially the federal government, alienation from politics, and lack of interest in participating in politics were rife. That is the social welfare consensus lived on without an active constituency. This is probably the norm for democratic political life, especially in the "peaceable kingdom." Given some capacity for the bureaucratic self-perpetuation of governments and especially government programs, the lack of an active political constituency is not a disadvantage, in principle. In a worsening economic context, however, this means that resistance to attacks on the welfare state will have an ad hoc, and for that reason potentially ineffective, quality.

In addition to these ambiguities, contradictions and weaknesses in public support for a welfare state in Canada, the hegemonic consensus at the end of the Trudeau era was limited by significant divisions in its perception by different social classes. We found substantial class differences in political attitudes (see chapter 5).

Not surprisingly the extent of class difference depends on the aspect of ideology considered. We found it useful to think of three layers of ideology. Two of these layers preoccupy mainstream political sociology: one refers to party support and party politics directly, and one, usually labelled "political culture," refers to political efficacy, trust, and political participation. Missing from the two, of course, is the real content of contemporary politics, which we have conceived in terms of the relationships between capital, labour, and the state. In the third layer of ideology, which deals with these relationships and the ways in which the welfare state defines them, we found significant divisions among classes.

At the same time, our surveys confirmed numerous other studies reporting the relative *in*significance of ideological divisions to party politics in Canada. At one level, therefore, the orthodox, non-class interpretation of electoral politics in Canada is perfectly correct. While we have little sympathy for the enterprise, conventional election studies can go on without fear that Marxist statisticians using survey data will discover the class roots of Canadian voting. That the absence of class in the discourse of electoral and party politics was coupled to the clarity of class divisions in public opinion regarding the welfare state represents a limit to the capacity of governing parties to sustain the latter. The lack of linkage between public opinion and party politics is a mark of the ideological and political weaknesses of labour, and of the welfare state in Canada during the Trudeau era.

The development of a more coherent ideological and political defense of the welfare state was further limited by another aspect of the Canadian political culture: the salience of regional identities and divisions over the "national question," that is the national identity of Quebec. These are clearly important elements of the Canadian political culture. Nevertheless the conventional explanation for the weakness of class differences in voting, the view that regionalism exerts a dominant effect on political culture in Canada, is clearly wrong. Regional differences in most aspects of political ideology are not in fact the result of the existence of multiple, distinctive regional political communities; to a very large extent they are differences only between French Quebec and English Canada outside of Quebec. Furthermore these differences have a definite ideological character.

A significant left-right polarization between French Quebec and English Canada has gone unobserved in the literature on political culture in Canada, presumably because ideological divisions are not systematically theorized or measured in studies of electoral politics. The left-right divisions between Quebec and English Canada, we have shown, are not the result of differences in the kinds of people living in Quebec and English Canada, at least as measured by their education, income, and a variety of other structural variables. Nor are they reducible to the relative deprivation of French Québécois, since the standard of living is lower in Atlantic Canada, where support for the left is much weaker, not stronger.

The relatively left-wing position of Quebec political culture is most convincingly interpreted in the context of the distinctive character of Quebec politics in the era of the Quiet Revolution and afterwards: the postwar focus of Quebec nationalism on the role of the Quebec state (i.e., the provincial government, regardless of the party in power) in institutionalizing the welfare state, and its doing so in the peculiar context of the need for a more systematic state response to the inequality between the dominant and minority language groups in Quebec produced by market forces.

The irony is that the hegemony of the welfare state project was perhaps best established in Quebec, especially in the direction of developing corporatist institutions. The particular dynamics of party politics and nationalism in Quebec, however, undermined the success of left-wing parties in that province, so that the Parti Québécois could serve as vehicle for social democratic politics in the 1970s, but in the next decade turn into a party hardly distinguishable from the Liberals in these terms. Further, the dynamics of Quebec nationalism have muted the clarity of ideological divisions in federal party politics in the rest of Canada as in Quebec.

By the early 1980s, therefore, our surveys show that the material limits and contradictions of the Canadian welfare state were reflected in the limits, contradictions, and class divisions of popular ideology. Further, our surveys confirm other evidence that by the end of the 1970s there was widespread public alienation from politics, a lack of political efficacy, and low levels of political participation, strongly linked to class differences. Importantly, however, in Canadians' minds none of these class-divided perspectives, nor the pervasive dissatisfaction with government, particularly the federal government, was linked to party politics in Canada. The welfare state was weak but not in crisis, if by that we mean the prospect of dramatic change brought about by organized popular resistance.

There was indeed a hegemonic order built around public support for the institutions of the Canadian welfare state, and this order survived, more or less intact ideologically, through the early 1980s. It was a limited hegemony, however, for the reasons summarized here, and the limitations help explain why an attack on the welfare state could be mobilized from the political right. Still, the likelihood of such mobilization and the rapid political turn to the right of the mid-1980s does not follow from our analysis of *public* ideology, where despite the contradictions and ambiguities we have discussed, left-leaning sentiments were more firmly entrenched than right-leaning sentiments. In order to pursue our understanding of these later developments we will have to turn to the implications of our analysis of elite ideology and public policy debates in the early 1980s.

ELITE IDEOLOGY AND THE AUTONOMY OF THE STATE

Relative to the class divisions in public opinion, we found marked ideological differences on the broad spectrum of political issues between the elite representatives of capital, labour, and the state. Our profile of elite ideology at the beginning of the 1980s makes much more intelligible the story of the subsequent collapse of the Liberal party electoral coalition, and Progressive Conservative party victories on platforms that ran against the drift of public opinion.

Nevertheless if elite answers to our surveys in 1977 and 1981 were marked by sectoral division, it is also true that they appear remarkably supportive of the welfare state, in comparison to the policies of the first and especially the second Mulroney governments. In the business elites' responses to our questions it is possible to foresee the ideological roots of the Mulroney years in support for free trade, opposition to foreign investment review, etcetera. But opposition to the welfare state was, at the time, more qualified than absolute. Missing from their views at the time was the bedrock opposition to the postwar settlement that increasingly came to dominate business ideology, as well as the federal and many provincial governments. Support for the essential policy framework of the Canadian welfare state still defined the dominant position among elites at the beginning of the 1980s. For elites, as for members of the general public, there was a consensus sustaining the welfare state.

Despite this consensus, our data bear no resemblance to the political worlds imagined in standard pluralist accounts of political accommodation or consensus among elites. Canadian labour elites were completely isolated, considerably to the left of their own constituency of trade union members in Canada. Labour elites were so different from business elites that there was virtually no overlap in the distributions of their opinions. Differences between labour and state elites and between business and state elites were not quite so extreme, but it is no exaggeration to say that they each occupied distinct and different ideological niches.

Canada's corporate executives overwhelmingly supported cutbacks to social expenditures and "tight money" policies to combat inflation, while almost unanimously opposing government investments in industry. And there was majority, although not at the time overwhelming, support for "free" trade with the U.S. Except for labour relations issues, where they are clearly more vulnerable than their more powerful counterparts, small-business owners held somewhat less extreme views. Only on civil liberties issues did corporate executives share in an elite consensus, and here small business was more conservative.

In a way that the business executives do not, the trade union leaders in our sample represent a mass constituency. So it is important to ask how representative of trade unionists are the political opinions of their leaders. Of course there is likely to be much more consensus on questions related to the *raison d'être* of unions – their representation of workers to employers. The more general comparison is interesting, of course, because trade unions are engaged in a more general confrontation with capital as well as in day-to-day conflicts in the workplace. The surveys are quite unambiguous on this point: trade union leaders take positions that, while clearly reflecting the interests of their constituents, are much more consistently left wing, even compared to the most militant sectors of the class they represent (though not, of course, to the left of individual militants).

In developing the questions in our surveys, we focused on what were at the time unresolved and contested political issues related to the preservation of the welfare state. For this reason it is not surprising that state elites really are in the middle of the ideological spectrum. But this should not detract from the concrete interpretation of what they said. At the beginning of the 1980s the state elites were divided in their views of a whole series of policy questions, including cutbacks in social programs, a guaranteed annual income, income inequality, and a variety of instances of state intervention in the economy. Still, in this period the dominant position among state elites was to favour a more activist regime of economic regulation, and the conservation, although not extension, of social programs. Only with respect to a lack of interest in and opposition to changes to strengthen organized labour did state elites reflect the position of business.

In our view these findings raise insuperable problems for much of elite theory as a viable political sociology. While elite theory correctly points to the need to consider elites as distinct groups, rather than merely the "tails" of distributions for samples of the entire public, the political positions of Canadian elites in the early 1980s are incompatible with notions of "elite liberalism," "elite integration," or "elite accommodation." Instead of suggesting support for theories of the liberal democratic state as a special terrain in which differences are worked out through bargaining and compromise on the part of elites who share an overriding ideological consensus, our data suggest that ideologically articulated class divisions, which are muted in the general public, are in some historical circumstances enormously amplified at the elite level. Although the argument for elite consensus and accommodation can be rescued by invoking the notion that there is an underlying agreement on the rules of the political game – essentially support for parliamentary government in the context of a market-driven society – this gives an extremely partial and biased view. Our data suggest that policy making takes place in the context of *unresolved* ideological conflict among elites, and this ideological conflict reflects the opposing interests of capital and labour.

It is still difficult to interpret our elite data from the vantage of pluralist theory even if, like most elite theorists, we simply read the labour elites out of the picture on the grounds that they do not, despite the promise of the theory, share effective power with other elites in capitalist democracies. The large differences between the opinions of business and the state elites are also difficult to square with a pluralist interpretation. Pluralists assume competing interests among sectorally distinct elites like politicians and business leaders, but they have tended to assume that such competition is restrained by a consensus on the fundamental value of a welfare state. Pluralist theory has not anticipated or theorized a crisis of the welfare state, except in terms of the stimulation of excess demand, and it provides no coherent way in which to understand divisions between political and business elites like those we have described. The only way of understanding such divisions, we have argued, is to view the ideas of elites as reflecting their places in capitalist society.

Thus we have elites without elite theory. We understand that sectors of society are in varying degrees represented, led, and controlled by elite groups, and that this conception is applicable to the very different kinds of organizations and institutions represented by capital, labour, and the state. Different recruitment processes govern the selection of elites within each sector and these are interesting in their own terms, but not very germane to our effort to map general ideological struggle. Only by theorizing their positions in class terms is it possible to understand the politics of elites. The politics of elites do not reflect their common situations – at the top of sectoral groups. Instead elites are class-identified actors playing out the structural conflicts in capitalist society.

It is possible to interpret the ideology of the state elites, and their conflict with business, in terms of longer- and shorter-term strategies for capitalist society. State and business elites really agree, but they have different views about the best tactics, especially at times where there appears to be no simple formula for smooth, continuing growth. The problem with this view is that the different policy positions of state and business elites involve real differences in the balance of power between capital and labour and in the extent to which market forces will be allowed to drive the society and economy. The rather tepid welfare-statism of the Canadian state elites who we interviewed was obviously not a formula for the overthrow of capitalism; but it was also not what the business elites wanted at the time, and proceeded to get in subsequent years.

The distinctive position of state elites, we have shown, is not a function of their social background, and cannot be explained in instrumental terms as the result of a progressive recruitment to state positions from lower- or middle-class backgrounds, despite the truth of this latter generalization. Rather it reflects the relative autonomy of capitalist states to define public policy at variance with the interests of capital, even when these are as clearly articulated as they were in Canada at this time.

This notion of the relative autonomy of the state is clearly different from comparable notions in pluralist theory. It has a meaning only in the context of an understanding of the role of the state in the regulation of class conflict in capitalist societies. Pluralist theory grants to the state a much more radical autonomy, rooted in the fundamental separation of state and civil society, politics and economics, and public and private life. The limits to such autonomy are derived only from the consensus that defines elite integration, a line of argument that is theoretically and empirically weak.

If the alternative conception of the relative autonomy of the state that we have invoked is theoretically richer, and provides a more adequate explanation of the data we have produced on elite ideological divisions, it remains somewhat imprecise. With hindsight, we can see the limits of such autonomy. When leading members of the capitalist class are as ideologically opposed to the direction of state policy as we show Canadian businessmen to have been at this time, liberal democratic governments that choose to govern in relative isolation from a distinct social base cannot continue long in that direction. The defeat of the Trudeau national project, shortly after the period in which our data were collected, is prefigured in our descriptions of public dissatisfaction with government, the extent of business hostility to government positions, the likely futility of government turning to the alternative support of labour elites (given the public opposition to enhancing the position of labour), and the difficulty of relying on the otherwise clear public support for welfare state policies in the absence of clear linkages of such support to the Liberal party.

At the same time, there was nothing automatic about the ability of business elites to mobilize opposition to the Trudeau government. The sudden and dramatic political change in the election of the first Mulroney government in 1984 cannot be understood as the capture of a political party and the government it subsequently formed by the capitalist class, no matter the strength of business allegiance with that party, no matter how impressive the financial resources it made available to it, and no matter how "instrumental" that government's policies may have subsequently appeared to be. How then does our analysis help understand the very real shift in Canadian politics that has occurred since 1984?

FAREWELL TO THE WELFARE STATE?

The first federal election after our surveys, in 1984, was something of an enigma. It does not reflect in any coherent way a response to the very sharp ideological conflict we have described among elites over public policy debates involving the protection and extension of the welfare state, and the evidence we have given of ideological and class divisions over such issues in public opinion. Rather than being a clear political realignment of class and ideological forces, it appears to confirm a number of points central to the common wisdom of Canadian politics as devoid of class and ideological content.

The landslide victory of the Progressive Conservative party and the events leading up to it appear, first, to provide clear evidence of the centrality of brokerage politics in Canada. Leadership changes in both parties prior to 1984 involved the selection of brokers, who were thought to be able to win elections because of their personal style, their pragmatic rather than programmatic orientation to politics, and their clear commitment to the liberal centre rather than to the ideological left and right represented in their respective parties. The 1984 election apparently further illustrated the irrelevance of ideology in Canadian politics. The poverty of ideological content in the election campaigns of the victor and the major loser was mirrored by the absence of ideological commitments or sophistication in the general public. At least this is a plausible interpretation of the massive, short-run fluctuations in public opinion support for the different parties between the elections of 1980 and 1984, as well as the eventually overwhelming majority vote from all sectors of the population for the programmatically ill-defined PCs.

Similarly the election of 1984 appears to have demonstrated the absence of class politics – and the failure of class-based appeals to voters – in Canada. The NDP argued that it represented "ordinary" people, as opposed to the "Bay Street" identity of both its major opponents, and the third party explicitly defended its status as a social democratic party with strong commitments to organized labour. But, despite its popularity in public opinion polls when the 1984 election was first called, only 19 percent of Canadians voted for the NDP, and despite gaining or holding key working class – dominated ridings, there was no evidence of disproportionate support for the NDP by the working class or any other group of ordinary people.

Finally, the election seemed to confirm, although less clearly in keeping with the conventional wisdom than for the other points mentioned, the importance of regionalism in Canadian politics. The "blue tide" swept from coast to coast, taking all regions in its wake, but this victory was achieved by very explicit appeals to regional dissatisfactions, by promises of cooperative rather than conflictual federal-provincial relations, and by deals with the provincial leaders (including "nationalists" in Quebec) and party organizations that played major roles in the federal Progressive Conservative campaign.

Against this quite conventional interpretation of the irrelevance of class and ideology to this transition, and of the apparent resurgence of brokerage politics, can our emphasis upon class and ideological conflicts, even if relatively hidden in the bosom of the state, make any contribution to an understanding of these events? Our general thesis is that the Trudeau era was indeed characterized by the development of increasingly significant class and ideological division, and that the Mulroney victory in 1984 and the subsequent reorientation of the federal government towards neo-conservatism, was a reflection rather than a denial of such developments.

Like the ambiguous politics of the Trudeau era, the 1984 election and subsequent changes must be seen in the context of a long period of economic malaise, if not outright crisis. Our surveys took place at a time when one could see the beginnings of the large federal deficits of the 1980s and the growing failure of Keynesian policies to effectively stimulate employment and investment. Unemployment rates were the most dramatic manifestation of the intensifying disorder and restructuring, moving from between 3.4 and 4.5 percent from 1966 to 1969, rising slightly to between 5.3 and 6.2 percent from 1970 to 1974, fluctuating between 7.4 and 8.3 percent between 1975 and 1981, but then jumping to 11.0 percent in 1982 and 11.9 percent in 1983. Such changes were not likely to decrease the need for social programs in the mass public, even if they decreased the inclination to pay for them in the highest strata of the class structure. Class divisions in support of the welfare state were likely therefore to have been more pronounced by the time of the 1984 election than when we measured them just prior to an official recession.

But such conflicts are subject to a complex process of mediation through ideological and political action. The economic dislocation was particularly severe during the period of our surveys, intensifying class and regional conflicts, and forcing the Liberal government of Prime Minister Trudeau to clarify a national policy that it had hitherto only intimated in contradictory and incoherent ways. This clarification of national policy was, however, deficient in a manner characteristic of liberal responses to crises in capitalist societies.

The emphasis on civil rights and bilingualism appealed to the liberal sense of justice as a question of individual opportunity, but failed to respond to Quebec's historic interest in the autonomy of a French society in English North America. The economic nationalism of the last Trudeau government may have had a substantial appeal to the general public and to sectors of the national bourgeoisie that it promoted, but it prompted also the increasingly generalized, and effectively coordinated and articulated, opposition of corporate capital and smaller businesses, through agencies like the Business Council on National Issues and the Canadian Federation of Independent Business. The latter was important, and extremely dangerous to the preservation of a Liberal electoral alliance, because of, as our surveys showed, the much greater public credibility of small business and because – unlike the large resource firms, foreign investors, and their allies in big business – small business had little direct stake in the sectors subject to Liberal government intervention. Of course the Liberal government was simply incapable of articulating a coherent national policy explicitly directed towards a definite class and ideological coalition. After Trudeau's resignation the Liberal government under Prime Minister John Turner backed away from ideological clarification and confrontation and the Progressive Conservative party seized the opportunity to avoid genuine ideological debate over issues, and advertised itself simply as the only option that would satisfy the public "desire for change." The public responded by voting for the only change it was offered, undefined though that offer was.

Eventually, therefore, the traditional, *diversified* class base of the Liberal party – and of our late-developing and timid version of a postwar welfare state – deserted the party, though not at first with a significant ideological realignment. In retrospect it is significant that the Mulroney government's attempt to cut old-age pensions produced widespread public opposition, but not its attacks on unemployment insurance and clawback of the family allowance. In the context of popular and elite ideology, as we have described it, we can see why the abandonment of welfare state initiatives by the Liberal party did not result in a shift towards the NDP, but instead paved the way for the Conservative party's victories in 1984 and 1988. There were significant weaknesses on the left, and significant strengths on the right. Where the public ideological consensus in support of the welfare state was relatively ambiguous and contradictory, the business attacks upon it were highly coherent and systematic. Where public support was weakly attached to political parties, if at all, business attacks were increasingly tied to attachments to the Progressive Conservative party. In the context of a massive cynicism about the competence of government, economic concerns translated easily into a rejection of the statism of social democratic ideology, and into a hope for business competence.

If these dynamics help explain the political shift initiated in 1984, they should not be exaggerated. The change did not involve a right-wing realignment of popular beliefs with business elite ideology, but rather a choice among alternatives in a political space monopolized by the major parties, each appealing in 1984 to business. Although we have no data to decide the question of ideological change prior to or following the 1984 election, the stability of opinion from 1977 through 1981 makes clear that the first electoral turn away from the Liberals in the election of the Joe Clark government did not reflect or produce any such realignment of public opinion. The 1984 election, remember, was fought with the promise of preserving past social policy commitments as a "sacred trust."

THE WELFARE STATE AND THE NATIONAL QUESTION AT THE MILLENNIUM

In accounting for political developments immediately subsequent to our 1977–81 surveys, we have argued that, as well as describing what seem like relatively enduring features of contemporary elite and public ideology in Canada, our surveys help to understand concrete political developments in the 1980s – at least using a common-sense, not too exact, yardstick. As the millennium approaches we wish we had survey data to describe how the ideological landscape has changed. For all we know there has been relatively little change in the relative positions of classes, regional divisions, and so on, but our surveys can say little about the gathering force of neo-conservatism in the period after our fieldwork.

We can see *a* basis for right-wing populism in the distrust of government and the ambiguity and reactionary elements of the general support for the Canadian welfare state, combined with the room for manouevre in the *dis*connectedness of public and elite ideology and ideological indistinctness of the parties. But these are not the determinant causes of the realignment in the political environment; we might find equally convincing portents of a leftward swing. The realization of a neo-conservative political project in Canada required a fiscal crisis and the agency of a well-organized right. Unhindered by serious attachments to ideological divisions in the general public, the elites of the political parties each took a step to the right: Conservatives became "Reformers"; Liberals became Conservatives; and the NDP, the last Liberals.

Lacking significant ideologically cohesive support in public opinion for a genuinely social democratic project and with a relatively weak partisan attachment in the working class, the NDP had no public policy counter to the drift of neo-conservative attack on the welfare state. In Ontario a new, almost accidentally elected, NDP government began with a series of conventionally Keynesian attempts at deficit "pump priming" to revitalize the heart of the Canadian economy weakened by the loss of over a million jobs. Far from recovering jobs and building the support of a working-class coalition, this policy contributed to rapidly escalating government debt, provoking threats of investment strike by the local business class and the lowering of credit ratings by the international financial community. In response the NDP government took a U-turn from deficit financing to deficit trimming, slashing public spending and the employment and wages of its constituency among public sector workers. Of course the breadth of the forces afflicting developed capitalist countries in the 1980s raises questions about whether, at the time, there was a political and economic space for a social democratic response. The left is fond of talking about the seizure of social democratic parties by the right, often by the parliamentary wing of the party in defiance of its membership. And students of the workings of such parties have no difficulty in describing just how these internecine battles unfold. What we quarrel with, however, is the idea that social democrats can appeal to an untapped radicalism among voters turned off by the limited party platforms on offer.

Thus we view the rightward realignment as conjunctural, rather than a fundamental shift in the ideological terrain. If active political engagement on the right and a fiscal crisis can produce a swing to the right, active political engagement and changed economic circumstances can do the reverse. The risk to the left is that the economic inequalities of a capitalist economy facilitate the institutionalization of political force on the right. Compare the resources and success of the Fraser Institute and the Business Council on National Issues to those of the Canadian Centre for Policy Alternatives and the Canadian Labour Congress. No political or economic theorem guarantees the success of either side, but resources count.

On the national question as well our surveys can help describe the environment, but not the complex trajectory of the subsequent events. In Quebec we found a political culture that was unique in two respects. Clearly predominant were the extraordinary differences over language between the peoples of Quebec and English Canada, accompanied by the distinct positions of the corresponding linguistic minorities. But there was also the divide in what we have referred to as the basic layer of political ideology, where the most important "regional" difference is also between Quebec and English Canada. In Canada, of course, elite deal making is the traditional solution to this kind of problem, even when there is deep public disagreement. Attempts at brokerage, however, are severely compromised in two directions. The first involves the social organization of Quebec nationalism. We have emphasized that the political parties' ideologically diffuse electoral constituencies make it easy for them to change positions, especially for the two parties with a traditional near-monopoly on the right to govern. It also reflects their lack of attachment to ideologically distinct constituencies. The same cannot be said for Quebec nationalism, which is directly represented in the party system, as well as in unions and cultural organizations in Quebec.

Second, in recent years the traditional, passive disengagement of the Canadian public has been coupled with dramatically lowered confidence in the efficacy and honesty of government. On the extreme right this is manifest in support for policies to reduce the legitimate terrain of the state, coupled with a hypocritical and opportunistic support for the direct "democracy" of referenda and the "recall" of elected officials. Accompanying this is an economistic view of the "rights" of individuals and communities that equates equality with identical treatment, and so does not conceive of collective rights or culture. On the more conventional right, of course, the turn against the state comes in the polite disguise of incremental changes to the tax regime, privatization of (especially unionized) "unprofitable" state activities that are said to be better managed as profit-making business, and the progressive reassignment of the responsibility for common interests, such as the environment and zoning, to lower levels of government more prone to the pressure of powerful business interests. Whatever the angle of attack, the neo-conservatives' success in confining and de-legitimizing the state – in strange resonance with traditionally left-wing anti-elitism – undercuts elite attempts to make deals over the national question. Hence Meech Lake, the Charlottetown Accord, and the national question that will not go away.

The commentary in these last sections of this chapter is more in the way of speculation than conclusion. We have engaged in such speculation because, like all historical information, our survey data have significance only in relation to imaginative hypotheses about their meaning. But such speculation is fruitless unless it requires that we get back to more detailed empirical work that sets out to map the political and ideological divisions and connections of the contemporary era, as we have tried to do for the past.

APPENDICES

Appendix A:
Implementing Marxist Concepts of Class and Comparing Alternative Class Structures

Because of imprecision in the theoretical specifications and limitations of the survey data, the implementation of three Marxist class categorizations using our survey data presented a number of problems. Although Marxist theories of class are inherently categorical so that boundaries between classes cannot be defined by arbitrary divisions of a continuous scale, any empirical implementation of these categories requires just such arbitrary divisions, giving rise to "boundary problems." While there is a temptation to conclude that these boundary problems have only developed since the passing of the golden age of social classes (somewhere in the nineteenth century) or outside the golden place of classes (surely England), this is not at all plausible. For example while the mean size of businesses has certainly increased, the distribution of the number of employees was as continuous in the nineteenth century as it is now – generating the same problem of distinguishing the petty bourgeoisie from the capitalist class proper.

One such boundary problem involves dividing the petty bourgeoisie, who must rely partly on selling the product of their own labour, from the bourgeoisie proper, who are reliant on the surplus value that they appropriate. In addition supervision must be distinguished from communication designed to coordinate the work process and a line must be drawn between the exercise of technical skills in the pursuit of predefined job tasks and their use in non-routine ways that require and involve genuine job autonomy. A related difficulty follows from the requirement that workers must be assigned to only one class category – even when different aspects of their work clearly place them in different class positions. Especially in bureaucratic organizations, a fair amount of supervision is carried out by workers who also spend a great deal of their time on non-supervisory tasks (and they may themselves be very closely supervised).

In describing this difficulty in implementing the class categorizations, a test of reasonableness may be applied to our class assignments, but there is nothing absolute about the particular measures we used. Because of ambiguities in the original theoretical formulations and the limitations of our data, it is probably fairer to refer to our empirical analysis as involving an interpretation rather than an operationalization of the theories. This point is especially important in our references to Erik Olin Wright's theory, since (in Wright et al. 1982) Wright and his colleagues have published the details of their own implementation of the theoretical scheme that he devised. A Canadian counterpart of Wright's American study was carried out in 1984 by Wallace Clement and John Myles; Donald Black and Myles (1986) have published an extensive comparison of the American, Canadian, and Swedish class structures, employing precisely similar methodology.

Without minimizing the empirical problems in defining social classes, it remains true that only major empirical or theoretical errors would result in our producing a seriously biased analysis of the relationship between class and ideology. Unreliability in the individual items dealing with political ideology are likely to contribute far more to error than would imprecision in the class definitions.

IMPLEMENTING THE THREE MARXIST CLASS CATEGORIZATIONS

Tables A-1 and A-2 show how the survey respondents were assigned to the class categories in accordance with the three different class definitions. Respondents were first divided into two groups on the basis of whether they owned a business. Business owners were further subdivided on the basis of information about the number of employees in the business. In Poulantzas's and Carchedi's categories, the upper bound of the petty bourgeoisie was set at four employees – capitalists with five or more workers were assigned to the bourgeoisie proper; in Wright's categories, business owners with between five and twenty-nine employees were assigned to the contradictory location for small employers and capitalists with thirty or more employees were assigned to the capitalist class.

Respondents who did not own a business were first categorized on the basis of their occupations and the industries in which they were employed. These allocations were further modified on the basis of the responses to questions about the respondent's role in planning the activities of his or her employment, the size of the business, and his or her position in the hierarchy of supervision. One example of the use of this additional information involves Wright's contradictory location for foremen and supervisors (to avoid sexist terminology they are referred to as supervisors henceforth). That location includes both non-owners of businesses who gave their occupations as foreman or supervisor *and* workers who did not say that they were foremen or supervisors as their occupation, but reported that their jobs involved considerable supervision of other workers. About one-tenth of the workers in skilled, high-autonomy, craft jobs, such as electricians and plumbers, reported that they had significant supervisory duties. It is likely that, in part, pride in their skills led these workers to emphasize their crafts in describing their occupations. Our survey data also showed that some workers in highly skilled occupations, such as tool and die making, which would normally involve a high degree of job autonomy, were very closely supervised, leading us to assign them to the working class rather than the contradictory location of semi-autonomous employees (in Wright's scheme).

Supervision plays a critical role in class identification in all three of the Marxist class theories, so that it was necessary to decide how much supervision was cause for reclassifying respondents who did not give supervisor or foreman as their occupations into a class category for supervisors. The problem was to separate routine coordination from the exercise of supervisory authority on the basis of our limited data. Guglielmo Carchedi, we note, tends to see the exercise of authority as more integrated into everyday work life than Nicos Poulantzas or Wright. Respondents who spent one-quarter or more of their time on supervision and who supervised five or more workers were reassigned from the working class to the new middle class in Carchedi's scheme; and workers who did any supervision of five or more workers were reassigned from the working class to the new petty bourgeoisie in Poulantzas's scheme and to the contradictory location for supervisors in Wright's scheme.

Because we did not think respondents would be able to give reliable reports on the responsibility for planning, supervisory authority, and supervision of their fathers and spouses, no attempt was made to refine the initial class designations based on business ownership and reported occupations. An analysis (discussed in more detail below) of how information about planning and supervision affects the class allocation of respondents suggests that our class assignments for respondents' fathers and spouses exaggerate the size of the working class by about 10 percent. Obviously the simpler measures for fathers and spouses are also somewhat less reliable than the class assignments for respondents. Table A-3 shows the class distribution of the population of working Canadians, on the basis of the three different Marxist theories, before and after the reclassification using information about the responsibility for planning and supervision in the work place.

The application of Poulantzas's theoretical approach to our Canadian data produces a working class that includes only about one-quarter of the working population, compared to just over one-half the population included in the new petty bourgeoisie. The traditional petty bourgeoisie and bourgeoisie proper each include about one-eighth of the population. Except for further decreasing the size of the working class, information about planning and supervision does little to alter the initial classification. While it is tempting to speculate that this class distribution reflects the decline of the traditional working class, with Poulantzas's definition of the working class as the criterion, in very few nations would the working class ever have constituted a majority of the population. In Canada the presence of a large farm population, which declined rapidly only after 1940 (Ornstein 1983c, 242), implies that the working class would never have constituted a majority of the population, according to Poulantzas's definition.

Table A-1
Definition of Social Classes Following Poulantzas and Carchedi

Business Ownership and Occupation	Under What Conditions	Social Class Following Poulantzas	Social Class Following Carchedi
OWNERS OF BUSINESSES			
Including joint owners and partners	Company employs 5 or more workers	Capitalist	
All occupations	Company employs fewer than 5 workers	Petty bourgeoisie	Petty bourgeoisie
NON-OWNERS OF BUSINESSES			
General managers, financial managers, all other managers, government administrators, producers, and directors	Company employs 5 or more workers and individual plans for entire company	Capitalist	Capitalist
	All others	New petty bourgeoisie	New middle class
Lawyers and ministers of religion, postmasters, inspectors and regulatory officers, personnel and purchasing officers, sport and recreation coaches, commissioned officers in the armed forces, supervisors and foremen, inspectors, testers, graders, police, and guards		New petty bourgeoisie	New middle class
Farmers, highly skilled, independent manual workers, technologists and technicians, manual occupations in material production	Supervise others*	New petty bourgeoisie	New middle class
	All others	Working class	Working class
Scientists, engineers, social scientists, physicians, and related occupations	Company employs 5 or more workers and individual plans for entire company	Capitalist	Capitalist
	All others	New petty bourgeoisie	
	Supervise others		New middle class
	All others		Working class

Table A-1
Definition of Social Classes Following Poulantzas and Carchedi (Continued)

Business Ownership and Occupation	Under What Conditions	Social Class Following Poulantzas	Social Class Following Carchedi
University teachers, artists, health-prescribing occupations, referees, farm management and management-related occupations, miscellaneous non-manual, high autonomy occupations, scientific occupations not elsewhere specified, performers, autonomous salespersons, protective service occupations, all other non-manual occupations	Supervise others All others	New petty boureoisie	New middle class Working class

* For Poulantzas, doing even minimal level of supervision places employed workers in the new petty bourgeoisie; for Carchedi, workers spending at least one-quarter of their time supervising five or more workers are recategorized into the new middle class.

According to Wright's scheme the working class constitutes 56 percent of the population and another 8 percent are in the contradictory location for semi-autonomous employees, which is distinguished from the working class only by their greater job autonomy. Including the 0.6 percent of the working population who are non-owning top managers of companies with thirty or more employees, business owners (including own-account workers who have no employees) constitute about 17 percent of the working population. Two-thirds of these business owners are in the petty bourgeoisie and the remainder are split equally between the capitalist class and the contradictory location for small employers. The contradictory locations for managers and technocrats and for supervisors respectively make up 7.0 and 10.9 percent of the workforce. Obviously Wright's theory of classes suggests a numerical balance among classes that is much more favourable to the working class than Poulantzas's, especially since at least some of the occupants of contradictory locations would gravitate towards the position of the working class in the course of political conflict. The information about workplace supervision and planning results in about 5 percent of the workforce being reassigned from the working class to the contradictory location for supervisors; in addition some semi-autonomous employees are reassigned to the working class, because they report being heavily supervised, or to the managerial and supervisory categories, because they do large amounts of supervision.

Table A-2
Definition of Social Classes Following Wright

Business Ownership and Occupation	Under What Conditions	Social Class or Contradictory Location
OWNERS OF BUSINESSES Including joint owners and partners		
All occupations	Company employs 30 or more workers	Capitalist
	Company employs 5 to 29 workers	Small employers
	Company employs fewer than 5 workers	Petty bourgeoisie
NON-OWNERS OF BUSINESSES General managers, financial managers, all other managers, government administrators, producers and directors	Company employs 30 or more workers and individual plans for entire company	Capitalist
	Company employs 5 or more workers and individual does some planning	Managers
	All others	Foremen, supervisors
Lawyers and ministers of religion	Do not plan strategy of entire firm (most lawyers are self-employed and are classified with business owners above)	Semi-autonomous workers
	All others	Managers
Postmasters	Do any planning	Managers
	All others	Foremen
Inspectors and regulatory officers, personnel and purchasing officers, sport and recreation	Do any planning	Managers
	Do no planning, do not supervise others,* not closely supervised	Semi-autonomous workers
	Do no planning, do not supervise others, closely supervised	Working class
	All others	Foremen, supervisors
Commissioned officers in the armed forces	Do no planning	Foremen
	All others	Managers

Table A-2
Definition of Social Classes Following Wright (Continued)

Business Ownership and Occupation	Under What Conditions	Social Class or Contradictory Location
Farmers	Supervise others	Foremen, supervisors
	Do not supervise others, closely supervised	Working class
	All others	Semi-autonomous workers
Scientists, engineers, social scientists, physicians, and related occupations	Company employs 30 or more workers and individual plans for entire company	Capitalist
	Not above and supervise others	Technocrats
	All others	Semi-autonomous workers
Supervisors and foremen	All	Foremen, supervisors
Inspectors, testers, graders	Supervise others[+]	Foremen, supervisors
	All others	Working class
Highly skilled, independent manual workers, university teachers, artists, health prescribing occupations, referees, miscellaneous non-manual and high autonomy occupations, scientific occupations not elsewhere specified, performers, autonomous salespersons, protective service occupations, technologists and technicians	Supervise others[+]	Foremen, supervisors
	Do not supervise others, not closely supervised	Semi-autonomous workers
	All others	Working class
Farm management and occupations related to management	Supervise others	Foremen, supervisors
	All others	Semi-autonomous workers
All other non-manual occupations	Supervise others	Foremen, supervisors
Manual occupations in material production, police and guards	All others	Working class

* defined as spending any time supervising five or more workers
+ checked on by supervisor once a week or less

Table A-3
The Size Distribution of Social Classes According to Three Different Theoretical Models,
Before and After Reclassification Using Information about Planning and Supervision

| | Class Categorization (percentage distribution of classes) | | | | | |
| | Poulantzas | | Wright | | Carchedi | |
Social Class	Before reclass-ification	After reclass-ification	Before reclass-ification	After reclass-ification	Before reclass-ification	After reclass-ification
Capitalists	11.3	13.8	2.2	2.8	11.3	12.0
Small employers	3.5	3.5				
Petty bourgeoisie	1.8	11.8	11.8	11.8	11.8	11.8
Managers and technocrats			7.0	7.0		
Supervisors			5.8	10.9		
New petty bourgeoisie	53.2	50.7				
New middle class					12.1	15.4
Semi-autonomous employees			7.7	8.1		
Working class	23.6	23.6	61.9	55.9	64.8	60.8
Total	99.9	99.9	99.9	100.0	100.0	100.0

According to Carchedi's theory, 60.8 percent of the workforce is in the working class and 15.4 percent is in the new middle class. In terms of numerical balance, therefore, Carchedi's classification is much closer to Wright's than to Poulantazas's. Wright and Carchedi both define a large working class and make no attempt to differentiate it. To accommodate what is known about ideological differences *within* the working class, for example between manual and non-manual workers, therefore, requires some additional specification of how the working class is economically and ideologically differentiated.

Although Marxists often criticize non-Marxist theories of class for relying too heavily on occupational distinctions, the characteristics of occupations figure strongly in Marxist theories and in attempts to implement them empirically. For example Carchedi assigns police and guards to the new middle class, instead of the working class, because their occupations involve the function of the global capitalist – despite the fact that the working conditions experienced by police and guards are often highly regimented. The larger question is not whether occupations have *any* relation to social class, but whether class categorizations are in significant measure different from occupational classifications. Table A-4 shows this relationship is actually quite weak.

Table A-4
Social Class by Occupation (Porter-Pineo-McRoberts Classification)

Social Class	Occupation (percentage distribution)					Number of cases
	Managers and professionals	Non-manual workers*	Manual workers+	Farmers	Total	
POULANTZAS						
Capitalists	76	15	5	4	100	254
Petty bourgeoisie	10	38	26	26	100	217
New petty bourgeoisie	14	65	20	0	100	929
Working class	0	6	91	3	100	430
WRIGHT						
Capitalists	73	25	2	0	100	51
Small employers	25	41	19	15	100	64
Petty bourgeoisie	10	38	26	26	100	217
Managers and technocrats	100	0	0	0	100	128
Supervisors	9	56	34	1	100	200
Semi-autonomous employees	34	31	29	6	100	148
Working class	7	46	46	1	100	1025
CARCHEDI						
Capitalists	72	18	6	4	100	219
Petty bourgeoisie	10	38	26	26	100	217
New middle class	24	40	35	1	100	282
Working class	9	47	43	1	100	1112
Total	19	41	35	5	100	1833

* includes "semi-professionals" and foremen
+ includes technicians, supervisors, and farm labourers

The exact strength of the relationship between class and occupation is a function of the class categorization employed. Because Poulantzas defines the working class to include all non-supervising production workers in manufacturing, the strongest relationship between class and occupation is obtained for his scheme. The relationship is much weaker for Wright's and Carchedi's class categories. Poulantzas's new petty bourgeoisie, which includes about half the working population, consists of 14 percent managers and professionals, 65 percent non-manual workers, and 20 percent manual workers. Interestingly the petty bourgeoisie includes approximately equal numbers of non-manual workers, manual workers, and farmers. If Poulantzas's class categories cannot be reduced to occupational distinctions, this reduction is even less possible for Wright and Carchedi. Using Wright's categories, only managers and technocrats (who are, naturally, entirely managers and professionals by occupation) and the bourgeoisie are drawn predominantly from a single occupation category. There are major manual *and* non-manual groups in five of the seven classes and contradictory locations defined by Wright and three of the four classes defined by Carchedi. It is therefore likely that the observed ideological differences between manual and non-manual workers will be manifest as ideological divisions between social classes, so an effort to examine this difference within classes is in order.

Examination of a more detailed sixteen-category classification of occupations designed by Peter Pineo and John Porter (1976) shows that the highest and lowest occupational categories are more homogeneous in terms of class than the categories in between (these results are not shown in a table). None of the *self-employed* professionals, who rank first in the Porter-Pineo classification and include lawyers and physicians, is classified into (Wright's) working class, whereas 37 percent of the professionals are in the working class. At the low end of the occupational categories, 91 percent of the "unskilled crafts" workers in our 1981 sample were assigned to the working class, compared to 86 percent of the semi-skilled and 67 percent of skilled crafts workers. At least a small proportion of the individuals in every occupational category turn out to be business owners. In terms of Wright's categories, again, the lowest-ranked occupational category of farm labourers (as distinct from the higher-ranked category of farmers in the Porter-Pineo classification) includes 13 percent petty bourgeois (that is they are actually farm *owners* with less than five employees), and 6 percent small employers, who have between five and twenty-nine employees. These results demonstrate that social classes cannot be reduced to occupational distinctions, even if the occupations are finely divided. In particular it is apparent the manual/non-manual distinction or any such simple classification of occupations is only moderately correlated with social class.

CLASS STRUCTURATION AND THE UTILITY OF ALTERNATIVE MARXIST CLASS CLASSIFICATION

Having outlined the application of three quite different Marxist models of social class using our national surveys, our analysis now takes a more empirical, some would say non-Marxist, turn. We now examine the extent of class structuration, comparing the three different Marxist conceptualizations. The findings of this analysis are of some intrinsic interest, since relatively little is known about the effects of social class, at least as it is measured using the concepts employed here. By demonstrating that one of the three concepts is clearly superior to the other two, these comparisons of the three class categorizations also reduce the length and complexity of the analysis of ideology and voting in chapters 5 and 6.

The differences among the three class theories are immediately apparent from the figures in table A-5, which gives the class distributions for men and women. Using Poulantzas's scheme, male workers are almost three times as likely as women to be classified into the working class (32 percent compared to 12 percent) while women are nearly twice as likely to be classified into the new petty bourgeoisie (71 versus 37 percent). Women are only about half as likely as men to be petty bourgeois or bourgeois.

Table A-5
Social Class by Gender

Social Class	Percentage Distribution in Classes		Percent women in class
	Men	Women	
POULANTZAS			
Capitalists	17	9	26
Petty bourgeoisie	14	8	27
New petty bourgeoisie	37	71	57
Working class	32	12	20
Total	100	100	40
WRIGHT			
Capitalists	4	2	23
Small employers	4	3	31
Petty bourgeoisie	15	8	27
Managers and technocrats	9	4	25
Supervisors	11	10	38
Semi-autonomous employees	10	5	24
Working class	47	68	49
Total	100	100	40
CARCHEDI			
Capitalists	14	8	28
Petty bourgeoisie	15	8	27
New middle class	17	13	33
Working class	54	71	47
Total	100	100	40

Wright's classification gives quite different and more intuitively pleasing results: 68 percent of women proved to be working class, compared to 47 percent of men; among the other categories, approximate parity obtains only for the contradictory location for supervisors – in this category, it is likely that a large proportion of the women supervise women workers. In all the other categories, the proportion of men is greater, including in all the categories for owners of businesses, and the managerial and semi-autonomous employees categories. Carchedi's classification gives results much more similar to Wright's than to Poulantzas's: 54 percent of the men and 71 percent of the women are working class, while men are about twice as likely as women to be classified into the bourgeoisie or petty bourgeoisie.

The analysis of the gender composition of classes suggests that Poulantzas's categories are unsatisfactory. Of course it is his exclusion of the female-dominated routine clerical and sales jobs from the working class that produces a working class that is 80 percent male. Despite the evidence that women have much lower wages than men and less managerial and supervisory authority in the workplace, the application of Poulantzas's theory suggests women are actually in a privileged position compared to men. Remember, the new petty bourgeoisie is said to enjoy privileges – in prospects for advancement for example – denied to the working class, which is *the* subordinate class in capitalism. Wright's and Carchedi's categorizations, on the other hand, show that one aspect of the situation of women is their subordination to men in the class structure. This subordination is not of such a magnitude, however, as to involve the exclusive or even predominant segregation of women in subordinate class positions. Thus the oppression of women cannot be reduced to class differences.

Table A-6 reveals that there are major differences in the age distributions of social classes. Here there is a surprising uniformity in the patterns observed for the three different class categorizations. Only the petty bourgeoisie includes more than a small percentage of individuals who are sixty-five years of age or more – 11 percent of its members are over sixty-five, compared to 3 percent or less for the other classes. There is a more general polarization between the propertied classes and non-propertied classes, with the latter being younger. In all the categorizations the working class has the lowest age distribution – between 26 and 32 percent of its members are between eighteen and twenty-four, depending on the classification – the intermediate non-owning classes, including the new petty bourgeoisie, semi-autonomous employees, and the new middle class, are intermediate in age, and the petty bourgeoisie and (to a lesser extent) bourgeoisie and small employers are the oldest.

Two processes are responsible for the observed relationship between social class and age: first, historical decline in the relative size of the owning classes and, second, mobility from the non-owning into the owning categories. This difference presumably reflects a combination of small-business owners' ability to delay retiring, if they choose, and the economic compulsion to continue working, perhaps because of inadequate pensions. Thirty-nine percent of the working respondents reported that, when they were about sixteen years of age, their fathers were business owners, roughly double the proportion of present-day business owners among the respondents. The age differences between social classes are sufficiently large to suggest the need to check whether observed class differences in ideology might reflect age differences.

Table A-7 shows the relationship between social class and education. Using Wright's or Carchedi's formulation, the petty bourgeoisie has the lowest level of education: only half its members completed high school and just 7 percent completed university. This finding is only partly the result of the higher age of the petty bourgeois respondents. Using Wright's scheme, the best-educated class is the bourgeoisie (with 42 percent university graduates), followed by the contradictory locations for managers and technocrats and for semi-autonomous employees (with 29 and 30 percent university graduates, respectively), followed by the small employers and supervisors (with 21 and 15 percent university graduates, respectively). The distribution of education of the working class is only slightly above that of the petty bourgeoisie: just 58 percent completed high school and 9 percent completed university. Poulantzas's restriction of the working class to manufacturing workers with no supervisory

Table A-6
Social Class by Age

Social Class	Mean age	Age (percentage distribution)					
		18–24	25–34	35–44	45–54	55 or older	Total
POULANTZAS							
Capitalists	41.2	3	37	25	25	10	100
Petty bourgeoisie	46.9	3	20	22	26	29	100
New petty bourgeoisie	38.9	19	29	23	16	13	100
Working class	35.8	32	25	18	14	11	100
WRIGHT							
Capitalists	43.9	0	20	28	33	19	100
Small employers	39.9	3	34	39	13	11	100
Petty bourgeoisie	46.9	3	20	22	27	29	100
Managers and technocrats	41.8	6	32	19	22	21	100
Supervisors	38.6	9	37	21	17	16	100
Semi-autonomous employees	37.4	16	34	22	14	14	100
Working class	35.6	27	26	21	16	10	100
CARCHEDI							
Capitalists	41.2	4	31	27	21	17	100
Petty bourgeoisie	46.9	3	20	22	27	29	100
New middle class	38.9	9	35	22	17	17	100
Working class	35.8	26	26	21	16	11	100
Total	38.2	18	28	22	18	14	100

authority produces a working class that contains only 40 percent high school gradu-ates and 1 percent university graduates. Thus differences in education are an impor-tant aspect of class structuration, even when the classes are not defined on the basis of occupations. Since education is a significant predictor of class location, it is impera-tive that we determine whether any observed class differences in ideology reflect un-derlying educational differentials.

Unlike education, income is the result and not the cause of class differences. In-come is the most important single indicator of class structuration, since it is such a powerful determinant of other aspects of class privilege such as the quality and own-ership of housing, nutrition, the use of leisure time, and so on. Table A-7 shows that there are large class differences in income. For all three class schemes the largest gap separates the bourgeoisie from the other classes and the working class is the lowest paid. Using Poulantzas's categorization, however, the difference between the working class and new petty bourgeoisie is a negligible $100 per year. This latter finding strikes another blow against the usefulness and internal consistency of Poulantzas's

Table A-7

Percent of High School and University Graduates, Mean Years of Educational Attainment, Mean and Standard Deviation of Rate of Pay and Family Income, and Home Ownership by Social Class

Social Class	Percent high school graduate	Percent university graduate	Mean years of education	Rate of Pay* ($1000/yr)		Household Income ($1000/yr)		Percent home-owners
				Mean	Standard deviation	Mean	Standard deviation	
POULANTZAS								
Capitalists	76	33	14.1	29.8	18.9	48.5	38.7	78
Petty bourgeoisie	49	7	11.1	20.8	17.4	32.5	24.1	84
New petty bourgeoisie	68	15	12.9	16.9	9.4	32.0	21.0	66
Working class	40	1	10.9	16.8	6.5	29.5	18.7	67
WRIGHT								
Capitalists	80	42	14.7	40.3	28.3	63.7	60.3	87
Small employers	59	21	12.5	27.8	18.2	53.5	36.1	84
Petty bourgeoisie	49	7	11.1	20.8	17.4	32.5	24.1	84
Managers and technocrats	89	29	14.2	26.2	13.0	39.3	30.8	73
Supervisors	70	15	12.9	20.6	11.1	33.1	18.1	66
Semi-autonomous employees	82	30	14.4	22.9	10.9	40.3	26.9	73
Working class	58	9	11.9	15.4	6.8	29.9	18.5	66
CARCHEDI								
Capitalists	72	27	13.7	29.0	19.5	47.5	38.7	80
Petty bourgeoisie	49	7	11.1	20.8	17.4	32.5	24.1	84
New middle class	73	22	13.5	22.2	12.6	36.0	25.6	68
Working class	60	10	12.1	16.1	7.6	30.8	20.0	66
Total	62	14	12.4	19.0	11.6	27.3	22.6	70

* adjusted to 40-hour week

formulation, since he repeatedly underlines the different conditions, including greater prospects for advancement, of the new petty bourgeoisie, relative to the working class.

With a mean rate of pay of $20,800 per year and mean family income of $32,500 per year, members of the petty bourgeoisie are only somewhat better off than members of the working class, according to all three class categorizations. In general, members of the petty bourgeoisie are not well rewarded for the uncertainty of their position or the capital that they have invested in their businesses, but (note the standard deviation of income is almost as large as the mean) some individuals in that class have very high incomes. Plainly, any ideological differences between the petty bourgeoisie and working class are not the result of income differences.

The bourgeoisie and (in Wright's categorization only) small employers enjoy greater income because of their position as owners of businesses. Supervisors and semi-autonomous employees are somewhat better paid than workers, but not as well paid as the managers and technocrats. An inspection of the differences in household income demonstrates that semi-autonomous employees are more likely than other groups to have other family members' earnings or other sources of income and/or to have steadier income (since unemployment and layoffs result in some workers who are highly paid having considerably lower annual incomes). This difference may reflect the fact that their spouses are more likely to work for pay. More extensive discussion of class differences in income may be found in Wright (1979), Hagen Koo and Doo-Seung Hong (1981), and Ornstein (1983a; 1983b).

Because pay and family income are such important elements of inequality, it is worth examining the relationship between class and income more carefully. Specifically, it is important to determine whether gender, education, and age differences between classes could account for the pattern of class difference in income observed in table A-7. We should be sceptical about class categorizations that do not exert some independent effect on income. The analysis in table A-8 shows that taking account of differences in the distributions of age, education, and gender somewhat decreases class differences in pay: between the capitalist and working classes the difference falls from $24,800 to $18,000; and between the small employers and the working class it falls from $12,600 to $10,100. Much greater absolute and proportionate reductions are found for the non-capitalist categories. For example the pay difference between the semi-autonomous workers and the working class drops from $7,000 to $2,500 when age, education, and gender are held constant. The implication of these findings is that rates of pay in the classes intermediate between capital and labour largely reflect differences in skills and seniority, and gender; the owners of business, on the other hand, are "rewarded" because of what they own.

These findings should not be taken as an indication that other variables have no effects on pay; large class differences in income can obviously coexist with, for example, gender differences. The difference in mean income between women and men only drops from $9,000 to $7,500 when the other variables are controlled; the difference between the (lowest) 18–24 and (highest) 55–64 age categories declines from

Table A-8
Mean Rate of Pay and Family Income by Social Class, Age, Education, and Gender

Independent Variable	Annual Rate of Pay in $1000		Family Income in Previous Year in $1000	
	Deviation from mean	Deviation from mean adjusted for all variables	Deviation from mean	Deviation from mean adjusted for all variables
SOCIAL CLASS				
Capitalists	21.1	15.8	29.6	23.3
Small employers	8.9	7.9	17.0	17.6
Petty bourgeoisie	2.1	1.3	.3	1.6
Managers and technocrats	7.0	3.5	6.4	2.5
Supervisors	1.5	.6	−1.0	−1.5
Semi-autonomous employees	3.3	.3	5.9	2.8
Working class	−3.7	−2.2	−4.1	−3.0
AGE				
18–24	−5.9	−3.2	−3.5	−.5
25–34	.1	−.9	−2.1	−4.3
35–44	1.0	.9	3.1	2.7
45–54	2.8	2.4	2.9	3.1
55–64	3.9	3.1	1.7	2.5
65 or older	−4.7	−6.2	−5.8	−4.2
EDUCATION				
Not elementary graduate	−3.7	−4.8	−8.5	−8.5
Elementary graduate	−2.2	−3.4	−7.3	−7.9
Some high school	−2.4	−2.2	−5.6	−5.7
High school graduate	−1.4	.3	−.2	1.1
Some post-secondary	−.5	−.1	.9	1.1
University graduate	9.8	7.3	15.4	13.5
GENDER				
Men	3.6	3.0	.9	.2
Women	−5.4	−4.5	−1.4	−.3
Percentage of variance explained		15.1		35.1

$9,800 to $6,300; and the difference between individuals with no high school and those with university degrees drops from $13,500 to $12,100. While class differences in income are not only the product of underlying age, education, or gender differences, these variables do have strong effects on income.

The corresponding analysis of the effects of class, age, education, and gender on *family* (as opposed to individual) income is also in table A-8. There are a number of important differences between the two sets of results. First, and not surprisingly, variables describing the respondent explain much less of the variance in his or her *family* income than in his or her rate of pay. Second, the effect of gender of respondent on family income is virtually nil, showing that the presence of other earners in the household results in women workers not living in lower-income households, even if women themselves have considerably lower earnings. Finally, the respondent's education is more strongly related to her or his household income than to her or his own income, suggesting that the education is related to standards of living – presumably because there are other earners in their households – even for individuals who are in marginal jobs or not in the labour force.

Giddens (1973) considers class background one of the major aspects of class structuration. Table A-9 shows the relationship between father's social class (when the respondent was about sixteen years of age) and respondent's class. There are striking differences among the classes. First, members of the bourgeoisie are disproportionately drawn from the ranks of managers and technocrats, although they are *not* more likely than average to come from the families of small employers or the petty bourgeoisie. Surprisingly, 45 percent of the bourgeoisie come from working-class origins, exactly the average for the population, which underlines the importance of education in the formation of the capitalist class.

The inheritance of business is greatest for small employers, 21 percent of whom come from small employer and 42 percent from petty bourgeois backgrounds. Thus the transmission of property is greater among the owners of middle-size business (five to twenty-nine employees) than among the owners and managers of larger businesses or smaller businesses. Forty-five percent of the petty bourgeoisie is drawn from petty bourgeois backgrounds, compared to 29 percent from the population. Finally, semi-autonomous workers are drawn disproportionately from bourgeois and manager and technocrat backgrounds. Over a generation there is a strong tendency for class privileges that do not involve actual business ownership to be converted into occupational pursuits that involve a high degree of personal autonomy, but not control of capital. The distribution of the backgrounds of managers and technocrats, supervisors, and the working class is quite typical of the population as a whole. While these patterns are complex, it is obvious that petty bourgeoisie small-employer parents are clearly most able to perpetuate their class positions. Entrance to the bourgeoisie proper, however, depends more on the educational credentials that are most likely to be acquired in privileged and managerial families.

We also examined the class composition of families in which the respondent has a current partner. Excluding the couples in which neither spouse is employed, in 48 percent of the households only the husband works, in 15 percent only the wife works, and in 37 percent both spouses work for pay. Among the 37 percent of households in which both spouses work, in 10.4 percent both spouses are working class and in another 2.3 percent both spouses are business owners or managers. In focusing exclusively on the husband's occupation, which is assumed to stand for the household's class, traditional studies of political attitudes deal unambiguously with about 80 percent of the households in which there are one or more working spouses. The greatest

Table A-9
Social Class by Father's Social Class

Respondent's Social Class	Social Class of Respondent's Father (percentage distribution)								
	Capitalists	Small employers	Petty bourgeoisie	Managers and technocrats	Supervisors	Semi-Autonomous employees	Working class	Total	Number of cases
Capitalists	2	1	25	15	5	7	45	100	51
Small employers	1	21	42	2	7	4	24	100	62
Petty bourgeoisie	2	9	45	3	6	3	32	100	206
Managers and technocrats	4	6	25	5	9	4	46	100	125
Supervisors	8	8	21	6	5	9	43	100	206
Semi-autonomous employees	9	10	24	9	6	7	36	100	144
Working class	2	6	27	3	6	6	50	100	1003
Total	3	7	29	4	6	6	45	100	1784

proportions of "inconsistent" households involve working-class wives and non-working-class husbands and working-class husbands with non-working-class wives, accounting for 12 and 4 percent, respectively, of all working couples. The remainder of the working couples involve a variety of different combinations of the classes of the spouses. There is thus a fairly high degree of class homogeneity within married couples – although there are certainly enough exceptions and enough theoretical reason for investigating the relationship between political ideology and household class composition.

From the various aspects of class structuration examined above, the most distinctive classes are the petty bourgeoisie and bourgeoisie. The petty bourgeoisie is distinguished by the relatively advanced ages of its members, by low levels of education, by the evidence that its members garner little financial advantage (compared to the working class) from their independence, and by relatively high levels of class inheritance. The bourgeoisie is distinguished by its high levels of education and income, but, surprisingly, not by virtue of having roots in business ownership in the previous generation. Ownership of a small business is much more likely the result of inheritance than ownership of a large business – perhaps because the education and skills required to run larger businesses are seldom acquired by people from petty bourgeois backgrounds. Supervisors appear relatively similar to the working class, while the middle classes are somewhat better paid and certainly better educated than the working class.

DECIDING AMONG THE THREE MARXIST MODELS OF CLASS

On the basis of our discussion of class structuration we decided to employ Wright's categorization in our analysis of ideology and voting. On a number of important counts the findings suggest shortcomings in Poulantzas's conceptualization. In particular the working class proves to be very largely male, in spite of the strong evidence of women's lower wages and confinement to occupations with relatively little job autonomy, and we find little evidence of the supposed material privilege of the new petty bourgeoisie. While the results of using Carchedi's classification are much more satisfactory, the lower level of detail means that the findings are not as interesting as those obtained with Wright's classification. Clearly, Wright's distinctions between supervisors and managers, between semi-autonomous employees and the working class, and between small employers and capitalists identify fairly significant differences in education, income, and class inheritance, which are concealed in Carchedi's simpler classification.

Our decision to employ Wright's categorization because it is more detailed and because this additional detail identifies significant differences in social background and material privilege is not proof that he has best "understood" the class structure of contemporary capitalism. Although it is not our own view, we should again point out that to many Marxists these empirical tests are inappropriate and irrelevant. Also we

Table A-10
Percentage Distribution of Combinations of Social Class of Husband and Social Class of Wife for Married Couples

Social Class of Husband	Social Class of Wife								
	Capitalists	Small employers	Petty bourgeoisie	Managers and technocrats	Supervisors	Semi-autonomous employees	Working class	Not employed	Total
Capitalists	–	–	.0	.1	.1	.1	.8	.8	1.8
Small employers	–	.6	.0	.1	.1	–	.8	.9	2.5
Petty bourgeoisie	–	.1	1.0	.1	.2	.2	2.1	5.6	9.2
Managers and technocrats	.1	–	.2	.5	.3	.2	1.6	3.4	6.2
Supervisors	.0	.0	.3	.2	.3	.2	2.1	3.5	6.6
Semi-autonomous employees	.1	.2	.1	.2	.3	.2	2.1	3.4	6.6
Working class	.2	.1	.6	.4	1.0	.5	10.4	19.3	32.7
Not employed	.1	.0	.7	.5	1.2	.6	8.4	23.0	34.6
Total	.4	1.0	2.9	2.0	3.5	2.0	28.2	59.9	100.0

– indicates no cases observed; .o indicates one or more cases observed, but number is below .o5 percent

should point out that we interpret this categorization in a manner not intended by Wright – in particular by considering the occupants of contradictory locations as fractions of two fundamental classes.

We believe, nevertheless, that Wright's model of class structure provides a useful means of empirically identifying the size and other characteristics of social classes in Canada, and that it is a useful means of examining the ideological and political significance of social class in Canada, as we do in chapters 5 and 6.

Appendix B:
Ideological Constraint:
The Structure of Public Ideology

The results in chapter 4 indicate a remarkable stability in the response distributions for questions in the 1977, 1979, and 1981 surveys, suggesting that individuals' opinions are very stable over time. These findings, however, are equally compatible with the presence of very high levels of individual *in*stability, so long as the individual changes in opinions cancel out. To properly evaluate the consistency of public opinion, it is necessary to examine the relationships between *individuals'* responses to conceptually related questions asked *at the same time* or their responses to identical questions asked *at different times*. The panel study design of the Quality of Life surveys allows both such analyses to be undertaken, and to address the extensive debate about the degree of consistency or "constraint" in public opinion.

As defined by Philip Converse (1964), constraint refers to the strength of the relationship between individuals' responses to conceptually related questions. Converse coined the term in the course of arguing that only a minority of Americans combine an understanding of political issues and of the positions of political parties required to vote in an informed way; a majority of voters, he concluded, have so little knowledge of and interest in politics that their responses to questions asked in surveys are essentially random. Analyzing data from two surveys conducted in the United States in the 1950s, Converse concluded:

It is our primary thesis that, as one moves from elite sources of belief systems downwards on such an information scale, several important things occur. First, the contextual grasp of "standard" political belief systems fades out very rapidly, almost before one has passed beyond the 10% of the American population that in the 1950s had completed standard college training ... The net result, as one moved downward, is that constraint declines across the universe of idea-elements, and that the range of relevant belief systems becomes narrower and narrower. (1964, 213)

David Butler and Donald Stokes's (1974, chap. 15) discussion of the British electorate leads them to quite similar conclusions.

An analysis of constraint in the Canadian general public is a prerequisite to our
analysis of political cleavages, and to our argument that such cleavages influence
public policy. If most respondents' answers to our survey questions are largely random error, we are not likely to discover systematic relations between political ideology and region, social class, or any other structural variables. Attention to Converse's
argument about constraint is also justified because its strongly anti-democratic implications run counter to our argument that popular, anti-establishmentarian interests
can and should influence state policy. Converse's argument legitimizes the domination of politics by higher-income, better-educated sectors of the population, for only
they have the conceptual skills necessary to understand contemporary politics. These
implications are strengthened by related research that argues that political elites and
the well educated are far more tolerant of dissent than the mass public (Stouffer 1955;
Lipset 1960; Hamilton 1972, chap. 11), a point taken up in the Canadian context in
chapter 5.

Our view is that public opinion is more consistent and stable than Converse predicts and that there is no upper-class monopoly on rationality or tolerance. To address
this issue we examine the relationships between individuals' responses to our survey
questions in the same survey as well as over time. We determine whether there is any
indication of an underlying left-right division in public ideology and also investigate
whether education and involvement in politics affect the extent of ideological constraint. We leave to later chapters the investigation of any class or elite bias in the acceptance of democratic values.

It would be nice to be able to compare our results to previous research on Canada,
but, with the exception of an argument by Richard Johnston about why it makes no
difference how large a proportion of the public exhibit constrained attitudes, we are
unable to find any substantial reference to the problem in the published literature.
Johnston argues,

If even a small proportion of the citizenry has real attitudes, those who have such attitudes will
cast the deciding votes. Response variation among those with no attitudes will be random and,
thus, usually, mutually cancelling. The exact extent to which those with real attitudes control the
play depends on means and variances in their attitudes and on the means and variances in the
distribution of non-attitudinal response. Because of the way in which random variation works,
there may be occasions in which those with non-attitudes unwittingly overturn the majority
preference among those with real attitudes, but these occasions should be rare. (1986, 220)

Even as qualified a statement as this simply cannot be sustained. As Johnston's own
discussion of a broad range of opinion data indicates, on relatively few issues is the
distribution of opinion so close to even that a small change in the opinions of constrained individuals will actually "cast the deciding votes." Johnston presents no evidence to sustain the questionable assumption that the public is made up partly of

constrained individuals and partly of individuals whose opinions are *entirely* random and who therefore choose alternative responses with exactly equal probabilities. Our own prejudice is to interpret the lack of previous attention to the problem of constraint in the Canadian literature as an aspect of the more general weakness of research on ideology and attitudes in this country.

Before discussing our data, we should consider the criticism directed at Converse's work (Nie and Anderson 1975; Pierce and Rose 1974; Achen 1975; Bishop, Tuchfarber, and Oldendick 1978; Sullivan, Piereson, and Marcus 1978; Erikson 1979; Judd and Milburn 1980; Judd, Krosnick, and Milburn 1981; a good summary is Pierce and Sullivan 1980). Converse's critics argue that his findings give a misleading impression of the level of constraint because of methodological artifacts in his data analysis and because his data were collected in the U.S. during an unusually apolitical period in American history.

The methodological problems in Converse's argument relate to the use of Pearson correlations between the responses to questionnaire items dealing with related issues as a measure of the level of constraint. The related concept of consistency is operationalized using similar correlations between responses to identical items at two or more points in time. Larger correlations are taken as an indication of greater constraint and consistency. The problem is that the *observed* correlations among items (i.e., the values measured with the actual survey data) tend to *under*estimate the true correlations. This is because the observed responses to items are imperfect indicators of the underlying traits of those responses, and because the indicators have some degree of unreliability and the correlations between indicators are attenuated, relative to the true correlations between the traits. The unreliability reflects imprecision in the wording of the questions and response categories, for example respondents are likely to differ in their interpretations of the "agree" and "strongly agree" response options. Also responsible for the misleadingly low correlations between items is the use of Pearson correlations to measure the relations between items, for which there are only two, three, or at most five valid responses. The limited number of responses results in lower observed correlations, relative to the values that would be obtained if responses were measured on a continuous scale.

A third objection to the use of correlations to measure constraint is theoretical rather than methodological. This involves the tendency to make unfounded assumptions about which combinations of responses indicate ideological consistency. A good example is our finding that many of the people who believe corporations are too powerful also believe that trade unions are too powerful. This combination of opinions may be seen as inconsistent, in Converse's terminology "unconstrained." As we have argued, however, this combination of attitudes can be interpreted as a consistent reflection of a petty bourgeois consciousness. Similarly, inconsistent responses to a question asked at two points in time may reflect changes in opinions between the two surveys.

One solution to these methodological dilemmas involves applying corrections to the observed correlations between items, which are used to measure the level of constraint in order to account for unreliability, the ordinal level of measurement, and temporal change (Achen 1975; Jidd and Milburn 1980; Jidd, Krosnick, and Milburn 1981). These corrections result in very much higher estimates of the relationships between items. Unfortunately there is considerable disagreement as to what constitute valid corrections to the observed correlations, particularly because it is possible to overestimate the inter-item correlations, which leads to *over*estimates of the level of constraint (Converse 1974).

In the context of this controversy over methodological issues, we proceeded cautiously in our analysis of the Quality of Life surveys. We concentrated on scales that combined the answers to a number of survey questions, and avoided analysis of individual survey items, on the grounds that individual questions – especially those with nuanced responses indicating degrees of opinion – involve too much verbal ambiguity to use as measures of attitudinal consistency. (Of course, this is different from arguing that the items are biased, that is that they are worded in such a manner as to give a misleading impression of the distribution of public opinion.) Second, we approached the problem in a number of different ways, hoping to find results that were consistent and to be able to argue that the findings were not methodological artifacts. Third, we focused on whether levels of constraint are related to education. Showing, contrary to Converse, that education is not related to constraint severely undermines justifications of the greater influence of more competent, better-educated citizens.

We employ an alternative to the conventional strategy for measuring constraint, which involves computing the correlations between individual questionnaire items for different groups within the population. Instead, using the 1981 survey data, we created an index measuring the consistency of each respondent's answers to fourteen questionnaire items identified (on the basis of a factor analysis) as reflecting a left-right dimension of ideology. The index measures the *variation* in an individual's responses, that is respondents who consistently chose right- or left-wing responses received low scores and respondents who gave a mixture of high and low responses received high scores.

If Converse's views are correct, there should be a strong, positive correlation between the measure of consistency and education. But the correlation is very close to zero (measuring education as years of attainment, $r = -.011$). There is also no pronounced difference between high school graduates and non-graduates or between university graduates and non-graduates. Furthermore the consistency variable was only weakly correlated with the five measures of political participation shown in table 4-10; the largest of these five correlations was only .039 (for the measure of whether the respondent had "worked with others in your community to try to solve some community problems").

A second analysis confirmed this finding that constraint is only very weakly related to education and political participation. Likert scales measuring support for social welfare effort, support for redistribution, and support for labour were created from the items shown, respectively, in tables 4-1, 4-2, and 4-5. Measures of the *in*consistency between the three pairs of scales were correlated with educational attainment and a scale of political participation, which was formed from the five items in table 4-10. Inconsistency in attitudes towards social welfare and redistribution had correlations, respectively, with education in years and the political participation scale of −.039 and −.044. Better-educated and more-politically active respondents are thus more likely to have consistent views, as predicted by Converse, but the differences are extremely weak (although statistically significant). The corresponding correlations with education and political participation for the consistency between support for government effort and support for labour are .003 and −.001, and for consistency between support for redistribution and support for labour are .033 and .007.

A third analysis of political consistency made use of the panel data and employed a similar analytic strategy. In each of the 1977, 1979, and 1981 surveys, a left-right scale was constructed from twelve items (all the items included in the consistency score except the ones concerning bilingualism and affirmative action, which were not included in all three surveys). The correlation between the 1977 and 1979 scales was .601, between the 1977 and 1981 scales was .573, and between the 1979 and 1981 scales was .632 (note, however, that due to losses from the panel and the inclusion of new respondents in 1979 and 1981, these correlations do not describe the same population.) These are very high correlations. Their strength is apparent when they are compared to the over-time correlations among measures of political participation, a "behavioural" measure. The correlation between the 1977 and 1979 participation levels is .570, between the 1977 and 1981 participation levels it is .534, and between the 1979 and 1981 participation levels it is .619.

The correlation between the squared *difference* between the 1977 and 1979 scales, which is a measure of attitudinal uncertainty and education, was −.079, again indicating a weak tendency for respondents with more education to have more consistent attitudes. The correlation between the squared difference and a scale of political participation was −.055. The corresponding correlations for the 1979-81 time period are very similar, −.082 and −.042.

These three analyses yield consistent and striking results. In Canada in the late 1970s political constraint and political consistency bare virtually no relationship to education or political participation. The level of ideological consistency over time is strikingly high, especially in view of the fact that the observed over-time correlations of about 0.6 are actually lower bounds of the true correlations. Whatever the hazards of drawing conclusions about the level of consistency on the basis of correlations, there can be no mistaking the finding that educational differentials in constraint are negligible.

This evidence about the level of constraint in the population provides a basis for further analysis of the relationships among different aspects of ideology and for an

Table B-1
Correlations among Scales Measuring Political Ideology

	Welfare Support	Redistribution	Labour	Discrimination	Protest	Participation	Efficacy	Power Deviation	Civil Liberties
Support for social welfare programs	1.000	.386	.230	.061	.108	.032	-.169	.078	.324
Support for redistribution	.386	1.000	.375	.230	.043	.081	-.295	.108	.241
Support for labour	.230	.375	1.000	.156	.016	.066	-.169	.069	.160
Opposition to discrimination	.061	.230	.156	1.000	-.188	.167	-.243	.043	.002
Legitimation of protest activities	.108	.043	.016	-.188	1.000	-.158	.094	.017	.186
Political participation	.032	.081	.066	.167	-.158	1.000	-.186	-.113	-.019
Political efficacy	-.169	-.295	-.169	-.243	.094	-.186	1.000	-.183	-.024
Deviation from present distribution of power	.078	.108	.069	.043	.017	-.113	-.183	1.000	.024
Support for civil liberties	.324	.241	.160	.002	.186	-.019	-.024	.024	1.000

analysis of regional, social class, and other structural cleavages in political ideology. The correlations among a series of indexes of ideology are given in table B-1. The largest correlations are between support for government effort and support for redistribution and between support for redistribution and support for labour, .386 and .375 respectively . The correlation of support for labour and support for welfare effort is only .230, which suggests that of the three measures, social welfare effort is less indicative of strong left-wing views. This supposition is strengthened by the finding that the correlations between opposition to discrimination against immigrants and support for redistribution, for labour, and for welfare effort are, respectively, .297, .156, and .061. Support for civil liberties is most strongly related to support for social welfare (r = .324), followed by support for redistribution (.241), and support for labour (.160). Surprisingly the correlation between support for civil liberties and opposition to discrimination (.002) is negligible.

The correlations among these five scales suggest that the various components that arguably make up a left-right dimension cohere only moderately strongly in the population. Although these results may be interpreted as evidence of weak ideological constraint, the previous results (especially the high consistency levels) and the particular pattern of correlations suggest only that various aspects of ideology are not strongly linked. For example we might generally expect, and the observed positive correlation between the scales indicates, that support for civil liberties would be strongest among individuals who believe that the state should redistribute income. However, some individuals may believe that protecting civil liberties is a substitute for greater equality of condition.

Table B-1 also shows that reactions to the political system are correlated with a number of aspects of ideology. Generally, people who are more left-wing are more likely to be politically *in*efficacious, that is they are less likely than average to believe they can affect what the government does. However, this does not carry over into left-wing respondents having stronger beliefs in the legitimacy of extra-parliamentary protest strategies – the correlation between welfare support and support for protest is only .108. Nor is there much of a relationship between political participation and ideological position. These last findings suggest that critics of present government policy are limited by conventional views about the appropriate means of effecting political change.

Factor analysis of support for government effort in different areas sheds further light on the structure of political ideology. Despite the substantial variation in public enthusiasm for various government programs (see table 4-1) it is possible that a single underlying dimension structures all the responses; each individual's opinions on the various issues might reflect her or his overall belief in the appropriateness of a high level of government activities. Alternatively, the single dimension may distinguish respondents who favour one type of spending (say expenditures for the poor, the unemployed, the retired, and injured workers) over another (say, for defence, eliminating pornography, and crime prevention). These two models do not exhaust the possible one-dimensional schemes that might explain the pattern of evaluations of government effort, and it is possible to imagine more complex schemes that group the various areas of government effort. The technique of factor analysis allows us to answer these questions about the dimensionality of public support for government effort.

Although many are close to zero, the correlations among the ratings of the twenty-one areas of government effort rated in the 1977 survey are almost entirely positive, which indicates that respondents tend not to see government spending in the various areas as requiring cuts in other areas. Still, some of the correlations are much greater than others. The correlation between support for protection of native rights and support for the business community, for example, is .03, compared to a correlation between support for health and medical care and for workers' compensation of .31. The first, and by far the strongest, factor obtained from the factor analysis measures overall support for government efforts – all the items load positively on this factor, although the loadings are greatest for social programs, such as support for the poor, daycare, and the retired, and weakest for non-social areas, such as support for the business community and defence.

The factor analysis divides the areas of government effort into four groups, as follows:

1. health and medical care, the unemployed, job creation, helping the poor, building public housing, eliminating discrimination against women, cutting inflation, daycare, education, helping the retired, and workers' compensation; social and non-social government effort;
2. maintaining national unity, crime prevention, cutting inflation, eliminating pornography, and national defence;
3. promoting bilingualism, creating more jobs, and foreign aid;
4. protecting the rights of native people, eliminating discrimination against women, protecting the environment, providing daycare, and decreasing regional inequality.

This factor structure suggests coherently structured dimensions of ideological cleavage in Canadian public opinion. The first dimension reflects attitudes towards social welfare programs; the second reflects attitudes towards national security and political order; the third reflects attitudes towards state relief of populations whose disadvantages have recognizably endured rather than eroded in the face of capitalist economic growth: the French-speaking population in Canada, the unemployed, and Third World countries; and the fourth reflects attitudes towards the new social movements of native people, women, environmentalists, and other issues, like regional equalization, involving values that question the conventional priorities of economic growth. The first, third, and fourth factors are moderately positively correlated with one another, while the second factor is weakly correlated with the first and is uncorrelated with the third and fourth factors.

Our data on Canadian public opinion, therefore, do not support the orthodox arguments for the lack of ideological constraint in the political attitudes of the general public. On the contrary, there is a reasonably high level of organization linking logically related opinions on issues at a given point in time, a very high level of consistency linking opinions over time, and only a very weak tendency for constraint and consistency to be greater for more-educated and politically active Canadians.

Appendix C:
Description of Scales Measuring
the Political Ideology of Elites

All the scales are formed by summing the responses to the items. Scale scores were calculated for all respondents who gave valid responses (i.e., not "don't know" or "no opinion" or "depends") to at least two-thirds of the items; in the scale calculation, for non-substantive responses the mean of the respondent's valid responses was substituted. Items marked with an asterisk were reversed before being added into the scales, because their "direction" was not the same as the other items. The scales are labelled to correspond to the trait common to each set of items and were formed on the basis of factor analyses.

A. Support for redistribution

Based on ratings of the following statements using the following responses: strongly agree (scored 5), agree (4), neither agree nor disagree (3), disagree (2), and strongly disagree (1).

1 There is too much of a difference between rich and poor in this country.
2 *Unemployment is high these days because it is too easy to get welfare assistance.
3 The government should provide jobs for Canadians who want to work but cannot find a job.
4 People with high incomes should pay a greater share of the total taxes than they do now.
5 Children who grow up in poor homes have much less chance to get ahead than children who grow up in more prosperous circumstances.
6 *In provinces where they now exist, rent controls should be abolished.

B. Support for government investment in industry

Rating of a number of present and possible policies intended to decrease foreign ownership, with the responses scored as in A.

1 Passage of the Foreign Investment Review Act.
2 Establishment of the Canada Development Corporation
3 Giving tax breaks to Canadian firms to allow them to grow faster than foreign firms.
4 Sponsorship of crown corporations in critical industries to compete with foreign firms, such as PetroCan.
5 Tax and other incentives to encourage Canadians to take over foreign firms.
6 Directing government spending to Canadian firms to increase their sales.
7 Takeover of some, but not all, of the multinational oil companies by crown corporations.
8 Nationalization of the Canadian operations of large multinational oil companies.
9 Laws to require foreign companies not now in Canada to form joint ventures with Canadian partners if they wish to start a business in Canada.
10 Legislation to force the sale of foreign-owned companies to Canadians.

C. Support for labour movement

Rating of the following statements, scored as in A.

1 During a strike, management should be prohibited by law from hiring workers to take the place of strikers.
2 Trade unions which are attempting to organize a bargaining unit should have the right to a list of names and addresses of the employees.
3 Postal workers should not have the right to strike.
4 Employees should be represented on the boards of the companies for which they work.
5 Workers' compensation payments should be increased to the level where they provide injured workers with the same income they had before being injured.

D. Support for socialized medicine

Rating of the following statements, scored as in A.

1 When doctors are allowed to bill more than the costs provided for in provincial health plans, the chances of poorer Canadians getting adequate health care are reduced.
2 Government should seek to increase the number of organized group practices with salaried physicians and paramedical personnel.
3 All provinces should adopt the policy of covering medical insurance by general income tax without imposing premiums.
4 All medical personnel should be put on salary.

5 Doctors who choose to bill for more than the costs provided for in provincial health insurance plans should be ineligible for participation in those plans.

E. Support for affirmative action and structural aid to minorities

The question is introduced with the statement that, "Various groups have proposed a number of additions to the protections of civil rights in Canada. Forgetting, for the moment, whether or not these items should be in the constitution, please tell me whether or not you support each of the following proposed changes to the law." Opinions of four policies were scored: yes (4); yes, with some qualification stated (3); no, with some qualification stated (2); no (1).

1 legislation to protect the rights of the disabled
2 the right of women to equal pay for work of equal value
3 protection of homosexuals from discrimination in employment
4 programs of affirmative action to favour the hiring and promotion of women and other minorities in order to redress historical traditions of discrimination.

F. Critical of foreign investment

Rating of the following statements, scored as in A.
1 *Foreign controlled firms import needed technology into Canada that would not otherwise be available.
2 The return of interest, dividends, fees and commissions by foreign firms to their home bases seriously hurts Canada's balance of payments.
3 *Foreign controlled firms do not act much differently from Canadian controlled firms in the same industries.
4 Foreign controlled firms' failure to carry out research and development in Canada injures the Canadian economy.
5 *Foreign controlled firms benefit Canada by taking risks their Canadian controlled counterparts will not.
6 *Foreign firms are not more likely than Canadian firms to import supplies and parts that could be made in Canada.
7 Foreign ownership results in our producing too many competing products in certain areas and this market fragmentation unnecessarily raises costs to consumers.
8 The economic power of foreign firms has stunted the development of Canadian companies.
9 *Foreign firms import capital that would otherwise be unavailable to Canada.

G. Increase the power of the federal government relative to the provincial governments

Using a card with a scale from 1 to 5, with 1 labelled "more power to provincial governments," 3 labelled "Balance of power should remain unchanged," and 5 labelled "more power to federal government," respondents were asked to give their opinions of the following policy areas: economic policy, education, immigration, energy policy, environmental protection, communications, social assistance, labour relations, language policy, health, civil rights.

Support for left-wing foreign policy

Now we would like to ask you some questions about foreign policy. Could you please give me your views on each of the following statements, using the responses on Card 4 (scored as in A).

1 *The most important objective of Canadian foreign policy ought to be to resist the spread of communism.
2 Present economic relations between rich and poor countries work largely to the detriment of the poor countries.
3 *At present, the Soviet Union is generally expansionist rather than defensive in its foreign policy aims.
4 *International agencies like the World Bank are right to impose conditions that encourage a good climate for foreign investment in borrowing countries.
5 The Canadian government should prohibit Canadian firms from investing in South Africa.
6 *Canadian commitments to NATO should be strongly increased.
7 Developed nations should allow their foreign aid to be spent where the recipients decide, rather than being tied to purchases in the donating nations.
8 The Western Allies should take stronger action to reduce the proliferation of nuclear weapons.
9 The Canadian government should set and enforce standards of business conduct to prevent Canadian firms from taking unfair advantage of customers and employees in Third World countries.
10 Canada should support socialist movements which overthrow dictatorial regimes.
11 The Canadian government should prohibit Canadian firms from investing in Chile.

References

Aberbach, Joel D., Robert D. Putnam, and Bert A. Rockman. 1981. Bureaucrats and Politicians in Western Democracies. Cambridge, MA: Harvard University Press.

Abercrombie, Nicholas, Stephen Hill, and Bryan S. Turner. 1980. The Dominant Ideology Thesis. London: George Allen and Unwin.

Abercrombie, Nicholas, and John Urry. 1983. Capital, Labour and the Middle Classes. London: George Allen and Unwin.

Abramson, Paul R., John H. Aldrich, and David W. Rohde. 1982. Change and Continuity in the 1980 Elections. Washington, DC: Congressional Quarterly Press.

Achen, Christopher. 1975. "Mass political attitudes and survey response." American Political Science Review 69:1218–31.

Acheson, Thomas W. 1972. "The national policy and the industrialization of the Maritimes, 1880–1910." Acadiensis 1:3–28.

Adams, Ian. 1971. The Real Poverty Report. Edmonton, AB: M.G. Hurtig.

Adamson, W.L. 1980. Hegemony and Revolution: A Study of Antonio Gramsci's Political and Cultural Theory. London: University of California Press.

Aglietta, Michel. 1979. A Theory of Capitalist Regulation: The US Experience. London: New Left Books.

Ake, Claude. 1967. A Theory of Political Integration. Homewood, IL: Dorsey Press.

Alford, Robert R. 1963. Party and Society: The Anglo-American Democracies. Chicago: Rand McNally.

Alford, Robert R., and Roger Friedland. 1985. Powers of Theory: Capitalism, The State and Democracy. New York: Cambridge University Press.

Almond, Gabriel, and Sidney Verba. 1963. The Civic Culture: Political Attitudes and Democracy in Five Nations. Princeton: Princeton University Press.

Althusser, Louis. 1969. For Marx. London: Allen Lane.

– 1971. Lenin and Philosophy, and Other Essays. New York: Monthly Review Press.

– 1977. Reading Capital. London: New Left Books.

Andrews, Frank M. 1976. Social Indicators of Well-being: Americans' Perceptions of Life Quality. New York: Plenum Press.

Apter, David Ernest. 1971. Choice and the Politics of Allocation. New Haven: Yale University Press.

– 1973. Political Change: Collected Essays. London: Cass.

– 1994. Political Development and the New Realism in Sub-Saharan Africa. Charlottesville, VA: University Press of Virginia.

Archer, Keith. 1987. "A simultaneous equation model of Canadian voting behaviour." Canadian Journal of Political Science 20:553–72.

Arendt, Hannah. 1965. The Human Condition. Chicago: University of Chicago Press.

Arrow, Kenneth. 1963. Social Choice and Individual Values. New York: Wiley.

Asher, Herbert B. 1983. "Voting behavior research in the 1980s: An examination of some new and old problems." In Ada W. Finifter, ed. Political Science: The State of the Discipline. Washington, DC: American Political Science Association.

Atwood, Margaret. 1972. Survival: A Thematic Guide to Canadian Literature. Toronto: Anansi.

Avineri, Schlomo. 1972. Hegel's Theory of the Modern State. London: Cambridge University Press.

Badgley, Robin F., and Samuel Wolfe. 1967. Doctors' Strike: Medical Care and Conflict in Saskatchewan. Toronto: Macmillan of Canada.

Banting, Keith. 1982. The Welfare State and Canadian Federalism. Montreal: McGill-Queen's University Press.

Banting, Keith, and Richard Simeon. 1983. And No One Cheered: Federalism, Democracy and the Constitution Act. Toronto: Methuen.

Barton, Allen H. 1974. "Consensus and conflict among American community leaders." Public Opinion Quarterly 38:507–30.

– 1984. "Determinants of elite policy attitudes." In Ronald H. Linden and Bert Rockman, eds. Elite Studies and Communist Politics: Essays in Memory of Carl Beck. Pittsburgh: University of Pittsburgh Press.

– 1985. "Background, attitudes and activities of American elites." In Gwen Moore, ed. Studies of the Structures of National Elite Groups. Greenwich, CT: JAI.

Bashevkin, Sylvia B. 1983. "Social change and political partisanship: The development of women's attitudes in Quebec, 1965–1979." Comparative Political Studies 16 (July):147–72.

– 1985. Toeing the Lines: Women and Party Politics in English Canada. Toronto: University of Toronto Press.

Baudrillard, Jean. 1981. For a Critique of the Political Economy of the Sign. St Louis, MS: Telos Press.

Becker, James F. 1973. "Class structure and conflict in the managerial phase." In two parts, Science & Society 37 (3):259–77; (4):437–53.

Beer, Samuel Hutchison. 1982. Britain against Itself: The Political Contradictions of Collectivism. New York: Norton.

Bell, Daniel. 1965. The End of Ideology: On the Exhaustion of Political Ideas in the Fifties. New York: Free Press.

– 1973. The Coming of Post-Industrial Society: A Venture in Social Forecasting. New York: Basic Books.

– 1976. The Cultural Contradictions of Capitalism. New York: Basic Books.

– 1977. "The future world disorder: The structural context of crises." Foreign Policy 27 (Summer):109–35.

Bellah, Robert Neelly, et al. 1985. Habits of the Heart: Individualism and Commitment in American Life. Berkeley: University of California Press.

Berelson, Bernard R., Paul F. Lazarsfeld, and William N. McPhee. 1954. Voting: A Study of Opinion Formation in a Presidential Campaign. Chicago: University of Chicago Press.

Bergeron, Michel. 1979. Social Spending in Canada: Trends and Options. Ottawa: Canadian Council on Social Development.

Berman, Marshall. 1981. All That Is Sold Melts into Air: The Experience of Modernity. New York: Simon and Schuster.

Beveridge, William Henry. 1909. Unemployment: A Problem of Industry. London: Longmans, Green.

– 1942. Social Insurance and Allied Services. London: His Majesty's Stationery Office.

Bhaskar, Roy. 1978. A Realist Theory of Science. Hassocks: Harvester Press.

Bishop, G.F., R. Oldendick, and A.J. Tuchfarber. 1978. "Effects of question wording and format on political attitude consistency." Public Opinion Quarterly 42:81–92.

Black, Donald, and John Myles. 1986. "Dependent industrialization and the Canadian class structure: A comparative analysis." Canadian Review of Sociology and Anthropology 23 (2):157–81.

Blake, Donald E. 1985. Two Political Worlds: Parties and Voting in British Columbia. Vancouver: University of British Columbia Press.

– 1988. "Division and cohesion: The major parties." In George Perlin, ed. Party Democracy in Canada. Scarborough, ON: Prentice-Hall Canada.

Blalock, Hubert M., Jr. 1968. "Theory building and causal inferences." In Hubert M. Blalock, Jr and Ann B. Blalock, eds. Methodology in Social Research. New York: McGraw-Hill.

Blau, Peter M., and Otis Dudley Duncan. 1967. The American Occupational Structure. New York: Wiley.

Blishen, Bernard, and Tom Atkinson. 1981. Regional and Status Differences in Canadian Values. Toronto: Institute for Behavioural Research.

Block, Fred. 1977. "The ruling class does not rule – notes on the Marxist theory of the state." Socialist Revolution 33:6–28.

Bottomore, Tom. 1966. Elites and Society. Middlesex: Penguin Books.

– 1975. Marxist Sociology. London: Macmillan.

Boyd, Monica, et al. 1985. Ascription and Achievement: Studies in Mobility and Status Attainment in Canada. Ottawa: Carleton University Press.

Braverman, Harry. 1974. Labor and Monopoly Capital. New York: Monthly Review Press.

Brodbeck, May. 1968. Readings in the Philosophy of the Social Sciences. New York: Macmillan.

Brodie, Janine. 1990. The Political Economy of Canadian Regionalism. Toronto: Harcourt, Brace, Jovanovich, Canada.

Brodie, Janine, and Jane Jenson. 1988. Crisis, Challenge and Change: Party and Class in Canada Revisited. Ottawa: Carleton University Press.

Bryce, Robert B. 1971. "Government policy and recent inflation in Canada." In Neil Swan and David Wilson, eds. Inflation and the Canadian Experience. Kingston, ON: Industrial Relations Centre, Queens University.

Bryden, Kenneth. 1974. Old Age Pensions and Policy-Making in Canada. Montreal: McGill-Queen's University Press.

Brym, Robert J. 1979. "Political conservatism in Atlantic Canada." In Robert J. Brym and James Sacouman, eds. Underdevelopment and Social Movements in Atlantic Canada. Toronto: New Hogtown Press.

– 1980. Intellectuals and Politics. Don Mills, ON: Oxford University Press.

– 1985. "The Canadian capitalist class, 1965–1985." In Robert J. Brym, ed. The Structure of the Canadian Capitalist Class. Toronto: Garamond.

Brym, Robert J., et al. 1989. "Class power, class mobilization, and class voting: the Canadian case." Canadian Journal of Sociology 14:25–44.

Burnham, Walter Dean. 1982. The Current Crisis in American Politics. New York: Oxford University Press.

Butler, David, and Donald Stokes. 1974. Political Change in Britain. 2d ed. London: Macmillan.

Cairns, Alan C. 1968. "The electoral system and the party system in Canada, 1921–1965." Canadian Political Science Review 1 (March):55–80.

– 1988. Constitutional Government and Society in Canada. Toronto: McClelland and Stewart.

– 1991. Disruptions: Constitutional Struggles from the Charter to Meech Lake. Toronto: McClelland and Stewart.

Callinicos, Alex. 1976. Althusser's Marxism. London: Pluto Press.

Campbell, Angus, Gerald Gurin, and Warren E. Miller. 1954. The Voter Decides. Evanston, IL: Row, Peterson Co.

Campbell, Angus, et al. 1960. The American Voter. New York: Wiley.

– 1966. Elections and the Political Order. New York: Wiley.

Campbell, Angus, Philip E. Converse, and Willard L. Rodgers. 1976. The Quality of American Life: Perceptions, Evaluations, and Satisfactions. New York: Russell Sage Foundation.

Campbell, Colin. 1983. Governments under Stress: Political Executives and Key Bureaucrats in Washington, London, and Ottawa. Toronto: University of Toronto Press.

Campbell, Robert. 1987. Grand Illusions: The Politics of the Keynesian Experience in Canada 1945–1975. Peterborough, ON: Broadview Press.

Carchedi, Guglielmo. 1975a. "On the economic identification of the new middle class." Economy and Society 4:1–86.

– 1975b. "Reproduction of social classes at the level of production relations." Economy and Society 4:361–417.

– 1975c. "The economic identification of state employees." Social Praxis 3:93–120.

Carroll, William K., John Fox, and Michael Ornstein. 1982. "The network or directorate interlocks among the largest Canadian firms." Canadian Review of Sociology and Anthropology 19 (1):44–69.

Clarke, Harold D., et al. 1979. Political Choice in Canada. Toronto: McGraw-Hill Ryerson.

– 1984. Absent Mandate: The Politics of Discontent in Canada. Toronto: Gage.

Clarkson, Stephen. 1982. Canada and the Reagan Challenge. Toronto: J. Lorimer in association with the Canadian Institute for Economic Policy.

Clement, Wallace. 1975. The Canadian Corporate Elite: An Analysis of Economic Power. Toronto: McClelland and Stewart.

– 1977. Continental Corporate Power: Economic Elite Linkages between Canada and the United States. Toronto: McClelland and Stewart.

– 1978. "A political economy of regionalism in Canada." In Daniel Glenday, Hubert Guindon, and Allan Turowetz, eds. Modernization and the Canadian State. Toronto: Macmillan.

– 1983. Class, Power and Property. Essays on Canadian Society. Toronto: Methuen.

Clement, Wallace, and John Myles. 1994. Relations of Ruling: Class and Gender in Postindustrial Societies. Montreal and Kingston: McGill-Queen's University Press.

Converse, Jean M., and Stanley Presser. 1987. Survey Questions: Handcrafting the Standardized Questionnaire. Beverly Hills, CA: Sage.

Converse, Phillip E. 1964. "The nature of belief systems in mass publics." In David Apter, ed. Ideology and Discontent. New York: Free Press.

– 1974. "Comment: The status of nonattitudes." American Political Science Review 68:650–60.

Coser, Lewis A. 1956. The Functions of Social Conflict. Glencoe, IL: Free Press.

Cox, Robert W. 1987. Production, Power and World Order: Social Forces in the Making of History. New York: Columbia University Press.

Craven, Paul, and Tom Traves. 1979. "The class politics of the national policy, 1872–1933." Journal of Canadian Studies 14 (3):14–38.

Crompton, Rosemary, and Jon Gubbay. 1978. Economy and Class Structure. New York: St Martin's Press.

Crozier, Michel, Samuel Huntington, and Joji Watanuki. 1975. The Crisis of Democracy: Report on the Governability of Democracies to the Trilateral Commission. New York: New York University Press.

Cuneo, Carl. 1978. "A class perspective on regionalism." In Daniel Glenday, ed. Modernization and the Canadian State. Toronto: Macmillan.

Czudnowski, Moshe M. 1982. "Introduction: A statement of the issues." In Moshe M. Czudnowski, ed. Does Who Governs Matter? DeKalb, IL: Northern Illinois University Press.

Dahl, Robert Alan. 1961. A Preface to Democratic Theory. Chicago: University of Chicago Press.

– 1970. After the Revolution: Authority in a Good Society. New Haven: Yale University Press.

– 1971. Polyarchy. New Haven: Yale University Press.

– 1982. Dilemmas of Pluralist Democracy. New Haven: Yale University Press.

– 1985. A Preface to Economic Democracy. Berkeley: University of California Press.

– 1989. Democracy and Its Critics. New Haven: Yale University Press.

Dahl, Robert Alan, and Charles E. Lindblom. 1963. Politics, Economics, and Welfare: Planning and Politico-Economics Systems Resolved into Basic Social Processes. New York: Harper.

Dahrendorf, Ralph. 1959. Class and Class Conflict in Industrial Society. Stanford, CA: Stanford University Press.

Davis, James A. 1982. "Achievement variables and class cultures: Family, schooling, job and forty-nine dependent variables." American Sociological Review 47 (5):569–86.

Davis, Mike. 1984. "The political economy of late imperial america." New Left Review 143:6–38.

Dawson, Robert MacGregor. 1963. Democratic Government in Canada. Toronto: University of Toronto Press.

Department of Finance, Canada. 1984. Economic Review. Ottawa.

Department of Labour, Canada. 1975. Strikes and Lockouts in Canada. Ottawa.

Dewey, John. 1930. The Quest for Certainty: A Study of the Relation of Knowledge and Action. London: Allen and Unwin.

Doern, G. Bruce, and Richard W. Phidd. 1983. Canadian Public Policy: Ideas, Structure, Process. Toronto: Methuen.

Downs, Anthony. 1957. An Economic Theory of Democracy. New York: Harper and Row.

– 1967. Inside Bureaucracy. Boston: Little, Brown.

Drache, Daniel, and Meric S. Gertler, eds. 1991. The New Era of Global Competition: State Policy and Market Power. Montreal: McGill-Queen's University Press.

Dye, Thomas. 1966. Politics, Economics and the Public. Chicago: Rand McNally.

Easterbrook, W.T., and Hugh G.J. Aitken. 1956. Canadian Economic History. Toronto: Macmillan of Canada.

Elkins, David, and Donald E. Blake. 1975. "Voting research in Canada." Canadian Journal of Political Science 8 (2):313–25.

Elkins, David J., and Richard Simeon, eds. 1980. Small Worlds: Provinces and Parties in Canadian Political Life. Toronto: Methuen.

Erikson, Robert S. 1979. "The SRC panel data and mass political attitudes." British Journal of Political Science 9:89–114.

Erikson, Robert, John H. Goldthorpe, and Lucienne Portocarero. 1979. "Intergenerational class mobility in three western countries: England, France and Sweden." British Journal of Sociology 30:415–41.

Evans, Peter B., Dietrich Ruechemeyer, and Theda Skocpol, eds. 1985. Bringing the State Back In. New York: Cambridge University Press.

Femia, Joseph. 1981. Gramsci's Political Thought: Hegemony, Consciousness and the Revolutionary Process. London: Clarendon Press.

Finkel, Alvin. 1979. Business and Social Reform in the Thirties. Toronto: Lorimer.

Fletcher, Joseph F. 1989. "Mass and elite attitudes about wiretapping in Canada – implications for democratic theory and politics. Public Opinion Quarterly 53 (2):225–45.

Fletcher, Joseph F., and H.D. Forbes. 1990. "Education, occupation and vote in Canada, 1965–1984." Canadian Review of Sociology and Anthropology 27 (4):441–61.

Fletcher, Joseph F., Peter H. Russell, and Paul M. Sniderman. 1991. "The fallacy of democratic elitism: Elite competition and commitment to civil liberties." British Journal of Political Science 21:349–70.

Forbes, Ernest K. 1979. The Maritime Rights Movement, 1919–1927: A Study in Canadian Regionalism. Montreal: McGill-Queen's University Press.

Fowke, Vernon Clifford. 1957. The National Policy and the Wheat Economy. Toronto: University of Toronto Press.

Freedman, Francesca. 1975. "The internal structure of the proletariat: A Marxist analysis." Socialist Revolution 26:41–83.

French, Richard D., and Richard Van Loon. 1984. How Ottawa Decides: Planning and Industrial Policy Making 1968–1984. Toronto: Lorimer.

Fromm, Erich. [1941] 1976. Escape from Freedom. New York: Holt, Rinehart and Winston.

Frye, Northrup. 1971. The Bush Garden: Essays on Canadian Imagination. Toronto: Anansi.

Frye, Northrup, and James Polk. 1982. Divisions on a Ground: Essays on Canadian Culture. Toronto: Lorimer.

Fukuyama, Francis. 1989. The End of History and the Last Man. New York: Free Press.

Fulford, Robert. 1983. Canada, A Celebration. Toronto: Key Porter.

Galbraith, John Kenneth. 1958. The Affluent Society. Boston: Houghton Mifflin.

– 1967. The New Industrial State. Boston: Houghton Mifflin.

Geras, Norman. 1972. "Marx and the critique of political economy." In Robin Blackburn, ed. Ideology in Social Science: Readings in Critical Social Theory. Glasgow: Fontana.

Gibbins, Roger. 1982. Regionalism: Territorial Politics in Canada and the United States. Toronto: Butterworths.

Giddens, Anthony. 1973. The Class Structure of the Advanced Societies. New York: Harper and Row.

– 1974. Elites and Power in British Society. London: Cambridge University Press.

Gidengil, Elisabeth. 1989. "Class and region in canadian voting: A dependency interpretation." Canadian Journal of Political Science 22:563–87.

– 1992. "Canada votes: A quarter century of canadian national election studies." Canadian Journal of Political Science 25 (2):219–48.

Githens, Marianne. 1983. "The elusive paradigm: Gender, politics and political behavior." In Ada W. Finifter, ed. Political Science: The State of the Discipline. Washington, DC: American Political Science Association.

Goldthorpe, John, in collaboration with Catriona Llewellyn and Clive Payne. 1989. Social Mobility and Class Structure in Modern Britain. 2d ed. Oxford: Clarendon Press.

Goldthorpe, John, et al. 1969. The Affluent Worker in the Class Structure. London: Cambridge University Press.

Gorz, Andre. 1982. Farewell to the Working Class: An Essay on Post-Industrial Socialism. London: Pluto.

Graham, Ron. 1986. One-Eyed Kings: Promise and Illusion in Canada. Toronto: Collins.

Granatstein, Jack L. 1975. Canada's War: The Politics of the Mackenzie King Government, 1939–45. Toronto: Oxford University Press.

– 1982. The Ottawa Men: The Civil Service Mandarins, 1935–1957. Toronto: Oxford University Press.

Greenberg, Edward S. 1980. The American Political System: A Radical Approach. Cambridge, MA: Winthrop.

Guest, Dennis. 1980. The Emergence of Social Security in Canada. Vancouver: University of British Columbia Press.

Gunn, John Alexander Wilson. 1995. Queen of the World: Opinion in the Public Life of France from the Renaissance to the Revolution. Oxford: Voltaire Foundation.

Gwyn, Richard J. 1985. The Forty-ninth Paradox: Canada in North America. Toronto: McClelland and Stewart.

Habermas, Jürgen. 1976. Legitimation Crisis. London: Heinemann.

Hall, Peter A. 1986. Governing the Economy: The Politics of State Intervention in Britain and France. New York: Oxford University Press.

Hall, Stuart. 1978. Policing the Crisis: Mugging, the State, and Law and Order. London: Macmillan.

– 1979. "The great moving right show." Marxism Today (January).

– 1985. "Authoritarian populism: A reply to Jessop et al." New Left Review 151.

Hall, Stuart, and Martin Jacques. 1983. The Politics of Thatcherism. London: Lawrence and Wishart, in association with Marxism Today.

Halsey, A.H., and Martin Trow. 1971. The British Academics. London: Faber.

Hamilton, Dwight, and Paul MacNames. 1996. "Fifty richest Canadians." Financial Post Magazine, January, 14–28.

Hamilton, Richard. 1972. Class and Politics in the United States. New York: Wiley.

Harvey, David. 1989. The Condition of Postmodernity: An Enquiry into the Origins of Cultural Change. Oxford and Cambridge, MA: Blackwell.

Heclo, Hugh. 1974. Modern Social Politics in Britain and Sweden; from Relief to Income Maintenance. New Haven: Yale University Press.

Heidenheimer, Arnold J, Hugh Heclo, and Carolyn Teich Adams. 1975. Comparative Public Policy: The Politics of Social Choice in Europe and America. New York: St Martin's Press.

Helvacioglu, Banu. 1992. "The thrills and chills of postmodernism: The western intellectual vertigo." Studies in Political Economy: A Socialist Review 38:7–34.

Higley, John, Desley Deacon, and Don Smart. 1979. Elites in Australia. London: Routledge and Kegan Paul.

Hirsch, Fred. 1978. The Political Economy of Inflation. Cambridge: Harvard University Press.

Hoare, Quintin, ed. 1977. Antonio Gramsci: Selections from Political Writings, 1910–1920. New York: International Publishers.

Hoare, Quintin, and Geoffrey Nowell Smith, eds. 1971. Selections from the Prison Notebooks of Antonio Gramsci. London: Lawrence and Wishart.

Hodson, Randy, and Robert L. Kaufman. 1982. "Economic dualism: A critical review." American Sociological Review 47:727–39.

Hunter, Alfred. 1982. "On class, status and voting in Canada." Canadian Journal of Sociology 7 (1):19–39.

– 1986. Class Tells: On Social Inequality in Canada. Toronto: Butterworths.

Inglehart, Ronald. 1977. The Silent Revolution: Changing Values and Political Styles. Princeton: Princeton University Press.

Irvine, William P. 1974. "Explaining the religious basis of Canadian partisan identity: Success on the third try." Canadian Journal of Political Science 7:560–3.

Irvine, William P., and H. Gold. 1980. "Do frozen cleavages ever go stale – The bases of the Canadian and Australian party systems." British Journal of Political Science 10 (April):187–218.

ISR. 1982. Sampling Report on the Quality of Life Survey. Toronto: Institute for Social Research.

Jackman, Mary R., and Robert W. Jackman. 1983. Class Awareness in the United States. Berkeley: University of California Press.

Jameson, Fredric. 1991. Postmodernism, or, the Cultural Logic of Late Capitalism. Durham, NC: Duke University Press.

Jamieson, Stuart. 1968. Times of Trouble: Labour Unrest and Industrial Conflict in Canada, 1900–66. Ottawa: Task Force on Labour Relations (Information Canada).

Jenson, Jane. 1986. "Gender and reproduction: Babies and the state." Studies in Political Economy 20 (Summer):9–46.

– 1989. " 'Different' but not 'Exceptional': Canada's permeable Fordism." Canadian Review of Sociology and Anthropology 26 (1):69–94.

Jessop, Bob. 1982. The Capitalist State: Marxist Theories and Methods. New York: New York University Press.

– 1989. "Conservative regimes and the transition to post-Fordism." In M. Gottdiener and Nicos Komninos, eds. Capitalist Development and Crisis Theory. New York: St Martin's Press.

– 1991. "Regulation theories in retrospect and prospect." Lecture to Political Science Seminar, York University, Toronto, ON.

Jessop, Bob, et al. 1984. "Authoritarian populism, two nations, and Thatcherism." New Left Review 147:32–60.

– 1985. "Thatcherism and the politics of hegemony: A reply to Stuart Hall." New Left Review 153:87–101.

Johnson, Leo. 1972. "The development of class in Canada in the twentieth century." In Gary Teeple, ed. Capitalism and the National Question in Canada. Toronto: University of Toronto Press.

Johnston, Richard. 1986. Public Opinion and Public Policy in Canada: Questions of Confidence. Toronto: University of Toronto Press.

– 1988. "The final choice: Its social, organizational and ideological basis." In George Perlin, ed. Party Democracy in Canada. Scarborough, ON: Prentice-Hall Canada.

Johnston, Richard, et al. 1992. Letting the People Decide: Dynamics of a Canadian Election. Montreal and Kingston: McGill-Queen's University Press.

Johnston, William, and Michael Ornstein. 1985. "Social class and political ideology in Canada." Canadian Review of Sociology and Anthropology 22:369–93.

Judd, Charles M., and Michael Milburn. 1980. "The structure of attitude systems in the general public: Comparisons of a structural equation model." American Sociological Review 45:627–43.

Judd, Charles M., Jon A. Krosnick, and Michael Milburn. 1981. "Political involvement and attitude structure in the general public." American Sociological Review 46:660–69.

Kariel, Henry S. 1970. Frontiers of Democratic Theory. New York: Random House.

Keynes, John Maynard. 1935. The General Theory of Employment, Interest and Money. New York: Harcourt Brace.

Kluegel, James R., and Eliot R. Smith. 1986. Beliefs about Inequality: Americans' Views of What Is and What Ought to Be. New York: Aldine de Gruyter.

Kluegel, James R., David S. Mason, and Bernd Wegener, eds. 1995. Social Justice and Political Change: Public Opinion in Capitalist and Post-Communist States. New York: Aldine de Gruyter.

Kluegel, James R., et al. 1995. "Accounting for the rich and poor: Existential justice in comparative perspective." In James R. Kluegel, David S. Mason, and Bernd Wegener, eds. Social Justice and Political Change: Public Opinion in Capitalist and Post-Communist States. New York: Aldine de Gruyter.

Koo, Hagen, and Doo-Seung Hong. 1981. "Class and income inequality in Korea." American Sociological Review 45:610–26.

Kopinak, Kathryn. 1979. "Gender differences in political ideology in Canada." Canadian Review of Sociology and Anthropology 24:23–38.

Kornberg, Allan, Joel Smith, and Harold D. Clarke. 1979. Citizen Politicians – Canada: Party Officials in a Democratic Society. Durham, NC: Carolina Academic Press.

Korpi, Walter. 1983. The Democratic Class Struggle. London: Routledge and Kegan Paul.

Kuhn, Thomas S. 1970. The Structure of Scientific Revolutions. Chicago: University of Chicago Press.

Laclau, Ernesto. 1977. Politics and Ideology in Marxist Theory: Capitalism, Fascism, Populism. London: New Left Books.

Laclau, Ernesto, and Chantal Mouffe. 1985. Hegemony and Socialist Strategy: Towards a Radical Democratic Politic. London: Verso.

Lakatos, Imre, and Alan Musgrave. 1974. Criticism and the Growth of Knowledge. Cambridge, U.K.: Cambridge University Press.

Lambert, Ronald D., et al. 1987. "Social class, left/right political orientations, and subjective class voting in provincial and federal elections." Canadian Review of Sociology and Anthropology 24:526–49.

Lambert, Ronald D., and James Curtis. 1993. "Perceived party choice and class voting." Canadian Journal of Political Science 26:273–86.

Lane, Robert Edwards. 1959. Political Life: Why and How People Get Involved in Politics. Glencoe, IL: Free Press.

– 1962. Political Ideology: Why the American Common Man Believes What He Does. New York: The Free Press of Glencoe.

Langille, David. 1987. "The business council on national issues and the Canadian state." Studies in Political Economy 24:41–85.

Larrain, Jorge. 1979. The Concept of Ideology. London: Hutchinson.

Lasch, Christopher. 1979. The Culture of Narcissism: American Life in an Age of Diminishing Expectations. New York: Warner Books.

Lash, Scott, and John Urry. 1987. The End of Organized Capitalism. Cambridge, U.K.: Polity.

Laux, Jeanne Kirk, and Maureen Appel Molot. 1988. State Capitalism: Public Enterprise in Canada. Ithaca: Cornell University Press.

Leys, Colin. 1983. Politics in Britain: An Introduction. Toronto: University of Toronto Press.

Lijphart, Arend. 1977. Democracy in Plural Societies: A Comparative Exploration. New Haven: Yale University Press.

Lindblom, Charles Edward. 1977. Politics and Markets: The World's Political Economic Systems. New York: Basic Books.

Lipietz, Alain. 1985. The Enchanted World: Inflation, Credit and the World Crisis. London: Verso.

– 1987. Mirages and Miracles. London: Verso.

Lipset, Seymour Martin. 1960. Political Man: The Social Bases of Politics. Garden City, NY: Doubleday.

Lipset, Seymour Martin, and Everett Carl Ladd. 1975. The Divided Academy: Professors and Politics. New York: McGraw-Hill.

Lockwood, David. 1975. "Sources of variation in working-class images of society." In Martin Bulmer, ed. Working-Class Images of Society. London: Routledge and Kegan Paul.

1989. The Blackcoated Worker: A Study in Class Consciousness. 2d ed. Oxford: Clarendon Press.

Loren, Charles. 1977. Classes in the United States. Davis, CA: Cardinal Pubs.

Lowi, Theodore J. 1969. The End of Liberalism: Ideology, Policy and the Crisis of Public Authority. New York: Norton.

Lucas, Rex. 1971. Minetown, Milltown, Railtown: Life in Canadian Communities of Single Industry. Toronto: University of Toronto Press.

Lukacs, Gyorgy. [1923] 1971. History and Class-Consciousness: Studies in Marxist Dialectics. Trans. Rodney Livingstone. Cambridge, MA: MIT Press.

MacIntyre, Alisdair. 1978. Against the Self-Images of the Age: Essays on Ideology and Philosophy. Notre Dame, IN: University of Notre Dame Press.

Macpherson, Crawford Brough. 1962a. Democracy in Alberta: Social Credit and the Party System. Toronto: University of Toronto Press.

– 1962b. The Political Theory of Possessive Individualism: Hobbes to Locke. Oxford: Clarendon Press.

– 1966. The Real World of Democracy. Oxford: Clarendon Press.

– 1973. Democratic Theory: Essays in Retrieval. Oxford: Clarendon Press.

– 1977. The Life and Times of Liberal Democracy. Oxford, U.K.: Oxford University Press.

Magnusson, Warren. 1990. "Critical social movements: De-centring the state." In Alain G. Gagnon and James Bickerton, eds. Canadian Politics: An Introduction to the Discipline. Peterborough, ON: Broadview Press.

Magnusson, Warren, and Rob Walker. 1988. "De-centring the state: Political theory and Canadian political economy." Studies in Political Economy, 26 (Summer):37–71.

Mahon, Rianne. 1977. "Canadian public policy: The unequal structure of representation." In Leo Panitch, ed. The Canadian State: Political Economy and Political Power. Toronto: University of Toronto Press.

– 1984. The Politics of Industrial Restructuring: Canadian Textiles. Toronto: University of Toronto Press.

Maier, Charles. 1987. Changing Boundaries of the Political: Essays on the Evolving Balance between the State and Society, Public and Private in Europe. Cambridge; New York: Cambridge and University Press.

Mallory, James Russell. 1971. The Structure of Canadian Government. Toronto: Macmillan of Canada.

Mann, Michael. 1970. "The social cohesion of liberal democracy." American Sociological Review 35:423–39.

– 1978. Consciousness and Action among the Western Working Class. London: Macmillan.

Manzer, Ronald A. 1985. Public Policies and Political Development in Canada. Toronto: University of Toronto Press.

Marcuse, Herbert. 1964. One Dimensional Man: Studies in the Ideology of Advanced Industrial Society. Boston: Beacon Press.

Markus, Gregory, and Philip Converse. 1979. "A dynamic simultaneous equation model of electoral choice." American Political Science Review 73:1055–70.

Marsh, Leonard. [1943] 1975. Social Security for Canada. Toronto: University of Toronto Press.

Marshall, Gordon. 1983. "Some remarks on the study of working-class consciousness." Politics and Society 12:263–301.

Marshall, Gordon, et al. 1989. Social Class in Modern Britain. London: Hutchinson.

Marshall, Thomas Humphrey. 1964. Class, Citizenship and Social Development. Garden City, NY: Doubleday.

Martin, Patrick, Allan Gregg, and George Perlin. 1983. Contenders: The Tory Quest for Power. Scarborough, ON: Prentice-Hall Canada.

Maslow, Abraham. 1954. Motivation and Personality. New York: Harper.

Matthews, Ralph. 1983. The Creation of Regional Dependency. Toronto: University of Toronto Press.

McCall Newman, Christina. 1982. Grits: An Intimate Portrait of the Liberal Party. Toronto: Macmillan of Canada.

McClosky, Herbert, Paul J. Hoffmann, and Rosemary O'Hara. 1960. "Issue conflict and consensus among party leaders and followers." American Political Science Review 5:406–27.

McClosky, Herbert, and Alida Brill. 1983. Dimensions of Tolerance: What Americans Believe about Civil Liberties. New York: Russel Sage.

McDonald, Lynn. 1969. "Religion and voting: A study of the 1968 federal election in Ontario." Canadian Review of Sociology and Anthropology 6:129–44.

McNaught, Kenneth William Kirkpatrick. 1976. The Pelican History of Canada. Markham, ON: Penguin.

McRoberts, Kenneth, and Dale Posgate. 1976. Quebec: Social Change and Political Crisis. Toronto: McClelland and Stewart.

Meiksins, Peter F. 1989. "A critique of Wright's theory of contradictory class locations." In Erik Olin Wright, et al. The Debate on Classes. London: Verso.

Meisel, John. 1973. Working Papers on Canadian Politics. Montreal: McGill-Queen's University Press.

– 1974. Cleavages, Parties and Values in Canada. London: Sage.

Mellos, Koula. 1978. "Developments in advanced capitalist ideology." Canadian Journal of Political Science 11:829–61.

Michels, Robert. 1966. Political Parties: A Sociological Study of the Oligarchical Tendencies of Modern Democracy. New York: Free Press.

Milbrath, Lester W. 1981. "Political participation." In Samuel L. Long, ed. The Handbook of Political Behaviour. New York: Plenum.

Miliband, Ralph. 1969. The State in Capitalist Society. London: Weidenfeld and Nicolson.

– 1977. Marxism and Politics. Oxford: Oxford University Press.

Miller, Nicholas. 1983. "Pluralism and social choice." American Political Science Review 77:734–47.

Mills, Charles Wright. 1956. The Power Elite. New York: Oxford University Press.

Monroe, Allan D. 1979. "Consistency between public preferences and national policy decisions." American Politics Quarterly 7:3–19.

– 1981. "Public opinion and ideology." In Samuel L. Long, ed. The Handbook of Political Behaviour. New York: Plenum.

Moody, Kim. 1987. "Reagan, the business agenda and the collapse of labour." In Ralph Miliband, Leo Panitch, and John Saville, eds. The Socialist Register. London: Merlin.

Mosca, Gaetan. 1965. The Ruling Class. New York: McGraw-Hill.

Moscovitch, Allan, and Glenn Drover. 1981. Inequality: Essays on Political Economy of Social Welfare. Toronto: University of Toronto Press.

Moscovitch, Allan, and Glenn Drover, eds. 1983. The Welfare State in Canada. Waterloo, ON: Wilfrid Laurier University Press.

Mouffe, Chantal, ed. 1979. Gramsci and Marxist Theory. London and Boston: Routledge and Kegan Paul.

Myers, Gustavus. 1914. History of Canadian Wealth. Chicago: C.H. Kerr and Company.

Naylor, R.T. 1972. "The rise and fall of the third commercial empire of the St Lawrence." In Gary Teeple, ed. Capitalism and the National Question in Canada. Toronto: University of Toronto Press.

– 1975. The History of Canadian Business, 1867–1914. Toronto: Lorimer.

Neuman, W. Russell. 1986. The Paradox of Mass Politics. Cambridge, MA: Harvard University Press.

Newman, Peter Charles. 1963. Renegade in Power: The Diefenbaker Years. Toronto: McClelland and Stewart.

Nie, Norman H., and Kristie Anderson. 1975. "Mass belief systems revisited: Political change and attitudes structure." Journal of Politics 36:540–91.

Nie, Norman H., Sidney Verba, and John Petrocik. 1979. The Changing American Voter. Cambridge, MA: Harvard University Press.

Niosi, Jorge. 1985. "Continental nationalism: The strategy of the Canadian bourgeoisie." In Robert J. Brym, ed. The Structure of the Canadian Capitalist Class. Toronto: Garamond.

Noelle-Neumann, Elizabeth. 1984. The Spiral of Silence: Public Opinion, Our Social Skin. Chicago: University of Chicago Press.

Nunn, Clyde, Harry Crockett, and J. Allen Williams. 1973. Tolerance for Nonconformity. San Francisco: Jossey-Bass.

O'Connor, James. 1973. The Fiscal Crisis of the State. New York: St Martin's Press.

O'Donnell, Guillermo, Philippe C. Schmitter, and Lawrence Whitehead. 1986. Transitions from Authoritarian Rule: Comparative Perspectives. Baltimore: Johns Hopkins University Press.

Offe, Claus. 1984. Contradictions of the Welfare State. Cambridge, MA: MIT Press.

– 1985. Disorganized Capitalism: Contemporary Transformations of Work and Politics. Cambridge, MA: Polity.

– 1987. "Challenging the boundaries of the political social movements since the 1960s." In Charles Maier, ed. Changing Boundaries of the Political: Essays on the Evolving Balance between State and Society, Public and Private in Europe. Cambridge and New York: Cambridge University Press.

Ogmundson, Rick. 1975a. "On the measurement of party class position: The case of Canadian federal political parties." Canadian Review of Sociology and Anthropology 12:565–76.

– 1975b. "On the use of party image variables to measure the political distinctiveness of a class vote: The Canadian case." Canadian Journal of Sociology 1:169–77.

– 1980. "Liberal ideology and the study of voting behaviour." Canadian Review of Sociology and Anthropology 17:45–54.

Ogmundson, Rick, and M. Ng. 1982. "On the inference of voter motivation: A comparison of the subjective class vote in Canada and the United Kingdom." Canadian Journal of Sociology 7:141–60.

Olsen, Dennis. 1980. The State Elite. Toronto: McClelland and Stewart.

Ornstein, Michael. 1983a. "Job income in Canada." In Robert V. Robinson and Donald J. Treiman, eds. Research in Social Stratification and Mobility, vol. 2. New York: JAI Press.

– 1983b. "The development of the Canadian class structure." In J. Paul Grayson, ed. Introduction to Sociology: An Alternate Approach. Toronto: Gage.

– 1983c. "Accounting for general wage differentials in Canada: Analysis of a 1981 survey." Ottawa: Labour Canada, Women's Bureau. Discussion Paper Series A, No. 2.

– 1985. "Canadian capital and the Canadian state: Ideology in an era of crisis." In Robert J. Brym, ed. The Structure of the Canadian Capitalist Class. Toronto: Garamond.

Ornstein, Michael, H. Michael Stevenson, and A. Paul M. Williams. 1980. "Region, class and political culture in Canada." Canadian Journal of Political Science 13 (2):227–72.

Page, Benjamin I., and Robert Y. Shapiro. 1983. "Effects of public opinion on policy." American Political Science Review 77:175–90.

Pammett, Jon. 1987. "Class voting and class consciousness in Canada." Canadian Review of Sociology and Anthropology 24:269–89.

Panitch, Leo. 1977. The Canadian State: Political Economy and Political Power. Toronto: University of Toronto Press.

– 1979. "Corporatism in Canada." Studies in Political Economy 1:43–92.

– 1981a. "Dependency and class in political economy." Studies in Political Economy 6:7–34.

– 1981b. "Liberal democracy and socialist democracy: The antinomies of C.B. Macpherson." In R. Miliband, Leo Panitch, and J. Saville, eds. The Socialist Register. London: Merlin.

– 1986. "The tripartite experience." In Keith Banting, ed. The State and Economic Interests. Toronto: University of Toronto Press 1986.

Panitch, Leo, and Donald Swartz. 1985. The Assault on Trade Union Freedoms: From Wage Controls to Social Contract. Toronto: Garamond Press.

Parkin, Frank. 1971. Class Inequality and Political Order: Social Stratification in Capitalist and Communist Societies. London: MacGibbon and Kee.

Parsons, Talcott. 1951. The Social System. Glencoe, IL: Free Press.

– 1977. Social Systems and the Evolution of Action Theory. New York: Free Press.

Parsons, Talcott, Robert Bales, and Edward Shils. 1953. Working Papers in the Theory of Action. New York: Free Press.

Parsons, Talcott, and Neil J. Smelser. 1956. Economy and Society: A Study in the Integration of Economic and Social Theory. Glencoe, IL: Free Press.

Phidd, Richard W., and G. Bruce Doern. 1978. The Politics and Management of Canadian Economic Policy. Toronto: Macmillan of Canada.

Phillips, Paul. 1979. "The national policy revisited." Journal of Canadian Studies 14 (3):3–13.

Pierce, John C., and David P. Rose. 1974. "Nonattitudes and American public opinion: The examination of a thesis." American Political Science Review 68:626–49.

Pierce, John C., and John L. Sullivan. 1980. The Electorate Reconsidered. Beverly Hills, CA: Sage.

Pineo, Peter C., John Porter, and Hugh A. McRoberts. 1977. "The 1971 census and the socioeconomic classification of occupations." Canadian Review of Sociology and Anthropology 14:91–102.

Porter, John. 1965. The Vertical Mosaic. Toronto: University of Toronto Press.

Poulantzas, Nicos. 1973. Political Power and Social Classes. London: New Left Books.

– 1974. Fascism and Dictatorship: The Third International and the Problem of Fascism. London: New Left Books.

– 1975. Classes in Contemporary Capitalism. London: New Left Books.

– 1976. "The capitalist state: Reply to Miliband and Laclau." New Left Review 95:63–83.

– 1980. State, Power, Socialism. London: Verso.

Pratt, Geraldine. 1987. "Class, home, and politics." Canadian Review of Sociology and Anthropology 24:39–57.

Pratt, Larry. 1982. "Energy: The roots of national policy." Studies in Political Economy 7:27–59.

Presthus, Robert Vance. 1973. Elite Accommodation in Canadian Politics. Toronto: Macmillan of Canada.

– 1974. Elites in the Policy Process. New York: Cambridge University Press.

Przeworski, Adam. 1985. Capitalism and Democracy. New York: Cambridge University Press.

Przeworski, Adam, and John Sprague. 1986. Paper Stones: A History of Electoral Socialism. Chicago: University of Chicago Press.

Putnam, Robert D. 1973. The Beliefs of Politicians: Ideology, Conflict and Democracy in Britain and Italy. New Haven: Yale University Press.

– 1976. The Comparative Study of Political Elites. Englewood Cliffs, NJ: Prentice-Hall.

Rea, K.J., and J.T. McCleod. 1976. Business and Government in Canada: Selected Readings. Toronto: Methuen.

Reid, Ivan. 1981. Social Class Differences in Britain. 2d ed. London: Grant McIntyre.

Riesman, David, with Nathan Glazer and Reuel Denney. 1953. The Lonely Crowd. New York: Doubleday.

Rinehart, James, and Ismael O. Okraku. 1974. "A study of class consciousness." Canadian Review of Sociology and Anthropology 11:197–213.

Roberts, K., et al. 1977. The Fragmentary Class Structure. London: Heinemann.

Robinson, Robert V., and Jonathan Kelley. 1979. "Class as conceived by Marx and Dahrendorf." American Sociological Review 44:38–58.

Roemer, John E. 1982. A General Theory of Exploitation and Class. Cambridge, MA: Harvard University Press.

Rotstein, Abraham. 1984. Rebuilding from Within: Remedies for Canada's Ailing Economy. Toronto: Lorimer.

Russell, Peter. 1982. "The effect of a charter of rights on the policy-making role of Canadian courts." Canadian Public Administration 25 (1):1–33.

– 1983. "The political purposes of the Canadian Charter of Rights and Freedoms." Canadian Bar Review. 61:30–54.

Scase, Richard. 1982. "The petty bourgeoisie and modern capitalism: A consideration of recent theories." In Anthony Giddens and Gavin Mackenzie, eds. Social Class and the Division of Labour: Essays in Honour of Ilya Neustadt. Cambridge: Cambridge University Press.

Schattschneider, Elmer Eric. 1960. The Semisovereign People: A Realist's View of Democracy in America. New York: Holt, Rinehart and Winston.

Schmitter, Philippe. 1979. "Still the century of corporatism?" In Philippe Schmitter and G. Lehmbruch, eds. Trends Towards Corporatist Intermediation. Beverley Hills, CA: Sage.

Schuman, Howard, and Michael P. Johnson. 1976. "Attitudes and behaviour." Annual Review of Sociology 2:161–207.

Schuman, Howard, and Stanley Presser. 1979. "The open and closed question." American Sociological Review 44:692–712.

Schwartz, Mildred. 1974. Politics and Territory: The Sociology of Regional Persistence in Canada. Montreal: McGill-Queen's University Press.

Schwarz, Bill. 1987. "The thatcher years." In Ralph Miliband, Leo Panitch, and John Saville, eds. The Socialist Register. London: Merlin.

Seliger, M. 1977. The Marxist Conception of Ideology: A Critical Essay. Cambridge and New York: Cambridge University Press.

Semmler, Willi. 1982. "Theories of competition and monopoly." Capital and Class 18:91–116.

Shalev, Michael. 1983. "Class politics and the Western welfare state." In Shimon E. Spiro and Ephraim Yuchtman-Yaar. Evaluating the Welfare State: Social and Political Perspectives. New York: Academic Press.

Shiry, John. 1976. "Mass values and system outputs: A critique of an assumption of socialization theory." In Jon Pammett and Michael Whittington. Foundations of Political Culture: Toronto: University of Toronto Press.

Simeon, Richard, and David Elkins. 1974. "Regional political cultures in Canada." Canadian Journal of Political Science 7 (3):397–437.

Simeon, Richard, and E. Robert Miller. 1980. "Regional variation in public policy."

Simeon, Richard, and Donald E. Blake. 1980. "Regional preferences: Citizens' views of public policy." In David J. Elkins and Richard Simeon, eds. Small Worlds: Provinces and Parties in Canadian Political Life. Toronto: Methuen Publications.

Simpson, Jeffrey. 1980. Discipline of Power: The Conservative Interlude and the Liberal Restoration. Toronto. Personal Library.

Slater, Philip Elliot. 1976. The Pursuit of Loneliness: American Culture at the Breaking Point. Boston: Beacon Press.

Smiley, Donald V. 1976. Canada in Question: Federalism in the Seventies, 2d ed. Toronto: McGraw-Hill Ryerson.

Sniderman, Paul M. 1981. A Question of Loyalty. Berkeley: University of California Press.

Sniderman, Paul M., et al. 1989. "Political culture and the problem of double standards: Mass and elite attitudes toward language rights in the Canadian Charter of Rights and Freedoms." Canadian Journal of Political Science 22:259–84.

Sniderman, Paul M., et al. 1996. The Clash of Rights: Liberty, Equality, and Legitimacy in Pluralist Democracy. New Haven: Yale University Press.

Stevenson, Garth. 1979. Unfulfilled Union: Canadian Federalism and National Unity. Toronto: Macmillan of Canada.

Stevenson, H. Michael, and Michael D. Ornstein. 1981. "Changing values and the politics of the quality of life." In Gunter Dlugos and Klaus Weiermair, eds. Management under Differing Value Systems. Berlin: Walter de Gruyter.

– 1982. On the Psychology of Political Change and Crisis: A Critique of New Themes in Bourgeois Political Sociology. Toronto: Institute for Behavioural Research.

Stevenson, H. Michael. 1987. "Ideology and unstable party identification in Canada: Limited rationality in a brokerage party system." Canadian Journal of Political Science 20 (4):813–50.

Stevenson, Paul. 1980. "Class and left-wing radicalism." Canadian Review of Sociology and Anthropology 14:269–84.

Stouffer, Samuel. 1955. Communism, Conformity, and Civil Liberties: A Cross-Section of the Nation Speaks Its Mind. Gloucester, MA: P. Smith.

Sullivan, John L., James Piereson, and George E. Marcus. 1978. "Ideological constraint in the mass public: A methodological critique and some new findings." American Journal of Political Science 22:233–49.

Taylor, M.G. 1978. Health Insurance and Canadian Public Policy: The Seven Decisions That Created the Canadian Health Insurance System. Montreal: McGill-Queen's University Press.

Therborn, Goran. 1978. What Does the Ruling Class Do When It Rules? London: New Left Books.

– 1980. The Ideology of Power and the Power of Ideology. London: New Left Books.

Tocqueville, Alexis de. 1966. Democracy in America. New York: Harper and Row.

Toole, David. 1989. "We've got their number." Financial Post Magnesia, May, 25–37.

Touraine, Alain. 1981. The Voice and the Eye: An Analysis of Social Movements. Cambridge: Cambridge University Press.

Traves, Tom. 1979. The State and Enterprise: Canadian Manufacturers and the Federal Government. Toronto: University of Toronto Press.

Trudeau, Pierre Elliott. 1968. Federalism and the French Canadians. Toronto: Macmillan of Canada.

Tucker, David F.B. 1980. Marxism and Individualism. Oxford: Basil Blackwell.

Underhill, Frank Hawkins. 1960. In Search of Canadian Liberalism. Toronto: Macmillan of Canada.

Vaillancourt, Pauline Marie. 1986. When Marxists Do Research. New York: Greenwood.

Van Parijs, Philippe. 1987. "A revolution in class theory." Politics and Society 15 (4):453–82.

Veltmeyer, Henry. 1979. "The capitalist underdevelopment of Atlantic Canada." In Robert J. Brym and James Sacouman, eds. Underdevelopment and Social Movements in Atlantic Canada. Toronto: New Hogtown Press.

Verba, Sidney, and Norman H. Nie. 1972. Participation in America: Political Democracy and Social Equality. New York: Harper and Row.

Walker, Pat, ed. 1979. Between Labour and Capital. Boston: South End Press.

Weber, Max. 1978. Economy and Society. 2 vols. Ed. Guenther Roth and Claus Wittich. Berkeley: University of California Press.

Westergaard, John, and Henrietta Resler. 1975. Class in a Capitalist Society. Harmondsworth, U.K.: Penguin.

Wilbur, J.R.H. 1968. Bennett New Deal: Fraud or Portent? Toronto: Copp Clark Publishing.

Williams, Glen. 1983. Not for Export: Towards a Political Economy of Canada's Arrested Industrialization. Toronto: McClelland and Stewart.

Wilson, John. 1974. "The Canadian political cultures: Towards a redefinition of the Canadian political system." Canadian Journal of Political Science 7:438–83.

Winch, Peter. 1958. The Idea of a Social Science and Its Relation to Philosophy. London: Routledge and Kegan Paul.

Wolfe, David. 1977. "The state and economic policy in Canada, 1968–75." In Leo Panitch, ed. The Canadian State. Toronto: University of Toronto Press.

– 1985. "The politics of the deficit." In The Politics of Economic Policy. Vol. 40. Toronto: University of Toronto Press in cooperation with the Royal Commission on the Economic Union and Development Prospects for Canada and the Canadian Government Publishing Centre, Supply and Services Canada.

Wood, Ellen. 1981. "Liberal democracy and capitalist hegemony: A reply to Leo Panitch on the task of socialist political theory." In Ralph Miliband and John Saville, eds. Socialist Register 1981. London: Merlin.

– 1973. in chapter 3, p. 14 probably a book – page quote from p. 257–258.

Wright, Erik Olin. 1976. "Class boundaries in advanced capitalist societies." New Left Review 98:3–41.

– 1979. Class Structure and Income Determination. New York: Academic Press.

– 1980a. "Class and occupation." Theory and Society 9:177–214.

– 1980b. "Varieties of Marxist conceptions of class structure." Politics and Society 9:323–70.

– 1985. Classes. London: Verso.

– 1996. Class Counts: Comparative Studies in Class Analysis. Cambridge: Cambridge University Press.

Wright, Erik Olin, et al. 1982. "The American class structure." American Sociological Review 47:709–26.

Wright, Erik Olin, et al. 1989. The Debate on Classes. London: Verso.

Wright, James D. 1981. "Political disaffection." In Samuel L. Long, ed. The Handbook of Political Behaviour. Plenum: New York.

Zipp, John F. 1978. "Left-right dimensions of federal party identification: A discriminant analysis." Canadian Journal of Political Science 11 (2):251–77.

Index